The Hulbert Guide to
Financial Newsletters

The Hulbert Guide to Financial Newsletters

MARK HULBERT

EDITOR, *"The Hulbert Financial Digest"*

FIFTH EDITION

 Dearborn
Financial Publishing, Inc.

While a great deal of care has been taken to provide accurate and current information, the ideas, suggestions, general principles and conclusions presented in this text are subject to local, state and federal laws and regulations, court cases and any revisions of same. The reader is thus urged to consult legal counsel regarding any points of law—this publication should not be used as a substitute for competent legal advice.

Publisher: Kathleen A. Welton
Associate Editor: Karen A. Christensen
Interior Design: Irving Perkins Associates
Cover Design: Michael Stromberg

Published by Dearborn Financial Publishing, Inc.

Printed in the United States of America

93 94 95 10 9 8 7 6 5 4 3 2 1

Library of Congress Cataloging-in-Publication Data

Hulbert, Mark
The Hulbert guide to financial newsletters / Mark Hulbert. —5th ed.
p.   cm.
Includes index.
ISBN 0-79310-619-2
1.   Investment analysis—Periodicals—Evaluation.   2. Investments—Periodicals—
Evaluation.   I. Title.
HG4529.H86   1992
332.6—dc20   92-35969
CIP

Acknowledgments

I have received help from an enormous number of people during my 12 years of monitoring investment newsletter performance—so many that I can't begin to acknowledge all of them here. It's just as well, since words cannot adequately express my gratitude for their assistance and support.

Nevertheless, there are a few whose work over the years I will try to acknowledge. Among *The Hulbert Financial Digest*'s current staff, I want to extend special recognition to Donna Westemeyer, the business manager, who started working for the HFD when it was only six months old and had just 1,000 subscribers. Its subsequent success is due in no small part to her commitment and abilities. Currently assisting Donna is John Kimble, who cheerfully keeps our subscribers happy (no mean feat, since the list of present and past subscribers now numbers nearly 100,000). I also want to acknowledge my great debt to David Timmerman, who beginning in 1991 began helping me calculate the performance ratings for each of the nearly 400 portfolios the HFD now monitors. Deb Smucker was the project manager for this edition of the *Guide*, compiling all the graphs that appear in this book. Other staff who have been of enormous assistance are Pat Timmerman and Mary Ann Ek.

I also want to thank James Davidson and William Bonner, who with me were the originators of the HFD back in 1980. (Their minority interest in the HFD was dissolved several years ago, however, so only I'm to blame for any mistakes.) Representing the HFD in all legal matters has been Michael Geltner, and James Wilkins III has done its accounting.

In 1990 the HFD formed an advisory board to advise me on methodological disputes which can (and often do) arise with newsletter editors. The members of this advisory board are Dr. Keith Johnson (associate professor of Finance at the University of Kentucky), Dr. John Markese (Director of Research at the American Association of Individual Investors), Dr. Donald Shannon, CPA (professor at DePaul University's School of Accountancy), Dr. Dave Upton, CPA (associate professor of Finance at Virginia Commonwealth University, and member of the Council of Examiners of the Institute of Chartered Financial Analysts), and Joel Wittenberg (president of the Wittenberg Investment Management, and former Branch Chief at the Office of Trading Practices, Division of Market Regulation, Securities and Exchange Commission; Joel also was my coauthor of the first edition of this *Guide*). Needless to say, responsibility for any mistakes remains mine.

My debt to Peter Brimelow, senior editor at *Forbes*, should be evident from the foreword. If at any time while reading this book you become overwhelmed with the sheer amount of statistical detail, you should turn to Peter's writings: He has a wonderful ability to find his way through this statistical thicket to focus on what is truly significant. A new edition of his book on investment newsletters (*The Wall Street Gurus: How You Can Profit From Investment Newsletters*) will be published in 1993, and I know from its first edition that it will be extremely valuable reading.

Finally, I want to thank the newsletter editors themselves—even though at one time or another many of them have wished that the HFD wasn't published. But my newsletter wouldn't exist if it were not for their willingness month after month to put their reputations, egos and fortunes on the line trying to beat the market. Lesser men and women wouldn't even try, and I take my hat off to them.

Mark Hulbert

Contents

Foreword

Every two weeks, I watch with a certain proprietorial pride as Mark Hulbert's column magically materializes via modem in *Forbes* magazine's computer system. I wrote what was perhaps the first major article to appear in the financial press about Hulbert and *The Hulbert Financial Digest* in 1981. I followed his work closely thereafter, and in 1986 made extensive use of it in my book on investment letters, *The Wall Street Gurus*. When I joined *Forbes*, later in 1986, I brought Mark along as a sort of dowry.

He wrote a few guest columns. And these were enough to cause the editor of *Forbes*, James W. Michaels, to reverse a lifetime's trenchantly-expressed skepticism about investment letters. He ordered Mark installed as a permanent columnist, and from this perch he has been serving us a sample of *The Hulbert Financial Digest* fare ever since.

To appreciate what a breakthrough this was for the investment letter community, you must realize that at that time *The Wall Street Journal* would not accept advertisements from them—and in fact had even refused to carry an advertisement for my book about them! Wall Street's attitude was equally dogmatic and dismissive. There has been a lot of progress since then. Investment letters get a lot more respect. Curiously, many of the individual letter editors forget this when screaming about Mark's assessment (always scrupulous) of their track records.

I would like to be able to claim credit for the Hulbert phenomenon. But that first story was actually the suggestion of another legendary editor, Alan Abelson of *Barron's*. "We've had a lot of inquiries about this guy who follows investment letters," he said to me after using *The Hulbert Financial Digest* ratings in one of his total-war columns attacking *The Granville Market Letter*'s Joe Granville, whose heavily publicized market calls were at that time making him the best-known investment letter writer in history. "Why don't you see if there's a story there?"

I took Mark to an elegant restaurant on Washington, D.C.'s Capitol Hill, where he then lived. Naturally, I could not know then that he was totally honest and there was no point in trying to lull him into a damaging admission about his rating system, nor that he was a vegetarian and *Barron's* expense account was going to be wasted on lettuce at $5.00 a leaf. I did realize immediately, however, that he was one of the most remarkable subjects I had ever interviewed.

I had mixed feelings about this, as a matter of fact. Mark was disgustingly young, just out of college (Haverford '77, Oxford '79) and he had done something truly astonishing: Not only was he providing the first-ever objective monitoring of investment letter performance, previously a cloud of confusion, conjecture and con tricks, but he was going to be able to use the results to solve the secret of the stock market—can it be beaten; and, if so, how.

(Over the years, screaming letter editors and formula-minded book reviewers have sometimes complained that I have nothing critical to say about Mark. This baffles me. I think he's the real thing, for God's sake. What am I supposed to do, make something up? To satisfy this apparently insatiable desire for symmetry, however, I will now report a fault: My wife thinks he's too nice with girlfriends.)

Before Hulbert—B.H. as it should be styled in the investment letter calendar—Wall Streeters and financial journalists tended to dismiss investment letters because some of them were written by lunatic self-promoters. There was a reason for this. Some letter writers are lunatic self-promoters. Wall Street itself, however, was in reality no less self-promoting, although it could afford subtler methods like prestige offices and paid endorsements by television stars. And the established orthodoxy among academics who study the stock market was "the efficient market hypothesis"—the view that the market reflects new information so fast that neither investment letters nor Wall Streeters could outguess it in the long run. This implies that the most logical course is to fire your investment adviser, buy a diversified portfolio and hold it through thick and thin.

Mark Hulbert's work has inclined him to different conclusions. These can be expressed as:

Hulbert's First Law:

It is E-X-T-R-E-M-E-L-Y hard to beat the market over time (Corollary: If anyone says he consistently makes spectacular profits, don't believe him.);
    And

Hulbert's Second Law:

It may be hard. But it can be done. (Corollary: We know who does it.)

This is in line with more recent work in academe, which focuses on the so-called "anomalies" in the efficient market, peculiar areas where the market does not seem to discount information immediately and which can be exploited to achieve superior returns.

Wall Street is at a disadvantage in finding these anomalies. For one thing, there is the conflict of interest: The stockbroker is concerned about commissions, the client about capital gains. Investment letters are prepared to give sell signals, which investment banks shrink from because it upsets their underwriting clients. For another, the inevitable bureaucracy of large organizations makes all innovation difficult. By contrast, investment letters can (and do) try anything they feel like immediately. They present every conceivable investment technique and style.

Investment letters are the guerrilla troops of the financial world—Wall Street irregulars. Mark Hulbert tracks their footsteps across the investment minefield. By following them, and halting if they terminate in a smoking crater, you can see what techniques work, and work for you (two different things). No more important work is being done anywhere in the investment industry today.

And if it seems surprising that this discovery was made by an ex-philosophy student with his personal computer, remember that two farm boys from Ohio invented the airplane.

Peter Brimelow
(Senior Editor of *Forbes* magazine and author of
*The Wall Street Gurus: How You Can Profit
from Investment Newsletters*)

Introduction

The number of Americans who invest in the stock market has increased dramatically in recent years. Not surprisingly, accompanying this growth has come an explosion in the investment advisory industry. Seemingly everyone is offering investment advice—commentators on television and columnists in the financial press, personal and business acquaintances, stockbrokers and investment advisory newsletters.

How are you to choose? While this book will help you choose among various investment advisory newsletters, you may be asking, "Why should I look to any newsletters at all?" This introduction discusses your range of options.

What about newspapers, television and the financial press as sources of investment advice? In recent years, they have greatly improved and expanded their coverage and analysis of the economy and of financial developments and trends. The Public Broadcasting Service's "Wall Street Week With Louis Rukeyser" is one of the most popular shows in all of television; CNBC, with its ever-present ticker tape running across the bottom of its broadcasts, is watched daily by millions of investors; *Barron's*, *The Wall Street Journal* and *Investor's Business Daily* are so widely followed and respected that a positive or negative report on a stock can move the stock up or down. Nevertheless, television programs, financial magazines and newspapers of general circulation are better thought of as good sources of factual information and investment ideas than of specific and systematic investment advice. As a rule, they do not recommend a specific model portfolio or provide consistent follow-up on the securities they mention.

Financial advice also may be forthcoming from personal or business acquaintances. Everyone from one's banker, accountant, lawyer, business partner, golf buddy, dentist or neighbor may volunteer investment advice. As with television and the financial press, however, personal and business acquaintances are better seen as sources of ideas than of systematic investment strategies. And, one suspects, the frequency with which those acquaintances boast about their winnings often is in inverse proportion to how much they actually are profiting from their investment genius.

Stockbrokers versus Newsletters

Two other, more traditional, and often more informed and more systematic, sources of investment advice are stockbrokers and investment newsletters. In deciding between them, the following factors should be kept in mind.

With respect to stockbrokers, you should realize that their incentives to make money for you sometimes conflict with their desire to make money for themselves. The source of this conflict is the fact that they are compensated on a commission basis: They are paid according to how many shares have been bought and sold by their clients, not according to how much money they have made for them. Of course, they also have an incentive to provide profitable advice (to gain more and wealthier clients), but it is an indirect and longer-term incentive as compared to the more direct and immediate incentive to earn commission income.

When a brokerage firm has a large inventory of stock it wishes to unload, for example, it is not uncommon for it to offer special compensation to its brokers who sell the most of those shares. Typically, this compensation includes an increased portion of the commission that is charged or bonuses such as an all-expense-paid trip to Hawaii. Does your stockbroker tell you how he is being compensated for pushing this stock, or why his firm is so eager to unload it?

Brokerage Firms' Research

Another factor that you should consider in comparing brokers with newsletters is that many firms forbid their brokers to make their own recommendations, requiring them instead to choose their recommendations from the "recommended list" compiled by that firm's research department. While the stocks on the recommended list may very well turn out to be more profitable than the stocks the brokers themselves would have chosen, this arrangement has several drawbacks. First, brokerage research departments rarely offer "sell" advice. Because brokers too easily begin to believe their own sales pitches, this may lead them to become permanently bullish on the market. Your broker therefore is likely to be far more silent on what or when to sell than about what or when to buy.

Another drawback to confining brokers to the recommendations of their firms' research departments is that you are just one of your broker's many clients and your broker is just one of his firm's many brokers. In all likelihood, therefore, you are nowhere near to being the first client of the firm to receive a new "buy" recommendation. In fact, a newly recommended stock's price most likely already will have been bid up substantially by the firm's major clients by the time you hear about it through your broker.

Finally, if the research of these firms is so valuable, why are they so reluctant to publish their performance results? What, for example, is the average gain or loss of those stocks recommended by Merrill Lynch? And is that better or worse than Dean Witter, Paine Webber, or their competitors? Don't you think that these firms would be sure to document their superior stockbrokering abilities if their advice was profitable?

In fact, there is at least some evidence to suggest that the recommendations of at least some firms' research departments are nowhere near to being as profitable as are those of the best-performing newsletters. From the beginning of 1986 through mid-1989, for example, *The Hulbert Financial Digest* (hereafter referred to in this *Guide* as the HFD) tracked the performance of the stock-rating system published by the *Merrill Lynch Stockfinder Research Service* (it ceased publication in mid-1989). While this service did not perform as poorly as many of the newsletters the HFD monitors, it did not do nearly as well as many others. Furthermore, it did not beat the market itself, lagging the Wilshire 5000's total return over this period by a margin of 61.1% to 63.3%.

Investment Newsletters

To be contrasted with brokers is the other important source of investment advice— advisory newsletters. Thousands of investment advisers are registered with the Securities and Exchange Commission (SEC), and a good estimate is that about 500 of them publish investment newsletters. No more than about two dozen of those, however, have more than 5,000 subscribers.

The performance incentives of investment newsletters differ from those of stockbrokers in several significant respects. First and foremost, investment newsletter editors charge directly for their advice. Consequently, the size of their subscriber base and their profitability are highly dependent upon the value of that advice; renewal rates for newsletters are extremely sensitive to their editors' success in devising a profitable strategy.

In addition, newsletters ordinarily have no immediate incentive to generate stock transactions. Unlike brokers, they are not compensated according to the number of shares their clients have bought or sold. Instead, their income is directly related to how many investors are convinced that the advice in the newsletter is profitable.

Finally, unlike with brokers, performance data are available for most of the widely followed investment newsletters. These figures, calculated by the HFD, enable you to select an adviser with a proven record from the many seeking attention (and your dollars) in the marketplace.

This book is based on the conviction that you would do well to consider newsletters as a source of investment ideas and strategy. Because their incentives differ from those of brokers, newsletters are a refreshing source of advice. They can make recommendations that are rare within the brokerage community and lead you in directions where brokers are unlikely to take you.

Just because newsletters operate under different incentives than stockbrokers do, however, does not mean that those incentives are all to the good—and an introduction to any comparison of newsletters would be amiss if it did not point them out. For example, some editors no doubt feel they must continually recommend new investments (even when market conditions are not optimum) in order to convince their subscribers that they are receiving their money's worth. Some editors have complained that they have lost subscribers during periods when their recommended strategy was to remain in cash, even when such a strategy proved to be more profitable than that advocated by most other newsletters. According to such editors, their subscribers felt they were not getting enough "action" for their subscription dollars; they felt that they did not pay someone several hundred dollars per year to be told to keep their money in cash. Potential newsletter subscribers therefore need to be on their guard against newsletters that generate more transactions than are paying off, after taking commissions and taxes into account. (By the same token, newsletter subscribers should be careful not to pressure newsletter editors into taking more "action" than is prudent.)

Exaggerated Advertising Claims

Another less-than-desirable consequence of the incentives under which newsletters operate is exaggerated advertising claims. As with any industry, the newsletter industry contains both honest and less-than-honest members, and it is too much to expect that each editor will be objective about his track record when such objectivity can be so devastating to his own fortunes. The HFD keeps a file of what appear to be exaggerated advertising claims, and the following are all-too-typical examples of what is in that file:

- a letter that "regularly" earns profits of 1,602% in just 48 months;
- a letter that turned $8,750 into $405,125 in only 13 weeks;
- a report on how you can "regularly" earn 4,000% annual profit;
- a report on how to earn "spectacular" profits of "950% better than the Dow" while "reducing your risks";
- an adviser who has helped subscribers earn "consistent profits of 922% during the last few years."

While the HFD has not tracked the performance of the newsletters making these specific claims, they strain credulity. During the 12 years the HFD has been tracking investment newsletters, no service has come close to living up to such claims. In fact, consistent average annual gains of more than 20% to 25% are extremely rare.

Even when a newsletter editor refers to his HFD performance rating, you can't be sure that he is telling the truth. In August 1991, for example, one of the newsletters tracked by the HFD claimed in its advertising that it was "Rated #1 by Hulbert," when in fact it was not, nor never had been, rated #1 in the HFD. The advertisement attempted to justify this phony claim by explaining that the newsletter was top-rated by the HFD among the "best-known 25 newsletters published in America." But this was hardly more convincing than the original phony claim, since all the newsletter did was define as "best-known newsletter" in America all those that had performed less well.

Clearly, newsletters' advertising is a poor source of information on which newsletters to choose. Can you look to registration with the SEC as a way to choose? No! Not all newsletters are registered with the SEC, and even if they were such registration would provide you very little protection. The SEC does not place any education, training or experience standards on becoming registered as an adviser (nor is it clear that any particular type of education, training or experience leads to better performance). In fact, almost anyone can become registered upon doing little more than filling out several forms and paying the modest filing fee. When it comes to choosing among investment newsletters, the answer is not more government regulation but more wariness among buyers.

In choosing among investment newsletters, you must examine their performance closely—and this is exactly what this *Guide* helps you do. Relying upon their advertising claims is too dangerous, and relying upon government regulation is misguided. By utilizing an objective rating system such as the one devised by the HFD, one can counteract the negative effects of newsletters' tendencies to exaggerate and derive maximum benefit from what those services do have to offer.

Newsletters and "Random Walks"

Another potential source of investor skepticism toward newsletters may be the debate among academics over whether the market can be beaten over long periods of time. (Of course, skepticism borne of such beliefs would extend to all sources of investment advice, not just to newsletters.) If the movement of security prices is random—as some contend—then there is no reason to pay for the advice of a newsletter. While the HFD believes the market can be beaten, it is important for investors to be aware of and familiar with this dispute.

The "random walk" theory and its closely related "efficient market hypothesis" are based in large part on the fact that the stock market very quickly and efficiently assimilates new information. Just think of all the different factors that might affect the profitability of a company over the next 15 years. Economists can and do debate endlessly about each one of these many factors, and not only do they disagree about the significance of each one, they are even less able to agree on how those factors interact with one another to affect the company's bottom line. How can any one of us know enough and be wise enough to correctly judge and weigh each one of these factors? The market, reflecting the best judgment of a large number of investors, more often than not will be hard to beat.

The random walkers make an even stronger claim. Even in the event that we knew how a particular development would affect a company's bottom line, it is unlikely we would hear about the news in time to profit from it. By the time you or I read about a company's new earnings report in the newspaper, for example, the stock's price has already adjusted to the news.

To the degree that information is quickly and efficiently reflected in the marketplace, it follows that at any given time a stock is neither "overvalued" nor "undervalued." Stock prices will go up or down over time, of course, but according to this theory, the path they take to get there will be a "random walk." Those who try to predict and profit from alleged trends in the market will inevitably meet with failure.

Is the Market Efficient for Every Stock?

The financial markets are indeed very efficient, and in disputing the conclusion of the efficient-market hypothesis we cannot deny their efficiency. But the markets are not equally efficient for all securities. With thousands of researchers from brokerage firms devoting themselves to scrutinizing IBM, for example, one would expect the market for IBM's stock to be far more efficient than the market for a stock of a small company that trades over the counter and has no following among the brokerage community. In the former case, there is very little likelihood that you or I could hope to discover some salient fact about IBM that has not already been analyzed hundreds of times—and thus is not already discounted in IBM's price. In the latter case, however, the likelihood is much greater. And, in fact, several academic studies have found that the average stock with no brokerage following has outperformed the average stock with such a following.

Apart from the presence or absence of a brokerage following, academic research has located a number of other areas where the market's efficiency is less than complete. These areas include companies that are in a strong capital position, stocks that are relatively low-priced, companies with relatively low market capitalization, stocks that are trading at a low price-earnings ratio, and companies with recent high profit increases.

Apart from these academic studies is the performance of stock-rating systems. Most prominent of such systems is that devised by *The Value Line Investment Survey* (published by Value Line, Inc.), which each week since 1965 has rated 1,500 stocks from Group 1 (the 100 best bets to outperform the market over the next six months to one year) to Group 5 (the 100 worst bets). It turns out that during each year since 1965 (with a few exceptions), those stocks rated "1" have outperformed those rated "2," which in turn have outperformed those rated "3," and so forth. This is a record one cannot ascribe to chance. Indeed, one of the early proponents of the "random walk" thesis has conceded as much. Fischer Black, who used to work at MIT and now works on Wall Street, has concluded from his analysis of the *Value Line* ranking system that, contrary to the assertion of the efficient-market hypothesis that the market cannot be beaten, "it does appear that there is hope that the traditional methods of portfolio management and security analysis can succeed."

The proof of the pudding is in the eating, of course, and the true test of the market's inefficiency is whether top-performing advisers can continue to beat the market into the future. After all, if past performance were completely unrelated to future performance, then we reluctantly would have to conclude that the market follows a random walk—and you could stop reading this book here. It would make just as much sense to follow an adviser with a terrible record as one who has beaten the market for a decade or more. But fortunately this isn't the case. As discussed in the chapter later in this *Guide* entitled "The Power of the Past," past performance *is* related to future performance. This perhaps is the most important evidence of all that the markets aren't totally random.

Just because the market isn't totally random and can be beaten, however, doesn't mean that it is easy to do so or that you should be sanguine about the prospects of finding a newsletter that will beat it. Indeed, as a cursory overview of this *Guide*'s appendices shows, very few newsletters beat the market over the 12 years through mid-1992. So while you should avoid the total skepticism of the random walkers, neither should you be a Pollyanna about beating the market. In addition to exciting you about the challenge of beating the market, a study of the markets and their efficiency should lead to a renewed respect for the market and how stiff a competitor it really is.

The Market's Efficiency and You

Why is this debate something you should be aware of? Because it points out what you should be looking for in a newsletter. To justify subscribing to a service and investing your assets according to its advice, a newsletter must show convincingly how and why there is reason to believe it can beat the market. The most important evidence in this regard is past performance, and the chapter "The Power of the Past" discusses what you should look for in a newsletter's past.

In addition to past performance, though, there are some other features of a newsletter's approach that you should be on the lookout for. Does it base its recommendations on an already proven method (such as a stock-selection method based on the criteria listed above) or on a method devised by it and on which sufficient research has been conducted to verify its effectiveness? Can the newsletter persuasively demonstrate that the factors on which it bases its advice have not already been discovered by other investors and thus already discounted by the market? You should approach newsletters with the attitude of the skeptic; make each service convince you that it has sufficiently increased the odds of beating the market to justify subscribing to it and risking your assets by following its advice.

Several examples illustrate what you should be on guard against. First, be on the lookout for advisers who do not follow their own logic and reasoning from issue to issue. Some newsletters, for example, will say that it is very bullish for the stock market that the economic data reported by the government appear to be so strong. Examine carefully what these advisers do if and when those data turn sour. Do they ignore it? Or, worse yet, do they reverse their logic and now conclude that the weak economic data are bullish too (arguing, for example, that it will reduce pressure on the Federal Reserve to tighten the money supply)?

To use another example, say that a newsletter places great weight on the so-called January Indicator ("How January goes, so goes the year") and on the basis of a conviction that January is going to be an "up" month recommends a bullish posture for the year as a whole. Watch what the newsletter does if January turns out to be a "down" month. If this service genuinely believes its own reasoning, it should turn bearish in February. Unfortunately, too many times the HFD sees that such services simply find other indicators to justify a bullish stance.

Such reasoning is a dead giveaway that the service in question has a predetermined view of the market that it will maintain regardless of what happens. Needless to say, following such advice can be dangerous. The profitability of such newsletters' advice will be purely random. If services can so easily disregard their own arguments of a previous month, then why should you accord that advice any greater respect?

How Accurate Is the January Indicator?

Newsletters' use of the January Indicator is a good example of another common pitfall— failure to conduct enough historical research on which to base a confident conclusion, or interpreting that research incorrectly. It turns out, according to this indicator's adherents, that it has an extremely impressive success ratio. But how has such a success rate been calculated? According to an analysis of the matter which appeared in the March 12, 1984, issue of *Barron's*, this success rate is based on erroneous reasoning.

In determining whether the market was up or down for the year—and thus whether the January Indicator was a success—such calculations examined the market's performance from January 1 to December 31, not from February 1 to December 31. Therefore, in years when the market went up 100 points in January and fell 90 points thereafter through December 31, the indicator was judged a success when in fact it was a failure. (It appeared to be a success because January was up and the year was up, even though you would have lost 90 points by acting upon the indicator.) When this bias is removed from the calculations, according to the *Barron's* article, January's record as an indicator is little better than random and, in any case, is worse than the records of four other months of the year! Needless to say, advice that is based on inadequate research holds no promise of being more profitable than random stock picks. You may or may not make money by following its advice, but whether or not you do has nothing to do with the reasons advanced by the newsletter.

The example of the January Indicator points up yet another thing to look for in judging various indicators. Look to see that an indicator has been tested in "real time," so to speak. The problem arises because it is all too easy—especially with the advent of computers, allowing more historical comparisons—to look back through history, picking and choosing among hundreds of potential indicators until one "discovers" one that has an "uncanny" record of accuracy. (Statisticians refer to this practice as "data snooping" or "data mining.") Such research is of dubious validity. Look to see whether or not an indicator has been tested over a different period of time than the one used initially to "discover" its existence. All too often, an indicator judged to be a success by non-real time tests begins to break down the moment you start to follow it.

Another way of safeguarding against data mining or snooping is to see if an alleged pattern or strategy makes sense. If a plausible theory can't be devised to explain why such a pattern should exist, it should increase your skepticism that the pattern is the result of little more than data mining. For example, much weight is given each January to the so-called "Super Bowl Indicator," based on the supposedly "uncanny" correlation between the stock market's behavior and the football conference of the team winning the Super Bowl. Regardless of how good the correlation may appear, however, you should be suspicious of this indicator until and unless you can offer a plausible explanation of why the Super Bowl should have any relation to the stock market.

Yet another type of reasoning that you need to guard against is the sort which appears to enjoy a strong foundation in historical research but which, upon examination, does not. In 1980, for example, several newsletters developed an argument based on the fact that every time in this century when a Republican President was in office during certain sets of circumstances, the market crashed. This appeared to be a strong, historically based argument, but what these letters did not tell you is that there was only one year in this century that fit its preconditions: 1930! The market did not do well in the years following 1930, of course, but a historical argument based on a sample size of just one has no validity whatsoever.

Conclusion

These examples, by pointing out what to avoid, also show what sort of approach to take to newsletters. Scrutinize them and their performance record in the HFD as well as the arguments they put forth. Adopt the attitude of the skeptic and make them convince you that they are worthy of your investment dollars. Just as you do not accept at face value every advertising claim you read, do not turn off your critical faculties and naively believe the hyperbole contained in investment newsletters' advertising. Beating the market is never easy, and it requires all the insight and hard-nosed analysis you can muster.

ONE

Questions and Answers About Newsletters

A good way to guide a diverse readership through this *Guide* is to start with a series of questions and answers about newsletters, pointing out which sections of the book are essential for all readers and which can be skipped by those already familiar with the subject being discussed.

I'm happy with my present full-service broker; why should I look to a newsletter for my investment advice?

If your broker is giving you enough profitable advice to justify paying full-service brokerage rates, then by all means stay with him. It may be, however, that if you were to analyze how much you actually pay for his advice (which is the difference between his and discount brokerage rates), your enthusiasm might wane. But even if your enthusiasm remains undiminished, you should still take a look at newsletters because they may provide you with better advice for your investment advisory dollars, or lead you in directions a broker is unlikely to lead you. (See the Introduction for a further discussion about the differences between newsletters and brokers.)

I'm too busy to manage my own investments. I much prefer to let my broker handle my account.

If you really are too busy to do it yourself, then some of the more active-trading newsletters may not be for you. But you can still tell your broker what investment strategy to pursue; for example, you could subscribe to a newsletter and have it mailed to him and instruct him to follow its advice.

In any case, not all newsletters require the same amount of attention in order to follow their advice. The newsletter the HFD calculates to have the best risk-adjusted performance for the 12 years through mid-1992, for example, is published only twice each month and has a brief hotline update once each week. Are you really so busy that you can't take the few minutes it takes each month to read the twice-monthly newsletter, call the weekly hotline, and call a discount broker when any changes are recommended?

Having said this, however, it is important for you to know how much time it will take to follow a given newsletter. It doesn't matter how good an adviser's track record may be if following it would require more time than you can afford to give. If you don't want to be calling a telephone hotline update every day or following the market on a minute-by-minute basis to see if contingent orders are activated, then don't spend your time wondering whether such a newsletter may be the one for you.

Accompanying our examination of each of the newsletters later in this *Guide* are a few words indicating how often the newsletter is published and how frequently it has a telephone hotline update (if at all). In addition, there is no substitute to taking out a trial subscription to each newsletter you are interested in and discovering for yourself just how much time would be required to follow its advice. Appendix D gives the addresses, subscription rates and telephone numbers of each of the monitored newsletters. As you will see, most have fairly inexpensive trial offers.

Which is the best investment newsletter?

This crucial question is not nearly as simple as it appears. To begin with, the question is poorly formulated. You might just as well ask, "Who is the best lawyer in the U.S.?" or "Who is the best physician?" Far more worthwhile is the question "Which adviser is the best for what I want to achieve?"

Because different subscribers are striving for different goals through their investing, there is no one single best investment adviser. An excellent options newsletter, for example, is of little use to someone for whom loss of capital is intolerable. Advisory newsletters specialize in various segments of the investment markets, and rarely will you find that the adviser who is best at calling turns in one area is also best in another.

What will this book do for me?

This book will help you formulate the most useful criteria with which to choose among investment strategies, and help you locate those services that best fulfill those criteria. Obviously, while proven performance is the single most important factor to consider when selecting an investment adviser, other considerations must be taken into account as well.

What is your risk threshold, for example? How much of a gambler are you? Do you roll the dice and participate in the office pool, or are you risk averse, unable to sleep nights when an investment moves only a few points against you? Is your worst nightmare receiving a margin call, or are you willing to risk a lot in the hopes of catching a really big winner? No amount of information about performance can decide for you what amount of risk you are willing to incur. That is something you must decide for yourself—taking into account your age, financial status, family situation, sense of security and so forth. Only after answering these questions can you pick a newsletter intelligently; even a well-performing newsletter may be inappropriate for you if it exceeds your risk threshold. A good place to start in your quest would be this *Guide*'s chapters on risk and asset allocation.

Another consideration is the clarity of the advice given. Some newsletter writers (as well as many other purveyors of financial advice, for that matter) are notorious for their ambiguous statements, talking out of both sides of their mouths at once. Some advisers, for example, will discuss in each issue both the bullish and bearish cases for the stock market, and in the next issue quote only that portion that makes them look clairvoyant. Others do not provide consistent follow-up advice on the stocks mentioned in earlier issues, instead mentioning just those that have performed the best in the interim.

The HFD specifically rates the clarity and completeness of the advice contained in each newsletter. For a complete listing of each newsletter's rating, you should turn to the end of the chapter on methodology.

I'm interested only in market timing for my mutual fund switch program, not stock selection. Which newsletters are best for me?

You should focus on the chapter on market timing, as well as on Appendix C, which ranks newsletters on the basis of their timing-only performances.

I once compared the HFD ratings with mutual fund performance and found that there were more high-performing funds than newsletters. Why shouldn't I just invest in mutual funds?

You still would have to decide which mutual funds to invest in, when to invest in them, and when to have your portfolio in money market funds or other cash equivalents. There are many newsletters that you would find beneficial in making those decisions.

In any case, comparisons between newsletters and mutual funds can be misleading. Funds are often parts of "families" of funds (for example, those in the Fidelity or Vanguard groups), and a fairer comparison with newsletters would be with the average of all funds within a family. With so many funds in these mutual fund families, it would be surprising if one or another of each family of funds was *not* at the top of the charts over any given quarter or year. But that doesn't mean the Fidelity or Vanguard groups have any particularly special investment genius. (Indeed, the particular genius of mutual fund families is a marketing rather than an investment genius; since one of their funds always will be at or near the top, their marketing campaigns can be little more than fill-in-the-blank affairs. You don't see Fidelity or Vanguard bragging about the *average* performance of their funds, however.)

Just as mutual fund families should be compared on the basis of some average, so should those newsletters that recommend more than one model portfolio. This is how all newsletters are ranked in the appendices at the end of this *Guide*. (The performance of each of their component portfolios is listed as well, but the HFD doesn't allow a newsletter to be ranked high on the basis of just one of many portfolios.)

Having said this, however, many (if not most) newsletter subscribers would do well to consider mutual funds as the vehicles for their investment strategies. Unless you have substantial amounts to invest in individual stocks, it is very difficult to achieve adequate portfolio diversification while keeping commissions at a tolerably low level. Through purchases of mutual funds, however, you can achieve that diversification for as little as the minimum purchase amount set by the fund.

I've read a lot recently about so-called "Dart Funds"—portfolios whose stocks were picked at random by the throw of a dart against the page of stocks in the newspaper. Some people claim that these funds stand just as much chance of success as newsletters do.

If you really believe this to be the case, then you have bought the wrong book. The premise behind this *Guide* is that you can increase your odds of beating the market by taking an objective, intelligent approach to the markets and to a major source of independent market advice: newsletters. Some newsletters have excellent tracks records, and you stand a better chance of profit by following them than by following those whose record is poorer. (The conditions under which past performance is a good guide to the future are discussed in the chapter "The Power of the Past.")

Ask yourself this question: If you had to choose between two newsletters, one with a consistent record of outperforming the market and one with a dismal performance, which would you choose?

You always say that we should concentrate on the long term. But how long is the long-term?

You should read the chapter on "The Power of the Past." There you'll read about several statistical studies on the length of time over which you must judge performance before it begins to provide a better-than-random guide to the future. Of course, you should always look at as much data as the HFD has for a newsletter. Performance over periods of three years or less, while suggestive, is not a particularly reliable guide to the future.

I recently received lots of direct-mail advertising about a particular newsletter that I don't see covered in this book. Is there something wrong with that newsletter that keeps you from following it?

There are many different reasons that could account for a newsletter's absence from the HFD Performance Ratings, so you can conclude nothing from that absence. Many popular newsletters, for example, do not provide model portfolios or sufficiently clear recommendations for the HFD to construct portfolios for them. So while they may be excellent at what they do provide (be it market commentary, philosophical discussions, political rhetoric or educational articles), the HFD cannot come up with a Performance Rating for them.

Another factor causing a newsletter to be absent from the HFD ratings could be that it is relatively new. The HFD adds newsletters to the list of those it monitors at the beginning of each year, so if a newsletter begins publishing after the beginning of a year, the earliest the HFD could begin following its performance would be the beginning of the following year. This *Guide* includes only those newsletters for which the HFD has at least 18 months' worth of performance data (i.e., those that were added to the list of those being monitored no later than January 1, 1991).

You also should be aware that the HFD insists on following a newsletter's performance in "real time," usually avoiding calculating its track record in past years when the HFD was not receiving the newsletter. The reason for this is that the HFD executes a recommended transaction at prices prevailing after the recommendation was received in the mail (or in trading following a telephone hotline, if the recommendation came via the telephone). To calculate a newsletter's performance for past years, the HFD would have to guess when a recommendation actually would have been received by a subscriber— something it usually is unwilling to attempt.

After all is said and done, however, a newsletter's absence may be due to nothing other than the fact that the HFD has not chosen to add it to the list of those monitored. Unfortunately, the HFD is not large enough to follow every newsletter, and the HFD will not add a new newsletter if it doesn't believe it can preserve its high standards of accuracy.

The HFD chooses among the many newsletters it could add according to the wishes of its subscribers. Other things being equal, the HFD tries to satisfy them first. If you have a particular newsletter you would like to see added, we invite you to let the HFD know (its address is 316 Commerce Street, Alexandria, VA 22314).

More and more newsletters are instituting telephone hotline updates. Should I seek out a newsletter that has a telephone update, or should I avoid them?

The average newsletter with a telephone hotline has performed no better than the average newsletter without one. In one study covering the five and one-half years from the end of 1984 through mid-1990, for example, the HFD found that newsletters with hotlines averaged a return of just over 10% a year. Those without hotlines averaged an annual return of just under 11%. Therefore, you shouldn't necessarily be upset if your newsletter doesn't have a hotline, nor should you automatically seek out one that does have one.

A newsletter's performance seems closely wound up with the personality of its editor. It bothers me to have my portfolio directed by someone I don't even know.

Such a concern is very understandable, but you never should think that you can remove the subjective and psychological component from investing. In the investment newsletter arena, you can respond to this concern by trying to find out as much as you can about the editor(s) of the newsletter(s) you are interested in.

One excellent way in which you can find out more about the editors of the best-performing newsletters is by reading an excellent book about them. It is Peter Brimelow's *The Wall Street Gurus: How You Can Profit from Investment Newsletters*. Brimelow devotes a chapter to each of the editors of the top-performing newsletters, and those chapters give you a wealth of insight that examining data in this *Guide* cannot.

I highly recommend Brimelow's book. (It was first published by Random House in 1986, and a new, updated edition is slated to appear in 1993 (by Dearborn Financial Publishing.)

How should I use the HFD's performance data? Should I switch between newsletters the way some investors switch into and out of mutual funds?

If new evidence develops that suggests your current newsletter is not for you, by all means you should switch to another. But as a general rule you should not switch back and forth between newsletters as cavalierly or as frequently as many mutual fund switchers do between their chosen mutual funds. Once you have chosen a good newsletter—after checking out its long-term track record, examining its risk level and assuring yourself that it is in accord with your own—then you probably should stick with it and give it a chance.

This isn't to say that the newsletter you have chosen will be the perfect one for you (as if any newsletter can fit that description). But the problem with constantly second-guessing your chosen newsletter (or with second-guessing your own investment system, for that matter) is that you most likely will be tempted to second-guess it at the worst possible times. Your emotions can be your own worst enemy in the investment arena, and the goal of a newsletter or investment system should be to impose a discipline that helps you to resist your temptations to second-guess. In other words, if you do switch newsletters, or strategies, do so with extreme care.

TWO

Newsletters and Asset Allocation

Asset Allocation, or Putting First Things First

You should read this chapter before you embark on your quest to find the right newsletter. There are some financial-planning questions you must answer first.

The need to focus first on these prior questions is illustrated by the following example: Consider a newsletter that recommends that you be 100% invested in the stock market. Does the newsletter's editor intend for you to liquidate everything you own—including your house, for example—in order for you to place 100% of all your assets in stocks? Of course not. What the editor means is this: Of those assets you have allocated to follow his advice, invest all of it in the stock market. In other words, you can't begin to make sense of this newsletter's advice until you have made your asset allocation decision.

What Exactly Is "Asset Allocation"?

Asset allocation may be crucial, but there is a lot of confusion about what exactly it entails. Of the three possible determinants of a portfolio's performance, for example, two sometimes are referred to as "asset allocation." To help focus on those questions you must answer first, therefore, a few definitions are in order.

Here are the three different possible determinants of portfolio performance:

INVESTMENT POLICY

This refers to the fundamental characteristics of your portfolio. Is it an all-equity portfolio, for example, or is it divided equally among stocks, bonds and gold? The factors you take into account in answering these questions have a lot to do with a number of financial-planning considerations (such as how risk averse you may be, the time horizon over which you are investing, etc.) and relatively little to do with your beliefs about whether or not stocks and bonds currently are over- or undervalued. "Investment policy" also is known as "passive asset allocation" because your answers to these questions don't change very often or by very much.

Investment *policy* is to be distinguished from investment *strategy*, which is the focus of the other two categories.

MARKET TIMING

This is the active attempt to exploit overall market moves by increasing or decreasing exposure to that market. For example, you may have decided—for a variety of investment *policy* reasons—to divide your IRA or pension plan equally between stocks and bonds. If you furthermore decide that stocks are overvalued right now, and that therefore you should only be 25% in stocks (keeping the other 25% in cash), then you are now engaging in market timing. This category is sometimes referred to as "active asset allocation" to distinguish it from "investment policy" and "passive asset allocation."

SECURITY SELECTION

This is the active attempt to pick securities that will do better than average. If, to refer back to the above example, you now have 25% of your pension plan invested in the stock market, you still must decide which stocks or mutual funds to invest in.

As these definitions make clear, "asset allocation" sometimes refers to "investment policy," and at other times to "market timing." The premise of this chapter can be restated in less confusing language as follows: You should settle upon your "investment policy" before you decide which newsletter to follow.

The Importance of Asset Allocation

The seminal academic work on the relative importance of these three factors was authored by Gary Brinson, L. Randolph Hood and Gilbert Beebower ("The Determinants of Portfolio Performance," in the July–August 1986 issue of *Financial Analysts Journal*). They examined the performance of 91 large pension plans over the period from 1974 to 1983, and developed a methodology to measure the impact of these three factors. Their conclusion: 93.6% of the variance in these pension plans' performances is explained by investment policy (or passive asset allocation). That leaves just 6.4% of the variance to be accounted for by the differing abilities of these pension fund managers to time the markets and pick individual securities.

As can be imagined, this study prompted a number of other academics and market participants to conduct similar studies over different time periods. Each of these additional studies (that I am aware of) reached more or less the same conclusion. In fact, Brinson himself revisited the subject five years later ("The Determinants of Portfolio Performance II: An Update," in the May–June 1991, issue of *Financial Analysts Journal*, co-authored with Brian Singer and Gilbert Beebower). His finding this time: 91.5% of the variance in long-term performances is accounted for by investment policy.

What does this mean? It means that *how* much you invest in the stock market is just as important, if not more so, than *what* you do with the assets allocated to the stock market.

I find that many have a difficult time accepting this conclusion, so I offer the following example to help illustrate its truth. Imagine that beginning in 1960 there are two investors, each one of whom is given $1,000 per year to invest in his retirement plan. Imagine furthermore that both decide to invest it in a stock-market index fund. The only difference between the two of them is that one of them is brilliant (or lucky) enough to pick absolutely the best price each year at which to invest his $1,000, whereas the other is so unlucky that he picks the absolute worst price each year.

How much more will the lucky investor have earned over 30 years than the unlucky one? Not as much as you think. According to Professor Geoffrey Hirt, chairman of DePaul University's finance department and the analyst who did the calculations to answer this question, the lucky investor will have realized an 11.08% compound annual rate of return, whereas the unlucky one will have achieved a 9.40% return. The conclusion readily follows: The most important factor in these investors' long-term performances was their investment *policy* of being fully invested in the stock market—not their differing investment *strategies* along the way.

Another way of stating this conclusion is this: Being an unlucky timer in the right market probably is more profitable than being a brilliant timer in the wrong market. Consider in the above example what would have happened if the brilliant (or lucky) timer in 1960 had chosen to focus on the bond market rather than on stocks. According to Ibbotson Associates of Chicago, long-term government bonds produced a 6.4% compound return over the 30 years through 1990, so even with great timing it's unlikely that the lucky bond-market timer would have done as well as the unlucky stock-market timer.

This discussion isn't to denigrate the role of market-timing newsletters, but instead to place their importance in context. After all, 1.68% per year may not sound like a lot, but it still compounds out to a significant amount: According to Professor Hirt, in the above example the lucky investor's portfolio would have been worth $224,377 at the end of 1990 while the unlucky investor's portfolio would have been worth $178,797.

The bottom line? Since newsletters are designed primarily to assist you with investment *strategy*, don't expect to get guidance from them about investment *policy*. You must decide yourself (perhaps in consultation with a financial professional) what your policy should be—how much you should invest in each market in the first place. And while settling upon your investment policy, don't forget that as much or more is riding on which policy you devise as on which newsletter you eventually choose to follow.

Asset Allocation Newsletters

At this point some of you might be wondering about the many asset allocation newsletters that are now being published. How do they relate to this debate? Aren't they designed to help you with investment policy as well as with strategy?

No. The asset allocation newsletters focus on the second of the two meanings of "asset allocation" defined above: They are active asset allocaters. In essence, they are market timers that focus on more than one market at once. That complicates their task enormously, and it's impressive that some are up to it. But complex as it is, what these asset allocation newsletters do still doesn't substitute for setting investment policy. I repeat: It's up to you to set your investment policy.

Once you have set your investment policy, however, the asset allocation newsletters can prove to be of assistance. Let's say, for example, that you have arrived at an investment policy calling for your portfolio over time to average being 60% invested in stocks and 40% in bonds, and now are looking for a market timer who can fine-tune these default percentages. The argument made by asset allocaters is that it isn't good enough in such a situation to pick two different timers, one who focuses on just the stock market and the other who focuses just on bonds. Instead, they argue, what is needed is a timer who takes both the stock and bond markets into account and assesses the relative attractiveness of each.

An example will show why an asset allocater will reach a different conclusion than market timers who focus on individual markets. Let's assume that instead of following an asset allocation newsletter, we have picked a stock-market timer and a bond-market timer of equal abilities, and that they have assessed each of their market's respective potentials as follows: The stock market's expected return over the next year is 6%, the bond market's 9%, and cash's return is expected to be 3%. The timer focusing on just the stock market may very well recommend being fully invested in the stock market, just as the bond-market timer will recommend being fully invested in bonds—since in both cases their alternative is the 3% return from cash. Yet an asset allocater who focuses on all three alternatives will see at once that bonds' expected return is greater than stocks', thus justifying a portfolio weighted heavier in bonds than in stocks.

How well do the asset allocation newsletters live up to their promise? Some of them do quite well. Since the beginning of 1988 the HFD has tracked the performance of a number of them on a pure-timing basis, and the results are reproduced in Tables 1-A (covering the four and one-half years through mid-1992) and 1-B (covering the two and one-half years through mid-1992). Those tables show that these letters do particularly well on a risk-adjusted basis—that is, when their performance is divided by their riskiness (see the chapter "Newsletters and Risk" for a discussion of the process the HFD uses to adjust performance for risk).

To measure the newsletters' timing, the HFD assumed that whatever was assigned to the stock market was invested in hypothetical shares of the Wilshire 5000 Value-

Weighted Total-Return Index, the bond market portion in the Shearson Lehman Treasury Index, the gold portion in gold bullion, and the cash portion in 90-day T-Bills. The number listed in the right-most column in these tables lists the number of switches generated by each asset allocater; a complete switch from being fully invested into being all in cash is counted as one switch.

As you are interpreting the results, avoid the temptation to judge an asset allocater's record solely by comparing it to the performance of just one of the individual markets. In Table 1-A, for example, you'll notice that on a total-return basis over the four and one-half years through mid-1992, none of the asset allocation newsletters beat a buy-and-hold in

Table 1-A
Asset Allocation Performance 1/1/88 to 6/30/92 (Total Return)

Newsletter	Gain/Loss	Number of Switches
Buy-and-Hold in Stocks (Wilshire 5000 Total Return Index)	+89.0%	
1. F.X.C. Investors Corp.	+59.3%	2.6
2. The Outlook	+59.2%	0.8
3. Donoghue's Moneyletter ("Venturesome" Portfolio)	+58.1%	5.7
Buy-and-Hold in Bonds (Shearson Lehman Treasury Index)	+56.6%	
4. The Peter Dag Investment Letter	+46.9%	4.4
5. The Garside Forecast (Aggressive Fund Switchers)	+46.5%	63.3
6. InvesTech Mutual Fund Advisor	+45.9%	4.0
7. Kinsman's Telephone Growth & Income Service (Mutual Fund Portfolio)	+40.7%	5.1
8. Fund Exchange (Aggressive Balanced Portfolio)	+36.7%	17.1
9. Fund Exchange (Conservative Balanced Portfolio)	+35.7%	16.8
10. Growth Fund Guide	+33.9%	2.6
T-Bill Portfolio	+33.7%	
11. Harry Browne's Special Reports (Permanent Portfolio)	+32.5%	0.0
Stocks/Bonds/Gold Composite (Equally Weighted)	+31.9%	
12. The Garside Forecast (Total Return Fund Switchers)	+26.6%	27.0
Buy-and-Hold in Gold (London's PM Fixing Price)	−29.4%	

stocks. Yet, since the "market" these allocaters were trying to beat is not comprised solely of stocks, it doesn't make sense to compare them to the stock market alone. It would be equally unhelpful to compare the asset allocaters' performance to a buy-and-hold strategy in gold, which it turns out that every one of the asset allocaters beat handily.

Instead, a more useful comparison is with a composite index, which incorporates all three markets that these allocaters are attempting to beat. Such a composite is included in Tables 1-A and 1-B, and you'll notice that the majority of asset allocation newsletters were able to beat it, on both a total-return and risk-adjusted basis.

Table 1-B
Asset Allocation Performance 1/1/88 to 6/30/92 (Risk-Adjusted)

Newsletter	Gain/Loss	Number of Switches
Buy-and-Hold in Bonds (Shearson Lehman Treasury Index)	+0.23%	
1. The Peter Dag Investment Letter	+0.22%	4.4
Buy-and-Hold in Stocks (Wilshire 5000 Total Return Index)	+0.18%	
2. F.X.C. Investors Corp.	+0.17%	2.6
3. The Garside Forecast (Aggressive Fund Switchers)	+0.17%	63.3
4. Donoghue's Moneyletter ("Venturesome" Portfolio)	+0.16%	5.7
5. The Outlook	+0.15%	0.8
6. InvesTech Mutual Fund Advisor	+0.11%	4.0
7. Kinsman's Telephone Growth & Income Service (Mutual Fund Portfolio)	+0.08%	5.1
8. Fund Exchange (Aggressive Balanced Portfolio)	+0.03%	17.1
9. Fund Exchange (Conservative Balanced Portfolio)	+0.03%	16.8
10. Growth Fund Guide	+0.01%	2.6
11. Harry Browne's Special Reports (Permanent Portfolio)	−0.01%	0.0
Stocks/Bonds/Gold Composite (Equally Weighted)	−0.01%	
12. The Garside Forecast (Total Return Fund Switchers)	−0.11%	27.0
Buy-and-Hold in Gold (London's PM Fixing Price)	−0.30%	

Table 2-A
Asset Allocation Performance 1/1/90 to 6/30/92 (Total Return)

Newsletter	Gain/Loss	Number of Switches
1. InvesTech Mutual Fund Advisor	+30.3%	1.8
Buy-and-Hold in Bonds (Shearson Lehman Treasury Index)	+27.9%	
2. F.X.C. Investors Corp.	+25.1%	0.9
Buy-and-Hold in Stocks (Wilshire 5000 Total Return Index)	+24.1%	
3. The Peter Dag Investment Letter	+24.1%	2.9
4. Personal Finance (Growth Portfolio)	+24.1%	1.5
5. Donoghue's Moneyletter ("Conservative" Portfolio)	+23.8%	1.7
6. Donoghue's Moneyletter ("Venturesome" Portfolio)	+23.6%	2.7
7. No-Load Mutual Fund Selections & Timing Newsletter (Asset Allocation Portfolio)	+22.9%	12.5
8. Donoghue's Moneyletter ("Moderate" Portfolio)	+22.6%	2.2
9. The Mutual Fund Letter ("All Weather" Portfolio)	+21.1%	0.7
10. Personal Finance (Income Portfolio)	+18.6%	1.7
11. Fund Exchange (Conservative Balanced Portfolio)	+18.3%	9.5
12. The Outlook	+17.4%	0.4
T-Bill Portfolio	+15.7%	
13. Fund Exchange (Aggressive Balanced Portfolio)	+15.5%	10.2
14. Kinsman's Telephone Growth & Income Service (Mutual Fund Portfolio)	+15.3%	4.4
15. The Timberline Investment Forecast (Aggressive Portfolio)	+15.0%	2.7
16. The Garside Forecast (Aggressive Fund Switchers)	+13.9%	23.4
17. The Timberline Investment Forecast (Average Risk Portfolio)	+13.7%	1.6
18. The Timberline Investment Forecast (Conservative Portfolio)	+13.4%	0.0
19. Harry Browne's Special Reports (Permanent Portfolio)	+13.4%	0.0
Stocks/Bonds/Gold Composite (Equally Weighted)	+12.5%	
20. Growth Fund Guide	+11.9%	1.1
21. The Garside Forecast (Total Return Fund Switchers)	+10.6%	14.2
Buy-and-Hold in Gold (London's PM Fixing Price)	−14.4%	

Newsletter	Gain/Loss	Number of Switches
Buy-and-Hold in Bonds (Shearson Lehman Treasury Index)	+0.29%	
1. The Peter Dag Investment Letter	+0.24%	2.9
2. InvesTech Mutual Fund Advisor	+0.20%	1.8
3. Donoghue's Moneyletter ("Conservative" Portfolio)	+0.17%	1.7
4. F.X.C. Investors Corp.	+0.12%	0.9
5. No-Load Mutual Fund Selections & Timing Newsletter (Asset Allocation Portfolio)	+0.12%	12.5
6. Donoghue's Moneyletter ("Moderate" Portfolio)	+0.10%	2.2
7. Donoghue's Moneyletter ("Venturesome" Portfolio)	+0.10%	2.7
8. The Mutual Fund Letter ("All Weather" Portfolio)	+0.09%	0.7
9. Personal Finance (Growth Portfolio)	+0.08%	1.5
Buy-and-Hold in Stocks (Wilshire 5000 Total Return Index)	+0.07%	
10. Personal Finance (Income Portfolio)	+0.07%	1.7
11. Fund Exchange (Conservative Balanced Portfolio)	+0.06%	9.5
12. The Outlook	+0.03%	0.4
13. Fund Exchange (Aggressive Balanced Portfolio)	0.00%	10.2
14. The Timberline Investment Forecast (Aggressive Portfolio)	−0.01%	2.7
15. The Timberline Investment Forecast (Average Risk Portfolio)	−0.04%	1.6
Stocks/Bonds/Gold Composite (Equally Weighted)	−0.05%	
16. Harry Browne's Special Reports (Permanent Portfolio)	−0.05%	0.0
17. The Timberline Investment Forecast (Conservative Portfolio)	−0.05%	0.0
18. The Garside Forecast (Aggressive Fund Switchers)	−0.06%	23.4
19. Growth Fund Guide	−0.06%	1.1
20. The Garside Forecast (Total Return Fund Switchers)	−0.20%	14.2
Buy-and-Hold in Gold (London's PM Fixing Price)	−0.27%	

THREE

Newsletters and Risk

There are two crucial reasons that you should be concerned about risk—even if you are fortunate enough to have discovered an adviser who has had a good track record up to this point. The first has to do with the length of time you are willing to tie up your assets following a particular strategy. As a general rule, riskier strategies need to be given more time in which to mature; if you may need to draw upon your assets in a few months' time—at which point a risky strategy may be in a "loss" position—you should choose very low-risk investments such as Treasury bills or money market funds. One of the major mistakes investors make is to pick a risky strategy and expect it to be profitable immediately. So even if you couldn't care less about risk for any other reason, you need to be aware of it as you contemplate the time horizon of your investments.

The second reason to be concerned about risk has nothing to do with your own risk preferences or how long you are willing to tie up your assets. It has to do with the likelihood that your chosen adviser will be able to repeat his past performance in the future. As a general rule, of two advisers with the same performance, the one who achieved his performance with lower risk is more likely to be able to do it again.

Investing and Gambling

In exploring both of these reasons to be concerned about risk, there is a fairly close analogy between taking risks through investing and taking risks through gambling. The situation of an investor's choosing among newsletters is much like that of someone who, after walking in on the middle of a poker game, is asked to bet on which of the present players will win. In such a case, would you automatically bet on the player with the largest pile of chips in front of him? Not necessarily. You would ask certain questions about the betting habits of the players. For example, how did the current leader win his chips? Did he win them with one "lucky" bet that overcame round after round of losing bets, or did he rack up his gains with a series of more consistent, though less spectacular, gains?

Unless you enjoy losing sleep at night, the same considerations are relevant to choosing an investment newsletter. Yet, curiously enough, when it comes to choosing an investment strategy, many people lose their well-founded instincts that protect them in gambling situations. Instead of asking which adviser has the most consistent record, too many investors want to know which one has made the most money, period. But such an attitude is tantamount to betting on the player with the highest pile of chips in front of him without any regard to how he won them. You might just as well bet your retirement money on the Irish Sweepstakes.

Measuring Risk

Statisticians have come up with a number of good measures of risk and consistency that allow us to use the insight gained from the poker example. One measure is known as the standard deviation, which measures the volatility of a given data series. This is the measurement the HFD uses to calculate the riskiness of each portfolio.

If a portfolio made 1% each and every month, for example, it would have exhibited no volatility at all. The standard deviation of its monthly gains and losses thus would be zero. In contrast, a portfolio that made 50% one month and then lost 50% another month would be extremely volatile, and would have a commensurately higher standard deviation. The risk rating that appears beside each graph later in the book is based on that portfolio's standard deviation of monthly performance over the 18 months through mid-1992 (normalized so that the Wilshire 5000 equals 100).

The three accompanying graphs show what kind of risk (or volatility or uncertainty) is represented by various levels of standard deviation. The portfolio plotted in the first graph is *Growth Stock Outlook*, the second is of the Wilshire 5000, and the third is *The*

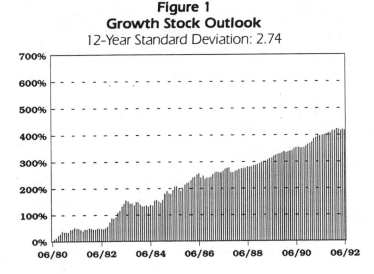

Figure 1
Growth Stock Outlook
12-Year Standard Deviation: 2.74

Figure 2
Wilshire 5000 Total Return Index
12-Year Standard Deviation: 4.71

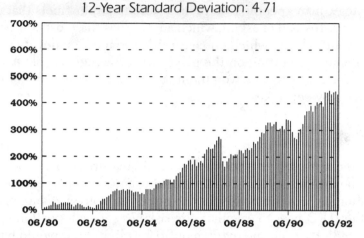

Figure 3
The Prudent Speculator
12-Year Standard Deviation: 11.84

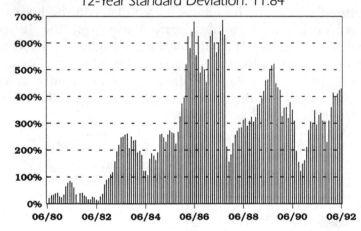

Prudent Speculator. Notice how the gyrations in the graph of *Growth Stock Outlook* are very small (the standard deviation of its monthly changes over the 12 years is 2.74) and those of *The Prudent Speculator* are huge (its standard deviation is 11.84). The Wilshire 5000's fluctuations are somewhere in between (its standard deviation is 4.71).

Are you comfortable with the market's risk? Only you can decide; no amount of performance research can tell you what level of risk you are comfortable with.

A word of warning: Do **not** confuse a newsletter's risk with its risk-adjusted performance (which is defined at greater length below). They are two entirely different things. On the one hand, a newsletter's *risk* is solely a function of its volatility. And, other things being equal, you should choose a newsletter with *lower* risk (unless you enjoy losing sleep). On the other hand, *risk-adjusted performance* refers to the relationship between performance and risk. And you should choose those advisers with the *highest* performance per unit of risk.

Thus, when you review each newsletter's risk level (reported beside each of the graphs that appear later in this book), remember that higher numbers reflect greater volatility and risk—and thus are something to be avoided if at all possible. When you compare newsletters' risk-adjusted performances in the appendices, in contrast, higher numbers reflect greater performance per unit of risk, and therefore are to be sought after.

Risk-Adjusted Performance

What, exactly, is "risk-adjusted performance?" An analogy can be helpful in understanding what it is. Imagine that you are comparing the fuel efficiency of two different automobiles, and that car #1 is able to travel 400 miles on a single tank of gas while car #2 is able to travel just 200 miles. Would you automatically conclude from this that car #1 had twice the fuel efficiency of car #2? Not at all. You first would need to know the capacity of each car's fuel tank. Fuel efficiency is a function not just of a car's range on one tank of gas, but the relationship between that range and the amount of fuel used. What if car #1's tank is three times larger than car #2's, for example? Then car #2 would be the more fuel efficient of the two, despite being able to travel only half as far as car #1 on one tank of gas.

The same goes for investment newsletters, but instead of miles per gallon the relevant basis of comparison is performance per unit of risk. Comparing two newsletters' total return without examining their risk is just as shortsighted as comparing cars' single-tank range without examining the size of their fuel tanks. A newsletter with 100% more risk should, over the long term, make more or less 100% more money. If it doesn't and instead makes, say, only 50% more, then that newsletter is less efficient in exploiting risk—even though it made more money and looks, at first blush, to be the better bet for future performance.

Here is the formula the HFD uses to adjust performance for risk:

$$\frac{(\text{Average Monthly Gain}) - (\text{Average Monthly T-Bill Rate})}{\text{Standard Deviation of Monthly Gains}}$$

For example, imagine a newsletter that made 1.5% per month on average over a period in which 90-day T-Bills averaged 0.5% per month. Assume further that the standard deviation of this newsletter's monthly gains or losses is 4.0. When applied to this newsletter, this formula equals 0.25, which means the newsletter was able to make 0.25% per month per unit of risk. The outcome of similar calculations for each newsletter the HFD follows appears in Appendices A, B and C. (This formula for adjusting performance for risk is known in academic circles as the Sharpe Ratio, after Stanford University's William Sharpe, who won a Nobel Prize for his contribution to finance theory.)

You'll notice from this formula that a newsletter receives credit for its performance only in the event it outperforms the T-Bill rate. There is good reason for this: If a newsletter can't do better than it could have by investing in T-Bills and incurring no risk at all, then it hasn't been compensated for undertaking risk. Its performance per unit of risk therefore is negative. In the risk-adjusted rankings that appear in the appendices, a positive number thus means the newsletter did better than the T-Bill rate, while a negative number means it did not.

Why It Is Important to Adjust Performance for Risk

The primary reason you should pay attention to risk-adjusted performance is that it increases your likelihood of investment success. Of two portfolios that have equal total returns, the one that achieved it with the least risk (or the most consistency) is a better bet for future performance. Why is this so, you may ask? It simply is a matter of probabilities, of playing the odds: The portfolio that has performed more consistently is that much less likely to have achieved its gain by luck alone. It is the same with the poker game: Of two players with the same number of chips, you would bet that the player who has won his chips in a more consistent fashion over many rounds will be the eventual winner; you wouldn't bet on the one who has achieved his winnings with one or two "lucky bets." (See also Chapter Five, "The Power of the Past," for a further discussion of the value of using risk-adjusted performances for choosing newsletters.)

Of course, you may say, in the real world there often are harder choices. Choosing between two advisers whose total returns are identical is easy—you simply take the one whose gain was achieved with lower risk. But what about two advisers with different total returns? It's in answering this question that the formula for risk-adjustment is indispensable: it places newsletters of widely varying performances and widely varying risk levels on one level playing field.

How should you use the risk-adjusted performance rankings in this book's appendices? Start at the top of those rankings, examining each newsletter in turn to see how risky it has been (by looking at the risk level that is reported beside the graph for it in the newsletter write-up section). Continue this process for each newsletter in turn, not stopping until you find the one or more newsletters whose risk levels correspond to your own preferences. In this way you can be assured that the newsletter(s) you come up with will be those that have done the best job of any at your chosen level of risk.

You can also approach this winnowing process in another way. For each newsletter you focus on, your goal should be to find an alternative that has been able either (1) to achieve a higher total return with the same amount of risk, or (2) to produce the same total return with less risk. If you find such an alternative, you should seriously consider shifting your focus to it, since it has been able to produce more return for the same amount of risk, or the same return for less risk. On either count, it is a better bet.

Eventually you will arrive at a group of newsletters for which it is impossible to find alternatives that satisfy either of these two conditions. You'll find that, among this select group, you are unable to find a newsletter with less risk that doesn't also have lesser performance. And conversely, you won't be able to find a newsletter that has a better total return that doesn't also incur more risk. At this point, the HFD can't help you any more. You'll have to decide for yourself where you stand on this trade-off between risk and return.

The goal of this book is to help you to arrive at this point. That is, the HFD's ratings can help make sure that if you are willing to undertake greater risk, then you do so with a newsletter that has good probabilities for greater gains. And in the event that you choose lower risk, those ratings can help you find the adviser who has done the best at that risk level.

FOUR

Newsletters, Market Timing and Taxes

A growing number of investors are interested in advisory newsletters for just one predominant purpose: advice on when to be in and out of the market. Whether they already are in a mutual fund family and simply want to receive advice on timing their switches, or whether they already know the stocks they want to buy when the "market is right," they are not interested in the particular stock or mutual fund recommendations that an adviser might make. Indeed, for all they care, their chosen adviser can be downright awful at picking individual stocks or funds—so long as he correctly advises on when to be in and out of the market.

If so, this chapter is for you. It discusses the search for the best market timers.

The Timing Scoreboard

It is not always obvious from the HFD's Performance Ratings which advisers are the best timers, however. This is not a defect of those ratings, of course, since they were designed to measure the worth of each adviser's total strategy—which in addition to timing advice includes recommendations about individual stocks, bonds, mutual funds, options or commodity futures contracts. It doesn't take much imagination to see how an adviser might be very good at timing the market but because of an ill-chosen individual recommendation end up at the bottom of the Performance Ratings. It would be unfortunate if this poor Performance Rating caused you to ignore this adviser's good timing advice.

For this reason the HFD created a Timing Scoreboard, which extracts the pure-timing component from each adviser's advice and measures just that. The Timing Scoreboard does this by constructing hypothetical portfolios for each adviser that are identical to those advisers' model portfolios—except for one crucial difference. Every time they recommend that their model portfolios purchase or sell individual stocks or mutual funds, their hypothetical "timing-only" portfolios buy or sell "shares" in the Wilshire 5000 (which is the index the HFD uses as a proxy for the stock market as a whole).

Before turning to the results of these calculations, there are several procedural details you need to keep in mind. First, no commissions are charged on any of these switches, on the assumption that the follower of the timing advice would use a no-load mutual fund. (This no-commission policy contrasts with the HFD's procedure for calculating newsletters' overall performances, of course, since in those ratings commissions *are* charged.) Second, the HFD assumed that all switches took place at the closing price on the day a subscriber could act on the advice (since that's when most mutual fund investors would be able to switch).

A third detail you need to keep in mind about the Timing Scoreboard concerns short selling. Since the majority of mutual fund investors can't actually go short the market, how should the Timing Scoreboard measure performance when a market timer recommends a short position? The HFD responded by constructing two different Timing Scoreboard portfolios for those advisers who actually recommended going short. The first of the two would go short in shares of the Wilshire 5000 upon receipt of a sell signal, while the second—mimicking the typical mutual fund investor—would instead go into cash. This is why the Timing Scoreboard contains two ratings for some advisers' timing systems: one that goes short on sell signals and the other that goes into cash on sell signals.

The bottom line: The differences in newsletters' performances in the Timing Scoreboard therefore can be traced to just one thing: Were they in and out of the market at the right times? An adviser who was in the market during rallies and in cash during declines will outperform the timer who missed the rallies and was invested during the declines.

The HFD's Timing Scoreboard is reproduced in Appendix C of this book. In addition to the newsletters' timing-only performances as described above, Appendix C also reports the number of switches that each newsletter's timing system generated during each time period. A switch from 100% invested in the market to 100% in cash is counted as one switch, so a round-trip is counted as two switches.

Appendix C also reports newsletters' timing-only performances on a risk-adjusted basis in addition to total return. The procedure for adjusting performance for risk is the same as is used for newsletters' overall performances, and is described in more detail in Appendix A and in the previous chapter, "Newsletters and Risk." In a nutshell, the risk-adjusted rankings report the ratio of performance above the T-Bill rate on the one hand, to risk on the other.

Gold- and Bond-Market Timing

The above discussion of market timing focused exclusively upon the stock market. But in recent years there has been a growing interest in timing the bond and gold markets as well. To respond to this interest, the HFD expanded its Timing Scoreboard to measure timing in these sectors. Appendix C includes these scoreboards for gold and bond timing, though for fewer time periods than it has for stocks.

The calculation of these gold- and bond-timing performances proceeded in the same way as for the stock market. The sole difference was the proxy used for the "market." With regard to stock-market timing, as mentioned above, the HFD used the Wilshire 5000. For calculations in the Gold Timing Scoreboard, the HFD uses the London P.M. Fixing Price, and for bonds the Shearson Lehman Treasury Index (which is a total-return index, taking into account all U.S. Treasury securities with maturities greater than one year).

Market Timers and Risk

An important pattern that emerges from the Timing Scoreboards in Appendix C is that more timers beat a bear market than a bull market. This is because during a bull market, by definition any time spent out of the market more likely will be a bullish than a bearish period for the market. Odds are, therefore, that such time in cash will cause a strategy to lose ground as compared to a buy-and-hold approach. But just the opposite holds true during a bear market, during which any time spent out of the market is likely to cause a strategy to gain ground vis-à-vis simply buying and holding.

Look, for example, at the proportion of timers beating the stock, bond and gold markets over the five and one-half years through mid-1992 (Appendices C-4, C-8 and C-12). Stocks and bonds both enjoyed strong bull markets over this period, and not surprisingly only a small percentage of them added value to a buy-and-hold (8 out of 46 in the stock market and 0 out of 8 in the bond market). In contrast, the gold market suffered a substantial decline over these five and one-half years, and 12 out of 14 gold timers beat a buy-and-hold. (This isn't to say that the gold timers who "beat the market" made more money than the stock or bond timers who lagged their markets, however.)

This suggests that we need an additional standard to judge timers' performances, especially during bull markets. Timers spend a significant time out of the market and in cash, and their portfolios thus incur substantially less risk than the market as a whole. To expect timers to beat a bull market is thus to hope that they will increase return *while reducing risk*. That's a tall bill to fill. A better (and fairer) measure of a market timer's value is to see if he sacrifices less return than he reduces risk. This additional standard should show that a timer is adding value if he makes 70% as much as the market with just 50% as much risk.

The HFD's risk-adjusted rankings provide this better measurement (see Appendix C). There you'll see that the proportion of timers adding value in the stock market is higher than when measured on the basis of total return. Indeed, it's as high as 40% to 50%.

Should you focus more on timers' total return or their risk-adjusted performances? The answer depends on how risk averse you are and the time horizon for which you are investing. If market volatility doesn't bother you (and it shouldn't if you are investing for the long term), then you should focus on timers' total return. But if you are particularly risk averse or are investing for a short-term time horizon, then you should focus primarily on timers' risk-adjusted performances.

Other Patterns

There are several other patterns in Appendix C that are worth bringing to your attention. One is that a greater proportion of newsletters have beaten the stock market with just their timing than with the totality of their advice. Over the 12 years through mid-1992, for example, 5 of 12 timers beat the market (Appendix C-1), as opposed to 4 of 20 newsletter portfolios (Appendix A-1). Over the nine and one-half years through mid-1992, 6 out of 20 timers beat the market, as compared to just 2 out of 36 newsletters (Appendices C-3 and A-3). This shows how difficult it is to do as well as the market itself when picking and choosing individual securities and paying commissions. There are exceptions, needless to say, but on balance the newsletters would have performed better had they invested in index funds and concentrated on market timing.

Another pattern has to do with the relationship between performance and the frequency of switching. You will notice from the Timing Scoreboards that those strategies that have made the most money over longer periods of time are not necessarily those that called for the greatest number of switches. Take a look at Appendix C-1, for example, which reports stock-market timers' performance over the last 12 years. The average number of switches recommended by the five timers who beat the market over the last 12 years is just under 18, or about one and one-half switches per year. In contrast, the average among those who lagged the market was nearly 27 switches (or more than two per year).

What this suggests is that switching often (though not always) reaches the point of diminishing returns quite quickly. This is an extremely crucial, and somewhat ironical, conclusion. Some investors, for example, conclude that because market timing and mutual fund switching can add value above and beyond a buy-and-hold strategy, lots of switches will add lots of value. The tables in Appendix C show that this often is not the case.

Timing and Taxes

One can't leave this discussion about the frequency of switching without also focusing on the impact such switching has on after-tax returns. This normally would be difficult to do, however, since the HFD's performance calculations do not take taxes into account. In a recent special study, though, the HFD did calculate the after-tax return of various timing systems, and discovered what our intuition probably already knows: On an after-tax basis, it is extremely difficult to beat the market.

The tax rates the HFD used in its study were those that would have applied in each of the years 1987-91 to an investor with $100,000 of gross annual income in constant 1984 dollars. Four exemptions were assumed, along with deductions equal to 15% of income. The HFD furthermore assumed that capital losses could be used to offset other taxable income, so losses were reduced by the amount of such benefit.

The investment vehicle the HFD used in the study was Vanguard's Index 500 Fund, a no-load fund that mimics Standard & Poor's 500 index. Income or capital gains taxes were paid as appropriate on the distributions this fund paid along the way. The HFD assumed that when the timers were out of the market and in cash, they were invested in 90-day T-Bills. Finally, all portfolios were liquidated at the end of 1991 and all taxes were paid.

The results appear in the accompanying table, with the timers ranked from best to worst in terms of after-tax return. In order to show the magnitude of the tax effect, the table also lists how much each of these timing strategies made on a pre-tax basis.

The primary conclusion to emerge from this investigation has to be how difficult it is for a timer in a taxable portfolio to beat buying and holding. Taxes simply are too much of a drag on performance, even for those timers who can add value on a pre-tax basis. Overall, just 3 of 29 timers beat the market on an after-tax basis over this five-year period. For example, look at the pre-tax and after-tax performances of *The Big Picture*'s "Short-Term Trading Guide." On a pre-tax basis it beat a buy-and-hold by 1.4% per year, but after taxes it is 0.2% behind.

These results very strongly suggest that the odds of success in market timing are much better in a tax-free or tax-deferred account.

Table 3
Newsletters' Timing-Only Performances
After-Tax Versus Pre-Tax
(1987 through 1991, annualized)

NEWSLETTER (Timing System)	Pre-Tax	After-Tax
Systems and Forecasts ("Time Trend III")	+19.4%	+13.3%
Investors Intelligence (Switch Fund Portfolio)	+18.4%	+12.5%
Market Logic	+15.5%	+11.2%
Buy-and-Hold	+15.0%	+11.0%
The Big Picture—Short-Term Trading Guide ("SGA")	+16.4%	+10.8%
Mutual Fund Forecaster	+14.4%	+10.6%
Fidelity Monitor (Growth Portfolio)	+14.1%	+10.2%
Telephone Switch Newsletter	+14.3%	+10.1%
Dow Theory Letters	+13.6%	+9.5%
The Marketarian Letter (Mutual Fund Portfolio)	+13.6%	+9.4%
The Value Line Investment Survey	+13.2%	+9.3%
Professional Tape Reader—Short-Term Model	+12.2%	+8.5%
Weber's Fund Advisor	+12.3%	+8.4%
Stockmarket Cycles	+12.4%	+8.3%
Professional Timing Service—"Supply/Demand Formula"	+11.5%	+8.3%
Mutual Fund Strategist—Intermediate Model	+11.8%	+8.3%
The Granville Market Letter	+11.8%	+8.2%
Bob Brinker's Marketimer	+11.7%	+8.1%
The Elliott Wave Theorist—Investors	+11.4%	+8.0%
Fund Exchange	+11.2%	+7.7%
InvesTech Mutual Fund Advisor	+11.3%	+7.6%
Zweig Forecast—Short-Term Trend Indicator	+10.5%	+7.6%
Professional Tape Reader—Long-Term Model	+10.6%	+7.4%
Personal Finance—ST Fund Trading Portfolio	+10.3%	+6.9%
The Garside Forecast ("Stock Bell Ringer")	+10.1%	+6.8%
The Dines Letter—Short-Term Trading Signals	+9.9%	+6.8%
Switch Fund Timing (Mutual Fund Portfolio)	+9.9%	+6.6%
Professional Tape Reader (Fund Timing Advice)	+9.4%	+6.3%
Bob Nurock's Advisory—Technical Market Index	+9.0%	+6.1%
T-Bill Portfolio	+6.8%	+4.6%
Professional Tape Reader—Intermediate Model	+2.2%	+1.4%

FIVE

The Power of the Past

This chapter addresses the $64,000 question: Is all of this worth it? Does it really make a difference if you follow an adviser with a great record rather than a dismal one? If you believe the skeptics, of course, it makes no difference: Since the markets behave randomly, an adviser with a terrible record is just as likely to do well in the future as a top-performing one. Therefore, choosing advisers on the basis of past performance is pointless.

Needless to say, this entire book is based on the conviction that past performance is a good guide to future performance. This chapter shows you that there is strong statistical support for this proposition. It turns out that we don't have to rely on just intuition in believing that past and future performances are correlated.

Not all past performances are equally good guides to the future, however. Indeed, the short-term periods focused on by most investors are of little or no value in choosing an adviser. To this extent, therefore, the random walkers are right: Investors who focus on the short term would do just as well flipping a coin. Thus, past performance is correlated with future performance only if it is interpreted correctly.

Following "Hot Hands"

Few would argue that performance over one day or one week is a meaningless guide to future performance. But what about gains turned in over one month, six months, one year or longer? At what point is there statistical reason to sit up and take notice?

When asked these questions, many investors guess that one year might be long enough. But it isn't. Investors who choose advisers solely on the basis of performance over the previous year would do very poorly.

To measure just how poorly, the HFD constructed a hypothetical portfolio that switched each year into the previous year's best performers. Therefore, on June 30, 1981—when the HFD had completed its first year of monitoring newsletter performance—this portfolio was divided into a number of equally sized segments, each of which began following the advice of one of the newsletters that had beaten the market over the 12 months from mid-1980 through mid-1981. One year later, on June 30, 1982, this portfolio switched again so as to begin following the advice of those letters that had beaten the market over the 12 months through mid-1982. A similar switch occurred on June 30 of every year thereafter. As of mid-1992, when the HFD had 11 years of data for this portfolio, it was ahead a dismal 51.2%.

How bad is this? Contrast it with the performance of another portfolio that is identical in every respect except that instead of investing in the one-year winners it invested in the one-year losers—those that failed to beat the market over the previous 12 months. This "losers" portfolio did more than four times better over this 11-year period, gaining 219.5%!

This doesn't mean you should invest with the losers rather than the winners, however. Over this 11-year period, the market itself gained 307.8%, significantly better than the "losers" portfolio. The correct conclusion is that one-year performances are an unreliable guide to the future.

The same conclusion was reached in a recent study of pension funds ("The Structure and Performance of the Money Management Industry," by Professor Josef Lakonishok of the University of Illinois, Professor Andre Shleifer of Harvard and Professor Robert Vishny of the University of Chicago, in *Brookings Papers on Economic Activity 1992: Microeconomics*). These professors discovered that pension funds that are in the bottom 25% of all funds for performance in Year 1 do significantly better on average in Year 2 than the funds in the top quartile for performance in Year 1. They conclude that if we had to choose a pension fund solely on the basis of performances over the past year, "picking a loser gives a higher subsequent return than picking a winner."

If one year is such an unreliable guide, then why does so much of the financial press focus on one-year performances? Even more amazingly, why do they focus on performances turned in over as short a period as one quarter or one month? Part of the answer lies in financial journalists' constant need to write about something new. If they were to focus only on those who beat the market over the last 10 years, for example, they wouldn't be able to find something new to write about every day or every week or even every month. The list of those advisers who have beaten the market over the last 10 years isn't very long, and the composition of this list doesn't change very frequently. The one thing a journalist knows is that if he focuses on performance over the previous month, quarter or year, he'll always have something to write about.

Your job is to resist the temptation to focus on who is doing well this month or quarter. Such a focus may make for good reading, but it is bad investment policy. If you pick investment letters on the basis of which ones beat the market over the recent past, the only thing you can be guaranteed of is that your subscription bill will go up.

What Is Long Enough?

If one year isn't long enough, what is? To find out, the HFD tested the predictive powers of various lengths of time longer than one year. On the basis of their performances in each of the different time periods being tested, the HFD ranked all newsletters' portfolios from top to bottom, and then checked to see if those rankings were in any way correlated.

A complete positive correlation would exist if each newsletter's rank was the same in both periods. That would mean that the newsletter ranked #1 in the first period would also be the top-ranked newsletter in the second period, and so forth. Such a perfect correlation would be great news for the investor, for it would provide assurance that the newsletter ranked #1 in the first period would be top-ranked in the second.

Though perfect correlations don't exist in the investment world, it should be possible to discover circumstances in which a positive correlation at least partially exists. And it should also be possible to avoid those circumstances in which no correlation exists, or worse yet, circumstances in which the correlation is negative—as we saw above that it is with one-year performances.

The statistical test the HFD used is known as Spearman's rank correlation coefficient. This coefficient ranges between -1.0 and 1.0, depending on whether the rankings in two periods are perfectly negatively or perfectly positively correlated. A 0.0 coefficient means that the two rankings are not correlated at all, either positively or negatively. In addition to testing the correlations that exist between rankings over different lengths of time, the HFD also tested whether the correlations are stronger when performance is adjusted for risk.

The results appear in the accompanying table. The third column reports the correlation coefficient between the rankings of newsletters' total return over the two time periods listed in the first two columns. For example, the ranking of newsletters on the basis of their total returns over the 1980–83 and 1983–86 period had a correlation coefficient of 0.015. Because this is so close to zero, this means that newsletter performance rankings over the 1980–83 period were virtually useless as a predictor of their performance rankings over the 1983–86 period.

The fourth column of the table shows the coefficients when the rankings in both periods are based on risk-adjusted performance. Thus, in contrast to the 0.015 coefficient when the 1980–83 total-return ranking is used to predict the 1983–86 total-return ranking, the risk-adjusted rankings had a coefficient of 0.052. The last column of the table reports the correlation when risk-adjusted performance rankings are used to predict total-return rankings; the correlation coefficient between the 1980–83 versus 1983–86 in this case is 0.075.

Table 4
Correlations Between Past & Future
Coefficient of Correlation Between Newsletter Rankings in First and Second Periods

First Period*	Second Period*	Total Return vs. Total Return	Risk-Adjusted vs. Risk-Adjusted	Risk-Adjusted vs. Total Return
1980–83	1983–86	0.015	0.052	0.075
1983–86	1986–89	0.097	0.101	*0.181*
1986–89	1989–92	0.099	*0.173*	0.075
1980–84	1984–88	*0.228*	*0.304*	*0.249*
1984–88	1988–92	0.102	*0.184*	0.106
1980–86	1986–92	0.180	*0.245*	*0.309*
1984–87	1987–92	0.077	0.129	*0.157*
1982–87	1987–92	*0.317*	*0.373*	*0.495*
1980–87	1987–92	*0.294*	*0.415*	*0.462*

*All periods beginning and ending on June 30.
Figures in *italic* represent a correlation coefficient that is significant at the 90% confidence level. Those also underlined are significant at the 95% confidence level.

What Do These Rank Correlations Mean?

Are these correlation coefficients significant? Figures in the table that are in *italic* represent coefficients that are significant at the 90% confidence level, while those also *underlined* are significant at the 95% confidence level.

A number of fascinating patterns emerge. First, performance is a more reliable guide to the future in the event that it is defined over a longer period of time. For example, in the various pairs of three-year periods that were studied, most of the correlation coefficients are not significantly different than zero. The four-year periods are more significantly correlated, and the two six-year periods more significantly still.

Second, risk-adjusted performance appears to be a better forecaster than total-return. In almost every case, the correlation coefficients in the right-most two columns are higher than those in the "total-return versus total-return" column. This shows why it is so important to judge an adviser's record alongside the risk he has incurred: If you focus on total return alone, you are vulnerable to following an adviser who may have achieved a great performance only by incurring dangerously high levels of risk—and who thus is a poor bet for future performance.

To be sure, few investors care very much whether they beat the market on a risk-adjusted basis; it's beating the market's total return that they care about. They thus aren't interested in predicting a newsletter's risk-adjusted performance; they want to be able to predict a newsletter's total return. This concern is addressed in the third column of the table. It shows that in trying to predict total return, risk-adjusted performance is a better measure than total return. In other words, even if you couldn't care less about risk-adjusted performance for every other reason, you still would benefit from using it to predict future performance.

Other Studies

These results are in line with what others have found in different parts of the advisory industry. One of the first such studies in the mutual fund industry was conducted by William Sharpe (who eventually won a Nobel Prize for his contributions to finance theory). Sharpe examined the correlation coefficient between rankings of mutual funds over the 1944–53 period and 1954–63 period. When these funds' risk-adjusted performances were used to predict subsequent risk-adjusted performances, the correlation coefficient was 0.360—quite similar to the coefficients the HFD found for newsletters. As Sharpe concluded, "These results show that differences in performance can be predicted, although imperfectly" ("Mutual Fund Performance," *Journal of Business*, January 1966, pp. 119–38).

The Lakonishok et al. study (mentioned before) likewise discovered that performance rankings are correlated when measured over periods longer than one year. Because their performance database covered just six years, they were unable to investigate the correlations between two periods longer than three years each. But even at three years they discovered significant positive correlations: "The gain from investing in [the three-year] winners relative to [the three-year] losers is 2.1% per year."

It is interesting that Lakonishok et al. found that three years is enough to provide at least the beginnings of a reliable guide to future performance for pension funds, whereas the HFD's research finds that three years are not enough for the newsletter universe. Nevertheless, both their study and the HFD's show that it is crucial that you focus on longer-term performance, and that one year definitely isn't long enough.

The Crash of 1987

Perhaps the most dramatic way of drawing these lessons comes from a review of newsletters' performances before and after the Crash of 1987. From a timing standpoint, the summer of 1987 would have been one of the worst times in recent history to have been picking a newsletter to follow the next five years. Nevertheless, you would have been able to do very well, thank you, by picking newsletters on the basis of their performances over the longer term.

The bottom three lines in the table tell the story. Picking a newsletter on the basis of performance over the previous three years would have been a poor idea, since the correlations are barely significant (if at all). However, if you nevertheless insisted on picking an adviser on the basis of performance over the previous three years, you would have increased your chances of success if you had focused on risk-adjusted performance rather than total return.

It would have been a far better idea, though, to pick a newsletter on the basis of its performance over the previous five or seven years. And it would have been a better idea still to choose a service on the basis of its risk-adjusted performance over these longer periods.

Conclusion

To be sure, there is still a lot of statistical "noise" in the data, since the correlations—though positive—are not overwhelming. But these results are sufficient reason for you to bear the following two rules in mind:

First, always look at performance over the longest period of time for which data are available. In the appendices that rank newsletters at the end of this book, always start by looking at the rankings covering the longest period of time. Look only at the rankings of shorter-term performance in the event that a rating over a longer period is not available, and keep in mind as you do so that your confidence level needs to fall as you pick an adviser on the basis of shorter-term performance.

Second, pay more attention to risk-adjusted performance than total return. This is easily done in the rankings that appear in this book's appendices, as the risk-adjusted rankings appear directly opposite the total-return rankings. Be especially on your guard for newsletters that perform high on a total-return basis but whose rank on a risk-adjusted basis is much lower.

SIX

Methodology

The following is an explanation of how *The Hulbert Financial Digest* (HFD) calculates Performance Ratings for investment newsletters. Understanding those procedures is an important part of making the most of this *Guide*, and you should take the time to go through the following explanations. Unfortunately, a certain amount of technical detail is unavoidable.

The ratings reflect the gains and losses of hypothetical model portfolios that were set up in accordance with the advice contained in each newsletter. In so doing, the HFD endeavored to be as faithful as possible to what each newsletter was telling its subscribers to do. Because of ambiguities in the investment advice provided by some newsletters, however, it often was difficult to know for sure every last detail of the portfolios the advisers wanted their subscribers to construct. To deal with each case of ambiguity impartially (since the HFD has no stake in one or another letter's doing well), the HFD set down in advance various rules and procedures that would be followed automatically in the event that a newsletter was silent or vague about this or that aspect of constructing a model portfolio. The purpose of this chapter is to acquaint you with those rules.

You should realize, however, that there is no one right way for a subscriber to deal with vague and ambiguous investment advice. One of the inevitable consequences of ambiguity is that different subscribers, each faithfully following such advice, may nevertheless invest their portfolios in quite different ways (with accordingly different results). To the extent that you would have interpreted a newsletter's advice differently than the HFD did, your results would vary from those the HFD publishes. This is not to say that the methodology chosen by the HFD is unfair or unrevealing; on the contrary, it is eminently fair. The point merely is that there is no one correct way to deal with ambiguities, and therefore you shouldn't assume that the HFD's resolution of them is the only way that could be chosen by fair and reasonable people.

The HFD's Rules

Most of the HFD's rules come into play only in the event that a newsletter is silent or vague about a particular portfolio matter. If a newsletter clearly and unambiguously deals with all aspects of translating its advice into a model portfolio, then the HFD follows that advice. As you read what follows, therefore, keep in mind that it applies primarily to newsletters that do **not** recommend specific model portfolios. (You'll find a listing of which newsletters do and don't at the end of this chapter.)

One other warning: The next time an adviser questions the HFD's interpretation of his advice, remember one thing above all else as you read what he has to say: The ambiguity in his advice does not have to exist. If an editor disagrees with the HFD's interpretation of his advice, then all he needs to do is say—clearly and unambiguously in his newsletter—what he wants a subscriber to do.

What are the rules the HFD follows when dealing with ambiguous advice? Basically, the HFD constructs portfolios for non-model-portfolio letters that have the following characteristics, unless the newsletter advises specifically to the contrary:

1. Is fully invested;
2. Employs no margin;
3. Gives equal weight to each position;
4. Includes just those securities most highly recommended at any given time.

If an editor wants to have a certain percentage of his subscribers' portfolios out of the market and in cash, if he wants positions to be purchased on a certain margin, or if he wants unequal allocation of the portfolio among its various components, and so on, then the HFD requires him to say so specifically in his newsletter.

Lies, Damn Lies and Statistics

Implicit in this approach is that the HFD takes a "total portfolio" approach to rating newsletters. In other words, the HFD believes that the best way to measure a newsletter's performance is by trying to decide how much to keep in cash, what weight to give to each position, and so on. To put it another way, it is not enough to say, "The average recommendation of newsletter ABC gained X%." Such a statement does not take into account the fact that a security's weight in a portfolio is a crucial factor affecting performance. How a stock behaves when there are only 10 stocks in the portfolio should have a different impact on a newsletter's track record than how it behaves when there are 100 stocks in a portfolio.

This is a crucial point about how statistics can be misleading, which an example can help illustrate. Let us suppose that a $10,000 portfolio starts out the year divided equally between two investments, each of which loses 10% of its value (or $500 each) before being closed out. The portfolio now is worth $9,000. Suppose next that the portfolio becomes half invested in a stock that gains 10%. Ignoring interest earned on the portion kept in cash, the portfolio now is worth $9,450.

If this portfolio's adviser simply reported the average percentage gain or loss of his recommendations, he would tell you that he lost 3.33% (which is the average of two 10% losses and one 10% gain). But in fact the portfolio is worth just $9,450, which is 5.5% less than its $10,000 starting value. While the discrepancy between 3.3% and 5.5% may not seem huge, imagine the distortions created in a portfolio with many stocks, and with many transactions made over a year's time.

When you total up your gains and losses at the end of the year, it is in terms of your actual portfolio: You have gained or lost a certain number of real dollars. It is only fair that newsletters' portfolios be judged by the same standard.

Rebalancing

Also implicit in the rules listed above is that the hypothetical portfolios set up by the HFD to track non-model-portfolio newsletters undertake transactions that no one subscriber to a newsletter is likely to undertake. To understand the need for these additional transactions, consider a service which recommends purchasing a new stock without also selling a currently held position. Where are you to get the money to buy the new stock? Undoubtedly, each subscriber will deal with this question differently, some selling out this or that security, some selling out partial positions in several securities, and some deploying new amounts of cash not previously invested according to the advice of the newsletter. Taking these various subscriber responses into account, what portfolio weight will the new recommendation have relative to other securities in the portfolio?

The least arbitrary response to this question is to assume that the new recommendation will have the same weight in the portfolio as the other securities in that portfolio (unless the newsletter specifically advises to the contrary). Therefore, after buying the new recommendation, the HFD undertakes a number of rebalancing transactions so that thereafter all securities in the portfolio enjoy equal weight. This means that if a stock has gained enough in value to have greater-than-equal weight, a portion of it is sold to bring it back into line with the others. And if a stock has declined in value so that it has less-than-equal weight, more shares are purchased to bring it back to the same weight as others. (Commissions are **not** charged on rebalancing transactions.)

New versus Old Subscribers

One way of thinking about the HFD's response to the above issue of rebalancing is to take the perspective of a new subscriber to the newsletter in question. Confronted with a list of recommended securities, the new subscriber intent on following the newsletter's advice will divide his assets equally among them—regardless of whether one of those recommendations is a newly rated "buy" that was unaccompanied by a "sell." The portfolio constructed by the HFD for this newsletter, after undertaking the various rebalancing transactions, will look just like the one constructed by the new subscriber. In general, other things being equal, the portfolios constructed by the HFD for non-model-portfolio letters will look like the ones constructed by new subscribers.

The different perspectives of the new and old subscriber also come into focus in the HFD's treatment of "buy"- and "hold"-rated securities. As pointed out in the above listing of the HFD's rules, the HFD constructs portfolios for non-model-portfolio letters out of those securities most highly rated by them. This means that if 50 stocks are on a recommended list, and of them 25 are rated "buy" and 25 are rated "hold," the portfolio the HFD constructs will include just the 25 "buys." And when a stock is downgraded from a "buy" to a "hold," the HFD's hypothetical portfolio will sell that stock. (The only exceptions to this rule come if and when a newsletter specifically says that their stocks rated "hold" are just as highly recommended as their stocks rated "buy," in which case the portfolios the HFD constructs include both the "buys" and the "holds.")

The HFD's orientation toward the new-subscriber perspective helps to explain this treatment of "hold"-rated securities. A new subscriber presumably will buy just those securities rated "buy," while longer-term subscribers may or may not own the securities rated "hold"—depending upon the length of time they have been subscribers and if they were following the newsletter's advice at the time those securities were rated "buy." How long should the HFD carry a "hold"-rated stock in a portfolio that is supposed to be representative of a wide variety of subscribers—three months, six months, one year or longer? Rather than legislate an arbitrary cutoff date for selling "hold"-rated securities that have been held for a certain period without an intervening "buy" recommendation, the HFD instead takes the perspective of the new subscriber and constructs the portfolios out of just the "buy"-rated securities.

To illustrate the pitfalls that would await the HFD if it were not to treat "hold"-rated securities in this way, consider a letter that on January 1, 1980, recommended IBM as a "buy." Assume further that it downgraded IBM to a "hold" on February 1, 1980, and has carried it as a "hold" in every issue up to the present. How many subscribers to that letter would have this stock in their portfolios today? If they faithfully followed the advice in the letter, only those who were subscribers during that one-month period during early 1980. For all other subscribers, the performance of IBM is irrelevant.

In any case, keep in mind that a newsletter's distinction between "buy" and "hold" becomes relevant only when the newsletter does not recommend a specific model portfolio. If it does, as explained above, then the HFD follows that portfolio, ignoring whether or not the newsletter also may rate some of the securities as "holds." So this whole debate over "buy" and "hold" arises only in the event that the newsletter has not been clear and complete in its advice to subscribers.

Replies to the Skeptics

Over the years the HFD has heard a number of objections to its treatment of "hold"-rated securities, and you should be aware of the HFD's replies. In that way you will know how to respond if and when particular newsletters use these objections as a way of dismissing their HFD Performance Ratings.

One criticism of the HFD's treatment of "holds" is, simply, that "hold" means "hold" and not "sell." But the point to bear in mind is that "hold" is a nebulous category, and that there is no way of avoiding treating "hold" as something other than "hold." To say that "hold" means "hold" is to miss the whole point; the point is that the meaning of "hold" itself is not clear.

Consider, for example, the consequences to new subscribers of deciding, in contrast to the HFD, to treat a "hold" as an equally high recommendation as a "buy." It would entail having them buy all of a newsletter's recommendations, the "holds" as well as the "buys." But if "hold" doesn't mean "sell," then why should it mean "buy"? In other words, the ambiguities surrounding "hold" would remain. Is a "hold" a "buy" or a "sell"? It has to be one or the other but can't be both.

Another objection to the HFD's treatment of "holds" is that it causes Performance Ratings for newsletters to be lower than otherwise. Howard Ruff of *The Ruff Times* articulates this objection as follows: "If I recommended Squibb as a buy at 64, and made it a hold at 70 until it reached 90, Hulbert's program would close me out at 70." But Ruff's criticism fails to focus on what the HFD does when, to use his example, Squibb is downgraded to a "hold" and is sold. The proceeds are not stuffed into a mattress, thus preventing Ruff from making more profits. Instead, *the HFD reinvests the proceeds into stocks Ruff is rating more highly at that time.* It is crucial to understand this point. The HFD's approach has the effect of keeping Ruff's portfolio invested in nothing other than the securities he most highly rates at any given time. He should be grateful.

An example from Ruff's own use of "buy" and "hold" illustrates this important point. In November 1988, after several months of highly recommending several Australian investments, Ruff's enthusiasm lessened. Explaining in his newsletter that "the Aussie dollar could slide if the greenback rallies" and conceding that he wasn't "convinced the U.S. dollar bull market is over," Ruff downgraded his recommendation on his Australian investments from "buy" to "hold."

Consider, thus, what happened to Ruff's portfolio when the HFD reoriented it out of these Australian investments into the other securities that Ruff liked better at that time. It was putting Ruff's best foot forward. The *only* way that the HFD's treatment of his portfolio could cause his performance to be worse would be for his Australian investments to perform better while rated "hold" than the securities he rated "buy." But if that is the case, Ruff shouldn't have downgraded them to a "hold" in the first place. The finger of blame should not be pointed at the HFD in such a case; put the finger of responsibility at Ruff himself. It was he, not the HFD, who believed that these Australian investments had less potential and therefore should be downgraded to a "hold."

What is true for Ruff is true for all the non-model-portfolio newsletters. In general, the HFD's approach to "buy" and "hold" would reduce a newsletter's performance only in the event that the newsletter's recommendations performed better while rated "hold" than while rated "buy." But why should that be the case? It is not the HFD, but the newsletters themselves, that have chosen to downgrade stocks to "hold" in the first place. It is their editors who have decided that other stocks, rated "buy," are better bets than those downgraded to "hold." The HFD simply is taking them at their word.

Finally, though, the point that needs to be emphasized is that all Ruff and the other editors of non-model-portfolio newsletters must do if they don't want to be followed in this way is to construct a model portfolio in their newsletters. Nothing is preventing them from doing so.

Further Replies to Skeptics

Another criticism the HFD has received over the years concerns the issue of rebalancing. As discussed above, for non-model-portfolio letters these rebalancing transactions entail selling off marginal portions of a portfolio's better performers and buying additional portions of a portfolio's poorer performers. Most commonly, editors have articulated their objection to this practice by arguing that it violates the cardinal rule to "let your profits run."

Of course, there is another investment cliché that runs "Buy low, sell high"—and is directly contradictory to these editors' cardinal rule. But the point is not which cliché is best; rather the point is that rebalancing is necessitated by ambiguous advice. If the editors want to let their subscribers' profits run, all they have to do is say so.

Consider the case of a newsletter just prior to the October 1987 crash that was recommending that 5% be invested in out-of-the-money put options. During the crash, of course, those puts skyrocketed; by mid-November, in fact, when the next issue of this newsletter appeared, those puts represented nearly 50% of the value of their portfolio. What was a subscriber to do upon reading in that new issue, "Continue to have 5% of your portfolios invested in put options"? Should he sell off the bulk of those put options to bring their percentage weight back down to 5%? Or does the adviser want the subscriber to continue to hold what was originally 5% but is now 50%? A case could be made for either course of action. Ambiguity has struck again.

Some newsletter editors, recognizing this ambiguity, have clarified their advice. They'll tell their subscribers, for example, that their puts, which originally represented 1% of their portfolio, now represent 5% of the portfolio, or whatever. If that is too heavy an investment in those puts, these advisers then would sell off a portion of them.

Similar options for clarifying their advice are open to any adviser, of course. All they must do is say what they mean and not keep the HFD (or their other subscribers) guessing.

Other Rules

In addition to the above rules—which deal with ambiguous advice—there are some which the HFD follows for all letters. For example, the HFD buys and sells recommended securities at their closing prices on the day the newsletter making the recommendation is received by the HFD in the mail. If the recommendation is made on a telephone hotline, then the trade is executed at the average of the security's high and low prices in the day's trading following the hotline update. These rules should ensure that the HFD's figures are based on prices you could have obtained.

Not all the recommendations contained on telephone hotlines are taken into account, however. The HFD follows hotline recommendations only in the event that (1) access to those hotlines is made available to a newsletter's regular subscribers at no additional subscription charge, and (2) the editor does not update the hotline more than once per day per portfolio. This latter condition means that some of the "900"-number hotlines are not called by the HFD, since many are updated three or four times per day.

In addition, the HFD debits a 1% commission on all purchases and sales (2% round-trip) of stocks and bonds, and charges a 0.05% round-trip commission for commodity futures contracts. Loads and redemption fees as set by each mutual fund, if any, also are debited. Dividends and mutual fund distributions are credited on the day the underlying security goes ex-dividend. Taxes are not included in the calculations.

With regard to options, the HFD began in 1990 to charge a 3% commission each way (6% round-trip), in contrast to a 1% commission each way for prior years. The HFD is in the process of recalculating prior years' ratings using the new option commission assumption, but as of press time this recalculation was not yet complete. Therefore, the gains and losses reported in this book assume a 1% commission each way on all option transactions for the years prior to 1990, and 3% thereafter. The HFD is not aware of any instance in which the change from 1% to 3% will significantly affect any newsletter's ranking.

The HFD's Clarity Ratings

Finally, listed below is the HFD's clarity rating for each of the newsletters it monitors, which rating is based on the clarity and completeness of each service's advice. The clarity ratings give you an indication of the extent to which the HFD had to resort to its methodology in resolving the ambiguities contained in the letter. An "A" rating is for the clearest letters, and these are the ones that recommended specific model portfolios, with relatively little or no ambiguity in their advice. Those rated "C"—the lowest rating—

had more ambiguity, and the ratings for those letters to that extent are more tentative. (In looking over the list, you should realize that in rating clarity, there is no completely objective way to determine that one newsletter is clearer than another. Because of this subjective component to rating clarity, you should be aware that they are based in part on the opinions of the HFD's editor.)

Newsletters and Portfolios Rated "A" for Clarity

(These newsletters and portfolios offer their advice in the form of model portfolios, specifically and completely covering all aspects of translating their advice into an actual portfolio.)

The Addison Report
AgBiotech Stock Letter
Better Investing
The Big Picture
The Blue Chip Correlator
Blue Chip Values
Bob Brinker's Marketimer
Bob Nurock's Advisory
The Cabot Market Letter
Cabot's Mutual Fund Navigator
California Technology Stock Letter
The Chartist (Actual Cash Account)
The Chartist Mutual Fund Timer
The Clean Yield
The Contrarian's View
Czeschin's Mutual Fund Outlook & Recommendations
The Dines Letter
Donoghue's Moneyletter
Equity Fund Outlook
Fast Track Funds
Fidelity Insight
Fidelity Monitor
Fund Exchange
Fund Kinetics
Fundline
Futures Hotline Mutual Fund Timer
Global Fund Timer
Graphic Fund Forecaster
Growth Fund Guide ("Model" accounts and "Valueratio" portfolios)
Growth Stock Outlook

Harmonic Research
Harry Browne's Special Reports
The Holt Advisory
Hussman Econometrics
InvesTech Market Analyst
InvesTech Mutual Fund Advisor
The Investor's Guide to Closed-End Funds
Investors Intelligence
Kinsman's Telephone Growth & Income Service
L/G No-Load Fund Analyst
MPT Fund Review
MPT Review
Margo's Market Monitor
Market Logic ("Actual Options" portfolio)
The Marketarian Letter
Medical Technology Stock Letter
Mutual Fund Investing
The Mutual Fund Letter
The Mutual Fund Strategist
Mutual Fund Technical Trader
The Ney Report
The No-Load Fund Investor
No-Load Mutual Fund Selections & Timing Newsletter
No-Load Portfolios
OTC Insight
The Oberweis Report
The Option Advisor
Overpriced Stock Service
The PAD System Report
Personal Finance (mutual fund portfolios)
The Peter Dag Investment Letter
Plain Talk Investor
The Princeton Portfolios
The Professional Tape Reader
Professional Timing Service
The Prudent Speculator
The Ruff Times ("Optimum Switch Hitter" portfolios)
The Scott Letter: Closed-End Fund Report
The Sector Funds Newsletter
Stockmarket Cycles
Strategic Investment (all portfolios other than "Speculative Strategy")
Switch Fund Timing

The Sy Harding Investor Forecasts
Systems and Forecasts
Telephone Switch Newsletter
Timer Digest
The Volume Reversal Survey
The Wall Street Generalist
Weber's Fund Advisor
Your Window Into the Future
The Zweig Forecast

Newsletters and Portfolios Rated "B" for Clarity

(These newsletters offer advice on how to allocate a model portfolio between cash and the market, but give discretion to subscribers in deciding what to buy or sell in order to bring their portfolios into line with that allocation. Usually that discretion comes in the form of a list of acceptable stocks or mutual funds to buy when a position in the market is recommended. The HFD constructs portfolios for such newsletters that have the recommended market allocation and whose market portion is divided equally among those recommended securities.)

Adrian Day's Investment Analyst
BI Research
The Chartist ("Traders' " Portfolio)
Dessauer's Journal
Dow Theory Forecasts
F.X.C. Investors Corp.
The Granville Market Letter
Growth Fund Guide (all portfolios other than "Model" accounts and "Valueratio" portfolios)
Income & Safety
The Insiders
The International Harry Schultz Letter
Investment Horizons
LaLoggia's Special Situations Report
Market Logic (Master [Stock] Portfolio)
Mutual Fund Forecaster
The Outlook
P. Q. Wall Forecast, Inc.
Personal Finance (stock and bond portfolios)
Richard E. Band's Profitable Investing
The Ruff Times ("The Back Page" portfolio)
The Value Line Investment Survey

The Value Line OTC Special Situation Service
The Wall Street Digest
The Wall Street Digest Mutual Fund Advisor

Newsletters and Portfolios Rated "C" for Clarity

(These newsletters typically offer no specific percentage allocation advice on the proper division of a model portfolio between cash and the market, and instead recommend a list of favored investments. The portfolios the HFD constructs for such newsletters are fully invested with no margin, and divided equally among those securities that are most highly recommended at any given time.)

Emerging & Special Situations
Equities Special Situations
Financial World
Ford Investment Review
The Garside Forecast
Individual Investor Special Situations Report
Investment Quality Trends
The Investment Reporter
Morningstar Mutual Funds
New Issues
**NoLoad Fund*X
On Markets
The R.H.M. Survey of Warrants, Options, & Low-Price Stocks
The Turnaround Letter
United & Babson Investment Report
United Mutual Fund Selector
Value Line Convertibles
Zweig Performance Ratings Report

Newsletters Tracked on the Basis of Just Their Timing

(The following newsletters don't make specific portfolio recommendations, and thus only can be followed on the basis of their timing recommendations.)

Crawford Perspectives
Dow Theory Letters
The Elliott Wave Theorist
The Market Mania Newsletter
The Timberline Investment Forecast

SEVEN

Analysis of Each Newsletter's Performance

If the reader has survived to this point, he has narrowed down the list of potential newsletters to a more manageable number. Nevertheless, it is unlikely that the list of potential newsletters has been narrowed down to just one service. What should be the next step?

The next step should be to review the analyses provided for each newsletter on the pages that follow. Each newsletter's strengths and weaknesses are discussed, and you will be able to gain more insight by reading those analyses than you could by seeing a line item in a table or appendix. Each newsletter's analysis is accompanied by a graph of its performance (or its portfolios' performances), comparing it to the market as a whole.

In addition to studying the newsletter write-ups that follow, you also should take out a trial subscription to those newsletters surviving the winnowing process described in the previous sections. Fortunately, as Appendix D shows, most newsletters have fairly inexpensive trial offers. (In fact, the per-issue cost of many newsletters is cheaper during the trial period than it is during a regular subscription. Therefore, most newsletters don't allow you to subscribe more than once to their trial offers.)

What should you be looking for during a trial subscription? A particularly crucial thing to look for is clarity of advice. As suggested in the previous chapter, you should look to see if the newsletter offers specific advice on all elements of constructing a portfolio. Does it tell you how much to keep out of the market in a money market fund, how much to put into their recommended investments, and so forth? Do you find that some of the securities that are recommended in one issue never get mentioned again, or is there complete follow-up advice provided for each stock in each issue—even for those stocks that happen to have gone down in price?

Another characteristic worth examining is the investment philosophy underlying the letter. As discussed in the Introduction, you should approach each letter with the attitude of the skeptic, making each one convince you that it sufficiently increases your odds of beating the market to justify risking your assets. If a letter cannot convince you that it does, then that is a good basis for further narrowing down the list of letters to which you would want to subscribe.

Alongside each of the graphs in the pages that follow you will find a small table which reports the newsletter's performance over various periods. For each of the performances the table reports the quintile of its rank among all newsletters that the HFD followed over this same period. If a portfolio's performance is in the top 20% of all newsletters the HFD was monitoring for that period, then we indicate that it is in the "First quintile;" if it is in the bottom 20%, then we indicate that it is in the "Fifth quintile."

In addition to reporting performance over various periods of time through mid-1992, the tables beside each graph also report the risk level of each letter. This risk measure is based on the standard deviation of the portfolio's monthly performances over the 18 months through mid-1992. It is normalized so that a 100 reading is equal to the Wilshire 5000's volatility over this period. A 50 thus would indicate that the portfolio has been half as volatile, while a 200 would mean it has been twice as volatile.

A Note on the Graphs

In the following section each newsletter's write-up is followed by at least one graph. Each graph shows the performance of one of the newsletter's portfolios together with the performance of the Wilshire 5000's Value-Weighted Total-Return Index. In each graph, the horizontal axis represents time and the vertical axis represents percent change. In order not to distort visually the performance of one newsletter over another (since not all newsletters have been tracked over the same periods of time), all graphs cover the same 12-year period through mid-1992 and the same range of percentage gain (from −100% to +1,200%).

In all cases, the Wilshire 5000 is plotted as the solid, upwardly sloping line, while the vertical bars represent the cumulative percentage gain of the newsletter over the period the HFD has followed it. The appearance of the Wilshire 5000's line is entirely dependent on when the HFD began following the newsletter, however, since the HFD has not followed all newsletters for the entire 12 years covered by each graph. Thus, the Wilshire 5000's line has been shifted upward or downward so that it crosses the 0% line at the point at which the newsletter began to be monitored by the HFD.

One consequence of drawing graphs in this way is that the plots of the performance for unvolatile newsletters cover only a small range of the graph, leaving much of it blank. While some may think this a waste of space, its effect is intended; it is a graphic way of illustrating the difference between a volatile and risky newsletter (whose performance would cover much of the graph) and a conservative newsletter (that leaves much of the graph untouched). The extremes of newsletter performance over the past twelve years range from a nearly 100% loss to a nearly 1,200% gain, which is why each graph covers such a large range.

A Note on the Wilshire 5000

In the write-ups and graphs that follow, you will see frequent mention of how the market behaved during the past 12 years, as measured by the Wilshire 5000 Value-Weighted Total-Return Index. In all cases, the performances referred to include the re-investment of dividends, and were calculated by Wilshire Associates of Santa Monica, California.

How the HFD Calculates Averages

Finally, your attention needs to be drawn to the average performance of those newsletters that recommend more than one portfolio. You should know that there are several different ways in which to calculate these averages, and that the way chosen by the HFD is not the only one.

For multi-portfolio letters, the HFD calculates an average performance for each month. The average performance for January, for example, is an average of that newsletter's portfolios' performances during January, and so on for each month. The average performance for the year is based on each of these average monthly performances.

The HFD could have, but did not, calculate a newsletter's average by waiting until the end of the year and taking an average of the service's individual portfolios' gains or losses for the year. Consider, for example, a newsletter with two portfolios, one of which gained 5% each and every month and another of which lost 3% each and every month. The first portfolio would have a yearly profit of 79.6%, whereas the second would have a loss of 31.6%. A simple average of the two would yield a 24% gain for the newsletter as a whole. The HFD's method, however, would calculate the average by first looking at the newsletter's average performance for each month, which is 1%. A portfolio that gains 1% each month would have a gain of 12.7% for the year. It is this latter figure that the HFD would report for such a newsletter.

One of the virtues of the HFD's procedure for calculating averages is the way it deals with newsletters that, at one time or another, add or delete one or more of their portfolios. (The HFD has to deal with such newsletters carefully, in order to make sure they derive no benefit from deleting those of its portfolios that have performed poorly. Such newsletters' averages must be calculated so that each of their component portfolios is given its proper weight.) If a newsletter has six recommended portfolios in a given month, for example, then the HFD calculates its average performance for that month on the basis of those six. If in a subsequent month it has only two portfolios, that's no problem: Its average performance for that later month will be based on just those two. When it comes time to calculate what that letter's average performance has been, the HFD multiplies together each of those average gains and losses—just as it does with any other multi-portfolio newsletter. In this way, the HFD's procedure gives proper weight to each component portfolio, regardless of whether the individual portfolios have existed for one month or for ten years.

You should keep this in mind when reviewing the appendices at the end of this volume. Sometimes you will see an average performance that seems totally unrelated to the component portfolios' performances listed below it. In such cases, most likely, one or more of the component portfolios that are included in the newsletter's average performance have not been in existence for the entire time period of comparison—and thus are not listed separately below the newsletter average.

The Addison Report

Address
P.O. Box 402
Franklin, MA 02038

Editor
Andrew L. Addison

Phone Number
508-528-8678

Subscription Rates
$ 35.00/3 months
$ 95.00/6 months
$175.00/year

Telephone Hotline
Yes

Money Management
Yes

The Addison Report

P.O. Box 402   Franklin, Massachusetts 02038

Andrew L. Addison, Publisher and Editor. Addison Investment Mgmt. Co.
Registered under the S.E.C. as an Investment Advisor ® Copyright.

QUICK TAKES

written on July 8, 1992   @S&P 410

Following last week's Discount Rate cut, monetary indicators are at their most bullish reading. Technical indicators are negative but beginning to improve, and sentiment indicators are positive. If there are positive divergences at the next market low (ideally below 3250 in the Dow and the 400 area in the S&P), then our indicators would project a rally back to the 3400-3450 area before year-end.

Bonds appear to have made a short-term top in the 103 area this week. After a consolidation, a rally back to the January high in the 104-106 area is possible.

Although its price action remains neutral as long as it remains below 350, bullion should outperform the other precious metals. North American gold stocks remain bullish, and should continue to outperform bullion on the upside.

THE BOND MARKET

Although we were too cautious towards the bond market, a near-term top appears to be forming. First, relative strength and stochastic indicators are at very overbought levels. Second, the September bond contract is back to resistance at its January high in the 103-103.5 area. Third, bonds continue to lag the T-notes to the upside. These indicators suggest that a "time-out" is coming. However, we do not expect September bonds to dip below 100.5 on any reaction.

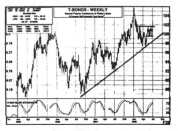

Longer-term, you can see that with last week's powerful price advance following the Fed's cut in the Discount Rate, the futures pushed through resistance in the 101.5 area. Pushing decisively out of a 5-month base between 97.5-101.5 generated upside projections to the 105-106 area. Also, momentum indicators continue to move higher with prices.

Action in the Dow Utilities and Electric Utility stocks is extremely bullish for bonds. With their decisive push through 216, the DJU advanced out of a 3-month base between 209-215. The Dow Utility Average has usually been a good leading indicator for the bond market (and stocks too).

In addition to strength in utilities, other interest-sensitive stocks are also displaying bullish price action. Bank and Insurance stocks are also pushing higher.

Another positive influence for bonds is the action of the CRB Index. An important leading indicator of inflationary sentiment, the CRB Index is resting near its 52-week low. Any decisive break below 204 would be very bearish for inflation and very bullish for bonds.

Sentiment indicators are mixed at best for bonds however. The put/call ratio on the bond futures remains at complacent levels. For the latest 10- and 30-day periods, the ratios are 90% and 97% respectively. Market Vane's tally of bullish sentiment is 50% for the latest week, and 51% on a 4-week basis.

Strategy: Bond investors are fully invested in the 4-year area. With the strong action in interest-sensitive stocks and last week's price breakout,

---

The Addison Report is published every three weeks by Andrew Addison and is supplemented by a telephone hotline that is updated each day. Each issue of his newsletter, as well as his hotline, advises the investor on what should be bought and sold from five separate model portfolios. The five portfolios include

two that focus on individual stocks (his "Speculative" and his "Conservative" portfolios) as well as three mutual fund switching portfolios (one each for the stock, gold and bond markets). Because these three fund portfolios were inaugurated in late 1991, they are not graphed separately in this book; nevertheless, their performance is reflected in what is reported for the newsletter's average.

The HFD has tracked Addison's two stock portfolios since the beginning of 1983. Over the subsequent nine and one-half years, his "Speculative" portfolio gained 174.8% and his "Conservative" portfolio gained 155.8%, in contrast to a 278.6% total return of the Wilshire 5000 index. Because his "Conservative" portfolio is less risky than his "Speculative" portfolio, both have the same performance on a risk-adjusted basis (though about half the market's performance).

The culprit in this underperformance appears to be Addison's stock selection. The HFD calculates that on a timing-only basis, for example, Addison's "Speculative" portfolio more nearly equaled the market's return (gaining 236.7% instead of 174.8%). This shows that Addison's recommended stocks did less well than the Wilshire 5000 during those times his "Speculative" portfolio owned them.

The HFD also has tracked Addison's timing advice for the gold and bond markets. For the three and one-half years through mid-1992, an investor who switched between gold bullion and cash on Addison's signals gained 22.8%, in contrast to a 25.3% gain for T-Bills alone and a 16.3% loss for bullion. A portfolio that over this same period switched between the Shearson Lehman Treasury Index and cash on Addison's bond-timing advice gained 41.6%, in contrast to 46.3% for the Shearson index. Owing to the fact that Addison's bond-timing advice incurred less risk than buying and holding, Addison's bond-timing performance equals the market's on a risk-adjusted basis—putting him in first place over this period among all bond-market timers the HFD followed.

The Addison Report (Average)

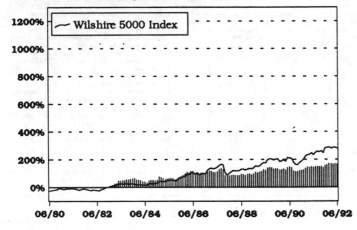

	Gain/Loss
1/1/91 to 6/30/92	+19.6%
(Third Quintile)	
1/1/89 to 6/30/92	+35.9%
(Third Quintile)	
1/1/87 to 6/30/92	+37.0%
(Fourth Quintile)	
1/1/85 to 6/30/92	+74.3%
(Fourth Quintile)	
1/1/83 to 6/30/92	+164.4%
(Second Quintile)	
6/30/80 to 6/30/92	(n/a)

Risk: 67% of market

The Addison Report (Speculative Portfolio)

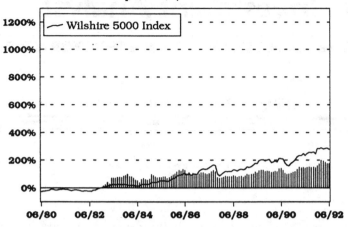

	Gain/Loss
1/1/91 to 6/30/92 (Second Quintile)	+29.7%
1/1/89 to 6/30/92 (Second Quintile)	+48.3%
1/1/87 to 6/30/92 (Fourth Quintile)	+45.3%
1/1/85 to 6/30/92 (Fourth Quintile)	+67.8%
1/1/83 to 6/30/92 (Second Quintile)	+174.8%
6/30/80 to 6/30/92	(n/a)

Risk: 99% of market

The Addison Report (Conservative Portfolio)

	Gain/Loss
1/1/91 to 6/30/92 (Third Quintile)	+16.9%
1/1/89 to 6/30/92 (Third Quintile)	+31.8%
1/1/87 to 6/30/92 (Fourth Quintile)	+36.5%
1/1/85 to 6/30/92 (Fourth Quintile)	+89.9%
1/1/83 to 6/30/92 (Second Quintile)	+155.8%
6/30/80 to 6/30/92	(n/a)

Risk: 74% of market

Chart: Wilshire 5000 Index, 06/80 – 06/92, scale 0% to 1200%.

Adrian Day's Investment Analyst

Address
Agora, Inc.
824 E. Baltimore St.
Baltimore, MD 21202

Editor
Adrian Day

Phone Number
800-433-1528

Subscription Rates
$49.00/year

Telephone Hotline
Yes

Money Management
Yes

Adrian Day's

Investment Analyst

Winning Recommendations for Today's Smart Investor

VOLUME 6, NUMBER 7   JULY 1992

THE YELLOW LIGHT FOR CAUTION IS STILL FLASHING--

EARN DOUBLE DIGIT YIELDS AND WAIT

Stock markets around the world have tumbled from their excessive overvaluations. More lies ahead. I'll tell you how to escape the carange, and what to do now.

Many think the market declines represent an opportunity to jump back in. I don't agree. True, some individual stocks have come back into buying ranges again. Generally, though, it's still a time for caution, and you should be holding money in cash-type and income vehicles. Now, I know that 3.5% interest at the bank is anathema to you (though a positive 3.5% sure looks better than a maybe 25% loss). So we'll look for alternatives. In this issue I'll tell you about:

> *Economy & Markets*

* 17 places you can still earn double-digit yields--or nearly--with minimal risk

* Solid stocks you can now buy again if you missed the first time; and

* Some more profits ripe for taking.

Before we get to that, let's look briefly at recent action in the markets. Stocks around the world have fallen, particularly the ones that were most overvalued: Japan is down 16% in the last month, 30% since the beginning of the year; Mexico is down 22% this month. There was a well-timed "sell" in the last issue. We have largely escaped the carnage. How?

* We hold only a small percentage of our portfolio in equities
* As stocks fell, other things went up, including foreign currencies, gold stocks and income vehicles
* We avoided the most dangerous areas, health stocks, and countries like Japan, Mexico, and Hong Kong
* Finally, our stocks didn't fall much; many went up.

This shows the beauty of our approach of sticking with value and solid diversification. Yes, you may miss a little on the upside, but you don't get hurt on the way down. Recently, I've been advising you to avoid the siren call of Japanese stocks, being recommended by many people. Just because a stock price is down, doesn't mean it represents value! Similarly, in

> **INSIDE:**
> Buy Latin America now?.....2
> Who'll win the election?...3
> The high yield approach....4
> Where to get 20%+ on bonds
>   again............5
> Banks that pay you 10-11%..6
> Two top futures funds open.7
> Some more portfolio sales..8

Adrian Day's Investment Analyst, edited by Adrian Day, is published monthly and supplemented by a Friday-evening telephone hotline update. For several years prior to starting his own publication, Day was co-editor of *Personal Finance* (with Richard Band, who now also has his own publication, *Richard E.*

Band's Profitable Investing, reviewed elsewhere in this book). The HFD began following *Adrian Day's Investment Analyst* at the beginning of 1990.

Day's investment approach is conservative, focusing primarily on the preservation of capital and speculating with relatively small amounts of his portfolio. His newsletter's model portfolio is diversified broadly among markets around the world and among different types of securities—everything from the common stocks of small Canadian gold-mining companies to South African government bonds, from mutual funds to Swiss annuities.

Over the time the HFD has tracked his performance, Day has become increasingly clear and specific about exactly how he would have subscribers allocate their portfolios among these many different investments. In 1990, in contrast, Day relatively rarely provided portfolio allocation advice in his newsletter. This proved to adversely affect his HFD performance rating: The HFD's methodological rules call for keeping portfolios fully invested unless specifically instructed to the contrary, and the investments Day recommended that year fared poorly. Since then, owing both to a more favorable climate for some of Day's recommendations and his clear and specific portfolio allocation advice, his performance has improved—though not

enough by mid-1992 to dig himself out of the hole created by his 1990 losses (see graph).

Another methodological difficulty in following Day's 1990 advice concerned the amount that was to be invested in cash equivalents. On several of the occasions on which he didn't advise the specific percentage he wanted to invest in cash, he nevertheless recommended that most ought to be. The HFD initially followed its then-in-effect policy that words like "most" mean the portfolio should have 50.1% invested in cash, on the theory that "most" means at least more than half. Subsequently, the HFD's advisory board reviewed terms such as "most" and reasoned that because "most" implicitly defines a range between 50% and 100%, the most neutral approach would be to interpret such terms to mean 75%. This policy is now being applied across the board. Upon recalculating Day's 1990 performance, his 1990 loss changed slightly from −27.5% to −26.9%, and it is this latter performance that is reflected in the graph below.

Adrian Day's Investment Analyst

	Gain/Loss
1/1/91 to 6/30/92	+21.3%
(Third Quintile)	
1/1/89 to 6/30/92	(n/a)
1/1/87 to 6/30/92	(n/a)
1/1/85 to 6/30/92	(n/a)
1/1/83 to 6/30/92	(n/a)
6/30/80 to 6/30/92	(n/a)

Risk: 63% of market

AgBiotech Stock Letter

Address
P.O. Box 40460
Berkeley, CA 94704

Editor
Jim McCamant

Phone Number
510-843-1842

Subscription Rates
$165.00/year

Telephone Hotline
No

Money Management
No

AgBiotech Stock Letter

July 1992   ISSUE NO: 48   DJIA: 3318.52

This Issue: Biological Control of Insects

INVESTMENT ENVIRONMENT

June was a difficult month for the stock market. While the correction in the DJIA was a modest one and off the all time highs, the NASDAQ Industrial Index was off sharply, bringing it down more than 20% from its February high. For June the DJIA was down 78 points or 2.3%. The Model Portfolio was down 13%, but remained up 3.0% for the year to date.

Investors are subject to a barrage of information and opinion, making it difficult to separate useful information from the noise. This process can be made easier by recognizing that predictions in some areas can never be much more than guesses. The short-term direction of the stock market clearly falls into the guess category. Like most investors, we find it helps to have a potential scenario for the market, but we react to the market's trend as it develops. So far, we have found no reliable method for making short-term market predictions. In contrast, the longer-term direction of the market is somewhat more predictable, and we often have a pretty clear idea about the course of the economy, which allows us to put the day-to-day economic news in perspective. When other investors get carried away by the short-term fluctuations in the economic news, it can provide investment opportunities.

In the last month we have grown increasingly confident that we are in a sustainable, but very slow, economic recovery. There may be some continued increase in unemployment, and the media is likely to worry about the recovery, but that will be just noise. This slow recovery is desirable for the stock market, because it will allow most corporations to improve profits, but the slow growth will keep inflation and interest rates down. The one danger would be if the Federal Reserve Board should decide to tighten prematurely and interest rates jumped. The recent low inflation numbers make this unlikely. However, none of this prevents a correction in the broad market like the one we have had in the NASDAQ so far this year. Our other concern is Japan, where the market and economy continue to decline. There is a significant danger of a financial panic in Japan, which would be severe enough to hurt financial markets world-wide.

The long-term economic outlook is significantly enhanced by the major move to free markets in the world. Free markets in Latin America have provided a big increase in U.S. exports, and this trend should continue. Soon the changes in Eastern Europe will

AgBiotech Stock Letter is published monthly by Jim McCamant; it is not supplemented with a telephone hotline. McCamant also is editor of the *Medical Technology Stock Letter* (reviewed elsewhere in this book), for which the HFD has a longer track record. The formats of McCamant's two newsletters are similar, and both focus on emerging companies in the genetic engineering/biotechnology arenas; the *AgBiotech Stock Letter* concentrates on those that have an agricultural angle.

Most of the companies that McCamant examines are very young and sometimes don't even have a proven product line. He believes that traditional technical analysis isn't very helpful in assessing such companies' prospects, not only because many possess little trading history but also because their volatility often is so high that any technical trading scheme would lead to frequent and unprofitable in-and-out trading. McCamant is convinced that the key to profiting from these emerging technologies is a willingness to stick with well-situated companies for more than just a month or two.

It's not that McCamant never trades; it's just that he takes a longer perspective than Wall Street's typical short-term horizon. He does engage in some market timing, building up cash if he believes that the biotechnology sector as a whole has become grossly over-valued. But more typically his model portfolio is close to being fully invested and infrequently traded.

The *AgBiotech Stock Letter* gained 103.0% over the two and one-half years through mid-1992, in contrast to a 24.1% total return for the Wilshire 5000. It's difficult to assess how much of this gain reflects McCamant's stock-picking abilities and how much is due to the fact that these months were very attractive for this industry in general. But one clue is provided by the newsletter's performance during 1990, when the Wilshire 5000 declined by 6.2%: Despite having much higher-than-average volatility, McCamant's portfolio dropped by just 3.3%.

AgBiotech Stock Letter

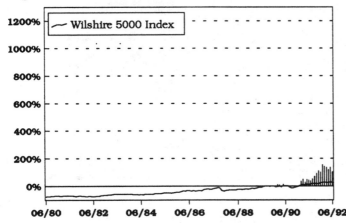

	Gain/Loss
1/1/91 to 6/30/92	+109.8%
(First Quintile)	
1/1/89 to 6/30/92	(n/a)
1/1/87 to 6/30/92	(n/a)
1/1/85 to 6/30/92	(n/a)
1/1/83 to 6/30/92	(n/a)
6/30/80 to 6/30/92	(n/a)

Risk: 316% of market

Address
P.O. Box 133
Redding, CT 06875

Editor
Tom Bishop

Subscription Rates
$80.00/year

Telephone Hotline
No

Money Management
No

BI Research
A Publication of BI Research, Inc.

P.O. Box 133, Redding, CT 06875   July 15, 1992

Vol. 12, No. 6   DJIA = 3331

(RLLY 18 3/4 Ask, OTC)

Year Ending-	6/88	6/89	12/90	12/91	12/92E
Revenues ($ millions)	19.7	33.4	81.6	94.1	127
Net Income ($ millions)	(.4)	2.2	5.0	6.1	8.5
Earnings Per Share	(.11)	.52	.70	.82	1.07
Avg. Shares (millions)		4.2	7.1	7.4	8.0

The fast food market was created about thirty years ago with
quick, simple, good food available on the go. By 1991 the fast food
market has grown to $78 BILLION. But in the rush to claim a share
of this rapidly growing market, many companies lost sight of the
original premise. "Fast" became "kindly step aside, your order will
be ready shortly." "Basic" became fajitas, pasta bars, and
croissants. And "quality" became questionable and inconsistent.
Our latest recommendation, "Rally's," is a drive-thru fast service
hamburger chain, that has reclaimed the market which is the very
roots of the fast food industry- truly fast service, accuracy in
filling orders, real value, all with quality products. Quick
service restaurants have emerged as the fastest growing segment of
the restaurant industry, representing 93% of the industry's traffic
growth in 1991. By capitalizing on that market Rally's has been the
fastest growing restaurant chain in America over the past two
years. In addition, it ranks amongst BusinessWeek's top 50 "Best
Small Growth Companies" (5/25/92) with three year average growth in
sales and profits and average return on equity of 73.9%, 98.4% and
16.7%. The BI RANK for Rally's is a solid 8.6 (where over 7 is buy
territory and over 10.0 is superb, but rare). Incidentally, this is
the one that got away from us for the last issue, but our patience
has been rewarded with a price $4 a share lower this time around!

The Company
Rally's is the industry's largest chain of double drive-thru
hamburger restaurants. It opened its first restaurant in 1985 and
as of 12/31/91 the Company operated 116 company owned stores and
franchised 217 stores in 60 markets in 22 states. Its 30% growth
target calls for it to open 35 more owned and 60 more franchised
stores this year. The Rally's concept combines drive-thru and
outside walk-up service with off-premise consumption of food and a

BI Research is published episodically, more or less once every five or six weeks, by Tom Bishop. There is no telephone hotline, though on occasion Bishop will send one-page "Flash Updates" between regular issues.

Bishop's approach is entirely fundamental. Each issue of his newsletter examines a new special situation in depth, usually involving two to three pages of analysis. The stocks tend to be from relatively unknown companies, and only rarely do they trade on a major exchange. The majority trade over-the-counter, while a handful have traded on the Vancouver Stock Exchange. Bishop's approach is to buy and hold these undervalued issues, not to trade them short-term.

In addition to the featured stock in each issue, Bishop offers follow-up analysis and buy-hold-sell advice on previous recommendations that are still open. There is no model portfolio as such, however. In accordance with its established methodology on such matters, therefore, the HFD constructs a portfolio for *BI Research* that includes just those stocks rated "buy." This "buy" list typically contains four to six stocks.

Up until mid-1987, furthermore, Bishop did not provide specific advice on the allocation of a portfolio between stocks and cash, and the HFD's portfolio for him therefore was fully invested. Beginning in 1987, however, Bishop did start recommending a specific per-

centage cash position, which was duly reflected in the portfolio the HFD set up to track its performance.

A portfolio substantially invested in a small number of stocks is relatively risky anyway, and Bishop's stock picks tend to be risky in the first place. Despite its risk, however, *BI Research* has been able to avoid any major stumble since the HFD began rating it in the beginning of 1984. Over the seven and one-half years through mid-1992, in fact, it was in second place among all the letters the HFD followed, gaining 497.5%, in contrast to the Wilshire's 197.6%. This is high enough that, even after taking into account the fact that it incurred about twice as much risk as the market, it beat the market on a risk-adjusted basis.

BI Research

	Gain/Loss
1/1/91 to 6/30/92	+135.5%
(First Quintile)	
1/1/89 to 6/30/92	+205.5%
(First Quintile)	
1/1/87 to 6/30/92	+302.0%
(First Quintile)	
1/1/85 to 6/30/92	+497.5%
(First Quintile)	
1/1/83 to 6/30/92	(n/a)
6/30/80 to 6/30/92	(n/a)

Risk: 184% of market

Better Investing

Address
National Association
of Investors
Corporation
1515 E. Eleven Mile
Rd.
Royal Oak, MI 48067

Editor
Donald Danko

Phone Number
313-543-0612

Subscription Rates
$ 2.00/1 issue
$17.00/year

Telephone Hotline
No

Money Management
No

Better Investing is edited by Donald Danko and published monthly by the National Association of Investors Corporation (NAIC), which is the parent organization of Investment Clubs of America. The NAIC has been in existence since 1951.

Their model portfolio, which is what the HFD tracks, is only one of many benefits that their subscribers receive from the magazine. The model portfolio is updated only once every three months, for example, and that update requires only one page in the 30-to-40 page magazine. The bulk of each magazine is devoted to general investment advice and information on specific stocks.

NAIC takes a long-term, value oriented approach to investing, in which technical analysis plays no role. Since the portfolio is updated just once every third issue, transactions in it occur no more often than once every three months, and sometimes less often than that. The model portfolio always contains 12 stocks and is fully invested. The typical holding period for a recommended stock is several years.

The HFD began following this model portfolio at the beginning of 1987, and over the five and one-half years through mid-1992 it gained 67.7%. This contrasts with a 93.3% gain for the Wilshire 5000. Because *Better*

Investing's model portfolio had above-average risk, it underperformed the market on a risk-adjusted basis as well.

The individual investment clubs that are members of NAIC appear to have a better record, at least over the long term. Under NAIC's tutelage, clubs are encouraged to focus on selecting individual stocks (usually "growth" stocks) to buy and hold for the long term. According to a 1991 NAIC survey of its 7,500 member chapters (which I have no reason to disbelieve), an impressive 61.9% of them bettered the S&P 500's total return over their lifetimes (which averaged about ten years). In contrast, only about a fifth of equity mutual funds beat the S&P 500 during the decade of the 1980s.

Better Investing

	Gain/Loss
1/1/91 to 6/30/92 (Third Quintile)	+26.1%
1/1/89 to 6/30/92 (Second Quintile)	+44.2%
1/1/87 to 6/30/92 (Second Quintile)	+67.7%
1/1/85 to 6/30/92	(n/a)
1/1/83 to 6/30/92	(n/a)
6/30/80 to 6/30/92	(n/a)

Risk: 128% of market

The Big Picture

Address
KCI Communications, Inc.
1101 King St.
Suite 400
Alexandria, VA
22314-2980

Editors
Stephen Leeb and
Walter Pierce

Phone Number
703-548-2400

Subscription Rates
$127.00/year

Telephone Hotline
Yes

Money Management
Yes

THE BIG PICTURE

VOLUME 31, ISSUE NO. 7 • JULY 1992   STEPHEN LEEB, EDITOR

TRADING STRATEGIES

The market's recent decline gave us a healthy profit in our short position in September S&P 500 futures. We closed out that position on a special hotline update on June 18. With stocks in oversold territory, a reflexive rally is now likely.

Our Master Key for Blue Chips is only marginally negative. Coupled with the possibility of another cut in interest rates by the Federal Reserve, standing on the sidelines is the most prudent course of action now.

STOCK TRADING PORTFOLIO
MASTER KEY: -0.87%

Position	Recomm. Price	Recent Price	Weighting
Cash	—	—	100%

BOND TRADING PORTFOLIO
MASTER KEY: -1.30%

Position	Recomm. Price	Recent Price	Weighting
Cash	—	—	100%

INSIDE THIS ISSUE

JUNKYARD GEMS	2
INDICATOR DIGEST	4
MODEL PORTFOLIO	6
HOT CORNER	7
SHORT REPORT	7
INSIDE VIEW	8

HOTLINE: 703-549-2793

SAME AS IT EVER WAS

As we predicted, the economy continues to improve steadily. But this growth, whether it's rapid or tepid, will be bearish for stocks. We're maintaining our cautious intermediate-term stance, but in the long term, especially for small stocks, we remain bullish.

Regardless of the numbers you choose to plug into your models—GDP, industrial commodity prices, employment data, personal income, auto sales—the economy has been, and remains, on an upward path.

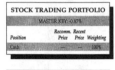

Faster growth will lead to higher inflation, causing stocks to plunge

Yet faster growth will lead to higher inflation, causing stocks to plunge. Lukewarm growth will lead to disappointing earnings and lower stock prices.

When price-to-earnings ratios (P/Es) are as high as they are today, the intermediate-term risk/reward equation turns against the bulls. But even if P/Es weren't so high, it would be hard to be bullish at this stage of the economic cycle.

Reviewing the economic data, it's evident that the recession ended sometime in the summer of 1991. That means we're about 10 months into the recovery. And this recovery jibes with the seven other recoveries we've had since 1955.

For example, let's look at two representative economic variables, capacity utilization and unemployment insurance claims.

As you can see from the first two columns of our table on the next page, 10 months into this recovery we're about where we were in past recoveries at the 10-month mark.

The same holds true for the Consumer Price Index. This broad-based measure of inflation is typically 3.5 percent at this point in the recovery. Today, the figure is 3 percent. In fact, you'd be hard pressed to find any key statistic of general economic activity that's markedly different this time around.

You could argue that broad-based M2 money supply growth is much slower this time around. But as our table shows, M1 money growth is much faster. No matter how you slice it, there just aren't any substantive differences between this and the other recoveries.

Don't believe press reports that assert this recovery is different—it's standard fare. All recoveries are marked by the same misperception.

Historical Perspective

What does an average recovery imply for stocks? As you can see from our table on the next page, in the 12 months following this point in the recovery, the market, as measured by the Stan-

At least six persons who now publish their own investment newsletters have formerly worked at *The Big Picture* (which used to be called *Indicator Digest*). In the fall of 1987, *Investment Strategist* was merged into *The Big Picture*, and its editor, Stephen Leeb, became the new editor. (Prior to Leeb, the newsletter's editor was Robert Cardwell.) Since then, Leeb also has become editor of *Personal Finance*, reviewed elsewhere in this *Guide*.

The Big Picture offers advice in several different categories. The service has two model portfolios, for example, one for traders and the other for investors. Both used to be just stock portfolios, but Leeb recently has begun to manage his "Trading" portfolio in an increasingly aggressive way, and today it trades only in stock index and bond futures. His "Model" portfolio continues to focus on individual stocks, however, and pursues a longer-term strategy.

The Big Picture also offers timing advice in the stock and bond markets. The timing system the HFD has been tracking the longest is a proprietary stock-market-timing indicator entitled the "Short-Term Trading Guide" (or SGA for short). This is a short-term model that is fairly active, generating about eight switches per year on average. The HFD also has data for a second timing model entitled the "Master Key" (which the newsletter used to call the "Master Technical Composite"); the model is used to generate signals for both the stock and the bond markets.

Overall, the HFD reports a mixed record for *The Big Picture*, with some parts beating the market and others lagging. From the beginning of 1983 through mid-1992, for example, the newsletter's "Model" and "Trading" portfolios gained an average of 102.8%, in contrast to 278.6% for the Wilshire 5000. The "SGA" timing model has a better record: A portfolio that switched between hypothetical shares of the Wilshire 5000 and T-Bills on SGA's signals almost equaled the market's return from the beginning of 1983 through mid-1992 (234.6% versus 278.6%). Since this hypothetical switching portfolio had less risk than buying and holding, however, it is ahead of the market on a risk-adjusted basis.

The HFD has less data for the "Master Key," but its record also is mixed. In the stock market it beat buying and holding from the beginning of 1989 through mid-1992, 65.8% to 60.3%. In the bond market, however, the "Master Key" lagged the Shearson Lehman Treasury Index, 16.2% versus 46.3%. (This bond-timing record takes into account timing signals issued by the newsletter prior to the formal creation of the "Master Key" for bonds, so it may not reflect how this model would have performed had it been in existence for the entire three and one-half years.)

The Big Picture (Average)

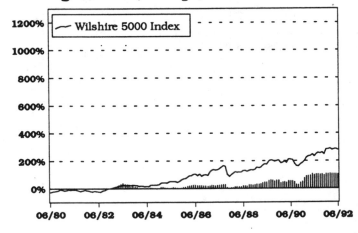

	Gain/Loss
1/1/91 to 6/30/92 (Second Quintile)	+36.8%
1/1/89 to 6/30/92 (Second Quintile)	+63.0%
1/1/87 to 6/30/92 (Second Quintile)	+76.6%
1/1/85 to 6/30/92 (Third Quintile)	+102.3%
1/1/83 to 6/30/92 (Third Quintile)	+102.8%
6/30/80 to 6/30/92	(n/a)

Risk: 122% of market

The Big Picture (Trading Portfolio)

	Gain/Loss
1/1/91 to 6/30/92 (First Quintile)	+51.4%
1/1/89 to 6/30/92 (First Quintile)	+93.9%
1/1/87 to 6/30/92 (First Quintile)	+110.5%
1/1/85 to 6/30/92 (Third Quintile)	+123.2%
1/1/83 to 6/30/92 (Third Quintile)	+123.9%
6/30/80 to 6/30/92	(n/a)

Risk: 187% of market

The Big Picture (Model Portfolio)

	Gain/Loss
1/1/91 to 6/30/92 (Third Quintile)	+22.1%
1/1/89 to 6/30/92 (Third Quintile)	+33.4%
1/1/87 to 6/30/92 (Fourth Quintile)	+42.8%
1/1/85 to 6/30/92	(n/a)
1/1/83 to 6/30/92	(n/a)
6/30/80 to 6/30/92	(n/a)

Risk: 78% of market

The Blue Chip Correlator

Address
P.O. Box 3576
Newport Beach, CA
92659

Editor
Steven G. Check

Phone Number
714-641-3579

Subscription Rates
$179.00/year

Telephone Hotline
Yes

Money Management
Yes

The BLUE CHIP CORRELATOR

Steven G. Check
(714) 641-3579

July 6, 1992

Check Capital Mgmt, Inc.
Vol. 6, No. 303 ©1992

Since our last issue, the Dow Jones Industrial Average has begun to give up some of its leadership role. For the month the Dow was down approximately 67 points, closing Thursday at 3330. The economic recovery so widely believed to be in place became suspect when it was announced that the June unemployment rate rose to 7.8%, its highest point since 1984. The Federal Reserve responded immediately by cutting the discount rate a half-point to 3%, its lowest level in 29 years!

Generally, when interest rates are cut, the Dow Jones Industrial Average soars. That was not the case this time. The Dow, which is heavily laden with cyclical stocks, pulled back on fears that earnings improvements may be below expectations in a subdued economic recovery. Money appears to be coming out of cyclical stocks and moving back into the more defensive long-term growth stocks that we concentrate on. For the month, as the Dow dropped approximately 2%, *The Blue Chip Correlator's* account rose slightly.

As promised in the last issue, on page 4 you will find the Blue Chip Value Index (BCVI) plotted *weekly* since the inception of *The Blue Chip Correlator*, September 14, 1986. I feel this is the most important graph that we have ever shown in the newsletter. The graph ties together stock valuations and interest rates, showing the undervalued and overvalued points in the stock market. I have seen graphs similar to this before, but never using a group of stocks like the ones that make up the Check 100. Usually the Dow or the S&P 500 is used. Unfortunately though, the earnings of the companies that make up the Dow or the S&P 500 are very volatile during recessions; and, consequently, their P/E's, and the graphs using the P/E's, become relatively meaningless. If, instead, an index of companies with stable earnings is used, such as the Check 100, the P/E's become meaningful and useful information can be extracted.

The BCVI graph clearly shows how overvalued the stock market became in 1987, prior to the crash. In an extremely dramatic manner, the stock market corrected its excesses in a period of one short month in October, 1987. After the crash, when investors were quite worried, the BCVI was stating to be fully invested. Subsequently, we had a strong bull market with the Dow rising from 1740 to 3000 in 1990.

The Persian Gulf conflict became the catalyst for another market decline. After the decline, the BCVI once again stated to become fully invested. The ensuing strong rally allowed us to profit handsomely. With the BCVI at its current value of 2.9, it is relatively close to its undervalued point. Consequently, we are bullish on the stock market and recommend a 90% invested position!

Dow Jones Data:

Recent Close: **3330**
Projected Low: **3220**
Projected High: **3770**

3 Month T-Bill: **3.29%**
30 Year T-Bond: **7.62%**

Market Position: **Bullish**
Since: **12/13/91**

Dow Jones Industrials

Past performance does not guarantee future results.

The Blue Chip Correlator is published monthly by Steven Check and is supplemented by a weekly telephone hotline update. Check bases his letter on the belief that "conservative growth stocks are the best investment for most investors," since hopefully they will provide "both safety as well as excellent return."

Check defines his universe of blue-chip stocks to be those of companies rated "A-" or better by Standard & Poor's, with earnings that have grown in at least 10 of the last 12 years, annual sales in excess of $1 billion, a high degree of institutional ownership, and a fairly valued price/earnings ratio (based, Check says, on current interest rates and the company's growth prospects). We would expect a portfolio based on such stocks to have below-average risk, and Check's does (about 22% less, in fact); but the riskiness of Check's portfolio is made even lower by the fact that he rarely has his portfolio fully invested.

The HFD began following *The Blue Chip Correlator* at the beginning of 1991, and over the 18 months through 1992 Check's model portfolio gained 14.4%. This contrasts to a 32.3% total return for the Wilshire 5000. The portfolio's below-average risk accounts for some of this underperformance, but not all of it: Even when adjusted for risk, the portfolio underperformed the market over this period.

The Blue Chip Correlator

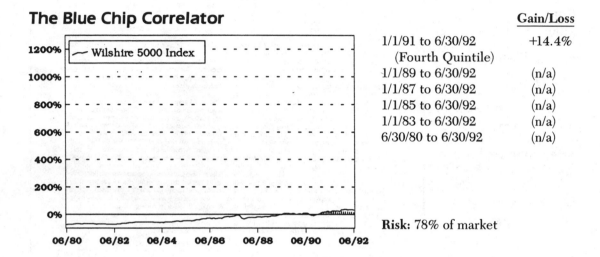

	Gain/Loss
1/1/91 to 6/30/92	+14.4%
(Fourth Quintile)	
1/1/89 to 6/30/92	(n/a)
1/1/87 to 6/30/92	(n/a)
1/1/85 to 6/30/92	(n/a)
1/1/83 to 6/30/92	(n/a)
6/30/80 to 6/30/92	(n/a)

Risk: 78% of market

Blue Chip Values

Address
680 N. Lake
 Shore Dr.
Tower Suite 2038
Chicago, IL 60611

Editor
Gerald Perritt

Phone Number
312-649-6940

Subscription Rates
$195.00/year

Telephone Hotline
No

Money Management
No

July 17, 1992   Volume 5, Number 9

Income Alternatives

In an effort to entice consumers to start spending, the Federal Reserve lowered interest rates once again. Last month, the Federal Reserve lowered its discount rate (the rate it charges member banks for loans) from 3.5 percent to 3.0 percent. Banks responded by lowering their prime interest rate (the interest rate charged to their best customers) from 6.5 percent to 6.0 percent. Bond traders in the secondary market rallied, which, in turn, has caused yields to decline. Overall, you can borrow money at cheaper rates.

For investors who use the interest on short-term instruments as their primary source of income, falling interest rates coupled with ongoing increases in consumer prices add up to disaster. Consider, for example, an individual who invested in money market instruments five years ago. Five years ago that individual was probably receiving $800 in annual interest for each $10,000 invested. Since then, consumer prices have expanded at a 4.5 percent annual rate. In other words, it now costs $125 to buy a market basket of goods that would have cost $100 five years ago. Today, an investor would receive less than $400 in annual interest for each $10,000 invested. Thus, investment income has declined by more than 50 percent while costs increased by 25 percent. That adds up to a 75 percent decrease in purchasing power. No wonder some so-called fixed-income investors are on the verge of panic.

What's the average income investor to do? First, here's what *not* to do: Don't Panic! Don't fall for some salesman's pitch that will lock you into high-risk investments. Don't invest in long-term bonds just because they are paying a higher yield than money market instruments. Don't invest that cash in highly touted junk bonds. Educated investors will calculate their time horizon for all funds and then reinvest their funds appropriately.

If your funds have a time horizon fewer than three years, consider investing in ARM mutual funds. Adjustable rate mortgage funds (ARMs) invest in renegotiable rate mortgages that are insured by an agency of the U.S. Government. Their portfolios have an average maturity of three years or less and you can cash out at any time without a penalty. We have listed two funds below that are excellent candidates.

Fund	Average Maturity	Yield	Phone
Benham Adj. Rate Mortgage	1.2 yrs.	6.0%	(800)321-8521
T. Rowe Price ARM Fund	0.9	6.5	(800)638-5660

If your funds have a time horizon of more than three years, consider assembling a portfolio of utility stocks. The average utility issue is paying more than 6.0% in dividend income and offers the opportunity for capital ap-

("Utility" continued on page 3)

Blue Chip Values (ISSN 1041-441X) is published 17 times a year by Investment Information Services, 680 N. Lake Shore Dr., 2038 Tower Offices, Chicago, IL 60611, publisher of *Investment Horizons* and *The Mutual Fund Letter* and the investment advisor of the Perritt Capital Growth Fund. The firm also manages investment portfolios for pension funds and individuals. ©Copyright 1992 by Investment Information Services. All rights reserved. The information has been obtained from sources believed to be reliable, but its accuracy cannot be guaranteed. Readers should not assume that recommendations made in the future will be profitable or equal past performance. Dr. Gerald Perritt, Editor. Annual subscription $195.

After this book entered into production, Gerald Perritt announced that he soon would stop publishing *Blue Chip Values*. Nevertheless, owing to the fact that he will continue to publish two other newsletters—*Investment Horizons* and *The Mutual Fund Letter*, reviewed elsewhere in this book—the performance of *Blue Chip Values* is relevant to the investor who is deciding which adviser to follow.

Perritt's approach in his several newsletters is similar. He is a long-term investor, and the positions in his model portfolios are held for longer periods than the positions in most other newsletters. He is a fundamentalist and most definitely is not a technician. The difference between his three services lies in the investments on which they focus. In contrast to *Blue Chip Values*, Perritt's mutual fund newsletter focuses on mutual funds, and *Investment Horizons* focuses on small, secondary stocks that are neglected by major institutions and brokerage research departments.

The HFD has been tracking *Blue Chip Values*'s two model portfolios since the beginning of 1989. Over the next three and one-half years, the Wilshire 5000's total return was a gain of 60.3%. In contrast, this newsletter's "Income & Growth" portfolio gained 59.5% and its "Growth" portfolio gained 58.3%. However, owing to the fact that both of these portfolios were substantially less risky than the market as a whole, this performance is quite impressive. Indeed, on a risk-adjusted basis this newsletter is well ahead of the market and is in second place over these three and one-half years among all letters the HFD followed.

Blue Chip Values (Average)

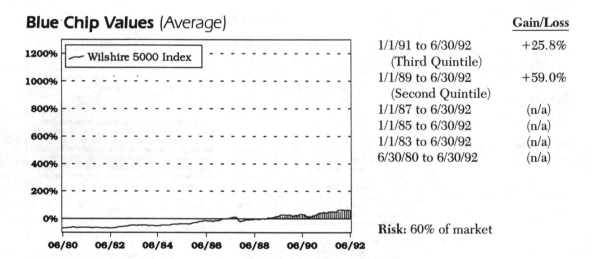

	Gain/Loss
1/1/91 to 6/30/92	+25.8%
(Third Quintile)	
1/1/89 to 6/30/92	+59.0%
(Second Quintile)	
1/1/87 to 6/30/92	(n/a)
1/1/85 to 6/30/92	(n/a)
1/1/83 to 6/30/92	(n/a)
6/30/80 to 6/30/92	(n/a)

Risk: 60% of market

Blue Chip Values (Income & Growth Model Portfolio)

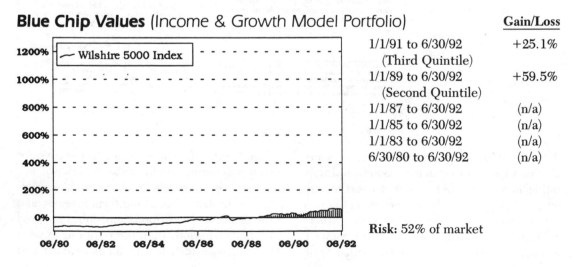

	Gain/Loss
1/1/91 to 6/30/92	+25.1%
(Third Quintile)	
1/1/89 to 6/30/92	+59.5%
(Second Quintile)	
1/1/87 to 6/30/92	(n/a)
1/1/85 to 6/30/92	(n/a)
1/1/83 to 6/30/92	(n/a)
6/30/80 to 6/30/92	(n/a)

Risk: 52% of market

Blue Chip Values (Growth Model Portfolio)

	Gain/Loss
1/1/91 to 6/30/92	+26.4%
(Third Quintile)	
1/1/89 to 6/30/92	+58.3%
(Second Quintile)	
1/1/87 to 6/30/92	(n/a)
1/1/85 to 6/30/92	(n/a)
1/1/83 to 6/30/92	(n/a)
6/30/80 to 6/30/92	(n/a)

Risk: 71% of market

Bob Brinker's Marketimer

Address
P.O. Box 7005
Princeton, NJ 08543

Editor
Robert J. Brinker

Phone Number
908-359-8838

Subscription Rates
$185.00/year

Telephone Hotline
No

Money Management
Yes

Bob Brinker's Marketimer

Volume VII, No. 7   July 6, 1992

"Ask no questions but the
price of votes."
...Samuel Johnson

STOCK MARKET TIMING   DJIA: 3318.52   S & P 500: 408.14

In recent weeks the stock market has experienced a health restoring short-term pullback. This correction is a positive development for the market in terms of its ability to sustain the primary bull trend. Our expectation for this pullback is an overall retrenchment of less than 10% as measured from the recent DJIA record high of 3413 and the earlier S & P 500 Index record high of 421.

We believe the key support level for the market at this time is the DJIA 3200-3275 range. We would regard any opportunity to buy into that range as very attractive. In the event the DJIA 3200 level is penetrated, we would view the DJIA 3100's as an exceptionally attractive area of accumulation. In either event, we view the market as a bargain below DJIA 3275.

Our 1992 objective for the DJIA remains in the 3400-3600 range. The probability of reaching or exceeding DJIA 3600 this year would be _enhanced_ by additional short-term weakness within the DJIA levels outlined above. In the absence of further near-term weakness, we believe the market will make new record highs but could fall short of the DJIA 3600 level on the next major rally.

The _Marketimer_ stock market timing model is bullish as we enter July. Our _Economic_ and _Monetary_ gauges are altogether favorable. Our _Valuation_ indicator, which was discussed in detail in our June edition, continues to point to a market that is fairly priced based on the current level of interest rates and inflation. Our _Sentiment_ indicator continues to improve as stock market weakness scares the nervous nellies out of the market during periods of weakness...thereby serving to enhance the position of the contrary indicators in the sentiment group.

One of the most favorable near-term developments for the stock market is the decline in long-term interest rates during recent weeks. The year-over-year percent change in 30-year Treasury bond yields has reached 7% as of late June... an indication that a major stock market top is most unlikely in the near future. Further interest rate declines at current stock market levels could trigger a major upside move in the stock market beginning this summer.

Subscribers who have followed the _Marketimer_ Model Portfolio strategies have outperformed the market during the last twelve months by spreading their equity money across the globe while avoiding Japan. We believe this global approach remains a valid means to superior performance...and our current allocations remain as follows: 70% USA, 10% New Asia, 10% Europe and 10% Emerging Markets. Specific selections and weightings are listed on page eight.

New subscribers who may be underinvested can purchase each of our 10% recommended foreign positions at current levels. In the USA, we recommend a dollar-cost-averaging approach with more aggressive accumulation advised on market weakness below DJIA 3275.

EDITOR: ROBERT J. BRINKER   P.O. Box 7005, Princeton, NJ 08543   (908) 359-8838   COPYRIGHT 1992 MARKETIMER

Bob Brinker's Marketimer is published monthly by Robert Brinker and is not supplemented by a telephone hotline update. However, Brinker will issue "Action Advisory" bulletins if and when he believes market conditions warrant it. In addition to editing this newsletter, Brinker hosts an investment call-in program each Saturday and Sunday on the ABC Radio Network (entitled "Bob Brinker's Moneytalk").

Brinker's letter primarily is intended to help the mutual fund investor both time the market and select individual funds (though Brinker also recommends individual stocks).

His approach involves a combination of both technical and fundamental analysis. Two pages of each eight-page newsletter are devoted to a review of the monetary, business, technical, valuation and supply/demand factors in the market and to a conclusion in which Brinker advises subscribers on the proper allocation of a portfolio between the stock market and cash. Four additional pages are devoted to analyzing specific no-load mutual funds, a fifth is devoted to individual stocks, and a sixth to reviewing the status of Brinker's four model mutual fund portfolios.

(Brinker's "Balanced" portfolio used to be designed for "telephone switch traders." However, in early 1990 he shifted this portfolio's focus, and thereafter it has been a balanced portfolio seeking both growth and income. The HFD treats the new portfolio as a successor of the old one in the graph that follows and in the Appendices at the end of this book.)

The HFD began monitoring Brinker's model portfolios at the beginning of 1987. On average over the five and one-half years through mid-1992, they gained 52.7%. The Wilshire 5000's total return over the same period, in comparison, was a gain of 93.3%. Brinker's portfolios were less risky than the market as a whole, but not by a large enough margin to make them beat the market on a risk-adjusted basis.

The HFD also has tracked the performance of Brinker's timing advice, by constructing a hypothetical portfolio that "bought" shares of the Wilshire 5000 when he was bullish and earned the T-Bill rate when he was bearish. Though this timing-only portfolio did better than his actual model portfolios (gaining 66.2% over this five-and-one-half-year period), it still did not beat the return that would have been achieved had he simply bought and held the average stock.

Bob Brinker's Marketimer (Average)

	Gain/Loss
1/1/91 to 6/30/92 (Third Quintile)	+26.3%
1/1/89 to 6/30/92 (Second Quintile)	+43.3%
1/1/87 to 6/30/92 (Third Quintile)	+52.7%
1/1/85 to 6/30/92	(n/a)
1/1/83 to 6/30/92	(n/a)
6/30/80 to 6/30/92	(n/a)

Risk: 68% of market

Bob Brinker's Marketimer
(Aggressive Growth Mutual Fund Portfolio)

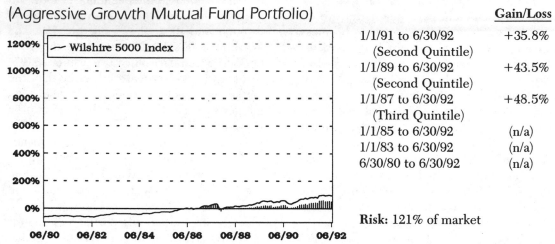

	Gain/Loss
1/1/91 to 6/30/92 (Second Quintile)	+35.8%
1/1/89 to 6/30/92 (Second Quintile)	+43.5%
1/1/87 to 6/30/92 (Third Quintile)	+48.5%
1/1/85 to 6/30/92	(n/a)
1/1/83 to 6/30/92	(n/a)
6/30/80 to 6/30/92	(n/a)

Risk: 121% of market

Bob Brinker's Marketimer
(Long-Term Growth Mutual Fund Portfolio)

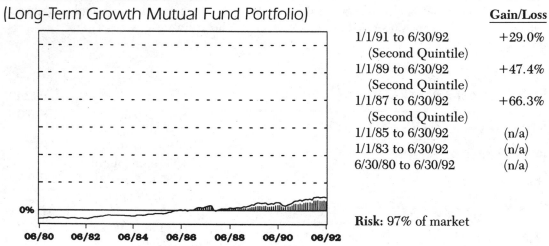

	Gain/Loss
1/1/91 to 6/30/92 (Second Quintile)	+29.0%
1/1/89 to 6/30/92 (Second Quintile)	+47.4%
1/1/87 to 6/30/92 (Second Quintile)	+66.3%
1/1/85 to 6/30/92	(n/a)
1/1/83 to 6/30/92	(n/a)
6/30/80 to 6/30/92	(n/a)

Risk: 97% of market

Bob Brinker's Marketimer (Balanced Portfolio)

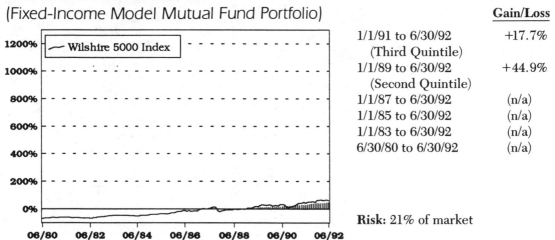

	Gain/Loss
1/1/91 to 6/30/92	+22.0%
(Third Quintile)	
1/1/89 to 6/30/92	+34.6%
(Third Quintile)	
1/1/87 to 6/30/92	+39.0%
(Fourth Quintile)	
1/1/85 to 6/30/92	(n/a)
1/1/83 to 6/30/92	(n/a)
6/30/80 to 6/30/92	(n/a)

Risk: 52% of market

Bob Brinker's Marketimer
(Fixed-Income Model Mutual Fund Portfolio)

	Gain/Loss
1/1/91 to 6/30/92	+17.7%
(Third Quintile)	
1/1/89 to 6/30/92	+44.9%
(Second Quintile)	
1/1/87 to 6/30/92	(n/a)
1/1/85 to 6/30/92	(n/a)
1/1/83 to 6/30/92	(n/a)
6/30/80 to 6/30/92	(n/a)

Risk: 21% of market

Bob Nurock's Advisory

Address
P.O. Box 988
Paoli, PA 19301

Editor
Robert Nurock

Phone Number
800-227-8883

Subscription Rates
$ 97.00/6 months
$247.00/year

Telephone Hotline
Yes

Money Management
No

ISSN 1050-9011   © Investor's Analysis, Inc. July 16, 1992

Interregnum

Investors face more than one interregnum!

This fancy word describes the period between two successive regimes during which there is a suspension of the normal functions of government. A possible Perot presidency provides the prospect of a political interregnum. If he wins in November, or garners enough votes to prevent either Bush or Clinton from getting an electoral majority, uncertainty during this period will be negative for stocks.

The term interregnum also describes a pause in a continuous series. In this sense, a potential downturn in the economy is of more immediate concern to investors.

Recent market action has reinforced an emphasis on fundamental earnings prospects. Potential earnings power has begun to lose its positive impact. Stock performance has become highly dependent on immediate results.

There are few winners of the week. Disasters du jour replace them. Any sign of disappointment leads to a sharp selloff. Losers don't bounce much. And, additional liquidation limits their rallies.

Now, it takes impeccable fundamentals for stocks to develop and maintain relative strength. When weak groups rally, the issues with the strongest earnings show the greatest participation. The balance bounce only modestly.

This reflects the high valuations recently placed on many stocks. Buoyed by recent investor optimism, their prices anticipate much greater than average earnings gains. Underlying this optimism is a high degree of confidence toward the economy.

Economy-o-my

Unfortunately, recently released economic data is troublesome. It has led to disappointment and concern. Many investors expected the strong early year upturn to continue, even if it was not at the same pace.

The declines in May homes sales and durable goods orders reported late last month warned of an impending slowdown. Then, the purchasing manager's index for June showed that the upturn was faltering. The Conference Board said consumer confidence fell slightly in June, after rising sharply over the previous four months. The June employment report finally delivered the coup de grace.

The Federal Reserve Board's cut in the Discount rate two weeks ago reflected its renewed concern about the economy. Recent prior comments from some of its influential members implied that the Fed had already lowered rates as much as it would for awhile. The swiftness

In Brief

Interregnum -
Political uncertainty diminishing short term. Expect revival in it as election approaches. Response to fundamental developments biased negatively. Economy renewed concern. Poor employment outlook expected to affect consumer confidence. Disinflation discouraging individuals and businesses. All point to difficult investment environment over coming months.

Technical Picture -
Recent rally aborted establishment of good bottom. Sentiment growing more optimistic. Further improvement in momentum needed to sustain upturn. Speculation increasing. E$P® on sell signal. Could give repeat sell if prices and breadth weaken next week. Overall background says renewed downturn likely.

Market Strategy/Tactics -
Cut in Discount rate leading to new optimism. Impact of lower rates has worn off. Valuations and yields imply expectations still exceed potential reality. Disinflationary environment could hurt stocks here as in Japan. Maintain very cautious posture. Expect short term downward reaction that could create better bottom or lead to bigger decline, depending upon background circumstances.

Next Issue - August 6, 1992

of its action showed how much slower business was than that which it expected.

The poor employment data shocked many economists into lowering their forecasts. Concern has begun to grow that it will take even lower rates to stimulate growth. That is because there has been only a limited effect from the string of interest rate reductions over the past two years.

Mis-Leading Indicators?
Contradicting this pessimism was the Commerce Department's index of leading indicators that rose 0.6% in May. This was its fifth consecutive monthly gain, and the largest increase since February.

The ratio of coincident to lagging indicators rose for the fifth month too, reinforcing the hopes for future

Investor's Analysis, Incorporated (215) 296-2411 Drawer 650 ■ Southeastern, PA 19399-0650

Bob Nurock's Advisory is published every three weeks by Robert Nurock and is supplemented by a twice-weekly telephone hotline. Nurock became well known in the 1970s and 1980s as one of the regular panelists on Public Television's "Wall Street Week With Louis Rukeyser" and the author of that show's

"Technical Market Index" (TMI). Though Nurock ended his association with that show in October 1989, he took the TMI with him and continues to report on its status in his newsletter and on his hotline.

The HFD's research suggests that one of the more valuable contributions Nurock has made is his TMI. On a pure timing basis, in fact, his TMI is in second place among those timing strategies the HFD monitored for the 12 years from mid-1980 to mid-1992. An investor who bought hypothetical shares of the Wilshire 5000 when the TMI was on a "buy," and who earned the T-Bill rate when it was on a "sell," made 499.9% over these twelve years, compared to a gain of 432.7% for buying and holding.

Nurock's model stock portfolio, in contrast, has underperformed the market. Over the seven and one-half years ending in mid-1992,

during which time the Wilshire 5000 gained 197.6%, Nurock's model portfolio gained 71.3%. And since its risk more or less equaled the market's, the portfolio underperformed the market on a risk-adjusted basis as well.

More recently, Nurock inaugurated two additional mutual fund portfolios, one for sector funds and the other for index funds. Over the three and one-half years through mid-1992, Nurock's sector funds portfolio gained 20.1% and his index funds portfolio gained 20.7%, in contrast to 60.3% for the market as a whole.

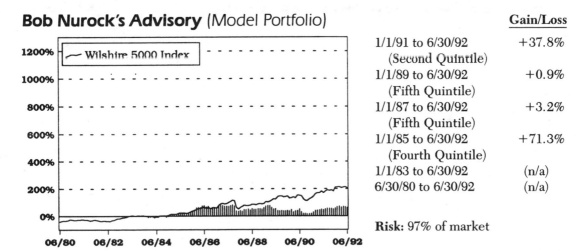

Bob Nurock's Advisory (Average)

	Gain/Loss
1/1/91 to 6/30/92	+17.6%
(Third Quintile)	
1/1/89 to 6/30/92	+6.5%
(Fifth Quintile)	
1/1/87 to 6/30/92	+8.9%
(Fifth Quintile)	
1/1/85 to 6/30/92	+80.7%
(Fourth Quintile)	
1/1/83 to 6/30/92	(n/a)
6/30/80 to 6/30/92	(n/a)

Risk: 44% of market

Bob Nurock's Advisory (Model Portfolio)

	Gain/Loss
1/1/91 to 6/30/92	+37.8%
(Second Quintile)	
1/1/89 to 6/30/92	+0.9%
(Fifth Quintile)	
1/1/87 to 6/30/92	+3.2%
(Fifth Quintile)	
1/1/85 to 6/30/92	+71.3%
(Fourth Quintile)	
1/1/83 to 6/30/92	(n/a)
6/30/80 to 6/30/92	(n/a)

Risk: 97% of market

Bob Nurock's Advisory (Index Mutual Funds Portfolio)

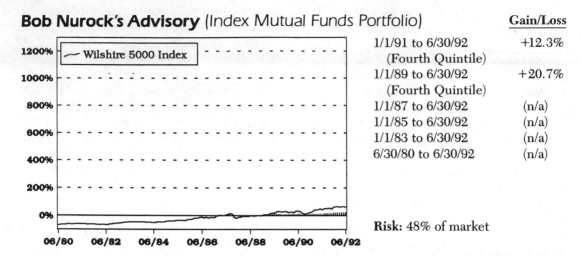

	Gain/Loss
1/1/91 to 6/30/92	+12.3%
(Fourth Quintile)	
1/1/89 to 6/30/92	+20.7%
(Fourth Quintile)	
1/1/87 to 6/30/92	(n/a)
1/1/85 to 6/30/92	(n/a)
1/1/83 to 6/30/92	(n/a)
6/30/80 to 6/30/92	(n/a)

Risk: 48% of market

Bob Nurock's Advisory (Sector Mutual Funds Portfolio)

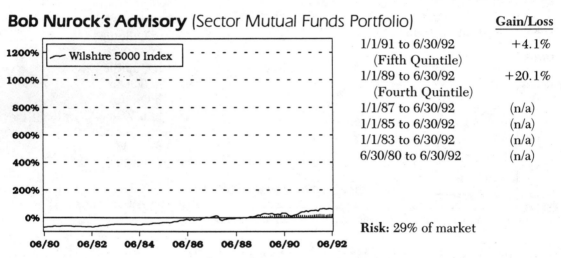

	Gain/Loss
1/1/91 to 6/30/92	+4.1%
(Fifth Quintile)	
1/1/89 to 6/30/92	+20.1%
(Fourth Quintile)	
1/1/87 to 6/30/92	(n/a)
1/1/85 to 6/30/92	(n/a)
1/1/83 to 6/30/92	(n/a)
6/30/80 to 6/30/92	(n/a)

Risk: 29% of market

The Cabot Market Letter

Address
P.O. Box 3044
Salem, MA 01970

Editor
Carlton Lutts

Phone Number
508-745-5532

Subscription Rates
$145.00/6 months
$250.00/year

Telephone Hotline
Yes

Money Management
Yes

Our 22nd Year

The Cabot Market Letter

Post Office Box 3044, Salem, Massachusetts 01970

Editors: Carlton G. Lutts and Timothy W. Lutts

Letter No. 738   July 10, 1992

Dow Industrials – 3324.08   Dow Transports – 1301.57

THE MARKET IS TRYING TO FOOL ALL OF US

PRESENT MARKET POSITION
This market, in its insidious way, is trying to fool all of us whenever it can. It will repeatedly dart and weave this way and that way in an attempt to get us to sell our stocks at exactly the wrong time. This act of thoughtlessly surrendering our stocks while under emotional pressure is called "capitulation." It's the give-up phase when you've reached the end of your rope marketwise. You are completely discouraged and are willing to sell many of your stocks "at any price."

We believe this capitulation phase for many investors occurred over a three-day period, specifically on June 17, 18 and 19, as the market dropped to a Dow level of 3250. Trading volume exceeded 200 million shares on each of those three days. The business news was bad, and many stocks dropped precipitously as investors simply dumped their stocks in disgust.

And now, this week, with the big news about the Federal Reserve Discount Rate cut from 3.5% to 3.0%, the market is testing all of us once again. Instead of shooting ahead on this bullish news as many expected, the market has sold off significantly over the past three days as it slides towards its June lows.

But instead of looking at the dismal gyrations of the market, we advise you to look at the bullish picture being painted by the daily new lows on the NYSE and on the NASDAQ. Our Two-Second Indicator hit its largest number of NYSE new lows (84) for the year in early April's market sell-off. Then on June 17, the market sold off sharply, recording 78 new lows, a somewhat smaller number in that series. Now, on the current market weakness the new lows reached a maximum of only 47 on Wednesday. Likewise on the NASDAQ, the new lows series for the recent sell-offs have been 468, 138 and yesterday an even smaller 109. So you see, the selling has become less intense on each new market sell-off. This pattern of fewer new lows on repeated sell-offs is always a prelude to higher market prices. Only patience is needed.

With the latest cut in the Discount Rate, the monetary picture has become even more bullish for the stock market. Let's look at the numbers, specifically, the ratio of the yield of 3-month T-bills to the yield of the S&P 500. History proves that it's a great time to buy stocks whenever the ratio of the yield on T-bills to the yield on the S&P 500 drops to below 1.75. And stocks can be safely held until this ratio exceeds 2.15, in other words, when the yield on T-bills is more than twice the yield on common stocks. A year ago in July, this ratio was 1.76, (5.56%/3.16%) a perfectly safe level. The market continued to move ahead. The yield on three-month T-bills has now dropped to an unattractive 3.2%. And yet the yield from dividends on the S&P 500 Average is currently 3.02%. Thus, the ratio of T-bill yields to the S&P 500 yield is just 1.06. This "almost equivalent" yield has never happened in our 25-year record of these two instruments. It means today an investor is provided with little incentive to be in T-bills when he can get the equivalent yield from common stocks, *along with a chance for capital appreciation.* Thus, this current exceedingly low ratio is very bullish for the stock market. Remember, money always goes where it's treated best. The flood of money has already pushed the Dow Utility Average to a new six-month high as conservative investors switch funds from T-bills and money market instruments into relatively safe utility stocks where current yields are better than 6%. Next, this money will send the broad market, as well, up to new highs.

WHAT TO DO NOW
Remain bullish and fully invested in our recommended stocks. The best thing you can do for yourself right now is to exercise patience while waiting for this market to start its next major advance. *(See page 2 for LATEST – FRIDAY MORNING)*

© 1992 Cabot Heritage Corporation

The Cabot Market Letter is published twice a month and is supplemented by a twice-weekly telephone hotline update. Editor Carlton Lutts's approach involves a combination of both fundamental and technical analysis. His stock selection relies heavily on a measure of relative strength, whereas his overall market timing involves a number of monetary, sentiment and fundamental indicators in addition to technical analysis.

Lutts's model stock portfolio has had streaks of brilliance interrupted by serious stumbles. It managed to keep its head above water during 1981's bear market, for example, and to shoot ahead along with the bull market in 1982, but in 1984's correction it shed nearly 23% of its value. Over the eleven and one-half years through mid-1992, Lutts's model portfolio gained 94.4%, in contrast to a 332.5% gain for the Wilshire 5000.

The primary culprit in this underperformance was Lutts's stock selection. A portfolio that invested in hypothetical shares of the Wilshire 5000 in the same proportion that his model portfolio invested in stocks made 265.2%. Though this wasn't equal to the market's 332.5% gain, it was significantly greater than his model portfolio's actual gain of just 94.4%.

Lutts's "Growth and Income" portfolio is a newer addition to his newsletter, and over the short time the HFD has followed it the portfolio has beaten the market. Over the 30 months through mid-1992, this portfolio gained 28.9%, in contrast to the Wilshire 5000's increase of 24.1%.

Lutts used to have a mutual fund portfolio in his newsletter, but this portfolio was assumed by his companion newsletter (*Cabot's Mutual Fund Navigator*) when it began publication. See the write-up for this other service next in this book.

The Cabot Market Letter (Average)

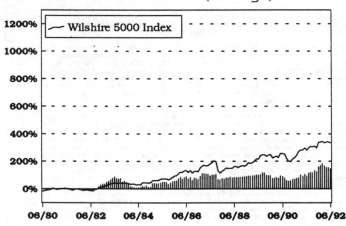

	Gain/Loss
1/1/91 to 6/30/92 (Second Quintile)	+44.4%
1/1/89 to 6/30/92 (Fourth Quintile)	+30.1%
1/1/87 to 6/30/92 (Third Quintile)	+46.3%
1/1/85 to 6/30/92 (Third Quintile)	+117.2%
1/1/83 to 6/30/92 (Fourth Quintile)	+80.0%
6/30/80 to 6/30/92	(n/a)

Risk: 160% of market

The Cabot Market Letter (Model Stock Portfolio)

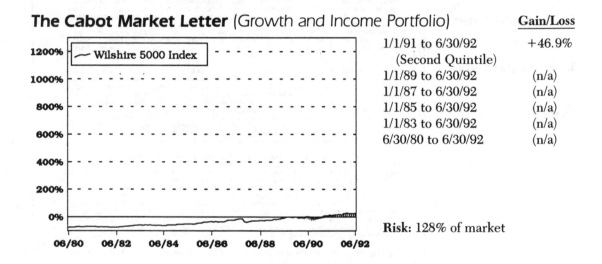

	Gain/Loss
1/1/91 to 6/30/92 (Second Quintile)	+39.9%
1/1/89 to 6/30/92 (Fifth Quintile)	+14.4%
1/1/87 to 6/30/92 (Fourth Quintile)	+16.0%
1/1/85 to 6/30/92 (Fourth Quintile)	+72.2%
1/1/83 to 6/30/92 (Fourth Quintile)	+42.8%
6/30/80 to 6/30/92	(n/a)

Risk: 213% of market

The Cabot Market Letter (Growth and Income Portfolio)

	Gain/Loss
1/1/91 to 6/30/92 (Second Quintile)	+46.9%
1/1/89 to 6/30/92	(n/a)
1/1/87 to 6/30/92	(n/a)
1/1/85 to 6/30/92	(n/a)
1/1/83 to 6/30/92	(n/a)
6/30/80 to 6/30/92	(n/a)

Risk: 128% of market

Cabot's Mutual Fund Navigator

Address
P.O. Box 3044
Salem, MA 01970

Editor
Timothy W. Lutts

Phone Number
508-745-5532

Subscription Rates
$86.00/year

Telephone Hotline
Yes

Money Management
Yes

Cabot's Mutual Fund Navigator

Your guide to investing for profits and safety in the best mutual funds

July, 1992   Volume 5, Issue 7

No Place Else To Go

The current bull market began in October 1990, a full 21 months ago. It was a bull market that had no fundamental reason to exist, according to experts. The country was in the grips of a recession, unemployment was high, and the Iraqi invasion of Kuwait cast a pall over all. Yet the bull market got under way for two big reasons. The first was psychological. The threat of a war in the desert had triggered a brutal and devastating four month market decline, turning legions of investors sour on the market. And finally, when the last seller had sold, the market was ready to move up again. The second was monetary. With the recession taking its toll on business and credit demand drying up, interest rates fell fast, with yields on 3-month T-bills falling from 7.91% to 7.18% in just five months. Because money always goes where it's treated best, we knew that wads of money in CDs, banks and other income invest- ments would be attracted to the stock market. Much of this money had been out of the market for over a decade, content with the double-digit yields available elsewhere. Thus, we reasoned its entry to the stock market would fuel a great advance. It did, and entirely without the help of fundamentals like rising corporate earnings.

It was fun, up until February anyway. Now the S&P 500 is down 3.1% for the year and the Investor's Business Daily mutual fund index is down 11.0%. As a result some investors have concluded the bull market is over and they've cashed in their chips. They're sitting in the safety of money market funds waiting for the next crash so they can say " I told you so." But we think they've made a big mistake. Because we're once again back where we were in October of 1990 ..... opportunitywise. True, there's no threat of war this time. But war's not a requirement for a bull market. We do have the necessary psychological environment, courtesy of a four-month market decline that's hurt virtually every stock but the automakers and the banks, and a populace that's so politically distrustful it's ready to elect an independent billionaire to the Presidency. And we still have the monetary environment. With money market funds now paying just 3.5%, the stock market (with an S&P 500 yield of 3.08% and the potential for capital appreciation) is still mighty attractive to a lot of new money. There's no place else to go.

Now we're not saying mutual fund investors are scared. In our opinion, you haven't done badly this year, with your funds declining just 11% on average. Contrast that with those individuals who invest directly in stocks. Those holding last year's winners, the high-tech growth stocks, have seen some of their holdings decline some 50% from their February peaks. That's the kind of decline that really hurts and makes you cash in your chips exactly when you should be standing pat. Yes, you're fortunate to own mutual funds, because the corrections don't bother you as much. It's easier to become a long-term investor when you own mutual funds. Thus, it's easier to take advantage of the power of compound growth. Sure, you forfeit the chance of getting rich quick in a hot stock. But no one ever acquired real wealth quickly. The biggest benefit of mutual funds is not the professional management, and it's not the automatic diversification. It's that mutual funds enable you to benefit from the long-term uptrend of the market, and that's the road to real wealth. So let the current correction run its course. By the time you receive this, the next big upmove may already be under way.

MARKET TIMING: Although the Dow Transports have closed below their Cabot Trend Line, the Industials remain above. So this indicator remains positive.

The closely watched Advance-Decline Line declined again in June, at one point falling for a rare thirteen consecu- tive days. That in itself is a sign of capitulation, a sign of the bottom of the correction. In fact, the decline only

(Market Timing continued on page 2)

HOTLINE NUMBER 508-745-1283

Cabot's Mutual Fund Navigator was started several years ago by Carlton Lutts as a companion service to his longer-lived *Cabot Market Letter*, and is edited by his son, Timothy Lutts. The newsletter is published monthly and is supplemented by a weekly telephone hotline update.

Two pages of each six-page issue are devoted to summarizing the status of Lutts's three model portfolios, one to market commentary, two to tables summarizing mutual fund performance, and a final one to in-depth reviews of individual mutual funds. Lutts's model portfolio advice is very clear, providing subscribers with precise instructions on what portion should be invested in the market and what portion withheld and kept in cash. As is the case for *The Cabot Market Letter*, the approach taken by this newsletter is a combination of both fundamental and technical analysis. Compared to the number of mutual fund newsletters that switch in and out of the market relatively frequently, Lutts has adopted a somewhat longer perspective.

The HFD has data for this newsletter's performance beginning in 1989. Its average performance over the next three and one-half years was a gain of 34.1%, in contrast to 60.3% for the Wilshire 5000. The best-performing of Lutts's three portfolios was his "Income" portfolio (with a 51.9% gain), while the poorest performer was his "Growth" portfolio (with a gain of 16.6%).

About half of Lutts's underperformance is due to market timing and about half is due to mutual fund selection. Had each of his recommended mutual funds performed as well as the market as a whole, for example, his growth portfolio would have gained 39.6% instead of 16.6%—though it still wouldn't have equaled the market's 51.9% gain.

Cabot's Mutual Fund Navigator (Average)

	Gain/Loss
1/1/91 to 6/30/92 (Second Quintile)	+33.7%
1/1/89 to 6/30/92 (Third Quintile)	+34.1%
1/1/87 to 6/30/92	(n/a)
1/1/85 to 6/30/92	(n/a)
1/1/83 to 6/30/92	(n/a)
6/30/80 to 6/30/92	(n/a)

Risk: 91% of market

Cabot's Mutual Fund Navigator (Income Portfolio)

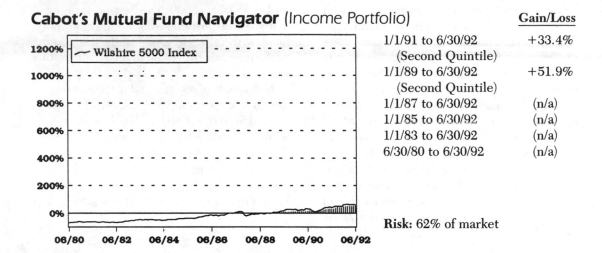

	Gain/Loss
1/1/91 to 6/30/92 (Second Quintile)	+33.4%
1/1/89 to 6/30/92 (Second Quintile)	+51.9%
1/1/87 to 6/30/92	(n/a)
1/1/85 to 6/30/92	(n/a)
1/1/83 to 6/30/92	(n/a)
6/30/80 to 6/30/92	(n/a)

Risk: 62% of market

Cabot's Mutual Fund Navigator (Growth & Income Portfolio)

	Gain/Loss
1/1/91 to 6/30/92 (Second Quintile)	+32.2%
1/1/89 to 6/30/92 (Third Quintile)	+34.5%
1/1/87 to 6/30/92	(n/a)
1/1/85 to 6/30/92	(n/a)
1/1/83 to 6/30/92	(n/a)
6/30/80 to 6/30/92	(n/a)

Risk: 98% of market

Cabot's Mutual Fund Navigator (Growth Portfolio)

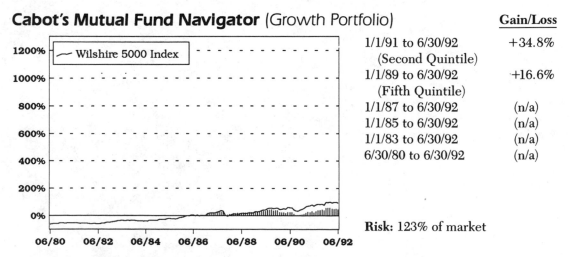

	Gain/Loss
1/1/91 to 6/30/92 (Second Quintile)	+34.8%
1/1/89 to 6/30/92 (Fifth Quintile)	+16.6%
1/1/87 to 6/30/92	(n/a)
1/1/85 to 6/30/92	(n/a)
1/1/83 to 6/30/92	(n/a)
6/30/80 to 6/30/92	(n/a)

Risk: 123% of market

California Technology Stock Letter

Address
Murenove, Inc.
P.O. Box 308
Half Moon Bay, CA
94019

Editors
Michael Murphy and
Lissa Morgenthaler

Phone Number
415-726-8495

Subscription Rates
$ 49.00/6 issues
$270.00/year

Telephone Hotline
Yes

Money Management
Yes

CALIFORNIA
Technology Stock Letter

AUTHORITATIVE INDEPENDENT ADVICE FOR HIGH-TECHNOLOGY INVESTING

JULY 10, 1992   CTSL INDEX: 215.14

THIS ISSUE: *Personal Digital Assistants*

ISSUE #267   DJIA: 3330.55

#1
1987
1988 - 1989
3 YEARS OVERALL

CTSL MARKET METER™

TODAY'S CLOSE 3330.55

HIGH 2480
FAIR VALUE 2018
LOW 1634

	High	Low
MARKET'S HISTORICAL		
Price/Earnings	18.0x	13.0x
Price/Book	1.9x	1.2x
Yield	3.2%	5.0%

THE CAPSULE OUTLOOK

Factors
Fundamentals.....
Valuation............
Technical............
Monetary............
Sentiment............

Forecasts
Economy.............
Stock Market......
Bond Market......
Gold Market.......

CONTENTS

MARKET REVIEW & OUTLOOK

If the recession is over, why hasn't the National Bureau of Economic Research (the official arbiter of these dates) declared it over? Just asking.

The answer, obvious to everyone except the White House, is that it's not clear the recession ever ended. Between the usual statistical noise and the revisions yet to come, the deliberate deception by the Bureau of Labor Statistics on the payroll employment numbers, and the way the government is "carrying" the banking system rather than forcing long-overdue writeoffs and restructurings, people have an uneasy feeling they're being conned for political purposes. As, indeed, they are.

* * * * *

The *California Technology Stock Letter* (*CTSL*) is published once every two weeks by Michael Murphy and Lissa Morgenthaler and ·is supplemented by a telephone hotline that typically is updated twice each week. The newsletter started in 1982 as a joint effort of Murphy and James McCamant, who subse- quently left to become editor on his own of *Medical Technology Stock Letter* (reviewed elsewhere in this volume). As a rule, the *California Technology Stock Letter* does not focus on medical technology companies.

CTSL's approach is predominantly funda- mental. A stock is recommended only after

Murphy and Morgenthaler examine industry trends, the company's particular product line and balance sheet, and so forth. However, from time to time they will look at a number of technical indicators, especially in their timing of short-term market swings.

CTSL's model portfolio was one of the severest casualties of the correction in secondary stocks that began in mid-1983 and lasted well into 1985 and 1986. It lost nearly half its value in 1984, for example, placing it at the bottom of the HFD's ranking for that year, and lost another 6% in 1985 when the market itself was gaining some 30%.

Beginning in 1986 the newsletter's editors announced their intention of managing the model portfolio more actively. That decision, coupled no doubt with a general improvement in the condition of the secondary sector, led to a marked improvement in its performance. CTSL's model portfolio gained 67.9% in 1987, for example, a year in which the Wilshire 5000 gained only 2.3%, ranking it third that year among all newsletters the HFD followed.

The improved performance since 1986 was sufficient to overcome the newsletter's earlier losses, but not enough by mid-1992 to bring the portfolio back to where it would have been if it had invested in the average stock. For the nine and one-half years from the beginning of 1983 through mid-1992, during which time the Wilshire 5000 gained 278.6%, CTSL's model portfolio gained just 40.6%. However, over the five and one-half years through mid-1992, CTSL beat the market 147.3% to 93.3%, which is good enough to earn it fifth place among all the newsletters the HFD tracked.

This marked reversal of fortunes poses one of the biggest challenges in interpreting performance. Statisticians tell us that there is no statistical reason to ignore CTSL's track record from 1983 to 1985 just because it is so much worse than in recent years, and that it is just as relevant as its more recent experience in predicting its future performance. Nevertheless, it is possible that there is a non-statistical reason—the editors changed methods, became wiser, etc.—to place more weight on CTSL's recent, and better, performance.

California Technology Stock Letter

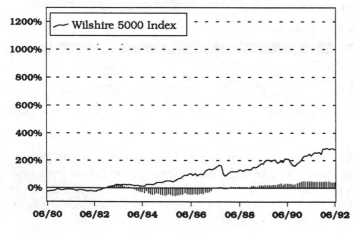

	Gain/Loss
1/1/91 to 6/30/92	+3.0%
(Fifth Quintile)	
1/1/89 to 6/30/92	+ 25.7%
(Fourth Quintile)	
1/1/87 to 6/30/92	+147.3%
(First Quintile)	
1/1/85 to 6/30/92	+165.6%
(Second Quintile)	
1/1/83 to 6/30/92	+ 40.6%
(Fourth Quintile)	
6/30/80 to 6/30/92	(n/a)

Risk: 46% of market

The Chartist

Address
P.O. Box 758
Seal Beach, CA 90740

Editor
Dan Sullivan

Phone Number
310-596-2385

Subscription Rates
$ 80.00/6 months
$150.00/year

Telephone Hotline
Yes

Money Management
Yes

THE CHARTIST

P.O. BOX 758, SEAL BEACH, CALIFORNIA 90740
EDITOR: DAN SULLIVAN

June 25, 1992   DJIA. 3284.01   UTL: 210.75   OTC: 548.32
92-12   TRAN: 1284.94   AMEX: 374.15   NYSE: 221.53

The Chartist
Actual Cash Account

HOTLINE #
(310) 431-3483

* Microsoft adjusted for 3 for 2 split.

STATUS AS OF 06/25/92   16:17 EASTERN

STOCK	STOCK SYMBOL	NUMBER SHARES	PURCHASE DATE	PURCHASE PRICE	CURRENT PRICE	GAIN [LOSS]	%CH
AMGEN	AMGN	626	01/29/91	24 1/8	56 3/4	$20,423.25	+ 135.2
ALZA CORP.	AZA	364	01/29/91	27 9/16	42 1/2	$5,438.16	+54.2
BIOMET, INC.	BMET	626	01/29/91	11 7/8	15	$1,959.38	+26.4
DELL COMPUTER	DELL	715	01/29/91	14 3/8	17 1/8	$1,969.83	+ 19.2
GENZYME CORP.	GENZ	531	01/29/91	28 5/8	42 3/4	$7,500.38	+49.3
IMCERA CORP.	IMA	556	01/29/91	27 1/8	30 1/8	$1,668.00	+11.1
MICROSOFT	MSFT	243 *	01/29/91	41 *	69 1/2	$6,925.50	+69.5
NOVELL, INC.	NOVL	737	01/29/91	20 1/2	51	$22,478.50	+ 148.8
PFIZER, INC.	PFE	341	01/29/91	44 1/4	71 1/2	$9,292.25	+61.6
READER'S DIGEST	RDA	501	01/29/91	30	46 3/8	$8,203.88	+54.6
UNITED HEALTHCARE	UNH	561	01/29/91	28	76 1/8	$26,998.13	+ 171.9
U. S. SURGICAL	USS	368	01/29/91	42 1/4	91	$17,940.00	+ 115.4
UST, INC.	UST	512	01/29/91	19 1/2	27 7/8	$4,288.00	+42.9

PURCHASE VALUE $169,551.39
CURRENT VALUE $304,636.63   TOTAL PROFITS $135,085.24

Above are all the open positions in the Chartist long term managed account. The account is NOT hypothetical. On each and every trade actual cash is deployed. Whenever, the Chartist makes recommendations concerning this account, they are placed on our Hotline at approximately 3:00 PM West Coast time. Absolutely no one has an unfair advantage in the utilization of the Hotline, because we do not act in behalf of ourselves, or this account, or any other account, until the day after our Hotline is activated. This gives everyone ample time to accept or reject the advice placed on the Hotline. Copies of the complete Track Record are available upon request.
For Managed Account Information please call (310) 596-2385   ($100,000 minimum)

ACTUAL CASH ACCOUNT UPDATE

The Chartist Hotlines were activated on Monday, June 22nd at approximately 3:00 p.m. West Coast time. The advice was strictly for long-term investors and concerned the Actual Cash Account. Long-term investors were advised to sell all of Conagra and one half of Biomet. Mailgrams confirming the Hotline advice were sent out to our special Mailgram subscribers the same day. We acted on the aforementioned advice in behalf of the Actual Cash Account the next day, Tuesday, June 23rd. We sold 625 shares of Biomet at 16 1/4 and 405 shares of Conagra at 24 1/2.

The partial profits on Biomet, after in and out commissions were factored in, amounted to $2,500.00, a gain of 33.0% on invested capital. The Actual Cash Account is still holding 626 shares of Biomet. The sale of Conagra, after commissions, resulted in a loss of $485.95, or -4.74% on invested capital.

The printout at the top of page two reflects the profits that have been taken by the Actual Cash Account since the beginning of this bullish cycle. Long-term investors

The Chartist is published twice each month by Dan Sullivan, who has been publishing this newsletter since the late 1960s. The service is supplemented by a telephone hotline that is updated twice each week and more often when needed. One of the things that makes Sullivan unique within the newsletter industry is that he is one of the very few who have created real-world portfolios to track their newsletters's advice. He offers brokerage statements to any subscriber who requests them.

As his newsletter's name suggests, Sullivan is a technician. Among the technical indicators he uses are a number of relative-strength gauges (for individual stock selection) and, for market timing, the percentage of stocks that fall above or below their 30-week moving averages. Unlike many technicians, however, Sullivan takes a relatively long-term view of investing. He typically holds stocks in his "Actual Cash Account" for several years, and even stocks in his "Traders" portfolio are held longer than positions in some of the shortest-term newsletters followed by the HFD.

The Chartist is in first place for performance over the 12 years from mid-1980 to mid-1992 among those newsletters the HFD tracked. This ranking is based on an average of its "Actual Cash Account," which the HFD began following in 1980, and its "Traders" portfolio, for which the HFD's data begin in 1983. This average performance is a gain of 665.2%, well ahead of the Wilshire 5000's 432.7%.

During the time that both of Sullivan's portfolios have existed, the "Traders" portfolio has been the better performer. Over the nine and one-half years through mid-1992, for example, the HFD reports that this portfolio gained 498.1%, as compared to 315.0% for his "Actual Cash Account" and 278.6% for the Wilshire 5000.

High relative-strength stocks tend to be among the biggest losers in a bear market, and Sullivan is aware of the crucial role that market timing plays in the long-term success of his approach. Sullivan accordingly is willing to forgo some bull-market gains in order to be out of the market during serious declines. Over the entire 12 years, for example, a portfolio that invested in hypothetical shares of the Wilshire 5000 in the same proportion as Sullivan's "Actual Cash Account" incurred only slightly more than half as much risk as the market as a whole.

The Chartist (Average)

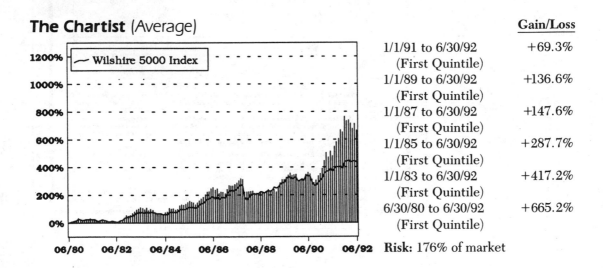

	Gain/Loss
1/1/91 to 6/30/92 (First Quintile)	+69.3%
1/1/89 to 6/30/92 (First Quintile)	+136.6%
1/1/87 to 6/30/92 (First Quintile)	+147.6%
1/1/85 to 6/30/92 (First Quintile)	+287.7%
1/1/83 to 6/30/92 (First Quintile)	+417.2%
6/30/80 to 6/30/92 (First Quintile)	+665.2%

Risk: 176% of market

The Chartist (Actual Cash Account)

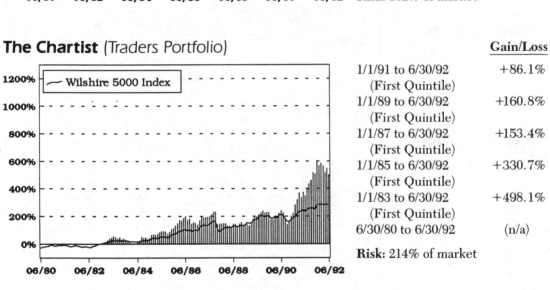

	Gain/Loss
1/1/91 to 6/30/92	+52.0%
(First Quintile)	
1/1/89 to 6/30/92	+107.0%
(First Quintile)	
1/1/87 to 6/30/92	+130.8%
(First Quintile)	
1/1/85 to 6/30/92	+228.5%
(First Quintile)	
1/1/83 to 6/30/92	+315.0%
(First Quintile)	
6/30/80 to 6/30/92	+514.0%
(First Quintile)	

Risk: 162% of market

The Chartist (Traders Portfolio)

	Gain/Loss
1/1/91 to 6/30/92	+86.1%
(First Quintile)	
1/1/89 to 6/30/92	+160.8%
(First Quintile)	
1/1/87 to 6/30/92	+153.4%
(First Quintile)	
1/1/85 to 6/30/92	+330.7%
(First Quintile)	
1/1/83 to 6/30/92	+498.1%
(First Quintile)	
6/30/80 to 6/30/92	(n/a)

Risk: 214% of market

The Chartist Mutual Fund Timer

Address
P.O. Box 758
Seal Beach, CA 90740

Editor
Dan Sullivan

Phone Number
310-596-2385

Subscription Rates
$ 55.00/6 months
$100.00/year

Telephone Hotline
Yes

Money Management
Yes

The Chartist
MUTUAL FUND TIMER

P. O. BOX 758, SEAL BEACH, CALIFORNIA 90740
EDITOR: DAN SULLIVAN   MANAGED ACCOUNTS: BILL MAIS

Forty-seventh Issue   July 9, 1992

Actual Cash Account
Chartist Mutual Fund Timer

Important: This is a real money account, it is not hypothetical. It buys and sells in concert with the Long-term Momentum Model.

* Important: Purchase price has been adjusted to reflect dividends and capital gains.

STATUS AS OF 07/08/92   13:00 EASTERN

FUND	PURCHASE DATE	PRICE*	AMOUNT INVESTED	CURRENT PRICE	GAIN LOSS	% CHANGE
FEDERATED GRO. TRUST	01/25/91	17.53	$26,385.80	20.88	+ $5,047	+ 19.1%
FINANCIAL DYNAMICS	01/25/91	7.16	26,385.80	9.01	+ 6,796	+ 25.8
JANUS TWENTY	01/25/91	15.19	26,385.80	21.74	+ 11,390	+ 43.2
T. R. PRICE NEW HORIZ	01/25/91	11.28	26,385.80	13.70	+ 5,657	+ 21.4
SELECTED AMERICAN	01/25/91	13.41	26,385.80	17.82	+ 8,681	+ 32.9

Equity Value	$169,501	Beginning Value (8/29/88)	$100,000
Money Mkt. Value	$8,695	Current Value	$178,196
Total Value	$178,196	Total Profits	$78,196
		Annualized Gain	+ 16.10%

Above are all the open positions in The Chartist long term Mutual Fund Timer Actual Cash Account. This is NOT hypothetical. On each and every trade actual cash is deployed. Brokerage commissions are accounted for and copies of our brokerage statements are available upon request. Whenever the Chartist Mutual Fund Timer makes recommendations concerning this account, they are placed on our Hotlines at approximately 3:00 PM West Coast Time. The Hotline numbers are for the exclusive use of the subscribers of the Chartist Mutual Fund Timer and are changed frequently. Absolutely no one has an unfair advantage in the utilization of the Hotline, because we do not act in behalf of ourselves, or any other account, until the day after our Hotline is activated. This gives everyone ample time to accept or reject the advice placed on the Hotline. Copies of the complete Track Record are available upon request.
For Managed Account Information please call (310) 596-2385

OUR ADVICE.....STAY 100% INVESTED

As we go to press, the Long-term momentum model is positive while the Short and Intermediate-term models are improving rapidly, but are still negative. We follow the Long-term model exclusively and advise our subscribers to do the same, so our advice is to stay 100% invested in the recommended equity funds. The Long-term momentum model, which has been in a positive mode since flashing a buy signal on January 24, 1991, came very close to flashing an all-out sell signal on June 22nd, and again on June 26th. This was not the first time that the Long-term model came close to rendering a sell signal. In the current cycle the Long-term model was in a caution mode on August 19, 1991, at the height of the Russian Coup. There was also a series of trading sessions in late November of last year that brought the Long-term model perilously close to a sell signal. Once again in early April, it appeared that a sell signal was imminent. On all of the aforementioned occasions the market rallied sharply just as the long-term momentum model was about to slip into negative territory. This doesn't surprise us because the model has many checks and balances which keep it uncannily attuned to the long-term primary trend

Since the last edition of the Chartist Mutual Fund Timer (6/10/92) the Dow has dropped 1.49%. However, this average is not of any great importance to us. The average that is important is the Russell 2000, which tracks the secondary market. Over the same period the Russell was much weaker than that Dow, losing 4.73%. This has been the situation since the middle of January. The Dow has been masking the deterioration

---

The Chartist Mutual Fund Timer is published monthly by Dan Sullivan and is supplemented by a daily telephone hotline update. It commenced publication in 1988, and the HFD began following it at the beginning of 1989.

Like Sullivan's other service (*The Chartist*, reviewed on the previous pages), *The Chartist Mutual Fund Timer* takes an exclusively technical approach to market timing and selection. In contrast to Sullivan's other newsletter, however, this one takes a somewhat shorter-term focus, recommending more frequent switches into and out of the market (between four and five per year, on average). Since Sullivan recommends no-load mutual funds, the higher commissions that normally would be associated with such an approach are not a problem. (Taxes, however, which the HFD's figures don't take into account, could be.)

The Chartist Mutual Fund Timer is one of the few services that beat the market over the three and one-half years through mid-1992, gaining 81.6%, as compared to 60.3% for the Wilshire 5000. In addition, this newsletter's gain was turned in with less risk than the market as a whole, so on a risk-adjusted basis it beat the market by an even larger amount.

The primary credit in beating the market goes to Sullivan's selection of mutual funds. On a timing-only basis, in fact, *The Chartist Mutual Fund Timer* did not beat the market: A portfolio that invested in hypothetical shares of the Wilshire 5000 in the same proportion as its model portfolio made 54.7% over these three and one-half years—slightly less than the Wilshire's 60.3% and substantially less than the 81.6% that portfolio actually gained.

The Chartist Mutual Fund Timer

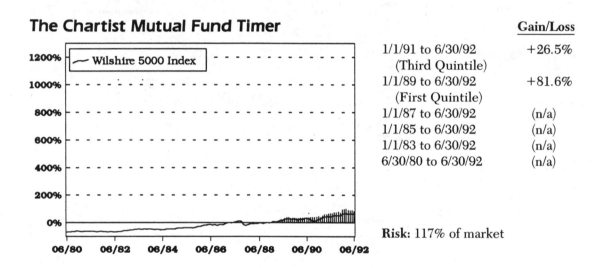

	Gain/Loss
1/1/91 to 6/30/92	+26.5%
(Third Quintile)	
1/1/89 to 6/30/92	+81.6%
(First Quintile)	
1/1/87 to 6/30/92	(n/a)
1/1/85 to 6/30/92	(n/a)
1/1/83 to 6/30/92	(n/a)
6/30/80 to 6/30/92	(n/a)

Risk: 117% of market

The Clean Yield

Address
Clean Yield
  Publications, Ltd.
P.O. Box 1880
Greensboro Bend, VT
  05842

Editor
Rian Fried

Phone Number
802-533-7178

Subscription Rates
$ 3.50/1 issue
$85.00/year

Telephone Hotline
No

Money Management
Yes

CLEAN YIELD
PRINCIPLES AND PROFITS WORKING TOGETHER

CLEAR VIEW: Not Yet

In their eagerness to trade with South Africa, many nations seem willing to accept at face value President F.W. de Klerk's assurances that the era of white minority rule is about to end. Trade sanctions are being relaxed or lifted by country after country.

For the first time in years, socially responsible investors and corporations disagree on the issue of South African investment. This split is highlighted by Lotus Development's intent to reenter the South African market.

Like many of our compatriots in the socially responsible investment community, we have been torn between our desire to help a democratic South Africa rebuild its economy and our concern that premature reinvestment might lead to renewed government intransigence.

For many of us, the resolution of this question of timing came at a June 14 meeting of our trade group, the Social Investment Forum. Max Sisulu, Chief Economist of the African National Congress, addressed the group and em-

phatically answered the question foremost in everyone's mind. Do not, he declared, drop the sanctions yet.

The correctness of Mr. Sisulu's advice has already been demonstrated. Until the South African government ceases

For the first time in years, socially responsible investors and corporations disagree on the issue of South African investment.

its attempts to divide blacks through atrocities such as the recent police-assisted massacre, there will be no stability. If South Africa wishes to fully rejoin the world community, it must bring its security forces to heel and move forward honestly toward the goal of bringing a democratic government into existence. Further attempts to preserve a white monopoly on power will be futile. All that political and police chicanery can produce is a bloodbath from which none will escape unscathed. ❦

GOING TO MARKET: Inflated Fears

Inflation fears and tighter interest rates triggered a sell-off in June. May's producer price index jumped a surprising 0.4% for its biggest gain in 19 months. If wholesale prices continue to rise, the consumer price index will also start to rise, a bad sign for interest rates and stocks. We believe that the 1990s will be an era of relatively low inflation; however, a short uptick in inflation now is quite possible because of the monetary policy the Federal Reserve has pursued—cutting interest rates fully in half over the past two years—and the economic recovery. Even though the recovery is anemic, it is still strong enough to spark a modest rise in inflation.

Signs of recovery came from the housing sector, where May starts were up 11%, and industrial production, which rose 0.6% for the fourth consecutive monthly increase. Despite the fact that May unemployment climbed to 7.5%, the total number of hours worked increased. When compared to the end of past recessions, a 7.5% unemployment rate is relatively low. The number of hours worked is a more reliable indicator of economic activity, so we do not think that the employment data is as bad as it appears on the surface. Raising doubts about the strength of the recovery, however, were May's durable goods orders, which fell 2.4%, and retail sales, which inched ahead by only .2%. Despite the

fact that the monthly economic data remains mixed, the overall picture is positive, and we expect the economy to continue to improve, albeit at a sluggish pace.

The good news is that secondary stocks generally do much better than the large caps when inflation ticks up. Currently, many secondary stocks offer excellent long-term value, especially in light of a slow-recovery scenario. We would be buyers of the secondary stocks at these levels and use rallies to sell the overvalued blue chips that led this market and are now quite vulnerable. ❦

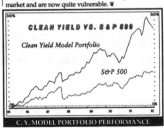

CLEAN YIELD VS. S&P 500

Clean Yield Model Portfolio

S&P 500

C. Y. MODEL PORTFOLIO PERFORMANCE

VOLUME 8   JULY 1992   NUMBER 5

The Clean Yield is published monthly by Rian Fried and is not supplemented by a telephone hotline update. It is the only newsletter among those monitored by the HFD that has "socially responsible" investments as its primary focus. In addition to a company's performance according to any of a number of social responsibility criteria, however, the newsletter also looks at a host of fundamental and technical indicators in constructing its model portfolio.

The newsletter's model portfolio is the focus of just one of the newsletter's six to eight pages a month, however. The other pages are devoted to a number of in-depth examinations of individual companies according to various criteria used by socially responsible investors, as well as to general philosophical discussions of those criteria.

Over the three and one-half years through mid-1992, during which time the Wilshire 5000 gained 60.3%, this newsletter's model portfolio gained 46.4%. Owing to the fact that the newsletter's model portfolio was slightly more risky than the market over this period, it underperformed the market on a risk-adjusted basis as well.

The Clean Yield

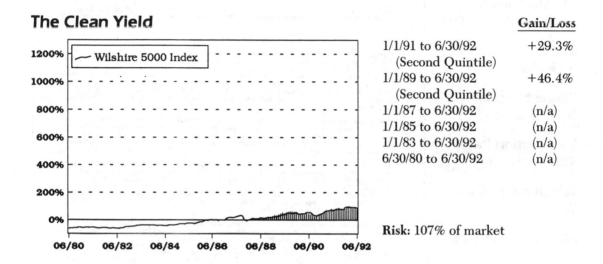

	Gain/Loss
1/1/91 to 6/30/92	+29.3%
(Second Quintile)	
1/1/89 to 6/30/92	+46.4%
(Second Quintile)	
1/1/87 to 6/30/92	(n/a)
1/1/85 to 6/30/92	(n/a)
1/1/83 to 6/30/92	(n/a)
6/30/80 to 6/30/92	(n/a)

Risk: 107% of market

The Contrarian's View

Address
132 Moreland St.
Worcester, MA 01609

Editor
Nick Chase

Phone Number
508-757-2881

Subscription Rates
$39.00/year

Telephone Hotline
Yes

Money Management
No

The CONTRARIAN'S view

Vol. VI, #11   June 32, 1992

- THE BEAR OF '93 -

People lied. Well, perhaps there's a nicer way to put it.... they misled the pollsters, because it wasn't fashionable to say you were going to vote for the "outsider", Ross Perot, for president (although many did). As the previous summer had worn on and the conventions had elected their nominees, Bush's popularity in the polls had slowly climbed, peaking at 39% just before the election, leading Perot at 31% and Clinton at 24%.... with Bush almost guaranteed to carry the large states and therefore win an electoral majority.

The stock market had responded kindly to a continuation of the status quo, first by rallying in early July to yet another discount-rate cut by the Federal Reserve, then continuing upward to break the 3600 barrier in early September. After that, it had drifted down to about 3490 as the uncertainty of the election approached.

Even the much-vaunted exit polls did not fully reveal what lay ahead.... it wasn't until the actual vote totals started rolling in that it became clear that the "discredited" (by the media) Ross Perot had actually won the Presidential election by a substantial margin.... 41% for Perot, 36% for Bush, 23% for Clinton. Seems like the voters were ready to throw the bums out, as there was also a substantial turnover in Congress (much of which had been accomplished in the primaries).

On Wednesday November 4, 1992, stocks soared upward 230 DJI points on the apparent belief that Ross Perot would and could actually clean up the mess in Washington, closing at 3723.56. This was the peak.

The next day, reality sank in. Ross Perot had won only 37% of the electors (that is, votes in the Electoral College). Bush had 34%, and Clinton 27%, with 2% of the electors uncommitted. The Constitution requires a clear majority (51%), so clearly a crisis was at hand. The posturing began. Some of the electors on Bush and Clinton slates felt they could not in good conscience go against the wishes of a majority of the American people, and they switched to Perot. A few of the Perot electors were bought off by the Bush and Clinton people (though not many, because they were a pretty dedicated bunch). As the early-December meeting of the Electoral College approached, the percentages were: Perot, 42%; Bush, 32%; Clinton, 25%, uncommitted 1%.

On Thursday November 5, 1992, stocks tanked 165 points, wiping out most of the previous day's gain, and the 1993-94 bear market was underway. Similar slides were seen in the rest of the world's stock markets, especially in Japan, where the Nikkei slid 8.1% to close just under 14000, a new multi-

(over, please)

The Contrarian's View is published eleven times per year by Nick Chase and is supplemented by a telephone hotline that typically is updated twice each week. (Chase refers to his hotline as a "warmline," and it is accessible only by computer modem.) Chase is relatively unique in the newsletter industry in that the portfolios his letter summarizes are his own personal portfolios.

Chase's stock-picking appears to be based entirely on fundamental analysis, with many of the positions purchased because of long-standing limit orders placed below the market. The cash positions in his model portfolios seem more to reflect the number of limit orders that have been filled than an explicit market-timing judgment on his part.

Chase does engage in market timing, however, even if his conclusions don't immediately translate into changes in his model portfolios. His market timing model is an active, trend-following system, having generated an average of one switch each month over the 18 months through mid-1992. Though the HFD calculates that this timing system essentially equaled the market's return over this period, it did so with substantially less risk.

On a risk-adjusted basis, therefore, Chase's timing handily beat the market.

In contrast to his pension-timing system, Chase's model portfolios on average are more risky than the market as a whole. The 18 months through mid-1992 were very favorable ones for his recommended securities, producing an average gain of 47.6% among the four portfolios, in contrast to 32.3% for the Wilshire 5000. Though their above-average risk accounts for some of this overperformance, it doesn't account for all of it: Even on a risk-adjusted basis, Chase's portfolios outperformed the market.

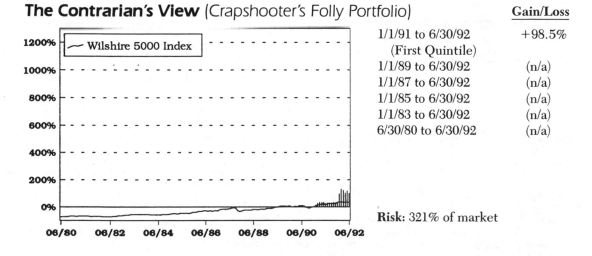

The Contrarian's View (Average)

	Gain/Loss
1/1/91 to 6/30/92	+47.6%
(Second Quintile)	
1/1/89 to 6/30/92	(n/a)
1/1/87 to 6/30/92	(n/a)
1/1/85 to 6/30/92	(n/a)
1/1/83 to 6/30/92	(n/a)
6/30/80 to 6/30/92	(n/a)

Risk: 113% of market

The Contrarian's View (Crapshooter's Folly Portfolio)

	Gain/Loss
1/1/91 to 6/30/92	+98.5%
(First Quintile)	
1/1/89 to 6/30/92	(n/a)
1/1/87 to 6/30/92	(n/a)
1/1/85 to 6/30/92	(n/a)
1/1/83 to 6/30/92	(n/a)
6/30/80 to 6/30/92	(n/a)

Risk: 321% of market

The Contrarian's View (Hedger's Delight Portfolio)

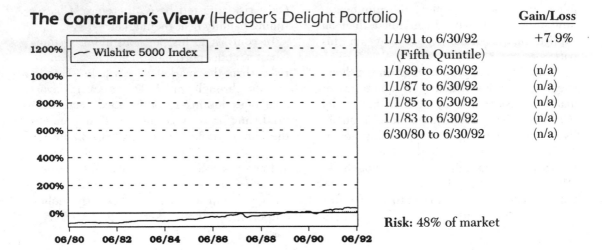

	Gain/Loss
1/1/91 to 6/30/92	+7.9%
(Fifth Quintile)	
1/1/89 to 6/30/92	(n/a)
1/1/87 to 6/30/92	(n/a)
1/1/85 to 6/30/92	(n/a)
1/1/83 to 6/30/92	(n/a)
6/30/80 to 6/30/92	(n/a)

Risk: 48% of market

The Contrarian's View (Present & Future Income Portfolio)

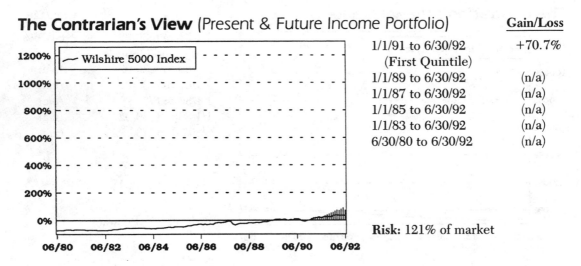

	Gain/Loss
1/1/91 to 6/30/92	+70.7%
(First Quintile)	
1/1/89 to 6/30/92	(n/a)
1/1/87 to 6/30/92	(n/a)
1/1/85 to 6/30/92	(n/a)
1/1/83 to 6/30/92	(n/a)
6/30/80 to 6/30/92	(n/a)

Risk: 121% of market

The Contrarian's View (IRA Portfolio)

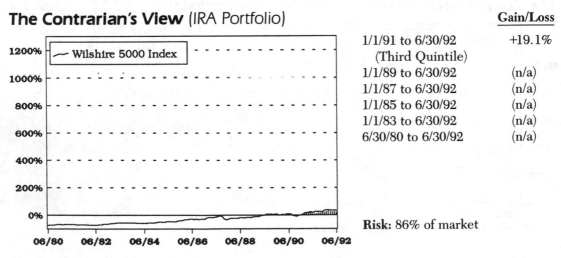

	Gain/Loss
1/1/91 to 6/30/92	+19.1%
(Third Quintile)	
1/1/89 to 6/30/92	(n/a)
1/1/87 to 6/30/92	(n/a)
1/1/85 to 6/30/92	(n/a)
1/1/83 to 6/30/92	(n/a)
6/30/80 to 6/30/92	(n/a)

Risk: 86% of market

Crawford Perspectives

Address
1456 Second Ave.
Suite 145
New York, NY 10021

Editor
Arch Crawford

Phone Number
212-744-6973

Subscription Rates
$ 85.00/3 issues
$250.00/year

Telephone Hotline
No

Money Management
No

CRAWFORD PERSPECTIVES

MARKET TIMING BY PLANETARY CYCLES AND TECHNICAL ANALYSIS SINCE 1977
205 EAST 78TH STREET NEW YORK, N.Y. 10021 (212) 628-1156

JULY 11, 1992
VOL.92-(1)

WE BELIEVE THE NEXT IMPORTANT MARKET MOVE WILL BE ......UP!!!

We made it through the Eclipse series without major incident in the stock market, which is more than we can say for California (state bankruptcy plus largest earthquake in decades) or Florida (20 inches of rain in 7 days) or numerous places hit by tornadoes, hail & drought. Last issue we warned of "...earthquake and weather abnormalities (June-July)." We also said we thought the market would break to the upside by the June 30th Solar Eclipse and that it would be a fakeout before going lower. The next day, July 1st, has been the high of the rally so far...BUT...the market broke DOWN before up and we are now suspecting that the DOWN was the FAKEOUT! We also suggested coming into the Solar Eclipse on the LONG (UP) side of the market but with close stop-loss orders. Since the market went down first, we were stopped out of all LONG positions on the 16th or 17th of June. We recommend to reposition on the UPSIDE on an hour print over 3360 on the Dow Industrials or 416 on the S&P 500 (cash) if it hasn't happened by the time you get this. If these LONG positions are filled, place stop-loss orders at DJIA 3260 (hourly) and S&P500 below 400 anytime. We also said last time: "Don't trade around the eclipses" because "normal trading patterns are often disrupted" leading to WHIPSAW markets... AND HOW! We essentially are the same place we were on June 10-11, one month ago, but with many a "choppy" move in between.

Technically, many of our indicators went deep enough 18-23 June to propose that an important bottom may already be past! It was certainly NOT across the board and that leaves us with a somewhat queasy feeling that maybe the LOW is past and maybe it isn't. That leads us to a BUY with the stipulations above, i.e. if those levels are overcome, and with close stops in case it's another Whipsaw. The most important position these days is to minimize RISK because with today's fundamental overvaluation levels, when she blows, she's gonna blow BIG (like another 1987)! The most positive valuation component is the BOND/STOCK YIELD ratio. At least from the short term Bond yield perspective, this measure shows the stock market to be a glaring undervalued BUY!! Other technical positives: the 10-day Advances-Declines (NYSE) failed to break the April 8 low of -3707, worst case so far = -3034 on June 22nd and yesterday's figure +2585 is the highest since January, and the NEW HIGHS have recovered sharply from the lows and the July 2nd figure of 105 is the highest since February 27th! Maximum NEW LOWS of 78 on June 17th also failed to break the April 8th number, 84, which was the highest since November 1st of 1990! Although much long-term deterioration persists, THIS MARKET IS NOT FALLING APART!! Joe Granville is remaining significantly bearish despite his CLIMAX indicator having given a number of Downside Non-confirmations since its maximum LOW -13 on May 15th. Even much bigger down days in the averages have failed to break this important indicator lower. Watch and see if and when Joe turns positive. He is a genius and his work is magnificent, even when he doesn't follow it! He's still looking for another killer wave down. ASTRONOMIC CYCLES also agree with another leg down (see chart last issue), but Intermediate moves in those cycle sums are not as reliable as Big Ones.

TELEPHONE UPDATE   1 900-PRODIGY $1/minute   TWICE DAILY   10 & 2 E.D.T.

Crawford Perspectives is published ten times a year by Arch Crawford. Crawford also has a telephone hotline update service, but since he charges extra for it, the HFD does not take its recommendations into account in calculating his performance. Because *Crawford Perspectives* is a timing service and does not have particular model portfolios, the HFD is unable to calculate a Performance Rating for it. Instead, the HFD's monitoring of its performance is limited to measuring its ability to time the stock market.

Crawford's approach to market timing is somewhat unique within the newsletter industry because his approach is based in part on astrology (or, to use his words, "planetary cycles"). He bases his market timing also on more conventional technical analysis. Whatever his method, it involves fairly active trading: Between the beginning of 1989 and the middle of 1992, he recommended a switch into or out of the market about once every two months on average. His resultant timing portfolios were about 10% to 15% less volatile or risky than buying and holding the market itself.

The HFD has performance data for this newsletter since the beginning of 1989. An investor who alternated between hypothetical shares of the Wilshire 5000 and T-Bills according to those of Crawford's signals that were published in his newsletter would have made 46.8% over the subsequent 42 months, in contrast to a 60.3% gain for a buy-and-hold. An investor who actually went short the market on Crawford's "sell" signals, instead of going into T-Bills, would have made just 23.4%. Part of this underperformance can be accounted for by his below-market risk, but not all of it: Even on a risk-adjusted basis, his timing has lagged the market.

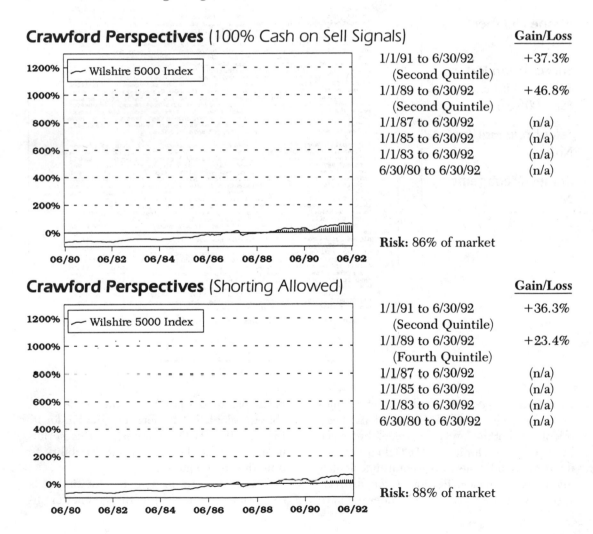

Crawford Perspectives (100% Cash on Sell Signals)

	Gain/Loss
1/1/91 to 6/30/92 (Second Quintile)	+37.3%
1/1/89 to 6/30/92 (Second Quintile)	+46.8%
1/1/87 to 6/30/92	(n/a)
1/1/85 to 6/30/92	(n/a)
1/1/83 to 6/30/92	(n/a)
6/30/80 to 6/30/92	(n/a)

Risk: 86% of market

Crawford Perspectives (Shorting Allowed)

	Gain/Loss
1/1/91 to 6/30/92 (Second Quintile)	+36.3%
1/1/89 to 6/30/92 (Fourth Quintile)	+23.4%
1/1/87 to 6/30/92	(n/a)
1/1/85 to 6/30/92	(n/a)
1/1/83 to 6/30/92	(n/a)
6/30/80 to 6/30/92	(n/a)

Risk: 88% of market

Czeschin's Mutual Fund
Outlook & Recommendations

Address
P.O. Box 1423
Baltimore, MD
   21203-1423

Editor
Robert Czeschin

Phone Number
410-558-1699

Subscription Rates
$147.00/year

Telephone Hotline
Yes

Money Management
No

Czeschin's

MUTUAL FUND
Outlook & Recommendations

New Recommendations Summary:

              Buy: Hopewell Holdings
                   New World Development

Investment Markets Outlook:

                  The Dow's best days are past

    Very likely, the best days for U.S. stocks have already past
-- at least for 1992. I say this for several reasons.

    In my view, much of the market's advance to its last closing
high of 3413 on 1 June has been a result of the Fed's low
interest rate policy -- as US investors sought higher yields than
what they could get on CDs and money funds.

    But notice what happened on 2 July -- when the U.S. Federal
Reserve cut the discount rate a full-half point. The Dow Jones
Industrial Average still fell 24 points. This was a signal that
U.S. share prices have gone about as high as they can on the
strength of lower interest rates alone.

    So if lower interest no longer do the trick, what will it
take for the market to reclaim the high ground above 3,300?
Well, a dramatic improvement in corporate earnings would probably
do. Unfortunately, that is also exceedingly unlikely. After
all, one of the reasons behind the recent interest rate cut was a
dramatic worsening in the prospects for rapid economic recovery.

                       Distant thunder

    While the bullish power of lower interest rates has waned,
bearish forces are gathering strength. One bearish factor is
declining foreign interest in U.S. stocks.

Czeschin's Mutual Fund Outlook & Recommendations is published episodically (more or less once a month on average) by Robert Czeschin, who supplements his newsletter with a weekly telephone hotline update.

Czeschin is based in Hong Kong, and he brings an international perspective to his newsletter and his model portfolios, each of which is well-diversified globally. Though most of Czeschin's portfolio recommendations are of mutual funds, at times he also advises holding securities other than mutual funds.

Czeschin's approach is based on his fundamental analysis of individual companies and his macroeconomic analysis of various nations' economies. Technical analysis apparently plays no part, with the possible exception of his so-called "Jaguar" portfolio: Czeschin recommends that all positions in this particular portfolio have a 20% trailing stop loss.

Czeschin places these trailing stop loss orders on this portfolio because it is the most speculative of his three. The hope, of course, is that in return for incurring this higher risk,

a follower of this portfolio will achieve a greater performance over time. At least for the 18 months through mid-1992, however, this hope went unrealized: Czeschin's "Jaguar" portfolio performed less well than his other two, less risky, portfolios.

Czeschin's best performer for these 18 months was his "Long-Term Growth" portfolio, followed closely by his "Income" portfolio—which nearly equaled the market's return with less than half the risk. Taking the gains of all three portfolios into account, along with their risk, Czeschin equaled the market's return on a risk-adjusted basis.

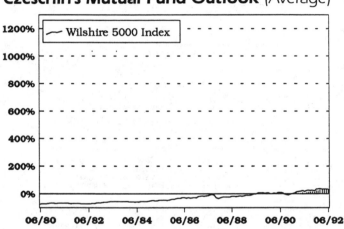

Czeschin's Mutual Fund Outlook (Average)

Gain/Loss

1/1/91 to 6/30/92	+27.4%
(Second Quintile)	
1/1/89 to 6/30/92 Gain:	(n/a)
1/1/87 to 6/30/92 Gain:	(n/a)
1/1/85 to 6/30/92 Gain:	(n/a)
1/1/83 to 6/30/92 Gain:	(n/a)
6/30/80 to 6/30/92 Gain:	(n/a)

Risk: 83% of market

Czeschin's Mutual Fund Outlook (Jaguar Portfolio)

Gain/Loss

1/1/91 to 6/30/92	+15.5%
(Fourth Quintile)	
1/1/89 to 6/30/92	(n/a)
1/1/87 to 6/30/92	(n/a)
1/1/85 to 6/30/92	(n/a)
1/1/83 to 6/30/92	(n/a)
6/30/80 to 6/30/92	(n/a)

Risk: 150% of market

Czeschin's Mutual Fund Outlook (Long-Term Growth Portfolio)

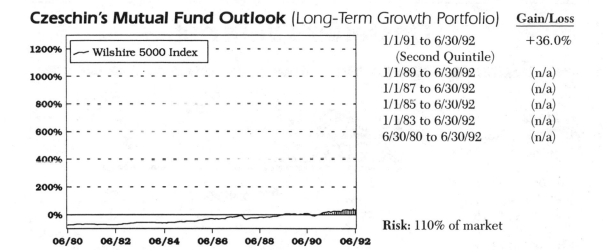

	Gain/Loss
1/1/91 to 6/30/92	+36.0%
(Second Quintile)	
1/1/89 to 6/30/92	(n/a)
1/1/87 to 6/30/92	(n/a)
1/1/85 to 6/30/92	(n/a)
1/1/83 to 6/30/92	(n/a)
6/30/80 to 6/30/92	(n/a)

Risk: 110% of market

Czeschin's Mutual Fund Outlook (Income Portfolio)

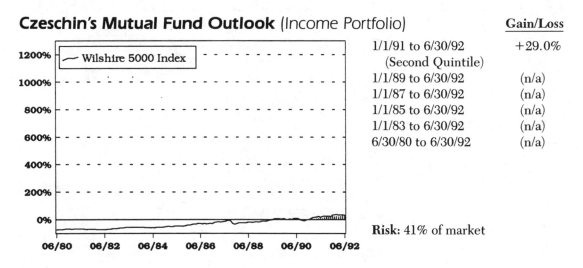

	Gain/Loss
1/1/91 to 6/30/92	+29.0%
(Second Quintile)	
1/1/89 to 6/30/92	(n/a)
1/1/87 to 6/30/92	(n/a)
1/1/85 to 6/30/92	(n/a)
1/1/83 to 6/30/92	(n/a)
6/30/80 to 6/30/92	(n/a)

Risk: 41% of market

Dessauer's Journal

Address
P.O. Box 1718
Orleans, MA 02653

Editors
John Dessauer and
Susanna Graham

Phone Number
508-255-1651

Subscription Rates
$ 35.00/2 months
$105.00/6 months
$195.00/year

Telephone Hotline
Yes

Money Management
Yes

Dessauer's Journal OF FINANCIAL MARKETS

AUTHENTIC DEVELOPMENTS FROM AN UNTRODDEN POINT OF VIEW   July 15, 1992

CURRENCIES AND STOCK PRICES

Americans, including many well educated, otherwise-sophisticated professionals, have the wrong idea when it comes to foreign stocks and currency markets. They understand the math but do not seem to fully grasp the complex interaction between currencies and foreign stock prices.

For example, some are concerned that the German mark might tumble when German interest rates finally come down. It is by no means certain the mark will fall. The U.S. dollar was supposed to collapse if U.S. interest rates fell below interest rates in Germany. However, when that day came the experts were wrong. The dollar has not collapsed in spite of the fact interest rates on dollars are now 5% lower than similar interest rates on German marks. The experts could be wrong again. The German mark may hold its ground even after German interest rates come down. But, there is the possibility that the German mark will fall versus the U.S. dollar.

For the sake of discussion, suppose the mark falls 25% versus the U.S. dollar. Mathematically, if all else remained the same, the value of German assets, including stocks, would decline by 25% in U.S. dollar terms. Supposedly American investors would suffer losses on German investments. The risk of a significant decline in the German mark is what stops some American investors from buying German stocks. They fear the mathematics of changes in the currency markets.

What is missing from this sort of risk analysis is real market experience. Not all German assets are the same. Americans holding cash in a German bank would suffer a 25% loss if the mark fell. Americans holding German bonds would also suffer, but not quite as much. The interest paid on the bonds would cushion them against the full impact of a fall in the currency. Holders of German stocks may not suffer at all. In fact, they could profit from a fall in the mark. This is one reason foreign stocks are more attractive than either foreign currencies or foreign bonds.

BRITISH PETROLEUM (NYSE, BP), $47¹/₈, YLD: 9.9%

BP plunged on fear of a dividend cut in the wake of the chairman's resignation. The dividend costs 900 million pounds per year, while earnings are roughly half that. To be fair, after adjusting for special charges, BP should earn 1 billion pounds, enough to just cover the dividend, with crude oil at $20 a barrel. But, BP also needs cash for capital improvements, etc. The market has been trying to guess how much the board will pay shareholders. At $47⅞ the market is priced for a 50% cut. Odds are the board will not be that severe and that BP's stock will return to the $60-$65 level soon after the next dividend announcement. BP is a buy.

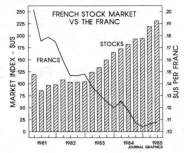

Even professional investors have trouble with this chart. They think it must be a fabrication. It isn't. The truth is that American investors enjoyed significant gains on French stocks during a time when the French franc was extremely weak.

In May 1981 Francois Mitterand managed to sweep national elections in France. Days before the elections the polls pointed in the opposite direction. For that reason both the French franc and French stocks held their ground until the election results were known. The French stock market plunged on the news of a Mitterand-socialist victory. American investors were reluctant to buy French stocks, even though they were trading at bargain prices in French franc terms. The French franc was expected to decline in value as a result of having a socialist government. Although not exactly for the expected reasons, the French franc did fall sharply in the years following Mitterand's shocking victory. At the end of 1984 the French franc had lost 48.5% of its 1981 value versus the U.S. dollar.

More shocking than the Mitterand election was the fact that, despite the steep fall in the currency, French stocks provided American investors with outstanding gains. The Morgan Stanley Capital International Perspective French stock index, expressed in U.S. dollars, climbed 170% between spring 1981 and summer 1985. In other words, the French stock market rose much more than the franc fell because French companies enjoyed benefits from the fall in the currency. A lower French franc made French companies more competitive. The price of goods and services from France declined. At the

To page 2

Dessauer's Journal is published every three weeks by John Dessauer and Susanna Graham and is supplemented by a twice-weekly telephone hotline update. Dessauer once worked for Citibank in Switzerland, and his letter always has taken an international perspective toward investing. His recommended portfolio

typically has devoted 30% to 40% of assets to non-U.S. securities. (Dessauer does offer portfolio advice for subscribers interested only in investing in U.S. securities, but the HFD tracks his "International" portfolio, since this is the preferred portfolio: It includes all his recommended securities and his asset allocation advice between U.S. and foreign stocks and bonds.)

One of the advantages of international diversification is a reduction in portfolio volatility and risk, and this has been true for *Dessauer's Journal*. According to the HFD, its risk level has been about 5% lower than the market's since 1982. Despite this lower risk, it has appreciated almost as much as the market, making it one of the better-performing newsletters on a risk-adjusted basis (sixth out of 36 letters the HFD tracked over the nine and one-half years through mid-1992).

Dessauer is more of a buy-and-hold inves-
tor than he is a trader. Most of the positions in his recommended portfolio, for example, are held for more than a year. His telephone hotline is used primarily for commentary on the markets, and rarely (if ever) to recommend short-term trades.

For the nine and one-half years from the beginning of 1983 through mid-1992, Dessauer's portfolio gained 255.5%, slightly behind the Wilshire 5000's total return of 278.6%. And as mentioned above, when his slightly below-market risk is taken into account, his performance comes even closer to matching the market's.

Dessauer's Journal

	Gain/Loss
1/1/91 to 6/30/92	+50.6%
(First Quintile)	
1/1/89 to 6/30/92	+51.4%
(Second Quintile)	
1/1/87 to 6/30/92	+72.4%
(Second Quintile)	
1/1/85 to 6/30/92	+193.9%
(Second Quintile)	
1/1/83 to 6/30/92	+255.5%
(First Quintile)	
6/30/80 to 6/30/92	(n/a)

Risk: 97% of market

The Dines Letter

Address
P.O. Box 22
Belvedere, CA 94920

Editor
James Dines

Subscription Rates
$115.00/6 months
$195.00/year

Telephone Hotline
No

Money Management
Yes

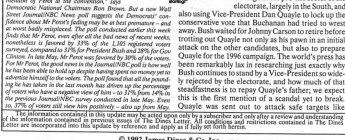

July 10, 1992 Vol 32, No 13
DJI: 3330.56
DJT: 1303.25
DJU: 218.64
London Gold PM Fix: . . . 348.30

The Dines Letter

PUBLISHED SINCE JANUARY 1960

The river continues on its way to the sea, broken the wheel of the mill or not. — **Kahlil Gibran**

TDL'S LATEST ON POLITICS:
How Will Perot Affect Stocks?

Ross Perot's Presidential campaign is spooking investors in Mexico. The once-booming Mexican Bolsa de Valores, which had held steady for three months, took a nosedive in mid-June, losing 15%, when Perot's campaign heated up. The Texas billionaire doesn't like the proposed North American Free Trade Agreement. BUSINESS WEEK, 29 Jun 92

The great rule of conduct for us, in regard to foreign nations, is in extending our commercial relations to have with them as little political connection as possible. So far as we have already formed engagements, let them be fulfilled with perfect good faith. Here let us stop. Europe has a set of primary interests which to us have none, or a very remote relation. Hence she must be engaged in frequent controversies, the cause of which are essentially foreign to our concerns. Hence, therefore, it must be unwise in us to implicate ourselves, by artificial ties, in the ordinary combinations and collisions of her friendships or enmities...Why, by interweaving our destiny with that of any part of Europe, entangle our peace and prosperity in the toils of European ambition, rivalship, interests, humor, or caprice? **George Washington**

In the convention that opens here next week, Democrats plan to target George Bush's weaknesses and largely ignore Mr Perot, confident in the belief that the independent's support will inevitably dwindle as Election Day nears. "I expect very little if any mention of Perot at the convention," says Democratic National Chairman Ron Brown. But a new Wall Street Journal/NBC News poll suggests the Democrats' confidence about Mr Perot's fading may be at best premature – and at worst badly misplaced. The poll conducted earlier this week finds that Mr Perot, even after all the bad news of recent weeks, nonetheless is favored by 33% of the 1,105 registered voters surveyed, compared to 31% for President Bush and 28% for Gov Clinton. In late May, Mr Perot was favored by 30% of the voters. For Mr Perot, the good news in the Journal/NBC poll is how well he has been able to hold up despite having spent no money yet to advertise himself to the voters. The poll found that all the pounding he has taken in the last month has driven up the percentage of voters who have a negative view of him – to 31% from 14% in the previous Journal/NBC survey conducted in late May. Even so, 37% of voters still view him positively – also up from May.

More important, Mr Perot remains the only one of the three candidates who is viewed more positively than negatively by the voters. Mr Bush is viewed negatively by 46%, positively by 35%; Mr Clinton, negatively by 38%, positively by 30%. WALL STREET JOURNAL, 9 Jul 92

Turgidly cosseted politicians immersed in the slatternly fen of politics appear to only dimly comprehend the marmoreal numenousness of candidate Ross Perot as a cynosure; indeed, British bookmakers are now quoting four-to-one odds against a Perot victory, which we consider an attractive gamble.

Early doctors used the word "recipe" from the Latin *recipere* which means "to take," and doctors still put RX (or recipe) on their prescriptions. George Bush's secret plans were to first establish that Perot's position was unknown, setting up an inviting highway for a smear, and then "redefining" Perot by planning to mock his "kook" preoccupation with soldiers missing in action – unfortunately, Boris Yeltsin yanked the rug out from under this particular recipe when he announced that US soldiers had indeed been spirited from Vietnam and Korea to China and then the Soviet Union. So Bush then decided to attack Perot for having made money, which is surely the wrong tack and which turned out to have been a crowd *pleaser.* Bush's private plan also included staking out the pro-life sector of the electorate, largely in the South, and also using Vice-President Dan Quayle to lock up the conservative vote that Buchanan had tried to wrest away. Bush waited for Johnny Carson to retire before trotting out Quayle not only as his pawn in an initial attack on the other candidates, but also to prepare Quayle for the 1996 campaign. The world's press has been remarkably lax in researching just exactly why Bush continues to stand by a Vice-President so widely rejected by the electorate, and how much of that steadfastness is to repay Quayle's father; we expect this is the first mention of a scandal yet to break. Quayle was sent out to attack safe targets like

"Kemosabel . . . The music's starting! The music's starting!"

The Dines Letter is published twice each month by James Dines and is not supplemented by a telephone update. Dines also publishes what he calls an "Interim Warning Service," which provides subscribers, for an additional subscription fee, with access to any change in Dines's thinking between issues.

Because regular subscribers to Dines's newsletter are not given access to the recommendations in this separate service, they are not taken into account in the HFD's calculations.

Dines calls himself the "original goldbug," having first recommended gold and gold shares in the 1960s. In the 1980s Dines didn't recommend selling gold until June 1982, however, when it was trading at around $300—well below its $875 peak set in early 1980. Since $300 more or less marked the low in gold, Dines has been roundly criticized for his timing. However, at that same time Dines argued that regardless of how gold would perform from there, the stock market would do even better. Subsequent events proved him right.

With Dines's shift from gold to stocks, he became much more short-term oriented. Prior to the shift, his "Supervised Lists" were rarely traded and contained mostly Treasury bills. Subsequently, they became actively traded and frequently owned options and low-priced stocks.

Dines's best-performing portfolio for the 12 years through mid-1992 was his "Growth" portfolio, which gained 558.2%, in contrast to the Wilshire 5000's 432.7%. While it alone is one of the best-performing portfolios of any

the HFD followed since 1980, when this portfolio's gain is averaged in with the performance of the other portfolios Dines also has recommended (several of which have been discontinued along the way), the 12-year performance of the newsletter as a whole drops to a gain of just 38.3%.

Since 1985, the HFD also has been tracking Dines's timing of the gold market, specifically the buy and sell signals he gives for gold's short term. An investor who switched between gold bullion and T-Bills according to those signals would have made 3.2% between the beginning of 1985 and mid-1992, in contrast to an 11.1% gain for bullion itself.

More recently still the HFD began tracking Dines's signals for the bond market. Over the three and one-half years through mid-1992, during which time the Shearson Lehman Treasury Index gained 46.3%, an investor switching between bonds and T-Bills on Dines's signals would have made 36.3%.

The Dines Letter (Average)

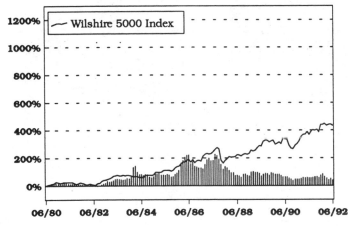

	Gain/Loss
1/1/91 to 6/30/92 (Fifth Quintile)	−5.8%
1/1/89 to 6/30/92 (Fifth Quintile)	−18.4%
1/1/87 to 6/30/92 (Fifth Quintile)	−39.5%
1/1/85 to 6/30/92 (Fifth Quintile)	−16.5%
1/1/83 to 6/30/92 (Fifth Quintile)	+18.1%
6/30/80 to 6/30/92 (Fifth Quintile)	+38.3%

Risk: 138% of market

The Dines Letter (Good Grade Portfolio)

	Gain/Loss
1/1/91 to 6/30/92 (Fifth Quintile)	−5.0%
1/1/89 to 6/30/92 (Third Quintile)	+34.9%
1/1/87 to 6/30/92	(n/a)
1/1/85 to 6/30/92	(n/a)
1/1/83 to 6/30/92	(n/a)
6/30/80 to 6/30/92	(n/a)

Risk: 155% of market

The Dines Letter (Long-Term Growth Portfolio)

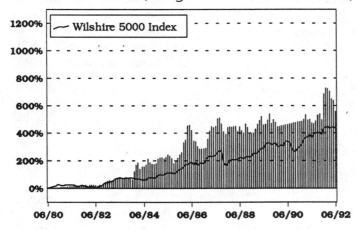

	Gain/Loss
1/1/91 to 6/30/92 (Fourth Quintile)	+13.0%
1/1/89 to 6/30/92 (Third Quintile)	+33.6%
1/1/87 to 6/30/92 (Second Quintile)	+70.1%
1/1/85 to 6/30/92 (Second Quintile)	+136.6%
1/1/83 to 6/30/92 (First Quintile)	+335.2%
6/30/80 to 6/30/92 (First Quintile)	+558.2%

Risk: 228% of market

The Dines Letter (Precious Metals Portfolio)

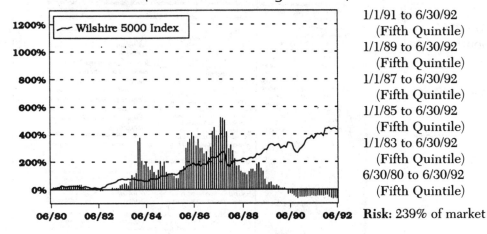

	Gain/Loss
1/1/91 to 6/30/92	−6.1%
(Fifth Quintile)	
1/1/89 to 6/30/92	+13.7%
(Fifth Quintile)	
1/1/87 to 6/30/92	(n/a)
1/1/85 to 6/30/92	(n/a)
1/1/83 to 6/30/92	(n/a)
6/30/80 to 6/30/92	(n/a)

Risk: 93% of market

The Dines Letter (Short-Term Trading Portfolio)

	Gain/Loss
1/1/91 to 6/30/92	−28.3%
(Fifth Quintile)	
1/1/89 to 6/30/92	−85.5%
(Fifth Quintile)	
1/1/87 to 6/30/92	−91.1%
(Fifth Quintile)	
1/1/85 to 6/30/92	−86.2%
(Fifth Quintile)	
1/1/83 to 6/30/92	−66.6%
(Fifth Quintile)	
6/30/80 to 6/30/92	−66.9%
(Fifth Quintile)	

Risk: 239% of market

Donoghue's Moneyletter

Address
290 Elliot St.
Box 91004
Ashland, MA
    01721-9104

Editor
Ann Needle

Phone Number
508-881-2800

Subscription Rates
$ 49.00/6 months
$127.00/year

Telephone Hotline
Yes

Money Management
Yes

July 1992 — first issue
Vol. 13, No. 13
ISSN: 0197-7083

Donoghue'$ MONEYLETTER®

Your Award-Winning Guide To Mutual Fund Profits

Moneyline

Donoghue's HOTLINE
900/773-4868
updated every
Tuesday and
Friday at
5 P.M.
(ET)

The Fed to the Rescue?

On July 2, the markets were treated to a pre-4th of July rally as the June employment data was released showing an unexpectedly large decline of 177,000 jobs and an increase in the unemployment rate to 7.8 percent. The markets had expected an increase of about 85,000 jobs and a civilian unemployment rate of 7.4 percent. **The unexpected news from the employment front has finally pushed the Fed to lower the discount rate to 3.0 percent, which should greatly benefit the bond and stock markets.**

The employment results suggest that hopes of a near-term rebound in the economy have faded. While this would normally cause selling in the stock markets, the initial reaction has been positive. Many analysts now feel that the Fed's actions will be beneficial for economic growth by opening the way for a capital infusion to business. Also, the cuts should lead to lower mortgage rates, which helps both the housing and construction in-

(continued on page 3)

Inside MONEYLETTER

◆ Moderate and Venturesome investors — anticipate a potential "buy" fund.
.... See page 3

◆ Go ahead and enjoy that "free lunch" at Schwab.
.... See page 7

◆ Donoghue Signal Portfolio investors should bend the rules when it come to "buys."
.... See page 8

☆☆ Next issue mails ☆☆
July 21

Insight

A New Ball Game
by Walter S. Frank, Chief Investment Officer

We're batting .500 when it comes to our outlook for 1992. We said in December that it would be tougher to make money in 1992 than in 1991 — right on. Then again, we also said that asset allocation would be the key to success in '92 — not so (at least so far). The key in the first half of this year was fund selection. Choose the right fund type (value) and you made money, otherwise you lost (aggressive growth).

What's ahead for the rest of the year and into the first quarter of '93? Well, slightly bloodied but unbowed, we're sticking to our guns, with one change. We now rank fund selection as equally important as asset allocation in determining performance over the next six to nine months. Put another way, it won't be enough to be in markets where the averages show gains, you will also have to be in funds which have a high correlation with the averages.

This sounds like a truism, but it isn't. With the exception of Japan, most stock markets are in long-term uptrends. But they have been picked over. Achieving above average performance is no longer a piece of cake. Only truly superior stock-picking ability can produce satisfactory results from here on.

Now for the good news. Despite all the gloom that's around now, we think the next six to nine months will prove to be better for patient investors than the last six. We don't see sensational gains ahead, but we think equity markets, both here and abroad, offer opportunities. The same holds true for the bond markets, at least in the near-term and maybe longer. Here's why...

We now rank fund selection as equally important as asset allocation in determining performance over the next six to nine months. Put another way, it won't be enough to be in markets where the averages show gains, you will also have to be in funds which have a high correlation with the averages.

Money: Cheap here, cheaper there

Behind all our thinking is the importance of trends in interest rates here and abroad. U.S. interest rates are low and, in the broad sweep of things, are close to hitting bottom. Abroad (in Europe at least) they're high. But, following the lead of the all-powerful German monetary authorities (the Bundesbank), we expect to see rates coming down in Europe, maybe late this year or early next year. The exact timing is not clear, but it doesn't really matter.

Here in the U.S., the importance of low interest rates cannot be overstressed. By all the usual rules of thumb, the U.S. market appears fully valued, if not over valued. But throw in interest rates and, as we see it, the market is still undervalued (yes, even at 3300).

(continued on page 2)

IBC Donoghue a service of IBC/Donoghue, Inc.   290 Eliot Street, Box 91004, Ashland, MA 01721-9104

Donoghue's Moneyletter, published by William Donoghue and edited by Ann Needle, is published twice monthly and supplemented by a twice-weekly telephone hotline.

Donoghue is best known for his early championing of money market funds and for his pioneering work in tracking and comparing yields of money-market mutual funds. Initially his newsletter focused on them, and only later did his newsletter's scope expand to include other mutual funds. Only more recently still did he start to translate his recommendations into particular model portfolios.

The model portfolio for which the HFD has

the most data has been in existence since the beginning of 1987, entitled the "Venturesome" model portfolio. It gained 59.2% over the five and one-half years through mid-1992, in comparison to a 93.3% total return for the Wilshire 5000. Over the three and one-half years for which the HFD has data for Donoghue's additional three portfolios (during which time the Wilshire 5000 gained 60.3%), his "Venturesome" portfolio did the best (gaining 42.9%), followed in order by his "Conservative" portfolio (+39.0%), his "Signal" portfolio (+37.8%), and his "Moderate" portfolio (+34.6%).

Because Donoghue's portfolios don't invest solely in the stock market, however, it's unfair to judge them solely according to whether they beat the Wilshire 5000. A better standard might be an unmanaged portfolio that is equally divided among the stock, bond and gold markets—the three markets Donoghue focuses on. Over the three and one-half years through mid-1992, such a portfolio gained 28.0%, or less than each of Donoghue's portfolios over this period.

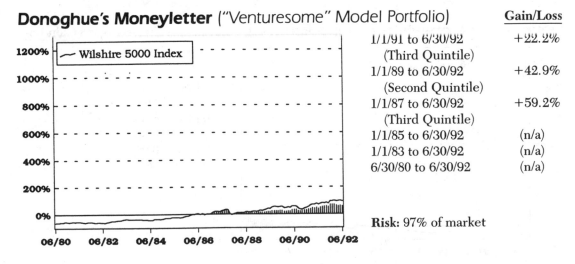

Donoghue's Moneyletter (Average)

	Gain/Loss
1/1/91 to 6/30/92 (Third Quintile)	+22.5%
1/1/89 to 6/30/92 (Third Quintile)	+39.2%
1/1/87 to 6/30/92 (Third Quintile)	+55.1%
1/1/85 to 6/30/92	(n/a)
1/1/83 to 6/30/92	(n/a)
6/30/80 to 6/30/92	(n/a)

Risk: 86% of market

Donoghue's Moneyletter ("Venturesome" Model Portfolio)

	Gain/Loss
1/1/91 to 6/30/92 (Third Quintile)	+22.2%
1/1/89 to 6/30/92 (Second Quintile)	+42.9%
1/1/87 to 6/30/92 (Third Quintile)	+59.2%
1/1/85 to 6/30/92	(n/a)
1/1/83 to 6/30/92	(n/a)
6/30/80 to 6/30/92	(n/a)

Risk: 97% of market

Donoghue's Moneyletter (Moderate Mutual Fund Portfolio)

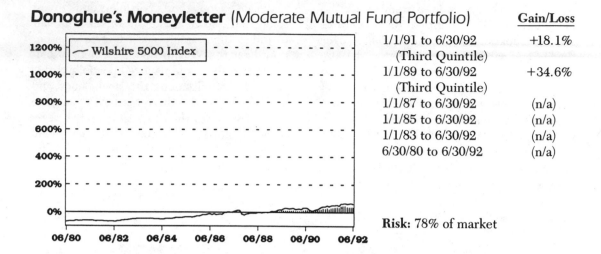

	Gain/Loss
1/1/91 to 6/30/92	+18.1%
(Third Quintile)	
1/1/89 to 6/30/92	+34.6%
(Third Quintile)	
1/1/87 to 6/30/92	(n/a)
1/1/85 to 6/30/92	(n/a)
1/1/83 to 6/30/92	(n/a)
6/30/80 to 6/30/92	(n/a)

Risk: 78% of market

Donoghue's Moneyletter (Conservative Mutual Fund Portfolio)

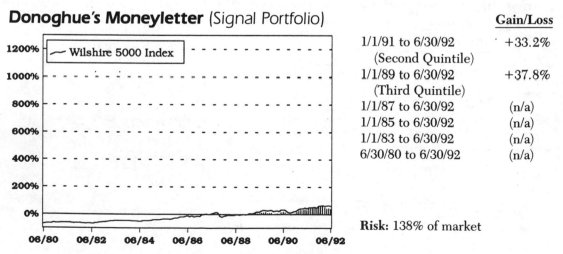

	Gain/Loss
1/1/91 to 6/30/92	+15.8%
(Fourth Quintile)	
1/1/89 to 6/30/92	+39.0%
(Third Quintile)	
1/1/87 to 6/30/92	(n/a)
1/1/85 to 6/30/92	(n/a)
1/1/83 to 6/30/92	(n/a)
6/30/80 to 6/30/92	(n/a)

Risk: 46% of market

Donoghue's Moneyletter (Signal Portfolio)

	Gain/Loss
1/1/91 to 6/30/92	+33.2%
(Second Quintile)	
1/1/89 to 6/30/92	+37.8%
(Third Quintile)	
1/1/87 to 6/30/92	(n/a)
1/1/85 to 6/30/92	(n/a)
1/1/83 to 6/30/92	(n/a)
6/30/80 to 6/30/92	(n/a)

Risk: 138% of market

Dow Theory Forecasts

Address
7412 Calumet Ave.
Hammond, IN
  46324-2692

Editor
Charles Carlson

Phone Number
219-931-6480

Subscription Rates
$233.00/year

Telephone Hotline
No

Money Management
No

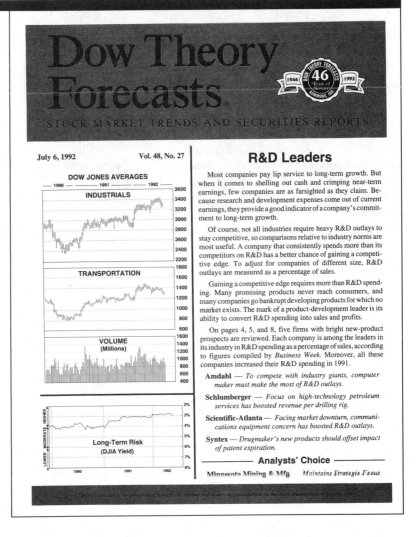

July 6, 1992   Vol. 48, No. 27

R&D Leaders

Most companies pay lip service to long-term growth. But when it comes to shelling out cash and crimping near-term earnings, few companies are as farsighted as they claim. Because research and development expenses come out of current earnings, they provide a good indicator of a company's commitment to long-term growth.

Of course, not all industries require heavy R&D outlays to stay competitive, so comparisons relative to industry norms are most useful. A company that consistently spends more than its competitors on R&D has a better chance of gaining a competitive edge. To adjust for companies of different size, R&D outlays are measured as a percentage of sales.

Gaining a competitive edge requires more than R&D spending. Many promising products never reach consumers, and many companies go bankrupt developing products for which no market exists. The mark of a product-development leader is its ability to convert R&D spending into sales and profits.

On pages 4, 5, and 8, five firms with bright new-product prospects are reviewed. Each company is among the leaders in its industry in R&D spending as a percentage of sales, according to figures compiled by *Business Week*. Moreover, all these companies increased their R&D spending in 1991.

Amdahl — *To compete with industry giants, computer maker must make the most of R&D outlays.*

Schlumberger — *Focus on high-technology petroleum services has boosted revenue per drilling rig.*

Scientific-Atlanta — *Facing market downturn, communications equipment concern has boosted R&D outlays.*

Syntex — *Drugmaker's new products should offset impact of patent expiration.*

—— **Analysts' Choice** ——

Minnesota Mining & Mfg   *Maintains Strategic Focus*

Dow Theory Forecasts is an independent investment adviser and makes no commissions on the stock transactions of its subscribers.

Dow Theory Forecasts was founded by LeRoy Evans in the 1940s, and to this day the operation remains in his family, in the hands of his sons. Along with Standard and Poor's newsletter *The Outlook*, *The Value Line Investment Survey*, and *The United & Babson Investment Report* (all reviewed elsewhere in this volume), this service is one of the oldest published in this country. It is a review of the financial markets and a source of investment ideas in addition to being a guide on which stocks should be bought and sold.

Dow Theory Forecasts maintains five different lists of recommended stocks, ranging from the conservative "Income" and "Investment" lists to the more aggressive "Speculative" and "Low-Priced and Special Situations" lists. These lists typically have between 20 and 50 stocks in them, and the service pinpoints a subset of stocks among each of them that are especially recommended for current purchase.

Up until early 1990, the newsletter did not specify the percentage division of each portfolio between stocks and cash. Until then, accordingly, the HFD constructed model portfolios for each of the newsletter's recommended lists that were fully invested at all times in those stocks that were especially recommended. Beginning in 1990, however, the newsletter began translating its market timing into specific percentage allocations for the market and cash, at which point the HFD began taking this additional advice into account.

Dow Theory Forecasts bases its market timing on its interpretation of the Dow Theory. In contrast to this reliance upon technical analysis, the newsletter's selection of individual stocks is based on a combination of factors, primarily fundamental (such as price-earnings multiples, the prospects for various industry groups, etc.).

The best-performing group of stocks offered by *Dow Theory Forecasts* is its "Investment" list, which gained 419.5% over the 12 years through mid-1992, essentially equaling the 432.7% total return of the Wilshire 5000 over the same period. The poorest performance of its lists was turned in by its "Speculative" stocks list at 215.9%. On average, the newsletter's portfolios have underperformed the market, on both a total-return and a risk-adjusted basis.

Dow Theory Forecasts (Average)

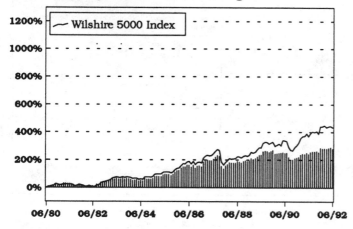

	Gain/Loss
1/1/91 to 6/30/92 (Third Quintile)	+20.9%
1/1/89 to 6/30/92 (Fourth Quintile)	+29.4%
1/1/87 to 6/30/92 (Third Quintile)	+52.8%
1/1/85 to 6/30/92 (Third Quintile)	+131.6%
1/1/83 to 6/30/92 (Second Quintile)	+168.7%
6/30/80 to 6/30/92 (Third Quintile)	+280.1%

Risk: 74% of market

Dow Theory Forecasts (Income List)

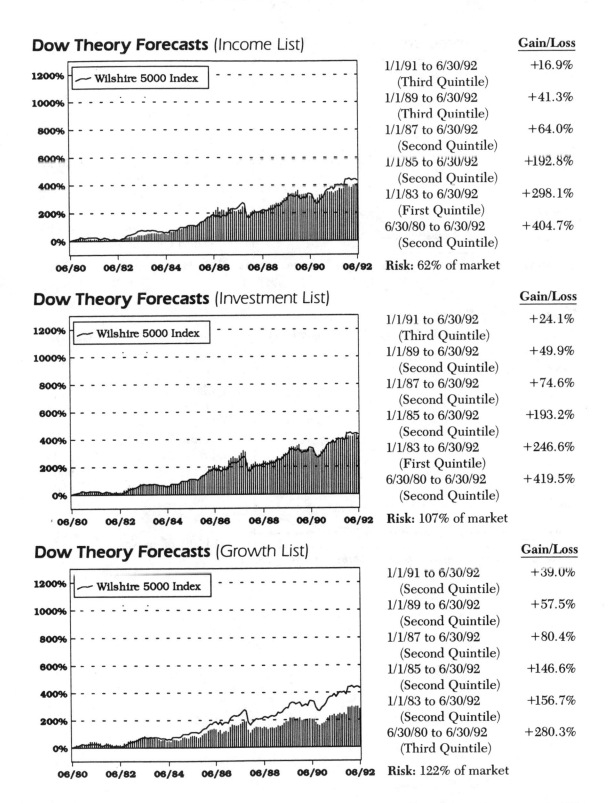

	Gain/Loss
1/1/91 to 6/30/92 (Third Quintile)	+16.9%
1/1/89 to 6/30/92 (Third Quintile)	+41.3%
1/1/87 to 6/30/92 (Second Quintile)	+64.0%
1/1/85 to 6/30/92 (Second Quintile)	+192.8%
1/1/83 to 6/30/92 (First Quintile)	+298.1%
6/30/80 to 6/30/92 (Second Quintile)	+404.7%

Risk: 62% of market

Dow Theory Forecasts (Investment List)

	Gain/Loss
1/1/91 to 6/30/92 (Third Quintile)	+24.1%
1/1/89 to 6/30/92 (Second Quintile)	+49.9%
1/1/87 to 6/30/92 (Second Quintile)	+74.6%
1/1/85 to 6/30/92 (Second Quintile)	+193.2%
1/1/83 to 6/30/92 (First Quintile)	+246.6%
6/30/80 to 6/30/92 (Second Quintile)	+419.5%

Risk: 107% of market

Dow Theory Forecasts (Growth List)

	Gain/Loss
1/1/91 to 6/30/92 (Second Quintile)	+39.0%
1/1/89 to 6/30/92 (Second Quintile)	+57.5%
1/1/87 to 6/30/92 (Second Quintile)	+80.4%
1/1/85 to 6/30/92 (Second Quintile)	+146.6%
1/1/83 to 6/30/92 (Second Quintile)	+156.7%
6/30/80 to 6/30/92 (Third Quintile)	+280.3%

Risk: 122% of market

Dow Theory Forecasts (Speculative List)

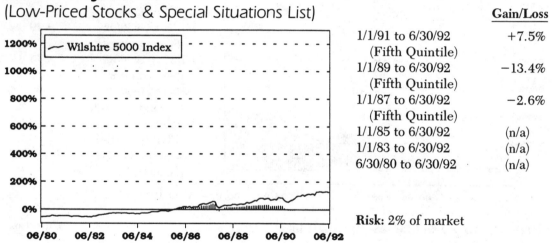

	Gain/Loss
1/1/91 to 6/30/92 (Fourth Quintile)	+16.6%
1/1/89 to 6/30/92 (Fourth Quintile)	+21.0%
1/1/87 to 6/30/92 (Third Quintile)	+52.3%
1/1/85 to 6/30/92 (Third Quintile)	+118.2%
1/1/83 to 6/30/92 (Third Quintile)	+132.2%
6/30/80 to 6/30/92 (Third Quintile)	+215.9%

Risk: 113% of market

Dow Theory Forecasts
(Low-Priced Stocks & Special Situations List)

	Gain/Loss
1/1/91 to 6/30/92 (Fifth Quintile)	+7.5%
1/1/89 to 6/30/92 (Fifth Quintile)	−13.4%
1/1/87 to 6/30/92 (Fifth Quintile)	−2.6%
1/1/85 to 6/30/92	(n/a)
1/1/83 to 6/30/92	(n/a)
6/30/80 to 6/30/92	(n/a)

Risk: 2% of market

Dow Theory Letters

Address
P.O. Box 1759
La Jolla, CA 92038

Editor
Richard Russell

Phone Number
619-454-0481

Subscription Rates
$150.00/6 months
$250.00/year

Telephone Hotline
No

Money Management
No

RICHARD RUSSELL'S **DOW THEORY LETTERS** INCORPORATED

Since 1958 •

Post Office Box 1759, La Jolla, California 92038
26 Letters Per Year • $250 annually

July 8, 1992   **LETTER 1099**

June 26   DJIA 3282.44; PTI 3484; A-D Ratio -11.18
July 2   DJIA 3330.32; PTI 3500; A-D Ratio -10.42
Dow Yield: 3.10%; Dow Price/Earnings: 69.2
Dow 200-day MA: 3182; Dow 30-day MA: 3336
Dow Times Book Value: 2.50; PTI 89-day MA: 3476
Percentage of Undervalued Blue-chips: 10%

ECONOMY: Whoops! Unemployment up to 7.8% in June (an eight-year high). Employment down by over 100,000 (that was a shock). Tool orders down 28% in May, durable goods down 2.5%, housing sales down 5.6% in May for their fourth decline in a row (sales declined 34.4% in the West, the sharpest drop on record), home prices down, car sales sputtering (GM's total 1992 sales are up only 1.7% from disastrous 1991 levels), Purchasing Agents' Index dropping back to 52.8%.

This is a recovery? The secret that Washington won't admit -- without rising home and car sales, there can't be a recovery.

On July 2 (reacting to the awful employment and unemployment news) the Fed panicked and dropped the discount rate a full half percent to 3%. With this latest act, the markets have to believe that the Fed has "shot its wad." There's nothing left on the downside, unless the Fed drives up with a dump-truck and gives money away.

STOCK MARKET: Ah, they never make it easy for you on Wall Street. The market rallied strongly from June 29 through July 1. Question: Is this it? Is this the true, bonafide, honest-to-gosh, revival of the long-sleeping bull market? Or is it the last hurrah, the final summer rally (remember 1972), the rally that rekindles optimism and brings the hopeful in for that last doomed surge prior to the top?

Let's face it, you pessimists, there's been no Dow Theory bear signal (the Dow never broke down). And my Primary Trend Index (PTI) never turned bearish. Furthermore, there's been a big surge in investor advisory pessimism (could it be totally misplaced?). Last but not least, our hero of the past two years, the Fed, continues to fight the "nothing economy" tooth and nail -- yep, fighting it with 24 assorted declines in the Fed Funds, the discount rate or the bank reserves.

THE BIG PICTURE: Obviously, I can't prove it, but I've been wondering if maybe we're seeing the beginning of a global bear market. Here are a few statistics that bother me: Australia's stock market is down 29% from its record high; France is down 6.8%; Germany down 9.6%; Italy down 48%; Japan down 60%; Spain down 24%; Sweden down 30%; UK down 4.4%; USA down only 3.6%. Finally, the *Economist's* World Index is down 12.3%.

Question: How is it that the US stock market has been doing so much better than the rest of the world's markets? Answer (or at least my theory): We start with the fact that the dollar's been collapsing. Consciously or unconsciously, US investors are saying, "I'd rather be in stocks than in dollars. At least stocks represent something of value; stocks represent actual equity in a real, live corporation. With the US running deficits of half a trillion dollars a year and George Bush shouting for even lower rates, I'm afraid of dollars. Frankly, if I'm going to lose money, I'd rather lose it in stocks."

Question: So who wants dollars? Answer: At present, only Americans, who are unfamiliar with trading or holding foreign currencies. Study these three-month Euro-currency rates: British sterling -- 10%, Dutch guilders -- 9 3/4%; Swiss franc -- 9 3/4%; D-mark -- 9 1/4%; French franc -- 10 1/8%; Danish krone -- 11%; Spanish peseta -- 12 3/4%. And the three-month return on the dollar -- around 3.5%. So if you like money, if you like a return on

your investment, why would you, as a knowledgeable international investor, want to be in dollars?

Let's face it, the US economy is still nowhere. The US continues to run huge deficits, but despite those deficits the US still can't really get out of recession. In a frenzy to re-inflate the economy, the Fed has ballooned bank reserves and driven down short-term interest rates to 20-year lows. But in doing so, the US has, among other things, sacrificed its currency.

Question: Where are the losses? Answer: The losses show up in two areas. The losses show up in the majority of stocks on all the US stock exchanges (for proof, check the chart of the advance-decline ratio on page 2). If you're a German or a Frenchman or a Swissman, you know well enough where the losses are. The losses are in anything denominated in dollars -- from houses to salaries to property to US stocks and bonds. Let me put it this way -- from an international standpoint, if it's expressed in dollars, it's probably worth less than it was a year ago.

Question: How long can all this go on before it finally sinks in to the consciousness of Americans? Say you're a foreign investor or a foreign bank or insurance company, and you own a slew of US securities. How long can you take these dollar losses without panicking? How long can you sit, white-knuckled, as you watch the dollar and your investments go down the drain?

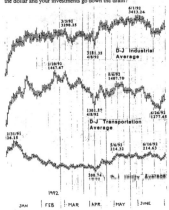

Dow Theory Letters is one of the oldest investment newsletters that has been edited continuously by one person, having been written by editor Richard Russell since 1958. Among Russell's many claims to fame are a series of articles in the early 1960s for *Barron's* explaining the Dow Theory, a well-

timed call in December 1974 that the 1973-74 bear market had finally come to an end, and another well-timed call in August 1987 that the bull market had come to an end.

Dow Theory Letters provides general market commentary and timing advice, and is not particularly well designed for the investor interested in specific advice on constructing a model portfolio. Beginning in 1981, Russell began publishing an "Investment Position" box in each issue, at which time the HFD began constructing a portfolio to track the recommendations Russell put in that box. At the end of 1986, however, the HFD gave up trying to do so. Over the six years that the HFD did track the recommendations Russell made in this box, the HFD calculated a gain of just 15.1%, in contrast to the 123.7% turned in by the Wilshire 5000. The reader should view this figure in the context of the fact that *Dow Theory Letters* often was not very specific or complete in its portfolio recommendations; this means that other reasonable subscribers could have translated Russell's advice in different ways and achieved different results than the HFD did.

The HFD also measures newsletters' pure-timing records, apart from their abilities to select individual stocks or mutual funds, and here *Dow Theory Letters*'s advice generally has been clearer and its recommendations have performed much better than those of other newsletters. In almost every issue Russell grades the stock market as either bullish or bearish, and the HFD's Timing Scoreboard measures these signals (and this is what is graphed in this book). For the 12 years ending in mid-1992, a portfolio that alternated between hypothetical shares of the Wilshire 5000 and T-Bills on Russell's signals gained 344.2%, in contrast to the market's gain of 432.7%. Owing to the fact that Russell's timing involved less risk than simply buying and holding, however, it outperformed the Wilshire on a risk-adjusted basis.

Russell received some much-deserved publicity for recommending that investors get out of the stock market in late August 1987, within days of what turned out to be that year's top. He looked very good on the day of the 1987 crash, but he did not get back into the market afterward. Indeed, he did not turn bullish again until August 1989, at which point the market was higher than when he had gotten out in August 1987.

Dow Theory Letters
(Grading of Primary Trend—100% Cash on Sell Signals)

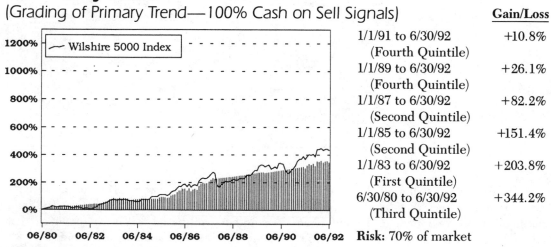

	Gain/Loss
1/1/91 to 6/30/92 (Fourth Quintile)	+10.8%
1/1/89 to 6/30/92 (Fourth Quintile)	+26.1%
1/1/87 to 6/30/92 (Second Quintile)	+82.2%
1/1/85 to 6/30/92 (Second Quintile)	+151.4%
1/1/83 to 6/30/92 (First Quintile)	+203.8%
6/30/80 to 6/30/92 (Third Quintile)	+344.2%

Risk: 70% of market

The Elliott Wave Theorist

Address
P.O. Box 1618
Gainesville, GA 30503

Editor
Robert Prechter

Phone Number
404-536-0309

Subscription Rates
$ 55.00/2 months
$233.00/year

Telephone Hotline
No

Money Management
No

ROBERT PRECHTER

THE ELLIOTT WAVE THEORIST

August 1992 issue
(July 31, 1992)

©

STOCK MARKET · New Classics Library · INTEREST RATES · P.O. Box 1618 · PRECIOUS METALS · Gainesville, GA 30503

$233 per year
12 Monthly Issues
plus Special Reports
and Interim Reports

DJIA WAVE STATUS: SUMMARY and OUTLOOK

WAVE DEGREE	DATE BEGAN	WAVE NUMBER	CURRENT DIRECTION	SIGNIFICANCE TO	OPTIMUM STRATEGY	TARGET	NEXT BEST COUNT
GRAND SUPERCYCLE	1789	FIVE	UP, PEAKING	U.S. SURVIVAL	PRESERVATION OF CAPITAL	3420-3700	THREE
SUPERCYCLE	JULY 8, 1932	(V)	UP, PEAKING	ECONOMIC CONDITIONS	PREPARE FOR DEPRESSION	3420-3700	---
CYCLE	MAR. 27, 1980	V	UP, PEAKING	INSTITUTIONAL INVESTOR	HOLD FOREIGN MONEY MARKET	3420-3700	---
PRIMARY	JULY 25, 1984	⑤	UP, PEAKING	INSTITUTIONAL TRADER	HOLD FOREIGN MONEY MARKET	3420-3700	---
INTERMEDIATE	OCT. 11, 1990	(5)	UP, PEAKING	INDIVIDUAL INVESTOR	HOLD FOREIGN MONEY MARKET	3420-3700	(3)
MINOR	JULY 23, 3:00	5	UP, PEAKING	INDIVIDUAL TRADER	SEE INSIDE FOR TACTICS	3420-3700	C
MINUTE	----	---	UP, PEAKING	OPTION/FUTURE TRADER	SEE INSIDE FOR TACTICS	----	---

THE BOTTOM LINE
Contrary to general investor expectations, time cycles strongly indicate a stock market bottom in October-November, near election day. If the long standing maximum bull market target of Dow 3600-3700 is to be achieved, it must happen in the next few weeks. The bond market should rise for another month or so before making a major top. Gold rallied nicely, as expected, but is due for a correction soon. Silver should collapse to new lows in August (or September at the latest), probably to near $3/oz., there registering a final bottom for its twelve year bear market.

ITEMS OF NOTE
THE ELLIOTT WAVE THEORIST was rated #1 in "percentage of profitable trades" (88.2%) and #1 in stock index trading gains for the first half of 1992 by Commodity Traders Consumer Report of Sacramento, California. THE ELLIOTT WAVE CURRENCY & COMMODITY FORECAST placed among the top four in currencies, metals and energy futures. EWT and EWCF are rated 3rd and 4th respectively out of 26 services for "net equity increase after commissions" for total futures trading.

There is still time to register for our International Conference on the Wave Principle, Advanced Tutorial and/or Basic Workshop to be held September 10-15 at the Stouffer PineIsle Resort on Lake Lanier Islands, Georgia. Space is limited for the tutorial, so be sure to register soon. For details, see the enclosed brochures or contact Elliott Wave International at (800) 336-1618 or (404) 536-0309.

Director of Research Dave Allman will join John Murphy, Ian McAvity, David Fuller, Gail Dudack, Richard Mogey and other well known speakers at the 5th World Conference of the International Federation of Technical Analysts, to be held October 14-17 at the Dublin Castle in Ireland. The seminar fee is 390 Irish Punts for IFTA members and 440 for non-members. For further details and a brochure, contact Michael Weir or Francis Fullen in Dublin at (353 1) 616997, or fax (353 1) 616133.

The Elliott Wave Theorist is edited by Robert Prechter and published monthly. A telephone hotline update is not provided as part of a subscription to the newsletter itself, but a thrice-weekly telephone update service is sold separately. Per its established methodol-ogy on such matters, the HFD tracks the advice contained in the newsletter only.

Prechter takes an entirely technical approach to the market, using his analysis of the "Elliott Wave" to time the equity, bond and gold markets. His newsletter does not offer

The Elliott Wave Theorist   **121**

specific recommendations of individual securities, which explains why the HFD only has a Timing Scoreboard rating for him and not a Performance Rating as well.

In each of the three markets he attempts to time, Prechter offers advice for both investors and traders. The difference has to do both with subscribers' aversion to risk and their willingness to switch into and out of the market frequently. His advice for investors typically involves far fewer switches than his advice for traders, for example, and rarely (if ever) are Prechter's investors advised to go short the market.

The HFD has the most performance data for Prechter's stock-market timing advice for investors. Over the 12 years through mid-1992 this advice has added value to a buy-and-hold, though barely: A portfolio that alternated between hypothetical shares of the Wilshire 5000 and T-Bills on Prechter's signals gained 434.0%, in contrast to 432.7% for buying and holding the Wilshire itself. But this portfolio was able to beat the market by incurring nearly 40% less risk than the market, so it beat the market handily on a risk-adjusted basis.

Prechter has been providing specific advice for stock market traders for less time, and this advice has significantly underperformed the market: The HFD reports a 2.9% loss over the seven and one-half years through mid-1992 for a portfolio that went long or short in hypothetical shares of the Wilshire 5000 on Prechter's advice, and otherwise earned the T-Bill rate. This contrasts with a 197.6% gain for buying and holding the Wilshire itself.

Prechter's gold-market timing has been similarly mixed, with his advice for investors beating the market and his advice for traders lagging. In the bond market, however, neither his bond-market timing advice for traders nor for investors beat simply buying and holding (see Appendices C-7 and C-11).

Procedural note: While the riskiness of Prechter's stock-market timing advice for investors is below the market's, it isn't really as low as what is listed in the accompanying chart (at just 2% of the market's risk). The risk level that is listed for this portfolio (as well as for all others in this book) is based on the standard deviation of its monthly returns from the beginning of 1991 through mid-1992. Since Prechter recommended that stock market investors remain in cash over this period, this portfolio's risk level accordingly is quite low. If we were to have based this portfolio's risk level on 12 years of volatility instead of 18 months, it would be reported as having 63% as much risk as the market.

The Elliott Wave Theorist
(Traders—May Go Short on Sell Signals)

	Gain/Loss
1/1/91 to 6/30/92	−32.2%
(Fifth Quintile)	
1/1/89 to 6/30/92	−51.6%
(Fifth Quintile)	
1/1/87 to 6/30/92	−40.7%
(Fifth Quintile)	
1/1/85 to 6/30/92	−2.9%
(Fifth Quintile)	
1/1/83 to 6/30/92	(n/a)
6/30/80 to 6/30/92	(n/a)

Risk: 126% of market

The Elliott Wave Theorist
(Investors—100% Cash on Sell Signals)

	Gain/Loss
1/1/91 to 6/30/92	+7.5%
(Fifth Quintile)	
1/1/89 to 6/30/92	+19.5%
(Fifth Quintile)	
1/1/87 to 6/30/92	+70.8%
(Second Quintile)	
1/1/85 to 6/30/92	+183.1%
(Second Quintile)	
1/1/83 to 6/30/92	+313.2%
(First Quintile)	
6/30/80 to 6/30/92	+434.0%
(First Quintile)	

Risk: 2% of market

Emerging & Special Situations

Address
Standard & Poor's Corp.
25 Broadway
New York, NY 10004

Editor
Robert Natale

Phone Number
800-852-1641

Subscription Rates
$ 45.00/3 months
$210.00/year

Telephone Hotline
Yes

Money Management
No

STANDARD & POOR'S

Emerging & Special Situations

July 17, 1992
VOL. 12, NO. 7 FOCUSING ON THE NEW ISSUE, SMALLCAP & MIDCAP 400 SECTORS OF THE STOCK MARKET

▶ OTC-NEW ISSUE MARKET REVIEW

Second Quarter Earnings Announcements Buttressing The Bullish Case

The U.S. economy continues to slowly recover. Over the next six months we expect the overall inflation rate, currently running at about 3%, to drift a little lower. Interest rates will bottom with the three month T-bill hitting 3%, and then moving to about 4% to 4.25% by the middle of next year.

As long as there is no fiscal stimulus, the recovery is apt to remain in low gear. Still, we continue to believe that operating profits for U.S.-based corporations will rise some 10% to 12% this year, with at least a similar gain possible in 1993. With interest rates remaining low through year end, we think stock prices could still mount a modest advance before election day.

S&P MIDCAP 400 INDEX VS. S&P 500 INDEX

If interest rates do start to trend higher in 1993, that could trigger the first major correction in stock prices since the current bull market began in early 1991. One hedge against this prospect would be to buy recovering REITs. Mature trusts with stable cash flows are likely to see their stock prices decline as interest

rates fall, but those with more troubled loan or asset portfolios would benefit substantially from faster economic growth and inflation. Our favorites in the latter category, in increasing order of risk and potential reward, are **MGI Properties, National Income Realty Trust, Banyan Mortgage Investment Fund** and **Property Capital Trust.**

Small Cap Stocks Could Do Well in Third Quarter

For the five weeks ended July 10, the S&P MidCap 400 declined 1.9%. The S&P 500 edged up 0.2% during the period. However, the more recent action of small to intermediate capitalization equities has been encouraging. Despite the cratering of several technology stocks, since the first of July, the MidCap 400 has done better than the S&P 500. We think the

S&P MIDCAP 400 INDEX VS. S&P 500 INDEX

Emerging & Special Situations is edited by Robert Natale and published monthly by Standard & Poor's Corp. Smaller between-issue mailings also are sent to subscribers, who in addition have access to a weekly telephone hotline. The newsletter is the successor to *New Issue Investor*, which Standard & Poor's began publishing in 1982. The name change occurred when the letter's focus expanded beyond initial public offerings, though this sector remains one of its primary emphases.

In addition to recommending one or two new special situations, each issue of *Emerg-*

ing & Special Situations also reviews all previously recommended positions, rating them a "buy," a "hold" or a "sell." The service does not recommend a particular allocation of a portfolio between stocks and cash, so per its established methodology on such matters, the HFD constructs a portfolio that is fully invested at all times in those stocks rated "buy."

The HFD has tracked this service's performance since the beginning of 1983, and for the nine and one-half years through mid-1992, the newsletter gained 121.6%. While this is well below the return of the Wilshire 5000 for the same period (+278.6%),

it should be remembered that the period since 1983 has been a poor one for initial public offerings.

Besides comparing *Emerging & Special Situations* to the market as a whole, therefore, another worthwhile comparison is with other newsletters that focus on the same sector of the market. Here *Emerging & Special Situations* compares more favorably. For example, the HFD also follows *New Issues* (reviewed elsewhere in this volume), and this other service gained 58.5% over the same period of time.

Emerging & Special Situations

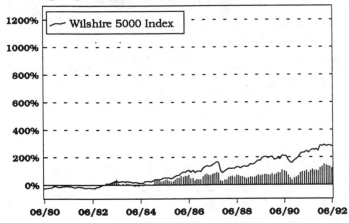

	Gain/Loss
1/1/91 to 6/30/92 (Second Quintile)	+45.0%
1/1/89 to 6/30/92 (Second Quintile)	+49.4%
1/1/87 to 6/30/92 (Third Quintile)	+60.0%
1/1/85 to 6/30/92 (Third Quintile)	+118.0%
1/1/83 to 6/30/92 (Third Quintile)	+121.6%
6/30/80 to 6/30/92	(n/a)

Risk: 142% of market

Equities Special Situations

Address
P.O. Box 1708
Riverton, NJ 08077

Editor
Robert J. Flaherty

Phone Number
800-237-8400 ext. 61

Subscription Rates
$150.00/year

Telephone Hotline
No

Money Management
No

Special Situations No. 400   **July 27, 1992**

Dear Friends:

LET THE SUNSHINE IN: When a big magazine like *Barron's* attacks a little magazine like our sister publication *Equities* in its July 6 issue, we must be doing something right. *Equities* is calling for passage of the Shareholder Protection Act and increased disclosure of the prepublication trading activities of secret short sellers. I hope everyone interested in continued short selling reforms will support our call to "let the sunshine in!"

I have personally written over 60 articles on abusive short selling and no one feels more strongly than I about the need for greater disclosure. I am at it again. Although our 1988 Short Symposium was not an economic success, it did do one thing. It focused on the need for reforms, many of which are reality or are awaiting SEC approval.

In many ways abusive short selling (where secret short sellers, mainly hedge funds, are permitted to prey upon the public because their accounts are so profitable) is a throwback to the 1920s. This is the age of disclosure, of instant information. Secret short sellers are a remnant of the past, or at least they should be. I look forward to the day when the short position leaps 218% as it did before *Barron's* recent blast on Conseco and *Equities* will not have to ask whodunnit.

The very first meeting of the ShortBuster Club will be on July 30th from 7:45 a.m. to 5:00 p.m. at New York City's Waldorf-Astoria Hotel. Any company who would like to join our list of presenters should call me at (212) 685-6244 or Ray Dirks at RAS Securities (800) 354-DIRK.

ONE MORE TIME: The special situation I originally chose for this month just didn't seem like the best relative value I saw. What excited me more was our January 1991 pick of International Mobile Machines, recommended back then at 4 1/4 and sold at 10 for a gain of 135%. After 20 years of persistence, IMM looks ready to pay off.

Equities Special Situations. Subscription price: $150/yr. $15 an issue. Published monthly since 1958 by OTC Review, Inc., 37E. 28th St., Suite 706, New York, NY 10016; also publishers of *Equities* magazine, subscription price: $42/yr.

The information presented in this publication is not to be construed as an offer to sell or a solicitation to buy any securities referred to herein. The information contained in this publication is considered reliable, but is not guaranteed as to accuracy or completeness. Errors are inevitable. The policy of OTC Review, Inc. is for our staff to avoid any pre-publication trading. Some companies written up may be advertisers in our sister publication, paid sponsors at our spring or winter corporate conferences or may buy reprints. However, our buy, sell or hold decisions will never be based on such events but on what we believe is best for our readers.

Equities Special Situations is published monthly by Robert J. Flaherty (the newsletter used to be called *OTC Review/Special Situations*). Flaherty also publishes a magazine entitled *OTC Review*, which covers the over-the-counter markets. According to Flaherty, both publications have been in existence since 1958. Flaherty's approach appears to be based entirely on fundamental analysis of companies that trade over-the-counter.

Each monthly issue of *Equities Special Situations* is devoted to the recommendation of one new special situation and to providing buy-hold-sell advice on previous recommendations that have yet to be closed out. Per the HFD's methodology on such matters, the HFD used to construct a model portfolio for this newsletter out of just those stocks rated "buy." However, in early 1990 the newsletter specifically recommended that all stocks, whether rated "buy" or "hold," should be considered on its list of highest recommendations—and the portfolio the HFD constructs for this newsletter thereafter included both its "buys" and its "holds." In addition, because the newsletter does not provide ex-

plicit allocation advice on the proper division of a portfolio between stocks and cash, the portfolio the HFD constructs is fully invested at all times.

Over the five and one-half years through mid-1992, this portfolio constructed by the HFD gained 34.3%, in contrast to 93.3% for the Wilshire 5000. Furthermore, because this portfolio had greater risk than the market, its risk-adjusted performance also is below the Wilshire's.

Equities Special Situations

	Gain/Loss
1/1/91 to 6/30/92	+46.2%
(Second Quintile)	
1/1/89 to 6/30/92	+10.6%
(Fifth Quintile)	
1/1/87 to 6/30/92	+34.3%
(Fourth Quintile)	
1/1/85 to 6/30/92	(n/a)
1/1/83 to 6/30/92	(n/a)
6/30/80 to 6/30/92	(n/a)

Risk: 180% of market

Equity Fund Outlook

Address
P.O. Box 1040
Boston, MA 02117

Editor
Thurman Smith

Phone Number
617-397-6844

Subscription Rates
$95.00/year

Telephone Hotline
No

Money Management
Yes

EQUITY FUND OUTLOOK

A Guide to the Best Managed No-load Growth Funds

July 1992

Prices updated
through
July 2

Equity Fund Research   P.O. Box 1040   Boston, Massachusetts   02117   617-397-6844

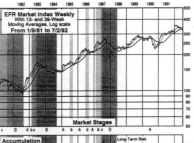

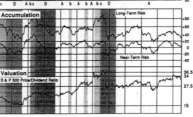

THE MARKET: Skepticism Warranted

The chart pattern above is very typical of how things look at the end of a secondary correction when the market drops slightly below its flattish but still rising 39-week moving average. This time the market average masks the wide diversion of behavior of the component stocks. The fund charts inside tell the real story: growth stocks rising to highs in the first quarter then declining beyond what would be the limit for a typical secondary correction; and value and cyclical stocks not yet completing a full correction, or in several cases rising from the mid-February high in the broad market.

In a still well-valued market such a divergence warrants an assumption that all stocks not yet fully corrected will do so soon. Uncertainty in the national political picture

may negate the usually positive election year cycle. And the 10-year cycle is still unfavorable through the summer as this is the second year of a decade.

THE FUNDS: Salvation through Variety

There is really no aggressive fund that inspires new purchases and quite a few with a marginal rating that tempt rotation to more resilient choices in other classes. **MIM Stock Appreciation** continues to deserve respect for maintaining an above average growth/risk relationship even as it has declined along with its classmates. Fewer funds in this group have both 39-week moving averages in downtrends than last month. If June 26th was the bottom for this correction, action in the next few weeks will point out funds with most potential in a general market recovery.

Fidelity Low Price leads the market-risk class. The fund charter now allows purchase of stocks selling less than $25, up from the original $15 ceiling. Manager Joel Tillinghast follows a value approach, embellished by an interest in potential earnings surprises. Now reopened to new investors, it is likely to get a sales charge this year.

Gloom to glory could be the model for **Fidelity Contrafund** which has the most admirable relative strength line of any fund we follow (page 6). Manager Will Danoff took over in 1990, continues the approach of Jeff Vinik (now heading Magellan) in seeking out distressed out-favor issues with a recent development suggesting potential for turnaround. With the fund now at $1.3 billion in assets this will be harder to do than when Vinik took over at only $100,000, but there has been no flagging off in relative efficiency as the fund has grown. Another fund for all investors, except perhaps the most conservative. A rare case where the 3% load may be justified.

New this issue is **Babson Enterprise II**. Like its namesake, it is managed by Peter Schliemann who looks for promising mid-cap and small cap issues, using the same general approach as for Babson Enterprise. So far, not so good, but as time goes on it probably will show

Recommended portfolio relative risk ranges			
	LOW	IDEAL	HIGH
Aggressive	97	110	123
Moderate	79	90	101
Conservative	62	70	78

Equity Fund Outlook is published monthly by Thurman Smith, and though Smith does not have a telephone hotline update, he will send out a special bulletin between issues if he believes conditions warrant. The newsletter focuses on both overall market timing and the selection of individual no-load mutual

funds, and Smith translates this advice into three separate model portfolios. The HFD began following the letter at the beginning of 1991.

Smith's approach is based on a combination of both technical and fundamental analysis. For his market timing, for example, he looks at several overbought/oversold indicators as well as the market's price/dividend ratio. In picking individual mutual funds, he rates funds according to their performance and volatility.

Smith's portfolio advice is a model of clarity: Subscribers are given advance notice of the precise date on which a transaction is to take place, and—unlike some editors of competing mutual fund newsletters—he gives followers of these portfolios two weeks between the sale of one fund and the purchase of its replacement. This means that subscribers have ample time to receive the check from the redeemed fund and reinvest the proceeds in the new fund.

Over the 18 months through mid-1992, Smith's three model portfolios produced an average gain of 28.8%, in contrast to a 32.3% total return for the Wilshire 5000. Because on average his portfolios were no less risky than the market as a whole, his newsletter's risk-adjusted performance lagged the Wilshire's by a similar margin.

Equity Fund Outlook (Average)

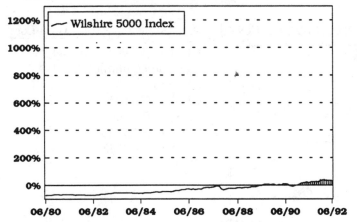

	Gain/Loss
1/1/91 to 6/30/92	+28.8%
(Second Quintile)	
1/1/89 to 6/30/92	(n/a)
1/1/87 to 6/30/92	(n/a)
1/1/85 to 6/30/92	(n/a)
1/1/83 to 6/30/92	(n/a)
6/30/80 to 6/30/92	(n/a)

Risk: 100% of market

Equity Fund Outlook (Aggressive Portfolio)

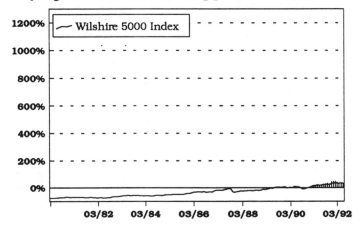

	Gain/Loss
1/1/91 to 6/30/92	+29.1%
(Second Quintile)	
1/1/89 to 6/30/92	(n/a)
1/1/87 to 6/30/92	(n/a)
1/1/85 to 6/30/92	(n/a)
1/1/83 to 6/30/92	(n/a)
6/30/80 to 6/30/92	(n/a)

Risk: 126% of market

Equity Fund Outlook (Moderate Risk Portfolio)

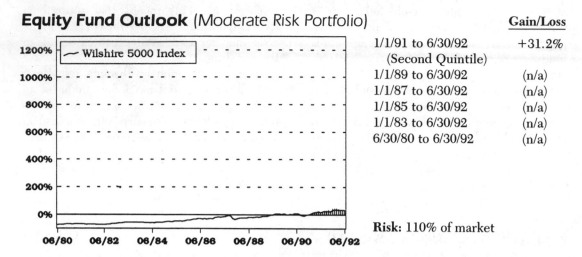

	Gain/Loss
1/1/91 to 6/30/92	+31.2%
(Second Quintile)	
1/1/89 to 6/30/92	(n/a)
1/1/87 to 6/30/92	(n/a)
1/1/85 to 6/30/92	(n/a)
1/1/83 to 6/30/92	(n/a)
6/30/80 to 6/30/92	(n/a)

Risk: 110% of market

Equity Fund Outlook (Conservative Portfolio)

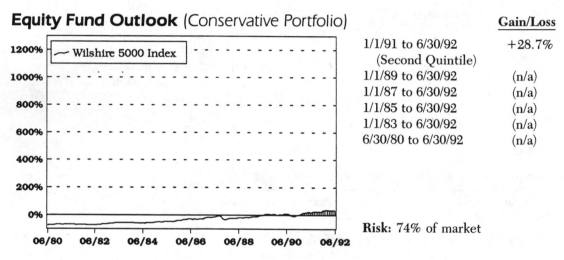

	Gain/Loss
1/1/91 to 6/30/92	+28.7%
(Second Quintile)	
1/1/89 to 6/30/92	(n/a)
1/1/87 to 6/30/92	(n/a)
1/1/85 to 6/30/92	(n/a)
1/1/83 to 6/30/92	(n/a)
6/30/80 to 6/30/92	(n/a)

Risk: 74% of market

F.X.C. Investors Corp.

Address
62-19 Cooper Ave.
Glendale, Queens, NY
11385

Editor
Francis X. Curzio

Phone Number
800-392-0992

Subscription Rates
$ 48.00/3 months
$290.00/year

Telephone Hotline
No

Money Management
Yes

F.X.C. INVESTORS CORP.
62-19 Cooper Avenue
Glendale, Queens, N.Y. 11385
(718) 417-1330

Volume 15
Number 14

INTERIM UPDATE: JULY 1992
14th "First Class Mailing"

INTEREST RATE CRASH CONTINUING

MAINTAIN 80% POSITION IN QUALITY INTEREST SENSITIVE SECURITIES

HUGE DEFLATIONARY TREND ON HORIZON

THE ECONOMY: Our predicted discount rate cut came 7/3/92. We have been in a recessionary climate since the Great Crash of September-October 1987. Throughout this time frame a few pockets of strength prevailed due to excessive government spending; a $400 billion Federal Budget Deficit and 10's of billions of State and Local Deficit spending. We believe a recessionary environment will prevail throughout the next 3 to 5 years and as such our choice is 80% of funds in F.X.C.'s Utility and Bond picks. Speculate with no more than 20% of your funds. After the Presidential election, massive cuts in government spending and increased taxes will enhance a deflationary scenario not witnessed since the Great Depression. Quality interest sensitive stocks and bonds should perform well given our deflationary outlook. Next year, the real estate crash will intensify, corporate profits will begin a multi-year decline and virtually all commodity prices will decline.

THE MARKET: We maintain our prediction of Dow Jones 3,500-3,700 by year end. December of last year when the Dow was 2,900 we predicted Dow Jones of 4,000 but changed our prediction in February 1992 to 3,500-3,700 due to stock splits in some of the Dow's components.

Boeing (BA $39.50 NYSE) received a $320 million order, including spare parts from Singapore Airlines for two 747-400's. 1992 orders currently total $9.4 billion for 111 aircraft. The House of Representatives approved 1.5 billion to build Boeing's V-22 aircraft, which takes off like a helicopter and flies like a plane. We maintain a buy on this quality blue chip Dow Jones stock. One of few companies that will see earnings per share increase throughout the next 3 to 5 years. Selling at 8 times earnings (P/E 8) vs. the Dow Jones P/E of over 20, downside risk appears limited vs. upside potential. BA has over three billion dollars in cash and five billion in cash and receivables. Long term debt is only $1.3 billion. Research and Development (R&D) costs should peak this year resulting in an upward surge in profits throughout the next few years.

F.X.C. Investors Corp. is published 24 times a year by Francis X. Curzio and is not accompanied by a telephone hotline. The HFD began following this newsletter in 1988, following a burst of publicity earned by Curzio because he had predicted a crash in advance of 1987's Black Monday. In fact, however, a subscriber should not look to his newsletter for short-term market timing, since Curzio concentrates on intermediate and longer-term market trends and asset allocation.

Curzio's recommended portfolio doesn't focus just on stocks, and consequently is less risky than the stock market. It therefore is not that surprising that Curzio underperformed the Wilshire 5000 over the three and one-half years through mid-1992 (53.1% versus 60.3%). On a risk-adjusted basis, however, Curzio did beat the Wilshire 5000.

A more insightful basis for measuring Cur-zio's asset allocation approach would be a comparison with an unmanaged portfolio that is equally divided among the major different asset categories (stocks, gold and bonds). Cur-zio handily beat such a portfolio. (See the chapter on asset allocation earlier in this book.)

F.X.C. Investors Corp.

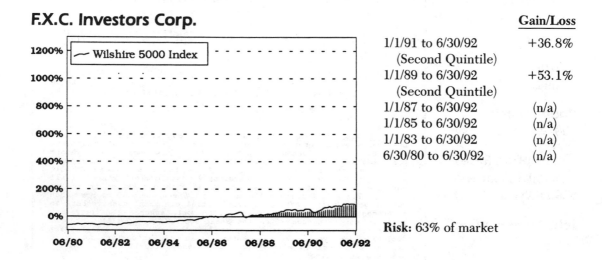

	Gain/Loss
1/1/91 to 6/30/92	+36.8%
(Second Quintile)	
1/1/89 to 6/30/92	+53.1%
(Second Quintile)	
1/1/87 to 6/30/92	(n/a)
1/1/85 to 6/30/92	(n/a)
1/1/83 to 6/30/92	(n/a)
6/30/80 to 6/30/92	(n/a)

Risk: 63% of market

Fast Track Funds

Address
5536 Temple City Blvd.
Temple City, CA 91780

Editor
Eli Pereira

Subscription Rates
$107.00/year

Telephone Hotline
Yes

Money Management
No

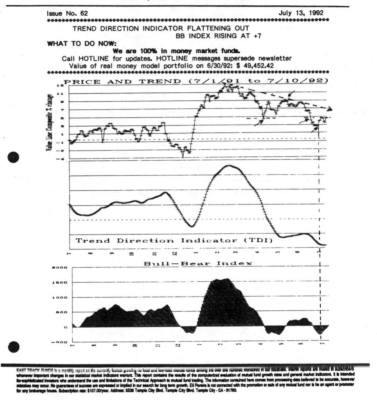

Fast Track Funds is published monthly by Eli Pereira and is supplemented by a telephone hotline that is updated as often as daily. It is designed to aid the investor both in timing the market as a whole as well as in the selection of individual mutual funds. Pereira's approach to both tasks is almost exclusively technical.

The HFD has been tracking Pereira's advice since the beginning of 1989. For the ensuing three and one-half years, the HFD reports a gain of 24.7%. This contrasts with a 60.3% gain for the Wilshire 5000 and a 25.3% return for 90-day T-Bills.

The culprit in Pereira's submarket performance is his timing rather than his selection of mutual funds. According to the HFD's calculations, a portfolio that switched on Pereira's signals between hypothetical shares of the Wilshire 5000 and T-Bills gained 17.4% over these three and one-half years. Since this is less than the 24.7% that the HFD reports for Pereira's actual portfolio, this shows that his recommended funds outperformed the market during the times he was invested in the market—and that it is his timing that caused him to underperform the market.

Fast Track Funds

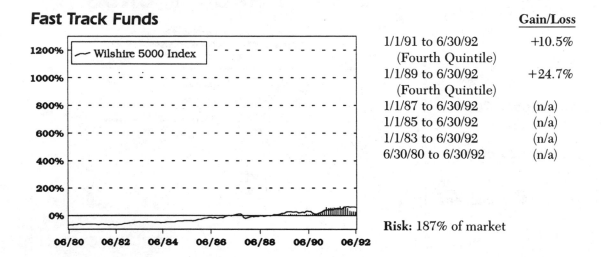

	Gain/Loss
1/1/91 to 6/30/92	+10.5%
(Fourth Quintile)	
1/1/89 to 6/30/92	+24.7%
(Fourth Quintile)	
1/1/87 to 6/30/92	(n/a)
1/1/85 to 6/30/92	(n/a)
1/1/83 to 6/30/92	(n/a)
6/30/80 to 6/30/92	(n/a)

Risk: 187% of market

Fidelity Insight

Address

Mutual Fund Investors
  Association
P.O. Box 9135
Wellesley Hills, MA
  02181-9135

Editor

Eric Kobren

Phone Number

617-235-4432

Subscription Rates

$39.00/4 months
$99.00/year

Telephone Hotline

Yes

Money Management

Yes

HOTLINE
(617) 237-8869

The Independent
Report on
Fidelity Funds
July 1992
Vol.8, No.7

Eric's Outlook

We did start to come out of recession during the first half of 1992. Consumer spending turned up; so did business spending. Residential real estate activity bottomed out, and cyclical industries showed signs of improvement.

But it was a far cry from past economic recoveries. Take business spending as an example. Companies have been playing it close to the vest. Spending was up, but there weren't many significant capital expenditures or significant rises in inventory levels, as in past recoveries. Instead of hiring new employees, businesses had existing employees work longer hours. Payrolls rose, but not enough to absorb new entrants into the work force. Unemployment actually inched up to 7.5% in May.

Andrew Midler, manager of Fidelity's **Growth & Income** fund (formerly of **Equity-Income II**) talks to dozens of company executives every day. He's convinced that June's economic figures will show that the recovery has stalled.

Where is economic growth coming from? Not from the service sector, which was long the engine of growth. Banks, insurance companies, and other service industries are consolidating and trimming fat. The latest casualty is Aetna (insurance), which is laying off 10% of its work force.

The economy will not pick up steam during the second half of 1992. Demand will remain weak. We may fall back into recession; more likely, we will hobble along at about a 2% annual growth rate for the remainder of the year.

Equity Markets

How will the securities markets react to this less-than-robust recovery? Not very well. Today's market is beating up any stock that falls short of its earnings estimates. And unfortunately, earnings disappointments will become commonplace as second

Outlook *cont'd on page 3*

Table of Contents

Fund Commentary 1
Eric's Outlook 1
Model Portfolios 2
Which Funds Should You Buy Now! 3
Europe Exchange 5
Scorecard 6
At a Glance: Growth and Income Funds 8
Eye on Equity-Income II 9
Fidelity Funds at Fidelity Brokerage 10
Money Market Rates: Not That Bad 10
Question & Answer 11
Dividend Update 11
Inside Fidelity 12
Message to Members 12

Fund Commentary

A faltering economy, some poor corporate earnings announcements, and the Fed's hesitancy to cut interest rates hurt the market in June. The S&P 500 index dropped 1.5% for the month; the Dow lost 2.1%; and the NASDAQ, after substantial losses in technology and health-related stocks, gave up 3.7%.

The declines put the S&P and NASDAQ into the loss column for the year, down 0.7% and 3.9% respectively. The Dow is still up 6.3%, the gains due largely to the disproportionate weighting of automotive and other cyclicals in this narrower index.

The month was good if you held financial services, gold, or utilities; it was less than good if you were in technology, energy, or health care.

Top Growth Funds (YTD Return %)	
Cap App	14.4%
Low-Priced Stock	10.9
Value	10.0
Destiny II	5.7
Destiny I	5.2

None of Fidelity's growth funds is entirely out of the poor-performing sectors. Only one, **Special Situations**, escaped the stigma of a down month; it was up a whopping 0.1%. Utility stocks represent about 31% of its assets. **Capital Appreciation**, with no exposure to technology, almost escaped; it was down just 0.1% in June. Losers for the month had "Growth" in their names. **Emerging Growth** was down 5.0%; **Growth Company** and **Retirement Growth** were down 3.6% and 3.7% respectively.

Top G&I Funds (YTD Return %)	
Convertible Secs	9.0%
Equity-Inc II	8.5
Puritan	7.2
Equity-Income	5.9
Asset Manager	5.9

For the year, Capital Appreciation kept well ahead, up 14.4%, while **Low-Priced Stock** stayed in the double digits (up 10.9%) even though it lost 2.4% in June. With technology and health care sickly, Emerging Growth and Growth Company could not stanch the hemorrhaging and lost 13.8% and 8.6%, respectively.

A weaker U.S. dollar helped the **D-Mark** and **Pound** currency funds advance 6.4% and 4.9% during June. The weaker dollar also helped foreign stock funds, but not enough. **Worldwide** did the worst (down 3.5%), and **Overseas** declined 2.4%. With the half-year results in, **International Opportunities** (up 10.4%) and **Europe** (up 8.7%) are competing with the domestic growth

Commentary *cont'd on page 4*

Fidelity Insight is published monthly by the Mutual Fund Investors Association and is edited by Eric Kobren. The service is supplemented by a weekly telephone hotline update. While the newsletter concentrates exclusively on the timing and selection of Fidelity's mutual funds, it is not associated with Fidelity itself.

Kobren's approach to both timing and selection is fundamental, and he takes a longer-term focus than most other mutual fund newsletters followed by the HFD. On the whole the newsletter has kept pace with the market and has beaten it when its below-market risk is taken into account.

Kobren recommends four different model portfolios of mutual funds, ranging from a conservative "Income & Preservation" portfolio to a more aggressive "Speculative" portfolio. Over the four and one-half years through mid-1992, Kobren's best performer was his "Growth" portfolio, which gained 109.9%, as compared to 89.0% for the Wilshire 5000. The poorest performer was his "Income & Preservation" portfolio, which gained 65.5%. Overall, averaging all portfolios (taking into account an additional portfolio that no longer is being recommended), Kobren gained 80.4%. When these portfolios' low risk is taken into account, *Fidelity Insight* beat the market over this period of time by a significant margin.

A significant factor in the 109.9% gain of the "Growth" portfolio was Kobren's selection of individual mutual funds. According to the HFD, if each of the funds in this portfolio had performed the same as the Wilshire 5000, it would have gained 71.5% over this period of time. The fact that it did better means that Kobren's particular fund picks outperformed the market during the times the portfolio owned them.

Fidelity Insight (Average)

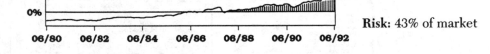

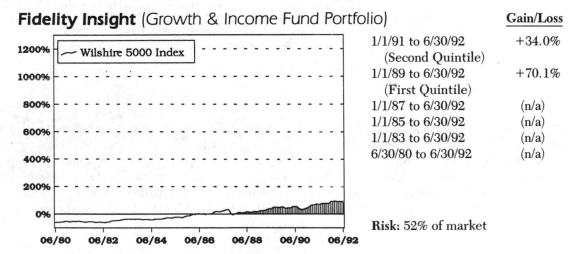

	Gain/Loss
1/1/91 to 6/30/92 (Second Quintile)	+30.5%
1/1/89 to 6/30/92 (Second Quintile)	+63.3%
1/1/87 to 6/30/92	(n/a)
1/1/85 to 6/30/92	(n/a)
1/1/83 to 6/30/92	(n/a)
6/30/80 to 6/30/92	(n/a)

Risk: 43% of market

Fidelity Insight (Growth & Income Fund Portfolio)

	Gain/Loss
1/1/91 to 6/30/92 (Second Quintile)	+34.0%
1/1/89 to 6/30/92 (First Quintile)	+70.1%
1/1/87 to 6/30/92	(n/a)
1/1/85 to 6/30/92	(n/a)
1/1/83 to 6/30/92	(n/a)
6/30/80 to 6/30/92	(n/a)

Risk: 52% of market

Fidelity Insight (Growth Portfolio)

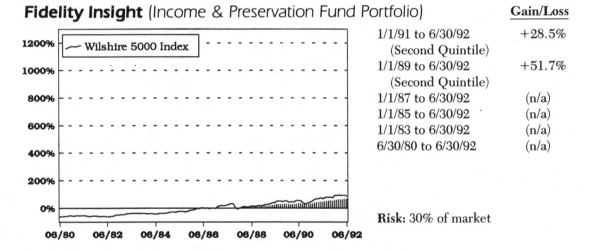

	Gain/Loss
1/1/91 to 6/30/92 (Second Quintile)	+33.5%
1/1/89 to 6/30/92 (First Quintile)	+79.6%
1/1/87 to 6/30/92	(n/a)
1/1/85 to 6/30/92	(n/a)
1/1/83 to 6/30/92	(n/a)
6/30/80 to 6/30/92	(n/a)

Risk: 42% of market

Fidelity Insight (Income & Preservation Fund Portfolio)

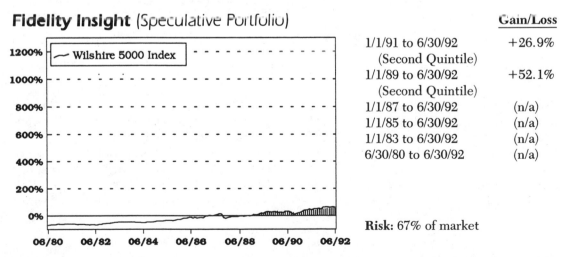

	Gain/Loss
1/1/91 to 6/30/92 (Second Quintile)	+28.5%
1/1/89 to 6/30/92 (Second Quintile)	+51.7%
1/1/87 to 6/30/92	(n/a)
1/1/85 to 6/30/92	(n/a)
1/1/83 to 6/30/92	(n/a)
6/30/80 to 6/30/92	(n/a)

Risk: 30% of market

Fidelity Insight (Speculative Portfolio)

	Gain/Loss
1/1/91 to 6/30/92 (Second Quintile)	+26.9%
1/1/89 to 6/30/92 (Second Quintile)	+52.1%
1/1/87 to 6/30/92	(n/a)
1/1/85 to 6/30/92	(n/a)
1/1/83 to 6/30/92	(n/a)
6/30/80 to 6/30/92	(n/a)

Risk: 67% of market

Fidelity Monitor

Address
P.O. Box 1294
Rocklin, CA
   95677-7294

Editor
Jack Bowers

Phone Number
800-397-3094

Subscription Rates
$48.00/5 months
$96.00/year

Telephone Hotline
Yes

Money Management
Yes

Fidelity Monitor

The Independent Newsletter
for Fidelity Investors

JULY 1992

Seeking Higher Yields

CD and money market yields are remaining at meager levels that don't even keep even with inflation. Clearly investors are anxious for a better return on their money, but in the short run the choices are limited. The stock market remains nervous and is still a bit on the expensive side, and bonds could see more interest rate pressures in months ahead.

But there are still some good ways to boost your yield without taking on a lot of additional risk. This month we look at several Fidelity bond funds that should be steady performers over the next 12 months. These funds are good alternatives to CDs or money markets because they are likely to do well no matter what happens to the stock market.

You may also want to consider our Income Model (see the top of the back page), which has a goal of earning 8% safely with a mix of the funds we've described below. In our Income Model we strive to keep the risk level low. While a loss is certainly possible in this model, so far it has logged a gain for every week since its introduction at the start of the year.

SHORT-TERM BOND

As its name implies, Short-Term Bond Portfolio buys short-term investment grade debt. If you want a simple alternative, this fund by itself is an excellent way to earn a higher yield without taking on much interest rate risk. Short-Term Bond currently yields 6.70%, almost twice what most money markets provide. The fund also takes steps to keep the share price more stable than other bond funds. In a recent meeting, manager Donald Taylor explained to us how he has reduced the fund's duration (a measure of interest rate sensitivity) to a very low 1.3 multiple. That means the fund is pretty well protected against rising rates; a 1% increase in short-term interest rates would result in an approximate decline of 1.3% in Short-Term Bond's share price. Not bad when you consider that most other bond funds would lose 2-3 times as much. Taylor's goal is to stay ahead of money market returns even if short-term rates go up.

We project about a 6-8% total return for Short-Term Bond over the next 12 months. Even in

Continued on page 2

Recommendations

Stocks declined during most of June as international markets sold off and the economy showed signs of losing momentum. But expectations of further easing for interest rates gave stocks a boost near the end of the month. The S&P 500 finished with a loss of 1.2%. Most growth funds did slightly worse because of a poor showing in smaller stocks.

GROWTH FUNDS

Buy: Contrafund, Capital Appreciation, Value, Magellan, Int'l Opportunities.

For a simple growth-oriented approach, follow our Growth Model which is tracked on page 8 and updated on our hotline.

Capital Appreciation, with a 0.1% decline, was the top domestic performer. Disciplined Equity and Value were close behind with losses of 1.0% and 1.3% respectively. At the bottom end was Emerging Growth which was down 5.0% due to a sharp selloff in small company stocks. Magellan lagged the S&P 500 with a 1.8% decline, but is still slightly ahead of the index on a year-to-date basis. Low Priced is now rated hold because we expect Capital Appreciation to perform better over the next year.

Among the internationals, only the currency funds managed a gain, thanks to a slide in the dollar. Deutsche Mark was up 6.4%, British Pound gained 4.9%, and Japanese Yen rose 1.9%. International Opportunities was among the better performing global stock funds; it declined 0.3% and is now our only buy in this group. Worldwide was down 3.5% and is now rated hold.

GROWTH & INCOME

Buy: Equity-Income II, Equity-Income I, Utilities Income, Puritan, Convertible Securities, Asset Manager, Balanced, Market Index.

Utilities Income was the only fund to gain for the month; it was up 1.0%. Asset Manager was even for the month and Balanced declined 0.3% (both funds were helped by their conservative positioning). Equity-Income II was off 0.7% but was still slightly ahead of the S&P 500. On the bottom end was the slightly more aggressive Growth & Income Fund with a 2.0% decline.

Continued on page 3

Fidelity Monitor is published monthly by Jack Bowers and is supplemented by a weekly telephone hotline update (which, by the way, is one of the few in the newsletter industry that is toll-free).

As its name suggests, *Fidelity Monitor* focuses exclusively on funds in the Fidelity family. While its "Select System Mutual Funds" portfolio invests exclusively in Fidelity's Select funds, its "Growth" and "Income" portfolios focus on other funds within the Fidelity family. (The HFD didn't begin following this latter portfolio until the beginning of 1992, so while its performance is reflected in what's reported for the newsletter's average, it is not graphed separately here.) The other major difference between the newsletter's portfolios is that the "Select" portfolio actively switches between different Select funds, while the other two switch rarely.

Bowers's approach appears to involve a combination of both fundamental and technical analysis. For his more long-term-oriented "Growth" and "Income" portfolios, fundamental analysis predominates, but the strategy he pursues for his "Select" portfolio appears to be more technically based.

The newsletter is in first place for the five and one-half years from the beginning of 1987 to mid-1992 among all mutual fund newsletters tracked by the HFD. In comparison to the 93.3% that the Wilshire 5000 gained over this period, the newsletter's average performance was a gain of 127.7%. Though both the "Select" and "Growth" portfolios had higher risk than the market itself, they still beat the Wilshire on a risk-adjusted basis.

Fidelity Monitor (Average)

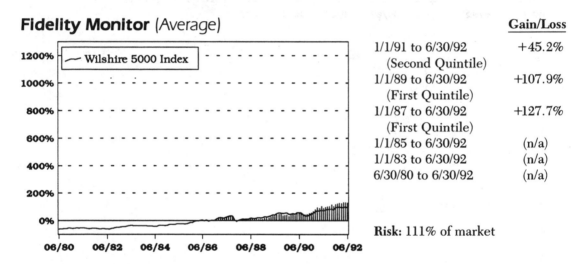

	Gain/Loss
1/1/91 to 6/30/92	+45.2%
(Second Quintile)	
1/1/89 to 6/30/92	+107.9%
(First Quintile)	
1/1/87 to 6/30/92	+127.7%
(First Quintile)	
1/1/85 to 6/30/92	(n/a)
1/1/83 to 6/30/92	(n/a)
6/30/80 to 6/30/92	(n/a)

Risk: 111% of market

Fidelity Monitor (Growth Mutual Funds Portfolio)

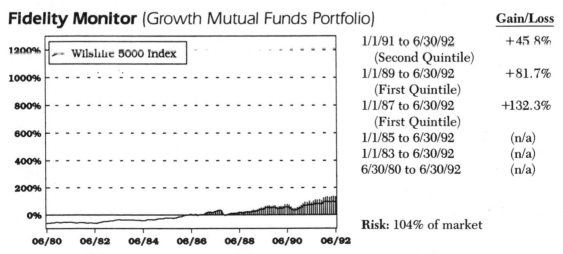

	Gain/Loss
1/1/91 to 6/30/92	+45.8%
(Second Quintile)	
1/1/89 to 6/30/92	+81.7%
(First Quintile)	
1/1/87 to 6/30/92	+132.3%
(First Quintile)	
1/1/85 to 6/30/92	(n/a)
1/1/83 to 6/30/92	(n/a)
6/30/80 to 6/30/92	(n/a)

Risk: 104% of market

Fidelity Monitor (Select System Mutual Funds Portfolio)

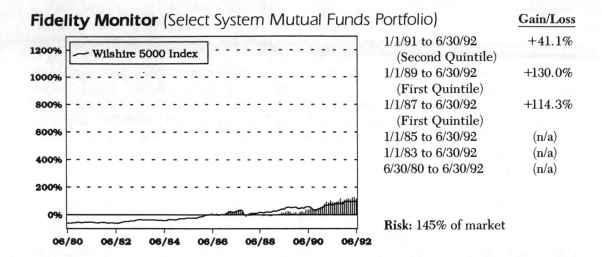

	Gain/Loss
1/1/91 to 6/30/92 (Second Quintile)	+41.1%
1/1/89 to 6/30/92 (First Quintile)	+130.0%
1/1/87 to 6/30/92 (First Quintile)	+114.3%
1/1/85 to 6/30/92	(n/a)
1/1/83 to 6/30/92	(n/a)
6/30/80 to 6/30/92	(n/a)

Risk: 145% of market

Financial World

Address
P.O. Box 10750
Des Moines, IA 50340

Phone Number
800-666-6639

Subscription Rates
$37.50/year

Telephone Hotline
No

Money Management
No

Financial World, the well-known biweekly business magazine, has been grading a large universe of stocks and mutual funds for several years. The service has no telephone hotline update.

The magazine does not advise subscribers on the proper allocation of a portfolio be-tween the market and cash, so the HFD constructs portfolios for it that are fully invested in each category of stocks or mutual funds. Furthermore, each category's portfolio is equally weighted among those securities that are rated most highly in that category.

In the individual stock portfolio, the magazine's highest grade is an "A+." Stocks are added to this portfolio when their grade is raised, and deleted as soon as their status is downgraded. *Financial World's* ranking of mutual funds is a bit more complex. In some issues funds are ranked on the same letter-grading scale as individual stocks. In other issues, however, the magazine gives a "star" to the highest-ranked funds, and at those times the HFD's portfolios are constructed out of the star-ranked funds.

The HFD has data for *Financial World's* stock-ranking system dating back to the beginning of 1985. Over the subsequent seven and one-half years through mid-1992, the HFD's portfolio of the magazine's "A+" stocks gained 86.2%. This contrasts with a 197.6% gain for the Wilshire 5000.

The HFD began tracking *Financial World's* mutual fund portfolios at the beginning of 1991. Over the subsequent 18 months none of them beat the Wilshire 5000. In contrast to the Wilshire's 32.3% gain over this period, these portfolios' performances ranged from a high of 21.6% for the "Balanced Fund" portfolio to a low of 2.4% for the "International Bond Fund" portfolio.

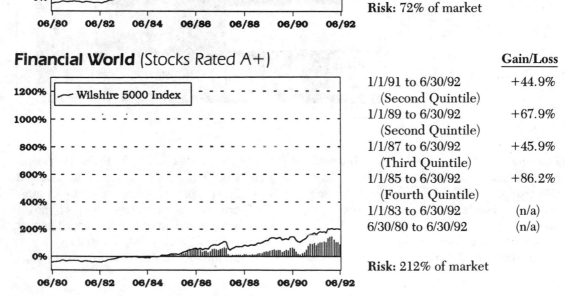

Financial World (Average)

	Gain/Loss
1/1/91 to 6/30/92 (Fourth Quintile)	+12.6%
1/1/89 to 6/30/92 (Fourth Quintile)	+30.4%
1/1/87 to 6/30/92 (Fifth Quintile)	+13.3%
1/1/85 to 6/30/92 (Fourth Quintile)	+44.6%
1/1/83 to 6/30/92	(n/a)
6/30/80 to 6/30/92	(n/a)

Risk: 72% of market

Financial World (Stocks Rated A+)

	Gain/Loss
1/1/91 to 6/30/92 (Second Quintile)	+44.9%
1/1/89 to 6/30/92 (Second Quintile)	+67.9%
1/1/87 to 6/30/92 (Third Quintile)	+45.9%
1/1/85 to 6/30/92 (Fourth Quintile)	+86.2%
1/1/83 to 6/30/92	(n/a)
6/30/80 to 6/30/92	(n/a)

Risk: 212% of market

Financial World (Balanced Fund Portfolio)

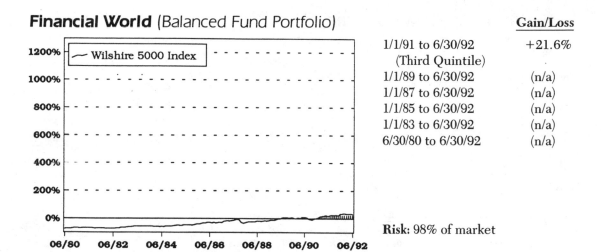

	Gain/Loss
1/1/91 to 6/30/92	+21.6%
(Third Quintile)	
1/1/89 to 6/30/92	(n/a)
1/1/87 to 6/30/92	(n/a)
1/1/85 to 6/30/92	(n/a)
1/1/83 to 6/30/92	(n/a)
6/30/80 to 6/30/92	(n/a)

Risk: 98% of market

Financial World (Corporate Bond Fund Portfolio)

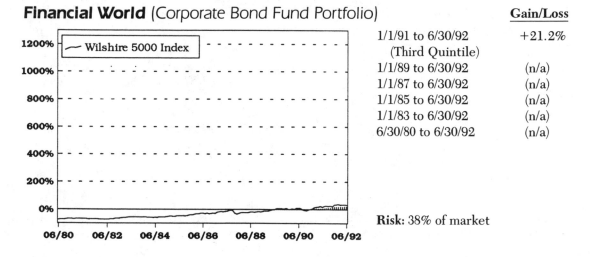

	Gain/Loss
1/1/91 to 6/30/92	+21.2%
(Third Quintile)	
1/1/89 to 6/30/92	(n/a)
1/1/87 to 6/30/92	(n/a)
1/1/85 to 6/30/92	(n/a)
1/1/83 to 6/30/92	(n/a)
6/30/80 to 6/30/92	(n/a)

Risk: 38% of market

Financial World (International Stock Fund Portfolio)

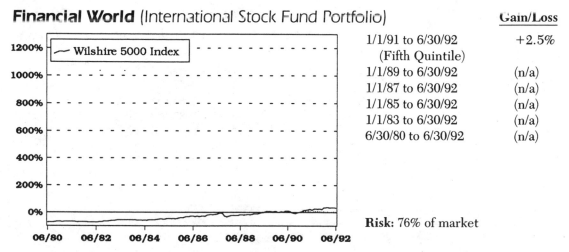

	Gain/Loss
1/1/91 to 6/30/92	+2.5%
(Fifth Quintile)	
1/1/89 to 6/30/92	(n/a)
1/1/87 to 6/30/92	(n/a)
1/1/85 to 6/30/92	(n/a)
1/1/83 to 6/30/92	(n/a)
6/30/80 to 6/30/92	(n/a)

Risk: 76% of market

Financial World (Growth & Income Fund Portfolio)

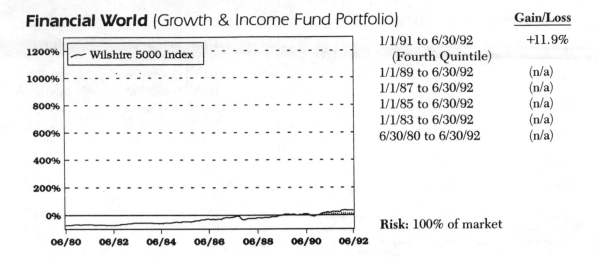

	Gain/Loss
1/1/91 to 6/30/92	+11.9%
(Fourth Quintile)	
1/1/89 to 6/30/92	(n/a)
1/1/87 to 6/30/92	(n/a)
1/1/85 to 6/30/92	(n/a)
1/1/83 to 6/30/92	(n/a)
6/30/80 to 6/30/92	(n/a)

Risk: 100% of market

Financial World (Long-Term Growth Fund Portfolio)

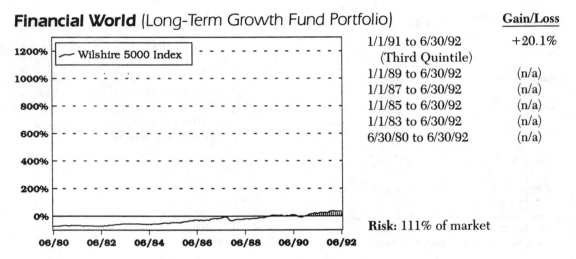

	Gain/Loss
1/1/91 to 6/30/92	+20.1%
(Third Quintile)	
1/1/89 to 6/30/92	(n/a)
1/1/87 to 6/30/92	(n/a)
1/1/85 to 6/30/92	(n/a)
1/1/83 to 6/30/92	(n/a)
6/30/80 to 6/30/92	(n/a)

Risk: 111% of market

Financial World (Aggressive Growth Fund Portfolio)

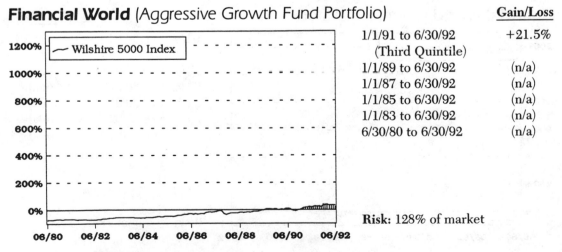

	Gain/Loss
1/1/91 to 6/30/92	+21.5%
(Third Quintile)	
1/1/89 to 6/30/92	(n/a)
1/1/87 to 6/30/92	(n/a)
1/1/85 to 6/30/92	(n/a)
1/1/83 to 6/30/92	(n/a)
6/30/80 to 6/30/92	(n/a)

Risk: 128% of market

Financial World (Sector Funds Portfolio)

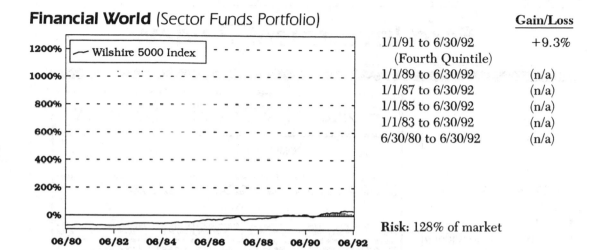

	Gain/Loss
1/1/91 to 6/30/92 (Fourth Quintile)	+9.3%
1/1/89 to 6/30/92	(n/a)
1/1/87 to 6/30/92	(n/a)
1/1/85 to 6/30/92	(n/a)
1/1/83 to 6/30/92	(n/a)
6/30/80 to 6/30/92	(n/a)

Risk: 128% of market

Financial World (U.S. Gov't Bonds Fund Portfolio)

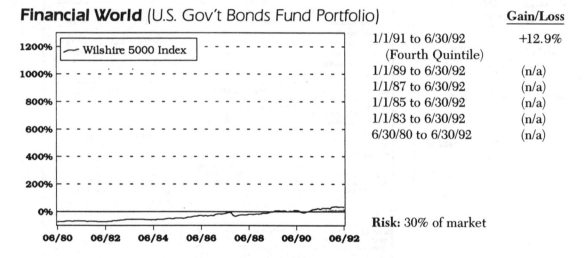

	Gain/Loss
1/1/91 to 6/30/92 (Fourth Quintile)	+12.9%
1/1/89 to 6/30/92	(n/a)
1/1/87 to 6/30/92	(n/a)
1/1/85 to 6/30/92	(n/a)
1/1/83 to 6/30/92	(n/a)
6/30/80 to 6/30/92	(n/a)

Risk: 30% of market

Financial World (International Bond Fund Portfolio)

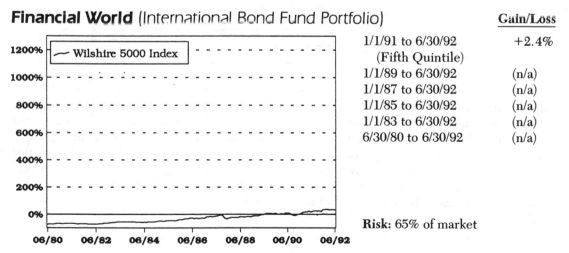

	Gain/Loss
1/1/91 to 6/30/92 (Fifth Quintile)	+2.4%
1/1/89 to 6/30/92	(n/a)
1/1/87 to 6/30/92	(n/a)
1/1/85 to 6/30/92	(n/a)
1/1/83 to 6/30/92	(n/a)
6/30/80 to 6/30/92	(n/a)

Risk: 65% of market

Ford Investment Review

Address
11722 Sorrento Valley Rd.
Suite I
San Diego, CA 92121

Editor
Ford Investor Services

Phone Number
800-842-0207

Subscription Rates
$120.00/year

Telephone Hotline
No

Money Management
No

FORD INVESTMENT REVIEW

COMMENTARY - JUNE 30, 1992

The stock market declined in June, with the Dow Jones Industrials losing 2.3% and the index of Ford stocks down 4.3%. Long term interest rates remained unchanged at 8.2%. The net effect decreased the Ford stock average price/value from 1.14 to 1.10, indicating that the typical stock remains somewhat overpriced.

****

Ford utilizes a proprietary dividend discount model to estimate the intrinsic value (VAL) of companies in our data base. The table below illustrates the impact that a given change in any of the 5 components of this model has upon the intrinsic value (the equally weighted Ford 2000 averages are used here to represent a "typical" company). The effect on the average price to value ratio (PVA), which is based upon this intrinsic value, is also shown. The table is followed by a brief description of these 5 model components.

	ENO	DIV	GRO	BDR	QTY	VAL	PVA	VAL change
Ford 2000 Averages (6/19/92)	1.93	.60	11	8.2	B	24.37	1.09	-
10% ENO increase	2.12	-	-	-	-	26.26	1.01	+ 7.8%
10% DIV increase	-	.66	-	-	-	24.93	1.07	+ 2.3%
10% GRO increase	-	-	12	-	-	27.08	0.99	+11.1%
100 basis point BDR decrease	-	-	-	7.2	-	28.81	0.92	+18.2%
QTY change from B to B+	-	-	-	-	B+	26.46	1.01	+ 8.6%

Ford intrinsic value calculation factors include: 1) the basic discount rate (BDR) which is set equal to the Moody's long-term AAA Corporate Bond Index; 2) the normal earnings (ENO) which are equal to the latest 12 months earnings per share adjusted for cyclical or non-recurring factors where necessary; 3) the dividend (DIV) reflecting the annual payout per share; 4) The growth rate (GRO) representing the estimated annual growth of earnings and dividends over the next 10 years; and 5) the quality rating (QTY) which adjusts the discount rate for perceived risk by increasing the BDR by 50 basis points for each incremental step downward in quality (e.g. B to B-).

Note that the information in the above table reflects average changes for the 2000 issues covered by Ford. Individual stocks and portfolios may react somewhat differently given the same input changes.

****

Ameritech, ConAgra, First of Amer Bank, and PHH were removed from the select stock list this month due to neutral earnings trends, while Wetterau was removed because its price is being determined by an acquisition offer. Added to the list are Adobe Systems (computer graphics software), Hewlett-Packard (instrumentation, computers), and Stride Rite (children's shoes).

SELECTED STOCKS

COMMON STOCK	QUALITY RATING	GROWTH RATE	PRICE/VALUE RATIO	DIVIDEND YIELD	EARNINGS TREND
ADOBE SYSTEMS	B	22	0.62	0.7	21
AMER BRANDS	A-	11	0.67	3.9	31
AMER MGMT SYSTEM	B	20	0.91	0.0	52
APPLE COMPUTER	A-	14	0.72	1.0	52
BECTON, DICKINSON	A-	13	0.91	1.6	29
BERGEN BRUNSWIG	B	13	0.86	2.1	43
CINCINNATI FINL	A-	12	0.84	2.4	47
DELUXE CORP	A	13	0.82	3.0	21
EATON VANCE	B	13	0.55	2.0	25
EQUIFAX	A-	15	0.67	3.2	21
HEWLETT-PACKARD	A	14	0.90	1.2	35
STRIDE RITE	B+	17	0.68	1.5	27

Ford Investment Review is published monthly by Ford Investor Services and is not supplemented by a telephone hotline update.

This service is primarily a stock-rating service, and the bulk of each monthly issue is devoted to a statistical summary of the relative attractiveness of hundreds of stocks according to any of a number of fundamental valuations. The newsletter also highlights a small number of these stocks (usually about a dozen) as specific recommendations. The turnover on this recommended list is fairly high: In a typical month three or four of the dozen stocks are sold and replaced with new ones.

The newsletter does not provide specific portfolio advice, so subscribers aren't told how much of their portfolios ought to be invested in these recommended stocks or whether or not they should have equal portfolio weight. Pursuant to its methodology on such matters, therefore, the HFD constructs a portfolio for *Ford Investment Review* that is fully invested and equally weighted among each of the service's recommended stocks.

The stocks that the newsletter recommends tend to have slightly-above-average risk: Over the two and one-half years through mid-1992, the portfolio the HFD constructed to track the service's advice had slightly more volatility than the Wilshire 5000. At the same time, however, the portfolio also gained about 10% more than the market (27.7% versus 24.1%), so on a risk-adjusted basis over these 30 months, its performance is more or less equal to the Wilshire's.

Ford Investment Review

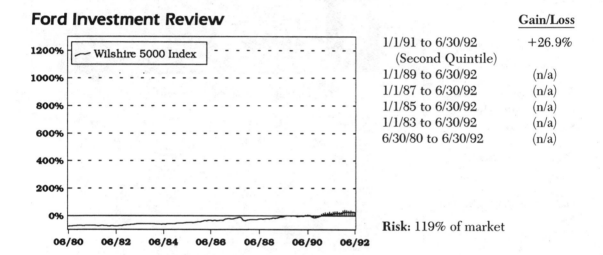

	Gain/Loss
1/1/91 to 6/30/92	+26.9%
(Second Quintile)	
1/1/89 to 6/30/92	(n/a)
1/1/87 to 6/30/92	(n/a)
1/1/85 to 6/30/92	(n/a)
1/1/83 to 6/30/92	(n/a)
6/30/80 to 6/30/92	(n/a)

Risk: 119% of market

Fund Exchange

Address
1200 Westlake Ave. N.
Suite 700
Seattle, WA 98109-3530

Editor
Paul Merriman

Phone Number
800-423-4893

Subscription Rates
$49.00/6 months
$99.00/year

Telephone Hotline
Yes

Money Management
Yes

Fund Exchange is published monthly by Paul Merriman and is supplemented by a hotline that is updated as often as daily in the event that there are changes in one of the newsletter's timing signals for the stock, bond, gold or international markets.

Merriman believes that it is just as important for the investor to diversify among several different market timers as it is to diversify among several different securities. He has taken this belief to heart, dividing his newsletter's model portfolios into several portions and managing only one of them according to his own signals and letting other managers direct the others.

In addition to monitoring Merriman's model portfolios, the HFD also has measured the performance of his newsletter's switches into and out of the stock, gold and bond markets. Overall those switches have added value to a buy-and-hold strategy in the gold market but have lagged a buy-and-hold approach in both stocks and bonds (see Appendix C).

Among the several model portfolios Merriman recommends, the best performers have been his "Aggressive Growth Margined" portfolio (up 182.2% over the seven and one-half years through mid-1992) and his "Conservative Growth Margined" portfolio (up 161.5%). Averaging all his portfolios, including several that Merriman has discontinued along the way, the newsletter's performance is a gain of 125.5%, in contrast to 197.6% for the Wilshire 5000.

On average, Merriman's portfolios have been less risky than the market as a whole, so his risk-adjusted performance has been better. However, it hasn't been sufficiently better for him to beat the market on a risk-adjusted basis over the entire seven and one-half years the HFD has tracked it.

Fund Exchange (Average)

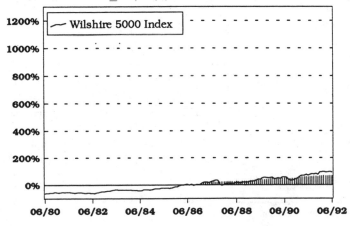

	Gain/Loss
1/1/91 to 6/30/92 (Third Quintile)	+17.1%
1/1/89 to 6/30/92 (Third Quintile)	+35.0%
1/1/87 to 6/30/92 (Second Quintile)	+74.9%
1/1/85 to 6/30/92 (Third Quintile)	+125.5%
1/1/83 to 6/30/92	(n/a)
6/30/80 to 6/30/92	(n/a)

Risk: 56% of market

Fund Exchange (Aggressive Balanced Portfolio)

	Gain/Loss
1/1/91 to 6/30/92 (Fourth Quintile)	+14.4%
1/1/89 to 6/30/92 (Third Quintile)	+31.7%
1/1/87 to 6/30/92 (Second Quintile)	+67.2%
1/1/85 to 6/30/92	(n/a)
1/1/83 to 6/30/92	(n/a)
6/30/80 to 6/30/92	(n/a)

Risk: 51% of market

Fund Exchange (Conservative Balanced Portfolio)

	Gain/Loss
1/1/91 to 6/30/92 (Fourth Quintile)	+10.9%
1/1/89 to 6/30/92 (Fourth Quintile)	+24.8%
1/1/87 to 6/30/92 (Third Quintile)	+54.3%
1/1/85 to 6/30/92	(n/a)
1/1/83 to 6/30/92	(n/a)
6/30/80 to 6/30/92	(n/a)

Risk: 38% of market

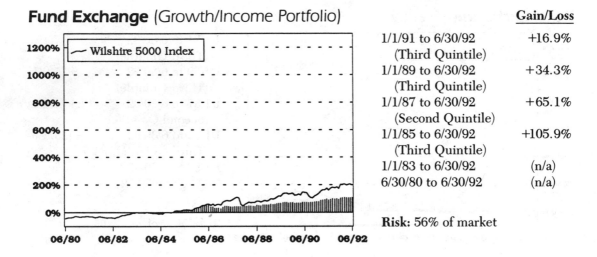

Fund Exchange (Growth/Income Portfolio)

	Gain/Loss
1/1/91 to 6/30/92 (Third Quintile)	+16.9%
1/1/89 to 6/30/92 (Third Quintile)	+34.3%
1/1/87 to 6/30/92 (Second Quintile)	+65.1%
1/1/85 to 6/30/92 (Third Quintile)	+105.9%
1/1/83 to 6/30/92	(n/a)
6/30/80 to 6/30/92	(n/a)

Risk: 56% of market

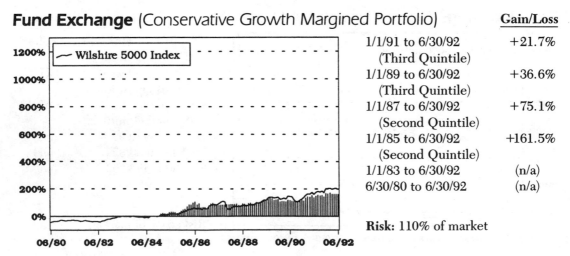

Fund Exchange (Conservative Growth Margined Portfolio)

	Gain/Loss
1/1/91 to 6/30/92 (Third Quintile)	+21.7%
1/1/89 to 6/30/92 (Third Quintile)	+36.6%
1/1/87 to 6/30/92 (Second Quintile)	+75.1%
1/1/85 to 6/30/92 (Second Quintile)	+161.5%
1/1/83 to 6/30/92	(n/a)
6/30/80 to 6/30/92	(n/a)

Risk: 110% of market

Fund Exchange (Aggressive Growth Portfolio)

	Gain/Loss
1/1/91 to 6/30/92 (Third Quintile)	+19.4%
1/1/89 to 6/30/92 (Third Quintile)	+37.5%
1/1/87 to 6/30/92 (Second Quintile)	+75.5%
1/1/85 to 6/30/92 (Third Quintilc)	+124.4%
1/1/83 to 6/30/92	(n/a)
6/30/80 to 6/30/92	(n/a)

Risk: 73% of market

Fund Exchange (Aggressive Growth Margined Portfolio)

	Gain/Loss
1/1/91 to 6/30/92 (Second Quintile)	+43.4%
1/1/89 to 6/30/92 (First Quintile)	+70.8%
1/1/87 to 6/30/92 (First Quintile)	+128.5%
1/1/85 to 6/30/92 (Second Quintile)	+182.2%
1/1/83 to 6/30/92	(n/a)
6/30/80 to 6/30/92	(n/a)

Risk: 143% of market

Fund Exchange (Fixed Income Bond Portfolio)

	Gain/Loss
1/1/91 to 6/30/92 (Third Quintile)	+20.1%
1/1/89 to 6/30/92 (Second Quintile)	+44.2%
1/1/87 to 6/30/92 (Second Quintile)	+74.3%
1/1/85 to 6/30/92 (Third Quintile)	+126.6%
1/1/83 to 6/30/92	(n/a)
6/30/80 to 6/30/92	(n/a)

Risk: 23% of market

Fund Exchange (Gold Mutual Funds Portfolio)

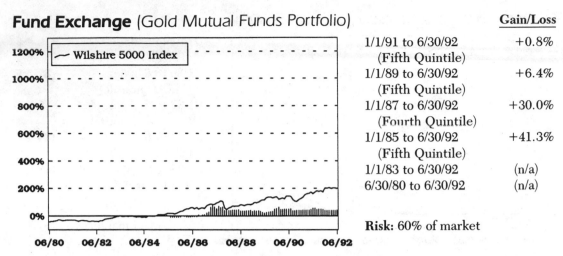

	Gain/Loss
1/1/91 to 6/30/92 (Fifth Quintile)	+0.8%
1/1/89 to 6/30/92 (Fifth Quintile)	+6.4%
1/1/87 to 6/30/92 (Fourth Quintile)	+30.0%
1/1/85 to 6/30/92 (Fifth Quintile)	+41.3%
1/1/83 to 6/30/92	(n/a)
6/30/80 to 6/30/92	(n/a)

Risk: 60% of market

Fund Exchange (International Mutual Funds Portfolio)

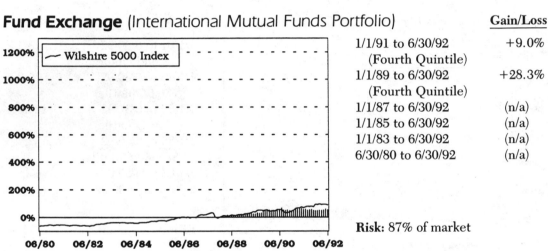

	Gain/Loss
1/1/91 to 6/30/92 (Fourth Quintile)	+9.0%
1/1/89 to 6/30/92 (Fourth Quintile)	+28.3%
1/1/87 to 6/30/92	(n/a)
1/1/85 to 6/30/92	(n/a)
1/1/83 to 6/30/92	(n/a)
6/30/80 to 6/30/92	(n/a)

Risk: 87% of market

Fund Kinetics

Address
17525 NE 40th St.
Suite E123
Redmond, WA 98052

Editor
Byron B. McCann

Phone Number
800-634-6790

Subscription Rates
$ 45.00/6 weeks
$175.00/year

Telephone Hotline
Yes

Money Management
No

Fund Kinetics™
Mutual Fund Switching with Confidence

WEEKLY RSO/SVI REPORT
No Switch - New Passing Rule in Effect!

VENTURE CATALYST, INC. 1532 7TH AVE. WEST, SEATTLE, WA 98119 • 206-282-7728

Week Ending July 2, 1992

Action Items

All-Funds Portfolio: Hold Select/Regional Banks. (FAST# 507).

Diversified Portfolio: Hold Global Bond (FAST# 451).

Market Timing

S&P 500 Index	411.77
S&P 500 Dividend Yield	3.02%
S&P 500 P/E Ratio	25.43
S&P 500 Earnings Yield	3.93%
90-Day T-Bill Yield	3.59%
SVI Indicator	1.39 (bullish)
All-Funds Portfolio	In the market

Performance Update

Below is an updated chart for the S&P 500 Index (with dividends reinvested). Column 2 provides updated price and relative strength charts for this week's top rated funds (alpha = 0.15/0.60).

S&P 500 Index

Fund Kinetics Commentary

We are introducing the **Passing Rule** into the system for the second half of 1992. We are using the 15% level which means that the new RSO% must pass the old RSO% by fifteen percent or more to trigger a switch (e.g., an RSO% of 4.00% for the current fund requires a new fund RSO% of 4.60% or higher to trigger a switch).

Our previous research report results, sent out with the April 10, 1992 edition of the newsletter, and the current frequency of switching compel us to implement the Rule before the end of the year. Please call us if you do not have a copy of the report and we shall send you one.

The Passing Rule *prevents* us from switching back into **Select/Savings & Loan** which we left last week. Instead we shall remain in **Select/Regional Banks** despite the fact that it did not rise as well as Savings & Loan for the week.

In the last issue, we mentioned that we would have stayed in Savings & Loan had the Passing Rule been in effect and that there would not be much of a difference staying in since the two funds' RSO%'s were close and that they were both in financial sectors. For those of you who stayed, you enjoyed a +6.40% gain for the week compared to +3.85% for Regional Banks (+4.47% net gain including our Monday switch effect.) Despite this we recommended the switch because we did not want to change aspects of the system before the half year mark. Now we feel free to do so.

One should realize that Savings & Loan could outperform our hold in Regional Banks and that we may switch out of Regional Banks as early as next week if the rankings so indicate. One should expect that the benefits from the Passing Rule will be achieved over the long run and that there will be many cases in the short term where switching would have been the better thing to do for any particular week.

We did benefit from a switching gain as last Monday's price for the fund sold rose +2.03% from Friday's compared to the cost of the fund we purchased which rose +1.42%. This was a case where we had a good net gain on the switch.

The important news of the week centered around the drop in the discount rate to 3.0% along with the rise in unemployment to 7.8% from 7.5%. This should lower Monday's Treasury Bill auction prices and cause an increase in the **SVI** . With yields so low, we remain bullish on equity funds as our primary vehicle.

The **S&P 500 Index** rose +2.06% for the week compared to our net rise of +4.47%. We are now up +6.49% for the year compared to -1.28% for the S&P.

We wish you all a Happy Independence Day celebration!

Fund Kinetics, published weekly by Byron McCann, is really two services in one. Each service consists of a two-page weekly bulletin and a telephone hotline update, and both recommend a model portfolio of mutual funds in the Fidelity family. They differ according to the investment approach each takes: The first of the two halves of the Fund Kinetics service is referred to as the "Weekly Erfer Report," and the second half is called the "Weekly RSO/RVI Report" ("Erfer" and "RSO/RVI" refer to McCann's two different rating systems for mutual funds).

The HFD began following the "Erfer" half

of this service at the beginning of 1991 and the "RSO/RVI" half at the beginning of 1992. Since this book includes graphs for portfolios that have been followed at least since the beginning of 1991, a separate graph doesn't appear for the "Weekly RSO/RVI Report,"— but its performance is included in the *Fund Kinetics* average.

McCann focuses on both overall market timing as well as the selection of individual mutual funds, but at least during the 18 months through mid-1992 both his model portfolios were fully invested. His portfolios have switched between funds somewhat more often than once per month on average, thus frequently incurring the redemption fees that Fidelity sometimes charges on funds held for less than 30 days.

Over the 18 months through mid-1992, *Fund Kinetics* on average gained 26.5%, in contrast to 32.3% for the Wilshire 5000. The newsletter's volatility during this period was higher than the market's, so on a risk-adjusted basis its performance also was below the market's.

Fund Kinetics (Average)

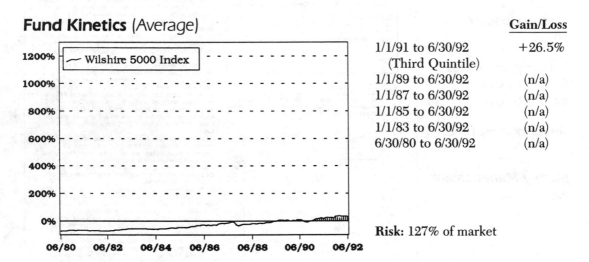

	Gain/Loss
1/1/91 to 6/30/92	+26.5%
(Third Quintile)	
1/1/89 to 6/30/92	(n/a)
1/1/87 to 6/30/92	(n/a)
1/1/85 to 6/30/92	(n/a)
1/1/83 to 6/30/92	(n/a)
6/30/80 to 6/30/92	(n/a)

Risk: 127% of market

Fund Kinetics (Weekly "Erfer" Report)

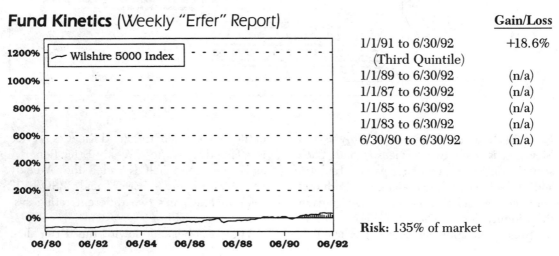

	Gain/Loss
1/1/91 to 6/30/92	+18.6%
(Third Quintile)	
1/1/89 to 6/30/92	(n/a)
1/1/87 to 6/30/92	(n/a)
1/1/85 to 6/30/92	(n/a)
1/1/83 to 6/30/92	(n/a)
6/30/80 to 6/30/92	(n/a)

Risk: 135% of market

Fundline

Address
P.O. Box 663
Woodland Hills, CA
91365

Editor
David Menashe

Phone Number
818-346-5637

Subscription Rates
$ 47.00/4 months
$127.00/year

Telephone Hotline
Yes

Money Management
Yes

Fundline Established 1968

ISSUE #290
August 1, 1992

DAVID H. MENASHE & CO. Registered Investment Adviser   P.O. BOX 663 • WOODLAND HILLS, CALIFORNIA 91365

Composite Fund Index $95.32 (as of July 29)
Trading Oscillator 63% Long-Term Indicator 57%

FIDELITY TOLL-FREE
#1-800-544-6666

ACTION ADVICE New buying should be undertaken only if you are a new subscribers wanting to follow **Model #3**, using 50% of your assets to buy the top two funds on the ranking table, retaining the balance as a cash reserve for future deployment. Otherwise, the ongoing portfolio requires no changes.

The **International funds** included in **Model #1** are subject to elimination due to their <u>unexpected</u> drop last week. <u>Explanations follow.</u> As a last-ditch precaution, we will probably recommend selling the **Overseas** fund should it drop below the critical $24 level, a level that has shown support on several such recent-forays. Therefore, <u>keep in frequent touch with the hotline for specific recommendations.</u> Also, for the record, on June 30 this model bought **Regional Banks** at $17.11 and **Transportation** at $15.03.

The market has been in a labored rally since the last short-term buy signal in late June. So far, so good. However, we mustn't be dazzled by the DJIA flirting once again with new highs. The broad market, as represented by the pattern of our Composite Fund Index, posted its high point in February and has been in a wishy-washy trend ever since.

Continued on page 2 . . . . .

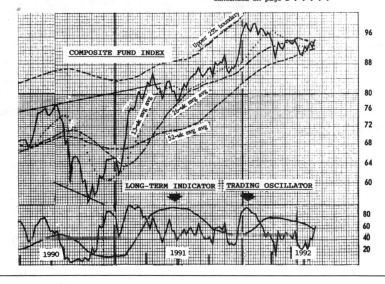

According to editor David Menashe, *Fundline* was established in 1968. It is a mutual fund selection and timing service that is published monthly, and is accompanied by a telephone hotline update. Menashe's approach to both market timing and mutual fund selection appears to be based primarily on technical analysis.

The HFD has been following *Fundline* since the beginning of 1986, though Menashe's two current portfolios date back only to the beginning of 1991. What is reported for the newsletter's average takes into account these two current portfolios as well as several previous ones that no longer exist.

Both of Menashe's current portfolios invest exclusively within the Fidelity family of funds. His "$100,000 Timing" portfolio fairly actively switches between various funds, whereas his "$100,000 No-Timing" portfolio switches just once per year. Over the 18 months through mid-1992, both these portfolios beat the market; in contrast to the Wilshire 5000's 32.3%, Menashe's "$100,000 No-Timing" portfolio gained 62.4% and his "$100,000 Timing" portfolio gained 39.4%.

The primary credit for this latter portfolio's beating the market goes to Menashe's individual fund recommendations: A portfolio that switched on Menashe's signals between hypothetical shares of the Wilshire 5000 and T-Bills gained just 20.2%—less than buying and holding and barely half the actual gain of this portfolio.

Overall, for the six and one-half years through mid-1992, *Fundline* beat the market—though barely. In contrast to a total return of 124.0% for the Wilshire 5000, *Fundline* gained 128.0%.

Fundline (Average)

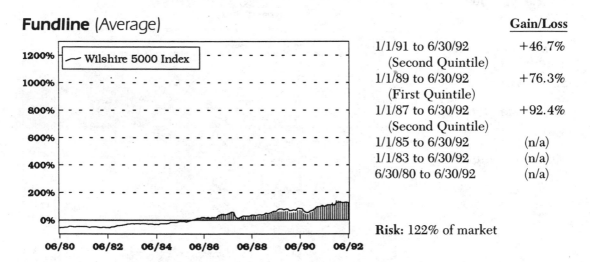

	Gain/Loss
1/1/91 to 6/30/92 (Second Quintile)	+46.7%
1/1/89 to 6/30/92 (First Quintile)	+76.3%
1/1/87 to 6/30/92 (Second Quintile)	+92.4%
1/1/85 to 6/30/92	(n/a)
1/1/83 to 6/30/92	(n/a)
6/30/80 to 6/30/92	(n/a)

Risk: 122% of market

Fundline ($100,000 Timing Portfolio)

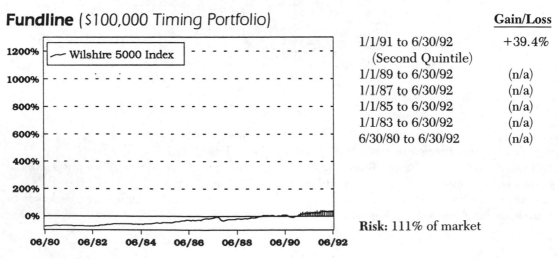

	Gain/Loss
1/1/91 to 6/30/92 (Second Quintile)	+39.4%
1/1/89 to 6/30/92	(n/a)
1/1/87 to 6/30/92	(n/a)
1/1/85 to 6/30/92	(n/a)
1/1/83 to 6/30/92	(n/a)
6/30/80 to 6/30/92	(n/a)

Risk: 111% of market

Fundline ($100,000 No-Timing Portfolio)

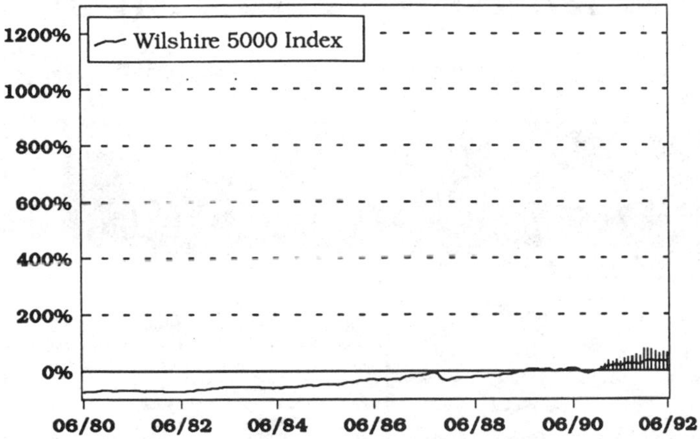

	Gain/Loss
1/1/91 to 6/30/92 (First Quintile)	+62.4%
1/1/89 to 6/30/92	(n/a)
1/1/87 to 6/30/92	(n/a)
1/1/85 to 6/30/92	(n/a)
1/1/83 to 6/30/92	(n/a)
6/30/80 to 6/30/92	(n/a)

Risk: 163% of market

Futures Hotline Mutual Fund Timer

Address
P.O. Box 6275
Jacksonville, FL 32236

Editor
Craig Corcoran

Phone Number
904-693-0355

Subscription Rates
$295.00/year

Telephone Hotline
Yes

Money Management
No

FUTURES HOTLINE MUTUAL FUND TIMER

A service designed to transmit the *'cold and bloodless'* verdicts of the markets to our clients. Edited by: Craig Corcoran

future facts

FUTURES	TRADING MODELS	SENTIMENT INDEX	MOMENTUM INDEX
STOCK INDEX	63%	Neutral	Neutral
TREASURY BOND	53%	Overly Optimistic	Overbought
GOLD	50%	Overly Optimistic	Neutral
CRUDE OIL	0%	Neutral	Neutral
GERMAN MARK	100%	Overly Optimistic	Overbought

FUTURES PORTFOLIO GAIN (LOSS) SINCE LAST ISSUE = $3,643.75

THE BUBBLE

"A bubble is kept inflated by one thing, confidence. The fall in the public's confidence has already caused the financial bubble of the 1980's to stop inflating and begin receding. As social psychology is the engine of booms and busts, the potential for the current malaise to result ultimately in a severe financial and economic contraction is very high."

Bob Prechter - Elliott Wave Theorist

For quite some time, we have monitored the progress of the stock market's mania bubble by way of the DJIA Price to Dividend Ratio, see chart below. Unlike earnings-based valuation indicators, which can be influenced by the changes of accountant opinions, dividends are an investor's cold cash measure of value and illustrate if stocks are either over or undervalued. As the chart shows, investors have become overconfident (similar to all prior major market peaks over the past 77 years) and willing to pay greater than 36 times cumulative dividends offered by stocks comprised within the Dow Industrial Average. The record shows that any DJIA decline of greater than 3% from these historical overvaluations signals that a multi-year top has been seen. Such an event occurred in June!

Issue #92.6
2 July 1992

CRAIG CORCORAN FUTURES, INC. P.O. BOX 725, ORANGE PARK, FL 32067 / 904-269-7456
Published monthly / Subscriptions: $295 annually

Futures Hotline Mutual Fund Timer is the product of an early 1990 marriage of two separate newsletters, both of which had been edited by Craig Corcoran. While the *Futures Hotline Mutual Fund Timer* is published every three weeks, a subscriber must call its daily telephone hotline number for updates (or receive them by fax or modem) in order to make maximum use of the service. (Much of the newsletter, in fact, is devoted to reviewing the recommendations that were made on the hotline.) There are two hotline updates per day: one for those interested in the newsletter's futures recommendations, and the other for those interested in the service's mutual fund recommendations.

The newsletter has two model portfolios: the "Model Futures" portfolio, which contains commodity futures contracts, and the "Asset Allocation" portfolio, which invests primarily in mutual funds though sometimes also will include individual stocks or options. This latter portfolio is the successor to several individual ones that were merged at the beginning of 1992; the pre-1992 performance that the HFD reports is based on an average of each of those individual portfolios.

The approach taken by Corcoran in constructing these two portfolios appears to be primarily technical and, especially in the case of the futures portfolio, very short-term oriented. While the same overall market analysis underlies both, their performance sometimes can diverge markedly. Over the four and one-half years through mid-1992, Corcoran's "Model Futures" portfolio lost 22.3% while his "Asset Allocation" portfolio gained 53.8%. Both underperformed the Wilshire 5000's 89.0% gain over this period.

Futures Hotline Mutual Fund Timer (Average)

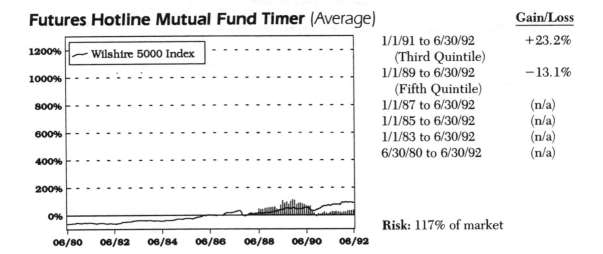

	Gain/Loss
1/1/91 to 6/30/92	+23.2%
(Third Quintile)	
1/1/89 to 6/30/92	−13.1%
(Fifth Quintile)	
1/1/87 to 6/30/92	(n/a)
1/1/85 to 6/30/92	(n/a)
1/1/83 to 6/30/92	(n/a)
6/30/80 to 6/30/92	(n/a)

Risk: 117% of market

Futures Hotline Mutual Fund Timer
(Model Futures Portfolio)

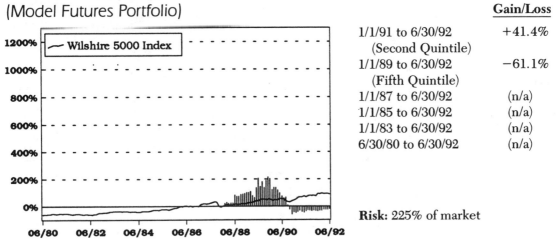

	Gain/Loss
1/1/91 to 6/30/92	+41.4%
(Second Quintile)	
1/1/89 to 6/30/92	−61.1%
(Fifth Quintile)	
1/1/87 to 6/30/92	(n/a)
1/1/85 to 6/30/92	(n/a)
1/1/83 to 6/30/92	(n/a)
6/30/80 to 6/30/92	(n/a)

Risk: 225% of market

Futures Hotline Mutual Fund Timer
(Asset Allocation Portfolio)

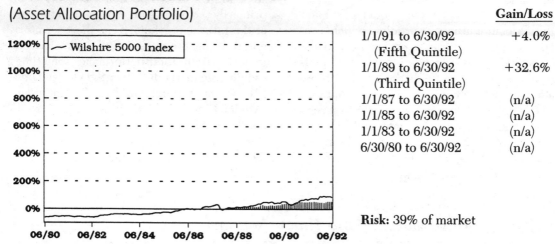

Gain/Loss

1/1/91 to 6/30/92 (Fifth Quintile)	+4.0%
1/1/89 to 6/30/92 (Third Quintile)	+32.6%
1/1/87 to 6/30/92	(n/a)
1/1/85 to 6/30/92	(n/a)
1/1/83 to 6/30/92	(n/a)
6/30/80 to 6/30/92	(n/a)

Risk: 39% of market

The Garside Forecast

the GARSIDE FORECAST

COUNTER FORCE THEORY

July 8, 1992   Volume XXIII Issue 14   Dow Jones Average 3292

Address
P.O. Box 1812
Santa Ana, CA 92702

Editor
Ben Garside

Phone Number
714-259-1670

Subscription Rates
$ 75.00/6 months
$125.00/year

Telephone Hotline
Yes

Money Management
No

CURRENT SYNOPSIS: Very Long Term – Bearish; Long Term – Bearish; Intermediate Term – Bearish; Short Term – Bullish; Very Short Term – mail advice too slow (call 1-900-446-9744).

INDICATOR SUMMARY: Positive Indicators: Market Barometer Strong (short term); Bell Ringers (intermediate term) Gold, Silver, Heating Oil, and Yen; Senticator (long term sentiment), Moneycator (long term interest sensitive). Negative Indicators: Bell Ringers (intermediate term) Stocks, Bonds, T-Bills, Crude Oil, D-Mark.

INDUSTRY GROUPS: Trend Ratings +5 to –5 (+ or – after number indicates direction of last change).

Aerospace +3 (–), Air Transport –5 (–), Aluminum +5 (+), Automobiles +3 (–), Banks—NYC +5 (+), Banks—Others +5 (+), Building Supplies +3 (–), Chemicals +3 (–), Computers –5 (–), Containers +1 (–), Cosmetics +3 (–).

Drugs –5 (–), Electrical Equipment –1 (–), Electronics +1 (–), Foods –5 (–), Gold Mining –3 (+), Hospital Management –5 (–), Hospital Supplies –3 (–), Household Furnishing –3 (–), Household Products +3 (–), Insurance –3 (–).

Leisure –3 (–), Liquor –3 (–), Machine Tools +1 (–), Machinery –1 (–), Metals +5 (+), Oils—Domestic –1 (+), Oils—International +3 (+), Oil Well Machinery +1 (+), Paper/Forest Products +1 (–), Pollution Control –5 (–), Publishing +1 (–).

Restaurants +3 (–), Retail—Department –5 (–), Retail—Food +1 (–), Retail—General +1 (–), Soft Drinks +5 (+), Steel/Iron –1 (–), Textiles +5 (+), Tobacco +1 (–), Toys and Games +3 (–), Truckers +1 (–).

GRAND TOTAL –8 (–) versus an early May '91 high of +148.

So far, so good — TGF of May 27th reviewed the total despair found at major bottoms in any supply/demand market. "That is what major bottoms are made of. It is almost impossible to think of a single 'reason' why that market would go up, and it is easy to find many reasons why it should continue to move lower.

"A good example of 'major bottom total despair' is the Gold Market. On the May 22nd edition of Wall Street Week the guest was a very well respected metal analyst. The very thought that WSW would have such a guest at this time is bullish for Gold. However, the 'total despair' comes from the fact that the guest could not think of a single reason why Gold would go up." Needless to say, it has done nothing but go up since then. The Gold Stock Index is up 7% from there and up 19% since its April low.

Whenever we have a Counter Force Theory Zone, it just plain takes time before you can look back and see how accurate its prediction was. Of course, that is particularly true of "Big Picture" turns. The importance of the 1991/early '92 Strong High Risk Year is becoming more obvious, but it will undoubtedly be years before we know its true importance. January early February was a Strong High Risk Monthly Zone, and the broader market averages have not seen those prices since. In fact, virtually every day one or more stocks get cut in half (or more) because of some disappointment.

The overall positions of our Bell Ringer Indicators is still on an Inflationary Alert. Only the D-Mark and Crude Oil Bell Ringers are on the deflationary side of the ledger. It would not take much to put Gold, Heating Oil, and the Yen on a deflation reading, but we cannot jump the gun — we will wait and see. Of course, if we get 5 Bell Ringers on the deflationary side that would make for a Deflation Alert. The relative short but accurate record of the Inflation/Deflation Alerts says the Dow will not go into a Bear Market until a Deflation Alert comes into being.

July/early August is still a Strong Counter Force Theory Low Risk Month but the SLR Weekly Zone given in the last letter has expanded to July 6-21.

TIMER DIGEST TIMER OF THE YEAR AWARDS 1982 - STOCKS, 1986 - GOLD, 1988 - STOCKS

The Garside Forecast is published every two weeks by Ben Garside and is supplemented by a daily telephone hotline update. Garside also updates a hotline service several times during each trading session, primarily for those interested in trading the stock index futures market. He devotes the bulk of his newsletter to timing a number of different markets, though he also makes specific stock recommendations.

In the timing arena, Garside's best performance from the beginning of 1985 through mid-1992 was in the gold market. An investor who invested in gold bullion when Garside's

"Gold Bell-Ringer" timing model was bullish, and earned the T-Bill rate when it was bearish, gained 43.8%, in contrast to just 11.1% for buying and holding gold itself. A portfolio that actually went short on Garside's sell signals, instead of into cash, did even better, gaining 50.1%.

In the bond market, Garside has lagged a buy-and-hold. An investor who held shares of the Shearson Lehman Treasury Index when Garside's bond "Bell Ringer" was on a "buy," and held T-Bills when it was bearish, gained 82.0% over the same seven-and-one-half-year period, compared to a gain of 124.0% for buying and holding. An investor who went short on Garside's sell signals lost 32.6% over the same period.

Garside also lagged a buy-and-hold in the stock market. Over these seven and one-half years a portfolio that alternated between the Wilshire 5000 and T-Bills on signals from Garside's stock "Bell Ringer" gained 91.2%, in contrast to 197.6% for buying and holding. A portfolio that actually went short on Garside's sell signals did even worse, losing 55.6%.

In addition to monitoring Garside's timing advice, the HFD also tracks a portfolio constructed out of his specific stock recommendations. This stock portfolio is fourth from the bottom among all newsletters the HFD has tracked over these seven and one-half years, losing 35.4%, in contrast to the Wilshire 5000's 197.6% gain. This portfolio suffered because Garside was predominantly bearish throughout the period.

The Garside Forecast

	Gain/Loss
1/1/91 to 6/30/92 (Fifth Quintile)	−24.8%
1/1/89 to 6/30/92 (Fifth Quintile)	−41.5%
1/1/87 to 6/30/92 (Fifth Quintile)	−49.7%
1/1/85 to 6/30/92 (Fifth Quintile)	−35.4%
1/1/83 to 6/30/92	(n/a)
6/30/80 to 6/30/92	(n/a)

Risk: 89% of market

Global Fund Timer

Address
P.O. Box 77330
Baton Rouge, LA
70879

Editor
Greg Cook

Phone Number
800-256-3136

Subscription Rates
$96.00/year

Telephone Hotline
Yes

Money Management
No

GLOBAL FUND TIMER

TIMING FOR MUTUAL FUND INVESTORS   BY DR. GREG COOK

July 1, 1992   Registered Investment Advisor   Issue No. 58

SIGNAL SUMMARY

S&P 500 (med)	BEAR
S&P 500 (long)	BULL
GOLD	BEAR
BONDS	BULL
ENERGY	BULL
INTERNATIONAL	BEAR

FUND RECOMMENDATIONS

The Gold Model issued a SELL signal on June 19, 1992. All positions in gold funds were closed on June 22.

The Medium Term S&P 500 composite model issued a SELL signal on June 10, 1992. All growth funds, except energy sector funds, were sold on June 11. The Long Term S&P 500 composite model has remained bullish since activating a BUY signal on April 10, 1992.

A BUY signal was issued by the Bond Model on March 24, 1992. The following bond funds are recommended: Benham Target 2020 (BTTTX), Vanguard U.S. Treasury Bond (VUSTX), Fidelity Flexible Bond (FBNDX), Financial U.S. Government Portfolio (FBDGX) and T. Rowe Price U.S. Treasury Long-Term (PRULX).

The Energy Model activated a BUY signal on April 10, 1992. The following energy funds are recommended: Fidelity Select Energy (FSENX), Financial Strategic Energy (FSTEX) and Vanguard Specialized Portfolio Energy (VGENX). The T. Rowe Price New Era fund (PRNEX), which invests in natural resource companies such as energy, paper & forest products and metals, is also recommended.

The International Model has been on a SELL signal since January 8, 1991.

GLOBAL PORTFOLIO - 75% money market funds and 25% energy funds.

U.S. PORTFOLIO - 60% money market funds, 20% energy funds and 20% bond funds.

CONSERVATIVE PORTFOLIO - 40% money market funds, 20% energy funds and 40% bond funds.

ZERO BOND PORTFOLIO - 100% bond funds.

SECTOR SURVEY

GOLD: -5 -4 -3 -2 -1 0 +1 +2 +3 +4 +5

The Gold Model slipped to a bearish -2 reading on June 19, 1992. The indicators that pushed the Gold Model into negative territory are based on the price of United Services Gold Shares (USERX). USERX, which invests entirely in South African gold mining shares, has taken a beating lately because of the racial violence in that country. The fund has lost 8.2% in the last four weeks.

Although racial unrest is bearish for South African gold mining stocks, it is bullish for gold bullion and non-South African mining concerns because of potential cutbacks in South African gold production. The result has been a two-tiered market where gold funds invested in South Africa have headed south, and funds invested in North American gold mines have held on to their gains.

We are trying to sort this divergence out. If this problem persists, it may be necessary to issue buy recommendations on individual gold funds that invest outside of South Africa. In the meantime, the bearish -2 reading in the Gold Model will be observed. No positions in gold funds are recommended.

S&P 500: -5 -4 -3 -2 -1 0 +1 +2 +3 +4 +5

Long Term: -5 -4 -3 -2 -1 0 +1 +2 +3 +4 +5

June was a difficult month for equities, particularly small stocks. The NASDAQ Composite (OTC-C) lost 6.4%, and in doing so, broke below its April low. The S&P 500 held up much better than the

GLOBAL FUND TIMER   Page 1

Global Fund Timer is published monthly by Greg Cook, who supplements his service with a telephone hotline update. Cook's investment approach is a combination of both technical and fundamental analysis, and he focuses on timing the domestic and international stock, gold and bond markets as well as on the selection of individual mutual funds.

Global Fund Timer contains four distinct model portfolios of mutual funds: a "Global" portfolio, which invests exclusively in the Fidelity family; a "U.S." portfolio, which invests exclusively in funds within the Financial family; a "Conservative" portfolio, which invests exclusively in Vanguard funds; and a "Zero Bond" portfolio, which invests exclusively in funds managed by Benham Capital Management. All four portfolios are managed fairly conservatively, with none as risky as the market during the 18 months ending in mid-1992.

On average over these one and one-half years, Cook's four model portfolios gained an average of 15.1%, in contrast to a 32.3% total return for the Wilshire 5000. While part of this underperformance can be accounted for by Cook's below-market risk, not all of it can:

Even on a risk-adjusted basis, *Global Fund Timer* underperformed the market.

The culprit in this underperformance appears to be market timing rather than security selection, since Cook's recommended funds have done better than the market. Over the 18 months through mid-1992, for example, Cook's "U.S." portfolio would have gained 14.9% had each of his recommended funds performed the same as the Wilshire 5000 (see Appendix C-6). In fact, however, this portfolio gained 21.1%, meaning that Cook's recommended funds outperformed the market.

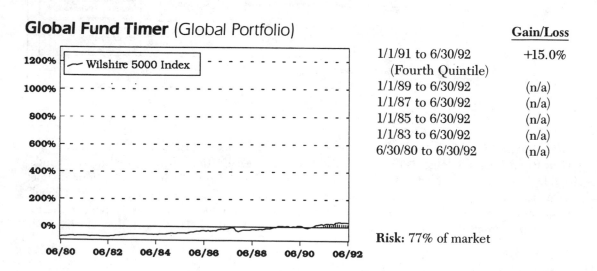

Global Fund Timer (Average)

	Gain/Loss
1/1/91 to 6/30/92	+15.1%
(Fourth Quintile)	
1/1/89 to 6/30/92	(n/a)
1/1/87 to 6/30/92	(n/a)
1/1/85 to 6/30/92	(n/a)
1/1/83 to 6/30/92	(n/a)
6/30/80 to 6/30/92	(n/a)

Risk: 61% of market

Global Fund Timer (Global Portfolio)

	Gain/Loss
1/1/91 to 6/30/92	+15.0%
(Fourth Quintile)	
1/1/89 to 6/30/92	(n/a)
1/1/87 to 6/30/92	(n/a)
1/1/85 to 6/30/92	(n/a)
1/1/83 to 6/30/92	(n/a)
6/30/80 to 6/30/92	(n/a)

Risk: 77% of market

Global Fund Timer (U.S. Portfolio)

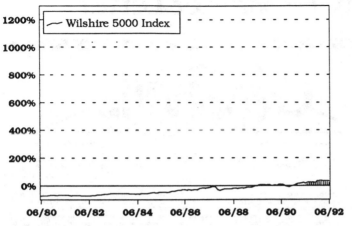

	Gain/Loss
1/1/91 to 6/30/92	+21.1%
(Third Quintile)	
1/1/89 to 6/30/92	(n/a)
1/1/87 to 6/30/92	(n/a)
1/1/85 to 6/30/92	(n/a)
1/1/83 to 6/30/92	(n/a)
6/30/80 to 6/30/92	(n/a)

Risk: 91% of market

Global Fund Timer (Conservative Portfolio)

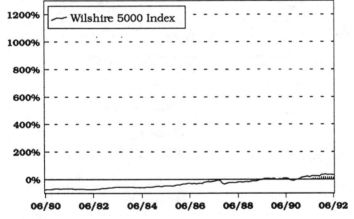

	Gain/Loss
1/1/91 to 6/30/92	+14.4%
(Fourth Quintile)	
1/1/89 to 6/30/92	(n/a)
1/1/87 to 6/30/92	(n/a)
1/1/85 to 6/30/92	(n/a)
1/1/83 to 6/30/92	(n/a)
6/30/80 to 6/30/92	(n/a)

Risk: 62% of market

Global Fund Timer (Zero Bond Portfolio)

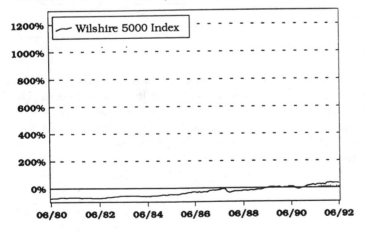

	Gain/Loss
1/1/91 to 6/30/92	+9.0%
(Fourth Quintile)	
1/1/89 to 6/30/92	(n/a)
1/1/87 to 6/30/92	(n/a)
1/1/85 to 6/30/92	(n/a)
1/1/83 to 6/30/92	(n/a)
6/30/80 to 6/30/92	(n/a)

Risk: 68% of market

The Granville Market Letter

Address
P.O. Drawer 413006
Kansas City, MO 64141

Editor
Joe Granville

Phone Number
816-474-5353

Subscription Rates
$ 85.00/3 months
$150.00/6 months
$250.00/year

Telephone Hotline
No

Money Management
No

© 1990 The Granville Market Letter, Inc. All Rights Reserved   P O DRAWER 413006, KANSAS CITY, MISSOURI 64141

Volume XXX, Number 25   July 2, 1992   Whole Number 1329
Written solely by Joseph E. Granville   Inspired by Karen Granville

NO SUMMER RALLY

Turn to three charts shown each day in *Investor's Business Daily*. We first look at the chart of the <u>Nasdaq Composite</u>. We see the major break below the 200-day trendline in early June taking the average down to the 543 level. Thus any strength now is what technicians call <u>the return move</u>. After breaking under a major trendline, the extent of the return move is back to that trendline. In the current case <u>we see that we can look for new upside resistance on any approach to the 580 level</u>.

The second chart is that of the <u>American Stock Exchange</u>. We see the major break below the 200-day trendline in early June taking the Amex Value Average down to the 374 level. Thus any strength now is what technicians call <u>the return move</u>. So here we see <u>the probable extent of the return move back to the 392 level where we would expect to see new upside resistance</u>.

The third chart is that of the <u>Mutual Fund Index</u>. We see the major break below the 200-day trendline in early April with the index continuing to fall to the 208 level by late June. The return move here would be a rally back to the 50-day trendline at the 218 level and then major upside resistance at the 225 level.

Now we draw our attention to Dow Industrials and Transports. <u>Right away we know that something is wrong with the current strength off the June lows</u>. In examining the chart shown in the *Wall Street Journal*, we see a band of chart upside resistance between 3340 and 3350 with the upside going very difficult after 3350. In the chart of the Dow Transports we see strong upside resistance in the 1350-1360 area with the going very difficult after 1360.

Now, all these five mentioned charts <u>have one thing in common</u>. Current strength predominantly consists of <u>OBV lower up designations</u>. Think of a giant downside zig-zag. It consists of higher ups, higher downs, lower ups, and then lower downs. All important market downlegs are preceded by lower ups. So then, <u>current strength is technically preparing the way for the summer downleg that I see ahead</u>.

We also know that something is radically wrong because major charts covering the Nsdaq, the American Stock Exchange, and the Mutual Funds do not break under their 200-day trendlines in bull markets.

We also know that somethng is very wrong because all the people that did not get you out of this market at the top last January are the ones that are telling you that they are still bullish and that the Dow is going to 4000 in 6-12 months. <u>And we also see that these are the same people now looking for a big summer rally</u>.

For openers, most of these people expect that the Fed will soon ease rates again. It is immaterial whether this is done or not. <u>My current numbers tell me that we are headed for a market disappointment regardless of what the Fed does</u>.

Joe Granville may be the most widely known newsletter editor. His "sell-everything" message in January 1981 sent the stock market reeling and made him a household name to many who otherwise were not familiar with the investment newsletter industry. He set off mini-crashes in several European stock markets in September 1981 by predicting bear markets on his visits to those countries. He claims (and I have no reason to disbelieve him) that he is the only investment newsletter editor to have his picture on the front page of *The New York Times*.

By the same token it also is widely known

that Granville failed to throw in the bearish towel after the 1982 bull market took off. In fact, he stubbornly remained bearish (but for minor exceptions along the way) until early 1986. He then turned bullish, and was bullish during the Crash of 1987. The HFD calculates that a portfolio of his stock recommendations lost 51.8% from mid-1980 to mid-1992, as compared to a 432.7% gain for the Wilshire 5000.

For the last several years Granville also has recommended individual put and call options in his newsletter, and since January 1985 the HFD has tracked a portfolio of them. On balance it has been a large loser, losing almost everything in 1985, 1986 and 1987. Though it was a big winner in 1989 (gaining some 1,200%), this was not nearly enough to overcome the earlier losses. This is well illustrated in the graph for this portfolio, since 1989's huge gain hardly shows up at all. Over the five and one-half years through mid-1992, this portfolio lost 94.7%.

More recently still Granville has created a stock portfolio for investors in addition to his stock portfolio for traders. This newer portfolio typically goes into cash when Granville is bearish as opposed to actually going short. Over the 18 months through mid-1992 that the HFD has data for both the "Investors'"

and "Traders'" stock portfolios, the "Traders'" portfolio gained 41.5% and the "Investors'" portfolio 36.9%.

Averaging these three portfolios' performances, along with several additional portfolios that Granville recommended at different points along the way that have since been discontinued, *The Granville Market Letter*'s performance ranks at the bottom among all letters followed since 1980. Even if the devastating losses of his options portfolio are ignored, Granville's performance since 1980 still would place him at the bottom of the list.

Granville recently has made much of the fact that he issued a "buy" signal immediately after the Crash of 1987 and that his HFD performance since then puts him near the top of the list. This is true as far as it goes (see Appendix A-5, for example), but overlooks the fact that Granville was bullish immediately prior to the crash as well. (In the last issue he wrote before the 1987 crash, for example, Granville announced that the correction that had begun the previous August had run its course, and he recommended a number of low-priced stocks.) If we extend the period of comparison just a few months to include the crash, Granville's performance is well below the market's.

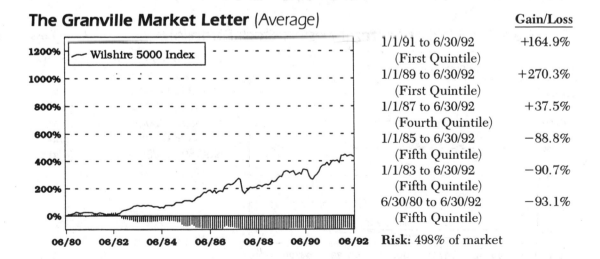

The Granville Market Letter (Average)

	Gain/Loss
1/1/91 to 6/30/92 (First Quintile)	+164.9%
1/1/89 to 6/30/92 (First Quintile)	+270.3%
1/1/87 to 6/30/92 (Fourth Quintile)	+37.5%
1/1/85 to 6/30/92 (Fifth Quintile)	−88.8%
1/1/83 to 6/30/92 (Fifth Quintile)	−90.7%
6/30/80 to 6/30/92 (Fifth Quintile)	−93.1%

Risk: 498% of market

The Granville Market Letter (Traders' Stock Portfolio)

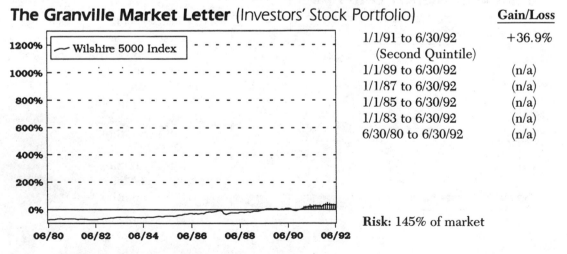

	Gain/Loss
1/1/91 to 6/30/92	+41.5%
(Second Quintile)	
1/1/89 to 6/30/92	+24.6%
(Fourth Quintile)	
1/1/87 to 6/30/92	+24.8%
(Fourth Quintile)	
1/1/85 to 6/30/92	−16.7%
(Fifth Quintile)	
1/1/83 to 6/30/92	−35.9%
(Fifth Quintile)	
6/30/80 to 6/30/92	−51.8%
(Fifth Quintile)	

Risk: 147% of market

The Granville Market Letter (Options Portfolio)

	Gain/Loss
1/1/91 to 6/30/92	+297.6%
(First Quintile)	
1/1/89 to 6/30/92	+211.8%
(First Quintile)	
1/1/87 to 6/30/92	−94.7%
(Fifth Quintile)	
1/1/85 to 6/30/92	−100.0%
(Fifth Quintile)	
1/1/83 to 6/30/92	(n/a)
6/30/80 to 6/30/92	(n/a)

Risk: 1,227% of market

The Granville Market Letter (Investors' Stock Portfolio)

	Gain/Loss
1/1/91 to 6/30/92	+36.9%
(Second Quintile)	
1/1/89 to 6/30/92	(n/a)
1/1/87 to 6/30/92	(n/a)
1/1/85 to 6/30/92	(n/a)
1/1/83 to 6/30/92	(n/a)
6/30/80 to 6/30/92	(n/a)

Risk: 145% of market

Graphic Fund Forecaster

Address
6 Pioneer Circle
P.O. Box 673
Andover, MA 01810

Editor
Fred W. Hohn

Phone Number
508-470-3511

Subscription Rates
$ 30.00/2 months
$145.00/year

Telephone Hotline
Yes

Money Management
Yes

Graphic Fund Forecaster

Up Index 55

Down Index 50

Volume 24 Number 14   Editor: Fred W. Hohn   July 3, 1992

Market Forecast ◊
Consolidation Starting

A few days of consolidation are likely after the good run-up this week. That's reflected by short term oversold sell signals on the stochastic oscillators and the poor response to the lowering of interest rates. Our Forecast Indexes are 55 Up and 50 Down, a neutral reading.

There is some question as to whether this rally will end prematurely, i.e., before the 21 day market averages move up for a week or more during the up period. After all, our GFF Stochastic Value is high and the associated spike value is also high (see page 2). These signs are normally associated with sell conditions for diversified funds. We don't know for sure, but believe recent market action is the first surge to a longer term summer rally. In that case, consolidation occurs after the first surge (could test recent lows) and then the second surge provides the better sell signal. The latter usually coincides with some of the market indices crossing the upper Bollinger Band lines.

Fundamental factors are in favor of an extended rally. Inflation is not a worry and the very low interest rates will generate more economic activity. We note the banks have lowered their prime rate to 6% when the Fed lowered the discount rate and Fed funds rate. That should result in lower interest rates reaching small businesses and the consumer, a vital ingredient to economic recovery.

Fund Chart and Data Trends
Performance Summary of 58 Funds

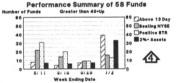

The TYS Fundletter has editor call hours Tuesday-Thursday, 7:30 to 8:30PM EDT. Call 1-508-470-3511   or write to TYS, P.O.Box 673, Andover, MA 01810

Last Week's Leaders

NO.	MUTUAL FUNDS LISTED IN 7 DAY ORDER (7/2)	7 DAY	15 DAY	PAGE
1	SELECT SAVINGS & LOAN	6.9%	5.0%	11
2	SELECT MEDICAL DELIVERY	5.9%	-8.3%	6
3	SELECT FINANCIAL SVCS.	5.8%	4.3%	11
4	SELECT BROKERAGE	5.5%	2.7%	11
5	STRATEGIC FINANCIAL	5.3%	2.5%	11
6	SELECT REGIONAL BANKS	5.2%	2.7%	11
7	SELECT BIOTECHNOLOGY	4.5%	-5.6%	6
8	SELECT HEALTH CARE	4.1%	-5.3%	6
9	STRATEGIC LEISURE	3.8%	1.4%	6
10	SELECT PAPER & FOREST	3.5%	2.6%	9

How far will the market drop during a consolidation period? It depends somewhat on economic news and trader reaction to mixed earnings reports. A quick look at previous consolidations shows the NYSE and Mid-Cap indices could easily drop 2 points. The DJIA could look for support about 3280 and the S&P 500 about 403. Larger declines will put us below recent basing areas.

On the positive side, recent advance/decline and Hi-Low action has been strong (see page 2), another reason we favor a resumption of the uptrend.

Fund Status

Stocks appear to have started another rolling move, this time out of some cyclicals and into defensive growth stocks. That's improved some growth funds and sector funds in the food and health areas. Of course, lower interest rates are powering the financial and utility funds. And the lower dollar is providing a temporary boost to the international funds. Our fund data trends are 4 Up.

What to Do Now

Hold on to financial and utility funds. Watch growth funds by checking their position relative to the mental stop points as technology groups were set back on Thursday. The Sample Portfolios will be monitored with RSI and moving average charts. They are subject to Hotline update.

Graphic Fund Forecaster is published every other week by Fred Hohn and is supplemented by a telephone hotline that is updated at least once each week (and at other times when needed). Hohn's approach is primarily technical, both to the timing of the market as a whole as well as to the selection of individual mutual funds.

Hohn currently recommends five model portfolios of mutual funds: two "Fidelity Select Fund" portfolios (#1 and #2, which, despite their names, don't always invest in

Fidelity's Select funds), two "Growth/International" portfolios (#1 and #2, which focus primarily, though not exclusively, on Fidelity funds other than the Select funds) and a "Financial Strategic" portfolio. (Hohn has recommended additional portfolios in the past which have since been discontinued; their performances are included in what is reported for the newsletter's average.)

Hohn uses the same timing model to manage each of these portfolios, and most of the time they switch into and out of stocks in tandem. The differences between the portfolios thus have to do with the funds they own. Not surprisingly, the riskiest portfolios are the two that focus on Fidelity's Select funds.

Averaging the performances of Hohn's portfolios, *Graphic Fund Forecaster* gained 42.8% over the four and one-half years through mid-1992, below the Wilshire 5000's total return of 89.0%. (The performances of the individual portfolios range from +59.2% on the high side to +17.4% on the low side.) On average these portfolios' risk was less than that of the market, but not by enough to make the newsletter's risk-adjusted performance equal to or better than the Wilshire's.

The culprit in this below-market performance, insofar as the HFD data allow a conclusion to be drawn, is Hohn's timing. If each of the funds in Hohn's "Growth/International Portfolio #1" had performed exactly as the Wilshire 5000, it would have gained 46.0% over this four-and-one-half-year period—essentially equaling the 48.1% performance for the portfolio itself. This means that Hohn's fund selections have done about as well as the Wilshire when he was invested in the market, and that he lagged a buy-and-hold because he wasn't in and out of the market at the right times.

Graphic Fund Forecaster (Average)

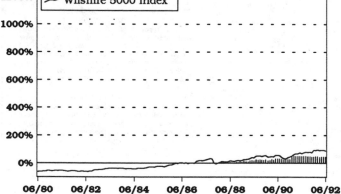

	Gain/Loss
1/1/91 to 6/30/92 (Fourth Quintile)	+13.3%
1/1/89 to 6/30/92 (Third Quintile)	+33.5%
1/1/87 to 6/30/92	(n/a)
1/1/85 to 6/30/92	(n/a)
1/1/83 to 6/30/92	(n/a)
6/30/80 to 6/30/92	(n/a)

Risk: 83% of market

Graphic Fund Forecaster (Growth/International Portfolio #1)

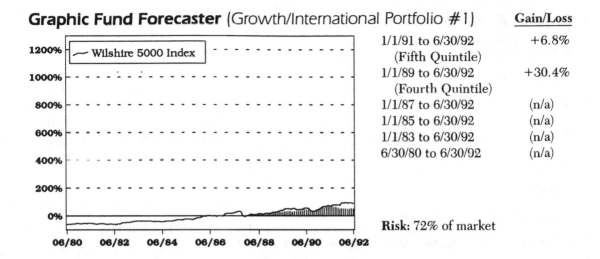

	Gain/Loss
1/1/91 to 6/30/92 (Fifth Quintile)	+6.8%
1/1/89 to 6/30/92 (Fourth Quintile)	+30.4%
1/1/87 to 6/30/92	(n/a)
1/1/85 to 6/30/92	(n/a)
1/1/83 to 6/30/92	(n/a)
6/30/80 to 6/30/92	(n/a)

Risk: 72% of market

Graphic Fund Forecaster (Growth/International Portfolio #2)

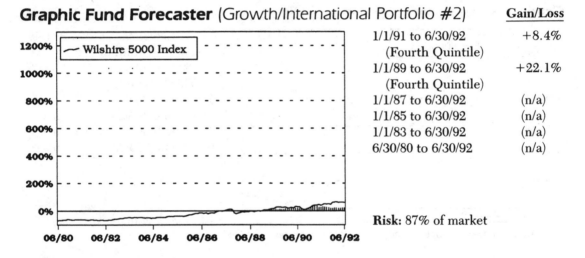

	Gain/Loss
1/1/91 to 6/30/92 (Fourth Quintile)	+8.4%
1/1/89 to 6/30/92 (Fourth Quintile)	+22.1%
1/1/87 to 6/30/92	(n/a)
1/1/85 to 6/30/92	(n/a)
1/1/83 to 6/30/92	(n/a)
6/30/80 to 6/30/92	(n/a)

Risk: 87% of market

Graphic Fund Forecaster (Fidelity Select Fund Portfolio #1)

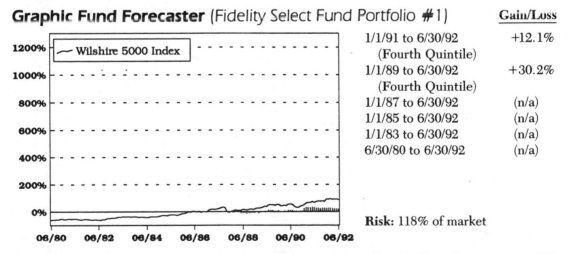

	Gain/Loss
1/1/91 to 6/30/92 (Fourth Quintile)	+12.1%
1/1/89 to 6/30/92 (Fourth Quintile)	+30.2%
1/1/87 to 6/30/92	(n/a)
1/1/85 to 6/30/92	(n/a)
1/1/83 to 6/30/92	(n/a)
6/30/80 to 6/30/92	(n/a)

Risk: 118% of market

Graphic Fund Forecaster (Fidelity Select Fund Portfolio #2)

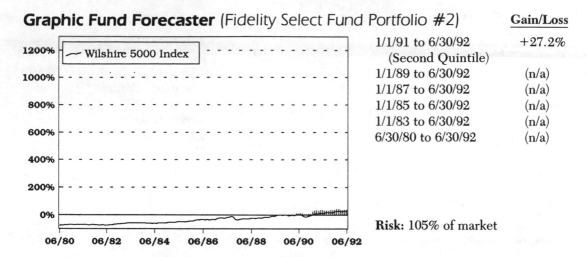

	Gain/Loss
1/1/91 to 6/30/92	+27.2%
(Second Quintile)	
1/1/89 to 6/30/92	(n/a)
1/1/87 to 6/30/92	(n/a)
1/1/85 to 6/30/92	(n/a)
1/1/83 to 6/30/92	(n/a)
6/30/80 to 6/30/92	(n/a)

Risk: 105% of market

Graphic Fund Forecaster (Financial Strategic Funds Portfolio)

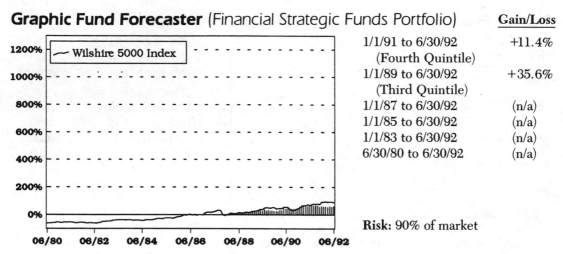

	Gain/Loss
1/1/91 to 6/30/92	+11.4%
(Fourth Quintile)	
1/1/89 to 6/30/92	+35.6%
(Third Quintile)	
1/1/87 to 6/30/92	(n/a)
1/1/85 to 6/30/92	(n/a)
1/1/83 to 6/30/92	(n/a)
6/30/80 to 6/30/92	(n/a)

Risk: 90% of market

Growth Fund Guide

Address
Growth Fund Research
  Building
Box 6600
Rapid City, SD 57709

Editor
Walter Rouleau

Phone Number
605-341-1971

Subscription Rates
$54.00/6 months
$89.00/year

Telephone Hotline
Yes

Money Management
No

JULY 1992   Our Twenty-Fifth Year   VOL. 25   NO. 1

IN REVIEW

Making Money With Mutual Funds - How can you tell when the stock market has reached the area of a major top?. page 2

Buy Rated GFG Funds - are Fidelity Asset Manager, Lindner, Lindner Dividend, Lexington Goldfund, Mathers, Price Capital Appreciation, Scudder Short Term Global Income, Strong Investment and all money funds listed in GFG..... page 3

Top Performing GFG Funds for June - were Financial Gold (+5.6%), Mathers (+1.5%), Lindner Dividend (+1.3%), Lexington Goldfund (+1.1%), Mutual Shares (+0.6%), Mutual Beacon (+0.3%) and Fidelity Asset Manager (0).   ..... page 5

Relative Strength Report - How have GFG funds performed in important up and down periods since mid-1990?.... page 6

Traders Corner - How have those who moved from CD's and money funds to very aggressive funds early this year made out?   ..... page 10

The Perot Factor - The stock market is going through a topping process that may be accelerated by the Perot Presidential candidacy.   ..... page 22

Funds For The Months Ahead - Here's a look at some funds that should help you preserve your purchasing power and, to the extent possible, make it grow in the months ahead.   ..... page 23

Also See

Growth Fund Guide has been published monthly since 1968 by Growth Fund Research; it is edited by Walter Rouleau. In 1986 it inaugurated a telephone hotline update that is made available to all regular subscribers. It is updated monthly, and more often as needed.

Growth Fund Guide maintains a "Select Supervised List of Funds," which is broken down into four categories: Aggressive Growth, Growth, Quality Growth and Special Situations. Eight or so pages of each 24-page issue are devoted to charting the price movement of the funds that appear on this supervised list. Within each of the four categories on their supervised list, *Growth Fund Guide* rates each fund on a scale from 1 to 5 (with 1 being the best rating). For purposes of tracking each of these four categories' performance, the HFD has constructed portfolios that contain just those funds most highly rated by the newsletter at any given point in time.

Growth Fund Guide also provides market-timing advice and specific recommendations on the proper division of a portfolio between the market and cash. They are not short-term market timers, however. Prior to the 1986 inauguration of their hotline, for example, their advice typically was to be fully invested. Since then they have recommended a fairly high cash position, which has not been altered very often or by very much.

The HFD has performance data for these four categories since June 1980. The best-performing of the four was the "Special Situations" portfolio, which gained 378.6%, in contrast to the Wilshire 5000's 432.7%. The poorest performer of the four was its "Aggressive Growth" portfolio, with a gain of 200.9%. On a risk-adjusted basis, the "Special Situations" portfolio equaled the market while the remaining three lagged.

Over the years, *Growth Fund Guide* also has maintained specific model accounts, though until recently it had not reported in each issue the composition of or changes in those accounts. The HFD began following their three model accounts in 1988. The three are a "Selected Core Account," a "Growth Model Account" and an "Aggressive Model Account." These portfolios typically contain the same funds as in *Growth Fund Guide's* "Selected Supervised List of Funds," though with varying portfolio allocations.

Beginning in 1989, the HFD also started following three additional portfolios that began being recommended by *Growth Fund Guide*. These three all are variants on an approach they refer to as "Valueratio," an approach which calls for the investors to vary their allocation to conservative and aggressive mutual funds according to the stock market's price/dividend ratio. Over the three and one-half years through mid-1992, these three portfolios were the best performers among the *Growth Fund Guide* portfolios the HFD follows.

The newsletter's average performance over the entire 12 years the HFD followed it (taking into account all ten of their portfolios and the different lengths of time each has been followed) was below the Wilshire 5000's, both on a total-return and risk-adjusted basis.

The culprits in this underperformance appear to be both market timing and stock selection. On a timing-only basis, the HFD reports that *Growth Fund Guide* gained 304.0% over these 12 years. This is better than the newsletter's average performance, which suggests that their actual fund picks did not equal the Wilshire's performance during the times they were owned. However, even this timing-only portfolio also underperformed the market.

Growth Fund Guide (Average)

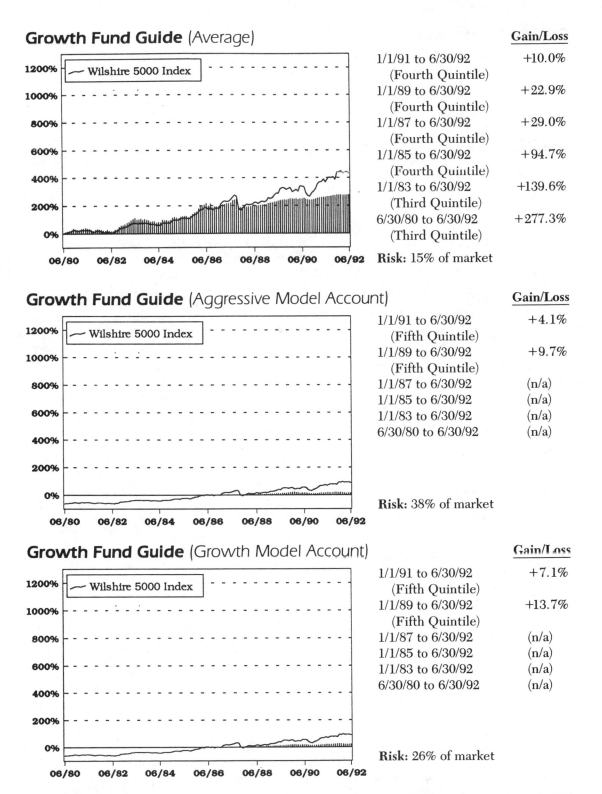

	Gain/Loss
1/1/91 to 6/30/92 (Fourth Quintile)	+10.0%
1/1/89 to 6/30/92 (Fourth Quintile)	+22.9%
1/1/87 to 6/30/92 (Fourth Quintile)	+29.0%
1/1/85 to 6/30/92 (Fourth Quintile)	+94.7%
1/1/83 to 6/30/92 (Third Quintile)	+139.6%
6/30/80 to 6/30/92 (Third Quintile)	+277.3%

Risk: 15% of market

Growth Fund Guide (Aggressive Model Account)

	Gain/Loss
1/1/91 to 6/30/92 (Fifth Quintile)	+4.1%
1/1/89 to 6/30/92 (Fifth Quintile)	+9.7%
1/1/87 to 6/30/92	(n/a)
1/1/85 to 6/30/92	(n/a)
1/1/83 to 6/30/92	(n/a)
6/30/80 to 6/30/92	(n/a)

Risk: 38% of market

Growth Fund Guide (Growth Model Account)

	Gain/Loss
1/1/91 to 6/30/92 (Fifth Quintile)	+7.1%
1/1/89 to 6/30/92 (Fifth Quintile)	+13.7%
1/1/87 to 6/30/92	(n/a)
1/1/85 to 6/30/92	(n/a)
1/1/83 to 6/30/92	(n/a)
6/30/80 to 6/30/92	(n/a)

Risk: 26% of market

Growth Fund Guide (Selected Core Account)

Gain/Loss

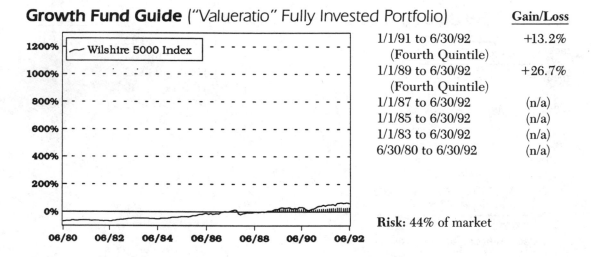

1/1/91 to 6/30/92	+6.9%
(Fifth Quintile)	
1/1/89 to 6/30/92	+23.2%
(Fourth Quintile)	
1/1/87 to 6/30/92	(n/a)
1/1/85 to 6/30/92	(n/a)
1/1/83 to 6/30/92	(n/a)
6/30/80 to 6/30/92	(n/a)

Risk: 10% of market

Growth Fund Guide ("Valueratio" Fully Invested Portfolio)

Gain/Loss

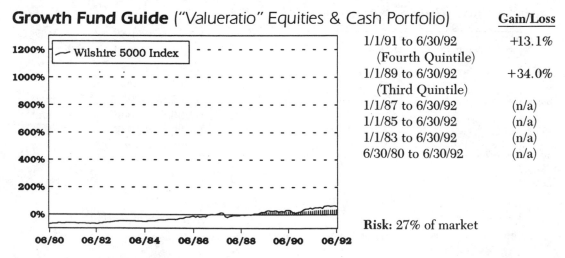

1/1/91 to 6/30/92	+13.2%
(Fourth Quintile)	
1/1/89 to 6/30/92	+26.7%
(Fourth Quintile)	
1/1/87 to 6/30/92	(n/a)
1/1/85 to 6/30/92	(n/a)
1/1/83 to 6/30/92	(n/a)
6/30/80 to 6/30/92	(n/a)

Risk: 44% of market

Growth Fund Guide ("Valueratio" Equities & Cash Portfolio)

Gain/Loss

1/1/91 to 6/30/92	+13.1%
(Fourth Quintile)	
1/1/89 to 6/30/92	+34.0%
(Third Quintile)	
1/1/87 to 6/30/92	(n/a)
1/1/85 to 6/30/92	(n/a)
1/1/83 to 6/30/92	(n/a)
6/30/80 to 6/30/92	(n/a)

Risk: 27% of market

Growth Fund Guide
("Valueratio" Equities, Cash & Leverage Portfolio)

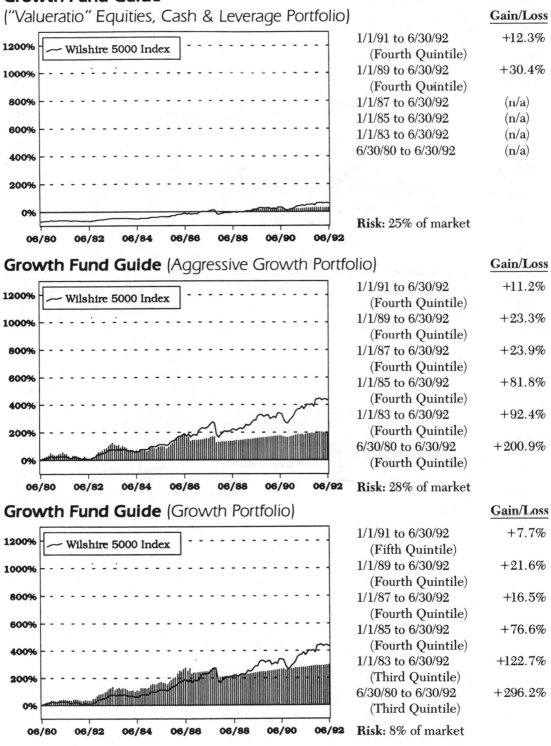

	Gain/Loss
1/1/91 to 6/30/92	+12.3%
(Fourth Quintile)	
1/1/89 to 6/30/92	+30.4%
(Fourth Quintile)	
1/1/87 to 6/30/92	(n/a)
1/1/85 to 6/30/92	(n/a)
1/1/83 to 6/30/92	(n/a)
6/30/80 to 6/30/92	(n/a)

Risk: 25% of market

Growth Fund Guide (Aggressive Growth Portfolio)

	Gain/Loss
1/1/91 to 6/30/92	+11.2%
(Fourth Quintile)	
1/1/89 to 6/30/92	+23.3%
(Fourth Quintile)	
1/1/87 to 6/30/92	+23.9%
(Fourth Quintile)	
1/1/85 to 6/30/92	+81.8%
(Fourth Quintile)	
1/1/83 to 6/30/92	+92.4%
(Fourth Quintile)	
6/30/80 to 6/30/92	+200.9%
(Fourth Quintile)	

Risk: 28% of market

Growth Fund Guide (Growth Portfolio)

	Gain/Loss
1/1/91 to 6/30/92	+7.7%
(Fifth Quintile)	
1/1/89 to 6/30/92	+21.6%
(Fourth Quintile)	
1/1/87 to 6/30/92	+16.5%
(Fourth Quintile)	
1/1/85 to 6/30/92	+76.6%
(Fourth Quintile)	
1/1/83 to 6/30/92	+122.7%
(Third Quintile)	
6/30/80 to 6/30/92	+296.2%
(Third Quintile)	

Risk: 8% of market

Growth Fund Guide (Quality Growth Portfolio)

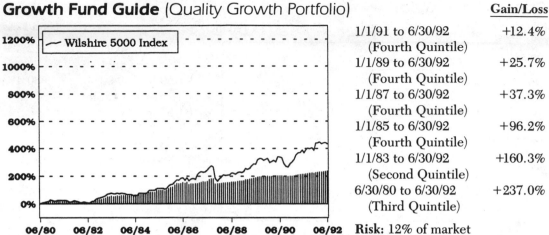

	Gain/Loss
1/1/91 to 6/30/92	+12.4%
(Fourth Quintile)	
1/1/89 to 6/30/92	+25.7%
(Fourth Quintile)	
1/1/87 to 6/30/92	+37.3%
(Fourth Quintile)	
1/1/85 to 6/30/92	+96.2%
(Fourth Quintile)	
1/1/83 to 6/30/92	+160.3%
(Second Quintile)	
6/30/80 to 6/30/92	+237.0%
(Third Quintile)	

Risk: 12% of market

Growth Fund Guide (Special Situations Portfolio)

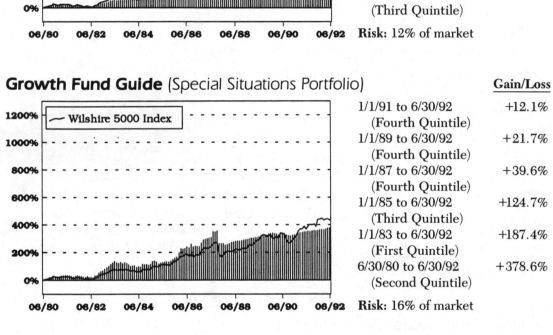

	Gain/Loss
1/1/91 to 6/30/92	+12.1%
(Fourth Quintile)	
1/1/89 to 6/30/92	+21.7%
(Fourth Quintile)	
1/1/87 to 6/30/92	+39.6%
(Fourth Quintile)	
1/1/85 to 6/30/92	+124.7%
(Third Quintile)	
1/1/83 to 6/30/92	+187.4%
(First Quintile)	
6/30/80 to 6/30/92	+378.6%
(Second Quintile)	

Risk: 16% of market

Growth Stock Outlook

Growth Stock Outlook

P. O. BOX 15381   CHEVY CHASE, MARYLAND   20825

Twice Monthly ● **$195⁰⁰ Per Year** Registered under the S.E.C. Investment Advisors Act. ● **TWENTY-EIGHTH YEAR**

JULY 15, 1992
VOL. 28, NO. 16

Charles Allmon, Editor

© Growth Stock Outlook, Inc., 1992
Reproduction Prohibited

"When you take into public ownership a profitable industry, the profits soon disappear. The goose that laid the golden eggs goes broody. State geese are not great layers."
– Margaret Thatcher, 1976

FRESH LOOK AT REAL ESTATE — Several years ago, when we first began commenting on the coming real estate debacle in the U.S., agreement was almost unanimous that we had taken leave of our senses. The slump is not over and probably will continue for some years, perhaps to the turn of the century. A glance at the accompanying graph explains the problem: there simply are not enough 18–34-year-olds to fuel a real estate boom, much less contribute to the present economy.

That portion of the construction industry dependent on new office buildings is dead in the water. Nationwide, there is a 10-year supply, and the vacancy rate varies from 15%—20%. From 1979 to 1991, office space doubled in the U.S., thanks to tax laws that encouraged construction which was not needed.

We have heard hundreds of tales of lost assets, and the debacle is not over. Most who read this probably have seen their residential real estate decline in value, perhaps 15% to 50%. New home sales are stalled around a seasonally adjusted annual rate of 525,000, lowest in over 40 years. And for good reason. There can be no economic boom without broad participation by the housing industry. You buy a home today for shelter and enjoyment. For most, you can forget the investment aspect. Admittedly, there are a few hot local real estate markets. But they are the exception as our citizens flee for their lives from big cities.

Lyle Gramley, chief economist for the Mortgage Bankers Association of America, said: "The improvement in housing will resume, but it's not going to resume at anything near the pace that's going to be needed to drag the whole economy along."

This brings us around to the stock market, which has discounted an enormous boost in corporate profits which may not be forthcoming. As this is written in late June, it certainly appears that housing has lost momentum. The bottom line is this: for the first time since World War II, 47 years ago, there will be no starring role for real estate in powering an economic recovery. What's holding up the stock market bubble? Who knows?

Change in Population of 20-to-34-year-olds (U.S.)

* Projected Population: Bureau of the Census

Source: Bureau of the Census, December 1991

THE GREAT MEETING OF POOH-BAHS!! — Well over 5,000 investors jammed the Riviera Hotel in Las Vegas in May to hear stock market pooh-bahs of every stripe. The conference was sponsored by Investment Seminars, Inc. (ISI) of Sarasota, Florida (Kim and Charles Githler). There was no broad consensus of bulls or bears (unfortunately). They were about evenly divided. This would imply to us that the stock market bubble may continue to inflate a bit longer.

As we listened to perhaps 30 of over 100 speakers, there was no "Grand Pooh-Bah." While attendees may have offered no consensus, we guessed that 85% of the speakers (pooh-bahs) were bullish. Fence sitters were considered bullish because fence sitters rarely make money in the stock market. Some pooh-bahs were wildly bullish: DJIA of 4400—4800 in 1993 was heard several times. Attendees hung on their every word, scribbling furiously to jot down names of hot stocks selling at 50—100 times earnings. And often no earnings! Value obviously was a dirty word. One oldster, a most energetic 89 years of age, who was wiped out in 1929, threw an arm across our shoulder and advised: "Hang in there, kid. This is 1929 all over again!" He admonished us to hold more cash than the almost 80% in our fund and managed accounts.

After speaking at investment conferences for a quarter century, we learned a most valuable lesson. Whenever investors see a lopsided consensus of speakers, they should do just the opposite. You never know when such a consensus will appear. We witnessed a lopsided consensus at an ISI conference in San Francisco in July 1982, and again in August 1987. Both were major market turning points.

About 1700 investors, perhaps a third of all participants, attended our four workshops. Some naturally were disappointed that we did not lob hot stock missiles at them. We offered only five solid companies and suggested they buy all five and hold for five years . . . or forget them and look for a hot stock pooh-bah promising utopia. We leave you with this thought: the good stock market advisory services can be counted on the fingers of one hand. But please do not ask us which five!!

Address
P.O. Box 15381
Chevy Chase, MD
20825

Editor
Charles Allmon

Phone Number
301-654-5205

Subscription Rates
$ 75.00/3 months
$195.00/year

Telephone Hotline
Yes

Money Management
Yes

Growth Stock Outlook is in its 28th year of publication, according to editor Charles Allmon. It is published twice each month and is supplemented by a Friday-evening telephone hotline update.

Allmon is a pure fundamentalist. He mocks those who rely on charts to make investment decisions, and claims that no one is able to time the market. Instead, he believes that the task of the adviser is to seek out undervalued situations to be bought and held for several years.

Though Allmon believes that market timing is impossible, his model portfolio has not been fully invested at all times, especially since 1986, during which time it had as much as 80% in cash. Though this would seem to be market timing in everything but name only, it just as much is a reflection of the fact that Allmon was unable to find a sufficient number of undervalued stocks to fill out a diversified portfolio. In contrast to Allmon, a number of other value-oriented advisers relaxed their criteria of value as the bull market went to vertigo-inducing heights. Unlike them, Allmon for the most part stuck to his guns.

Allmon's portfolio nevertheless has been close to the top of the HFD's rankings for the period since 1980, in large part due to a very strong performance in the early 1980s. His portfolio gained 417.4% over the 12 years through mid-1992, ranking him sixth among all newsletters the HFD monitored for this period. And since his portfolio incurred relatively little risk in the process, his newsletter is in first place over these 12 years on a risk-adjusted basis.

Over the five and one-half years through mid-1992, however, owing to the fact that he had such a high cash position, Allmon lagged the market: He gained 51.0% during a time the Wilshire 5000 itself gained 93.3%. How significant is it that Allmon's best years came earlier in the 1980s rather than later? Statisticians tell us that there is none: There is no statistical reason for us to favor another adviser over Allmon just because the other's best years came more recently.

There's evidence from another quarter that we shouldn't be too quick to overlook Allmon because his recent performance has lagged the market: His stock picks themselves have beaten the market. According to the HFD, a portfolio that always remained fully invested in Allmon's stock recommendations would have made 104.1% from the beginning of 1987 through mid-1992, in contrast to 93.3% for the Wilshire 5000 and 51.0% for Allmon's actual portfolio.

Growth Stock Outlook

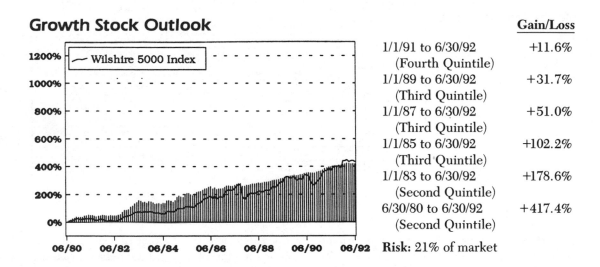

	Gain/Loss
1/1/91 to 6/30/92 (Fourth Quintile)	+11.6%
1/1/89 to 6/30/92 (Third Quintile)	+31.7%
1/1/87 to 6/30/92 (Third Quintile)	+51.0%
1/1/85 to 6/30/92 (Third Quintile)	+102.2%
1/1/83 to 6/30/92 (Second Quintile)	+178.6%
6/30/80 to 6/30/92 (Second Quintile)	+417.4%

Risk: 21% of market

Harmonic Research

Address
650 Fifth Ave.
New York, NY 10019

Editor
Mason S. Sexton

Phone Number
212-484-2065

Subscription Rates
$720.00/year

Telephone Hotline
Yes

Money Management
Yes

Harmonic Research

August 5, 1992
Volume 8, Issue 6
ISSN   088-8574

FORECASTS

U.S. Stock Market

The market is in the final "blow-off" rally of the entire Bull market move from the 1982 low. Maximum upside potential is another ten percent, but any high in late September /early October between S&P 427 and 461 especially 432 or 441 is most likely The Top.

Long-Term Bonds

The late July high in the Bond contract at 106 came in on maximum momentum suggesting at least a retest or marginal new high will present itself as an excellent shorting opportunity. The time frames for a trend change are August 8 - 10 and near month end.

INTRODUCTION

In our June issue we discussed the likelihood that the Perot candidacy, which was enjoying unprecedented popular support at that time with a substantial lead in national opinion polls, was likely to experience a "backlash". Little did we know that such a backlash would be so complete and devastating to the candidate and his campaign.

We attended the MAR conference on managed futures money in Chicago this past week. With over 800 attendees it was the biggest conference by far in the history of the managed futures business despite the last twelve months being one of the most difficult periods in the industry's young history. One of the keynote speakers compared Ross Perot to a good commodity trader in that he "saw a trend and jumped on it ... as soon as the trend started to reverse he got out." Maybe that is why Mr Perot is a billionaire but not much of a politician.

In our Annual Forecast issue back in January our models (see below) had predicted highs in January and February, lows in April and June and a strong rally beginning in mid-June to late-July which would end in September. That appears to be what is happening as we are seeing the expiration of numerous important long-term cycles which govern interest rates and equity prices. There is a distinct 45 and 90 year cycle in interest rates which does not run out until after this September. In stocks the ten year cycle from the low and the five year cycle from high runs out this month with the 30 and 60 year cycles having already expired. Finally, most of the long-term commodity cycles finish this Fall or in early 1993 suggesting that the deflationary environment which has been so favorable to long-term bond prices is approaching its end as well.

As detailed below, once we are able to identify the final ninety-day "blow-off" in the major averages which then shows resistance at one of our pre-determined up-side objective levels, we should be at one of the great put buying/shorting opportunities of all time. Stay tuned!

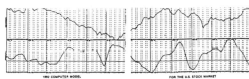

1992 COMPUTER MODEL   FOR THE U.S. STOCK MARKET

Harmonic Research is published monthly by Mason Sexton and is supplemented by a telephone hotline that is updated daily. Because Sexton charges subscribers an extra fee for access to that hotline, the HFD normally would not follow it in calculating a performance rating for the newsletter. However, owing to the fact that the HFD received a number of requests from subscribers to track the newsletter, and also to the fact that it would not be possible to construct a performance rating for the newsletter without calling the hotline, the HFD decided to make an exception in this case. Though Sexton's approach is primarily technical, he also pays "attention to the eclipse cycle and harmonics of the solar year."

Around the time the HFD began following *Harmonic Research* in early 1988, Sexton inaugurated three very specific model portfolios, one each for stocks, options and futures. By early 1989, however, the clarity and completeness of Sexton's advice for the options portfolio had became insufficient for the HFD to continue tracking it. (For the year 1988, the HFD reports that Sexton's model options portfolio lost 65.3%.) During 1989, further-

more, the HFD—for similar reasons— stopped tracking Sexton's stock portfolio. Over the two years 1988 and 1989, the HFD reports that it lost 28.1%, in contrast to the Wilshire 5000's 52.4% gain. What the HFD reports for the newsletter's average takes into account these two discontinued portfolios.

This means that there is only one portfolio left from Sexton's original three that the HFD still can follow. Over the four and one-half years through mid-1992, *Harmonic Research*'s "Futures" portfolio lost 59.1%, in contrast to the Wilshire 5000's gain of 89.0%.

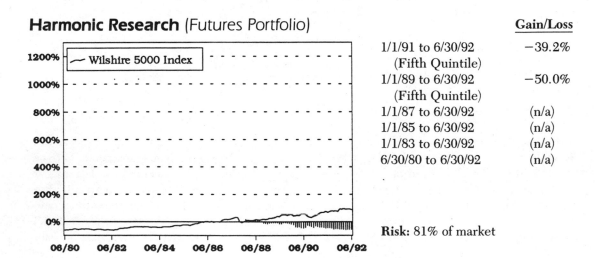

Harmonic Research (Average)

	Gain/Loss
1/1/91 to 6/30/92	−39.2%
(Fifth Quintile)	
1/1/89 to 6/30/92	−48.1%
(Fifth Quintile)	
1/1/87 to 6/30/92	(n/a)
1/1/85 to 6/30/92	(n/a)
1/1/83 to 6/30/92	(n/a)
6/30/80 to 6/30/92	(n/a)

Risk: 81% of market

Harmonic Research (Futures Portfolio)

	Gain/Loss
1/1/91 to 6/30/92	−39.2%
(Fifth Quintile)	
1/1/89 to 6/30/92	−50.0%
(Fifth Quintile)	
1/1/87 to 6/30/92	(n/a)
1/1/85 to 6/30/92	(n/a)
1/1/83 to 6/30/92	(n/a)
6/30/80 to 6/30/92	(n/a)

Risk: 81% of market

Harry Browne's Special Reports

Address

P.O. Box 5586
Austin, TX 78763

Editor

Harry Browne

Phone Number

800-531-5142

Subscription Rates

$ 5.00/1 issue
$225.00/year

Telephone Hotline

Yes

Money Management

No

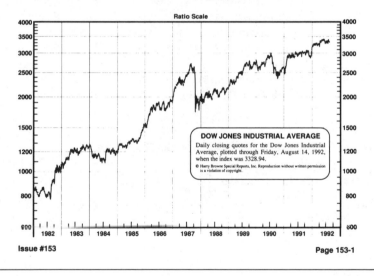

Harry Browne's SPECIAL REPORTS

BOX 5586, AUSTIN, TEXAS 78763   (800) 531-5142. (512) 453-7313   FAX: (512) 453 2015

FRONT PAGE

August 19, 1992   File under: **Front Page**

Although the 1990-1991 recession is officially over, the country's climb back toward prosperity is widely perceived as being too slow. The article "Economic Recovery & the Money Supply" in this issue attempts to explain why this is so, where we are now, and where we may be headed.

If you find yourself worrying which way the economy is going — and avidly reading such articles, hoping to find a definitive answer — it may mean that you're invested in too many assets that would be hurt by one economic outcome. If so, you need to create a safer position — by diversifying your portfolio sufficiently so that it will survive any economic outcome.

In addition to the article on the economic recovery, this issue includes the customary Investment Outlook, graphs, and tables.

Next Issue

The next issue is scheduled tentatively for Friday, September 11.

Model Permanent Portfolio

On Friday, August 14, the newsletter's model Permanent Portfolio had a value of $133,175.55 — a loss of 1.0% so far in 1992. Recent advances in the stock and bond markets have been helpful.[1]

[1]The portfolio was started on December 31, 1987, with $100,000.

Ratio Scale

DOW JONES INDUSTRIAL AVERAGE
Daily closing quotes for the Dow Jones Industrial Average, plotted through Friday, August 14, 1992, when the index was 3328.94.
© Harry Browne Special Reports, Inc. Reproduction without written permission is a violation of copyright.

Issue #153   Page 153-1

Harry Browne's Special Reports is published episodically, about ten times a year. While it does not have a formal telephone hotline per se, Browne does have what he calls a "stop-loss" service that is updated after he makes a recommendation in his newsletter. Subscribers are to call this number to see if Browne has changed any of the sell parameters he previously had established for his portfolio's positions.

At the center of Browne's approach to investing is the need to separate one's portfolio into two parts: one a core, or "permanent," portfolio that is held for the long term and does not change composition frequently or drastically, and the other a speculative, or "variable," portfolio that attempts to capitalize on particular market opportunities.

For most of the time between 1981 (when the HFD began monitoring his newsletter) and mid-1992, Browne did not recommend a particular permanent portfolio, instead presenting a number of sample permanent portfolios. The idea for a permanent portfolio was that it should be sufficiently hedged to avoid large losses regardless of what happens, be it deflation, hyperinflation or long-term sustainable economic growth. Beginning in 1988, however, Browne began presenting a model permanent portfolio in his letter. Over the four and one-half years through mid-1992 it gained 31.8%, in contrast to an 89.0% gain for the Wilshire 5000, a 56.6% gain for the Shearson Lehman Treasury Index and a 29.4% loss for gold bullion. This portfolio essentially equaled a composite portfolio that each year was equally weighted in the stock, bond and gold markets.

Much of Browne's contribution to the investment debate during the 1980s was his exploration of economic scenarios that were not given much credence by the consensus of investment advisers. During the early 1980s, for example, the prevailing wisdom was that a "soft landing" from the inflationary excesses of the 1970s was impossible: Either deflation or hyperinflation was inevitable. Browne repeatedly reminded his subscribers that these were not the only alternatives, and he gradually increased the probabilities he gave to a "soft landing." Hindsight shows that Browne successfully made the transition to the new investment climate of the 1980s.

Even Browne's variable, or speculative, portfolio is fairly conservative, according to the HFD's calculations, and it rarely has stood out in performance summaries of shorter periods of time. But in classic tortoise-and-hare fashion, Browne's portfolio at times has ranked high for performance over longer periods of time, especially on a risk-adjusted basis. For the entire eleven and one-half years through mid-1992 that the HFD has followed this portfolio, however, it gained just 96.7%—even less than T-Bills' return over this period.

Harry Browne's Special Reports (Average)

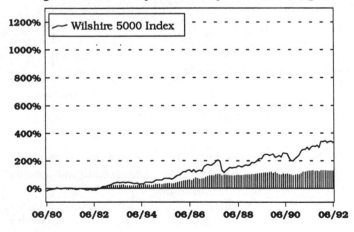

	Gain/Loss
1/1/91 to 6/30/92	+14.0%
(Fourth Quintile)	
1/1/89 to 6/30/92	+14.1%
(Fifth Quintile)	
1/1/87 to 6/30/92	+36.1%
(Fourth Quintile)	
1/1/85 to 6/30/92	+84.5%
(Fourth Quintile)	
1/1/83 to 6/30/92	+107.5%
(Third Quintile)	
6/30/80 to 6/30/92	(n/a)

Risk: 45% of market

Harry Browne's Special Reports

(Variable [Speculative] Portfolio)

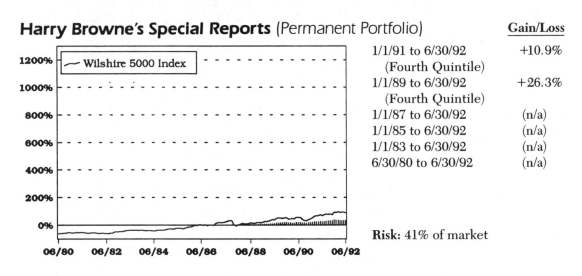

	Gain/Loss
1/1/91 to 6/30/92	+16.6%
(Fourth Quintile)	
1/1/89 to 6/30/92	+1.9%
(Fifth Quintile)	
1/1/87 to 6/30/92	+18.2%
(Fourth Quintile)	
1/1/85 to 6/30/92	+60.3%
(Fourth Quintile)	
1/1/83 to 6/30/92	+80.2%
(Fourth Quintile)	
6/30/80 to 6/30/92	(n/a)

Risk: 79% of market

Harry Browne's Special Reports (Permanent Portfolio)

	Gain/Loss
1/1/91 to 6/30/92	+10.9%
(Fourth Quintile)	
1/1/89 to 6/30/92	+26.3%
(Fourth Quintile)	
1/1/87 to 6/30/92	(n/a)
1/1/85 to 6/30/92	(n/a)
1/1/83 to 6/30/92	(n/a)
6/30/80 to 6/30/92	(n/a)

Risk: 41% of market

The Holt Advisory

The Holt Advisory

Address
P.O. Box 2923
West Palm Beach, FL 33409

Editors
Thomas J. Holt and
Frank Ventura

Phone Number
800-289-9222

Subscription Rates
$185.00/year

Telephone Hotline
No

Money Management
Yes

THE NEWSLETTER FOR DECISION MAKERS

July 3, 1992

Issue #613

Strategies in a nutshell:

Primary Portfolio: Shift 10% to Benham's European Gov't Bond Fund.

Gold investors: Hold current positions.

Balanced Hedge Strategy: If you haven't done so already based on last issue's recommendations, exit Coastal, Dravo, Eastern Enterprises and sell short Lockheed.

CONTENTS

This is the slowest recovery since World War II. First-time claims for unemployment benefits have increased to 422,000. Sales of existing homes have dropped for the second straight month. A record 252,000 individuals and companies filed for bankruptcy last quarter, while delinquent loans soared to the highest level in three years. And the U.S. trade deficit increased to $7 billion in April, the worst since late 1990.

Meanwhile, a report issued by American Business Econometrics concluded that the Dow should be near the 1500 level —a full 55% lower. That's not so unreasonable because the S&P 500 is trading at 25 times earnings, while the average price/earnings ratio since 1970 is 13.

So be sure to stay mostly with cash and safe assets, in anticipation of a steep market sell-off during the second half.

In the **Primary Portfolio**, you should have taken profits on **Eastern Enterprises**. Now we'd like to make one more change to the portfolio: Place 10% of your funds in **Benham's European Government Bond Fund** (800-321-8321) —an intermediate fund holding European government bonds. This will increase your yield and give you added protection against a possible dollar decline. (See last question, page 8.)

As a result, although individual accounts may vary somewhat, you should aim for the following allocation: At least **30%** in 3-month Treasury bills or a Treasury-only money fund; about **25%** in medium-term Treasury notes or a Treasury note fund; a maximum of **20%** in gold shares, such as **Battle Mountain, Hecla, Homestake** and **Placer Dome**; **10%** in a short-term global fund such as **Scudder Short-Term Global Income Fund**; **10%** in **Benham European Government Bond Fund**; plus up to **5%** allocated to shares such as **Sprint**, with any unused amounts in Treasury bills or equivalent.

(We also recommend a similar shift to the **Benham European Government Fund** if you're following our **Primary Mutual Fund Portfolio**.)

Our **Balanced Hedge Strategy**—updated in detail in this issue—is positioned nicely for aggressive investors seeking capital gains regardless of the market's general direction. After exiting three of our long positions with gains and adding a short position, we now are ready for a market decline, with additional capital set aside for more opportunities later.

The **Balanced Mutual Fund Portfolio** is also doing well as the shorts in biotech and health sciences funds continue to rack up profits for us. Hold both long and short funds for now.

Weiss Research, P.O. Box 2923, West Palm Beach, FL 33402 (407) 684-8100

The Holt Advisory is the successor publication to two previous newsletters published by Thomas Holt, *The Holt Investment Advisory* and *The Holt Executive Advisory*. The merger of the two occurred in late 1986, before which time the HFD tracked the performance of the recommendations contained in *The Holt Investment Advisory*.

Martin Weiss began editing *The Holt Advisory* in 1988. Weiss made a number of changes to the portfolios recommended by the newsletter, making them much clearer and also less risky. Since then he has become very well known for his rating of the stability of insurance companies and other financial institutions and has become less involved in the editing of *The Holt Advisory*.

These changes in editorship present difficulties in interpreting past performance (just as it does when a mutual fund changes managers). While the graphs and appendices in this *Guide* treat *The Holt Advisory's* current performance as a continuation of its performance under previous editors, you should be aware of this shift of editors and strategies— and hence the possibility that the newsletter's more recent performance is not as comparable to earlier performance as it would be if the newsletter had been edited by the same adviser.

The dominant feature of *The Holt Advisory's* investment approach during the 1980s was a persistent bearishness on stocks. For much of the first half of the decade, for example, the newsletter's recommended investment posture was to allocate 50% of investable assets to short sales. Not surprisingly, given the unprecedented bull market during the 1980s, such a posture was unprofitable. For the 12 years through mid-1992, the HFD calculates that this newsletter's advice led to a loss of 62.4%, as compared to a gain of 432.7% for the Wilshire 5000.

Under Weiss's editorship, *The Holt Advisory* inaugurated three model portfolios. One, called the "Primary" portfolio, is a very conservative strategy that to date has invested the bulk of its assets in Treasury securities and only a few percent in gold stocks and utilities. A second portfolio, pursuing what Weiss calls his "Guaranteed Gold & Treasury Strategy,"

divides its assets equally between Treasury securities and gold stocks. Finally, the third portfolio, pursuing a "Balanced Hedge Strategy," has divided its assets more or less equally between stocks held long and short.

Unfortunately, Weiss hasn't always repeated in every issue the portion of these portfolios that he recommends should be kept in cash. Pursuant to its methodology on such matters, therefore, the HFD kept these portfolios fully invested during those months when no cash position was recommended (see the discussion of the HFD's methodology earlier in this book). Weiss subsequently pointed out to the HFD that in some of his issues in which he didn't specify a percentage to be kept in cash, he at least did say that the "bulk" of these portfolios should be. In response, the HFD at first decided that "bulk" meant at least 50% should be kept in cash and, more recently, decided that since "bulk" implicitly defines a range between 50% and 100% in cash, Weiss's recommendation should be interpreted to mean that 75% should be kept in cash. The figures in this book reflect this latter interpretation of "bulk."

In early 1992, because of ambiguous advice such as "bulk" and owing to the fact that Weiss began updating their status less and less frequently, the HFD discontinued tracking his "Primary" portfolio and "Guaranteed Gold & Treasury Strategy" (though their performances are included in what is reported for the newsletter's average). This leaves just the "Balanced Hedge Strategy," which the HFD currently tracks. For the two and one-half years through mid-1992, this portfolio lost 16.5%, in contrast to a 24.1% gain for the Wilshire 5000.

The Holt Advisory (Average)

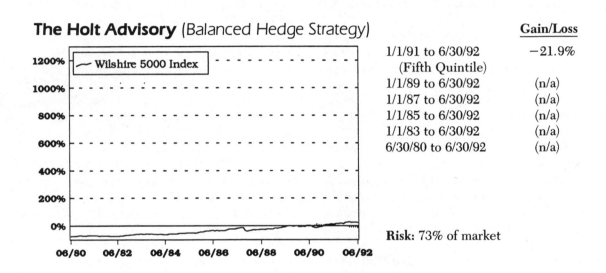

	Gain/Loss
1/1/91 to 6/30/92 (Fifth Quintile)	−14.6%
1/1/89 to 6/30/92 (Fifth Quintile)	−29.8%
1/1/87 to 6/30/92 (Fifth Quintile)	−45.2%
1/1/85 to 6/30/92 (Fifth Quintile)	−54.0%
1/1/83 to 6/30/92 (Fifth Quintile)	−57.9%
6/30/80 to 6/30/92 (Fifth Quintile)	−62.4%

Risk: 49% of market

The Holt Advisory (Balanced Hedge Strategy)

	Gain/Loss
1/1/91 to 6/30/92 (Fifth Quintile)	−21.9%
1/1/89 to 6/30/92	(n/a)
1/1/87 to 6/30/92	(n/a)
1/1/85 to 6/30/92	(n/a)
1/1/83 to 6/30/92	(n/a)
6/30/80 to 6/30/92	(n/a)

Risk: 73% of market

Hussman Econometrics

Address
P.O. Box 3199
Farmington Hills, MI
48333

Editor
John Hussman

Phone Number
800-487-7626

Subscription Rates
$ 99.00/6 months
$195.00/year

Telephone Hotline
Yes

Money Management
No

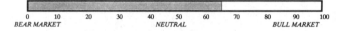

HUSSMAN ECONOMETRICS

Value-oriented market timing and comprehensive security selection for maximum profits

VOLUME 5   NUMBER 7   JULY 2, 1992

MARKET MODEL FORECASTS
Precise Econometric forecasts of upcoming market action

FORECAST	PERCENT CHANGE	S&P 500 TARGET	DJIA TARGET
12 MONTHS	+5.63%	431.12	3505.35
6 MONTHS	+13.34%	462.59	3761.21
3 MONTHS	+7.91%	440.42	3581.01
CURRENT (6/30)		408.14	3318.52

MARKET BAROMETER 66% : BULL MARKET
A snapshot of the primary trend, measured as the probability that stocks are currently in a bull market

0	10	20	30	40	50	60	70	80	90	100
BEAR MARKET					NEUTRAL				BULL MARKET	

FOR THE RECORD
A visual performance review of newsletter features

This month we feature the record of our Multi-Fund Portfolio (see page 5 for current holdings), up over +134% since its inception in 9/88. The lighter bars track the Multi-Fund Portfolio. The darker bars track the S&P 500 Index.

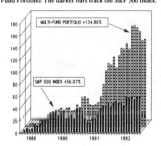

"Buy. Our econometric market forecasts have improved dramatically in the past month, and the Market Models are now positive for every forecast horizon out to 12 months. This suggests that the market is probably at the best buying point we will see in 1992. Among the bullish factors fueling our positive outlook, short term interest rates are now at the lowest level in two decades, placing stocks at fair value despite 3% dividend yields. Industrial production continues to increase, generating good prospects for earnings growth. Market sentiment, a contrary indicator, is extremely pessimistic, particularly in the OTC market. Short interest on the Nasdaq has surged to record highs. Finally, inflation continues to ease. This is likely to spur a significant decline in long term interest rates, which will be more bullish than short term cuts in the Discount Rate could ever be. We have closed our OEX hedge, and recommend a margined **140% invested position in recommended stocks.**"

Hussman Econometrics is published monthly by John Hussman, who supplements the newsletter with a weekly telephone hotline update. Econometrics is a statistical tool that enables the adviser to incorporate in one systematic model a large number of individual indicators. One of the first investment news-letter publishers to use econometrics was The Institute for Econometric Research, and Hussman says he owes "considerable credit" to Norman Fosback of that Institute. (Five of the Institute's newsletters are reviewed elsewhere in this book.)

Regardless of how much credit Hussman

owes Fosback, their econometric models are quite different. Hussman's model ventures no forecasts beyond 12 months into the future, for example, while Fosback's will forecast the market's movement over the next five years. And even for periods of one year and less, their two models generate significantly different forecasts. In a study for *Forbes* in which I compared their 3-month, 6-month and 12-month forecasts (covering the period from 1988 to 1990), I found that Hussman's forecasts were more accurate.

In addition to five model portfolios of individual stocks and mutual funds that are tracked by the HFD, Hussman's service also provides advice for traders of options and stock index futures. (This latter advice isn't tracked because it isn't provided in the context of a model portfolio.) Three of Hussman's five model portfolios are featured in the accompanying graphs since the HFD has at least 18 months of performance data for them; the remaining two, though not graphed separately, are included in the figures for Hussman's average.

Much of Hussman's impressive performance over the 18 months through mid-1992 can be attributed to his aggressive use of margin, but not all. Even on a risk-adjusted basis, *Hussman Econometrics* is well ahead of the market.

Hussman Econometrics (Average)

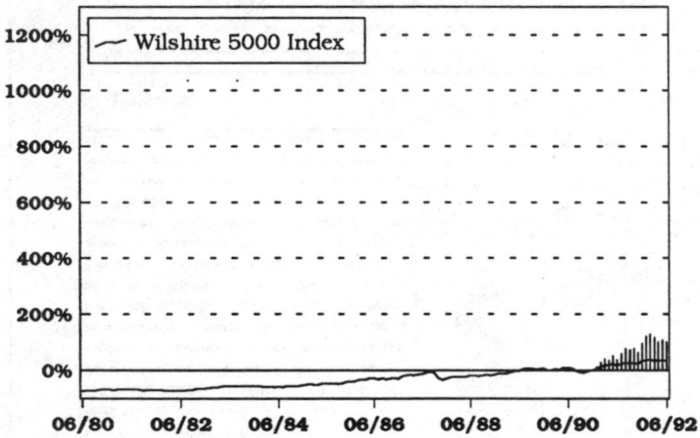

	Gain/Loss
1/1/91 to 6/30/92	+98.5%
(First Quintile)	
1/1/89 to 6/30/92	(n/a)
1/1/87 to 6/30/92	(n/a)
1/1/85 to 6/30/92	(n/a)
1/1/83 to 6/30/92	(n/a)
6/30/80 to 6/30/92	(n/a)

Risk: 240% of market

Hussman Econometrics (Diversified Stock Portfolio)

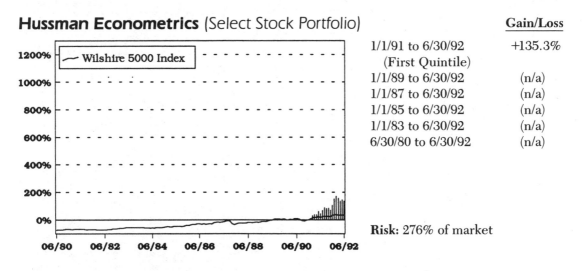

	Gain/Loss
1/1/91 to 6/30/92	+129.2%
(First Quintile)	
1/1/89 to 6/30/92	(n/a)
1/1/87 to 6/30/92	(n/a)
1/1/85 to 6/30/92	(n/a)
1/1/83 to 6/30/92	(n/a)
6/30/80 to 6/30/92	(n/a)

Risk: 285% of market

Hussman Econometrics (Select Stock Portfolio)

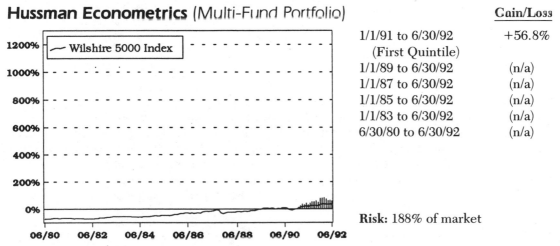

	Gain/Loss
1/1/91 to 6/30/92	+135.3%
(First Quintile)	
1/1/89 to 6/30/92	(n/a)
1/1/87 to 6/30/92	(n/a)
1/1/85 to 6/30/92	(n/a)
1/1/83 to 6/30/92	(n/a)
6/30/80 to 6/30/92	(n/a)

Risk: 276% of market

Hussman Econometrics (Multi-Fund Portfolio)

	Gain/Loss
1/1/91 to 6/30/92	+56.8%
(First Quintile)	
1/1/89 to 6/30/92	(n/a)
1/1/87 to 6/30/92	(n/a)
1/1/85 to 6/30/92	(n/a)
1/1/83 to 6/30/92	(n/a)
6/30/80 to 6/30/92	(n/a)

Risk: 188% of market

Income & Safety

Address
The Institute for
 Econometric
 Research
3471 N. Federal Hwy.
Ft. Lauderdale, FL
 33306

Editors
Norman Fosback and
 Glen King Parker

Phone Number
800-327-6720

Subscription Rates
$49.00/year

Telephone Hotline
Yes

Money Management
No

INCOME & SAFETY®
The Consumer's Guide to High Yields

Norman G. Fosback, Editor

Glen King Parker, Publisher

Issue No. 132   July 10, 1992

Most Attractive Funds

The most attractive funds in each income category are below. See article at right for recommended portfolio maturities in the current environment.

Money Market Funds

Tax Status	Best Buys	Safety Rating	Yield Forecast	30-Day Yield
Taxable	Capital Preservation	AAA+	0	3.4%
Taxable	Fidelity Spartan U.S. Govt.	AAA	+2	4.0%
Taxable	Vanguard Prime	AA	+2	3.8%
Taxable	Fidelity Spartan Money Market	A	+2	3.9%
Tax-Free	Federated Tax-Free	AAA	0	2.7%
Tax-Free	Vanguard Muni Bond MM	AA	+2	3.0%
Tax-Free	Calvert Tax-Free	A	+2	3.2%

Buys

Tax Status	Best Buys	Safety Rating	Yield Forecast	30-Day Yield
Taxable	Dreyfus 100% U.S. Treasury LP	AAA	+2	3.7%
Taxable	Fidelity Spartan U.S. Treasury	AAA	+2	3.8%
Taxable	Benham Government Agency	AAA	+1	3.5%
Taxable	Vanguard Federal	AAA	+1	3.8%
Taxable	Kemper Government	AAA	0	3.7%
Taxable	Merrill Lynch Government	AAA	0	3.7%
Taxable	Federated Trust U.S. Treasury	AAA	0	3.6%
Taxable	Vanguard U.S. Treasury	AAA	0	3.7%
Taxable	Pacific Horizon Treasury	AAA	0	3.5%
Taxable	American Expr. Government	AAA	0	3.6%
Taxable	Fidelity U.S. Government	AAA	0	3.6%
Taxable	Zweig Government	AAA	0	3.7%
Taxable	Merrill Lynch Institutional	AAA	+1	3.8%
Taxable	Merrill Lynch Ready Assets	AA	+1	3.6%
Taxable	Dreyfus Worldwide Dollar	A	+2	3.9%
Taxable	Evergreen Money Market	A	+2	3.9%
Taxable	American AAdvantage Mileage	A	+2	3.9%
Tax-Free	Scudder Tax-Free	AAA	0	2.6%
Tax-Free	Smith Barney Tax-Free MF	AAA	0	2.5%
Tax-Free	Nuveen Tax-Exempt Money Mkt.	AA	+1	2.6%
Tax-Free	Fidelity Tax Exempt	AA	+1	2.8%
Tax-Free	Lehman Provident Muni-Fund	AA	+1	2.7%

Taxable and tax-free money funds are ranked first by Safety Rating and then by expected yield

Long-Term Income Funds

Type	Best Buys	Yield
Treasury	Vanguard U.S. Treasury Long Term	7.6%
Treasury-Zero	Benham Target 2010	7.8%
Treasury-Zero	Benham Target 2015	7.8%
Govt. Agency	USAA Income	7.7%
Ginnie Mae	Scudder GNMA	8.1%
Corp. AA+	Scudder Short Term Bond	7.4%
Corp. AA	Babson Bond Long	7.8%
Corp. AA–	Vanguard Investment Grade Corp.	8.1%
Corp. BB	Vanguard High Yield Corp.	9.8%
Corp. CCC+	Northeast Investors Trust	11.0%
Pfd. Stock	Vanguard Preferred	7.5%
Tax-Free	Price – Tax-Free High Yield	6.5%

Buys

Type	Best Buys	Yield
Treasury-Zero	Benham Target 2005	7.7%
Govt. Agency	Fidelity Spartan Government Income	7.4%
Govt. Agency	Fidelity Mortgage Securities	7.2%
Ginnie Mae	Vanguard GNMA	7.9%
Ginnie Mae	Benham GNMA	7.8%
Corp. B+	Financial – High Yield	9.4%
Corp. B	Price – High Yield	9.5%
Corp. B	GIT Income Maximum	9.4%
Corp. CC+	Fidelity Spartan High Income	10.1%
Tax-Free	Fidelity Aggressive Tax-Free (1.0% load)	6.8%
Tax-Free	Fidelity Massachusetts Tax-Free	6.4%
Tax-Free	Fidelity High Yield Tax-Free	6.3%
Tax-Free	Dreyfus California Tax-Exempt	6.2%
Tax-Free	Fundamental – California Muni	6.2%

Current Outlook

An unwelcome jump in election-year unemployment spooked the Federal Reserve into cutting its discount rate to 3%, a level last seen when JFK was in the White House. The Fed's dramatic action drove money market yields to two-decade lows, but had much less impact on long-term interest rates.

Considering that the economy has been growing, albeit fitfully, for 15 months or more, the Fed's stance of aggressive monetary ease increasingly looks more political than essential to the nation's economic health. As disappointing as recent growth rates are compared to past decades, it may well be that structural constants now limit long-run potential GNP growth to less than 3% a year.

From this point on in the economic cycle, Fed decisions on short-term rates are not going to have as much impact on long-term rates as are *[Continued on Page 2]*

New Recommendations

LONG-TERM: In the Treasury-Zero Coupon category, *Benham Target 2005* has been lowered from "Best Buy" to "Buy". In the Government Agency sector, *Columbia Fixed Income*, a "Buy" last month, is now marked "Hold." Among Ginnie Mae funds, *Lexington GNMA* and *Price – GNMA* are lowered from "Buy" to "Hold," while *Benham GNMA* is a new "Buy."

Turning to the corporate sector, we recommend sale of *Flagship Corporate Cash*, which is converting from a Preferred Stock fund to a Utility fund. In the Municipal arena, *Dreyfus California Tax-Exempt* garners a new "Buy" recommendation.

MONEY MARKET: Our money fund recommendations are unchanged from June. *Dreyfus BASIC Money Market*, an interesting new alternative in the "A"-Safety Rating category, is analyzed on Page 3.

Tax-free funds remain the investment of choice for high-bracket taxpayers, even though yields continue to fall.

Announcement

We are implementing an all-new and significantly improved Hot Line system today, which includes many new features. Please see Page 4 for details.

 See the enclosed letter for your confidential Hot Line number and current Hot Line Report #

A Service of The Institute for Econometric Research, 3471 North Federal, Fort Lauderdale, Florida 33306
For Subscriber Services and Information, Call Toll-Free 800-442-9000

Income & Safety is one of several newsletters published by The Institute for Econometric Research, which is run by Norman Fosback and Glen Parker. Four of their other newsletters also are reviewed in this volume: *Market Logic, Mutual Fund Forecaster, The Insiders* and *New Issues. Income & Safety* is published monthly, but is supplemented by a weekly telephone hotline update.

Income & Safety focuses on mutual funds that invest in fixed-income securities, ranging from money market funds to junk bond funds. The service offers overall timing advice for the fixed-income market as well as advice on the selection of individual mutual funds. Much of the newsletter is devoted to a statistical summary of each of several hundred such funds.

The service defines its model portfolio to include all mutual funds in their statistical universe that they rate "hold" or higher—typically 60 or more funds. That part of their advice is clear enough, but it is less clear how a follower of this model portfolio is supposed to incorporate the newsletter's market-timing advice. In mid-1991, for example, the newsletter became bearish on the overall bond market and recommended that subscribers move out of long-term bond funds into short-term vehicles. Yet the newsletter continued to rate a number of their long-term bond funds as "hold" or higher—and hence, by im-

plication, to be owned by their model portfolio. (The HFD chose to move the service's portfolio out of long-term funds and into cash.)

The HFD calculates that the newsletter produced a 9.9% return over the 18 months through mid-1992, in contrast to a 17.8% total return for the Shearson Lehman Treasury Index. The culprit in this underperformance is the service's market timing rather than its selection of individual funds. Had each of *Income & Safety's* model portfolio funds performed exactly as the Shearson index did, its model portfolio would have gained just 7.6% instead of its actual 9.9%—suggesting that their recommended funds actually did better than the average.

Income & Safety

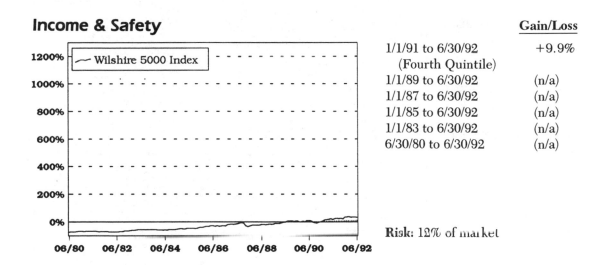

	Gain/Loss
1/1/91 to 6/30/92	+9.9%
(Fourth Quintile)	
1/1/89 to 6/30/92	(n/a)
1/1/87 to 6/30/92	(n/a)
1/1/85 to 6/30/92	(n/a)
1/1/83 to 6/30/92	(n/a)
6/30/80 to 6/30/92	(n/a)

Risk: 12% of market

Individual Investor Special Situations Report

Address
38 E. 29th St.
4th Floor
New York, NY 10016

Editor
Gordon Anderson

Phone Number
212-689-2777

Subscription Rates
$ 12.50/1 issue
$165.00/year

Telephone Hotline
No

Money Management
No

RECOMMENDATION

The continuing evolution of the discount stock brokerage has fundamentally altered the brokerage industry. In recent years, investors have swarmed the discount segment, in search of lower trading commissions than traditional firms charge.

Discounters now account for nearly one-fourth of all the retail trading activity occuring in the United States, according to the New York-based research firm Mercer, Inc. More important, a sea change in investors' thinking is apparently taking place: Nearly four percentage points of that market share gain has come in the past year alone.

Discount brokers, increasingly competitive with the full-service firms, will pick up the lion's share of the industry's future growth, at least as far as individual investor trading is concerned. Moreover, demographic trends portend a coming era when small investors dominate the market. In fact, individuals have been the driving force on Wall Street since the Desert Storm rally began in early 1991. This has profound positive ramifications for discounters, whose only lord and master is the small investor.

One of the best-positioned discount brokers is Quick & Reilly Group, Inc. One of the so-called Big 3 national discounters (along with Charles Schwab and Fidelity Investments), Q&R is showing dramatic sales and earnings gains, and increasing market share. Yet the stock--whose trading patterns are closely tied to trends in the market as a whole--looks quite undervalued.

Quick & Reilly has had exceptional growth over the last four years, posting a compound annual pre-tax income growth of 38%. Its most recent quarter was no exception. An increase in the firm's customer base, and the surge in trading activity by small investors resulted in the company's second highest quarterly earnings ever (surpassed only by the preceding quarter).

For the first quarter of fiscal 1993, net income rose 41% to $6.8 million, or $0.69 per share, versus $4.7 million, or $0.52 per share, in the first quarter of fiscal 1992. First-quarter revenues increased 42%, to $46.5 million from $32.7 million a year earlier.

The combination of earnings momentum and the Fed-

eral Reserve's recent discount rate cut, make Q&R stock an attractive value play. Trading near its 52-week low at eight times earnings, the negative condition of the current market has depressed Q&R shares. This, we believe, presents investors with an excellent opportunity to buy on weakness. The stock, with a book value of $14.63 per share, should outperform the market over the next six to 12 months-- especially if stock market volume increases--and move back up into the low-30s.

Management is confident the company will increase its client customer base, even in a market downturn. The biggest opening is a growing population of clients who are unhappy with recommendations and service provided by their full-priced brokers. Investing has fundamentally changed--more and more individual investors are making their own investment decisions, and are unwilling to pay for advice they do not need or use. Discounters like Quick & Reilly are the beneficiaries.

Quick & Reilly differentiates itself from other discounters by giving clients individual personal account executives. And, Q&R offers new clients a risk-free service guarantee, whereby the company will refund its fee to clients if they are not satisfied with its service.

We are expecting Quick & Reilly's revenues to increase to $175 million for fiscal 1993 compared to $154 million in fiscal 1992. Earnings should rise to $3.00 per share from $2.44 in the prior year.

Q&R is arguably the most cost conscious of all the discounters. In fact, the company's low expense structure produces wider profit margins than its rivals, and insulates Q&R from market downturns better than most. In the most recent quarter, for example, Q&R posted a pre-tax profit margin of 26%, compared to 20% for Schwab.

Quick & Reilly hopes to double its customer base over the next three years, through a new advertising campaign and aggressive branch office expansion. In the first quarter of fiscal 1993, the brokerage division saw a 75% increase in new accounts opened versus the same period last year despite decreased trading volume in this time frame. In addition to Q&R's brokerage operations, the company's clearing and specialist subsidiaries have demonstrated strong

Individual Investor Special Situations Report is published monthly by Jonathan Steinberg, the son of the famous Wall Street investor Saul Steinberg. The service does not include a telephone hotline.

The newsletter is devoted entirely to stock selection: No market-timing advice is provided at all. One new special situation is provided each month, and buy-hold-sell advice is provided on all previous recommendations.

Because there is no recommended model portfolio, the HFD constructs one for the newsletter that is fully invested and equally divided among all those stocks that the service rates as "buy." Consult the discussion of the HFD's methodology earlier in this book for an explanation of why the HFD follows non-model-portfolio letters in this way.

The stocks on which Steinberg focuses tend to be secondary stocks trading over-the-counter, and it therefore is not surprising that a portfolio that is fully invested in them is quite volatile. Over the 18 months through mid-1992, in fact, the portfolio the HFD constructed was more than three times as volatile (or risky) as the average stock.

At least over the one and one-half years through mid-1992, Steinberg's letter was well rewarded for incurring this risk—gaining 101.8%, in contrast to 32.3% for the market as a whole. When this performance is adjusted for its high risk, however, its gain is only slightly ahead of the market itself (see Appendix A-6).

Individual Investor Special Situations Report

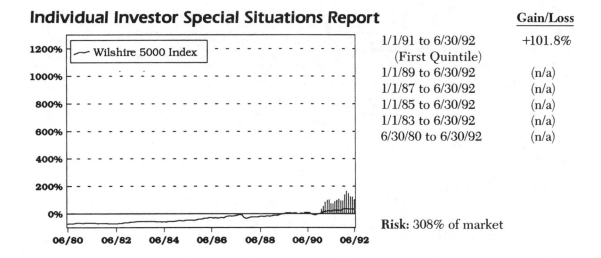

	Gain/Loss
1/1/91 to 6/30/92	+101.8%
(First Quintile)	
1/1/89 to 6/30/92	(n/a)
1/1/87 to 6/30/92	(n/a)
1/1/85 to 6/30/92	(n/a)
1/1/83 to 6/30/92	(n/a)
6/30/80 to 6/30/92	(n/a)

Risk: 308% of market

The Insiders

Address
The Institute for
 Econometric
 Research
3471 N. Federal Hwy.
Ft. Lauderdale, FL
 33306

Editors
Norman Fosback and
 Glen King Parker

Phone Number
800-327-6720

Subscription Rates
$49.00/year

Telephone Hotline
Yes

Money Management
No

THE INSIDERS

America's Most Knowledgeable Investors

Norman G. Fosback, Editor   Glen King Parker, Publisher

Issue No. 286   See the enclosed letter for your current confidential Insider Line # and Report #.   July 3, 1992

Flash Indexes Jump Into Bullish Territory

The Flash Index has jumped back into the favorable zone. A 59% reading is the strongest in six months, and once again shows a majority of recent insider traders on the buy side.

The Flash Index measures insider trades executed during the latest 30 calendar days, and for the most part reflects trades reported to the SEC within the last one or two weeks. Many more trades covering that latest 30 days will be reported by insiders in later weeks. In other words, the Flash Index is based on a relatively small number of trades, and is therefore more erratic than the Insider Indicator presented in the chart below. An even more volatile and more sensitive measure of recent insider trading is a Flash Index we maintain for the latest *20-day* period. Currently, this index shows an overwhelming 70% of insiders executing trades on the buy side. But the sample size here is only a fourth that of the 30-day Flash Index.

What all this means is that the most recent trends of insider trading are very favorable, but that our readings are based on a limited sample. *We therefore prefer to await further confirmation of these readings before moving to a more aggressively bullish market posture.* At this juncture,

many more stocks appear to be vulnerable because they have low and bearish Insider Ratings of 0, 1, and 2, than those that have upside potential because they have Ratings of 10, 9, or 8. Therefore, be selective in your buying, and don't hesitate to trim stocks with low Insider Ratings from your portfolio.

Buy Favorites

We featured **USF&G** (NYSE – FG, 13½) in our January 24 issue earlier this year at 7⅜. We concluded, "This stock is extremely speculative and is not formally recommended, but it is an interesting situation for turnaround-oriented accounts."

The stock has now nearly doubled, as the turnaround continues to evolve. Just as significantly for those of you that bought these shares, you still have the insiders on your side because they are still buying.

USF&G is the thirteenth largest property/casualty insurer in the U.S. A big money maker in the 1970s and 1980s, the company has been awash in red ink in the '90s. The losses, however, are narrowing. Some analysts see

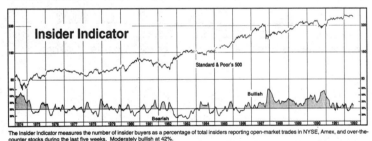

The Insider Indicator measures the number of insider buyers as a percentage of total insiders reporting open-market trades in NYSE, Amex, and over-the-counter stocks during the last five weeks. Moderately bullish at 42%.

A Service of The Institute for Econometric Research, 3471 North Federal, Fort Lauderdale, Florida 33306
For Subscriber Services and Information, Call Toll-Free 800-442-9000

The Insiders is published every two weeks by The Institute for Econometric Research, whose president is Norman Fosback and chairman is Glen Parker. The Institute also publishes a number of other investment newsletters, including several that are reviewed elsewhere in this *Guide*: *Market Logic, New Issues, Mutual Fund Forecaster,* and *Income & Safety*. The newsletter is supplemented by a weekly telephone hotline update.

Norman Fosback was a student of finance at Portland State University before assuming his post at the Institute, and it was at Portland

State that one of the seminal academic studies into insider buying and selling was conducted. That research showed that the markets could be beaten by following the lead of corporate insiders, and Fosback capitalizes on that and other research in formulating the investment approach of *The Insiders*.

Though most of the academic studies on insider buying and selling have focused just on stock selection, Fosback uses insider trading data as a market-timing tool as well. According to Fosback, on average over long periods of time 35% of all insider transactions in the open market are purchases. His theory is that whenever the actual current percentage of purchases is above that level, it is bullish—and when below, bearish. Each issue of his newsletter, as well as his weekly telephone hotline, indicate what the current insider purchase percentages are.

Each issue of *The Insiders* also ranks a large number of stocks on a 1-to-10 rating scale. In addition, each issue reports on the status of its model portfolio, a relatively infrequently traded collection of all stocks that have formally been recommended by *The Insiders* and that have yet to be closed out. It is this portfolio that the HFD tracks.

Over the seven and one-half years through mid-1992, this portfolio gained 118.9%, in contrast to the Wilshire 5000's 197.6%. The portfolio also was more risky (volatile) over this period, so it underperformed the market on a risk-adjusted basis by an even larger margin.

The Insiders

	Gain/Loss
1/1/91 to 6/30/92 (First Quintile)	+72.5%
1/1/89 to 6/30/92 (Third Quintile)	+38.6%
1/1/87 to 6/30/92 (Second Quintile)	+71.2%
1/1/85 to 6/30/92 (Third Quintile)	+118.9%
1/1/83 to 6/30/92	(n/a)
6/30/80 to 6/30/92	(n/a)

Risk: 188% of market

The International
Harry Schultz Letter

Address
P.O. Box 622
FERC
CH-1001, Lausanne
Switzerland

Editor
Harry Schultz

Phone Number
32 16 533684

Subscription Rates
$275.00/year

Money Management
No

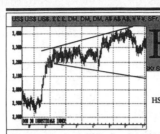

"The leading international, monetary, socio, geo-political & philosophical newsletter"

— For THINKING humanoids —
Written in the abbreviated spelling of tomorrow

Single copy price US$50, DM76, SFr68, £26, DFI85, A$67, C$60

HSL 541 - Covering events to occur in July-August, 1992 & beyond

Tho everyone watches the US Dow Jones Industrial Average, no one seems to have seen the megaphone chart pattern it has formed over the last 6mos. It's a classic bear market forecaster. No chart pattern **always** works. Tho odds favor a break down, it's a coilspring for a **big** move (vital details in US mkt section).

Big picture

A pendulum too far. At every period in history when society moved to an extreme, when the "madness of crowds" took over, it was confusing &/or frustrating for people who thot they understood common sense, to cope with the news **each day**, which seemed to depart from logic. Such people then began to doubt their own premises, in a sea of new era "thinking". Today is one of those periods. News headlines in just **one** day's newspaper include the following departure from common sense: "Russia will safeguard freedom, Yeltsin vows". "US may (unilaterally) deactivate more missiles". "UN's Leader asks for standing (UN army) peace force.". "Ireland votes for Maastricht 2-1". "Serbs Pound Sarajevo in total attack". "Weinberger quizzed re Irangate". "ANC blames de Klerk for township massacre". "Help Yeltsin escape the gun at his head" (columnist Jim Hoagland). "US Fed to help Russia build bank system" "DJIA up as Europe fetes Irish Referendum". All the above is a mixture of insanity, lies & fantasy. Yet it was the menu served up to readers of the IHTribune (& most other papers) on June 20,1992. The poor public is pounded by this typical nonsense day after day until it achieves credibility. Hitler/Goebels contended that lies repeated often enough attain the status of truth. So does **nonsense**. In essence it's mostly designer-brain washing.

The Americans are **hugging 2 ferocious bears**, thinking they are **tame**. Both can cause fatalities. Bear #1: Yeltsin, who the US sees as a big teddy bear with no teeth, & promises of domesticity. Bear #2: a stock mkt **bear mkt** wearing the **mask** of a smiling **bull** mkt, offering promises of higher numbers. Bear #1 is a professional liar, who has spent his lifetime lying. He has not stopped construc-

tion of the Russian war machine, has in fact stepped up its production of nuclear submarines, intercont'nl missiles & aircraft carriers, while refusing to give up its strategic military bases in the Kuriles, Cuba & SoVietnam. He is mum on the secret underground warehouses of grain, while begging for foreign aid. He refuses payment on all past Russ loans, while making new ones. Bear #2 is **also** a liar. While the DJIA index jiggles arpund near its all time high, most other mkt indicators topped out months ago, including the advance decline index which reflects ALL US stks. And the US public has bought mutual funds as never before in history, yet the mutual funds index only moves **downhill**. The mask worn by bear #2 continues to fool the masses in the biggest madness of crowds drama of the century.

The **majority** of the world's nations are locked into depression. A minority are in recession, that is now chronic. Only a handful are outside recession. The Anglo nations are trapped in a vicious circle of capital consumption, public & private, which continues to grow at the expense of investment & longterm growth potential.

As Dr. Kurt Richebacher (Mendelssohn Strasse 51, D-6000 Frankfurt 1, Germany), a superlative economist, puts it: The US Fed money easing has stimulated **financial speculation** but is totally ineffective in stimulating the **real economy**. Money/credit growth, essential to sustainable recovery, has deteriorated to unprecedented lows. And the view that **restructuring** in US, Cda, Oz (slashing jobs & loss-plants) will help the economy is illusion. It helps profits for some companies but for the economy to grow requires **expanding** plant & equip & jobs. **Downsizing** results in **general impoverishment**. Dr. R smiles at attempts to impress the public by **annualizing** economic statistics. He says: Scanning for evidence of recovery in the US case, we see not the slightest improvement in monetary conditions. There's the same gulf btwn soaring **M1** & dormant **broad** money growth, btwn exploding budget deficit & dormant private credit, & btwn **hype** in the stock mkt & **distress** in the real economy. There's an unrealized gigantic **flight of money** out of the real economy & into stocks & bonds, asset inflation's last hurrah.

The International Harry Schultz Letter is published monthly by Harry Schultz. Schultz is based in Europe, and his letter is one of the few (though increasing) number of invest-

ment newsletters that approach investing from a global perspective.

Schultz's service focuses on a myriad of topics in addition to investing, ranging from his political commentary about many Western nations to his complaints that there is a conspiracy to ignore a safer airplane design. Schultz's investment recommendations are equally broad in scope, ranging in type from stocks and bonds to commodity futures, and in geographical location from the U.S.-based exchanges to those in virtually every country that has them.

For several reasons, the HFD does not attempt to follow each and every recommendation made by Schultz in his letter. Often this is because his recommendations are too ambiguous for us to interpret. For example, at times Schultz will give more than one piece of advice on the same stock, as when he said in 1987 that holders of Rustenburg Platinum should place stops at "30, 34 & 40." Another time in 1987 he advised that holders of his recommended stocks raise all their stop loss levels by writing "it's 330 AM when I write this section; too tired to move up stops for the list; hope U'll do it yourself" (sic).

Over the years Schultz has highlighted specific subsets of his recommendations, for which regular follow-up advice usually is provided and advice is relatively clear. One such subset has been a portfolio of U.S. stocks, another is a portfolio of non-U.S. stocks, and a third is a portfolio the HFD has constructed out of Schultz's trading advice for gold and silver futures. Because Schultz does not recommend a particular margin level for his gold and silver futures recommendations, this last portfolio was constructed by the HFD without the use of margin.

Over the 12 years through mid-1992, the HFD calculates that Schultz's portfolio of U.S. stocks gained just 55.3%, as compared to 432.7% for the Wilshire 5000. The HFD has less data for the other two Schultz portfolios, but their record is mixed. Schultz's list of foreign stocks has lagged the market over the five and one-half years ending in mid-1992, for example, gaining 14.1%, compared to the Wilshire 5000's 93.3% gain. Over the same period, the portfolio the HFD constructed out of Schultz's gold- and silver-trading advice has done better, gaining 25.5%, compared to a 12.1% loss for gold bullion.

The Int'l Harry Schultz Letter (Average)

	Gain/Loss
1/1/91 to 6/30/92 (Fifth Quintile)	+4.4%
1/1/89 to 6/30/92 (Fifth Quintile)	+18.7%
1/1/87 to 6/30/92 (Fourth Quintile)	+20.2%
1/1/85 to 6/30/92 (Fifth Quintile)	+43.9%
1/1/83 to 6/30/92 (Fourth Quintile)	+67.3%
6/30/80 to 6/30/92 (Fourth Quintile)	+84.2%

Risk: 38% of market

The Int'l Harry Schultz Letter (U.S. Stocks on the "List")

	Gain/Loss
1/1/91 to 6/30/92 (Fifth Quintile)	−14.7%
1/1/89 to 6/30/92 (Fourth Quintile)	+21.8%
1/1/87 to 6/30/92 (Fifth Quintile)	+10.7%
1/1/85 to 6/30/92 (Fifth Quintile)	+28.6%
1/1/83 to 6/30/92 (Fourth Quintile)	+41.0%
6/30/80 to 6/30/92 (Fifth Quintile)	+55.3%

Risk: 96% of market

The Int'l Harry Schultz Letter (Foreign Stocks on the "List")

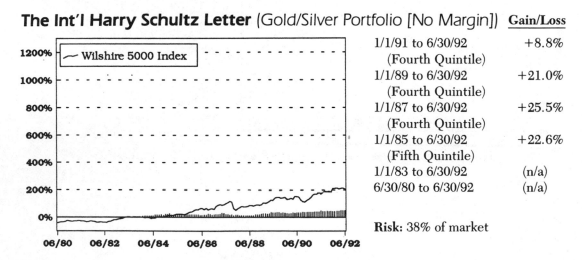

	Gain/Loss
1/1/91 to 6/30/92 (Third Quintile)	+20.6%
1/1/89 to 6/30/92 (Fifth Quintile)	+8.5%
1/1/87 to 6/30/92 (Fifth Quintile)	+14.1%
1/1/85 to 6/30/92	(n/a)
1/1/83 to 6/30/92	(n/a)
6/30/80 to 6/30/92	(n/a)

Risk: 77% of market

The Int'l Harry Schultz Letter (Gold/Silver Portfolio [No Margin])

	Gain/Loss
1/1/91 to 6/30/92 (Fourth Quintile)	+8.8%
1/1/89 to 6/30/92 (Fourth Quintile)	+21.0%
1/1/87 to 6/30/92 (Fourth Quintile)	+25.5%
1/1/85 to 6/30/92 (Fifth Quintile)	+22.6%
1/1/83 to 6/30/92	(n/a)
6/30/80 to 6/30/92	(n/a)

Risk: 38% of market

InvesTech Market Analyst

Address
2472 Birch Glen
Whitefish, MT
  59937-3349

Editor
James B. Stack

Phone Number
406-862-7777

Subscription Rates
$ 99.00/7 months
$175.00/year

Telephone Hotline
Yes

Money Management
No

MARKET ANALYST

V92I09   *TECHNICAL AND MONETARY INVESTMENT ANALYSIS*   JULY 10, 1992

4 Weeks Ending July 8th, 1992:	HIGH	LOW	LAST
Financial			
Discount Rate	3.50%	3.50%	3.50%
Federal Funds	3 7/8%	3 1/8%	3 1/8%
90-day T-Bills	3.68%	3.21%	3.22%
Stock Market			
DJIA	3354.90	3274.12	3293.26
DJTA	1346.23	1277.65	1289.61
DJUA	217.64	209.69	217.64
NASDAQ	569.52	547.84	557.57
Silver (SEP)	4.17	3.90	3.91
Gold (AUG)	348.40	342.30	348.40

SLEEPLESS NIGHTS

1992 - it's been a rough first half for the stock market. The DJIA was the only popular average that was up (+3.9%), while the NYSE Index lost 2% and the AMEX, DJ Transports, and OTC Nasdaq each slipped 4-5%. Those meager losses aren't bad except in comparison to the unrealistic level of investor expectations. Over the past decade, investors have grown accustomed to a 30% gain being a *"decent year in the market"*... a 15% gain being *"mediocre"*... and no gain or a loss (heaven forbid!) as *"a lousy bear market."* Rest assured, we have not experienced a bear market this year (although those investors holding a few of the air pocket stocks listed inside might disagree). Instead, it has been a series of trendless gyrations – or relentless whipsaws for anyone gullible enough to jump on the latest 35pt spurt or dip in the DJIA.

Yet throughout this period, investors have found an endless supply of worries to lose sleep over: *Is the U.S. Dollar going to collapse? Has a bear market already begun? Is the debt bubble about to burst? Has the Federal Reserve lost control? Are we heading into a 1930's style depression? Have interest rates hit their bottom?*

We've kept you posted on our expectations for the market, economy, and interest rates. And for the most part, this outlook has been on target. Inside this issue, we provide a new update on our stance and likely changes in the weeks ahead. The desperate cut in the Discount Rate, along with the upcoming election toss-up could have a significant impact on the markets. In addition, we have sent our computers back in time to study and answer those questions which are likely to be at the top of your list:

- What have 7 consecutive cuts in the Discount Rate done to the stock market in the past?
- If this was the FINAL cut in the Discount Rate, how soon could we expect the first uptick in interest rates?
- In this Presidential Election Year, is the stock market more likely to peak BEFORE or AFTER the election?
- Based on past history, what might be the maximum downside risk between now and election day?

InvesTech Market Analyst is published every three weeks by James Stack and is supplemented by a telephone hotline that is updated at least twice each week. This newsletter, along with *InvesTech Mutual Fund Advisor*, are the successor publications to *InvesTech Market Letter*, which Stack previously published and which included both a stock and a mutual fund section. These sections now appear in the separate newsletters. (The HFD's historical track records for both portfolios give them credit for the time they were recommended by the same newsletter.)

Stack's approach involves a combination of

both fundamental and technical analysis, including a number of proprietary indicators his research has produced. A hallmark of Stack's approach is an objective analysis of his indicators along with a willingness to shift his investment stance when he believes the indicators warrant it. In September 1985, for example, Stack advised subscribers to get out of the stock market in anticipation of an imminent bear market. Stack was not alone in prematurely announcing the end of the bull market, but he set himself apart from some other advisers by throwing in the towel and reinvesting in stocks when it was obvious that the bull market still had more life. And at the top of the bull market in the summer of 1987, a time when there was a preponderance of bullish news, Stack began getting out of stocks; by the day of the crash, his portfolio mostly was in cash.

Over the seven and one-half years through mid-1992, this service's model portfolio gained 141.8%, which compares to a 197.6% gain for the Wilshire 5000. However, this below-market performance was turned in with below-market risk, so its risk-adjusted performance is better—though, as it turns out, not by enough to beat the market over this period.

InvesTech Market Analyst

	Gain/Loss
1/1/91 to 6/30/92	+19.9%
(Third Quintile)	
1/1/89 to 6/30/92	+36.7%
(Third Quintile)	
1/1/87 to 6/30/92	+78.3%
(Second Quintile)	
1/1/85 to 6/30/92	+141.8%
(Second Quintile)	
1/1/83 to 6/30/92	(n/a)
6/30/80 to 6/30/92	(n/a)

Risk: 85% of market

InvesTech Mutual Fund Advisor

Address
2472 Birch Glen
Whitefish, MT
   59937-3349

Editor
James B. Stack

Phone Number
406-862-7777

Subscription Rates
$ 99.00/7 months
$175.00/year

Telephone Hotline
Yes

Money Management
No

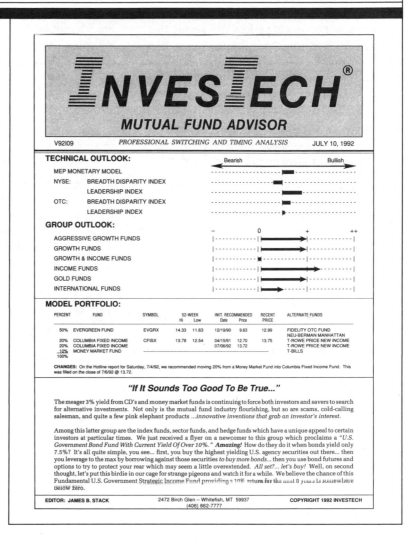

The *InvesTech Mutual Fund Advisor* is published every three weeks by James Stack, who also publishes the *InvesTech Market Analyst* (reviewed elsewhere in this volume). It is accompanied by a telephone hotline that is updated at least twice each week.

Of the two services published by Stack, this one has had the better record. Since the beginning of 1986 (when the HFD began following the *InvesTech Mutual Fund Advisor*) through mid-1992, for example, Stack's mutual fund advice gained 164.7% whereas his model portfolio of individual stocks gained 82.2%. Over this same period the Wilshire 5000 gained 124.5%.

The explanation for this difference is that Stack's mutual fund recommendations did better than his stock picks. We know this because on a timing-only basis, these two portfolios performed almost identically: A portfolio that invested in hypothetical shares of the Wilshire 5000 in the same proportion as Stack's mutual fund portfolio gained 105.6% over this six-and-one-half-year period, whereas his stock portfolio gained 100.4%. From this we can conclude that Stack's mutual fund picks did better than the Wilshire during the time he owned them, while his stock picks did worse.

InvesTech Mutual Fund Advisor

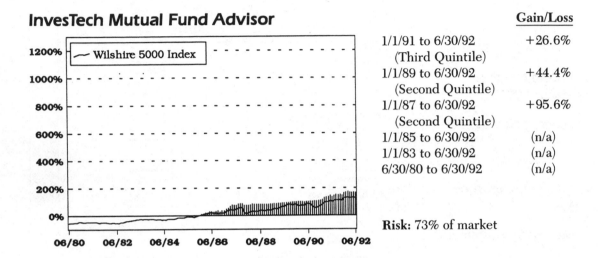

	Gain/Loss
1/1/91 to 6/30/92	+26.6%
(Third Quintile)	
1/1/89 to 6/30/92	+44.4%
(Second Quintile)	
1/1/87 to 6/30/92	+95.6%
(Second Quintile)	
1/1/85 to 6/30/92	(n/a)
1/1/83 to 6/30/92	(n/a)
6/30/80 to 6/30/92	(n/a)

Risk: 73% of market

Investment Horizons

INVESTMENT
HORIZONS

| June 26, 1992 | Volume 10, Number 12 |

Semi-Annual Portfolio Review

Address
680 N. Lake
 Shore Dr.
Tower Suite 2038
Chicago, IL 60611

Editor
Gerald Perritt

Phone Number
800-326-6941

Subscription Rates
$195.00/year

Telephone Hotline
No

Money Management
Yes

As is usually the case, small firm stocks came roaring out of the starting gate at the beginning of the year. In fact, the month of January turned out to be one of the better months for small firm stocks since October 1983. During January of this year, the *Investment Horizons'* equal-weighted index of small firm stocks rose 13 percent. The index then tacked on a 4.3 percent gain during February. After that, the bottom fell out of the market. From its peak in mid-February, the value of the index has fallen by 10.5 percent.

While we expected that small cap stocks would continue to outperform large cap stocks, we didn't think it would happen the way it did. So far this year, our recommended portfolio has declined by 1.8 percent while the large cap-dominated S&P 500 Index has declined by 3.3 percent. Of course, the year is far from over. While a struggling economy and a presidential election whose results are up in the air are negatives overhanging the stock market, we believe that small cap stocks will finish the year on a higher note. Our belief is founded on the assumption that the economy will continue to grow throughout the year and begin to pick up steam early next year. If correct, small firm stocks should post higher than expected earnings comparisons during the second half of the year, buoying investor enthusiasm for small cap stocks. Make no mistake about it, the small cap rally is still intact. In fact, a 12 to 15 percent price correction in this segment of the market is a healthy sign.

As is usually the case, our recommended list of stocks produced both big winners and losers. During the first half of the year, our big winners included: Air Express International (+62.8%), Respironics (+44.0%), Lindsay Manufacturing (+30.3%), Aceto (+26.8%), American Filtrona (+25.3%) and Quaker Chemical (+22.2%). A round of negative earnings surprises took its toll on a number of stocks including: Genovese Drug Stores (-43.6%), EMCON Associates (-36.1%), J&J Snack Foods (-34.5%), Home Intensive Care (-33.3%), Porta Systems (-32.3%) and Frenchtex (-22.2%). The divergence in short-term performance is the reason we have always stressed portfolio diversification. In any growth stock portfolio, about 20 percent of its stocks produce about 80 percent of its long-term gains. In other words, you can expect three to five stocks in a 20-stock portfolio to shoulder most of the performance burden.

At present, our recommended list contains 42 companies. Thirty-two are rated a buy, eight hold and we have recommended the sale of two stocks (Bowl America and Rauch Industries). Both of these stocks have produced handsome gains since their initial recommendation. However, revenue growth of both firms has slowed con-

("Semi" continued on page 190)

Investment Horizons focuses on small emerging growth firms that are not extensively followed by professional security analysts and institutional investors. Issues are mailed twice monthly. Copyright by Investment Information Services Inc., G.W. Perritt, Chairman. All rights reserved.

Investment Horizons is published twice each month by Gerald Perritt and is not supplemented by a telephone hotline update. Perritt also edits two other newsletters reviewed in this book: *The Mutual Fund Letter* and *Blue Chip Values*. *Investment Horizons* is different from the other two in that in this service Perritt focuses on stocks that are for the most part neglected by major institutions or brokerage research departments.

Perritt brings a strong academic background to his editing of this newsletter, and his investment approach is an attempt to exploit several of the well-known exceptions (or "anomalies") to the otherwise very efficient market. One of those anomalies is that stocks with little or no institutional following tend to do better, over long periods of time, than stocks that do have such a following.

Like many academics, Perritt formally eschews any attempts to time the stock market. Nevertheless, at no point during the time the HFD has tracked Perritt have his model portfolios been fully invested. Furthermore, in the wake of the October 1987 crash, Perritt increased his cash reserves. Thus, at least *de facto*, he is engaged in market timing.

For much of the period since 1983, secondary stocks have lagged behind blue chips, and the stocks Perritt recommended were no exception. Over the five and one-half years through mid-1992, according to the HFD, the newsletter produced a return of 50.1%, in contrast to 93.3% for the Wilshire 5000. Had each of the stocks Perritt recommended performed as well as the Wilshire during the time he owned them, then the newsletter would have gained 59.0%.

Investment Horizons

	Gain/Loss
1/1/91 to 6/30/92 (Fourth Quintile)	+15.9%
1/1/89 to 6/30/92 (Fourth Quintile)	+27.3%
1/1/87 to 6/30/92 (Third Quintile)	+50.1%
1/1/85 to 6/30/92	(n/a)
1/1/83 to 6/30/92	(n/a)
6/30/80 to 6/30/92	(n/a)

Risk: 62% of market

Investment Quality Trends

Address
7440 Girard Ave.
Suite 4
La Jolla, CA 92037

Editor
Geraldine Weiss

Phone Number
619-459-3818

Subscription Rates
$175.00/6 months
$275.00/year

Telephone Hotline
No

Money Management
No

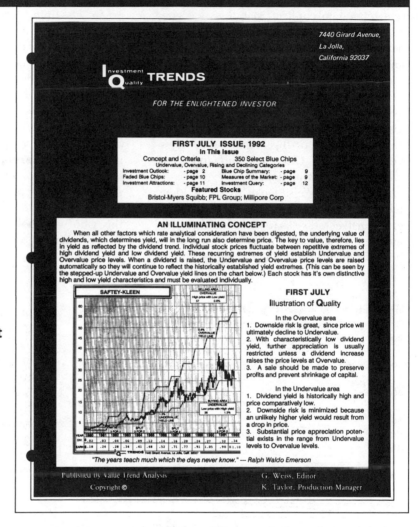

Investment Quality Trends is published twice monthly by Geraldine Weiss and is not supplemented by a telephone hotline. The service is one of the longer-lived newsletters still in publication, having been in existence since 1969. In late 1988, Weiss (with *San Diego Tribune* investment columnist Janet Lowe) wrote a book detailing this newsletter's investment approach, entitled *Dividends Don't Lie* (Dearborn Financial Publishing).

Investment Quality Trends is a simple and elegant application of the belief that the stock investor is, in effect, buying a stream of dividend payments. To buy low and sell high, therefore, one should purchase stocks whose dividend yield is the highest (one for which the investor is paying the least per dollar of dividends) and sell or avoid stocks whose yield is the lowest. A number of academic studies have tended to confirm that this is a good long-term stock selection tool, even though there may be significant shorter periods of time during which the strategy may not lead to above-market returns.

One's intuition also would suspect that a 6% dividend yield might be one thing when the prime rate also is 6%, and quite another when the prime is two or three times that. However, *Investment Quality Trends* does not make any such distinctions.

In each issue Weiss looks at the dividend yield of around 350 blue-chip stocks, her universe constructed so as to include those companies rated at least an "A" by Standard & Poor's for quality, and which have had a long and relatively consistent pattern of dividend payouts. Weiss's computer then divides this universe of stocks into four groups: those that are "Undervalued," those in "Rising Trends," those that are "Overvalued," and those that are in "Declining Trends." Beginning in October 1987, Weiss specifically defined her model portfolio to include all stocks in the "Undervalued" and "Rising Trend" categories. (Prior to that, the portfolio the HFD constructed to follow her advice included only those stocks in the "Undervalued" category.)

Over the six and one-half years through mid-1992, the portfolio the HFD constructed to track *Investment Quality Trends* gained 154.7%, beating the Wilshire 5000's 124.5%. Furthermore, since the newsletter achieved this gain with below-market risk, it handily beat the market on a risk-adjusted basis.

Investment Quality Trends

	Gain/Loss
1/1/91 to 6/30/92 (Second Quintile)	+41.5%
1/1/89 to 6/30/92 (First Quintile)	+76.7%
1/1/87 to 6/30/92 (First Quintile)	+114.8%
1/1/85 to 6/30/92	(n/a)
1/1/83 to 6/30/92	(n/a)
6/30/80 to 6/30/92	(n/a)

Risk: 90% of market

The Investment Reporter

Address
133 Richmond St. W.
#700
Toronto, Ontario
Canada, M5H 3M8

Editor
Canadian Business
Service

Phone Number
416-869-1177

Subscription Rates
$257.00/year

Telephone Hotline
Yes

Money Management
No

THE INVESTMENT REPORTER

CANADIAN BUSINESS SERVICE / a division of MPL Communications Inc.
Since 1941   133 Richmond Street West, Toronto M5H 3M8 Telephone: (416) 869-1177

Volume LII, No. 27	July 10, 1992	Pages 221 to 224

Resource revival favors Noranda

Some investors fear that the Edper group (of which giant Noranda Inc. is a key part) is liable to follow Olympia & York into receivership. We see some crucial differences between Edper and O & Y—see box. We also see bright economic prospects for Noranda.

It's the investor fashion nowadays to dismiss resource-sector stocks as being in a 'commodity business'. These are businesses in which prices, demand and so on are out of producers' hands. All they can do to improve their lot is cut costs.

Following this line of thought has paid off in the past decade. During that time, the prosperity of all resources industries has, on the whole, waned. That's especially so in the past five years; prices of resource-sector stocks have worked their way downward since the summer of 1987.

This may be about to change. The best resource stocks are cheap in relation to assets. As the economy recovers these next few years, supply tightness could develop and push up resource prices, along with share prices of these companies.

NORANDA INC. $17 (*Quality rating: Conservative*) is one of the world's biggest natural-resources companies. The company operates in three groups: forest products (50% of revenue), mining and metals (46% of revenue), and oil and gas (4% of revenue). Wholly-owned Noranda Minerals has interests in 28 mines and 10 metallurgical plants. It produces base and precious metals. Its subsidiaries include 64%-owned Brunswick Mining and Smelting, 51%-owned Kerr Addison Mines, 50%-owned Falconbridge, and 46%-owned Hemlo Gold Mines.

Noranda Forest Products Inc., 82%-owned, operates in all aspects of the forest-products business; its assets include 50% of MacMillan Bloedel, another of our Key stocks. Noranda carries out its oil and gas operations through wholly-owned Canadian Hunter Exploration, and Hunter's subsidiaries, 33%-owned Norcen Energy Resources, and 51.2%-owned North Canadian Oils.

Noranda's per-share profit peaked at $3.14 in 1988, and fell to $2.19 the following year. In 1989, the company raised its dividend to $1 from $0.90. It has kept on paying $1 yearly ever since, although profit

slumped to $0.36 a share in 1990, and the company reported a $1.04 a share loss last year. Revenues, meanwhile, have hovered around $9 billion.

Noranda's profit returned in this year's first quarter, thanks mainly to gains of $17 million, mostly from the sale of Hemlo shares. (In February, 1992,

Caveat Edper

Bramalea's troubles have deepened long-standing investor fears that the Edper group has hidden problems like those at Olympia and York. If so, we'd probably know by now. But Edper is more diversified than O & Y, and more inclined to give outsiders a financial stake that sharpens their interest. To top it off, Edper has no Canary Wharf.

We've shied away from what we might call the Edper paper-shufflers: Edper itself, Hees, Dexleigh, Canadian Express and Pagurian. We have advised investing in the operating companies—Royal Trustco, Noranda, Trilon, Trizec, Noranda Forest, MacMillan Bloedel, Labatt and Bramalea. This in where we think the hidden values reside.

Edper stocks have suffered lately because they are leveraged, and involved in cyclical industries (minerals and real estate), or ambitious undertakings (Royal Trust's international expansion). These factors will work in their favor when things turn around, assuming they last that long.

We advise, as always, that you diversify your portfolio in a variety of ways. One is to avoid too much exposure to any single investment group like Edper. If you invest in Noranda for a Resource holding, complement it with CP Forest rather than Noranda Forest.

Investment Reporter Quality ratings (safest to riskiest):
Very Conservative; Conservative; Average; Higher Risk; Speculative
©1992 MPL Communications Inc. and Marpep Publishing Limited GST# R121844328
Reproduction allowed only on written permission. Information presented herein, while obtained from sources we believe reliable, is not guaranteed.

The Investment Reporter is published weekly by the Canadian Business Service, a division of Marpep Publishing, Ltd., of Toronto, Canada. A Friday-evening telephone hotline update is made available to all subscribers.

Each weekly issue of *The Investment Reporter* examines a group of stocks in depth, provides overall market commentary, and reports on the value of a number of different Canadian stock and industry indices. Beginning in mid-1991 it also began to provide regular advice on the stocks of U.S. companies. Its investment approach is primarily fundamental, and it takes a relatively long-term view of investing.

The HFD's performance calculations for *The Investment Reporter* are based on recommendations contained in a monthly supplement, entitled *The Investment Planning Guide*. This monthly supplement recommends Canadian stocks in five different risk categories (ranging from "Very Conservative" to "Speculative") and U.S. stocks in four different categories (ranging from "Very Conservative" to "Higher Risk"). The composition of these lists changes very rarely, and when it does it often involves the transfer of a stock from one of the lists to another. (The newsletter's lists of U.S. stocks are not graphed separately in this book, owing to the fact that the HFD didn't begin following them until the beginning of 1992; their performances are included in what is reported for the newsletter's average, however.)

The Investment Reporter does not recommend a specific division of its portfolios between stocks and cash, so the HFD constructs a portfolio for each of the categories that is fully invested at all times. Over the eight and one-half years through mid-1992 that the HFD has data, the best-performing of the five portfolios of Canadian stocks was the newsletter's "Speculative" list, which gained 190.9%. The worst performance of the five was turned in by its "Average Risk" list, with a gain of 99.0%. Over this period, the average gain of these portfolios (along with the newly inaugurated U.S. stock portfolios) was 159.0%, which is below the 206.6% gain for the Wilshire 5000.

The risk levels of each of these five portfolios are not quite in line with what one would expect. To be sure, the "Very Conservative" list is the least risky. But the riskiest of the five over the 18 months through mid-1992 was the service's "Average Risk" rather than its "Speculative" list.

The Investment Reporter (Average)

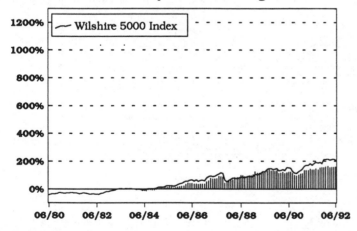

	Gain/Loss
1/1/91 to 6/30/92 (Third Quintile)	+24.8%
1/1/89 to 6/30/92 (Fourth Quintile)	+28.4%
1/1/87 to 6/30/92 (Second Quintile)	+91.5%
1/1/85 to 6/30/92 (Second Quintile)	+175.1%
1/1/83 to 6/30/92	(n/a)
6/30/80 to 6/30/92	(n/a)

Risk: 90% of market

The Investment Reporter
(Portfolio of Very Conservative Stocks)

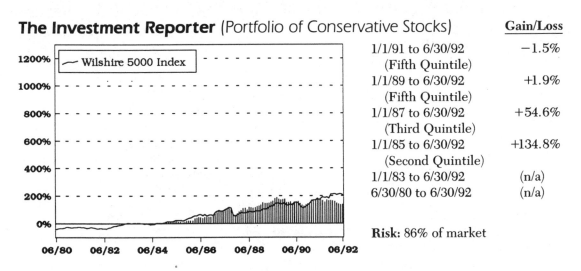

	Gain/Loss
1/1/91 to 6/30/92	+5.2%
(Fifth Quintile)	
1/1/89 to 6/30/92	+11.0%
(Fifth Quintile)	
1/1/87 to 6/30/92	+63.6%
(Second Quintile)	
1/1/85 to 6/30/92	+112.5%
(Third Quintile)	
1/1/83 to 6/30/92	(n/a)
6/30/80 to 6/30/92	(n/a)

Risk: 72% of market

The Investment Reporter (Portfolio of Conservative Stocks)

	Gain/Loss
1/1/91 to 6/30/92	−1.5%
(Fifth Quintile)	
1/1/89 to 6/30/92	+1.9%
(Fifth Quintile)	
1/1/87 to 6/30/92	+54.6%
(Third Quintile)	
1/1/85 to 6/30/92	+134.8%
(Second Quintile)	
1/1/83 to 6/30/92	(n/a)
6/30/80 to 6/30/92	(n/a)

Risk: 86% of market

The Investment Reporter (Portfolio of Average Risk Stocks)

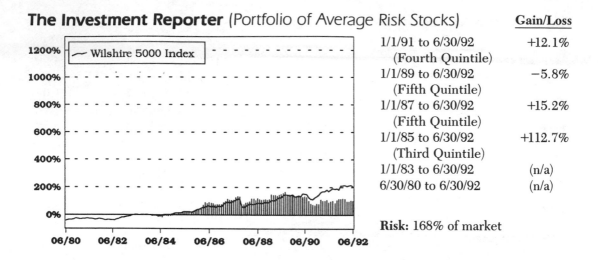

	Gain/Loss
1/1/91 to 6/30/92 (Fourth Quintile)	+12.1%
1/1/89 to 6/30/92 (Fifth Quintile)	−5.8%
1/1/87 to 6/30/92 (Fifth Quintile)	+15.2%
1/1/85 to 6/30/92 (Third Quintile)	+112.7%
1/1/83 to 6/30/92	(n/a)
6/30/80 to 6/30/92	(n/a)

Risk: 168% of market

The Investment Reporter (Portfolio of Higher Risk Stocks)

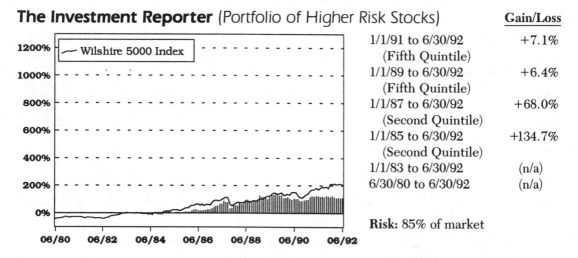

	Gain/Loss
1/1/91 to 6/30/92 (Fifth Quintile)	+7.1%
1/1/89 to 6/30/92 (Fifth Quintile)	+6.4%
1/1/87 to 6/30/92 (Second Quintile)	+68.0%
1/1/85 to 6/30/92 (Second Quintile)	+134.7%
1/1/83 to 6/30/92	(n/a)
6/30/80 to 6/30/92	(n/a)

Risk: 85% of market

The Investment Reporter (Portfolio of Speculative Stocks)

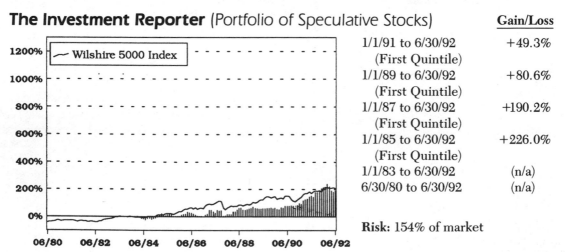

	Gain/Loss
1/1/91 to 6/30/92 (First Quintile)	+49.3%
1/1/89 to 6/30/92 (First Quintile)	+80.6%
1/1/87 to 6/30/92 (First Quintile)	+190.2%
1/1/85 to 6/30/92 (First Quintile)	+226.0%
1/1/83 to 6/30/92	(n/a)
6/30/80 to 6/30/92	(n/a)

Risk: 154% of market

The Investor's Guide to Closed-End Funds

Address
Thomas J. Herzfeld
    Advisors, Inc.
P.O. Box 161465
Miami, FL 33116

Editor
Thomas J. Herzfeld

Phone Number
305-271-1900

Subscription Rates
$ 60.00/2 months
$325.00/year

Telephone Hotline
No

Money Management
Yes

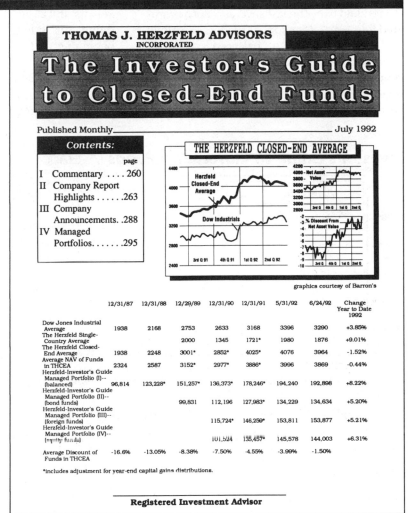

THOMAS J. HERZFELD ADVISORS
INCORPORATED

The Investor's Guide to Closed-End Funds

Published Monthly _____ July 1992

Contents:

THE HERZFELD CLOSED-END AVERAGE

graphics courtesy of Barron's

	12/31/87	12/31/88	12/29/89	12/31/90	12/31/91	5/31/92	6/24/92	Change Year to Date 1992
Dow Jones Industrial Average	1938	2168	2753	2633	3168	3396	3290	+3.85%
The Herzfeld Single-Country Average			2000	1345	1721*	1980	1876	+9.01%
The Herzfeld Closed-End Average	1938	2248	3001*	2852*	4025*	4076	3964	-1.52%
Average NAV of Funds in THCEA	2324	2587	3152*	2977*	3886*	3996	3869	-0.44%
Herzfeld-Investor's Guide Managed Portfolio (I)-- (balanced)	96,814	123,228*	151,257*	136,373*	178,246*	194,240	192,898	+8.22%
Herzfeld-Investor's Guide Managed Portfolio (II)-- (bond funds)			99,831	112,196	127,983*	134,229	134,634	+5.20%
Herzfeld-Investor's Guide Managed Portfolio (III)-- (foreign funds)				115,724*	146,259*	153,811	153,877	+5.21%
Herzfeld-Investor's Guide Managed Portfolio (IV)-- (equity funds)				101,524	135,457*	145,578	144,003	+6.31%
Average Discount of Funds in THCEA	-16.6%	-13.05%	-8.38%	-7.50%	-4.55%	-3.99%	-1.50%	

*includes adjustment for year-end capital gains distributions.

Registered Investment Advisor

The Investor's Guide to Closed-End Funds is published monthly by Thomas J. Herzfeld and is not supplemented by a telephone hotline update. Because the HFD measures this newsletter's performance on the basis of portfolios that take up just two of the 40 or more pages in each issue, readers should be aware that there is more provided in Herzfeld's newsletter than portfolio advice alone. Readers also should be aware that the portfolios recommended in the newsletter are actual portfolios managed by Herzfeld on a day-by-day basis. Since the HFD executes all transactions on the date of receipt of the monthly newsletter, the performances calculated by the HFD will be different from those reported by Herzfeld.

Herzfeld over the last several years has created four separate model portfolios: "Portfolio #1" (which pursues a "balanced" strategy); "Portfolio #2" (designed primarily for income); "Portfolio #3" (focusing on overseas investments); and "Portfolio #4 (which invests only in the U.S. equity market). On aver-age over the three and one-half years through mid-1992, these portfolios gained 39.0% in contrast to the Wilshire 5000's 60.3%.

The HFD calculates that Herzfeld's approach has been substantially less risky than the market as a whole, which partially explains why it didn't make as much as the market itself. Even on a risk-adjusted basis, though, it didn't beat the market from the beginning of 1989 through mid-1992. However, it is in seventh place among 118 newsletters on a risk-adjusted basis over just the 18 months from the beginning of 1991 through mid-1992 (see Appendix A-6).

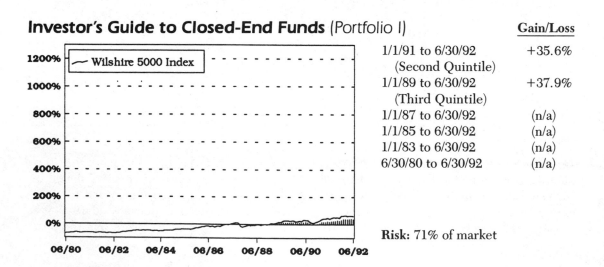

Investor's Guide to Closed-End Funds (Average)

	Gain/Loss
1/1/91 to 6/30/92 (Second Quintile)	+28.9%
1/1/89 to 6/30/92 (Third Quintile)	+39.0%
1/1/87 to 6/30/92	(n/a)
1/1/85 to 6/30/92	(n/a)
1/1/83 to 6/30/92	(n/a)
6/30/80 to 6/30/92	(n/a)

Risk: 59% of market

Investor's Guide to Closed-End Funds (Portfolio I)

	Gain/Loss
1/1/91 to 6/30/92 (Second Quintile)	+35.6%
1/1/89 to 6/30/92 (Third Quintile)	+37.9%
1/1/87 to 6/30/92	(n/a)
1/1/85 to 6/30/92	(n/a)
1/1/83 to 6/30/92	(n/a)
6/30/80 to 6/30/92	(n/a)

Risk: 71% of market

Investor's Guide to Closed-End Funds (Portfolio II)

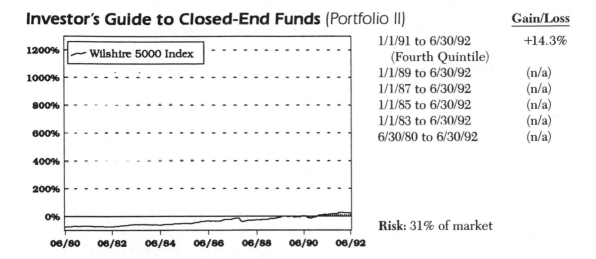

	Gain/Loss
1/1/91 to 6/30/92	+14.3%
(Fourth Quintile)	
1/1/89 to 6/30/92	(n/a)
1/1/87 to 6/30/92	(n/a)
1/1/85 to 6/30/92	(n/a)
1/1/83 to 6/30/92	(n/a)
6/30/80 to 6/30/92	(n/a)

Risk: 31% of market

Investor's Guide to Closed-End Funds (Portfolio III)

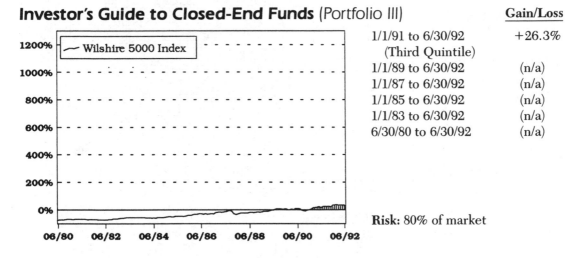

	Gain/Loss
1/1/91 to 6/30/92	+26.3%
(Third Quintile)	
1/1/89 to 6/30/92	(n/a)
1/1/87 to 6/30/92	(n/a)
1/1/85 to 6/30/92	(n/a)
1/1/83 to 6/30/92	(n/a)
6/30/80 to 6/30/92	(n/a)

Risk: 80% of market

Investor's Guide to Closed-End Funds (Portfolio IV)

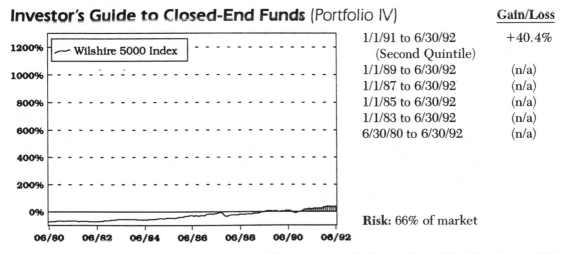

	Gain/Loss
1/1/91 to 6/30/92	+40.4%
(Second Quintile)	
1/1/89 to 6/30/92	(n/a)
1/1/87 to 6/30/92	(n/a)
1/1/85 to 6/30/92	(n/a)
1/1/83 to 6/30/92	(n/a)
6/30/80 to 6/30/92	(n/a)

Risk: 66% of market

Investors Intelligence

Address
Chartcraft, Inc.
P.O. Box 2046
30 Church St.
New Rochelle, NY
10801

Editor
Michael Burke

Phone Number
914-632-0422

Subscription Rates
$ 30.00/2 months
$175.00/year

Telephone Hotline
Yes

Money Management
No

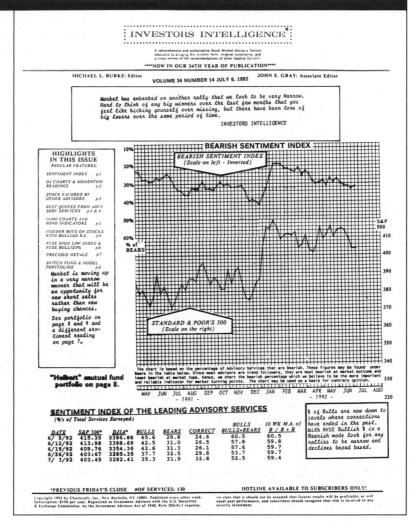

Investors Intelligence is published every two weeks by Chartcraft, Inc., and is supplemented by a telephone hotline. It was started nearly 30 years ago, making it one of the oldest newsletters being published today. It was edited for a number of years by Abraham Cohen; after his death several years ago, the editorship was assumed by Michael Burke.

Investors Intelligence is best known for originating the "Bearish Sentiment Index," which measures bullishness and bearishness among stock market advisory newsletters.

Based on the contrarian theory that the majority of advisers typically are wrong, especially at major market turning points, this service turns bullish as advisory bearishness reaches extremes, and vice versa. A large number of investment newsletters also rely on and make reference to the *Investors Intelligence* tally of advisory sentiment.

Few indicators are flawless, and this one is no exception. The majority of investment newsletter editors, even if they are wrong at market turning points, typically are right during the periods between market turning points. For much of the bull market beginning in 1982, for example, advisory sentiment was at historically extreme bullish levels—and those who followed it in a contrarian way missed much of the bull market. For the record, however, it should be stressed that *Investors Intelligence* does not advise focusing on this one indicator alone. Indeed, in devising its own portfolios, it looks at a number of additional indicators.

At the beginning of 1987, the HFD began following this newsletter's switch fund portfolio. It was out of the market during the October 1987 crash, and it turned in one of the best performances for that year. Over the five and one-half years through mid-1992, during which time the Wilshire 5000 gained 93.3%, this portfolio gained 125.3%. The major credit for beating the market goes to the newsletter's market timing: An investor who invested in hypothetical shares of the Wilshire 5000 in the same proportion that this portfolio invested in mutual funds would have gained 136.1% over this period. This shows that *Investors Intelligence*'s actual fund picks for this portfolio slightly underperformed the market during the times the portfolio owned them.

More recently, the HFD began following four more portfolios recommended by *Investors Intelligence*. Two invest in individual stocks (a "Long-Term" and a "Low-Priced" portfolio) and two invest in mutual funds (both in Fidelity funds, one focusing on international funds and the other on bond funds). Over the two and one-half years through mid-1992 for which the HFD has data for these two stock portfolios, the "Long-Term" portfolio gained 40.4% and the "Low-Priced" portfolio lost 11.9% (in contrast to a 24.1% gain for the Wilshire 5000). Over the 18 months through mid-1992 for which the HFD has data for these two additional fund portfolios, the one focusing on international funds gained 6.0% and the one investing in bond funds gained 23.5% (in contrast to a 32.3% gain for the Wilshire 5000 and a 17.8% gain for the Shearson Lehman Treasury Index).

Investors Intelligence (Average)

	Gain/Loss
1/1/91 to 6/30/92 (Third Quintile)	+23.8%
1/1/89 to 6/30/92 (Fourth Quintile)	+30.2%
1/1/87 to 6/30/92 (First Quintile)	+101.4%
1/1/85 to 6/30/92	(n/a)
1/1/83 to 6/30/92	(n/a)
6/30/80 to 6/30/92	(n/a)

Risk: 71% of market

Investors Intelligence (Fidelity Portfolio [Equity])

	Gain/Loss
1/1/91 to 6/30/92 (Fifth Quintile)	+5.8%
1/1/89 to 6/30/92 (Second Quintile)	+45.6%
1/1/87 to 6/30/92 (First Quintile)	+125.3%
1/1/85 to 6/30/92	(n/a)
1/1/83 to 6/30/92	(n/a)
6/30/80 to 6/30/92	(n/a)

Risk: 50% of market

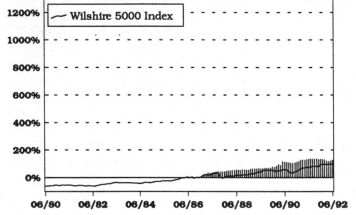

— Wilshire 5000 Index

Investors Intelligence (Long-Term Portfolio)

	Gain/Loss
1/1/91 to 6/30/92 (Third Quintile)	+26.5%
1/1/89 to 6/30/92	(n/a)
1/1/87 to 6/30/92	(n/a)
1/1/85 to 6/30/92	(n/a)
1/1/83 to 6/30/92	(n/a)
6/30/80 to 6/30/92	(n/a)

Risk: 93% of market

— Wilshire 5000 Index

Investors Intelligence (Low-Priced Portfolio)

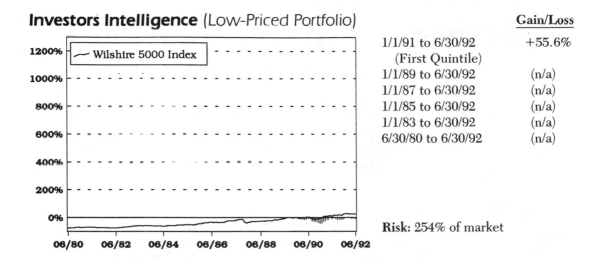

Risk: 254% of market

Investors Intelligence (Fidelity Portfolio [International])

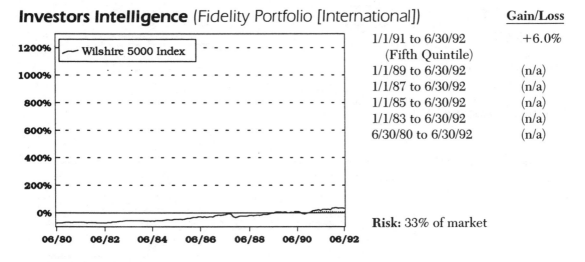

Risk: 33% of market

Investors Intelligence (Fidelity Portfolio [Bond])

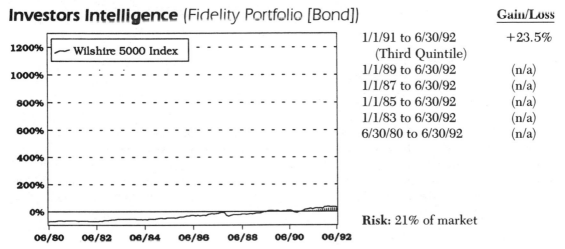

Risk: 21% of market

Kinsman's Telephone Growth & Income Service

Address
P.O. Box 2107
Sonoma, CA
95476-2107

Editor
Robert Kinsman

Phone Number
707-935-6504

Subscription Rates
$145.00/year

Telephone Hotline
Yes

Money Management
Yes

Robert Kinsman's
Telephone GROWTH & INCOME SERVICE
Your Instant-Access Advisor

VOLUME 2, NUMBER 7   JULY 1992

REVERTING TO THE PAST?

Let's be blunt about it. The July 2 cut to 3% in the FED's key discount rate re-raises the specter of 1929-31. The economy doesn't seem to be responding any better to rate cuts lately than it did then. The jobless picture in both periods underscores this.

Here are the facts. The FED cut the discount rate in eight steps from 6% in Nov. 1929 to 1.5% in May 1931 -- a 75% slash in 18 months. Those actions have since been termed "pushing on a string" because they had about that effect on the economy.

In the past 18 month stretch the FED has cut the discount rate from 7% to 3%, almost 60%, and the string analogy seems again right.

Why isn't the economy being stimulated by the rate cuts now? Is something happening that is very similar to the 1930s? After all, rate cuts have worked in bringing us out of eight straight recessions since WW II.

Key Factors

First, the economy is responding **some** now. The economic numbers clearly do not show a continuing slide. There was a true rebound in the first quarter and more recent figures show a flatter, but still upward tilt.

Unfortunately, the economy was flat by mid-1931, too.

A second factor is the **type** of recession we are now in. It isn't the standard post-WW II bust from an inflation or business boom. It's what's being called a "balance sheet" recession: One where individuals, corporations and the government are over-leveraged with debt.

That was a key element in the Thirties Depression, too. Inflation was **not** a problem going into that debacle. Nor was business over-extended. But stock margin was, and so was aggregate debt.

When the combination of rising interest rates in August 1929, the stock market Crash of October, and later world banking system contractions led to a business downturn, there wasn't the wherewithal to rebound. Money wasn't being borrowed at almost any interest rate.

That inability to respond is running a very close parallel to current conditions, even though the reasons differ in the two periods.

One bottom line: It appears that now as then, interest rate cuts aren't the whole answer to what ails the economy. They may help, but they need a boost.

Another parallel: Fighting inflation was the watchword for FED policy in the early Thirties. You will find it mentioned frequently in FED and government officials' statements of the day.

This was despite the fact that the Consumer Price Index was virtually unchanged from 1922 to 1929-30.

The irony is that aside from the Gulf War's brief inflation spurt, the inflation growth rate has been declining for the past two years. And still FED governors, including Chairman Greenspan, state they want it reduced.

> No question, then, that certain key economic parallels between today and the early Thirties are striking.

The Oddity

The notable oddity between the two periods is that stock prices have recently been close to highs where they were plunging in the days of 1930-31.

That's easily explainable, if potentially mistaken now.

The reason is post-WW II history. In eight recessions and recoveries, lower interest rates have always equated with higher stock prices. Never mind that they didn't in the Thirties. Nearly all the economists and stock analysts now working were trained in the post-War era. Experience, not their studies, has taught the strongest lesson.

What's more, there is strong theory that says this should be so. (You can check it in my "...Always A Bull Market" book, pp. 56-60.) In short words, it says that declining interest rates mathematically cause higher stock **values**.

Of course, translating values into prices requires another step. In the Thirties that didn't happen because while values were increasing, prospects for better company earnings and balance sheets weren't. So they got increasingly better values at increasingly lower prices -- a double-barreled dive.

Kinsman's Telephone Growth & Income Service is published monthly by Robert Kinsman and is supplemented by a telephone hotline that is updated at least once each week (and more often when needed). It is the successor to a previous newsletter Kinsman published, *Kinsman's Low-Risk Growth Letter.*

Kinsman's approach is a combination of both fundamental and technical analysis. He orients his advice to those for whom preservation of capital is paramount. Kinsman recommends several model portfolios in his newsletter. One, a "Growth & Income" portfolio, is the one for which the HFD has the most data (dating back to mid-1980). A second portfolio is a mutual fund switch plan which pursues more or less the same asset allocation strategy as Kinsman's "Growth & Income" portfolio. Kinsman used to recommend an "Aggressive" portfolio, which, though it exists no longer, is included in what the HFD reports for the newsletter's average.

The HFD reports a gain of 134.9% for Kinsman's "Growth & Income" portfolio for the twelve years through mid-1992, in contrast to a 432.7% gain for the Wilshire 5000 and a 159.4% gain for T-Bills. The fact that the portfolio underperformed the average stock is not that surprising, owing to its very low risk. However, because it also underperformed risk-free T-Bills, this portfolio's risk-adjusted performance actually is negative.

The HFD has data for Kinsman's mutual fund portfolio beginning in 1988. Over the four and one-half years through mid-1992, his mutual fund portfolio gained 25.9%, in contrast to an 89.0% gain for the Wilshire 5000 and a 33.7% gain for T-Bills.

Kinsman's Telephone Growth & Income Service (Average)

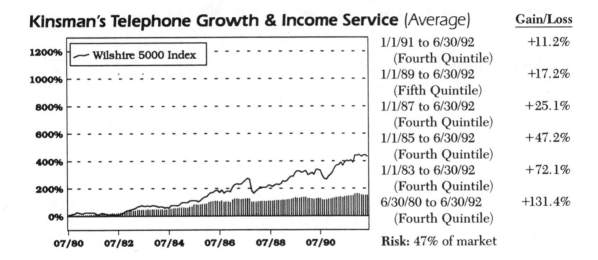

	Gain/Loss
1/1/91 to 6/30/92 (Fourth Quintile)	+11.2%
1/1/89 to 6/30/92 (Fifth Quintile)	+17.2%
1/1/87 to 6/30/92 (Fourth Quintile)	+25.1%
1/1/85 to 6/30/92 (Fourth Quintile)	+47.2%
1/1/83 to 6/30/92 (Fourth Quintile)	+72.1%
6/30/80 to 6/30/92 (Fourth Quintile)	+131.4%

Risk: 47% of market

Kinsman's Telephone Growth & Income Service
(Growth & Income Portfolio)

	Gain/Loss
1/1/91 to 6/30/92 (Fourth Quintile)	+9.6%
1/1/89 to 6/30/92 (Fifth Quintile)	+16.0%
1/1/87 to 6/30/92 (Fourth Quintile)	+23.6%
1/1/85 to 6/30/92 (Fourth Quintile)	+49.4%
1/1/83 to 6/30/92 (Fourth Quintile)	+74.7%
6/30/80 to 6/30/92 (Fourth Quintile)	+134.9%

Risk: 47% of market

Kinsman's Telephone Growth & Income Service
(Mutual Fund Switch Portfolio)

	Gain/Loss
1/1/91 to 6/30/92 (Fourth Quintile)	+12.7%
1/1/89 to 6/30/92 (Fifth Quintile)	+18.2%
1/1/87 to 6/30/92	(n/a)
1/1/85 to 6/30/92	(n/a)
1/1/83 to 6/30/92	(n/a)
6/30/80 to 6/30/92	(n/a)

Risk: 52% of market

L/G No-Load Fund Analyst

Address
300 Montgomery St.
Suite 621
San Francisco, CA
  94104

Editors
Ken Gregory and
  Craig Litman

Phone Number
415-989-8513

Subscription Rates
$169.00/year

Telephone Hotline
No

Money Management
Yes

L/G No-Load Fund Analyst

300 Montgomery Street, Suite 621, San Francisco, CA 94104 (415) 989-8513

JULY 1992 — Volume 4, Number 7

L/G No-Load Fund Analyst is published monthly by Ken Gregory and Craig Litman. The service does not include a telephone hotline update.

Much of the service is devoted to a comprehensive summary of the approach and past performance of each of a number of no-load mutual funds. One of the unique features of their analysis of these funds is their measurement of risk in unconventional ways. Gregory and Litman feel that the standard academic definition that equates risk with volatility is inadequate, and they prefer instead to define risk as the probability of loss. Their risk measurements thus show the percentage of time that each fund has shown a loss when held for various lengths of time.

Gregory and Litman construct four model portfolios of mutual funds. Their portfolios "A" and "B" are the most conservative, and they are designed to have a "very low probability" of loss over any two-year period. Their portfolio "C" is intended to be more of a total-return portfolio, and their portfolio "D" is designed to be fully invested most of the time. All four portfolios have below-average volatility, however: even their portfolio "D" has been 10% less volatile than the Wilshire 5000.

Over the two and one-half years through mid-1992, these four portfolios gained an average of 21.5%, which contrasts with a gain of 24.1% for the Wilshire 5000. If we take into account the fact that Gregory and Litman's portfolios incurred significantly less risk than the market as a whole, however, their performances equaled the market's.

L/G No-Load Fund Analyst (Average)

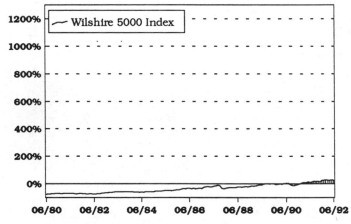

	Gain/Loss
1/1/91 to 6/30/92	+25.6%
(Third Quintile)	
1/1/89 to 6/30/92	(n/a)
1/1/87 to 6/30/92	(n/a)
1/1/85 to 6/30/92	(n/a)
1/1/83 to 6/30/92	(n/a)
6/30/80 to 6/30/92	(n/a)

Risk: 60% of market

L/G No-Load Fund Analyst (Portfolio A)

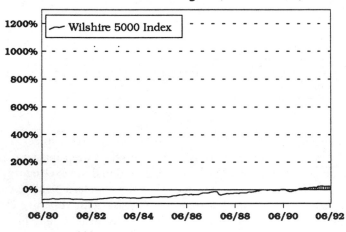

	Gain/Loss
1/1/91 to 6/30/92	+24.7%
(Third Quintile)	
1/1/89 to 6/30/92	(n/a)
1/1/87 to 6/30/92	(n/a)
1/1/85 to 6/30/92	(n/a)
1/1/83 to 6/30/92	(n/a)
6/30/80 to 6/30/92	(n/a)

Risk: 35% of market

L/G No-Load Fund Analyst (Portfolio B)

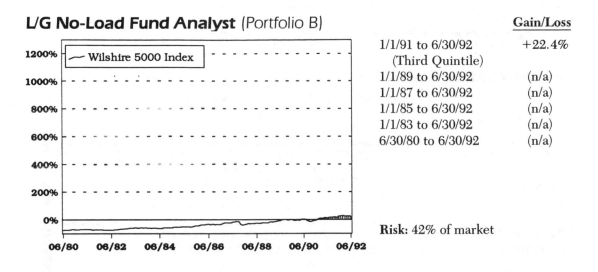

	Gain/Loss
1/1/91 to 6/30/92	+22.4%
(Third Quintile)	
1/1/89 to 6/30/92	(n/a)
1/1/87 to 6/30/92	(n/a)
1/1/85 to 6/30/92	(n/a)
1/1/83 to 6/30/92	(n/a)
6/30/80 to 6/30/92	(n/a)

Risk: 42% of market

L/G No-Load Fund Analyst (Portfolio C)

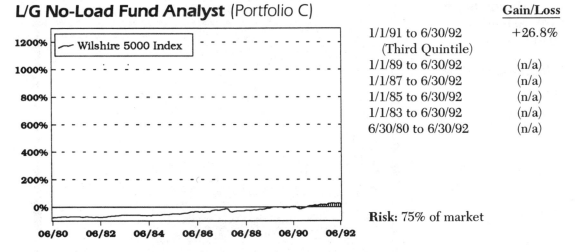

	Gain/Loss
1/1/91 to 6/30/92	+26.8%
(Third Quintile)	
1/1/89 to 6/30/92	(n/a)
1/1/87 to 6/30/92	(n/a)
1/1/85 to 6/30/92	(n/a)
1/1/83 to 6/30/92	(n/a)
6/30/80 to 6/30/92	(n/a)

Risk: 75% of market

L/G No-Load Fund Analyst (Portfolio D)

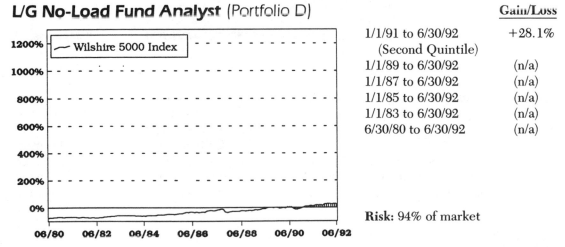

	Gain/Loss
1/1/91 to 6/30/92	+28.1%
(Second Quintile)	
1/1/89 to 6/30/92	(n/a)
1/1/87 to 6/30/92	(n/a)
1/1/85 to 6/30/92	(n/a)
1/1/83 to 6/30/92	(n/a)
6/30/80 to 6/30/92	(n/a)

Risk: 94% of market

LaLoggia's Special Situation Report

Address
P.O. Box 167
Rochester, NY 14601

Editor
Charles LaLoggia

Phone Number
716-232-1240

Subscription Rates
$125.00/6 months
$230.00/year

Telephone Hotline
No

Money Management
No

LaLoggia's

SPECIAL SITUATION REPORT AND STOCK MARKET FORECAST

July 17, 1992

P.O. Box 167, Rochester, N.Y. 14601   6 Months: $125   1 Year: $230

Gaming And Gold Stocks Are The Best Bets As The Economy Begins To Weaken Again

What's wrong with the stock market? Why are most stocks far below their 1991 highs even though the Fed has once again cut the discount rate, taking short-term rates to their lowest levels in 30 years? Why are **30-year** Treasury Bonds stuck at their same levels of March 1989, when 3-month Treasury Bills were yielding 9%? Why is gold sneaking higher, and why have certain gold stocks broken out to new highs? The answer to all of these questions, we believe, is that some sort of economic crisis is brewing which will probably become apparent after the election. The Fed has now used up virtually all of its interest rate ammunition, yet the latest series of economic numbers clearly show that the economy remains mired in recession.

Plunging Money Supply Growth Means the Economic News Will Get Worse As Election Day Approaches

The unemployment rate jumped sharply last month, housing is turning down again, auto sales are still weak and retail sales are not even keeping up with inflation. Meanwhile, the money supply growth rate is plunging once again, a strong clue that the economic numbers will get worse as we approach the election. Our opinion is that a new economic crisis, probably involving renewed weakness in real estate, will emerge after the election. We do not share the view that "the worst is over" for the banking system, and we believe the next round of real estate price weakness will cause major problems for insurance companies such as CIGNA (CI) and AETNA (AET), both of which are on our short sale list and both of which have major exposure to commercial real estate. We believe renewed economic weakness will cause tax receipts to fall far below expectations, pushing the federal deficit sharply higher and leading to rising interest rates at the worst possible time for the economy. (As an aside, we believe lower tax revenues will force more states to legalize video lottery and casino gambling in order to raise revenues -- see page 3). The bottom line here is that if the economy were going to recover it would have done so already. The

LaLoggia's Special Situation Report is published every three weeks by Charles LaLoggia and is not supplemented by a telephone hotline update.

LaLoggia is perhaps best known for the niche he has created within the newsletter industry: focusing on those companies that are likely takeover targets. Several years ago LaLoggia initiated a portfolio in his letter entitled "Master List of Takeover Candidates" and the HFD has been monitoring this portfolio since the beginning of 1984 (the portfolio has since expanded beyond takeover stocks, but this remains one of its focuses). Over the subsequent eight and one-half years the portfolio gained 117.2%, in contrast to a 206.6% gain for the Wilshire 5000.

The major culprit in this underperformance appears to be LaLoggia's timing advice. A portfolio that invested in hypothetical shares of the Wilshire 5000 in the same proportion as LaLoggia's "Master List" invested in individual stocks gained 122.5% over these eight and one-half years, only slightly more than the portfolio actually gained and still well less than the 206.6% gain of the Wilshire 5000.

More recently LaLoggia has created a second portfolio, this one a trading portfolio. Unlike his other portfolio, which is based almost entirely on fundamental analysis of the individual companies, this trading portfolio is based exclusively on LaLoggia's technical analysis. Over the six and one-half years through mid-1992, the trading portfolio gained 25.3% in contrast to a 124.5% gain for the Wilshire 5000.

LaLoggia's Special Situation Report (Average)

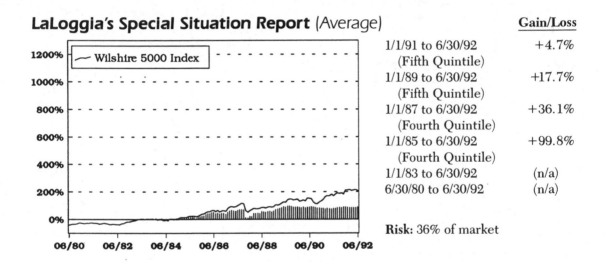

	Gain/Loss
1/1/91 to 6/30/92	+4.7%
(Fifth Quintile)	
1/1/89 to 6/30/92	+17.7%
(Fifth Quintile)	
1/1/87 to 6/30/92	+36.1%
(Fourth Quintile)	
1/1/85 to 6/30/92	+99.8%
(Fourth Quintile)	
1/1/83 to 6/30/92	(n/a)
6/30/80 to 6/30/92	(n/a)

Risk: 36% of market

LaLoggia's Special Situation Report
(Master List of Recommended Stocks)

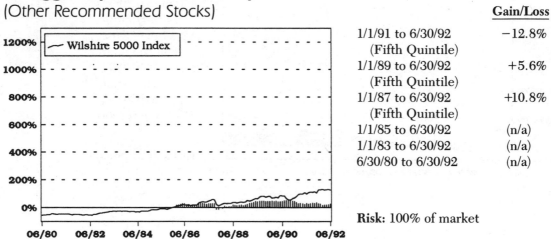

	Gain/Loss
1/1/91 to 6/30/92 (Third Quintile)	+23.9%
1/1/89 to 6/30/92 (Fourth Quintile)	+28.1%
1/1/87 to 6/30/92 (Third Quintile)	+60.7%
1/1/85 to 6/30/92 (Third Quintile)	+131.9%
1/1/83 to 6/30/92	(n/a)
6/30/80 to 6/30/92	(n/a)

Risk: 51% of market

LaLoggia's Special Situation Report
(Other Recommended Stocks)

	Gain/Loss
1/1/91 to 6/30/92 (Fifth Quintile)	−12.8%
1/1/89 to 6/30/92 (Fifth Quintile)	+5.6%
1/1/87 to 6/30/92 (Fifth Quintile)	+10.8%
1/1/85 to 6/30/92	(n/a)
1/1/83 to 6/30/92	(n/a)
6/30/80 to 6/30/92	(n/a)

Risk: 100% of market

MPT Fund Review

Address
P.O. Box 5695
Incline Village, NV
89450

Editors
Bruno Terkaly and
Treanna Allbaugh

Phone Number
702-831-1396

Subscription Rates
$39.00/2 months
$95.00/year

Telephone Hotline
No

Money Management
Yes

MPT Fund Review
Specializing in Modern Portfolio Theory

P.O. Box 5695• Incline Village, Nevada 89450-5695 • (510) 527-5116 • Hotline (914) 278-3009
Publisher Navellier & Associates Inc. Editors: Bruno Terkaly & Treanna Allbaugh

July 1992

MPT Fund Review's Index portfolio gained 60% in 1991, versus only 24% for the Dow Jones Industrial Average, according to *Hulbert Financial Digest* ratings.

Investment Outlook & Strategy

Bonds Rally on Interest Rate Cut
The Federal Reserve's discount rate cut on July 2nd ignited an enormous rally for both bonds and utility stocks. The current discount rate of 3.0% is the lowest rate in almost 30 years. Bonds and utilities have rallied impressively since April and should help lead the overall stock market higher. *Bonds and utility averages are among the best leading stock market indicators.* Normally, the overall stock market rallies within six weeks of the start of an impressive bond market rally. Based on historical trends, the stock market should have rallied strongly in late May or early June. Instead, most stocks were subjected to relentless selling pressure in June. Last month's sell-off occurred on low volume, which is indicative that most of the selling pressure has been exhausted. An explosive stock market rally is now long overdue.

The lower discount rate prompted banks to lower their prime rate to 6.0%, the lowest rate in 15 years. The Discount rate is the interest rate which the Federal Reserve charges other member banks. The Prime rate is the interest rate which banks charge their best corporate customers.

Second Quarter Earnings to be Released
The other reason stocks are likely to rally strongly in July is that the second quarter earnings that will be released, commencing in mid-July, are anticipated to be far better than Wall Street's expectations. The first quarter earnings were characterized by the best earnings growth in four years and the best earnings "surprises" in more than two years. After a correction of more than 20% in the OTC Industrials since February, bearish sentiment is now rampant on Wall Street. There are far too many pessimistic predictions now circulating on Wall Street and the environment is perfect for tremendous second quarter earnings surprises that will exceed Wall Street's estimates.

About the only industry sectors that might disappoint Wall Street are the large capitalization cyclical stocks that rallied so impressively earlier this year. Outside of Goodyear Tire and a few other large capitalization special situations, most large cyclical stocks will not be characterized by impressive earnings growth until the third and fourth quarters, so there will be very little additional good news to drive these large capitalization stocks higher. Since these large cyclical stocks have outrun their near-term earnings expectations, investors will naturally turn to the small capitalization growth

stocks to resume leading the stock market.

Growth Stocks to Strengthen: Bullish
Growth-related strategies have been out of favor most of this year and it is highly unusual for growth strategies to underperform the stock market for more than a three-to-four month period. Consequently, stock selection strategies based on earnings growth are now overdue to resume outperforming the stock market. Most of the downside risk associated with growth stocks has been exhausted.

Heavier Volume Will Indicate a Rally
The key to the resurgence in growth stocks is for volume to expand. The trading volume in many small capitalization stocks has become dangerously thin in the past few months as many stocks drifted lower on precipitously light trading volume. What most small growth stocks need is for something to "spark" interest in these stocks and cause the trading volume to expand.

The most logical spark is likely to be the positive second quarter earnings that will be released during a six-week period from mid-July through August. A very small trading volume increase in late June and early July caused the OTC Industrials to surge over 4% in only three trading days! In other words, many small growth stocks are on the brink of an explosive rally and all that is needed to ignite the rally is an increase in trading volume.

The lowest long-term and short-term interest rates in nearly three decades have many consequences for the stock market. First, the stock market's main competitor for capital, the bond market, is less attractive due to bonds' lower yields. Second, as interest rates fall, price/earnings ratios rise, allowing stocks to continue appreciating. Third, the low interest rate environment is ideal for spurring economic growth and fueling corporate earnings growth.

(continued on page 4)

MPT Fund Review's Annualized Return	
Index portfolio	28%
Aggressive portfolio	24%
Selective portfolio	19%
Balanced portfolio	16%
S&P 500 Index	14%

MPT Fund Review is published monthly and is not supplemented by a telephone hotline update. It is edited by Bruno Terkaly and Treanna Allbaugh and is published by Navellier & Associates (which publishes *MPT Review*, reviewed elsewhere in this *Guide*).

MPT Fund Review initially focused exclusively on mutual funds, but more recently has expanded the scope of its model portfolios to include both mutual funds and stocks. In addition to the four model portfolios graphed separately here, the newsletter used to have a fifth portfolio that focused on income; while it has been discontinued, its performance is included in what is reported for the newsletter's average.

Like its sister publication *MPT Review*, this newsletter's rating system focuses on risk-adjusted performance (or return per unit of risk). For example, a stock or mutual fund will be rated higher than another in the event that it has gained more than the second with no more risk, or has gained just as much as the second with less risk. Each issue of *MPT Fund Review* ranks a universe of about 100 mutual funds according to their risk-adjusted performance over the past year. Their model portfolios are constructed out of the funds and stocks rated highest by their ranking system, consistent with maintaining adequate portfolio diversification.

Over the three and one-half years through mid-1992, *MPT Fund Review*'s average performance was a gain of 59.3%, just barely below the 60.3% gain for the Wilshire 5000. The newsletter also underperformed the market slightly on a risk-adjusted basis.

Over this period of time, its best-performing portfolio was its "Optimal Aggressive Strategy" portfolio, with a gain of 70.2%, and its poorest performer was its "Optimal Balanced Strategy," with a gain of 42.5%.

MPT Fund Review (Average)

	Gain/Loss
1/1/91 to 6/30/92 (Second Quintile)	+36.5%
1/1/89 to 6/30/92 (Second Quintile)	+59.3%
1/1/87 to 6/30/92	(n/a)
1/1/85 to 6/30/92	(n/a)
1/1/83 to 6/30/92	(n/a)
6/30/80 to 6/30/92	(n/a)

Risk: 129% of market

MPT Fund Review (Optimal Selective Strategy)

	Gain/Loss
1/1/91 to 6/30/92 (Second Quintile)	+32.5%
1/1/89 to 6/30/92 (Second Quintile)	+48.4%
1/1/87 to 6/30/92	(n/a)
1/1/85 to 6/30/92	(n/a)
1/1/83 to 6/30/92	(n/a)
6/30/80 to 6/30/92	(n/a)

Risk: 139% of market

MPT Fund Review (Optimal Balanced Strategy)

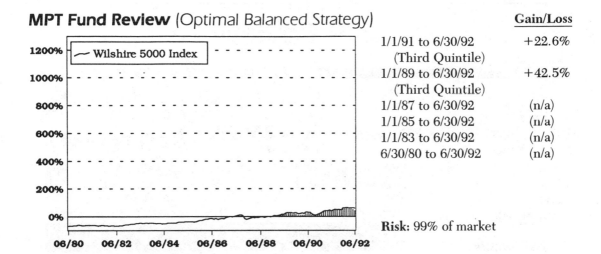

	Gain/Loss
1/1/91 to 6/30/92	+22.6%
(Third Quintile)	
1/1/89 to 6/30/92	+42.5%
(Third Quintile)	
1/1/87 to 6/30/92	(n/a)
1/1/85 to 6/30/92	(n/a)
1/1/83 to 6/30/92	(n/a)
6/30/80 to 6/30/92	(n/a)

Risk: 99% of market

MPT Fund Review (Optimal Aggressive Strategy)

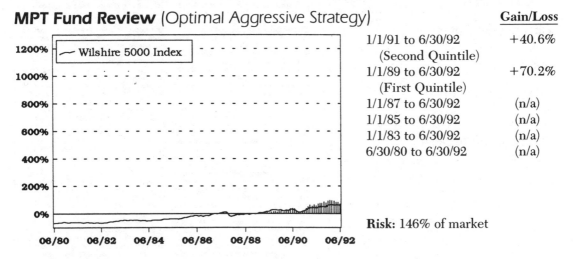

	Gain/Loss
1/1/91 to 6/30/92	+40.6%
(Second Quintile)	
1/1/89 to 6/30/92	+70.2%
(First Quintile)	
1/1/87 to 6/30/92	(n/a)
1/1/85 to 6/30/92	(n/a)
1/1/83 to 6/30/92	(n/a)
6/30/80 to 6/30/92	(n/a)

Risk: 146% of market

MPT Fund Review (Optimal Index-Plus Strategy)

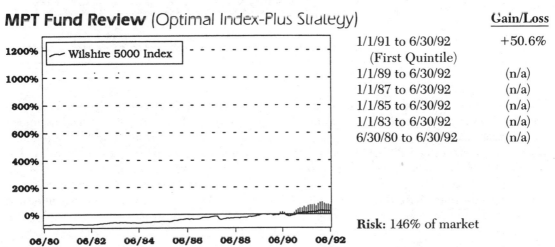

	Gain/Loss
1/1/91 to 6/30/92	+50.6%
(First Quintile)	
1/1/89 to 6/30/92	(n/a)
1/1/87 to 6/30/92	(n/a)
1/1/85 to 6/30/92	(n/a)
1/1/83 to 6/30/92	(n/a)
6/30/80 to 6/30/92	(n/a)

Risk: 146% of market

MPT Review

Address
P.O. Box 5695
Incline Village, NV
89450

Editor
Louis Navellier

Phone Number
702-831-1396

Subscription Rates
$ 59.00/2 months
$245.00/year

Telephone Hotline
Yes

Money Management
Yes

Louis Navellier's
MPT Review
Specializing in Modern Portfolio Theory

The Nation's #1 Advisory Service (**up 954%**) from 1985 through 1991 as rated by *The Hulbert Financial Digest*

P.O. Box 5695 • Incline Village, Nevada 89450-5695 • (702) 831-7800
Available Electronically via NewsNet (215-527-8030)
Available by Fax & Electronically through Compuserve via Investors News Forum (505-474-0098)

July 1992

Investment Outlook & Strategy

The Federal Reserve's Discount Rate cut on July 2nd ignited an enormous rally for both bonds and utility stocks. Bonds and utilities have rallied impressively since April and should help lead the overall stock market higher. Bonds and utility averages are among the best leading stock market indicators. Normally, the overall stock market rallies within six weeks of the start of an impressive bond market rally. Based on historical trends, the stock market should have rallied strongly in late May or early June. Instead, most stocks were subjected to relentless selling pressure in June. Last month's sell-off occurred on low volume, which is indicative that most of the selling pressure has been exhausted. An explosive stock market rally is now long overdue.

The other reason stocks are likely to rally strongly in July is that the second quarter earnings that will be released, commencing in mid-July, are anticipated to be far better than Wall Street's expectations. The first quarter earnings were characterized by the best earnings growth in four years and the best earnings "surprises" in more than two years. After a correction of more than 20% in the OTC Industrials since February, bearish sentiment is now rampant on Wall Street. There are far too many pessimistic predictions now circulating on Wall Street and the environment is perfect for tremendous second quarter earnings surprises that will exceed Wall Street's estimates. About the only industry sectors that might disappoint Wall Street are the large capitalization cyclical stocks that rallied so impressively earlier this year. Outside of Goodyear Tire and a few other large capitalization special situations, most large cyclical stocks will not be characterized by impressive earnings growth until the third and fourth quarters, so there will be very little additional good news to drive these large capitalization stocks higher. Since these large cyclical stocks have outrun their near-term earnings expectations, investors will naturally turn to the small capitalization growth stocks to resume leading the stock market.

Growth-related strategies have been out of favor most of this year and it is highly unusual for growth strategies to underperform the stock market for more than a three-to-four month period. Consequently, stock selection strategies based on earnings growth are now overdue to resume outperforming the stock market. Most of the downside risk associated with growth stocks has been exhausted. The key to the resurgence in growth stocks is for volume to expand. The trading volume in many small capitalization stocks has become dangerously thin in the past few months as many stocks drifted lower on precipitously light trading volume. What most small growth stocks need is for something to "spark" interest in these stocks and cause the trading volume to expand. The most logical spark is likely to be the positive second quarter earnings that will be released during a six-week period from mid-July through August. A very small trading volume increase in late June and early July caused the OTC Industrials to surge over 4% in only three trading days! In other words, many small growth stocks are on the brink of an explosive rally and all that is needed to ignite the rally is an increase in trading volume.

The lowest long-term and short-term interest rates in nearly three decades have many profound consequences for the stock market. First, the stock market's main competitor for capital, namely the bond market, will help stocks as more investors in search of higher yields allocate more of their capital to stocks. Second, as interest rates fall, price/earnings ratios rise, allowing stocks to continue appreciating. Third, the low interest rate environment is ideal for spurring economic growth and fueling corporate earnings growth. One of the most striking characteristics about the current interest rate environment is that the yield spread between short-term and long-term interest rates is over 400 basis points, which is also a record. This dramatic yield spread, caused by low inflation and very low short-term interest rates, holds the (continued on page 14)

MPT Review is published monthly by Louis Navellier and supplemented by a telephone hotline that is updated once per week and more often if necessary. Navellier does not use the hotline to make portfolio changes, however.

Prior to publishing *MPT Review*, Navellier was editor of *OTC Insight* (also rated in this volume). In July 1986 James Collins joined with Navellier to produce *OTC Insight*, in a partnership that lasted one year. Navellier has published *MPT Review* on his own since August 1987, during which time Collins has published *OTC Insight* by himself. Navellier and

Collins have agreed that the performance for *OTC Insight* up until its August 1987 issue belongs exclusively to Navellier and *MPT Review*, and that the *OTC Insight* record beginning with the August 1987 issue belongs exclusively to Collins. The figures reported in this book reflect this agreement.

Not surprisingly, *MPT Review* and *OTC Insight* take similar approaches to investing: Both favor stocks that have gained the most over the previous year with the least amount of volatility. *MPT Review*, however, has expanded its focus to include exchange-listed stocks in addition to those trading over-the-counter.

Navellier keeps his model portfolios fully invested at all times and does not engage in any explicit market timing. However, he attempts to increase or decrease the average beta (riskiness) of his recommended stocks as perceived market risk changes.

MPT Review has had an outstanding track record. Despite suffering through the Crash of 1987 in a fully invested posture, the newsletter is in first place for performance over the seven and one-half years through mid-1992 that the HFD tracked it. The HFD calculates

its average performance to be a gain of 821.7%, in contrast to 197.6% for the Wilshire 5000. Though Navellier's strategy is riskier than the market, it also is in first place over this period on a risk-adjusted basis.

Keep in mind, however, that Navellier's portfolios could be big losers during a bear market (high relative-strength stocks, which Navellier's approach favors, tend to be big losers when the market falls). During just the month of October 1987, for example, *MPT Review* lost 35.6%. Navellier's system doesn't promise to make money in a bear market, but he hopes he can beat the market over an entire cycle. You probably ought to be prepared to invest for at least that time horizon before following this newsletter.

Navellier recommends 12 separate model portfolios in his newsletter, divided into three risk categories ("Conservative," "Moderate Risk," and "Aggressive"). Owing to the fact that the four portfolios within each risk category (which vary only according to total dollar size) have very similar performances, it is their average performances that are graphed in this book.

MPT Review (Average)

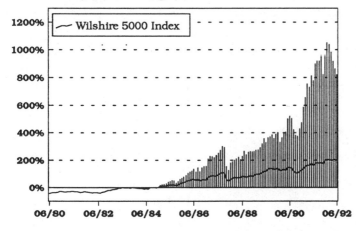

	Gain/Loss
1/1/91 to 6/30/92 (First Quintile)	+60.9%
1/1/89 to 6/30/92 (First Quintile)	+154.0%
1/1/87 to 6/30/92 (First Quintile)	+261.7%
1/1/85 to 6/30/92 (First Quintile)	+821.7%
1/1/83 to 6/30/92	(n/a)
6/30/80 to 6/30/92	(n/a)

Risk: 226% of market

MPT Review (Conservative Portfolio Average)

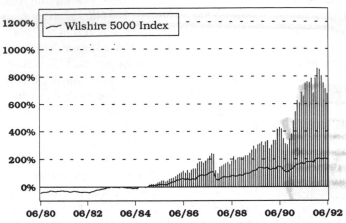

	Gain/Loss
1/1/91 to 6/30/92 (First Quintile)	+61.0%
1/1/89 to 6/30/92 (First Quintile)	+145.6%
1/1/87 to 6/30/92 (First Quintile)	+236.1%
1/1/85 to 6/30/92 (First Quintile)	+673.2%
1/1/83 to 6/30/92	(n/a)
6/30/80 to 6/30/92	(n/a)

Risk: 226% of market

MPT Review (Moderately Aggressive Portfolio Average)

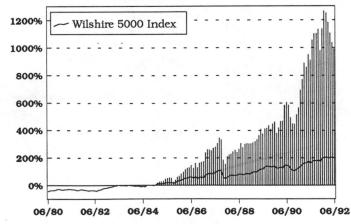

	Gain/Loss
1/1/91 to 6/30/92 (First Quintile)	+57.8%
1/1/89 to 6/30/92 (First Quintile)	+145.7%
1/1/87 to 6/30/92 (First Quintile)	+248.4%
1/1/85 to 6/30/92 (First Quintile)	+810.8%
1/1/83 to 6/30/92	(n/a)
6/30/80 to 6/30/92	(n/a)

Risk: 225% of market

MPT Review (Aggressive Portfolio Average)

	Gain/Loss
1/1/91 to 6/30/92 (First Quintile)	+64.1%
1/1/89 to 6/30/92 (First Quintile)	+171.1%
1/1/87 to 6/30/92 (First Quintile)	+302.3%
1/1/85 to 6/30/92 (First Quintile)	+990.7%
1/1/83 to 6/30/92	(n/a)
6/30/80 to 6/30/92	(n/a)

Risk: 229% of market

Margo's Market Monitor

Address
P.O. Box 642
Lexington, MA 02173

Editor
Bill Doane

Phone Number
617-861-0302

Subscription Rates
$ 25.00/4 issues
$125.00/year

Telephone Hotline
No

Money Management
Yes

"MARGO" PARRISH
EDITOR

WILLIAM S. DOANE
CONTRIBUTING EDITOR

Margo's Market Monitor

P.O. BOX 642 LEXINGTON, MASS. 02173
REGISTERED WITH THE S.E.C. AS AN INVESTMENT ADVISOR

Issue Number 285   July 10, 1992

    The Stock Market. We began the last issue with the caption, "Nearing an Over-sold." That issue was one day away from the exact interim low on the Dow Jones Transportation Average and one day away from an important low on the Utility Average. In fact the Utility Average, as we've so often commented, invariably acts as a harbinger of things to come in the Industrial Average.

    The Bellwether Utility Average. Because utility companies borrow so much money, the fortunes of the companies are very sensitive to changes in the cost of borrowing money--interest rates. Low rates will, of course, favorably affect their bottom line. Their common stocks, therefore, are quick to reflect changes in not only the level but also the direction of interest rates. It is not only the changes, but more importantly, the perceived changes that influence the behavior of the Utility Average. The price action of the Dow Jones Utility Average, therefore, reflects the opinions and expectations of a whole mass of astute investors. It often anticipates changes weeks, sometimes months in advance. Since the stock market, in general, thrives on low (and trending lower) interest rates and is dampened by high and rising rates, the action of the Utility Average is a helpful tool in analysis, especially during times when the trend in the Industrial sector is cloudy, murky or otherwise uncertain. Our present opinion is, therefore, that although longer-term negatives have not gone away shorter-term positives suggest that the market is oversold and that a recovery move of some importance could get underway at any moment. This would be in keeping with the historical tendency for prices to rally (in Election years) from the mid summer into the fourth quarter.

    The Investor's Daily Mutual Fund Index. This graph shows, of course, that the average mutual fund is down over 8% for the year. But, unlike other averages, this very representative index shows the weakness that has persisted, in a very orderly fashion, since the beginning of the year. The downward trendline is very well defined. Now, should this trendline be broken (exceeded on the upside) at any time between now and our next letter, it would be, in our opinion confirmatory evidence that a recovery is underway. Stated another way. There is evidence at the present time to recommend nibbling on common stocks. Should you see in your morning paper a 220 reading or better, on this Mutual Fund Index, it would warrant a more aggressive stance. We will also act on this signal by taking a 60% invested position in our Fidelity Select Model (see page three).

Margo's Market Monitor is published twice each month by William Doane and is not supplemented by a telephone hotline. The name derives from the fact that the newsletter was started (and edited for several years) by Margo Ballantine, who no longer is associated with the newsletter. Doane, who formerly was coordinator of technical research for the Fidelity family of mutual funds, began working at the newsletter in May 1985.

Margo's Market Monitor has two model portfolios, one constructed out of individual stocks and the other out of funds in Fidelity's family of Select funds. One other difference between the two is that the stock portfolio does not switch into or out of the market as actively as the mutual fund portfolio. While it has not always been fully invested, it rarely has more than a small percentage in cash.

The "Fidelity Select Funds" portfolio, in contrast, switches into and out of the market fairly actively—the equivalent of once every three or four months on average. This was not the original intent for this portfolio; it was designed always to be invested in the Fidelity Select fund trading at the highest premium to its 39-week exponentially weighted moving average. Due to this approach's disappointing performance, however, Doane decided to add a subjective market-timing component to this mechanical system.

The HFD has the most data for this newsletter's stock portfolio, from the beginning of 1984 through mid-1992. Over these eight and one-half years, this portfolio gained 44.7% in contrast to the Wilshire 5000's 206.6%. Because it incurred more risk than the market in the process, it underperformed the Wilshire on a risk-adjusted basis as well. The HFD began tracking this newsletter's mutual fund portfolio at the beginning of 1986. Over the subsequent six and one-half years, it gained 55.8%, as compared with the Wilshire's 124.5%.

Margo's Market Monitor (Average.)

	Gain/Loss
1/1/91 to 6/30/92	−4.4%
(Fifth Quintile)	
1/1/89 to 6/30/92	−6.4%
(Fifth Quintile)	
1/1/87 to 6/30/92	+25.8%
(Fourth Quintile)	
1/1/85 to 6/30/92	+80.3%
(Fourth Quintile)	
1/1/83 to 6/30/92	(n/a)
6/30/80 to 6/30/92	(n/a)

Risk: 82% of market

Margo's Market Monitor (Common Stock Portfolio)

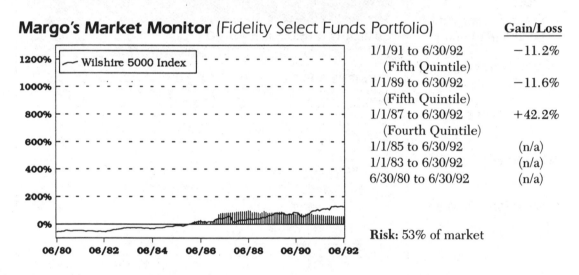

	Gain/Loss
1/1/91 to 6/30/92	+1.8%
(Fifth Quintile)	
1/1/89 to 6/30/92	−3.3%
(Fifth Quintile)	
1/1/87 to 6/30/92	+0.9%
(Fifth Quintile)	
1/1/85 to 6/30/92	+53.5%
(Fourth Quintile)	
1/1/83 to 6/30/92	(n/a)
6/30/80 to 6/30/92	(n/a)

Risk: 138% of market

Margo's Market Monitor (Fidelity Select Funds Portfolio)

	Gain/Loss
1/1/91 to 6/30/92	−11.2%
(Fifth Quintile)	
1/1/89 to 6/30/92	−11.6%
(Fifth Quintile)	
1/1/87 to 6/30/92	+42.2%
(Fourth Quintile)	
1/1/85 to 6/30/92	(n/a)
1/1/83 to 6/30/92	(n/a)
6/30/80 to 6/30/92	(n/a)

Risk: 53% of market

Market Logic

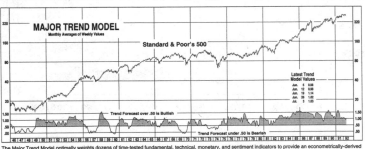

Address
The Institute for
  Econometric
  Research
3471 N. Federal Hwy.
Ft. Lauderdale, FL
  33306

Editors
Norman Fosback and
  Glen King Parker

Phone Number
800-327-6720

Subscription Rates
$95.00/year

Telephone Hotline
Yes

Money Management
No

Market Logic is published twice each month by The Institute for Econometric Research, whose president is Norman Fosback and whose chairman is Glen King Parker. The Institute also publishes a number of other investment newsletters, including several that are reviewed elsewhere in this book: *New Issues, Mutual Fund Forecaster, Insiders* and *Income & Safety*. The newsletter is supplemented by a telephone hotline that is updated twice each week.

In an industry that generally scorns academic approaches to investments, *Market Logic* stands out for having conducted a large amount of rigorous research into the markets and for being an interface between the academic and investment communities. Editor Norman Fosback received academic training at Portland State University's Investment Analysis Center, and both Fosback and co-editor Glen King Parker continue to stay abreast of developments in academia.

Market Logic's approach shuns short-term trading. Stocks held in its "Master" portfolio typically are held for more than five years. Even its "Actual Option" portfolio holds options for longer periods of time than many other services hold stocks.

The HFD has tracked both of these portfolios for 12 years, during which time the Wilshire 5000's total return was a gain of 432.7%. In contrast, this service's "Master" portfolio gained 339.2% and its "Actual Option" portfolio gained 217.4%. Both underperformed the market on a risk-adjusted basis as well.

The reason *Market Logic's* "Master" portfolio underperformed the market, to the extent that the HFD's data provide an explanation, is stock selection. Indeed, if every one of the stocks in *Market Logic's* "Master" portfolio had performed as well as the Wilshire 5000, the portfolio would have done much better—gaining 478.2% and outperforming the market itself. So *Market Logic's* timing did add value.

(Methodological note: In calculating this or any multi-portfolio service's average performance, the HFD normally gives equal weight to each portfolio. Beginning in 1986, however, *Market Logic* recommended that subscribers place 90% of their funds in their "Master" portfolio and no more than 10% in their "Actual Option" portfolio. The performance figure the HFD reports for this service's average reflects this 90:10 weighting thereafter.)

Market Logic (Average)

	Gain/Loss
1/1/91 to 6/30/92 (Second Quintile)	+45.7%
1/1/89 to 6/30/92 (Fourth Quintile)	+31.0%
1/1/87 to 6/30/92 (Fourth Quintile)	+41.9%
1/1/85 to 6/30/92 (Third Quintile)	+107.0%
1/1/83 to 6/30/92 (Third Quintile)	+139.4%
6/30/80 to 6/30/92 (Third Quintile)	+299.7%

Risk: 121% of market

Market Logic (Actual Option Portfolio)

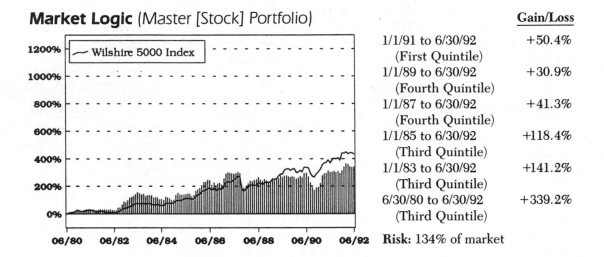

	Gain/Loss
1/1/91 to 6/30/92 (Fifth Quintile)	+7.6%
1/1/89 to 6/30/92 (Fourth Quintile)	+25.3%
1/1/87 to 6/30/92 (Fourth Quintile)	+32.2%
1/1/85 to 6/30/92 (Fourth Quintile)	+73.6%
1/1/83 to 6/30/92 (Third Quintile)	+108.5%
6/30/80 to 6/30/92 (Third Quintile)	+217.4%

Risk: 2% of market

Market Logic (Master [Stock] Portfolio)

	Gain/Loss
1/1/91 to 6/30/92 (First Quintile)	+50.4%
1/1/89 to 6/30/92 (Fourth Quintile)	+30.9%
1/1/87 to 6/30/92 (Fourth Quintile)	+41.3%
1/1/85 to 6/30/92 (Third Quintile)	+118.4%
1/1/83 to 6/30/92 (Third Quintile)	+141.2%
6/30/80 to 6/30/92 (Third Quintile)	+339.2%

Risk: 134% of market

The Market Mania Newsletter

Address
P.O. Box 1234
Pacifica, CA 94044

Editor
Glenn Cutler

Phone Number
415-952-8853

Subscription Rates
$119.00/year

Telephone Hotline
Yes

Money Management
No

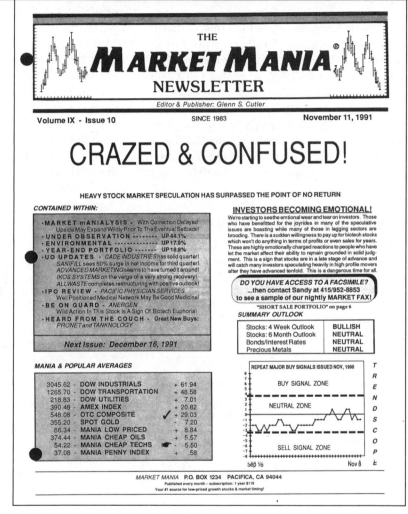

The Market Mania Newsletter used to be published every three weeks and was supplemented by a thrice-weekly telephone hotline update. In early 1992, however, editor Glenn Cutler discontinued the newsletter portion of his service, leaving just the hotline as an ongoing service.

Cutler's hotline provides timing advice in the stock, gold and bond markets, and that's what the HFD follows. In the equity arena, a portfolio that switched between the Wilshire 5000 and T-Bills on Cutler's signals for the "Long-Term Mutual Fund Investor" gained 23.3% over the two and one-half years through mid-1992. This contrasts with a 24.1% gain for the Wilshire 5000. However, owing to the fact that Cutler's timing-only portfolio was less risky than the market while almost equaling its return, it beat the Wilshire on a risk-adjusted basis.

In the gold arena, a portfolio that switched between bullion and T-Bills on Cutler's signals gained 33.6% over the four and one-half years through mid-1992, in contrast to a gain of 33.7% for T-Bills alone and a loss of 29.4% for bullion. A portfolio that actually went short on Cutler's sell signals (instead of going into cash) did even better, gaining 45.2%.

Cutler's bond market timing did not beat a buy-and-hold, however. A portfolio that switched between the Shearson Lehman Treasury Index and T-Bills on Cutler's signals gained 45.9% over this same four-and-one-half-year period, in contrast to 56.6% for the Shearson index itself. A portfolio that actually went short on Cutler's sell signals (instead of going into cash) did worse, gaining just 14.0%.

At the time that Cutler discontinued his newsletter in late 1991, the HFD had eight years of performance data for his model portfolios. Over the period from the beginning of 1984 through the end of 1991, during which time the Wilshire 5000 gained 211.1%, these portfolios lost an average of 25.9% according to the HFD.

The Market Mania Newsletter
(Long-Term Mutual Fund Investor)

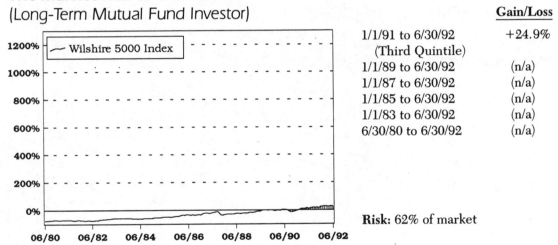

	Gain/Loss
1/1/91 to 6/30/92	+24.9%
(Third Quintile)	
1/1/89 to 6/30/92	(n/a)
1/1/87 to 6/30/92	(n/a)
1/1/85 to 6/30/92	(n/a)
1/1/83 to 6/30/92	(n/a)
6/30/80 to 6/30/92	(n/a)

Risk: 62% of market

The Marketarian Letter

Address
P.O. Box 1283
Grand Island, NE
68802

Editors
Gerald Theisen and
Jeff Helleberg

Phone Number
800-658-4325

Subscription Rates
$125.00/6 months
$225.00/year

Telephone Hotline
Yes

Money Management
Yes

THE MARKETARIAN LETTER
"Technical Timing For Today's Investments"

Date:	JULY 15, 1992	
Dow Industrials:	3,358	
Marketarian Index	11,340	
Monetary Matters		Page 3
Indicator Survey		3
Industry Group Review		4-5
Mutual Fund Timing		5
Model Portfolio		6-7
Summary		8

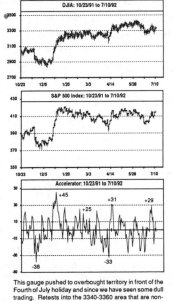

This gauge pushed to overbought territory in front of the Fourth of July holiday and since we have seen some dull trading. Retests into the 3340-3360 area that are non-confirmed would be short term bearish.

HOLDING PATTERN

The DJIA corrected to just under the 3280 level since our last newsletter and during the ensuing days we have had a shallow rally. A new round of rate cuts by the Federal Reserve contributed to this but the latest bout of easing was met with little enthusiasm so far. In view of that, it can be interpreted to be a market that is still overvalued and correcting and the lack of a strong broadly based rally keeps us cautious.

In retrospect, it is not really that surprising that the market has experienced this type of year coming after such strong gains in 1991. Thus, all we can do is be a bit patient here and keep a larger than normal amount of cash on the sidelines until conditions improve. The market has a tendency to behave like this more often than not and especially so the past few months as it has been like watching paint dry.

That will change one of these days and based on several of our longer term momentum gauges the major trend is still bullish and the likelihood of a decent summer rally is still possible.

The year 1984 behaved much the same way as we are seeing now especially in the summer. During that year the market lulled many investors to sleep prior to an explosive advance in a short period of time in early August. The DJIA tacked on ten percent that month and of course if the DJIA rose the same today percentage wise, it would get a lot of attention. While no one knows if it could be similar, the technical configurations that have been building are very similar.

But this year is different because of the three viable candidates in the race for the Presidency. While the market is holding up at least in terms of the DJIA, the subtle internal deterioration keeps us somewhat off balance as to which candidate is the most "market friendly".

We base many of our views on proven indicators that have relied on historical tendencies. If the economy does continue to improve, economically sensitive stocks will pick up momentum and may then begin to rival the gains seen in 1991.

You can only take what the market will give you as forcing trades during less then favorable indicator periods has too many risks

Subscription Rates: 1 year: $225.00/6 months: $150.00/3 months: $75.00/Air Mail Foreign: Add 20% US Funds
Editorial Address: 216 North Cedar, Grand Island, NE 68801 (308) 381-2121
Subscription Address: P.O. Box 1283, Grand Island, NE 68802-1283 (800) 658-4325   PUBLISHED BY MARKETARIAN, INC.

The Marketarian Letter is the successor to *The Lynn Elgert Report*, which was published by Lynn Elgert, Gerald Theisen and Jeff Helleberg. In the summer of 1989, Elgert left to begin his own newsletter (*The Lynn Elgert Letter*), and the former *Lynn Elgert Report* became *The Marketarian Letter*. The HFD has received different accounts from Elgert on the one hand and Theisen and Helleberg on the other concerning who deserves credit for the investment advice provided prior to their split. Since it has no way of determining who within an advisory organization is responsible for individual recommendations, the HFD remains neutral on this question. But you need to be aware of the newsletter's history in interpreting its performance prior to the summer of 1989.

The Marketarian Letter has three portfolios, two of which invest in mutual funds (one for shorter-term traders and the other for longer-term investors) and the third which invests primarily in stocks (though on occasion this portfolio also contains stock index or bond futures as well as options). Its approach to all three portfolios appears to involve a combination of fundamental and technical analysis.

The HFD has the most data for the non-mutual fund portfolio. Over the seven and one-half years through mid-1992, according to the HFD, it gained 62.4%, in contrast to the Wilshire 5000's 197.6%. The "Mutual Fund Portfolio for Traders" has done better, gaining 92.2% over the five and one-half years through mid-1992, in contrast to the Wilshire 5000's 93.3%. The HFD began following this newsletter's "Mutual Fund Portfolio for Investors" at the beginning of 1991, and over the next 18 months it performed quite similarly to the newsletter's fund portfolio for traders.

Taking all three portfolios into account, the HFD calculates a gain of 121.4% over the seven and one-half years through mid-1992, as compared to 197.6% for the Wilshire 5000. While the newsletter's portfolios are less risky than the market as a whole, they aren't so low in risk that the newsletter beats the market on a risk-adjusted basis.

The Marketarian Letter (Average)

	Gain/Loss
1/1/91 to 6/30/92 (Second Quintile)	+38.0%
1/1/89 to 6/30/92 (Fourth Quintile)	+26.8%
1/1/87 to 6/30/92 (Third Quintile)	+53.1%
1/1/85 to 6/30/92 (Third Quintile)	+121.4%
1/1/83 to 6/30/92	(n/a)
6/30/80 to 6/30/92	(n/a)

Risk: 85% of market

The Marketarian Letter (Model Portfolio)

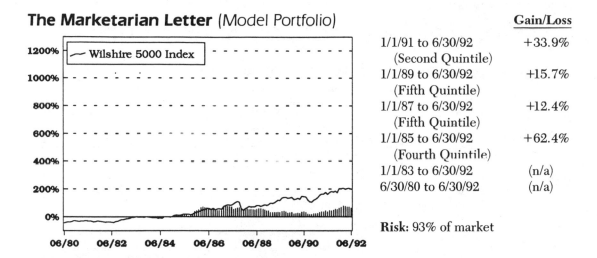

		Gain/Loss
1/1/91 to 6/30/92	(Second Quintile)	+33.9%
1/1/89 to 6/30/92	(Fifth Quintile)	+15.7%
1/1/87 to 6/30/92	(Fifth Quintile)	+12.4%
1/1/85 to 6/30/92	(Fourth Quintile)	+62.4%
1/1/83 to 6/30/92		(n/a)
6/30/80 to 6/30/92		(n/a)

Risk: 93% of market

The Marketarian Letter (Traders' Fund Portfolio)

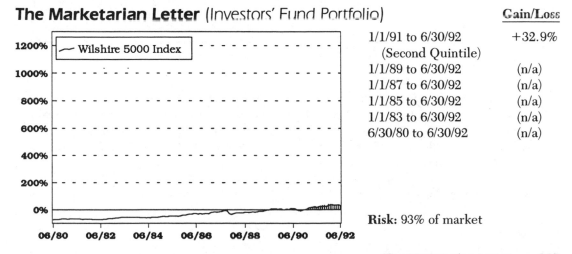

		Gain/Loss
1/1/91 to 6/30/92	(Second Quintile)	+33.1%
1/1/89 to 6/30/92	(Fourth Quintile)	+29.3%
1/1/87 to 6/30/92	(Second Quintile)	+92.2%
1/1/85 to 6/30/92		(n/a)
1/1/83 to 6/30/92		(n/a)
6/30/80 to 6/30/92		(n/a)

Risk: 88% of market

The Marketarian Letter (Investors' Fund Portfolio)

		Gain/Loss
1/1/91 to 6/30/92	(Second Quintile)	+32.9%
1/1/89 to 6/30/92		(n/a)
1/1/87 to 6/30/92		(n/a)
1/1/85 to 6/30/92		(n/a)
1/1/83 to 6/30/92		(n/a)
6/30/80 to 6/30/92		(n/a)

Risk: 93% of market

Medical Technology Stock Letter

Address
P.O. Box 40460
Berkeley, CA 94704

Editor
Jim McCamant

Phone Number
510-843-1857

Subscription Rates
$ 65.00/3 months
$320.00/year

Telephone Hotline
Yes

Money Management
No

Medical Technology Stock Letter

July 9, 1992 **ISSUE NO: 203** **DJIA: 3324.08**

This Issue: Contrast Imaging Agents

PULSE OF THE MARKET

Over the last two weeks, the stock market rallied, corrected and then bounced up again today. For the two weeks the DJIA is up 40 points or 1.2%. The Model Portfolio is up 6.0%, and the Aggressive Portfolio is up 7.6%.

The sharp rise in unemployment in June reported last week returned investor's focus to the economy. The media immediately began to question the length of the recovery and quoted some economists who now expect another downturn. The initial monthly numbers are often misleading. They usually are revised later, and the seasonal adjustments can distort them. The seasonal factors are particularly tricky for the employment numbers in June, when students leaving school increase those seeking jobs. Allowing for such errors, we consider the recent numbers consistent with the very slow recovery we have been predicting. The increase in automobile sales in the last part of June was evidence that the economy is still moving ahead, and it supports the report by the National Association of Purchasing Managers that new orders were strong in June.

One result of the weak economic numbers is that investors are showing a renewed interest in growth stocks. Growth stocks had a large correction from their first quarter highs and are now primed for another advance. The drug stocks took a beating as the move away from growth stocks was reinforced by bad news from a number of individual drug companies. We think this weakness helped put pressure on all of the healthcare stocks. We do not expect a big move in medical technology stocks in the second half, but we are convinced that the stage is set for selective strength. The large biotech stocks have been market leaders since their lows in April. As we predicted, Chiron has led the way with more than a 60% advance off its low.

INVESTMENT SCAN: Contrast Imaging Agents

Contrast imaging agents are an interesting specialty market which has received only limited interest from the investment community. This sector grew rapidly in the late 1980's. When Sterling Drug was acquired by Eastman Kodak, its largest selling product was a contrast agent, Isovue. In 1990 when Squibb was acquired by Bristol-Myers, its second largest product was a contrast agent. Rapid development of contrast agents for ultrasound and MRI in addition to X-rays should create substantial growth over the next five years. In this Issue, we will discuss this sector and the three public companies which have major efforts underway in this area.

Background

Contrast imaging agents allow a doctor to get more useful information from a diagnostic procedure and have emerged as a very attractive market in the last seven years. Historically contrast agents have been used to provide clarity in

The *Medical Technology Stock Letter* is published every two weeks by Jim McCamant and is supplemented by a telephone hotline that is updated weekly. McCamant at one time was co-editor with Michael Murphy of the *California Technology Stock Letter* (see review for this elsewhere in this *Guide*) but subsequently they decided to go their separate ways, Murphy retaining the original letter without a focus on medical technology stocks and McCamant initiating the new letter.

It was fortuitous timing for McCamant, as the medical technology sector performed handsomely over the subsequent several years, handily beating the Wilshire 5000. And even though his recommended stocks were a big casualty in the Crash of 1987, the newsletter remains ahead of the market over the longer term.

Most of the companies that McCamant examines are very young and sometimes don't even have a proven product line. He believes that traditional technical analysis isn't very helpful in assessing such companies' prospects, not only because many possess little trading history but also because their volatility often is so high that any technical trading scheme would lead to frequent and unprofitable in-and-out trading.

McCamant is convinced that the key to profiting from these emerging technologies is a willingness to stick with well-situated companies for more than just a month or two. His model portfolio undertakes few transactions,

and even his "Aggressive" portfolio, which more actively trades than his model portfolio and which also uses margin, holds stocks for longer than many other newsletter model portfolios.

Over the period of time when both of McCamant's portfolios have existed, his "Aggressive" portfolio has been the better performer. Over the three and one-half years through mid-1992, for example, the "Aggressive" portfolio gained 311.1%, as compared to 274.4% for the model portfolio. Both performances are well ahead of the Wilshire 5000's 60.3%, even on a risk-adjusted basis.

Taking both portfolios into account, and weighting them appropriately for the fact that one has existed longer than the other, the *Medical Technology Stock Letter* is one of just nine newsletters (out of 55 tracked by the HFD) that beat the market over the seven and one-half years through mid-1990.

Medical Technology Stock Letter (Average)

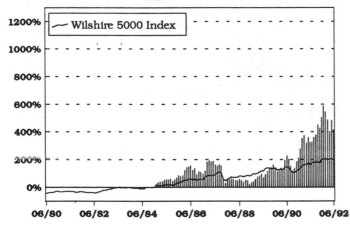

	Gain/Loss
1/1/91 to 6/30/92	+66.0%
(First Quintile)	
1/1/89 to 6/30/92	+289.1%
(First Quintile)	
1/1/87 to 6/30/92	+163.7%
(First Quintile)	
1/1/85 to 6/30/92	+413.6%
(First Quintile)	
1/1/83 to 6/30/92	(n/a)
6/30/80 to 6/30/92	(n/a)

Risk: 301% of market

Medical Technology Stock Letter (Model Portfolio)

	Gain/Loss
1/1/91 to 6/30/92 (First Quintile)	+82.9%
1/1/89 to 6/30/92 (First Quintile)	+247.4%
1/1/87 to 6/30/92 (First Quintile)	+135.4%
1/1/85 to 6/30/92 (First Quintile)	+358.5%
1/1/83 to 6/30/92	(n/a)
6/30/80 to 6/30/92	(n/a)

Risk: 315% of market

Medical Technology Stock Letter (Aggressive Portfolio)

	Gain/Loss
1/1/91 to 6/30/92 (Second Quintile)	+48.8%
1/1/89 to 6/30/92 (First Quintile)	+311.1%
1/1/87 to 6/30/92	(n/a)
1/1/85 to 6/30/92	(n/a)
1/1/83 to 6/30/92	(n/a)
6/30/80 to 6/30/92	(n/a)

Risk: 305% of market

Morningstar Mutual Funds

Address
53 West Jackson Blvd.
Suite 460
Chicago, IL 60604

Editor
John Rekenthaler

Phone Number
800-876-5005

Subscription Rates
$395.00/year

Telephone Hotline
No

Money Management
No

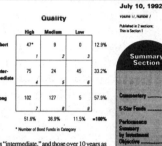

M⊙RNINGSTAR Mutual Funds

July 10, 1992

VOLUME 17, NUMBER 7

Published in 2 sections;
This is Section 1

Dressing Up Those Bonds
Fixed-income style boxes highlight this issue's additions and alterations.

by John Rekenthaler, Editor

This issue brings three improvements to *Morningstar Mutual Funds*. Most of this essay will discuss the biggest change, the addition of fixed-income style boxes. As we shall see, the methodologies underlying these boxes differ from those used with equity funds, but the end results are alike: a convenient, easy-to-use tool that permits fund shoppers to make quicker comparisons. We've also upgraded two graphs. First, we've added a "portfolio average" calculation to each bond-fund credit graph, so that investors may readily assess a fund's overall quality. And we've replaced the "net-assets" bar graph with a bar graph that illustrates a fund's relative annual performance. Unlike the first two items, this feature will henceforth appear on all fund pages, not solely on fixed-income pages.

Details, Details
While creating bond-fund style boxes proved trickier than we would have liked, the starting points were very easy. Whereas equity-fund style boxes classify each fund according to two stock-specific criteria, *investment type* (value, blend, or growth) and *company size* (large, medium, or small), fixed-income style boxes obviously must address important bond characteristics. And what could be more crucial than the two pillars of fixed-income performance, interest-rate sensitivity and credit quality? Thus, we split fixed-income funds into three *maturity* groups (short, intermediate, or long) and three *quality* groups (high, medium, or low). As with equity style boxes, nine possible combinations exist, ranging in this case from short maturity/high quality for the safest funds to long maturity/low quality for the riskiest.

Of the two starting points, interest-rate sensitivity poses the greatest difficulties. Had we access to clean, consistently calculated duration statistics, we would have used them. At this stage, we don't. So we have settled instead for the simpler, if less accurate, measure of effective weighted maturity. Specifically, funds with effective weighted maturities at or below four years qualify as "short," those from four years to

Quality

	High	Medium	Low	
Short	47*	9	0	12.9%
	1	*2*	*3*	
Intermediate	75	24	45	33.2%
	4	*5*	*6*	
Long	102	127	5	57.9%
	7	*8*	*9*	
	51.6%	36.9%	11.5%	=100%

Maturity (left axis label)

* Number of Bond Funds in Category

10 years as "intermediate," and those over 10 years as "long." We derive these figures by interviewing fund management and from quarterly fund surveys. In the rare instance that neither is available, we calculate them from the most recently available portfolio.

We opted for effective rather than nominal maturity because of the latter's all-too-frequent limitations. Nominal maturities work fine for Treasuries and other nonmortgage governments; with rare exception, such issues survive as long as their official maturities. Few other bonds are as straightforward, though. For example, corporate and municipal bonds sport call or put features that may abruptly shorten their lifespans. Mortgage-backed securities feature rolling call provisions in the form of homeowner prepayments. Finally, by adjusting their coupons so often, floating-rate notes tend to act like short-term securities no matter what their maturity dates.

Effective maturities solve some but not all of these problems. They work quite well with mortgage, put, and floating-rate bonds. Although nobody knows exactly when a mortgage pool will expire, its eventual life expectancy can be roughly estimated. Similarly, the effects of a bond's put or floating-rate features may be approximated by treating its effective maturity not as the date of the bond's retirement, but instead as the occasion of its next put or coupon adjustment. However, effective maturities still fail to describe the implications inherent in many corporate and municipal bonds' call options. Because these calls won't occur if interest rates rise steeply enough, they're uncertain and are therefore ignored in effective-maturity calculations. Such calculations may thus oversate corporate and muni fund maturities. One may estimate how much of a portfolio is susceptible to call by examining its average weighted price

Summary Section

Commentary 1
5-Star Funds 3
Performance Summary by Investment Objective 4
Index .... 5 - 27
Highest/Lowest Total Return by Time Period .... 28 - 31
Investment Objective Averages 32

continued

Morningstar Mutual Funds is published every other week by Morningstar, Inc.; Don Phillips is listed as publisher and John Rekenthaler as editor. It is not supplemented by a telephone hotline.

This newsletter gives every appearance of being modeled after the *Value Line Invest-* *ment Survey.* Just as the *Value Line Investment Survey* does for individual stocks, *Morningstar Mutual Funds* provides an exhaustive statistical analysis of each of hundreds of individual stock and bond mutual funds, devoting a full page to reviewing and graphing each fund. And like *Value Line*'s five-step ranking system for stocks, *Morningstar* has a five-step ranking system for mutual funds—from 1-Star (worst) to 5-Star (best).

The newsletter does not advise subscribers on the proper allocation of a portfolio among stocks, bond and cash, nor does it say whether subscribers ought to have more allocated to one fund than to another. The HFD thus constructs model portfolios for the newsletter that are fully invested and equally weighted among their highest recommendations. One portfolio is constructed out of their 5-Star equity funds and another out of their 5-Star bond funds. (As this edition of the *Guide* goes to press, however, *Morningstar* has announced plans to begin a new service entitled *The 5-Star Investor*, which will help subscribers translate their rating system into individual portfolios. The HFD intends to begin tracking this new newsletter when it does appear.)

One other factor has a big impact on the performance rating the HFD calculates for *Morningstar Mutual Funds*: The list of this service's 5-Star funds includes both load and no-load funds. This means that the portfolios the HFD constructs to track the newsletter's performance incur substantial loads every time a load fund is added to the list of 5-Star funds.

Whatever the cause, neither of this newsletter's two portfolios beat the market over the 18 months through mid-1992. *Morningstar*'s portfolio of 5-Star equity funds gained 18.4% (in contrast to 32.3% for the Wilshire 5000) and its portfolio of 5-Star bond funds gained 10.6% (in contrast to 17.8% for the Shearson Lehman Treasury Index). While both portfolios had below-average risk, they still underperformed the market even when their performance was adjusted for risk.

Morningstar Mutual Funds (Average)

	Gain/Loss
1/1/91 to 6/30/92	+14.7%
(Fourth Quintile)	
1/1/89 to 6/30/92	(n/a)
1/1/87 to 6/30/92	(n/a)
1/1/85 to 6/30/92	(n/a)
1/1/83 to 6/30/92	(n/a)
6/30/80 to 6/30/92	(n/a)

Risk: 53% of market

Morningstar Mutual Funds (Equity & Hybrid Funds [5-Star])

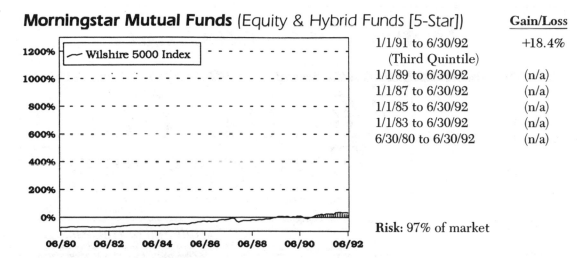

	Gain/Loss
1/1/91 to 6/30/92	+18.4%
(Third Quintile)	
1/1/89 to 6/30/92	(n/a)
1/1/87 to 6/30/92	(n/a)
1/1/85 to 6/30/92	(n/a)
1/1/83 to 6/30/92	(n/a)
6/30/80 to 6/30/92	(n/a)

Risk: 97% of market

Morningstar Mutual Funds (Bond Funds [5-Star])

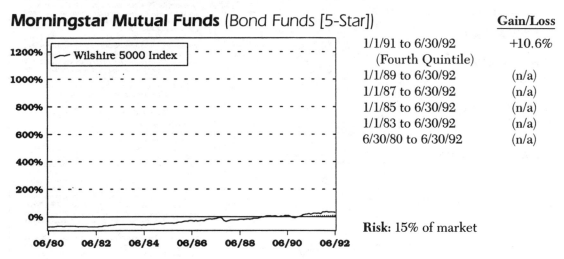

	Gain/Loss
1/1/91 to 6/30/92	+10.6%
(Fourth Quintile)	
1/1/89 to 6/30/92	(n/a)
1/1/87 to 6/30/92	(n/a)
1/1/85 to 6/30/92	(n/a)
1/1/83 to 6/30/92	(n/a)
6/30/80 to 6/30/92	(n/a)

Risk: 15% of market

Mutual Fund Forecaster

Address
The Institute for
Econometric
Research
3471 N. Federal Hwy.
Ft. Lauderdale, FL
33306

Editors
Norman Fosback and
Glen King Parker

Phone Number
800-327-6720

Subscription Rates
$49.00/year

Telephone Hotline
Yes

Money Management
No

MUTUAL FUND FORECASTER®

Profit Projections and Risk Ratings for Traders and Investors

Norman G. Fosback, Editor

Glen King Parker, Publisher

Issue No. 90

July 2, 1992

Half Full or Half Empty?

Half-full proponents point to the fact that despite gla-cially slow upside progress, all of the popular averages, including the Dow and indexes of all NYSE and Amex stocks, are within a few percentage points of new record highs. Indeed, a handful of mutual funds hit all-time highs this week (see Page 12).

The half-empty argument is that despite the Dow's strength, the more representative S&P 500 actually peaked 5½ months ago, and is now down on the year to date; that the most broadly-based market indexes last established new highs three months ago; and that major sectors of the market have deteriorated sharply.

The fact of the matter is that investors that have kept some of their assets in money *[Continued on Page 2]*

BEST BUY RECOMMENDATIONS
(Mutual funds with highest Profit Projection for each Risk Rating)

Risk Rating	Mutual Funds	1-Year Profit Projection	Combined Sales/Red. Fees
Very High	20th Century Ultra	+ 28%	None
High	Janus Twenty	+ 25%	None
Medium	General American Inv. (closed-end)	+ 24%	–
Low	Financial – Industrial Income	+ 19%	None
Very Low	Dodge & Cox Balanced	+ 16%	None

BUY RECOMMENDATIONS
(Mutual funds with high Profit Projections in each Risk Rating)

Risk Rating	Mutual Funds	1-Year Profit Projection	Combined Sales/Red. Fees
Very High	Berger – One Hundred	+ 27%	None
Very High	Pasadena Growth	+ 25%	5.8%
Very High	Keystone Am. Hartwell Emg. Growth	+ 24%	5.0%
Very High	Pacific Horizon Aggressive Growth	+ 23%	4.7%
Very High	AIM – Constellation Growth	+ 23%	5.8%
Very High	20th Century Growth	+ 23%	None
Very High	ABT – Emerging Growth	+ 23%	5.0%
Very High	Keystone America Omega	+ 23%	5.0%
High	Fidelity Growth Company	+ 23%	3.1%
High	Kaufmann	+ 23%	0.2%
High	Quest for Value Capital (closed-end)	+ 22%	–
High	Kemper Growth	+ 22%	6.1%
High	Fortis Growth	+ 22%	5.0%
High	Seligman Capital	+ 21%	5.0%
High	IDS Growth	+ 21%	5.3%
High	Composite Northwest 50	+ 21%	4.7%
Medium	Founders Special	+ 23%	None
Medium	Vanguard – World U.S. Growth	+ 22%	None
Medium	IDS New Dimensions	+ 22%	5.3%
Medium	Fidelity Contrafund	+ 21%	3.1%
Medium	Janus	+ 21%	None
Medium	Venture – New York Venture	+ 21%	5.0%
Medium	Fidelity Magellan	+ 20%	3.1%
Medium	Thomson – Growth "B"	+ 20%	1.0%
Medium	IDS Strategy Aggressive	+ 20%	5.3%
Medium	Liberty All Star Equity (closed-end)	+ 20%	–
Medium	Stein Roe Stock	+ 20%	None
Medium	Fidelity Growth & Income	+ 20%	2.0%
Low	Fidelity OTC	+ 19%	3.1%
Low	IAI – Regional	+ 18%	None
Low	IDS Stock	+ 17%	5.3%
Low	Scudder Growth & Income	+ 17%	None
Low	Nicholas	+ 17%	None
Low	Berger – One Hundred One	+ 17%	None
Very Low	United Retirement Shares	+ 16%	9.3%
Very Low	Merrill Lynch Capital "A"	+ 16%	6.4%
Very Low	Putnam Growth & Income	+ 16%	6.1%
Very Low	Shearson Portf. Premium Total Return	+ 15%	5.3%
Very Low	Phoenix Balanced	+ 15%	5.0%

Profit Projections are before sales and redemption fees, and are based upon our current one-year market forecast of a +18% total return.
Sales and redemption fees may be reduced for large transactions or on investments held for an extended period.

Recommendations

INVESTORS: *Financial – Industrial Income* and *Dodge & Cox Balanced*, a pair of no-load funds with low and very low Risk Ratings, respectively, have earned new "Best Buy" recommendations. The previous "Best Buys," *AIM – Charter* and *Gabelli Asset*, have been lowered to "Hold." The other "Best Buys" – *20th Century Ultra, Janus Twenty,* and *General American Investors* – are unchanged.

TRADERS: A maximum of 50% of portfolio trading commitments should be maintained in the following six funds that have high One-Year Profit Projections: *20th Century Ultra* (One-Year Profit Projection, +28%), *Berger – One Hundred* (+27%), *Janus Twenty* (+25%), *General American Investors* (+24%), *Founders Special* (+23%), and *Quest for Value Capital* (+22%).

GOLD: The Gold Price Model is bullish, and no-load gold funds continue to earn top recommendations. However, we anticipate that the Gold Model may revert to a bearish mode later this month. Any change in the Model's status will be reported on the *Hot Line.*

Hot Line: See Page 5 of this issue for details of our all-new Hot Line system to go into effect on July 10. See the enclosed letter for the current Hot Line number.

A Service of The Institute for Econometric Research, 3471 North Federal, Fort Lauderdale, Florida 33306
For Subscriber Services and Information, Call Toll-Free 800-442-9000

Mutual Fund Forecaster is one of several newsletters published by The Institute for Econometric Research, whose chairman is Glen Parker and whose president is Norman Fosback. (Four of these other newsletters are reviewed elsewhere in this *Guide*.) The newsletter is published monthly and supplemented by a weekly telephone hotline.

The centerpiece of the *Mutual Fund Forecaster* is a set of profit projections for each of a large number of mutual funds (both load and no-load). These profit projections are a function of each fund's past volatility and the Institute's estimate of where the market will be in a year's time. If they estimate that the market will be up by 20%, for example, and a fund historically has been 50% more volatile than the market, then—with a few additional modifications—that fund's profit projection will be about 30%.

Mutual Fund Forecaster divides up its universe of mutual funds into five risk categories, ranging from very low risk to very high risk, and in each issue reports the fund within each category that has the highest profit projection. The resultant five funds are given "Best Buy" status.

For switch-fund traders for whom load funds would be inappropriate, the newsletter recommends a set of no-load and very low-load funds whose profit projections are the highest. This subset often overlaps with the list of five "Best Buy" funds, but is not the same. A portfolio of these funds for switch-fund traders is what the HFD considers to be representative of this newsletter's performance. *Mutual Fund Forecaster* also offers market-timing advice in addition to recommending individual mutual funds. This advice is based on the same econometric model used by *Market Logic* (see the review of this newsletter elsewhere in this volume).

Over the six and one-half years through mid-1992 for which the HFD has data, the portfolio the HFD tracks for this newsletter gained 124.9%, as compared to 124.5% for the Wilshire 5000. However, because this performance was achieved with above-average risk, the service's risk-adjusted performance is below the market's.

Mutual Fund Forecaster

	Gain/Loss
1/1/91 to 6/30/92	+48.9%
(First Quintile)	
1/1/89 to 6/30/92	+74.4%
(First Quintile)	
1/1/87 to 6/30/92	+95.9%
(First Quintile)	
1/1/85 to 6/30/92	(n/a)
1/1/83 to 6/30/92	(n/a)
6/30/80 to 6/30/92	(n/a)

Risk: 120% of market

Mutual Fund Investing

Address
7811 Montrose Rd.
Potomac, MD 20854

Editor
Jay Schabacker

Phone Number
800-777-5005

Subscription Rates
$177.00/year

Telephone Hotline
Yes

Money Management
Yes

Jay Schabacker's

Mutual Fund Investing ®

Phillips Publishing, Inc.
Actionable Information for the '90s ®

YOUR KEY TO KNOWLEDGE, ACTION, AND PROFITS

July 1992
Vol.8, No.9

Dear Mutual Fund Investor,

If you are not yet in my favorite cyclical funds—or you're still overweighted in money markets and bonds—use the recent pullback as an excellent buying opportunity to scoop up a bargain before the next rise. You see, just when most fund managers have lost heart and raised cash (as they have recently)—that's when the stock market usually bounces back. So stay with the program.

Of course, patience is a little easier to practice when you're on the right side of the investment trends—as we have been this year. Many of our value cyclical funds have placed in the winner's circle for the first half of 1992, including Fidelity Value, Lindner Fund, Mutual Beacon, Fidelity Select Industrial Materials. While the S&P500 has dropped by 2.4% since January, these funds have gained almost 10% year-to-date.

Right now, cash in aggressive stock funds is at its highest level in 15 months (at 10.3%). Bearish sentiment (another good contrary indicator) is also high. All of this makes me cautiously optimistic about the future of U.S. stocks for the next 12 months. Which U.S. stocks make the most sense? With an economic recovery unfolding, and inflation and interest rates likely to rise, your best buys are <u>still</u> in the value cyclical funds I've been recommending since January.

At the same time, our funds outside the U.S. stock area are also working nicely —so don't leave them out of your program. Use <u>global income</u> funds for higher yields, <u>short-term bonds</u> for reasonable yields with low risks, <u>money markets</u> for a no-risk way to ride interest rates <u>up</u>, and <u>international stocks</u> for some double-digit growth in the next 12 months. Our strategy beats the high risks of being 100% in the U.S. stock market and the low yields of being 100% in money market funds.

CONTENTS

Looking Ahead to the Second Half of '92

There are still a lot of short-term question marks ahead for the U.S. market— not least of which is the presidential election and the unnerving possibility that our next president will wind up being picked by the House of Representatives. This uncertainty is just one more reason to focus on three key action items this month:

(1) <u>Get your portfolio in balance</u>. On pages 4-5, I offer some tips on how to make all the pieces of your mutual fund program work together to reap better rewards with less risk. That means 50% in stocks, 20% bonds, 10% internationals, 20% cash.

(2) <u>Buy value, avoid hype</u>. Don't be tempted by higher yields in long bonds and don't be hoodwinked by blockbuster profits that are yesterday's news. Go for the best no-load fund families, highly rated short-term bond funds, dividend-oriented and value cyclical stock funds, and fully diversified international stock funds.

(3) <u>Tune up your funds</u>. Make sure that within each section of your mutual fund portfolio you have the highest quality funds you can find. Use my Top purchase Candidates on page 3 as your shopping list.

With these three actions in place (and you may have done all three already!), you'll be safely positioned with a winning program for the second half of 1992.

Mutual Fund Investing is published monthly and is edited by Jay Schabacker. It is supplemented by a telephone hotline that is updated at least twice each week. Very rarely, however, does Schabacker use the hotline to make transactions in his newsletter's model portfolios.

Schabacker recommends three different model portfolios in his newsletter. Two, his "Balanced Growth" and "Growth With Income" portfolios, are fairly conservative; they typically contain a large cash position and are diversified among several different asset categories. The third is an "IRA/Long Term

Growth" portfolio, which typically remains fully invested and attempts to exploit strength in different market sectors.

Given the low risk of this newsletter's first two portfolios, it is not particularly surprising that they have underperformed the market as a whole. Over the six and one-half years through mid-1992 for which the HFD has data, Schabacker's "Balanced Growth" portfolio gained 87.1% and his "Growth With Income" portfolio gained 62.4%—in contrast to

the Wilshire 5000's gain of 124.5%. Though both portfolios were significantly less risky than the market as a whole, they still underperformed the market on a risk-adjusted basis.

The HFD has less data for the third portfolio, which is a newer addition to the newsletter. Over the two and one-half years through mid-1992, this portfolio gained just 2.2%, in contrast to the Wilshire 5000's 24.1%.

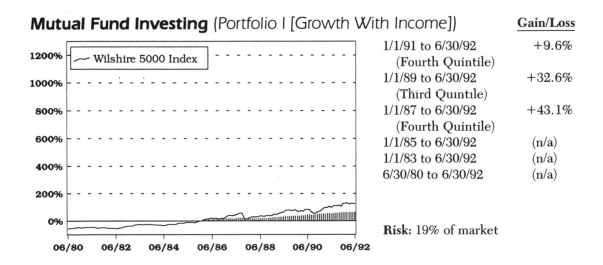

Mutual Fund Investing (Average)

	Gain/Loss
1/1/91 to 6/30/92	+9.3%
(Fourth Quintile)	
1/1/89 to 6/30/92	+25.7%
(Fourth Quintile)	
1/1/87 to 6/30/92	+40.5%
(Fourth Quintile)	
1/1/85 to 6/30/92	(n/a)
1/1/83 to 6/30/92	(n/a)
6/30/80 to 6/30/92	(n/a)

Risk: 39% of market

Mutual Fund Investing (Portfolio I [Growth With Income])

	Gain/Loss
1/1/91 to 6/30/92	+9.6%
(Fourth Quintile)	
1/1/89 to 6/30/92	+32.6%
(Third Quintile)	
1/1/87 to 6/30/92	+43.1%
(Fourth Quintile)	
1/1/85 to 6/30/92	(n/a)
1/1/83 to 6/30/92	(n/a)
6/30/80 to 6/30/92	(n/a)

Risk: 19% of market

Mutual Fund Investing (Portfolio II [Balanced Growth])

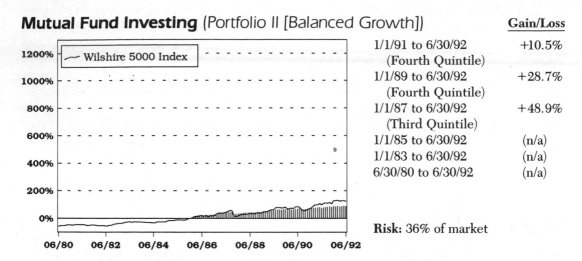

	Gain/Loss
1/1/91 to 6/30/92	+10.5%
(Fourth Quintile)	
1/1/89 to 6/30/92	+28.7%
(Fourth Quintile)	
1/1/87 to 6/30/92	+48.9%
(Third Quintile)	
1/1/85 to 6/30/92	(n/a)
1/1/83 to 6/30/92	(n/a)
6/30/80 to 6/30/92	(n/a)

Risk: 36% of market

Mutual Fund Investing (Portfolio III [IRA/Long Term Growth])

	Gain/Loss
1/1/91 to 6/30/92	+7.5%
(Fifth Quintile)	
1/1/89 to 6/30/92	(n/a)
1/1/87 to 6/30/92	(n/a)
1/1/85 to 6/30/92	(n/a)
1/1/83 to 6/30/92	(n/a)
6/30/80 to 6/30/92	(n/a)

Risk: 70% of market

The Mutual Fund Letter

Address
680 N. Lake
Shore Dr.
Tower Suite 2038
Chicago, IL 60611

Editor
Gerald Perritt

Phone Number
800-326-6941

Subscription Rates
$99.00/year

Telephone Hotline
No

Money Management
Yes

Gerald Perritt's

Volume 9, Number 7

the Mutual Fund Letter

Wealth-Building Strategies for the Astute Investor

A Recipe for Winning Big on Wall Street

Begin with a portfolio of small firm stocks, add a value discipline and stir in an ample amount of patience. That's the recipe for obtaining better-than-average stock market returns.

The risk-adjusted excess returns provided by small firm stocks was first uncovered in the late 1970s by Rolf Banz, a University of Chicago doctoral student. Mr. Banz found that while large company stocks delivered investment returns consistent with that predicted by their beta risk, small firm stocks had been providing investors with more returns than could be explained solely in terms of their risk. Doctoral student Banz had found a cafeteria on Wall Street that had been offering up free lunches for more than a half-century.

Prior to the Banz discovery of the "small firm effect" (as it came to be called), most academics firmly embraced the "efficient market hypothesis" (EMH). According to the EMH, common stock returns are tied to risk and nothing else. In an efficient market no investor can gain an advantage over another by either investing in undervalued stocks or shunning overvalued ones. According to the EMH, if you want greater returns, you must pay for them by assuming a greater amount of investment risk. The EMH states that there are no free lunches served up on Wall Street.

The free lunch being served up by small firm stocks is no hors d'oeuvre, it's an entire banquet. Since 1940, for example, small firm stocks have returned 15.7 percent compounded annually versus an 11.8 percent compound annual return for the large cap-dominated Standard & Poor's 500 Index. The 3.9 percent additional annual return provided by small caps is no trivial amount. For example, $1,000 invested in the S&P 500 Index at the beginning of 1940 would have grown to $330,000 by the end of 1991. A similar investment in small cap stocks would have grown to $1.96 million. During eight of the last 52 years, small cap stocks have returned more than 50 percent. Of course, small firm stock investors have had to endure some testy

moments as well. During 1973, small firm stocks lost 31 percent of their value. They then declined another 20 percent the following year. And during 1990, their prices plummeted nearly 22 percent (the sixth worst decline on record).

More than 90 open-end mutual funds claim to invest in the small firm sector of the stock market. These funds sport such names as: emerging growth, discovery, capital development, opportunity and small cap. However, according to Banz's definition of small cap (today, any company whose equity market value is below $115 million), only about a dozen of these funds invest the bulk of their assets in the small firm sector of the market. Some funds have missed their target by a wide mark. For example, the average equity caps of American Capital Emerging Growth, Fidelity Emerging Growth, Kemper Small Cap and Twentieth Century Vista funds exceed $1 billion. Even the long-time small cap devotee, the T. Rowe Price New Horizons Fund, has invested the bulk of its assets in firms with equity caps more than $700 million.

The problem faced by small cap fund managers is the illiquidity that exists in the small firm sector of the market. The 2,000 or so small cap stocks that are nationally traded

("Recipe" continued on back page)

Inside This Issue...

July 1992/1

The Mutual Fund Letter is published monthly by Investors Information Services, Inc., and is edited by Gerald Perritt, a former finance professor at DePaul University who, prior to assuming his current duties, worked closely with the American Association of Indi-vidual Investors (AAII). While at AAII Perritt was co-author of their annual editions of *The Individual Investor's Guide to No-Load Mutual Funds*, which was (and still is) regarded as one of the better such guides in the industry. In addition to *The Mutual Fund Letter*,

Perritt publishes *Investment Horizons* and *Blue Chip Values* (both followed by the HFD and reviewed elsewhere in this volume).

Perritt is a fundamentalist who shuns technical analysis. His investment approach focuses on exploiting a number of inefficiencies in the otherwise very efficient market, such as buying stocks (or mutual funds) of low-capitalization companies, or stocks that have little or no institutional following, etc. Perritt also believes that it is not possible to time the market consistently, and formally eschews any attempt to do so. However, his model portfolios have not universally been fully invested, especially during late 1987 as he built up some cash, so at least some implicit timing is taking place.

The Mutual Fund Letter has constructed and maintains five very clear model portfolios, one each for four different categories of risk ("Highly Aggressive," "Moderately Ag-gressive," "Growth & Income," and "Income") and a fifth (an "All Weather" portfolio) that focuses on asset allocation. The best-performing of these over the six and one-half years through mid-1992 for which the HFD has data was the "Growth & Income" portfolio, with a gain of 81.3%, while the poorest performance was turned in by the "Income" portfolio, with a gain of 67.3%. These performances compare with a 124.5% gain for the Wilshire 5000 over the same period. Over the three and one-half years for which the HFD has data for the "All Weather" portfolio, it gained 34.0%, in contrast to the Wilshire 5000's 60.3%.

It is noteworthy that these gains were produced with significantly less risk than that of the average stock. When these performances are adjusted for their low risk, they are much closer to the market's, though still behind by a slight amount.

The Mutual Fund Letter (Average)

	Gain/Loss
1/1/91 to 6/30/92 (Fourth Quintile)	+16.5%
1/1/89 to 6/30/92 (Third Quintile)	+35.3%
1/1/87 to 6/30/92 (Third Quintile)	+53.4%
1/1/85 to 6/30/92	(n/a)
1/1/83 to 6/30/92	(n/a)
6/30/80 to 6/30/92	(n/a)

Risk: 41% of market

The Mutual Fund Letter (Highly Aggressive Portfolio)

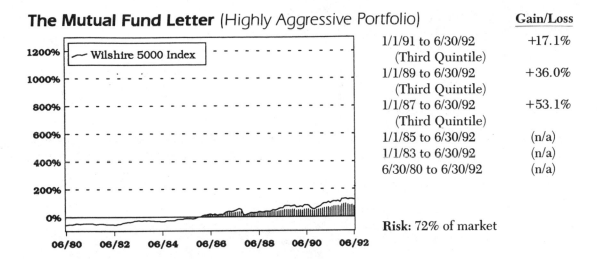

	Gain/Loss
1/1/91 to 6/30/92 (Third Quintile)	+17.1%
1/1/89 to 6/30/92 (Third Quintile)	+36.0%
1/1/87 to 6/30/92 (Third Quintile)	+53.1%
1/1/85 to 6/30/92	(n/a)
1/1/83 to 6/30/92	(n/a)
6/30/80 to 6/30/92	(n/a)

Risk: 72% of market

The Mutual Fund Letter (Moderately Aggressive Portfolio)

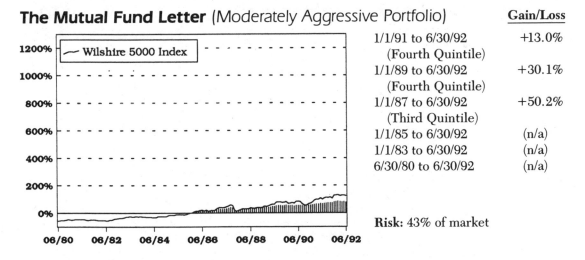

	Gain/Loss
1/1/91 to 6/30/92 (Fourth Quintile)	+13.0%
1/1/89 to 6/30/92 (Fourth Quintile)	+30.1%
1/1/87 to 6/30/92 (Third Quintile)	+50.2%
1/1/85 to 6/30/92	(n/a)
1/1/83 to 6/30/92	(n/a)
6/30/80 to 6/30/92	(n/a)

Risk: 43% of market

The Mutual Fund Letter (Growth & Income Portfolio)

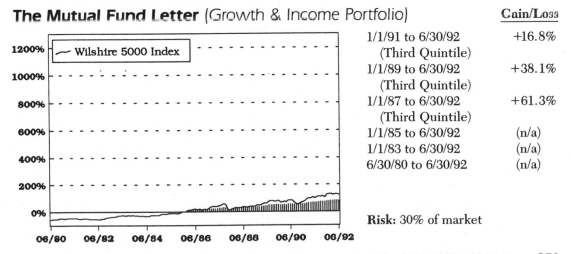

	Gain/Loss
1/1/91 to 6/30/92 (Third Quintile)	+16.8%
1/1/89 to 6/30/92 (Third Quintile)	+38.1%
1/1/87 to 6/30/92 (Third Quintile)	+61.3%
1/1/85 to 6/30/92	(n/a)
1/1/83 to 6/30/92	(n/a)
6/30/80 to 6/30/92	(n/a)

Risk: 30% of market

The Mutual Fund Letter (Income Portfolio)

	Gain/Loss
1/1/91 to 6/30/92	+18.4%
(Third Quintile)	
1/1/89 to 6/30/92	+37.7%
(Third Quintile)	
1/1/87 to 6/30/92	+48.6%
(Third Quintile)	
1/1/85 to 6/30/92	(n/a)
1/1/83 to 6/30/92	(n/a)
6/30/80 to 6/30/92	(n/a)

Risk: 24% of market

The Mutual Fund Letter (All Weather Portfolio)

	Gain/Loss
1/1/91 to 6/30/92	+16.6%
(Fourth Quintile)	
1/1/89 to 6/30/92	+34.0%
(Third Quintile)	
1/1/87 to 6/30/92	(n/a)
1/1/85 to 6/30/92	(n/a)
1/1/83 to 6/30/92	(n/a)
6/30/80 to 6/30/92	(n/a)

Risk: 52% of market

The Mutual Fund Strategist

Address
P.O. Box 446
Burlington, VT 05402

Editor
Charles Hooper

Phone Number
802-658-3513

Subscription Rates
$ 52.00/3 months
$ 94.00/6 months
$149.00/year

Telephone Hotline
Yes

Money Management
Yes

--------- The Mutual Fund Strategist ---------

Post Office Box 446   Burlington, Vermont 05402

July 1992

PULSE OF THE MARKET: (July 6, 1992) June was a correction month for the U.S. stock market with losses in the major market indices ranging from 1.7% for the S&P 500 to 3.7% for the NASDAQ Composite. The average mutual fund monitored in our *Diversified Growth Portfolio* declined 3.1%. Many of the more aggressive diversified growth funds, however, experienced setbacks in the 4% to 6% range, and a few of the sector funds lost 7% to 9%. At month's end, though, the market appeared to be on a rebound with the Dow Industrials gaining 2.2% and the NASDAQ Composite increasing 3.9% during the three-day period from June 29th to July 1st. When the Fed once again lowered interest rates on July 2nd, the stage was set for a nice summer rally - but there was a spoiler: The number of unemployed in the U.S. reached the highest level in June since 1984. Concern over the likelihood of a third dip in the recession and the distinct possibility that the presidential race may be thrown into the House of Representatives could keep a lid on the market for several months. We may have seen the shortest summer rally in history!

Status of Timing Models

Intermediate Trend Timing Model	Sell	(04/20/92)
International Funds Timing Model	Sell	(06/22/92)
Bond Funds Timing Model	Buy	(04/09/92)
Precious Metals Funds Timing Model	Buy	(07/01/92)

The current status of our timing models is provided on our weekend telephone hotline update. Unscheduled updates are also provided whenever the status of a timing model changes.

Major Stock Market Indices

	June 1992	Last 12 Months	Relative Strength
Dow Jones Industrial Average	- 2.3%	+ 12.2%	+ 4.2
NASDAQ Composite Index	- 3.7	+ 17.1	+ 2.6
NYSE Composite Index	- 2.0	+ 8.6	+ 3.2
S&P 500 Index	- 1.7	+ 8.0	+ 3.2
Value Line Composite Index	- 3.7	+ 4.2	+ 0.7
Wilshire 5000 Index	- 2.3	+ 9.2	+ 3.0

Money Market Funds

Average 30-day simple yield for taxable money market funds as of June 30, 1992, was 3.44%.

Performance Results (Average of Model Portfolios)

1985	1986	1987	1988	1989	1990	1991
+30.0%	+25.1%	+23.5%	+12.4%	+24.7%	+11.7%	+23.1%

(Source: The Hulbert Financial Digest, 316 Commerce Street, Alexandria, VA 22314)

The Mutual Fund Strategist is a mutual-fund-selection and market-timing newsletter, published monthly by Charles Hooper. It is supplemented by a telephone hotline that is updated at least once each week and more often when needed.

As of mid-1992, *The Mutual Fund Strate-gist* had two model portfolios, a "Diversified Growth" and a "Sector" portfolio, both of which the HFD has data for beginning in 1988. Over the years, though, Hooper has recommended a number of additional model portfolios that subsequently were discontinued. Though these portfolios' performances are not graphed separately in this book, they are reflected in what is reported for the newsletter's average—the HFD's data for which starts at the beginning of 1985.

Over the seven and one-half years through mid-1992, this newsletter's average performance was a gain of 234.1%, which compares to a 197.6% gain for the Wilshire 5000. Among those mutual fund letters tracked by the HFD, this is the only one over this period that beat the market.

A large part of Hooper's above-market performance can be attributed to his selection of individual mutual funds. On a pure timing basis, in fact, Hooper has slightly underperformed the market. Over these same seven and one-half years, an investor who switched between hypothetical shares of the Wilshire 5000 and T-Bills upon signals from Hooper's "Intermediate Timing Model" gained 188.9%—slightly behind a buy-and-hold and further behind his newsletter's actual performance. This indicates that Hooper's particular mutual fund picks did much better than the market during the times his portfolios owned them.

The Mutual Fund Strategist (Average)

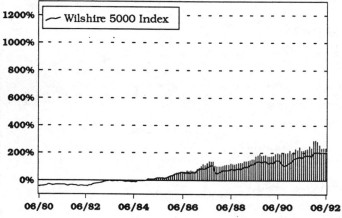

	Gain/Loss
1/1/91 to 6/30/92 (Fifth Quintile)	+6.3%
1/1/89 to 6/30/92 (Second Quintile)	+48.1%
1/1/87 to 6/30/92 (First Quintile)	+105.5%
1/1/85 to 6/30/92 (First Quintile)	+234.1%
1/1/83 to 6/30/92	(n/a)
6/30/80 to 6/30/92	(n/a)

Risk: 156% of market

The Mutual Fund Strategist (Diversified Growth Portfolio)

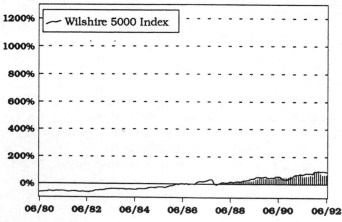

	Gain/Loss
1/1/91 to 6/30/92 (Fifth Quintile)	+5.8%
1/1/89 to 6/30/92 (Second Quintile)	+47.9%
1/1/87 to 6/30/92	(n/a)
1/1/85 to 6/30/92	(n/a)
1/1/83 to 6/30/92	(n/a)
6/30/80 to 6/30/92	(n/a)

Risk: 146% of market

The Mutual Fund Strategist (Sector Portfolio)

	Gain/Loss
1/1/91 to 6/30/92 (Fifth Quintile)	+6.5%
1/1/89 to 6/30/92 (Second Quintile)	+53.3%
1/1/87 to 6/30/92	(n/a)
1/1/85 to 6/30/92	(n/a)
1/1/83 to 6/30/92	(n/a)
6/30/80 to 6/30/92	(n/a)

Risk: 171% of market

Mutual Fund Technical Trader

Address
P.O. Box 4560
Burlington, VT
05406-4560

Editor
Stephen Parker

Phone Number
802-658-5500

Subscription Rates
$48.00/year

Telephone Hotline
Yes

Money Management
Yes

MUTUAL FUND TECHNICAL TRADER

JULY 15, 1992   DIVERSITY IN THE FACE OF ADVERSITY

Stormy Seas Ahead

You should strongly consider sitting on the sidelines in ultra safe investments over the next 6 to 8 months while current market, economic, and political uncertainties are resolved. You should also consider increasing the percentage of your portfolio in non-U.S. dollar denominated assets such as European bonds which command much higher interest rates than those offered in the United States.

One of the problems facing investors is the overvalued nature of U.S. stocks which offer very little upside appreciation potential and considerable downside risk due to the prospect for low economic growth over at least the next three years. U.S. bond prices could also suffer from the declining value of the U.S. dollar, low monetary growth rates, and increasing inflationary pressures.

Over the past 10 months, the Federal Reserve has aggressively pursued a strategy to bring down short-term interest rates in an attempt to stimulate economic growth. The latest move by the Federal Reserve was on Thursday, July 2, when the Fed lowered the discount

and Fed fund rates each by one half a percentage point to 3.0 and 3.25 percent respectively. The Fed lowered interest rates in response to a dismal June unemployment figure which rose to 7.8 percent, the highest level since 1984.

The current 3.25 percent Fed fund rate is the lowest level since 1963. So far, the lowering of interest rates by the Feds has produced little effect on stimulating any meaningful economic growth, but has set into motion strong economic forces which will eventually lead to much higher rates of inflation.

The Bush administration and Congress pressured Federal Reserve Chairman Alan Greenspan into lowering the discount rate from the current 3.5 percent level to an unbelievably low level of 3.0 percent. Ironically, Greenspan had previously stated that the Federal Reserve would not consider another cut in the discount rate in view of positive economic growth, but then reversed its earlier position when recently released unemployment figures for June showed another sharp and unexpected increase.

The Bush administration is using the Federal Reserve as an expedient scapegoat to mask its own incompetence and inability to formulate effective long-term solutions to reverse the current economic decay taking place in the United States.

Stock prices on Wall Street have appreciated sharply over the past 18 months despite the recession and the bleak outlook for future economic growth. The stock market advance is primarily due to the Federal Reserve's ongoing cut in interest rates and the belief by investors that three or more consecutive interest rate cuts mark the

beginning of an economic recovery and major upward move in stock market prices. Investors' belief in the timing of the current economic recovery and the recent buying of stock is based almost entirely upon previous recoveries in which similar interest rate cuts by the Federal Reserve awakened new bull markets.

Wall Street investors have come to accept and revere the power of the Federal Reserve which is aptly expressed in the adage, "Don't fight the Fed." This means that investors are wise to adopt trading strategies which are not contrary to the current monetary policy being promoted by the Federal Reserve. Historically, stock market prices tend to decline when the Fed tightens credit, and conversely, rise when the Fed eases credit by pushing interest rates down.

This time investors should adopt a contrary approach to the Federal Reserve's policies because the current economic recovery is significantly different from previous recoveries in that firstly, the United States faces the onerous burden of paying off a three trillion dollar federal budget deficit. Secondly, the industrial base of the United States, which is vitally necessary in generating needed tax revenues, is shrinking as U.S. based manufacturing is downsized and/or forced to move outside the United States.

The erosion of the U.S. industrial base is not likely to reverse itself any time soon, given the current excess global capacity and high labor costs in the United States. The U.S. cannot count on the service industry to replace the industrial base because the service industry provides mostly incremental earnings

(continued on page 2)

Table of Contents

Mutual Fund Technical Trader is published monthly by Stephen Parker, who supplements the service with a weekly telephone hotline update. The service is devoted both to timing the overall market as well as to picking individual mutual funds (both open and closed-end funds).

The newsletter's name notwithstanding, Parker relies on both technical and fundamental analysis. His market timing does appear to be entirely technical, based on the position and direction of an exponential moving average of the NYSE Composite. But his selection of individual funds is based heavily on his analysis of macroeconomic trends both in the U.S. and overseas. Parker believes that success in the 1990s will require investors to place a greater emphasis on emerging markets around the world, and each of his model portfolios has a heavy investment in non-U.S. markets.

The HFD began following the *Mutual Fund Technical Trader* at the beginning of 1991, at which time it had five recommended model portfolios. Two of those have since been discontinued, though their performance is included in what is reported here for the service's average. Each of the three remaining model portfolios has above-average risk, including its "Conservative Income & Growth/Moderate Risk" portfolio.

Despite their above-average risk, the newsletter's portfolios have underperformed the market over the 18 months through mid-1992, gaining 25.4% versus the market's 32.3%. This means that the newsletter underperformed the market on a risk-adjusted basis as well.

The culprit in this underperformance appears to be the newsletter's market timing, not its selection of individual funds. On a timing-only basis over these 18 months, for example, the newsletter's "Aggressive Growth/High Risk" portfolio gained 22.0%, in contrast to an actual gain of 37.7% (see Appendix C-6). This shows that Parker's recommended funds outperformed the Wilshire 5000 during those times this portfolio was invested in the market.

Mutual Fund Technical Trader (Average)

	Gain/Loss
1/1/91 to 6/30/92	+25.4%
(Third Quintile)	
1/1/89 to 6/30/92	(n/a)
1/1/87 to 6/30/92	(n/a)
1/1/85 to 6/30/92	(n/a)
1/1/83 to 6/30/92	(n/a)
6/30/80 to 6/30/92	(n/a)

Risk: 101% of market

Mutual Fund Technical Trader (Aggressive Growth/High Risk)

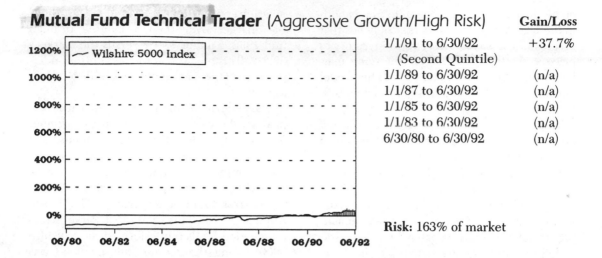

	Gain/Loss
1/1/91 to 6/30/92 (Second Quintile)	+37.7%
1/1/89 to 6/30/92	(n/a)
1/1/87 to 6/30/92	(n/a)
1/1/85 to 6/30/92	(n/a)
1/1/83 to 6/30/92	(n/a)
6/30/80 to 6/30/92	(n/a)

Risk: 163% of market

Mutual Fund Technical Trader (Growth/Short-Term Risk)

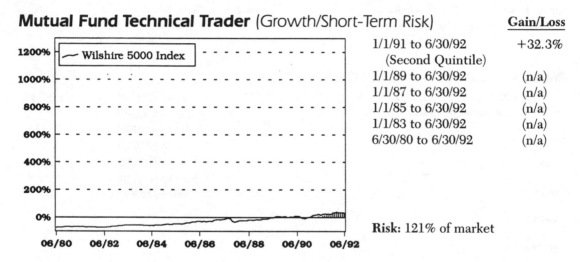

	Gain/Loss
1/1/91 to 6/30/92 (Second Quintile)	+32.3%
1/1/89 to 6/30/92	(n/a)
1/1/87 to 6/30/92	(n/a)
1/1/85 to 6/30/92	(n/a)
1/1/83 to 6/30/92	(n/a)
6/30/80 to 6/30/92	(n/a)

Risk: 121% of market

Mutual Fund Technical Trader (Conservative Income & Growth)

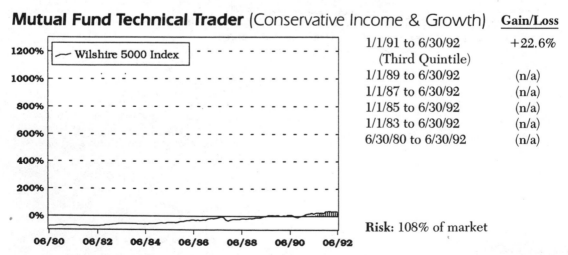

	Gain/Loss
1/1/91 to 6/30/92 (Third Quintile)	+22.6%
1/1/89 to 6/30/92	(n/a)
1/1/87 to 6/30/92	(n/a)
1/1/85 to 6/30/92	(n/a)
1/1/83 to 6/30/92	(n/a)
6/30/80 to 6/30/92	(n/a)

Risk: 108% of market

Address
The Institute for
Econometric
Research
3471 N. Federal Hwy.
Ft. Lauderdale, FL
33306

Editors
Norman Fosback and
Glen King Parker

Phone Number
800-327-6720

Subscription Rates
$95.00/year

Telephone Hotline
Yes

Money Management
No

NEW ISSUES

The Investor's Guide to Initial Public Offerings

Norman G. Fosback, Editor   *Glen King Parker, Publisher*

Creative Technology Blasts onto Multimedia Scene

CREATIVE TECHNOLOGY anticipates an early August offering at $10 to $13. We recommend purchase at $13 or below.

"Multimedia" is a new buzzword in the personal computer field. The term describes the integration of video and audio technology with computers. For example, using **CREATIVE** multimedia computer software and hardware, novice PC users can create full-blown presentations that bring moving pictures, dazzling graphics, and hi-fidelity sound to a world once limited to columns of numbers. The new technology could revolutionize the way people interact with computers.

Firmly entrenched in the vanguard of this fast-growing trend, Creative Technology sells a line of sound and video multimedia products for IBM-compatible personal computers. Best known for its popular *Sound Blaster* audio platform (which has sold nearly one million units and comprises 90% of revenues), the firm's business strategy is to supplant high-end and high-cost video and audio technologies with widely-available PC products that deliver similar functionality at rock-bottom prices.

The company's soaring revenue is nearly picture-perfect, and profit-growth is stepping to an even faster beat.

CREATIVE TECHNOLOGY – 1901 McCarthy Boulevard, Milpitas, CA 95035; (408) 428-6600.
Offering of 4,800,000 common shares @ $10-$13 per share: 3,600,000 shares (75%) by the company and balance by existing stockholders. Managing underwriters: Goldman, Sachs, 85 Broad Street, New York, NY 10004, (212) 902-1000; Alex. Brown & Sons, 135 E. Baltimore, Baltimore, MD 21202, (301) 727-1700; and Robertson, Stephens, 1 Embarcadero, San Francisco, CA 94111, (415) 781-9700.
After the offering, 39,600,000 shares will be outstanding and book value will equal $1.13 per share. Latest 12-month revenues are $1.73 per share for a Price/Revenues ratio of 5.8-7.5, and 12-month pro forma earnings equal 47 cents per share for a P/E of 21-28. No dividend. Proposed symbol: CREAF.

Year Ended	Revenues	Net Income	Profit Margin	Earn./Share
June 30, 1987	$ 2,473,000	$ 4,000	0.2%	$ .00
June 30, 1988	4,163,000	49,000	1.2%	.00
June 30, 1989	5,392,000	81,000	1.5%	.01
June 30, 1990	7,479,000	975,000	13.0%	.04
June 30, 1991	24,769,000	8,400,000	33.9%	.24*
Three Months Ended				
Mar. 31, 1991	$ 6,784,000	$2,288,000	33.7%	$ .07
June 30, 1991	7,985,000	2,920,000	36.6%	.08
Sep. 30, 1991	8,572,000	2,266,000	26.4%	.06
Dec. 31, 1991	24,692,000	6,847,000	27.7%	.19
Mar. 31, 1992	27,432,000	6,487,000	23.6%	.18**

(*$.21 pro forma; **$.16 pro forma; on shares to be outstanding.)

Issue No. 167   July 10, 1992

Announcement
We are implementing an all-new and significantly improved *Hot Line* system today, which includes many new features. Please see Page 3 for details.

We are somewhat surprised at the modest pricing of the offering, a multiple of just 21 to 28 even though profits are going through the roof. One reason may be the price weakness prevailing in already-public computer and technology stocks. Another might be the fact that Creative is a Singapore company, and most of the company's property, technology, and personnel reside in that nation.

But overall, the few risks are more than offset by a multitude of potential rewards. Among PC enthusiasts, Creative's popular *Sound Blaster* is regarded as without peer on a price/performance basis. Moreover, the company's strategy to leverage this already successful product line into other areas of the burgeoning multimedia market is promising. Lastly, the offering's conservative pricing will be no match for just a few more quarters of swelling sales and earnings. Buy at $13 or better.

G-Tech Fairly Priced

G-Tech is the largest operator and supplier of on-line lottery systems in the world, with annual revenues of $350 million. G-Tech went private three years ago in a $306-million leveraged buy-out at $16.25 a share. It now plans to go public again with a $170-million offering priced at $17 to $20. At 26 to 31 times earnings, the offering is fairly priced, neither under nor overvalued.

Since New Jersey established the first on-line lottery in 1975, the industry has expanded enormously. Last year, approximately $15 billion of lottery tickets were sold in the U.S., and another $13 billion were sold internationally. G-Tech says that during the last five years, it has been awarded 28 of the 39 on-line lottery [Continued on Page 2]

A Service of The Institute for Econometric Research, 3471 North Federal, Fort Lauderdale, Florida 33306
For Subscriber Services and Information, Call Toll-Free 800-442-9000

New Issues is published monthly by The Institute for Econometric Research, whose chairman is Glen Parker and whose president is Norman Fosback. The Institute publishes a number of other investment newsletters, four of which are reviewed elsewhere in this *Guide*.

As this newsletter's name suggests, *New Issues* focuses on the market for initial public offerings. Academic research has discovered that one of the inefficiencies in the otherwise very efficient stock market is the valuation of new issues; over long periods of time, such research has found, an investor who buys new issues at their initial offering price will eventually outperform the market as a whole. In *New Issues*, by screening the new-issue market for the best bargains, Fosback and Parker are hoping to improve even on this academically approved strategy.

Though Fosback and Parker provide market-timing and portfolio allocation advice in their other publications, they don't explicitly apply such advice to *New Issues*. The HFD therefore constructs a portfolio for this newsletter that always is fully invested and equally weighted among all their open positions. Not surprisingly, a fully invested portfolio in initial public offerings is risky; the portfolio the HFD has constructed has been significantly more volatile than the Wilshire 5000.

The 1980s were not particularly hospitable to the new-issue market, however, so the HFD may not have enough data to properly test their approach. Nevertheless, for the nine and one-half years through mid-1992, the HFD reports a gain of just 58.5% for this newsletter's recommendations, in contrast to a gain of 278.6% for the Wilshire 5000. This puts the newsletter in 25th place out of the 36 for which the HFD has continuous performance data over this period.

This *Guide* also reviews another newsletter that focuses at least in part on the new-issue market and for which the HFD has a track record over the same period: *Emerging & Special Situations*. Over these nine and one-half years, *Emerging & Special Situations* gained 121.6%, in contrast to *New Issues*'s 58.5%.

New Issues

	Gain/Loss
1/1/91 to 6/30/92 (First Quintile)	+63.0%
1/1/89 to 6/30/92 (Second Quintile)	+67.3%
1/1/87 to 6/30/92 (Second Quintile)	+91.3%
1/1/85 to 6/30/92 (Third Quintile)	+104.8%
1/1/83 to 6/30/92 (Fourth Quintile)	+58.5%
6/30/80 to 6/30/92	(n/a)

Risk: 194% of market

The Ney Report

Address
P.O. Box 92223
Pasadena, CA 91109

Editor
Richard Ney

Phone Number
818-441-2222

Subscription Rates
$195.00/6 months
$295.00/year

Telephone Hotline
Yes

Money Management
Yes

THE Ney Report

July 2, 1992   *Success in the market depends on buying when specialists buy and selling when they sell.*   Volume 17, No. 2

MARKET SUMMARY

What you have been watching for the past few weeks is a merchandising operation in which Exchange insiders dropped prices to accumulate stock at wholesale and have now rallied to sell short so they could move lower to accumulate more stock.

The foundation for the rally of the past week was laid with the sharp decline on heavy volume that began with the Dow at 3354 on June 16th and ended with an intra-day decline of 43 points to close the Dow at 3242 on June 22nd. In the course of this decline, investors bowed to the command of the specialist system and dumped almost a billion shares of stock into specialist and Exchange insider portfolios. Specialists then advanced the Dow last Monday and closed up +37.45. They kept the public out of the market Tuesday by opening the Dow down (and closed it down 1.34).

To be sure, all that changed with the Dow's advance on Wednesday from the opening until it closed up 35.61. This, of course, was attributed by the WSJ today to "speculation that interest rates are headed lower." After Wednesday's advance, investors were anxiously waiting to see how the Dow opened this morning. Imagine the joy in Mudville, therefore, when the prime rate was dropped and the Dow was advanced 20 points during the first half hour. The one thought that entered the investor's mind was that the Dow was launched on a pilgrimage to much higher price levels.

I have witnessed many impressive instances of how effectively specialists are able through their control of

stock prices, to control investor behavior. But there is nothing to compare to a back-to-back advance to the accompaniment of lower rates. For most investors the rally represented the chest of gold at the end of the rainbow. They charged into the market and volume soared to a very heavy 41 million shares <u>for the first half hour</u>! It was a feeding frenzy. In my judgment specialists were not unloading stock so much as selling short to supply demand. As a result of the short selling I expect a further decline (see Timing section).

As it was meant to, the rally and the decline in rates threw a pall of apprehensiveness over traders who had sold short on expectations of a major decline. They, therefore, threw in their orders to cover their short positions, not realizing specialists always rally prior to any decline that might enable short sellers to establish a profit (which, of course, would come out of specialist's pockets). One can only imagine their reaction to the bewildering turnabout in fortune when they saw the Dow drop 24 points during the next half hour.

Another reason I expect a pullback (after a further rally probably Monday) is because there are a number of stocks in which specialists have begun but have not yet completed their accumulations. They could, of course, do that even though the Dow is not dropped (when they dropped Bristol Myers 7 1/2 points on 10 million shares to close at 66 7/8 as the Dow was being advanced to a close above 3400). In any event, following the pullback, the portents for the future are excellent.

Published since 1976 by Richard Ney & Associates Asset Management, P.O. Box 92223, Pasadena, CA 91109
Richard Ney, Chairman • Telephone: (818) 441-2222 • Mei-Lee, President

The Ney Report is published twice each month by Richard Ney and is supplemented by a telephone hotline that is updated several times each week. The portfolios the HFD tracks for this newsletter first were recommended by another service Ney used to publish, *The Ney Mutual Fund Report*. When this mutual fund newsletter ceased publication in early 1990, these portfolios were taken over by *The Ney Report*.

Ney believes that the stock markets are dominated by the action of specialists on the exchanges, and therefore that the key both to the market's direction and to which individual stocks are best to buy and sell can be discovered by studying specialists' behavior. In addition to advising investors on mutual fund timing and selection, Ney's newsletter and hotline also make recommendations concerning individual securities.

Over the four and one-half years through mid-1992 for which the HFD has data, Ney's three mutual fund portfolios produced an average gain of 33.4%, in contrast to an 89.0% gain for the Wilshire 5000 and a 33.8% gain for T-Bills. These performances were turned in with less risk than that associated with the

average stock, but because they underperformed the T-Bill rate, their risk-adjusted performances are negative.

The culprit in these portfolios' lagging the market appears primarily to be Ney's market timing. For example, if each of the funds in his "Growth" portfolio had performed exactly as did the Wilshire 5000, the portfolio would have gained 24.2% instead of 32.3%. This shows that Ney's particular fund recommendations actually did better than the market during the times he owned them.

The Ney Report (Average)

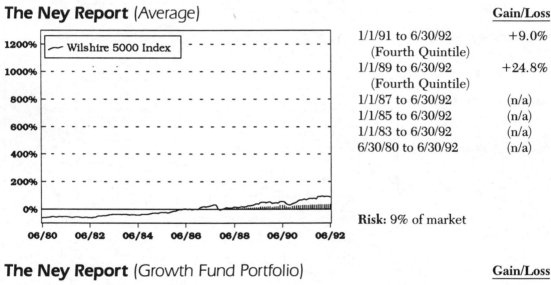

	Gain/Loss
1/1/91 to 6/30/92	+9.0%
(Fourth Quintile)	
1/1/89 to 6/30/92	+24.8%
(Fourth Quintile)	
1/1/87 to 6/30/92	(n/a)
1/1/85 to 6/30/92	(n/a)
1/1/83 to 6/30/92	(n/a)
6/30/80 to 6/30/92	(n/a)

Risk: 9% of market

The Ney Report (Growth Fund Portfolio)

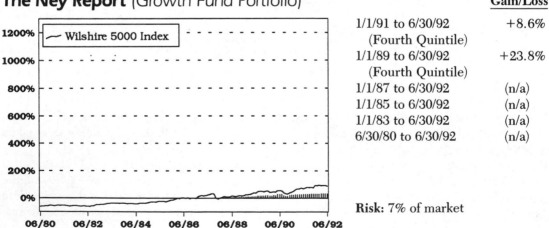

	Gain/Loss
1/1/91 to 6/30/92	+8.6%
(Fourth Quintile)	
1/1/89 to 6/30/92	+23.8%
(Fourth Quintile)	
1/1/87 to 6/30/92	(n/a)
1/1/85 to 6/30/92	(n/a)
1/1/83 to 6/30/92	(n/a)
6/30/80 to 6/30/92	(n/a)

Risk: 7% of market

The Ney Report (Growth & Income Fund Portfolio)

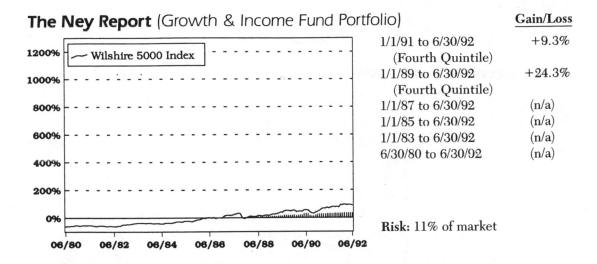

	Gain/Loss
1/1/91 to 6/30/92	+9.3%
(Fourth Quintile)	
1/1/89 to 6/30/92	+24.3%
(Fourth Quintile)	
1/1/87 to 6/30/92	(n/a)
1/1/85 to 6/30/92	(n/a)
1/1/83 to 6/30/92	(n/a)
6/30/80 to 6/30/92	(n/a)

Risk: 11% of market

The Ney Report (Income Fund Portfolio)

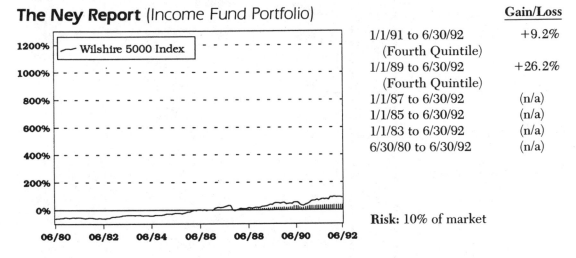

	Gain/Loss
1/1/91 to 6/30/92	+9.2%
(Fourth Quintile)	
1/1/89 to 6/30/92	+26.2%
(Fourth Quintile)	
1/1/87 to 6/30/92	(n/a)
1/1/85 to 6/30/92	(n/a)
1/1/83 to 6/30/92	(n/a)
6/30/80 to 6/30/92	(n/a)

Risk: 10% of market

**NoLoad Fund*X

Address
235 Montgomery St.
Suite 662
San Francisco, CA
94104

Editors
Burton Berry and
Janet Brown

Phone Number
415-986-7979

Subscription Rates
$ 27.00/3 months
$114.00/year

Telephone Hotline
No

Money Management
Yes

DAL Investment Co. Publication

NoLoad FUND*X

A Monitoring System for the Enterprising Investor

Volume 17 • Issue 7

July 1992

Includes 686 Funds • Annual Subscription $114

Following The Stars*

Top Ranking Funds at 6/30/92 In Descending Order

	Class 1			
Months in Star Box Con se- utive Past Qtr.	Most Speculative Growth Funds	Total % Assets in ($Mil) Cash	FvX Year Score	
4	15.08 **Financial Str Fin Svc	$239	8	
1	11.60 **Sherman Dean	3	2	
6	11.30 **American Heritage	27	28	
4	10.90 **Fidelity Low Price Stk	840	20	
1	10.70 **Fairmont	17	3	

	Class 2			
Months in Star Box Con se- utive Past Qtr.	Speculative Growth Funds	Total % Assets in ($Mil) Cash	FvX Year Score	
2	13.80 **Price New Asia	$239	6	
2	13.63 **20th Century Internat'l	187	10	
2	11.93 **Babson-S Internat'l	18	8	
1	9.08 **Price European Stk	139	13	
4	7.83 **Babson-Enterprise (r)	166	10	

	Class 3 (Recommended)			
Months in Star Box Con se- utive Past Qtr.	Higher Quality Growth Funds	Total % Assets in ($Mil) Cash	FvX Year Score	
1	11.20 **Century Shares	$162	3	
8	10.13 **Fidelity Equity Inc II	1,206	14	
1	10.13 **Vanguard Windsor (r)	8,492	8	
1	10.05 **Mutual Qualified	1,132	8	
1	9.68 **Mutual Beacon	430	9	
6	9.60 **Berwyn	34	7	

	Class 4			
Months in Star Box Con se- utive Past Qtr.	Total Return Funds	Total % Assets in ($Mil) Cash		
4	12.90 **Lindner Dividend	$381	6	
6	11.10 **Fidelity Convertible Sec	269	6	
3	10.25 **Legg Mason Total Ret	69	22	
1	8.68 **Fidelity Utilities Inc	7/9	7	
1	7.98 **Vanguard Wellesley	2,389	3	

How Funds Are Ranked

Each month funds in Classes 1 - 4 (pages 4 - 8) are ranked by their FvX Scores. The five winners appear above. So, if there is a tie:

FvX Score is an average of the 12, 6, 3, and 1 month total return results in column 5 - 8 on the inside pages. Stars are placed beside the funds in each Class having the highest returns in each column.

One ✱ point is added to the fund's average for each star earned during the four periods. After the bonus for stars is added to the average, the Star funds are re-ranked from best to worst. FvX Rank, followed by the Score, is listed in column 1 in front of the name of each fund. Funds ranked ✱5 make this StarBox.

LoLoads, Page 13, are not included in these rankings but are included in the Special Report rankings on page 16.

NoLoad Fund Highlights for 12-Months Ending 6/30/92: (Column 5)

	% of Class Outperforming S&P500	12 Mo. Total Return
Class 1	43%	40.9%
Class 2	43	26.2
Class 3	42	26.0
Class 4	58	31.3
		13.3
		17.7

Best of Class	
Financial Str Fin Svc	
20th Century Int'l	
Fidelity Eq Inc II	
Berger 101	
S&P 500	
DJIA	

Worst of Class	12 Mo. Total Return
United Serv Gold	-36.1%
A dtutcer	.202
Matters	.35
Evergreen Globl RE	-3.3

LoLoad Fund*X FOOTNOTES

SYMBOLS & FOOTNOTES
SCOREBOARD - Leading Market Barometers, Money & Capital Markets ... 15
SPECIAL REPORT ... 15,16

Class 5 - U.S. Government & Tax-Exempt Bond Funds ... 10, 11
Class 6 - Diversified Money Market Funds ... 12
Class 6 - U.S. Government & Tax Exempt Money Market Funds ... 13

	Page
REPORT - Markets, Following the Stars*, Industry News, Q & A's	2, 3, 14
FUND DATA - Performance, Rank, Score, Yield, Assets, Dividends & Capital Gains	
Class 1 - Most Speculative Growth Funds	4
Class 2 - Speculative Growth Funds	5, 6
Class 3 - Higher Quality Growth Funds	6, 7
Class 4 - Total Return Funds	8
Class 5 - Corporate Bond Funds	9

INSIDE:

**NoLoad Fund*X is published monthly and is edited by Burton Berry and Janet Brown. There is no telephone hotline.

**No Load Fund*X basically is a rating service for the major no-load (and a few very low-load) mutual funds, providing a monthly review of those funds' performance over the previous month and for various longer periods as well. In presenting these ratings, **NoLoad Fund*X breaks the mutual funds into different risk categories and highlights the top number (usually five) of funds in each that currently have the best performance.

Though Berry does not give the specific

formula with which he ranks the mutual funds in each category, he does provide an overall outline. The ranking is based on an average of each fund's twelve-, six-, three- and one-month results, with credit given to a fund if in any of those four periods it was in the top five.

Berry recommends that subscribers select one of the categories of risk and purchase the top-rated fund. They should continue to hold that fund as long as it remains in the top five, after which time they should switch into the newly top-ranked fund in that category. As long as certain funds and types of funds perform well for more than a very short period of time (such as the international funds did for several years in the 1980s), this strategy can do quite well.

The HFD tracks Berry's strategy, which he calls the "Follow the Stars" strategy, by constructing a portfolio for each category out of those top funds that currently are highlighted. That portfolio changes each month to the extent that Berry's highlighted funds change—which means that its composition changes in most, though not all, months. Because these categories do not contain money market funds, these portfolios are fully invested at all times. Berry points out, however, the best-performing funds in a bear market will be those that have built up a cash position, so his strategy does lead to at least some market timing.

The HFD has data for three categories of Berry's funds since mid-1980. The best-performing category was his "Class 3," which Berry has entitled his "Higher Quality Growth Funds." Over the twelve years through mid-1992, this portfolio gained 632.6%, outperforming the 432.7% total return of the Wilshire 5000. Berry's "Class 2" (which he defines as "Speculative Growth Funds") gained 373.3% over this same period, while his "Class 1" ("Most Speculative Growth Funds") gained 129.5%.

Several years ago Berry also created a new category, his "Class 4," for total return mutual funds. Over the five and one-half years through mid-1992, the highlighted funds in this category gained 45.5%, in contrast to 93.3% for the Wilshire 5000.

Using the same methodology for four different categories of funds, therefore, Berry was able to beat the market in just one of them. While statisticians would argue that this calls the methodology's worth into question, Berry believes that it is significant that his methodology worked in the case of his "Class 3." Beginning in late 1989, in fact, Berry announced that henceforth his newsletter's model portfolio would be just the highlighted funds in this one category. The performance the HFD reports for the newsletter's average from that point on, therefore, will be based on just this one category.

Time will tell whether the success of Berry's methodology in his "Higher Quality Growth Funds" category will continue. Since late 1989, however, the point at which Berry said that this category would be his model portfolio, it has underperformed two of Berry's three other categories.

NoLoad Fund*X (Average)

	Gain/Loss
1/1/91 to 6/30/92 (Third Quintile)	+25.9%
1/1/89 to 6/30/92 (Second Quintile)	+45.5%
1/1/87 to 6/30/92 (Third Quintile)	+48.2%
1/1/85 to 6/30/92 (Second Quintile)	+142.8%
1/1/83 to 6/30/92 (Second Quintile)	+176.8%
6/30/80 to 6/30/92 (Third Quintile)	+334.7%

Risk: 91% of market

NoLoad Fund*X (Portfolio of "Class 1" Funds)

	Gain/Loss
1/1/91 to 6/30/92 (First Quintile)	+65.6%
1/1/89 to 6/30/92 (Second Quintile)	+67.9%
1/1/87 to 6/30/92 (Fourth Quintile)	+42.9%
1/1/85 to 6/30/92 (Fourth Quintile)	+101.2%
1/1/83 to 6/30/92 (Fourth Quintile)	+73.7%
6/30/80 to 6/30/92 (Fourth Quintile)	+129.5%

Risk: 170% of market

NoLoad Fund*X (Portfolio of "Class 2" Funds)

	Gain/Loss
1/1/91 to 6/30/92 (Second Quintile)	+26.9%
1/1/89 to 6/30/92 (Third Quintile)	+41.9%
1/1/87 to 6/30/92 (Third Quintile)	+47.0%
1/1/85 to 6/30/92 (Second Quintile)	+133.7%
1/1/83 to 6/30/92 (Second Quintile)	+184.9%
6/30/80 to 6/30/92 (Third Quintile)	+373.3%

Risk: 122% of market

NoLoad Fund*X (Portfolio of "Class 3" Funds)

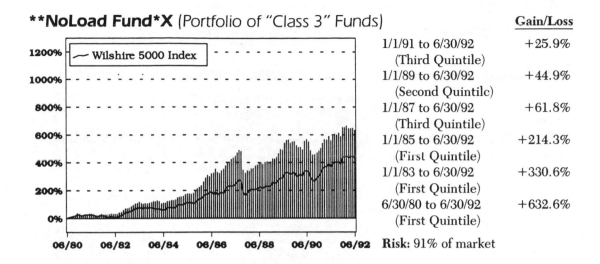

	Gain/Loss
1/1/91 to 6/30/92 (Third Quintile)	+25.9%
1/1/89 to 6/30/92 (Second Quintile)	+44.9%
1/1/87 to 6/30/92 (Third Quintile)	+61.8%
1/1/85 to 6/30/92 (First Quintile)	+214.3%
1/1/83 to 6/30/92 (First Quintile)	+330.6%
6/30/80 to 6/30/92 (First Quintile)	+632.6%

Risk: 91% of market

NoLoad Fund*X (Portfolio of "Class 4" Funds)

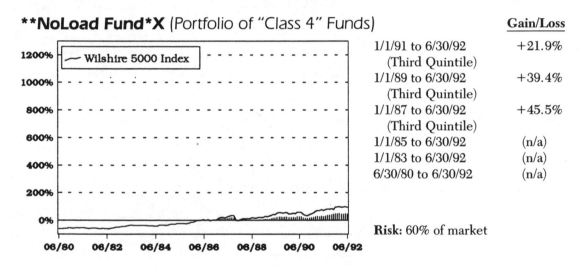

	Gain/Loss
1/1/91 to 6/30/92 (Third Quintile)	+21.9%
1/1/89 to 6/30/92 (Third Quintile)	+39.4%
1/1/87 to 6/30/92 (Third Quintile)	+45.5%
1/1/85 to 6/30/92	(n/a)
1/1/83 to 6/30/92	(n/a)
6/30/80 to 6/30/92	(n/a)

Risk: 60% of market

The No-Load Fund Investor

Address
P.O. Box 283
Hastings-on-Hudson,
   NY 10706

Editor
Sheldon Jacobs

Phone Number
914-693-7420

Subscription Rates
$105.00/year

Telephone Hotline
No

Money Management
Yes

ISSN # 0736-6256

THE NO-LOAD FUND INVESTOR

JULY 1992

Second quarter: modest declines

As a result of a 2.3% loss in June, the average equity fund ended the April-June quarter off 1% compared to a 0.3% decline in the first quarter. Small company funds declined 7.9% in the second quarter, health funds declined 6.9%, and the average aggressive growth fund declined 6.5%. Biggest winners in the second quarter were the finance funds, up 5.1%. Next were the internationals, up 4.4%, and the golds, up 4.2%. Among individual funds, **Fidelity Select S&L**, **Fidelity Pound Performance** and **Regional Banks** ranked one, two and three. There were 10 internationals in the top 20, three golds. Worst fund for the quarter was the **Prudent Speculator Leveraged Fund**, off 20.8%.

For 1992 year-to-date, **Fidelity Select Automotive** remains the number one fund, **Oakmark** the number one diversified equity fund, and **Price New Asia**, the number one international fund. The worst fund in the half was the **USAA Aggressive Growth Fund**, off 23.4%. Five of the top six funds in June were golds. The worst fund was **Financial Energy**, off 10.4%.

International funds have potential

International funds were underperformers last year, but so far this year their modest gains have looked good beside the declines in the domestic funds. If you delete Pacific Basin funds holding Japanese stocks, they're up 3.2%. We think the internationals have good potential. The following chart shows that a number of major European countries have lower price/earnings ratios and higher yields than does the U.S. Only Japan is less attractive.

continued on page 14

Funds that have never had a losing year

With the market at high levels, it is certainly comforting to own a fund with an exemplary performance record—a fund that has never had a down year. But is it the best strategy? We've done some research and find the answer is that, as usual, you will pay a price for the greater downside protection these "all-weather" funds provide.

Our analysis studied the performance of diversified equity funds over the last eleven years, a period selected to include 1981, a down year. (The next down year prior to 1981 was 1974, and to have included that would have made our fund universe too small.) This 11-year period was unusually favorable for stocks; but still, there were three calendar years when the average fund suffered small to moderate losses: 1981, 1984, and 1990. In addition, a number of funds ended 1987 with losses. Consequently, out of 128 diversified funds in our *Handbook* universe (all agg-gr, growth, gr-inc and income funds eleven or more years old) only *seven* funds had gains in each and every year. The seven funds, their ranks and overall gains are:

**Funds that gained every calendar year
1981-1991**

Fund	Rank among 128 funds	11-yr gain
Endowments	26	388.8%
Mairs & Powers Income	53	315.2
Pax World	55	311.9
Federated Stock & Bond	61	296.8
Beacon Hill Mutual	80	249.3
Stralem	90	221.3
Analytic Optioned Equity	99	206.9

If there is a common denominator among these equity funds, it's that many of them hold a significant portion of their portfolios in fixed-income investments. No doubt this is a major reason why they achieved positive returns each year. The average bond fund gained in all of the 11 years studied. This may not be the case in the next ten years.

Let's compare this to other funds that had occasional down years in this period. Number one among the 128 funds was the **CGM Capital Development Fund**, up 912.4%; second was **Fidelity Magellan**, up 863.2%; the tenth ranked fund was **Twentieth Century Select**, up 467.1%.

continued on page 15

Covers 617 no- and low-load stock and bond funds, more than any other newsletter.

The No-Load Fund Investor is published monthly by Sheldon Jacobs and is not supplemented by a telephone hotline update. It has been published since 1979.

For a number of years, *The No-Load Fund Investor* was published quarterly and was primarily a reference service for the no-load mutual funds (and a well-regarded one at that). In 1985 Jacobs increased his publishing frequency to monthly and began listing in each issue those funds in various risk categories that he rated most attractive for current purchase. Subsequent to that Jacobs began publishing specific portfolio allocation advice on how subscribers should divide their assets between the market and cash.

The HFD has data for *The No-Load Fund Investor* from the beginning of 1986, and the figure for its average performance reflects the track records for several portfolios that have since been discontinued. Over the subsequent six and one-half years through mid-1992, according to the HFD, this average was a gain of 91.5%, in contrast to the Wilshire 5000's gain of 124.5%.

All of Jacobs's portfolios have been substantially less risky than the market as a whole, so underperforming the market at least to some degree is not that surprising. But even when taking their low risk into account, they still have underperformed the market on a risk-adjusted basis.

The primary culprit in this underperformance appears to be Jacobs's allocation advice. If each of the funds in his "Wealth Builder" portfolio had performed exactly as the Wilshire 5000, then over these six and one-half years it would have gained 94.2% instead of 98.4%. This shows that Jacobs's recommended funds actually did slightly better than the market during those times his portfolio owned them—and that the reason the portfolio didn't beat the market was that it was less than fully invested.

In addition to publishing his newsletter, Jacobs also publishes an annual *Handbook for No-Load Fund Investors*, a well-regarded and comprehensive reference tool covering the no-load mutual fund industry. Jacobs frequently offers the *Handbook* at a reduced price to subscribers of his newsletter.

The No-Load Fund Investor (Average)

Gain/Loss	
1/1/91 to 6/30/92	+30.5%
(Second Quintile)	
1/1/89 to 6/30/92	+48.9%
(Second Quintile)	
1/1/87 to 6/30/92	+60.7%
(Third Quintile)	
1/1/85 to 6/30/92	(n/a)
1/1/83 to 6/30/92	(n/a)
6/30/80 to 6/30/92	(n/a)

Risk: 65% of market

The No-Load Fund Investor (Wealth Builder Portfolio)

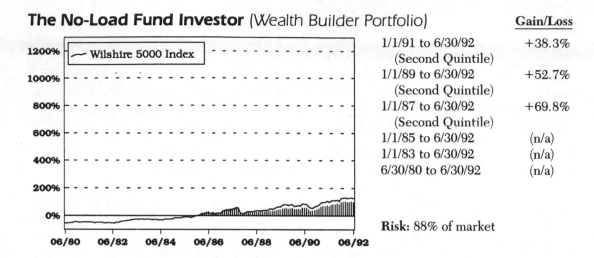

Gain/Loss	
1/1/91 to 6/30/92	+38.3%
(Second Quintile)	
1/1/89 to 6/30/92	+52.7%
(Second Quintile)	
1/1/87 to 6/30/92	+69.8%
(Second Quintile)	
1/1/85 to 6/30/92	(n/a)
1/1/83 to 6/30/92	(n/a)
6/30/80 to 6/30/92	(n/a)

Risk: 88% of market

The No-Load Fund Investor (Pre-Retirement Portfolio)

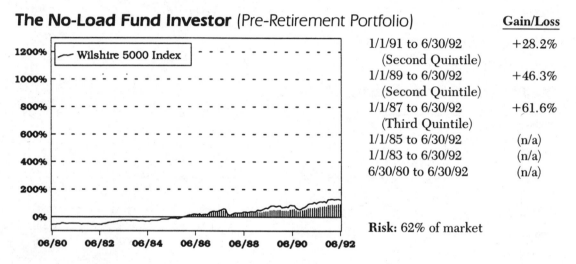

Gain/Loss	
1/1/91 to 6/30/92	+28.2%
(Second Quintile)	
1/1/89 to 6/30/92	+46.3%
(Second Quintile)	
1/1/87 to 6/30/92	+61.6%
(Third Quintile)	
1/1/85 to 6/30/92	(n/a)
1/1/83 to 6/30/92	(n/a)
6/30/80 to 6/30/92	(n/a)

Risk: 62% of market

The No-Load Fund Investor (Retirement Portfolio)

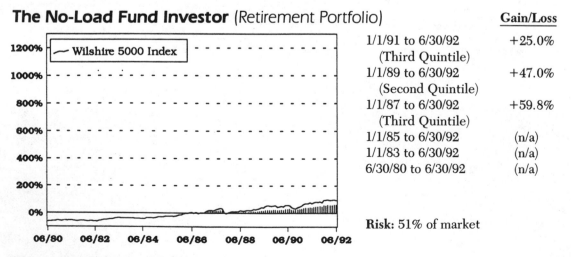

Gain/Loss	
1/1/91 to 6/30/92	+25.0%
(Third Quintile)	
1/1/89 to 6/30/92	+47.0%
(Second Quintile)	
1/1/87 to 6/30/92	+59.8%
(Third Quintile)	
1/1/85 to 6/30/92	(n/a)
1/1/83 to 6/30/92	(n/a)
6/30/80 to 6/30/92	(n/a)

Risk: 51% of market

No-Load Mutual Fund
Selections & Timing Newsletter

Address
1120 Empire Central Pl.
Suite 315
Dallas, TX 75247

Editor
Stephen L. McKee

Phone Number
800-800-6563

Subscription Rates
$ 50.00/3 months
$180.00/year

Telephone Hotline
Yes

Money Management
Yes

No-Load Mutual Fund
Selections & Timing Newsletter

1120 Empire Central Place, Suite 315, Dallas TX 75247

A service of
Investment Selections & Timing, Inc.   214-634-2366   Stephen L. McKee, Editor

We strive to provide the most return with the least risk given your objectives.

| VOLUME: Nine | NUMBER: Seven | DATE: July 7, 1992 |

The Chicken or The Egg?

Which came first, 0% interest rates or the recovery?

As I talked about in my *Recessions & Recoveries Report*, will the excesses of the eighties have to be fully purged in the depths of depression before economic expansion takes hold?

Congress can't spend its way out of the problem this time, besides it's an election year. The Fed appears intent on finding the answers by peering into the rear-view mirror. As questioned more closely elsewhere, why are they using a lagging indicator, employment, to set interest rate policy? Unfortunately, the latest round of loosening appears to be more of a political response than an economic one. So, in addition to getting his job back next year, Mr. Greenspan may also receive the unintended side effect of greater inflation and higher interest rates.

But, the problem isn't so much at the Fed. and with short-term interest rates. It's that they are once removed from the consumer, who is really the engine of any recovery, leading the way with housing related items and keeping up with the Jones. The consumer is ready today to move into the recovery, having already reduced the rate of growth in installment credit from 80% in the eighties to below 0% today. Moreover, the ratio of installment credit to income is below levels achieved in the last half of the 1980's. It's not the consumer, but the financial intermediaries and Congress that stand in the way of recovery.

Lower short-term interest rates help recoveries, but they can't sustain them. We need two things to happen: 1) Confidence must increase a bit more and 2) Long-term rates must decline substantially further.

People have to go out and consume, buy houses and cars. They have to spend and borrow. And, they need confidence in which to do all of that.

But, all they hear is that their neighbor is out of work, their savings are earning only 2.75%, their division is retrenching and international sales are slowing. Meanwhile, they still pay 16-21% on their credit cards, they wish they could cash out of their limited partnerships of the eighties and they find that their newest investment, mutual funds, are actually down from six months ago.

Furthermore, 20 years ago when the Fed Fund's rate was also at 3.25%, T-Bonds were below 6% and AAA bonds were at 7.25%. Today, the Fed Fund's rate is again at 3.25%, but T-Bonds are at 7.6% and AAA bonds are at, whoops, sorry I couldn't find any to quote.

What we need is for Congress to reestablish the tax benefits of debt and real estate losses, we need to be able to refinance our homes at 6.5% for 30-years, have our consumer installment debt at 8.5% and inflation running below 3%.

Ahh, for the good old days.

MARKET COMPOSITE BAROMETER
Bullish > 0   Bearish < 0

The Market Composite Barometer is a consensus of seven, long-term oriented, technical indicators. These include the major trend measures of the stockmarket, the level and flow of cash reserves, the actions of N.Y.S.E. Specialists and public, the degrees of investor sentiment and the internal divergences of the markets. The Barometer is designed to signal the major bullish and bearish periods in the domestic stockmarket. Invest in and stay with the top-performing equity funds in the risk class that meets your objectives when the Barometer crosses above or is above the zero line. Sell and avoid equity funds when the Barometer drops below or is below the zero horizontal reference line.

No-Load Mutual Fund Selections & Timing Newsletter is published monthly by Stephen McKee, who supplements the service with a telephone hotline that is updated several times each week. As indicated by the service's name, the newsletter focuses on both fund selection as well as market timing, and the markets that McKee attempts to time are the stock, gold and bond markets. McKee's investment philosophy appears to be based primarily (though not exclusively) on technical analysis.

McKee offers very clear advice on three model portfolios of no-load funds: a "Sector" portfolio that is constructed solely of the Fidelity family's Select funds; an "Asset Allocations" portfolio that trades among domestic and international stock and bond funds as well as precious metals funds; and an "Equity, Intermediate Term" portfolio that focuses on just the U.S. equity market. All three portfolios have below-average risk; even the "Sec-

tor" portfolio, which is the riskiest of the three, has been 14% less volatile than the Wilshire 5000.

Given this below-market risk, it is not particularly surprising that the newsletter has not beaten the Wilshire 5000 (gaining 22.6%, in contrast to the Wilshire's 32.3% over the 18 months through mid-1992). Even on a risk-adjusted basis, however, which takes into account this below-market risk, the newsletter underperformed the market.

No-Load Mutual Fund Selections & Timing Newsletter
(Average)

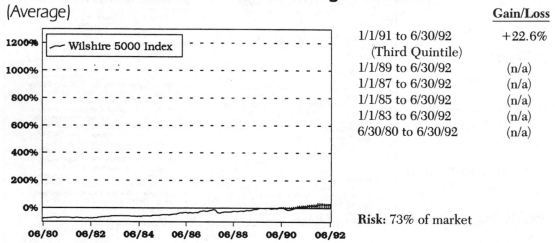

	Gain/Loss
1/1/91 to 6/30/92	+22.6%
(Third Quintile)	
1/1/89 to 6/30/92	(n/a)
1/1/87 to 6/30/92	(n/a)
1/1/85 to 6/30/92	(n/a)
1/1/83 to 6/30/92	(n/a)
6/30/80 to 6/30/92	(n/a)

Risk: 73% of market

No-Load Mutual Fund Selections & Timing Newsletter
(Asset Allocations Model Portfolio)

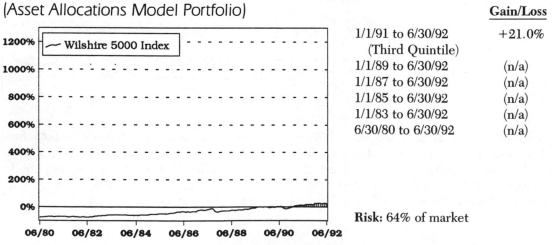

	Gain/Loss
1/1/91 to 6/30/92	+21.0%
(Third Quintile)	
1/1/89 to 6/30/92	(n/a)
1/1/87 to 6/30/92	(n/a)
1/1/85 to 6/30/92	(n/a)
1/1/83 to 6/30/92	(n/a)
6/30/80 to 6/30/92	(n/a)

Risk: 64% of market

No-Load Mutual Fund Selections & Timing Newsletter
(Sector Funds Portfolio)

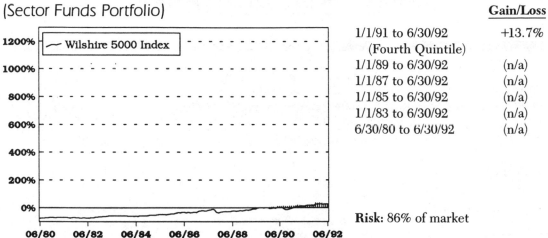

	Gain/Loss
1/1/91 to 6/30/92	+13.7%
(Fourth Quintile)	
1/1/89 to 6/30/92	(n/a)
1/1/87 to 6/30/92	(n/a)
1/1/85 to 6/30/92	(n/a)
1/1/83 to 6/30/92	(n/a)
6/30/80 to 6/30/92	(n/a)

Risk: 86% of market

No-Load Mutual Fund Selections & Timing Newsletter
(Intermediate Term Portfolio)

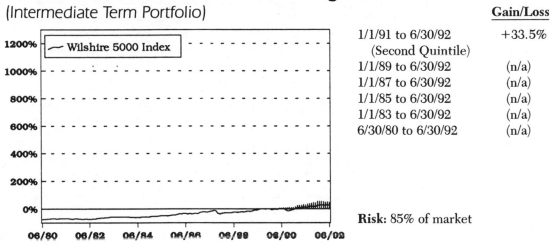

	Gain/Loss
1/1/91 to 6/30/92	+33.5%
(Second Quintile)	
1/1/89 to 6/30/92	(n/a)
1/1/87 to 6/30/92	(n/a)
1/1/85 to 6/30/92	(n/a)
1/1/83 to 6/30/92	(n/a)
6/30/80 to 6/30/92	(n/a)

Risk: 85% of market

No-Load Portfolios

Address
8635 W. Sahara
Suite 420
The Lakes, NV 89117

Editors
William Corney and
Leonard Goodall

Subscription Rates
$69.00/year

Telephone Hotline
Yes

Money Management
No

NO - LOAD PORTFOLIOS
the newsletter for the busy professional

Volume VII, No. 7
July 6, 1992

Market Summary

If you made money in the stock market in the first six months of 1992, we know two things about you: (1) you probably owned larger blue chip stocks, and (2) you were lucky! The Dow Jones Industrial Average closed on June 30 at 3318.52, up 4.7% in 1992. This hides the fact that most stocks were down during the period. The Standard and Poor's 500 declined 2.2% and the NASDAQ (smaller stocks) was down 3.9%.

There is little reason to believe the last half of the year will see much improvement. The economy is recovering <u>very</u> slowly. Corporate earnings are now growing, but not at a rate that can give much of a boost to the stock market. Add to this the uncertainties of a presidential election year, and you have a market which is likely to continue its lackluster performance for several months. Our *Conservative* and *Aggressive Growth* portfolios on page two are now invested in 50 percent and 75 percent money market funds respectively, reflecting the uncertainty in the market (a <u>sell</u> recommendation means move the money from the stock fund to its related money market fund).

One bright spot for investors in recent months has been bond funds. Declining interest rates have helped boost the value of bonds. This emphasizes once again the importance of our basic philosophy--diversification. A good mix of stock and bond funds, and money market funds when appropriate, is the best way to get balanced growth in the long run and protection from market volatility in the meantime.

Last week the market was hit with the news that joblessness climbed to 7.8 percent. The Federal Reserve responded by cutting the discount rate to 3 percent, an astounding *29 year low* (where were you 29 years ago?) Other interest rates followed the discount rate down, including the T-bill rate (now 3.23 percent) and the 30 year bond rate (now 7.62 percent). These low rates can't help but stimulate the economy. The only question is how long it will take to do so. In the meantime, investors may tire waiting for, as Alice said, "a case of jam tomorrow, but never jam today." The proof of the recovery will be in earnings improvements, and that is what market participants will likely demand as the months roll on. One negative for low rates is the U.S. dollar. The dollar's buying power is weak, as foreign investors would rather have their money in financial instruments of currencies that provide a greater rate of return. This means overseas vacations for us are more costly, while foreigners find our prices to be rock bottom cheap.

The technical condition of the market is neutral at best. Our big 10 indicators remain stuck at 20 percent positive and eighty percent negative. To get the indicators back on track will take better valuation (higher earnings or a lower price level) combined with a clear price uptrend for the broad market.

No-Load Portfolios is published monthly by William Corney and Leonard Goodall, both of whom are professors at the University of Nevada. The service is supplemented by a telephone hotline, though portfolio changes are rarely made on that hotline.

As one might expect given Corney's and Goodall's academic background, the service is closer to the buy-and-hold end of the investment spectrum than most mutual fund newsletters. Nevertheless, they have resisted academia's predisposition against technical analysis, and they include a number of technical indicators in their market-timing model—

along with a number of fundamental and monetary indicators as well.

The newsletter contains three model portfolios that the HFD has tracked since the beginning of 1991. Two of the three focus on the U.S. equity market and follow Corney and Goodall's timing models: their "Aggressive Growth" and their "Conservative" portfolios. The third, their "Income" portfolio, is designed always to be fully invested in various fixed-income funds, so the focus in this portfolio is solely on fund selection.

The newsletter's timing models were bearish for much of the 18 months through mid-1992, which accounts for the fact that its model portfolios were heavily invested in cash and had low risk; even its "Aggressive" portfolio had 37% less volatility than the Wilshire 5000. Given this low risk, it isn't surprising that the newsletter underperformed the market over this period, gaining 17.4% versus the market's 32.3%. This is why it's important to look also at risk adjusted performance; when this newsletter's low risk is taken into account, then it actually slightly beat the Wilshire 5000 over these 18 months.

No-Load Portfolios (Average)

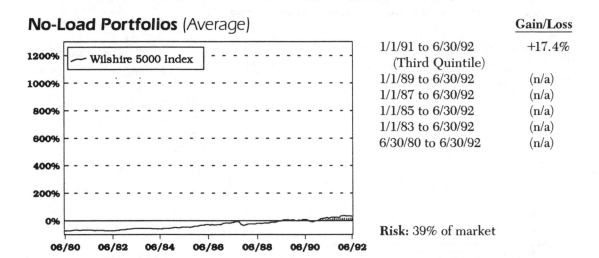

	Gain/Loss
1/1/91 to 6/30/92	+17.4%
(Third Quintile)	
1/1/89 to 6/30/92	(n/a)
1/1/87 to 6/30/92	(n/a)
1/1/85 to 6/30/92	(n/a)
1/1/83 to 6/30/92	(n/a)
6/30/80 to 6/30/92	(n/a)

Risk: 39% of market

No-Load Portfolios (Aggressive Growth Portfolio)

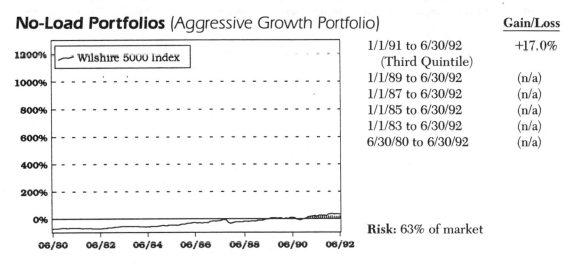

	Gain/Loss
1/1/91 to 6/30/92	+17.0%
(Third Quintile)	
1/1/89 to 6/30/92	(n/a)
1/1/87 to 6/30/92	(n/a)
1/1/85 to 6/30/92	(n/a)
1/1/83 to 6/30/92	(n/a)
6/30/80 to 6/30/92	(n/a)

Risk: 63% of market

No-Load Portfolios (Conservative Portfolio)

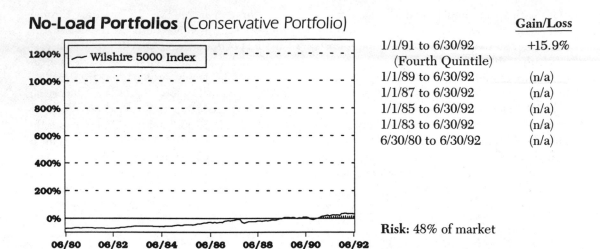

	Gain/Loss
1/1/91 to 6/30/92	+15.9%
(Fourth Quintile)	
1/1/89 to 6/30/92	(n/a)
1/1/87 to 6/30/92	(n/a)
1/1/85 to 6/30/92	(n/a)
1/1/83 to 6/30/92	(n/a)
6/30/80 to 6/30/92	(n/a)

Risk: 48% of market

No-Load Portfolios (Income Portfolio)

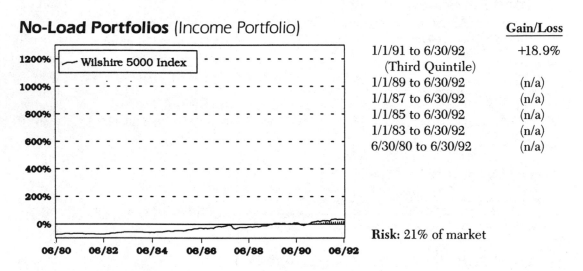

	Gain/Loss
1/1/91 to 6/30/92	+18.9%
(Third Quintile)	
1/1/89 to 6/30/92	(n/a)
1/1/87 to 6/30/92	(n/a)
1/1/85 to 6/30/92	(n/a)
1/1/83 to 6/30/92	(n/a)
6/30/80 to 6/30/92	(n/a)

Risk: 21% of market

OTC Insight

Address
Insight Capital
    Management, Inc.
P.O. Box 127
Moraga, CA 94556

Editor
James Collins

Phone Number
800-955-9566

Subscription Rates
$ 39.00/2 months
$195.00/year

Telephone Hotline
Yes

Money Management
Yes

OTC INSIGHT
Monthly Report on Over-the-Counter Growth Stocks

July 1992

Jim Collins, C.F.A.

Mr. Collins has seen a wide variety of markets during his 25 years of investment experience. He spent twenty of these years developing quantitative investment techniques at some of the most successful financial companies in the country. He holds an MBA from Harvard, a Bachelors degree from Georgia Tech, is a Chartered Financial Analyst and a graduate of the Pacific Coast Banking School.

Investment Performance Overview

During June the average loss for *OTC Insight's* eighteen model portfolios was -3.75%. The Buy List/*OTC Insight* Index was off -5.97% and the Exceptionally Attractive stock list lost -8.20% for the month. This compares to a loss of -5.17% for NASDAQ Industrial Index.

OTC INSIGHT is #1 for 1991. According to the Hulbert Financial Digest, the average gain on the model portfolios for 1991 was +148.7%; for the 3-year period ending 12/31/91, +303.6%. Insight Capital is #1 according to Money Manager Verified Ratings. Our conservative growth portfolio gained 112% during 1991.

Stock Ideas

Cerner Corporation (CERN) develops and supports information systems for clinical healthcare providers, such as hospitals, HMO's and reference laboratories. Headquartered in Kansas City, Missouri, the company has 505 employees. Telephone: (816) 221-1024.

Products/Services Cerner develops, markets, and supports medical and clinical information systems for the healthcare industry. The company is a leader in the trend toward automating healthcare services in nursing, pharmacy, laboratory, radiology, and internal medicine disciplines. Utilizing a centralized network architecture, Cerner develops software applications that serve the unique needs of different medical disciplines, while maintaining cross-functional information processing. The company's systems allow for quick and accurate access to patient information. Cerner systems automate test result preparation, and monitor costs, productivity, and resource use.

Recent Developments Cerner recently announced an agreement with the Henry Ford Health System of Detroit to provide the healthcare group with Cerner's RadNet radiology system. The Ford healthcare group includes the Henry Ford Hospital and 25 suburban outpatient facilities.

Cerner has established a "vision center" at its corporate headquarters which is used to demonstrate the company's information systems under actual patient care scenarios.

Cerner is followed by analysts at Smith Barney, Alex Brown, Piper Jaffray, and Kidder Peabody.

It should not be assumed that recommendations made will be profitable or will equal past performance. The information in this publication is collected from various sources believed to be reliable but cannot be guaranteed in any way. Neither *OTC Insight*, Insight Capital Management, Inc., nor its employees shall be liable in any manner for losses of any kind.

OTC Insight is published monthly by James Collins and Insight Capital Management (ICM). Up until mid-1986 this newsletter was edited by Louis Navellier, at which time he joined forces with Collins and ICM. This partnership dissolved in mid-1987, and Navellier is now publishing a newsletter of his own,

MPT Review (see review of this newsletter elsewhere in this *Guide*).

Collins and Navellier have agreed that the performance for *OTC Insight* up until its August 1987 issue belongs exclusively to Navellier and *MPT Review*, and that the *OTC Insight* record beginning with the August

1987 issue belongs exclusively to Collins. The figures reported in this book reflect this agreement.

OTC Insight (like *MPT Review*) concentrates on the application of modern portfolio theory to stocks that trade over-the-counter. The newsletter does not attempt to time the market, and it keeps its model portfolios more or less fully invested at all times. However, the newsletter will increase or decrease the average beta (volatility or riskiness) of those models as perceived market risk waxes and wanes.

OTC Insight's performance since August 1987 has been impressive. Over the 59 months from the beginning of August 1987 through mid-1992, the average performance of the newsletter's portfolios has been a gain of 170.3%. This contrasts with a gain of "just" 47.9% for the Wilshire 5000.

OTC Insight also has outperformed *MPT Review* over these 59 months. In contrast to *OTC Insight*'s 170.3%, the average gain of *MPT Review*'s model portfolios over this period was 147.7%. However, *MPT Review*'s portfolios were about 15% less risky or volatile than *OTC Insight*'s portfolios, so on a risk-adjusted basis these two newsletters' performances are almost identical.

Keep in mind, however, that Collins's portfolios could be big losers during a bear market (high relative-strength stocks, which Collins's approach favors, tend to be big losers when the market falls). During the month of October 1987, for example, OTC Insight lost 37.3%. Collins's system doesn't promise to make money in a bear market, but he hopes he can beat the market over an entire cycle. You probably ought to be prepared to invest for at least that time horizon before following this newsletter.

Collins recommends 18 separate model portfolios in his newsletter, divided into three risk categories ("Conservative," "Moderate Risk," and "Aggressive"). Owing to the fact that the six portfolios within each risk category (which vary only according to total dollar size) have very similar performances, it is their average performances that are graphed in this book.

OTC Insight (Average)

	Gain/Loss
1/1/91 to 6/30/92 (First Quintile)	+104.5%
1/1/89 to 6/30/92 (First Quintile)	+231.8%
1/1/87 to 6/30/92	(n/a)
1/1/85 to 6/30/92	(n/a)
1/1/83 to 6/30/92	(n/a)
6/30/80 to 6/30/92	(n/a)

Risk: 264% of market

OTC Insight (Conservative Portfolio Average)

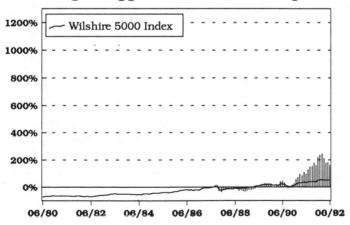

	Gain/Loss
1/1/91 to 6/30/92	+105.1%
(First Quintile)	
1/1/89 to 6/30/92	+228.4%
(First Quintile)	
1/1/87 to 6/30/92	(n/a)
1/1/85 to 6/30/92	(n/a)
1/1/83 to 6/30/92	(n/a)
6/30/80 to 6/30/92	(n/a)

Risk: 260.7% of market

Chart legend: Wilshire 5000 Index. Y-axis: 0% to 1200%. X-axis: 06/80 to 06/92.

OTC Insight (Moderately Aggressive Portfolio Average)

	Gain/Loss
1/1/91 to 6/30/92	+101.2%
(First Quintile)	
1/1/89 to 6/30/92	+216.7%
(First Quintile)	
1/1/87 to 6/30/92	(n/a)
1/1/85 to 6/30/92	(n/a)
1/1/83 to 6/30/92	(n/a)
6/30/80 to 6/30/92	(n/a)

Risk: 262% of market

Chart legend: Wilshire 5000 Index. Y-axis: 0% to 1200%. X-axis: 06/80 to 06/92.

OTC Insight (Aggressive Portfolio Average)

	Gain/Loss
1/1/91 to 6/30/92	+107.3%
(First Quintile)	
1/1/89 to 6/30/92	+263.8%
(First Quintile)	
1/1/87 to 6/30/92	(n/a)
1/1/85 to 6/30/92	(n/a)
1/1/83 to 6/30/92	(n/a)
6/30/80 to 6/30/92	(n/a)

Risk: 269% of market

Chart legend: Wilshire 5000 Index. Y-axis: 0% to 1200%. X-axis: 06/80 to 06/92.

The Oberweis Report

Address
841 N. Lake
Aurora, IL 60506

Editor
James D. Oberweis

Phone Number
708-801-4766

Subscription Rates
$ 99.00/year
$249.00/1 year by fax

Telephone Hotline
Yes

Money Management
Yes

Hamilton Investments Inc.   Member New York Stock Exchange.   Subscriptions
A Household International Company   Other Principal Exchanges and SIPC $99/Year by mail
                                                                            $249/Year by FAX

HAMILTON INVESTMENTS

THE OBERWEIS REPORT ™
A Monthly Review

Portfolio Performance Summary
(Since Origin: September 27, 1976)   **JULY 1992**

		$Change	%Change	Compound Growth Rate	Theoretical $1 Grew To:
Model Theoretical Portfolio (original investment - $50,000)		+2,791,430	+5583%	29.2%	$56.83
Dow Jones Industrial Average	3282.44	+2273pts	+225%	7.8%	$3.25
S & P 500 Index	403.45	+297pts	+278%	8.8%	$3.78
NASDAQ Composite	547.84	+456pts	+494%	12.0%	$5.94

Note: While past performance does not guarantee future success, we believe investing in rapidly growing companies will produce superior investment results. Dividends and commissions are ignored in performance calculations. The theoretical portfolio contains many high beta growth stocks which tend to be more volatile than DJIA stocks. Tax consequences must be carefully considered. Changes in our theoretical portfolio and current quote prices are made on the last Friday of each month. (This issue as of close of 6/26/92).

MEGASTOCKS V

In the March "Oberweis Report" we listed our eight guidelines for identifying "megastocks", stocks with the potential to rise in value several hundred percent over the next few years. Such stocks are normally appropriate only for investors willing to assume above average risk. In the April, May and June issues we discussed our first six guidelines in greater detail and in this issue we would like to focus on our final two guidelines. They are:

7. Believe the tape!

8. Carefully review the company's balance sheet, paying particular attention to footnotes in order to identify unusual items which may indicate future problems.

If you are looking for stocks with the greatest investment potential, we believe you should start with the companies which are most successful in the marketplace - those whose sales and profits are growing at 30%, 40%, 50% or faster. Our first two guidelines discuss this important requirement. Our second two guidelines relate to how an investor can then make value judgements among such rapid growth companies. Our third two guidelines focus on the immediate past and on the future. This month's two guidelines are final checks after we've discovered an apparently attractive investment opportunity.

If a company shows consistent rapid growth in both earnings and revenues, has attractive P.E. and P.S. ratios, strong recent trends, and a product or service which offers excellent future growth prospects, yet its stock is underperforming the market, **don't buy it.** If everything looks good fundamentally, the stock should be rising faster than the market. An easy way to check its relative performance over the last 12 months is to look at its relative strength, a number published daily in Investor's Business Daily newspaper and other publications. The number tells us how a particular stock is performing compared to the S&P 500. A relative strength of 90 means that a particular stock is doing better than 90% of the stocks in the S&P 500 with the most recent quarter being given a double weighting. If everything looks strong fundamentally for a particular stock, but it has a low relative strength, something may be wrong. Our analysis may be missing something or insiders may know something we don't. Generally it's best under such circumstances to wait awhile before buying the stock. If the fundamentals are as strong as we believe, the relative strength should begin to improve and we can buy the stock then, even though we may miss the first few points of a move. But frequently by waiting we may learn more and find that we have avoided a disaster. For this reason, **no matter how good a company looks on paper, if its stock is declining in a steady or rising market, don't buy it.** Buy companies with relative strengths of 75 or higher, preferably higher.

The last check is a review of the company's balance sheet. Sometimes very unusual items may be discovered such as a huge increase in receivables or inventories, unrelated to the sales increase. Or some unusual item may be referred to in the footnotes. We are not necessarily looking for unleveraged companies. Leverage tells us how a company is financed, not whether a business is successful. A successful, growing business can be financed primarily through equity, debt or any combination thereof. **In the case of a very successful company, some leverage may be a positive rather than a negative but that leverage does increase the risk level.**

Finally, it's especially important when investing in emerging growth companies to follow the Golden Rule of Investing - Diversify, diversify, diversify. If you follow these guidelines over long periods of time, at least 5 to 10 years, I believe you will be able to achieve above average investment results.

Hamilton Investments, is owned by Household International. It is a separate corporation from Household Bank, f.s.b. and the investments recommended, offered, or sold by it are not obligations of, guaranteed by, or insured by Household Bank or FDIC.

The Oberweis Report is published monthly by Hamilton Investments, a brokerage firm based in Illinois. It is edited by Jim Oberweis. Though there is no telephone hotline per se, subscribers can call the brokerage firm on the Saturday following the last Friday of each month to receive the recommendations contained in the latest issue of *The Oberweis Report*. They also can choose to receive each month's issue by facsimile.

Oberweis is a fundamentalist. Each issue of the newsletter contains a handful of new special situations, along with a review of those previously recommended situations that have yet to be sold. Oberweis is not a market timer, and he seeks to keep his model portfolio fully invested at all times by keeping the dollar amount of each month's purchases more or less equal to the amount of the sales. However, the portfolio the HFD constructs to follow Oberweis's advice has, during some years, built up a significant margin position—owing to the fact that the real-time prices at which the HFD was able to execute recommended purchases and sales were worse than the month-end prices that Oberweis used for his newsletter's calculations.

Most of the stocks Oberweis recommends are secondary issues that trade over-the-counter. Despite the fact that this sector of the market lagged the blue chips over the last half of the 1980s, Oberweis was able to beat the market. Over the four and one-half years through mid-1992, for example, Oberweis's model portfolio gained 221.8%, in contrast to the Wilshire 5000's 89.0%. To be sure, Oberweis's portfolio was more than twice as risky as the average stock, but even so it still beat the market on a risk-adjusted basis.

Because Oberweis's portfolio is fully invested at all times, you should not expect it to make money during a bear market. While his impressive performance holds out the hope that his approach can beat the market over an entire market cycle, you should be prepared to follow the service for at least that length of time.

The Oberweis Report

	Gain/Loss
1/1/91 to 6/30/92 (First Quintile)	+85.7%
1/1/89 to 6/30/92 (First Quintile)	+191.5%
1/1/87 to 6/30/92	(n/a)
1/1/85 to 6/30/92	(n/a)
1/1/83 to 6/30/92	(n/a)
6/30/80 to 6/30/92	(n/a)

Risk: 229% of market

On Markets

Address
31 Melkhout Crescent
Hout Bay 7800
South Africa

Editor
Tony Henfrey

Phone Number
+27 21 7904259

Subscription Rates
$ 50.00/3 months
$100.00/6 months
$185.00/year

Telephone Hotline
No

Money Management
No

Tony Henfrey

ON MARKETS

Incorporating Tony Henfrey's GOLD LETTER and THE BIG PICTURE

No. 312   FRIDAY 10TH JULY 1992

* INDUSTRIAL PRODUCTION continues to rise but should peak sometime around April 1993 and thereafter fall until the 8 year cycle low due in 1999 (chart 1). UNEMPLOYMENT is still rising giving no sign whatsoever that the economy is picking up -- but then it is a lagging indicator (chart 2). The sluggish recovery compared with strongly rising M1 growth is keeping MONEY VELOCITY in a downtrend (chart 3) - until it turns up there is theoretically no pressure on interest rates or inflation to rise. But the INFLATION RATE (chart 4) has indicated that it has bottomed and that it should go up for the rest of the year. Short term interest rates are still falling but the 91 DAY TREASURY BILL rate (chart 5) is incredibly oversold and is unlikely to go below the 1971 support level of 3.5%

* The DOW JONES BOND INDEX is still in a rising trend (chart 6) but the divergence between it and its indicators is alarming -- long term rates are perceived to have bottomed and with short term rates unlikely to fall any lower, the upside pressure on bond prices could soon evaporate.

* The DOW JONES INDUSTRIAL INDEX (chart 7) is still rising against all the odds on the technicals, in defiance of logic and at various with normal measures of value. The fact that its recent high is not matched by transports and utilities is a major negative

* The US DOLLAR measured against the GERMAN MARK (chart 8) is behaving very weakly and whilst it may rally in the short term it appears that it is just a matter of time before major support levels are taken out allowing the decline to be extended. The BRITISH POUND and the GERMAN MARK appear to have the best potential against the dollar.

* GOLD BULLION (chart 9) is trying very hard to reverse direction -- if it should be standing above $355 at the end of July, there is every chance that it should continue to rise to at least test the $420 resistance level. Measured against the dollar, gold has the potential to rise (chart 10).

* SOUTH AFRICAN GOLD SHARES INDEX (chart 11) is still declining but about to encounter major support which hopefully should hold. The political situation continues to trouble investors and gold shares have often proved to be good buys (not "good-byes") when the news is at its bleakest.

* Commodity prices as reflected by the CRB Commodity index have likely bottomed -- COPPER (chart 12) looks quite exciting and should outperform most other commodities -- this is probably supporting evidence of the fact that the economy is trying to move higher over the next 9 to 12 months.

P.O. Box 26796, Hout Bay 7800 South Africa.
Telephone: National (021) 727128 — International + 27 21 727128. Fax: National (021) 727127 — International + 27 21 727127.

On Markets is published 12 times a year by Tony Henfrey. This newsletter is the product of a fall 1988 marriage between two other newsletters Henfrey used to publish—*Tony Henfrey's Gold Letter* and *The Big Picture* (no relation to the current newsletter of that name). In addition to continuing his earlier service's focus on the gold markets, this new letter focuses on the major trends in a wide variety of additional markets as well.

The HFD began tracking *Tony Henfrey's Gold Letter* in 1982. The letter contained several categories of recommendations, but the one the HFD tracked was a portfolio he called his "Long-Term Gold Share" portfolio. This portfolio was also broken into several sub-portfolios according to the currency in which a subscriber's assets were denominated. The one the HFD tracked to represent Henfrey's advice was the one oriented to investors whose assets were denominated in U.S. dollars. This portfolio was taken over by *On Markets* and is what the HFD continues to track.

During some periods of time Henfrey's advice for this model portfolio has been admirably clear, with follow-up provided in each issue. During other times, however, especially when the gold market was performing poorly, mention of this portfolio became episodic at best. In fact, the HFD does not even have a performance figure for this portfolio for 1986, owing to the fact that in that year the portfolio hardly ever was mentioned. In the accompanying graph and in this *Guide*'s appendices, Henfrey's track record is included on the assumption that he earned the T-Bill rate during 1986.

This portfolio's best year was 1982, when it topped the performance sweepstakes with a gain of 93.3%. However, it also was a big loser in other years. For the ten and one-half years through mid-1992, in fact, assuming the newsletter earned the T-Bill rate during 1986, the portfolio lost 28.6%, in contrast to a gain of 349.4% for the Wilshire 5000 and a loss of 14.0% for gold bullion.

On Markets

	Gain/Loss
1/1/91 to 6/30/92	−33.7%
(Fifth Quintile)	
1/1/89 to 6/30/92	−37.5%
(Fifth Quintile)	
1/1/87 to 6/30/92	−36.8%
(Fifth Quintile)	
1/1/85 to 6/30/92	−51.9%
(Fifth Quintile)	
1/1/83 to 6/30/92	−63.1%
(Fifth Quintile)	
6/30/80 to 6/30/92	(n/a)

Risk: 326% of market

The Option Advisor

Address
Box 46709
Cincinnati, OH 45246

Editors
Bernard Schaeffer and
    Robert Bergen

Phone Number
800-327-8833

Subscription Rates
$66.00/6 months
$99.00/year

Telephone Hotline
Yes

Money Management
No

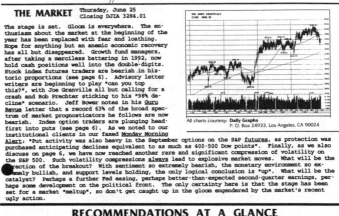

The Option Advisor®

A publication of
Investment Research Institute, Inc.

July, 1992/Volume 12, Issue 7

THE MARKET Thursday, June 25
Closing DJIA 3284.01

The stage is set. Gloom is everywhere. The enthusiasm about the market at the beginning of the year has been replaced with fear and loathing. Hope for anything but an anemic economic recovery has all but disappeared. Growth fund managers, after taking a merciless battering in 1992, now hold cash positions well into the double-digits. Stock index futures traders are bearish in historic proportions (see page 6). Advisory letter writers are beginning to play "can you top this?", with Joe Granville all but calling for a crash and Bob Prechter sticking to his "98% decline" scenario. Jeff Bower notes in his Guru Revue letter that a record 63% of the broad spectrum of market prognosticators he follows are now bearish. Index option traders are plunging headfirst into puts (see page 6). As we noted to our institutional clients in our faxed Monday Morning Alert: "Put activity was also heavy in the September options on the S&P futures, as protection was purchased anticipating declines equivalent to as much as 400-500 Dow points". Finally, as we also discuss on page 6, we have now reached another rare and significant compression of volatility on the S&P 500. Such volatility compressions always lead to explosive market moves. What will be the direction of the breakout? With sentiment so extremely bearish, the monetary environment so extremely bullish, and support levels holding, the only logical conclusion is "up". What will be the catalyst? Perhaps a further Fed easing, perhaps better-than-expected second-quarter earnings, perhaps some development on the political front. The only certainty here is that the stage has been set for a market "meltup", so don't get caught up in the gloom engendered by the market's recent ugly action.

All charts courtesy: **Daily Graphs**
P. O. Box 24933, Los Angeles, CA 90024

RECOMMENDATIONS AT A GLANCE

Portfolio	Underlying Stock	Ticker Symbol	Closing Price 06/25	B = Buy; W = Write	Expiration Month	Striking Price (P = Put)	Closing Price 06/25	Options Exchange	Maximum Entry Price	Target Profit	Closeout Date	Volume/Liquidity Class	Delta
A G G R E S S I V E	Barnett Banks Inc.	BBI	36	B	Oct.	35	2-5/8	A	3	100%	09/04	C4	65%
	Delta Airlines Inc.	DAL	53-3/4	B	Jan.	60	2-1/2	C	3	100%	12/04	B4	30%
	General Electric	GE	77-1/4	B	Dec.	80	3-1/4	C	3-1/2	100%	11/06	C2	45%
	Medtronic Inc.	MDT	74	B	Nov.	70P	3-5/8#	C	3-7/8	100%	09/28	D6	35%
	Merrill Lynch & Co.	MER	48-3/8	B	Jan.	50	4-1/4	A	4-1/2	100%	12/04	A4	50%
	PepsiCo Inc.	PEP	34-1/2	B	Oct.	35P	2-1/8	C	2-1/8	150%	08/31	C4	50%
C O N S E R V A T I V E	Intel Corp.	INQ	54-3/8	B	Aug.	55P	3-3/8	A	2-3/8	80%	08/21	C6	50%
				W	Aug.	50P	1-1/4	A	N/A	N/A	08/21	B4	25%
	Schlumberger Ltd.*	SLB	61-5/8	B	Aug.	60	3-3/8	C	2-5/8	75%	08/21	C6	65%
				W	Aug.	65	1-5/8	C	N/A	N/A	08/21	B4	35%
	Sears, Roebuck*	S	39-5/8	B	Oct.	40	2-1/4	C	1-7/8	80%	10/16	B6	50%
				W	Oct.	45	11/16	C	N/A	N/A	10/16	C1	25%

Also included in Option Income Portfolio. See page 3
asked price

Deltas calculated using software from Montgomery Investment Group (215) 688-2508.

The Option Advisor is published monthly and is edited by Bernard Schaeffer and Robert Bergen. It is supplemented by a telephone hotline that is updated at least once each week.

As its name suggests, *The Option Advisor* concentrates on the options market; it has three model portfolios. The strategy for its "Aggressive" portfolio involves the unhedged purchase of call or put options; its "Conservative" portfolio invests in option spreads or strangles; and its "Option Income" portfolio simultaneously purchases various stocks and writes call options against them.

The HFD began following The *Option Advisor* in 1983, during which year the newsletter's portfolios lost an average of more than 83%. The newsletter has done somewhat better in the years since. While its "Aggressive" portfolio has continued to lose money (down 54.1% from January 1984 through mid-1992), its "Conservative" portfolio has gained 70.2%. One of the unfortunate consequences of large percentage losses, however, is that the gain turned in by the "Conservative" portfolio is hardly enough to erase 1983's loss (see graph); for the entire nine and one-half years for which the HFD has data, this portfolio still is showing a loss of 71.9%.

The Option Advisor's "Income Option" portfolio hasn't been in existence as long as the newsletter's other two portfolios, and the HFD began following it at the beginning of 1989. Over the subsequent three and one-half years, it gained 18.3%, in contrast to a 60.3% gain for the Wilshire 5000. Part of this underperformance can be explained by its low risk; however, because the portfolio also underperformed the T-Bill rate over this period, it had a negative risk-adjusted performance.

Overall, taking into account all three of its portfolios, the newsletter lost 65.2% from the beginning of 1983 through mid-1992. Over this same period, the Wilshire 5000 gained 278.6%.

The **Option Advisor** (Average)

	Gain/Loss
1/1/91 to 6/30/92	+5.9%
(Fifth Quintile)	
1/1/89 to 6/30/92	−5.2%
(Fifth Quintile)	
1/1/87 to 6/30/92	+14.3%
(Fifth Quintile)	
1/1/85 to 6/30/92	+3.8%
(Fifth Quintile)	
1/1/83 to 6/30/92	−65.2%
(Fifth Quintile)	
6/30/80 to 6/30/92	(n/a)

Risk: 162% of market

The Option Advisor (Conservative Portfolio)

	Gain/Loss
1/1/91 to 6/30/92 (Fifth Quintile)	−7.2%
1/1/89 to 6/30/92 (Fifth Quintile)	−74.6%
1/1/87 to 6/30/92 (Fifth Quintile)	−65.5%
1/1/85 to 6/30/92 (Fifth Quintile)	−32.8%
1/1/83 to 6/30/92 (Fifth Quintile)	−71.9%
6/30/80 to 6/30/92	(n/a)

Risk: 317% of market

The Option Advisor (Aggressive Portfolio)

	Gain/Loss
1/1/91 to 6/30/92 (Fifth Quintile)	−3.3%
1/1/89 to 6/30/92 (Fourth Quintile)	+31.1%
1/1/87 to 6/30/92 (Fifth Quintile)	+6.5%
1/1/85 to 6/30/92 (Fifth Quintile)	−64.0%
1/1/83 to 6/30/92 (Fifth Quintile)	−92.3%
6/30/80 to 6/30/92	(n/a)

Risk: 235% of market

The Option Advisor (Option Income Portfolio)

	Gain/Loss
1/1/91 to 6/30/92 (Third Quintile)	+19.4%
1/1/89 to 6/30/92 (Fifth Quintile)	+18.3%
1/1/87 to 6/30/92	(n/a)
1/1/85 to 6/30/92	(n/a)
1/1/83 to 6/30/92	(n/a)
6/30/80 to 6/30/92	(n/a)

Risk: 64% of market

The Outlook

Address
Standard & Poor's
   Corp.
25 Broadway
New York, NY 10004

Editor
Arnold Kaufman

Phone Number
800-852-1641

Subscription Rates
$ 29.95/12 issues
$280.00/year

Telephone Hotline
No

Money Management
No

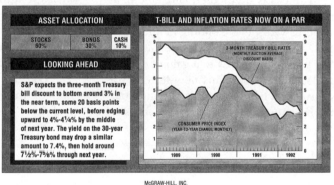
The Outlook is published weekly by Standard & Poor's Corp. and is edited by Arnold Kaufman. Having been published for over 50 years, *The Outlook* is one of the longest-lived newsletters being published today. It also has one of the larger circulations of any investment newsletter, and along with *Dow Theory Forecasts* and *The Value Line Investment Survey* (both of which are reviewed elsewhere in this volume), is one of the most frequently found newsletters in the financial sections of this country's libraries.

The advice and recommendations contained in *The Outlook* have evolved over the years. Up until 1989, for example, *The Outlook*'s stock recommendations appeared in four "Master Lists," one each of "Foundation Stocks," "Growth Stocks," "Speculative Stocks" and "Income Stocks." The HFD tracked each one of these four lists as separate portfolios. In 1989, however, *The Outlook* started publishing a stock-ranking system called the "Stock Appreciation Ranking System" (or STAR, for short). Because the HFD decided that this ranking system was a better reflection of *The Outlook*'s stock-selection abilities, the HFD started following just it. The figures the HFD reports for the newsletter's average performance up until then reflect the average of *The Outlook*'s master lists.

The STAR system segregates stocks into five different categories. The stocks with a 5-star ranking are those thought to have the greatest profit potential, and it is these the HFD places in the portfolio constructed to track *The Outlook*'s performance. This portfolio also reflects the market allocation advice provided in the newsletter; the portion assigned to stocks is divided equally among all 5-star stocks.

For the 12-year period ending in mid-1992, the HFD reports a gain for this newsletter of 266.0%, which compares to a gain of 432.7% for the Wilshire 5000. This newsletter's volatility (risk) has been less than the market's, but not by enough to make its risk-adjusted performance as good as the market as a whole. For the three and one-half years through mid-1992 during which time the HFD has data for the STAR system itself, the HFD reports a gain of 31.6% (versus the Wilshire 5000's total return of 60.3%).

Part of the STAR system's underperformance can be traced to *The Outlook*'s market timing, and part to the stock-selection method itself. A portfolio that followed just the newsletter's timing advice (by dividing between hypothetical shares of the Wilshire 5000 and T-Bills) would have made 42.6% over these three and one-half years, in contrast to 60.3% for buying and holding. The fact that *The Outlook*'s stock portfolio did even less well than this timing-only portfolio (gaining 31.6%) means that the newsletter's 5-star stocks underperformed the Wilshire 5000 during the times they enjoyed a 5-star ranking.

The Outlook has more to offer than the STAR system, however, and is regarded by many investors as a good source of investment ideas in addition to specific portfolio advice. For example, the newsletter also contains articles on a wide variety of financial planning topics. As suggested by the chapter on asset allocation that appears earlier in this *Guide*, *The Outlook*'s asset allocation advice may be one of the more valuable contributions it makes.

The Outlook (Average)

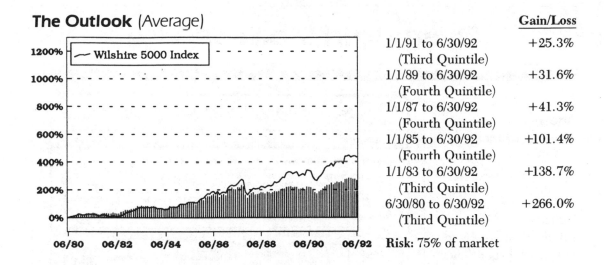

	Gain/Loss
1/1/91 to 6/30/92 (Third Quintile)	+25.3%
1/1/89 to 6/30/92 (Fourth Quintile)	+31.6%
1/1/87 to 6/30/92 (Fourth Quintile)	+41.3%
1/1/85 to 6/30/92 (Fourth Quintile)	+101.4%
1/1/83 to 6/30/92 (Third Quintile)	+138.7%
6/30/80 to 6/30/92 (Third Quintile)	+266.0%

Risk: 75% of market

The Outlook (Stock Appreciation Ranking System [5-Stars])

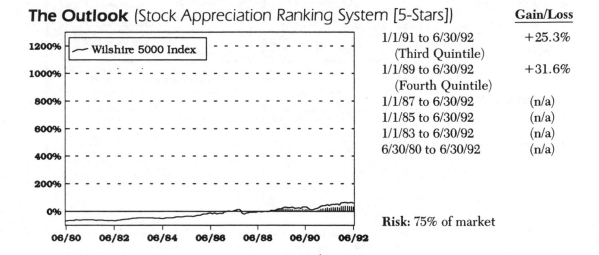

	Gain/Loss
1/1/91 to 6/30/92 (Third Quintile)	+25.3%
1/1/89 to 6/30/92 (Fourth Quintile)	+31.6%
1/1/87 to 6/30/92	(n/a)
1/1/85 to 6/30/92	(n/a)
1/1/83 to 6/30/92	(n/a)
6/30/80 to 6/30/92	(n/a)

Risk: 75% of market

The Outlook   297

Overpriced Stock Service

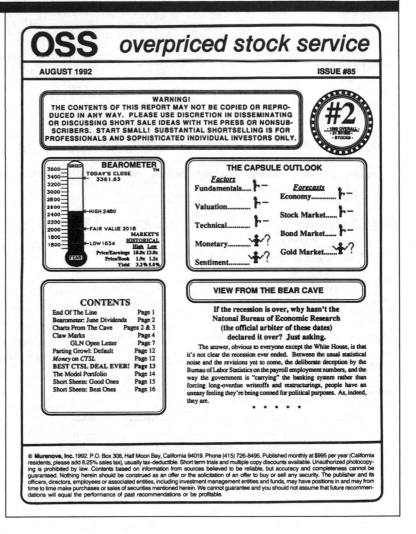

Address
Murenove, Inc.
P.O. Box 308
Half Moon Bay, CA
    94019

Editors
Michael Murphy and
    Lissa Morgenthaler

Phone Number
415-726-8495

Subscription Rates
$495.00/year

Telephone Hotline
Yes

Money Management
Yes

Overpriced Stock Service is published by Michael Murphy and Lissa Morgenthaler, both of whom also edit the *California Technology Stock Letter* (reviewed elsewhere in this volume). The newsletter is supplemented by a telephone hotline that is updated at least twice each week.

This newsletter is unique within the investment newsletter industry in that it focuses exclusively on finding good candidates for short selling. Though newsletters typically don't share Wall Street's bias against saying anything negative about a company's stock, relatively few newsletters recommend that their subscribers actually sell a stock short. And those few services that do offer short-selling advice usually do so in a portfolio that also owns some long positions. Not *Overpriced Stock Service*.

Murphy and Morgenthaler do offer some market-timing advice in their newsletter, so their model portfolio isn't always invested in short sales to the maximum extent possible. But their focus is more on selecting good short-sale candidates than it is on market timing. And, given the premise of their newsletter, I would guess they will continue to offer short-sale candidates in virtually every kind of market.

If this is the case, their performance most likely will continue to be a function of the overall market's direction—as it has up until mid-1992. In 1990, for example, the first year in which they offered a model portfolio, the market declined and their portfolio finished in second place among all newsletters the HFD tracked (with a gain of 35.7%). Over the next 18 months, in contrast, the market was very bullish and their model portfolio was a big loser. For the entire two and one-half years through mid-1992, their model portfolio lost 92%, as compared to a 24% gain for the Wilshire 5000.

Overpriced Stock Service

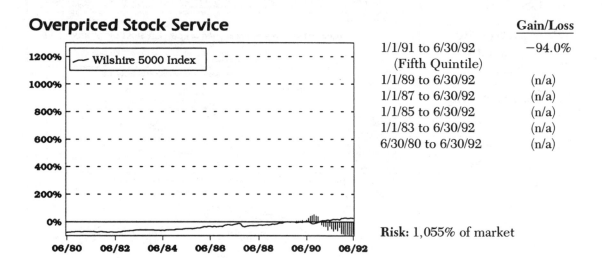

	Gain/Loss
1/1/91 to 6/30/92	−94.0%
(Fifth Quintile)	
1/1/89 to 6/30/92	(n/a)
1/1/87 to 6/30/92	(n/a)
1/1/85 to 6/30/92	(n/a)
1/1/83 to 6/30/92	(n/a)
6/30/80 to 6/30/92	(n/a)

Risk: 1,055% of market

P. Q. Wall Forecast, Inc.

Address
P.O. Box 480601
Denver, CO
  80248-0601

Editor
P. Q. Wall

Phone Number
303-455-1523

Subscription Rates
$ 99.00/3 months
$198.00/year

Telephone Hotline
Yes

Money Management
Yes

P.Q. WALL FORECAST, INC.

July 1992 Issue
Vol. 4 - No. 7
P.O. Box 480601 • Denver, CO 80248-0601

DJIA 3282.41
June 26, 1992
(303) 455-1523

NON-SUBSCRIBERS OR DAY TRADERS: 1-900-SUNLIGHT GETS YOU P.Q.'S REAL TIME MARKET COMMENTS FOR $2 A MINUTE, UPDATED FOUR TIMES DAILY AT 10:10, 12:30, 3:00 AND 5:00 P.M. NEW YORK TIME.

900# NOTE: FOR THOSE OF YOU WHO CAN'T GET THE 900 NUMBER DUE TO LOCATION, BUILDING LOCKOUT, ETC., CALL US AT (303) 455-1523. WE WILL MAKE ALTERNATE ARRANGEMENTS FOR YOU.

A TIP... THE 900 NUMBER AIMS, IN MOST CASES, TO HAVE THE TOTAL CALL LESS THAN 60 SECONDS. WHEN YOU HEAR, "THE NEXT UPDATE WILL BE..." HANG UP INSTANTLY.

CALLERS OF THE 4 TIMES DAILY 900 NUMBER. Since December you have noticed the "warning" preceding each call. You get 18 free seconds for that warning. I practised until I could give it in 4 seconds. Result: extra 14 seconds of message free up front. You are now getting 74 seconds of message for $2 instead of the old 60 seconds. I try very hard not to exceed the $2 limit unless for a good reason.

The P.Q. Wall Forecast, monthly with interim bulletins: $198 annually, with daily telephone update, $498; six mos, with daily telephone update, $285; two-issue trial w/daily telephone update, $99; three-issue trial w/o phone update, $99. Send check to P.Q. Wall Forecast, P.O. Box 480601, Denver, CO 80248-0601, or call 303-455-1523 to charge by credit card. We accept MasterCard, American Express and Visa. CO residents add 3.7% sales tax, Denver residents add 7.2%.

THEY CRUMBLED FROM THE DOOM IN JUNE — NOW THEY MUST DIE IN JULY

Finding it probable that the entire ten year bull market would end right here in spoke 5, we even attempted last issue to sort out the interior subsegment rhythms in order to predict the exact day of the final high and printed this top of page 7.

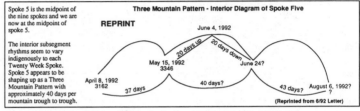

Three Mountain Pattern - Interior Diagram of Spoke Five

Spoke 5 is the midpoint of the nine spokes and we are now at the midpoint of spoke 5.

REPRINT

The interior subsegment rhythms seem to vary indigenously to each Twenty Week Spoke. Spoke 5 appears to be shaping up as a Three Mountain Pattern with approximately 40 days per mountain trough to trough.

June 4, 1992
20 days up   20 days down
May 15, 1992
3346
April 8, 1992
3162
37 days
40 days?
June 24?
43 days?   August 6, 1992?
                      ?

(Reprinted from 6/92 Letter)

The actual all time intraday print high was 3422.02 on June 3 so the updated diagram shows how close we were:

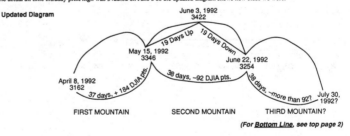

Updated Diagram

June 3, 1992
3422
19 Days Up   19 Days Down
May 15, 1992
3346
June 22, 1992
3254
April 8, 1992
3162
37 days, + 184 DJIA pts.
38 days, −92 DJIA pts.
38 days, −more than 92?   July 30, 1992?

FIRST MOUNTAIN   SECOND MOUNTAIN   THIRD MOUNTAIN?

(For Bottom Line, see top page 2)

P. Q. Wall Forecast, Inc. is published monthly by P. Q. Wall. It is supplemented by a telephone hotline (what Wall calls his "Nine-Word Number") that is updated as often as daily, whenever there is a change in Wall's forecasts for the stock, gold or bond markets. Wall also authors an additional daily telephone hotline for which he charges extra, as well as a "900"-number hotline that is updated four times each day and is available to subscribers and non-subscribers alike. Pursuant to the HFD's procedures on such matters, the HFD's performance rating for *P. Q. Wall Forecast, Inc.* is based on advice contained in the newsletter and Wall's "Nine-Word Number" hotline.

Wall says that his approach to investing is difficult to characterize. While it has similarities to technical analysis and cycle theory, Wall claims that such resemblances are superficial. In fact, he says, he tries to apply the insights gained from quantum physics and the theory of relativity to economic and historical events, because those events "show field characteristics" involving human motive. Understanding the markets, therefore, requires "an art beyond mere science" and "hence may not be fully accessible to the limited pattern recognition of narrow observers, even those of high intellect."

Subscribers to Wall's newsletter are advised to switch back and forth between the long and short sides of the market and are given recommendations of specific stocks to purchase or sell short. Over the 18 months through mid-1992, such a portfolio lost 38.7%, according to the HFD, in contrast to a 32.3% gain for the Wilshire 5000.

The primary culprit in this underperformance appears to be Wall's stock selection. A portfolio that went long and short in hypothetical shares of the Wilshire 5000 according to Wall's stock-market signals would have gained 14.0% over these 18 months, in contrast to the 38.7% loss that occurred when going long and short in Wall's specific stocks.

P.Q. Wall Forecast, Inc.

	Gain/Loss
1/1/91 to 6/30/92	−38.7%
(Fifth Quintile)	
1/1/89 to 6/30/92	(n/a)
1/1/87 to 6/30/92	(n/a)
1/1/85 to 6/30/92	(n/a)
1/1/83 to 6/30/92	(n/a)
6/30/80 to 6/30/92	(n/a)

Risk: 147% of market

The PAD System Report

Address
P.O. Box 554
Oxford, OH 45056

Editor
Daniel Alan Seiver

Phone Number
513-529-2863

Subscription Rates
$ 35.00/3 months
$195.00/year

Telephone Hotline
Yes

Money Management
No

THE PAD SYSTEM REPORT

Vol. 8, No. 7   July 21, 1992
VL MAP: 80%   S+P 500 414 DJ 3303

SIX CUTS TO ZERO

The stock market is addicted to Federal Reserve easing. It gets "high" after a half-point or full-point cut in the discount rate, sometimes staying "up" for months. And then the "addict" needs another easing. Can the Fed keep cutting the discount rate? We calculate that, at most, the Fed can cut the discount rate six more times, at a half-point per shot, which would bring the discount rate to zero. Then what?

The Fed keeps easing because the rickety recovery has not responded to previous easings. Why not? Consumers are holding back, working off excessive debt, while dreading the pink slip. Businesses are also cautious, many with too much debt, others with weak sales which cannot justify new hires or new investments in plant and equipment. All levels of government, federal, state, and local, face fiscal difficulties which will force them to cut spending or employment or both. And the export sector, which has been a source of strength, now faces weak demand in all of our biggest markets: Japan, Germany, and Canada. Monetary policy cannot do it all alone.

We doubt that Ross Perot had a workable plan to save the economy and cut the deficit. While Clinton-Gore may not have a plan to cut the deficit, they do have a plan to save the economy, which should not be dismissed out of hand. Spending on infrastructure and education will stimulate the economy in the short run, and will have growth-enhancing effects in the long-run. The Clinton-Gore plan will do more for the economy than a cut in the capital gains tax. Wall Street should not fear a Democratic victory in November.

[Continued on Page 8]

INSIDE: Boeing Aircraft..Page 5   Telmex..page 6

THE PAD SYSTEM REPORT IS PUBLISHED 12-18 TIMES A YEAR BY PATIENCE & DISCIPLINE INC. P. O. BOX 554 OXFORD OHIO 45056. PRES: DANIEL A. SEIVER. ANNUAL SUBSCRIPTIONS $195 (3 MO TRIAL: $35). SUBSCRIPTIONS NOT ASSIGNABLE WITHOUT CONSENT; PRO-RATA REFUNDS ON ANNUAL SUBSCRIPTIONS GIVEN WITHOUT QUESTION. PATIENCE AND DISCIPLINE IS REGISTERED AS AN INVESTMENT ADVISER WITH SEC.

The PAD System Report is published monthly by Daniel Seiver, a professor of economics at Miami University in Ohio. The newsletter is supplemented by what Seiver calls a "Messageline," which is updated episodically—at least every month and more often if Seiver recommends a change in his model portfolios.

The acronym "PAD" stands for "Patience and Discipline," and this is the key to Seiver's investment philosophy. Both his market timing and security selection are based on applying predetermined rules and formulae to publicly available information. For Seiver, long-term investment success is not a function of some magic or proprietary model but of the discipline not to deviate from an investment plan and the patience to follow it through thick and thin.

In addition to the two model portfolios graphed separately in this book, *The PAD System Report* used to have a third model portfolio (entitled "The Moderate Version"), which has since been discontinued. Furthermore, an additional model portfolio was inaugurated at the beginning of 1992 (entitled "The Income Version"). These two additional portfolios' performances are reflected in the newsletter's average, even though they are not graphed separately.

Overall for the three and one-half years through mid-1992, the newsletter produced a gain of 40.9%, in contrast to 60.3% for the Wilshire 5000. Owing to the fact that its risk (or volatility) was higher than that of the market over this period, its risk adjusted performance also was below the market's.

The PAD System Report (Average)

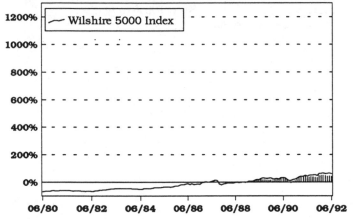

	Gain/Loss
1/1/91 to 6/30/92	+29.4%
(Second Quintile)	
1/1/89 to 6/30/92	+40.9%
(Third Quintile)	
1/1/87 to 6/30/92	(n/a)
1/1/85 to 6/30/92	(n/a)
1/1/83 to 6/30/92	(n/a)
6/30/80 to 6/30/92	(n/a)

Risk: 127% of market

The PAD System Report
(Model Portfolio A [The Aggressive Version])

	Gain/Loss
1/1/91 to 6/30/92	+14.2%
(Fourth Quintile)	
1/1/89 to 6/30/92	+19.6%
(Fourth Quintile)	
1/1/87 to 6/30/92	(n/a)
1/1/85 to 6/30/92	(n/a)
1/1/83 to 6/30/92	(n/a)
6/30/80 to 6/30/92	(n/a)

Risk: 185% of market

The PAD System Report
(Model Portfolio C [The Conservative Version])

	Gain/Loss
1/1/91 to 6/30/92	+42.5%
(Second Quintile)	
1/1/89 to 6/30/92	+91.1%
(First Quintile)	
1/1/87 to 6/30/92	(n/a)
1/1/85 to 6/30/92	(n/a)
1/1/83 to 6/30/92	(n/a)
6/30/80 to 6/30/92	(n/a)

Risk: 106% of market

Personal Finance

Address
1101 King St.
Suite 400
Alexandria, VA 22314

Editor
Stephen Leeb

Phone Number
703-548-2400

Subscription Rates
$39.00/year

Telephone Hotline
Yes

Money Management
Yes

Personal Finance

Stephen Leeb, Editor · Volume XIX, Number 13 · July 8, 1992

MARKETWATCH

President Bush recently urged the Federal Reserve to lower short-term interest rates. This is like a coach urging an athlete to take massive doses of steroids. Initially his performance might improve, but only at the expense of his long-term health.

If the Fed bows to political pressures, the dollar will fall. Stocks and bonds may bounce initially, but don't chase those rallies—the gains (and then some) will evaporate rapidly.

We haven't given up on stocks, but until the correction is past, we'll remain extremely selective. As we point out in the article to your right, foreign stock markets have more potential than the U.S. market. We also expect precious metals (see second article) to glitter in the next 6-12 months.

The fact is, we're bracing ourselves for higher inflation. The President, of course, argues that the Fed is free to focus on growth because inflation is no longer a concern. At first glance his argument seems to make sense. But first glances can be deceptive.

As we show on p. 154, inflation always declines in the first part of an economic recovery. What's different this time is that the decline has been less than in previous recoveries. Moreover, if history is any guide, the economy is now at a point where inflationary pressures will begin to pick up slightly. This is no time for complacency.

We base these views on forecasting models that rely on historical trends. If the economy does slow dramatically in the next month or two, we'll join the ranks of those urging lower rates. But right now, our models point to growth that's accelerating, not waning.

Stephen Leeb

PERSONAL FINANCE

OPEN THE DOOR TO CLOSED-END FUNDS

Put contrary opinion to work for you, to find values in closed-end funds that invest in both America and Europe.

BY JON OSTRIKER

With our 12-month forecast for the stock market in negative territory, where can an investor turn for profits? One option is closed-end funds that invest in the United States and Europe.

Below, we highlight the best plays in closed-end stock funds that are begging to be bought. For income investors, we highlight a bond fund that's particularly attractive. We also look at closed-end bond funds that are overpriced and ripe for shorting.

Some of the best buys are in European closed-end funds (CEFs). Today's economy is truly global, so you're doing yourself a great disservice if you ignore the rare buying opportunities that Europe currently has to offer.

The deep discounts of some of the closed-end funds investing in Europe reflect investor concern over potential problems there. European economies have been under a cloud for months, largely for two reasons: high German interest rates that are putting a lid on economic expansion, and the rejection by Danish voters of the European treaty on economic and political union.

However, voters in Ireland recently reaffirmed the treaty. And the core supporters of European integration—Germany, France, Holland and Luxembourg—are likely to move toward closer economic ties, with or without a formal treaty. In the ensuing uncertainty, German and Dutch markets are still attractive because of their central bankers' staunch anti-inflation stance.

European bourses are doing considerably better than ours. Compare year-

> **CLOSED-END EUROPE FUNDS ARE SELLING AT DEEP DISCOUNTS**

to-date stock market performance, as shown in the table on the next page. France, Germany and Switzerland handily beat the broader U.S. market.

Our market is also more expensive than European markets, based on price-to-earnings ratios. But despite the better relative performance and more attractive values in Europe, American investors remain wary about the European investment scene.

True, European economies have been kept on a tight leash by high German interest rates—their currencies are tightly linked to the dominant Deutsche mark. Nevertheless, as a harbinger of friendlier monetary policy to come, the British, French, and Irish central banks moved in early May to reduce key lending rates in their respective countries.

Watch The Discount

When public pessimism mounts, as it has about Europe, closed-end funds'

PAGE 145

Personal Finance is published every other week by KCI Communications and is edited by Stephen Leeb. It is supplemented by a daily telephone hotline. Leeb assumed the post of editor at the beginning of 1990; prior to Leeb, *Personal Finance* was edited by Richard Band, and before Band, co-edited by Band and Adrian Day. (Both Band and Day now edit newsletters of their own, and Leeb also edits *The Big Picture*; all three of these additional newsletters are reviewed elsewhere in this *Guide*.)

A number of the articles that appear in *Personal Finance* are written by contributing editors, and additional pages of the newsletter are devoted to summarizing what other advisers are saying. Though these articles typically contain specific investment recommendations, they are not formally considered to be official recommendations of *Personal Finance*.

In addition to articles by contributors, the newsletter contains four model portfolios that the HFD tracks, two that invest in individual stocks and bonds (a "Growth" and an "Income" portfolio) and two that invest in mutual funds (one for the short-term trader and the other for the long-term investor). Leeb's approach to these portfolios involves a combination of both technical and fundamental analysis.

The HFD has the most performance data for this newsletter's "Growth" and "Income" portfolios. Over the eight and one-half years through mid-1992, its "Income" portfolio did

better—gaining 226.0%, as compared to 67.5% for the "Growth" portfolio and 206.6% for the Wilshire 5000's total return. This performance of the "Income" portfolio is doubly worthwhile, because not only did it beat the market, but it did so with less risk.

The HFD's data for the two mutual fund portfolios begin in 1989. Over the subsequent three and one-half years through mid-1992, the newsletter's mutual fund portfolio for long-term investors gained 45.2% and its portfolio for short-term fund traders gained 45.9% (in contrast to the Wilshire 5000's 60.3%).

Overall, taking all four portfolios' gains into account and the fact that two of the portfolios haven't existed as long as the others, this newsletter's average performance from the beginning of 1984 to mid-1992 was a gain of 135.4%, as compared to 206.6% for the Wilshire 5000.

Personal Finance (Average)

	Gain/Loss
1/1/91 to 6/30/92 (Third Quintile)	+23.5%
1/1/89 to 6/30/92 (Second Quintile)	+49.3%
1/1/87 to 6/30/92 (Third Quintile)	+60.1%
1/1/85 to 6/30/92 (Second Quintile)	+166.4%
1/1/83 to 6/30/92	(n/a)
6/30/80 to 6/30/92	(n/a)

Risk: 53% of market

Personal Finance (Mutual Fund Portfolio [Long-Term])

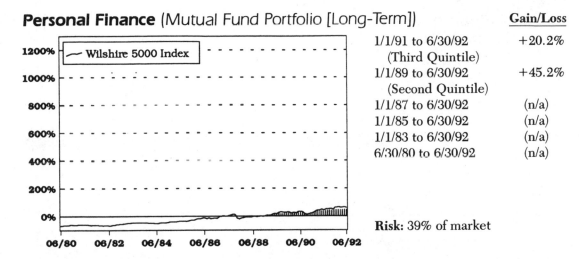

	Gain/Loss
1/1/91 to 6/30/92 (Third Quintile)	+20.2%
1/1/89 to 6/30/92 (Second Quintile)	+45.2%
1/1/87 to 6/30/92	(n/a)
1/1/85 to 6/30/92	(n/a)
1/1/83 to 6/30/92	(n/a)
6/30/80 to 6/30/92	(n/a)

Risk: 39% of market

Personal Finance (Mutual Fund Portfolio [Short-Term])

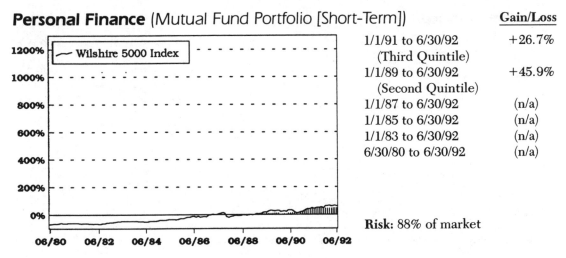

	Gain/Loss
1/1/91 to 6/30/92 (Third Quintile)	+26.7%
1/1/89 to 6/30/92 (Second Quintile)	+45.9%
1/1/87 to 6/30/92	(n/a)
1/1/85 to 6/30/92	(n/a)
1/1/83 to 6/30/92	(n/a)
6/30/80 to 6/30/92	(n/a)

Risk: 88% of market

Personal Finance (Growth Portfolio)

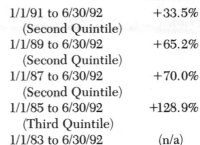

	Gain/Loss
1/1/91 to 6/30/92 (Second Quintile)	+33.5%
1/1/89 to 6/30/92 (Second Quintile)	+65.2%
1/1/87 to 6/30/92 (Second Quintile)	+70.0%
1/1/85 to 6/30/92 (Third Quintile)	+128.9%
1/1/83 to 6/30/92	(n/a)
6/30/80 to 6/30/92	(n/a)

Risk: 79% of market

Personal Finance (Income Portfolio)

	Gain/Loss
1/1/91 to 6/30/92 (Fourth Quintile)	+13.6%
1/1/89 to 6/30/92 (Third Quintile)	+40.7%
1/1/87 to 6/30/92 (Third Quintile)	+54.0%
1/1/85 to 6/30/92 (First Quintile)	+208.0%
1/1/83 to 6/30/92	(n/a)
6/30/80 to 6/30/92	(n/a)

Risk: 19% of market

The Peter Dag Investment Letter

The Peter Dag Investment Letter
THE RIGHT ADVICE • AT THE RIGHT TIME • DEPEND ON IT

Vol. 92 No. 15   July 6, 1992   65 Lakefront Drive, Akron, Ohio 44319   ISSN 0196-9323

30-SECOND INVESTMENT UPDATE

US stock market. Good trading opportunity ahead. Short-term and long-term buy signals still in effect. Too many bearish commentators.

Foreign stock markets. Momentum is down. The Swiss market is the strongest.

The economy. A sudden and worrisome string of bad news points to slower growth ahead.

Commodities. Mostly flat. The trend in industrial commodities is still up.

Crude oil. Stabilizing around $22.

Money supply. Continues to slow down. Very discouraging. Not a good sign for the economy.

Short-term interest rates. Down.

Yield curve. Very steep, reflecting the continuing efforts of the Fed to inject liquidity.

Real interest rates. Real short-term rates will stay low. Inflationary in the long run?

Monetary policy. The Fed has been too cautious. It has been easing too little, too late.

Inflation. Low growth in the money supply and a weakening economy could bring inflation rates close to 2%.

Bonds. Soaring. They are definitely an outstanding investment in this period of disinflation.

Inflation hedge stocks. Hold.

US dollar. Weak, due to low interest rates and a weak economy. Attracting foreign investment in the US. Encouraging capital flight from the US.

RECOMMENDED ASSET ALLOCATION

The following table shows the percent of your capital allocated to each asset. This percentage should be interpreted as the probability that each asset will outperform the others. The higher the probability, the lower is the risk associated with investing in a specific asset.

	7/6	6/22
Stocks	0%	0%
Inflation hedge stocks:		
Gold stocks	5%	5%
Energy stocks	10%	10%
Bonds	70%	70%
Money market instruments ..	15%	15%

US STOCK MARKET

Stocks are up a slim 5.6% since May of last year, and up 4.4% per year (compound) since August 1987. Although the S&P 500 is down only 1.8% since January 3, over-the-counter stocks are down a sharp 11.5% since then. We show these data to

MONEY SUPPLY M1
(% CHG, 3 & 6 MOS)

Fig. 1. Liquidity has been soaring.

The Peter Dag Investment Letter is published every three weeks by George Dagnino, and has no telephone hotline update.

Dag recommends two model portfolios, one that concentrates solely on mutual funds within the Vanguard family of funds, and a second that consists of individual stocks. For both portfolios his advice is very clear: Subscribers are told exactly what percentage of their portfolio should be devoted to each security, and what to sell to get the proceeds to purchase new recommendations. (Owing to the fact that Dag's stock portfolio wasn't inaugurated until late 1991 and the HFD didn't

---

Address
65 Lakefront Dr.
Akron, OH 44319

Editor
George Dagnino

Phone Number
800-833-2782

Subscription Rates
$ 75.00/3 months
$250.00/year

Telephone Hotline
No

Money Management
Yes

begin following it until the beginning of 1992, it isn't graphed separately in this book. But its performance is included in what is reported for the newsletter's average.)

Dag's mutual fund portfolio is one of the least risky of any monitored by the HFD. Over the time the HFD has been following it, a large percentage of Dag's portfolio consistently has been invested in a money market fund or in one of Vanguard's fixed-income funds. With such low risk one would not expect the portfolio to beat a buy-and-hold in the stock market, and this indeed is the case. Over the nine and one-half years through mid-1992, it gained 127.0%, as compared to

278.6% for the Wilshire 5000. However, Dag's mutual fund portfolio beat the T-Bill portfolio's 93.5% return over this same period—meaning that subscribers derived some additional value for undertaking the slight amount of risk in Dag's portfolio.

Rather than beating the market on a total-return basis, a much more realistic goal for a low-risk strategy such as Dag's would be to beat it on a risk-adjusted basis. While Dag has not done so over the nine and one-half years through mid-1992, he has done so over the period from the beginning of 1987 through mid-1992.

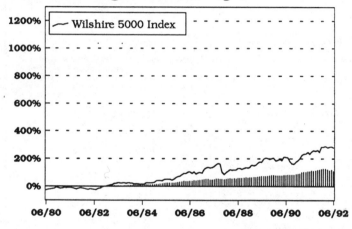

The Peter Dag Letter (Average)

	Gain/Loss
1/1/91 to 6/30/92 (Fourth Quintile)	+10.5%
1/1/89 to 6/30/92 (Fourth Quintile)	+28.7%
1/1/87 to 6/30/92 (Fourth Quintile)	+43.6%
1/1/85 to 6/30/92 (Fourth Quintile)	+86.1%
1/1/83 to 6/30/92 (Third Quintile)	+108.1%
6/30/80 to 6/30/92	(n/a)

Risk: 57% of market

The Peter Dag Letter (Model Vanguard Fund Portfolio)

	Gain/Loss
1/1/91 to 6/30/92 (Third Quintile)	+20.5%
1/1/89 to 6/30/92 (Third Quintile)	+40.5%
1/1/87 to 6/30/92 (Third Quintile)	+56.6%
1/1/85 to 6/30/92 (Third Quintile)	+103.0%
1/1/83 to 6/30/92 (Third Quintile)	+127.0%
6/30/80 to 6/30/92	(n/a)

Risk: 35% of market

Plain Talk Investor

Address
1500 Skokie Blvd.
Suite 203
Northbrook, IL 60062

Editor
Fred Gordon

Phone Number
708-564-1955

Subscription Rates
$135.00/year

Telephone Hotline
No

Money Management
No

PLAIN TALK INVESTOR

Your practical guide to market success

July 9, 1992   No. 173
DJIA: 3324.08

DIRTY TRICKS

I have it on good authority (if you must know, I read it in a tabloid at the supermarket checkout): The C.I.A. has a tape of a Ross Perot agent spying on Bill Clinton in the Rose Garden, as Slick makes eyes at the First Lady (well, not *his* first, second or third lady, possibly), while the President, having no agenda, plucks an American Beauty, a flower belonging, as H. Ross might proclaim, "to the American people!" (Have I offended everybody equally?) Election business as usual: Dirty tricks!

One of the dirtiest economic tricks came from the Labor Department, flashing news that 7.8% are jobless as of June (near 10 million), up from May's 7.5%, a startling job loss of 117,000. Dashing cold water on an already tepid recovery, the report nudged a beleaguered President Bush one step closer to the end of the unemployment line.

The downbeat numbers were a quick wake up call for Fed chief Alan Greenspan and Friends: The Fed moved quickly to breathe some life into a gasping recovery, slashing its discount rate—the Fed's loan charge to member banks—to 3% from 3 1/2%, the biggest one-day whack in 10 years, and the lowest pricetag since mid-'63. The Fed also cut the Fed funds rate—banks' inter-bank charges for overnight loans—from 3.75% to 3.25%.

The flip-side of ever-lower rates is the long-running dirty trick played upon millions of retirees and pensioners, their CD and money market yields now squeezed thinner still.

The Fed has now fired its biggest gun—rate cuts—24 times in three years and we're growing ever so slowly, if that. In a debt-burdened economy, rife with job insecurity, consumer confidence, understandably, continues to stall. And the consumer—two-thirds of the Gross Domestic Product— remains the necessary ingredient in any meaningful recovery.

Interestingly, the market added 72 points in the three days *prior* to the Fed's axing of rates; then, ex post facto, shed 59 the following three days. ("Buy the rumor, sell the news," as Wall Street trader's wisdom goes.)

More interest rate cuts to come? I'd make the bet: The Fed, sensing little inflation and

Unemployment's K.O. Punch

Monthly unemployment rate.

7.8%

'91 '92

J J A S O N D J F M A M J

The New York Times

Unexpectedly high unemployment profiles a stalled recovery and prods the Fed to cut interest rates.

One of America's 1991 "Top Ten Long Term Timers" (Timer Digest, Jan. '92)

© 1992 PLAIN TALK INVESTOR   (MORE)

Plain Talk Investor is published every three weeks by Fred Gordon. It is not supplemented by a telephone hotline update. Gordon's approach involves a combination of both fundamental and technical analysis, though he seems to place more importance on the former: Two to three pages of each issue are devoted to his analysis of the market's major trend, and the factors he refers to are almost entirely fundamental.

Technical analysis apparently plays more of a role in Gordon's stock selection, especially in picking stocks for his "High Risk/High Reward" portfolio. He also uses technical analysis to place a stop-loss below each stock's perceived support level. Gordon has an additional, less risky, "Personal-Best" portfolio, which is invested more for the long term than is his higher-risk portfolio.

Gordon's "High Risk/High Reward" portfolio typically invests a greater percentage of assets in each recommendation than does his "Personal-Best" portfolio (10% versus 5%). This fact alone increases the portfolio's riskiness, and in addition the securities recommended for this portfolio are riskier in and of themselves (at times Gordon has recommended warrants and options for this portfolio, as well as stocks).

This additional risk has not paid off for this portfolio, at least since 1985. For the seven and one-half years through mid-1992, in fact, the "High Risk/High Reward" portfolio gained only 8.7%, as compared to the Wilshire 5000's gain of 197.6%. Gordon's "Personal-Best" portfolio did better, gaining 109.5%, though still not beating the market.

The primary culprit in this underperformance appears to be Gordon's stock selection. If each of the stocks he recommended for these portfolios had done as well as the Wilshire 5000 during the times they held them, then both these portfolios would have performed much better (132.5% instead of 109.5% for his "Personal Best" portfolio and 122.0% versus 8.7% for his "High Risk/High Reward" portfolio). On a risk-adjusted basis, these timing-only performances are only slightly below the Wilshire's.

Plain Talk Investor (Average)

Gain/Loss	
1/1/91 to 6/30/92	+13.3%
(Fourth Quintile)	
1/1/89 to 6/30/92	+33.1%
(Third Quintile)	
1/1/87 to 6/30/92	+46.3%
(Third Quintile)	
1/1/85 to 6/30/92	+54.1%
(Fourth Quintile)	
1/1/83 to 6/30/92	(n/a)
6/30/80 to 6/30/92	(n/a)

Risk: 128% of market

Plain Talk Investor (Personal-Best Stock Portfolio)

	Gain/Loss
1/1/91 to 6/30/92 (Third Quintile)	+18.6%
1/1/89 to 6/30/92 (Third Quintile)	+32.8%
1/1/87 to 6/30/92 (Fourth Quintile)	+44.4%
1/1/85 to 6/30/92 (Third Quintile)	+109.5%
1/1/83 to 6/30/92	(n/a)
6/30/80 to 6/30/92	(n/a)

Risk: 92% of market

Plain Talk Investor (High Risk/High Reward Portfolio)

	Gain/Loss
1/1/91 to 6/30/92 (Fifth Quintile)	+7.3%
1/1/89 to 6/30/92 (Fourth Quintile)	+31.4%
1/1/87 to 6/30/92 (Fourth Quintile)	+44.9%
1/1/85 to 6/30/92 (Fifth Quintile)	+8.7%
1/1/83 to 6/30/92	(n/a)
6/30/80 to 6/30/92	(n/a)

Risk: 177% of market

The Princeton Portfolios

Address
301 N. Harrison
Suite 229
Princeton, NJ 08540

Editor
Michael Gianturco

Phone Number
212-288-8424

Subscription Rates
$225.00/year

Telephone Hotline
Yes

Money Management
Yes

PRINCETON
PORTFOLIOS
Investing in Science
Professionally managed individual portfolios invested in the
securities of exceptional growth companies in science and technology.

August 4, 1992

I am still reading occasionally that "the market" is flirting with a new all time high. This can only mean the Dow Jones 30 Industrials. The broad market has long since crashed, and is in the process of making a recovery.

This year the science and technology stocks, as a broad group, lost -23.2 percent of their value between their January 7 peak and their June 26 trough. These numbers are based on the Pacific Stock Exchange's Technology Index, which averages in all different kinds of technology companies. The biotech sector made a much deeper trough in late April; the computer bottomed in July. For the whole PSE average, the only worse dropout in recent memory was the -27 percent collapse owing to the invasion of Kuwait in 1990.

Yet in this same 6-month period of 1992, the DOW stocks lost just 1 percent. Strength in the DOW has masked, for the casual observers and for many in the press, the severe damage done by the recession to the smaller stocks and to the broader markets.

Both the DOW and the smaller stocks are now rallying, and the technology group has gained about 7 percent from its bottom five weeks ago. I believe the DOW will now flatten out, and will be outperformed by the technology growth stocks as the economy strengthens.

I diversify our portfolios on the basis of technology. The investment risk is spread across the fields of biotechnology, computer hardware, software, semiconductors, laser-related technologies, and conventional pharmaceuticals. All these companies are relative new or transitional, so each buy is a bet on their ability to survive and grow.

In the years I have been watching technology stock portfolios, beginning in 1978, this diversification across different technologies has worked for us to damp the swings in the portfolios. For example, when the biotechs and pharmaceuticals are down, some other group -- typically computers -- has been reliably up and coming.

This year it did not help. The speculative bubble in biotech burst and, two months later, the computer industry began to shake out. It does this periodically, but the effects of the shakeout have been aggravated by the recession. In sum, the science and technology group turned down in

301 N. Harrison, Suite 229 • Princeton, NJ 08540 • (609) 497-0362

The Princeton Portfolios, edited by Michael Gianturco, is the successor publication to *High Technology Investments*, which Gianturco also edited prior to its name change. Over the years the service has become increasingly an electronic one, to the point now that a subscriber needs a computer with a modem hookup in order to receive the newsletter.

Among those services the HFD follows that concentrate on the high-technology sector, *The Princeton Portfolios* is one of the better performers, though it has lagged the market. For the nine and one-half years through mid-1992, for example, this service's average performance was a gain of 146.7%, as compared to 278.6% for the Wilshire 5000. By comparison, another service which focuses on the technology sector (*California Technology Stock Letter*) gained just 40.6% over this same period of time.

One indication of the difficulties associated with picking stocks within the technology sector is the fact that on a timing-only basis,

Gianturco performed much better. If each of the stocks in his "Long-Term Portfolio #2" had performed as well as the Wilshire 5000 during the time this portfolio owned it, the portfolio's nine-and-one-half-year return would have been 208.1% instead of 129.8%. And if this timing-only portfolio's below-average risk is taken into account, it actually beat the market.

The Princeton Portfolios (Average)

	Gain/Loss
1/1/91 to 6/30/92 (Fifth Quintile)	+1.2%
1/1/89 to 6/30/92 (Fifth Quintile)	+6.5%
1/1/87 to 6/30/92 (Fourth Quintile)	+42.6%
1/1/85 to 6/30/92 (First Quintile)	+208.4%
1/1/83 to 6/30/92 (Third Quintile)	+146.7%
6/30/80 to 6/30/92	(n/a)

Risk: 196% of market

The Princeton Portfolios (Long-Term Portfolio #1)

	Gain/Loss
1/1/91 to 6/30/92 (Second Quintile)	+27.0%
1/1/89 to 6/30/92 (Fourth Quintile)	+28.2%
1/1/87 to 6/30/92 (Second Quintile)	+70.2%
1/1/85 to 6/30/92 (First Quintile)	+203.4%
1/1/83 to 6/30/92 (Third Quintile)	+140.9%
6/30/80 to 6/30/92	(n/a)

Risk: 196% of market

The Princeton Portfolios (Long-Term Portfolio #2)

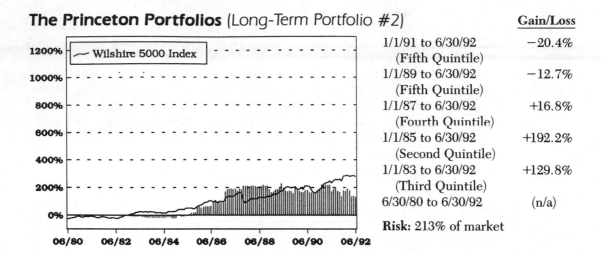

	Gain/Loss
1/1/91 to 6/30/92 (Fifth Quintile)	−20.4%
1/1/89 to 6/30/92 (Fifth Quintile)	−12.7%
1/1/87 to 6/30/92 (Fourth Quintile)	+16.8%
1/1/85 to 6/30/92 (Second Quintile)	+192.2%
1/1/83 to 6/30/92 (Third Quintile)	+129.8%
6/30/80 to 6/30/92	(n/a)

Risk: 213% of market

The Professional Tape Reader

Address
P.O. Box 2407
Hollywood, FL 33022

Editor
Stan Weinstein

Subscription Rates
$210.00/6 months
$350.00/year

Telephone Hotline
Yes

Money Management
No

"The Tape Tells All"   Published & Edited by: *STAN WEINSTEIN*

THE PROFESSIONAL
TAPE READER®

RADCAP, Inc.   P.O. Box 2407   Hollywood, FL 33022

Issue No. 496 July 10, 1992	DISTRIBUTION

TREND OVERVIEW	
Long Term	Neutral but Weakening
Intermediate Term	Moderately Negative
Short Term	Neutral

We stressed in our last issue that "we still feel that <u>extreme</u> caution is called for as the Dow continues to trace out a major top formation, while the majority of stocks outside of the blue chip universe are already in their own private bear markets." Nothing that we've seen in the past 2 weeks has caused us to alter that view, so don't be thrown off by the DJ Industrial's wild gyrations which are camouflaging what's *really* going on! While so many others are focusing on the market's oversold condition and the likelihood of a summer rally, we are far more concerned with the big picture which is <u>very</u> worrisome. Even though the Dow is still close to its all-time high, an incredible number of stocks have broken down from significant top formations and have had serious 'accidents.' Just look at these charts of Honeywell and Symantec (there are plenty of others which are in a similar position), and you'll see just what we're talking about. In a truly healthy bull market, you simply don't see so many 'explosions' taking place on the tape. This is a sign of both technical weakness and a lack of liquidity under the market (and it's especially worrisome because, once the Dow too turns negative and gives the Street 'a wake up call,' then this lack of liquidity is likely to be felt on a broad front). So while there are still a few areas on the long side that interest us (such as Electric Utilities, Insurance, and Telephone Utilities for investing, and both Biotechnology and Drugs for trading), more and more stocks are undergoing distribution (as they form major tops), and the simple reality is that the technically healthy universe continues to shrink. We, therefore, do <u>not</u> feel that it makes sense to be fully invested at this point simply because it's an election year and the Fed is being so accommodating.

Here's why we feel as we do. First of all, it's worrisome that our proprietary NYSE Survey is still in such horrid shape (it has actually weakened even further). On a healthy advance, 75%-80% of all issues should move into Stages 1 & 2 (the technically healthy phases). Not only are we nowhere near those sort of positive readings, but in recent weeks this gauge has weakened to the point where now less than 35% of all groups are in Stages 1 & 2. This simply isn't the way to put a broad-based and sustainable advance together! Therefore, even though the market is oversold

and is likely to do some further upside testing, we do not expect rallies to be really healthy at this point so caution is most definitely still the tactic of the day. Another cause for concern is that more and more market averages are starting to top out and break below their respective 30 week moving averages (which is a sign of serious long term technical weakness). Look at this chart of the DJ Transportation Average, and you'll see yet another cause for long term concern. First of all, this important index is now below its 30 week moving average (which is another long term negative indication). Secondly, a major negative divergence has formed in this gauge as the 1992 high never bettered the '89 peak despite the series of new DJ Industrial all-time highs. History shows us that such massive non-confirmations lead to serious trouble. Finally, this gauge has displayed very poor relative strength in recent weeks and has headed lower even as the DJI has rallied. This simply *isn't* the way to start a broad-based and sustainable advance. In addition to the above long term problems, it's also negative that our Momentum Index (a 200 day Advance-Decline moving average for the NYSE issues) is now in very poor shape. On a really healthy advance, this gauge should move far into positive territory but, currently, it's heading lower and is on the verge of breaking into negative territory. This is yet another clear-cut sign that, beneath the surface, the overwhelming majority of stocks are being distributed and are running into technical trouble, while the Dow continues to paint a rosy picture. Add into the long term equation the fact that, as narrow as the Dow's universe is (after all, how can just 30 stocks truly represent the entire market?), there's incredible selectivity taking place even within the blue chip average. Note that despite the series of new DJI

continued on page 8

The Professional Tape Reader is published every two weeks by Stan Weinstein and is supplemented by a telephone hotline that is updated twice each week. Weinstein's approach to the markets is almost exclusively technical. In addition to providing specific advice for model stock and mutual fund portfolios, he grades the status of the shorter- and longer-term trends of the stock, gold and bond markets.

Over the twelve years through mid-1992, Weinstein's model stock portfolio had a gain of 48.5%, compared to 432.7% for the Wilshire 5000. The HFD has less data for his mutual fund portfolio, but it has done better—especially on a risk-adjusted basis. Over the six and one-half years through mid-1992, it gained 70.9%, in contrast to 124.5% for the Wilshire 5000—but with substantially less risk. Indeed, on a risk-adjusted basis Weinstein's mutual fund portfolio beat the market over this period.

The HFD also measures the timing record of Weinstein's switches into and out of the stock, gold and bond markets, and the reader is referred to Appendix C for the full details. For the twelve years through mid-1992, the

HFD calculates that Weinstein's mutual fund allocation advice in the stock market gained 238.9% on a pure timing basis, as compared to 432.7% for buying and holding. When this timing-only portfolio's low risk is taken into account, it almost (but not quite) equals the market's return.

In the gold market, Weinstein's timing beat a buy-and-hold over the four and one-half years through mid-1992 (though it failed to equal the return of a money market fund). In the bond market, his timing failed to beat a buy-and-hold strategy.

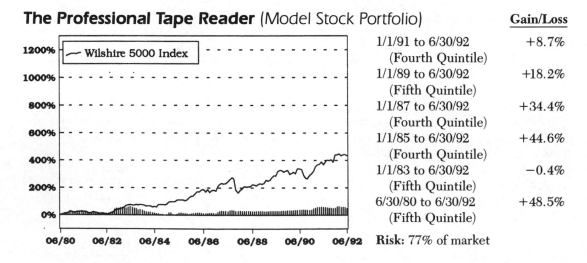

The Professional Tape Reader (Average)

	Gain/Loss
1/1/91 to 6/30/92 (Fourth Quintile)	+11.3%
1/1/89 to 6/30/92 (Fourth Quintile)	+24.7%
1/1/87 to 6/30/92 (Third Quintile)	+47.6%
1/1/85 to 6/30/92 (Fourth Quintile)	+62.6%
1/1/83 to 6/30/92 (Fifth Quintile)	+12.0%
6/30/80 to 6/30/92 (Fifth Quintile)	+67.0%

Risk: 51% of market

The Professional Tape Reader (Model Stock Portfolio)

	Gain/Loss
1/1/91 to 6/30/92 (Fourth Quintile)	+8.7%
1/1/89 to 6/30/92 (Fifth Quintile)	+18.2%
1/1/87 to 6/30/92 (Fourth Quintile)	+34.4%
1/1/85 to 6/30/92 (Fourth Quintile)	+44.6%
1/1/83 to 6/30/92 (Fifth Quintile)	−0.4%
6/30/80 to 6/30/92 (Fifth Quintile)	+48.5%

Risk: 77% of market

The Professional Tape Reader (Mutual Fund Portfolio)

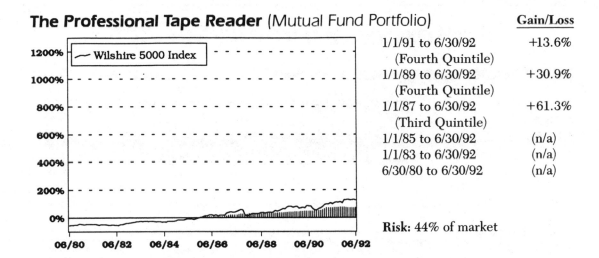

	Gain/Loss
1/1/91 to 6/30/92	+13.6%
(Fourth Quintile)	
1/1/89 to 6/30/92	+30.9%
(Fourth Quintile)	
1/1/87 to 6/30/92	+61.3%
(Third Quintile)	
1/1/85 to 6/30/92	(n/a)
1/1/83 to 6/30/92	(n/a)
6/30/80 to 6/30/92	(n/a)

Risk: 44% of market

Professional Timing Service

Address
P.O. Box 7483
Missoula, MT 59807

Editor
Curtis J. Hesler

Phone Number
406-543-4131

Subscription Rates
$100.00/6 months
$185.00/year

Telephone Hotline
Yes

Money Management
No

$185 A YEAR • MARKET REPORT MONDAY, WEDNESDAY & FRIDAY • P.O. BOX 7483, MISSOULA, MT 59807 • (406) 543-4131   #9207/7-3-92

FORGET THE DOW

For years we have admonished traders - especially mutual fund traders - about forgetting the Dow Industrials. It will never be a good guide for profitable mutual fund trading.

Here is why we have been in money market funds for all but 36 days this year. This is a chart of the Piper Jaffray Value Fund, which I trade in my personal account. It's very representative of most of the other funds I follow and use.

The chart is also representative of what the "real" market has been doing this year and shows why most investors have not been profitable. Outside of the December - January rally, prices have been falling all year. In fact, many funds I follow (including this one) are now selling for less than they did when we went long last December.

The Mutual Fund Index published by *Investor's Daily* shows the average mutual fund down by 11.3%. Bob Farrell of Merrill Lynch indicated that 40% of all stocks are down 30% since the first quarter. Think about that! You would need a 42.8% gain just to get even again. I hope your investments are doing better than that.

Spending so much time this year in dull old cash accounts has been the correct thing to do thus far, and the

Dynamo has done a splendid job in guiding us. However, things never stay the same for long in the stock market, and our technical indicators are beginning to improve.

First of all, we had a Supply/Demand Formula buy signal in the Dow Industrials on June 29 at 3290. The Dow has been on a sell since March.

Appel's "new high/new low index," which we showed you in the June mid-month letter, has now settled back to just over the 30% level.

Officially we need the index to fall under 30% and then move back over 30% for a buy signal, but we are setting up for that eventuality. Count new highs/new lows as at least a potential technical positive.

Another positive technical development is the market is near oversold levels in the Moving Balance Index. That's not been seen since last December. Such levels often precede strong rallies.

As we go to press, the Dynamo is close to a buy signal ... but it's not there yet. I suspect that once the second quarter window dressing bounce is over in early July, we will sell off again to test the June lows. Once that test is over (mid to late July), expect the Dynamo to take us back into equity funds.

What will drive stocks higher in an overvalued market? Two things: 1) short covering, and 2) the paradox of cash.

Professional Timing Service is published monthly by Curtis J. Hesler. The subscription is supplemented by a two-page mid-month bulletin and a telephone hotline that is updated three times each week. Prior to Hesler's becoming editor in early 1984, this newsletter was edited by Larry Williams.

Hesler's approach involves a number of various indicators, most of which are technical. One of his major market-timing systems is called the "Supply/Demand Formula." For the twelve years ending in mid-1992, an investor who went long or short in hypothetical shares of the Wilshire 5000 when this

"Formula" generated buy and sell signals for the DJIA would have made just 45.4%. In contrast, an investor who simply bought and held would have made 432.7%. If an investor followed Hesler's "Formula" by going into cash on sell signals instead of actually going short, however, he would have beaten the market with a 436.5% gain over these twelve years.

Hesler also provides specific timing signals for mutual fund traders, and the HFD has followed them on a pure-timing basis since the beginning of 1987. Over the subsequent five and one-half years, on a pure-timing basis, these signals produced a 67.2% gain, in contrast to 93.3% for the Wilshire 5000. However, during late 1987 Hesler introduced a new system to time mutual fund switches (which he called his "Dynamo") and it has done much better: If we measure Hesler's mutual fund timing from the beginning of 1988 instead of the beginning of 1987, he beat the market by a 100.4% to 89.0% margin over the period through mid-1992.

Up until 1987 the specific stock recommendations contained in *Professional Timing Service* were not part of a specific model portfolio. Per its established methodology, therefore, the HFD constructed one for it that was fully invested in the letter's open recommendations. Beginning in 1987 Hesler created a number of very specific model portfolios, one each for investors, traders and mu-

tual funds, though only the mutual fund portfolio survived for more than a year or two. Taking all these portfolios into account, the HFD reports that *Professional Timing Service* gained just 26.6% over the ten and one-half years through mid-1992, compared to 349.4% for the Wilshire 5000.

Since the beginning of 1985, the HFD also has been tracking a portfolio constructed out of Hesler's recommendations of gold futures trades. Since Hesler doesn't tell subscribers how much of their gold futures portfolio ought to be invested in these futures, or with what margin, the HFD has constructed this portfolio on the assumption that it becomes fully invested when a recommendation is made, with no margin. (The investor should keep this in mind when interpreting the results, since rarely is a commodities portfolio fully invested and since it frequently will use margin.) In any case, the portfolio constructed out of Hesler's recommendations of particular gold futures contracts gained 31.2% over the seven and one-half years through mid-1992, in contrast to an 11.1% gain for gold bullion and a 61.7% gain from a portfolio of 90-day T-Bills.

Finally, the HFD has tracked *Professional Timing Service*'s bond market timing since the beginning of 1989. Over the subsequent three and one-half years through mid-1992, this timing failed to beat the return of buying and holding.

Professional Timing Service (Average)

	Gain/Loss
1/1/91 to 6/30/92 (Fourth Quintile)	+13.6%
1/1/89 to 6/30/92 (Fifth Quintile)	+19.4%
1/1/87 to 6/30/92 (Fifth Quintile)	+11.9%
1/1/85 to 6/30/92 (Fifth Quintile)	+30.8%
1/1/83 to 6/30/92 (Fifth Quintile)	+29.8%
6/30/80 to 6/30/92	(n/a)

Risk: 34% of market

Professional Timing Service (Gold Futures Trading Portfolio)

	Gain/Loss
1/1/91 to 6/30/92 (Fifth Quintile)	−7.9%
1/1/89 to 6/30/92 (Fifth Quintile)	−13.1%
1/1/87 to 6/30/92 (Fifth Quintile)	+4.7%
1/1/85 to 6/30/92 (Fifth Quintile)	+31.2%
1/1/83 to 6/30/92	(n/a)
6/30/80 to 6/30/92	(n/a)

Risk: 43% of market

Professional Timing Service (Mutual Fund Model Portfolio)

	Gain/Loss
1/1/91 to 6/30/92 (Second Quintile)	+38.7%
1/1/89 to 6/30/92 (First Quintile)	+85.2%
1/1/87 to 6/30/92 (Second Quintile)	+92.2%
1/1/85 to 6/30/92	(n/a)
1/1/83 to 6/30/92	(n/a)
6/30/80 to 6/30/92	(n/a)

Risk: 81% of market

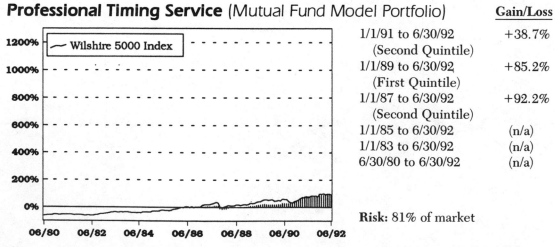

The Prudent Speculator

The Prudent Speculator

P.O. Box 1767, Santa Monica, CA 90406 (310) 315-9888

| TPS 309, July 7, 1992 | Established in 1977 | ISSN 0743-0809 |

Address
P.O. Box 1767
Santa Monica, CA
90406-1767

Editor
Al Frank

Phone Number
310-315-9888

Subscription Rates
$ 45.00/3 months
$175.00/year

Telephone Hotline
No

Money Management
Yes

Current Overview and Approaches

At last, alas, the Federal Reserve woke up and smelled the smoke of an economy threatening to crash and burn. Ironically, the economy is probably stronger than June employment and unemployment figures indicate. The half-point decreases in both the Federal Reserve's Discount and Federal Funds rates are very positive for both the economy and the stock market, practically insuring a "summer rally" in each. If not, the Fed is certain to ease yet again in a probably vain effort to help reelect President Bush. Now we have another historical precedent of seven consecutive Discount rate cuts. The previous four times have all led to higher blue chip prices over subsequent months.

Lower interest rates and continuing low inflation should support a volatile but positive summer rally. Bad employment figures and reduced confidence should be overcome by strength in construction and autos. BOLD, MODERATE SPECULATORS and CONSERVATIVE INVESTORS should be more bullish than bearish, while taking profits in overvalued stocks. See Page 2 for more commentary.

Review of Indexes

	Dow Jones Industrials*	Composite Index*	Hypothetical Cash Values*	TPS Portfolio Equity
For the past 3+ weeks:				
Close 6/30/92	3318.53	224.33	$ 465,641	$ 204,982
Close 6/ 5/92	3398.69	227.88	$ 471,309	$ 216,126
Changes	- 80.16	- 3.55	-$ 5,668^	-$ 6,144^^
Percentages	- 2.36%	- 1.56%	- 1.20%	- 2.84%^^
For the past six months:				
Close 12/31/91	3168.83	229.44	$ 549,766	$ 245,671
Changes	+ 149.60	- 5.11	+$ 69,311^	+$ 61,632^^
Percentages	+ 4.72%	- 2.23%	+ 14.49%^	+ 29.32%^^
For the life of TPS:				
Close 3/11/77	947.72	54.72	$ 16,200	$ 8,006
Changes	+2370.81	+169.61	+$ 348,049^	+$ 159,152^^
Percentages	+ 250.16%	+309.96%	+ 432.46%^	+ 838.72%^^

*These columns do not count dividends or reinvestments made with proceeds from tenders and buyouts. TPS Portfolio Equity Analysis reflects Al Frank's actual margined portfolio. Hypothetical Cash Values represents TPS Portfolio as if all stocks had been bought for cash; the values are actual but the performance is hypothetical. ^Changes include stocks traded. Equity Analysis includes margin cost, dividends, and paid commissions. ^^Changes include cash paid in or taken out. Note: TPS performance is based on a long-established, margined portfolio; current recommendations will have different results.

General Review & Observations

"Too little, too late" must be mitigated by "Better late than never" in a cliché analysis of the big picture. The mismanagement of financial institutions and the economy is almost unbelievable, but the core is solid and we will ultimately muddle through these leaderless times. Ironically, astute stock market players will profit (yet again) even as the average working persons in America will suffer a continuing decline in their standard of living. The recent interest rate cuts are the best tonic the economy and the market could expect.

After this letter goes to the printer, I will try to refinance my home mortgage. If successful, I will have several hundred dollars a month more of elective income. I expect my experience will be repeated by tens of thousands of home buyers. Also, many potential home buyers will become eligible to qualify for mortgages at these lower interest rates. Countless businesses and our federal, state and local governments will benefit as their cost of capital (borrowing) is decreased.

The Prudent Speculator (formerly *The Pinchpenny Speculator*) is published monthly by Al Frank. It used to be supplemented by a telephone hotline but is no longer.

Frank started the letter, among other reasons, to report on the status of his personal portfolio, transactions in which are listed in each issue. Frank also publishes in each issue a list of "currently recommended stocks." The HFD's performance rating is based on Frank's personal portfolio.

Frank advocates the aggressive use of margin and follows this advice in his own portfolio. This obviously has been a major factor in his performance in the 12 years since 1980. In fact, if he hadn't used margin, his portfolio would have performed significantly less well. You should keep this in mind when interpreting the fact that Frank only slightly underperformed the market over these 12 years on a total-return basis (428.9% versus 432.7% for the market). On a risk-adjusted basis, he lagged the market by a greater margin.

Frank is a value-oriented investor, and like most such investors, he generally has frowned on market timing and technical analysis. In the late 1980s, however, he began to try his hand at market timing, claiming that by using technical analysis he could reduce margin, build up cash reserves, and purchase index put options to hedge his portfolio in the event that market risk grew high enough. However, Frank had not undertaken any of these moves by the time of the crash in October 1987 and his portfolio lost nearly 60% that month. Indeed, his portfolio was one of the largest losers that month among those followed by the HFD, shedding nearly 60% of its value.

Prior to the 1987 crash and that 60% loss, *The Prudent Speculator* was in first place for performance over the period from mid-1980. And Frank's reaction to the crash, we now know with the benefit of hindsight, was correct: He bought stocks to the maximum ex-

tent possible immediately following the crash. Yet, even though the market has recovered, Frank's portfolio has not. Over the five and one-half years through mid-1992 (which includes the 1987 crash), the HFD reports that *The Prudent Speculator* actually lost 4.2%, in contrast to a 93.3% gain for the Wilshire 5000. From this we can conclude that the culprit in Frank's lagging the market was not his market timing but his stock picking.

Because the model portfolio the HFD tracks is Frank's personal portfolio, there will be some discrepancies between his actual performance and what the HFD reports. One source of this discrepancy can be traced to the margin level in the portfolio the HFD constructs to track Frank's performance. As an ongoing portfolio, Frank need keep the equity value of his personal portfolio no higher than the 30% maintenance level; in contrast, the HFD starts out each year with Frank's portfolio at the 50% margin level (since a new subscriber would not be able to leverage his portfolio as much as Frank's is). Another source of discrepancies is the fact that Frank often withdraws cash from the portfolio for personal use; the HFD, in contrast, assumes that no cash is withdrawn (or added) during the year.

The Prudent Speculator

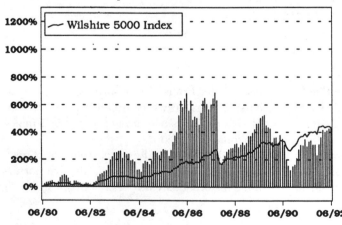

	Gain/Loss
1/1/91 to 6/30/92 (First Quintile)	+103.1%
1/1/89 to 6/30/92 (Fourth Quintile)	+ 25.3%
1/1/87 to 6/30/92 (Fifth Quintile)	−4.2%
1/1/85 to 6/30/92 (Fourth Quintile)	+ 81.6%
1/1/83 to 6/30/92 (Second Quintile)	+172.7%
6/30/80 to 6/30/92 (First Quintile)	+428.9%

Risk: 283% of market

The R.H.M. Survey of Warrants, Options & Low-Price Stocks

Address
172 Forest Ave.
Glen Cove, NY 11542

Editor
Mark Fried

Phone Number
516-759-2904

Subscription Rates
$150.00/6 months
$280.00/year

Telephone Hotline
No

Money Management
No

THE R·H·M SURVEY
of WARRANTS · OPTIONS & LOW-PRICE STOCKS

VOL. XLI No. 28   July 17, 1992

Consumer Prices
Year–to–year percent change

Although the recent move by the Federal Reserve, slashing its key lending rates, stole most of the thunder, investors would have been well advised to cheer the latest news on the inflation front. The Labor Department's report on June Producer Prices -- of particular interest given that measure's concerning 0.4% jump in May -- revealed a slim 0.2% rise. Even more impressive was word that the core PPI, which disregards volatile food and energy prices, actually declined 0.1% -- the first monthly drop in core Producer Prices in more than five years! Backed up some days later by the Consumer Price Index, which limited its increase to 0.3% (please see chart courtesy of The Wall Street Journal), Fed Governors and the incumbent presidential candidate can rest easy -- at least for the moment -- in the conviction that rip roaring price inflation won't be a player in this economic rebound.

What controlled inflation means to the financial markets is fairly obvious. First, the lack of inflationary pressure is likely to keep the skittish Fed Board in an accommodative mood, ensuring a continuation of steady or falling interest rates. Lower rates, as noted in last week's Survey, drive millions of dollars from banks and bonds into stocks and foster a generally bullish attitude on the part of investors. Second, price stability

encourages consumer spending -- a necessary ingredient if this recovery is to take hold. Finally, low inflation helps the dollar retain its value (and its integrity), not just at home but in important international markets.

That said, while we acknowledge the pessimists who point out that the current lack of inflation -- fairly unique during economic comebacks -- is symptomatic of just how sluggish things are, we think low inflation sets the stage for a fairly steady improvement in stocks in the near-term and we remain cautiously bullish.

Software Stocks Revisited

Subscribers will remember our rave review of the computer software industry and the related recommendation of three low-priced stocks last February 14. Indeed, the software group was at that time the top choice of many a mutual fund and brokerage house -- having enjoyed a sensational second half of 1991 -- and few expected anything different for 1992. Sadly, the fiercely competitive price cutting which dominated computer hardware sellers most of this year, squeezing the biggest names, crippling mid-sized competitors and forcing out many upstarts, ultimately led to similar repercussions on the software side (please note chart courtesy of Investor's Business Daily).

Although second quarter earnings are just beginning to trickle in, pessimistic projections from industry leaders the likes of spreadsheet specialist Lotus, publishing software maker Aldus and graphics expert Quarterdeck Office Systems suggest that margins will be lower across the board.

If there is a silver lining for our subscribers, it may be that while the three software makers in our recommended box have seen their share of profit-taking, each of them are leaders in a niche market where they are unlikely to be challenged, and we believe their fortunes will recover more quickly than the sector as a whole.

$280 Full-Year, $150 Half-Year

The R.H.M. Survey of Warrants, Options & Low-Price Stocks is published weekly by Mark Fried. The service has been published for quite some time: Its 1992 issues were listed as Volume 41. Fried took over as editor in 1991 upon the death of his father, Sidney, who had edited it until then.

From late 1989 through mid-1992, the newsletter was supplemented by a "900"-number telephone hotline service, with updates coming as often as several times a day. This hotline service was designed for those trading stock index options, with a new message coming on-line whenever Fried felt conditions warranted. Since the HFD's policy is not to follow the portfolio advice contained on a telephone hotline that is updated more than once per day, the HFD did not take into account the recommendations made on this "900"-number hotline.

In addition to providing advice in each of the three categories of warrants, options and low-priced stocks, *The R.H.M. Survey* is particularly valuable as a reference source for a large number of warrants that trade in the U.S. and Canada. Each issue of the *Survey* reports each warrant's price and its exercise terms, and no doubt many market professionals subscribe to this service to obtain this statistical detail.

The *Survey's* investment recommendations are derived from a combination of both fundamental and technical analysis. When it comes to analyzing the prospects for warrants and low-priced stocks, fundamental factors are paramount. A heavy emphasis in his list of recommended low-priced stocks over the past several years, for example, has been on gold-

and silver-mining companies, due to anxieties about the future of the world's monetary system. The newsletter's approach to options, in contrast, appears to be entirely technical. One options-trading strategy on which the newsletter relies heavily is to dollar-cost-average the purchase of out-of-the-money index calls and puts with one to two months left before expiration. The expectation is that while many of the options purchased by this strategy will expire worthless, a sharp market move in either direction will more than make up for these losses and still produce a handsome profit.

Fried does not organize his recommendations in these three categories into a portfolio, so the HFD constructs one for him that is fully invested and equally divided among all open recommendations. (The newsletter's index option recommendations were part of this portfolio except during the two-and-one-half-year period in which the service had its "900"-number hotline). For the eleven and one-half years through mid-1992, the portfolio the HFD constructed out of the *Survey's* recommendations lost 66.4%. Over the same period of time the Wilshire 5000 gained 332.5%.

The R.H.M. Survey of Warrants, Options & Low-Price Stocks

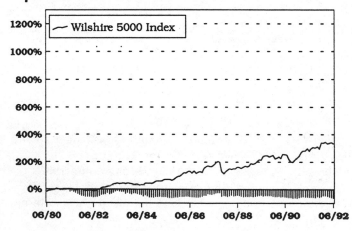

	Gain/Loss
1/1/91 to 6/30/92	−1.8%
(Fifth Quintile)	
1/1/89 to 6/30/92	−25.7%
(Fifth Quintile)	
1/1/87 to 6/30/92	−29.7%
(Fifth Quintile)	
1/1/85 to 6/30/92	−13.0%
(Fifth Quintile)	
1/1/83 to 6/30/92	−45.3%
(Fifth Quintile)	
6/30/80 to 6/30/92	(n/a)

Risk: 240% of market

Richard E. Band's Profitable Investing

Address
7811 Montrose Rd.
Potomac, MD 20854

Editor
Richard E. Band

Phone Number
301-424-3700

Subscription Rates
$99.00/year

Telephone Hotline
Yes

Money Management
No

Phillips Publishing, Inc.
Actionable Information for the '90s ®

Richard E. Band's

Profitable Investing®

Your guide to financial success.

August 1992
Vol.3, No.11

Dear Subscriber:

<u>This means war</u>! Are you as upset as I am about today's incredibly low yields on CDs, money market funds and the like? When I open my monthly bank statements, I don't know whether to laugh or scream.

Imagine, 3% interest (or less) on a savings account. Fortunately, I'm only 41 years young and not yet trying to <u>live</u> on those rates. But how, I ask you, are retired people supposed to make ends meet on such a pittance?

Let's face facts: In an attempt to "save" the U.S. economy from a triple-dip recession—and George Bush from defeat at the polls—the <u>Federal Reserve has declared war on savers</u>. As in any war, however, you can always find ways to outfox the enemy if you look closely enough.

<u>Why You Don't Have to Settle for 3%</u>

In this month's visit, I want you to meet a short-term government fund that still yields a lush 8% with a high degree of safety. If you've waited too long to take your money out of low-yielding bank accounts, this fund may be the answer to your prayers.

I've also located a fund that buys healthy loans from the government's Resolution Trust Corp. at a deep discount—for yields of 16% and up. Now you and I can cash in on this ultimate insider's game for as little as $15 per share.

Of course, in our quest for greater income, we mustn't overlook opportunities for long-term growth of principal. For months, I've patiently waited for the chance to recommend one of my favorite blue chip stocks—you might even call it a "green" chip, because the company is making a tidy profit from cleaning up the environment.

Now, at long last, the stock is ready for you to buy (at a 27% discount to its February high). I project we'll double our money with this beauty in three years or so—almost regardless of the Dow's near-term bobbing and weaving.

Finally, by popular demand, I'll show you how to launch a fully diversified, low-risk investment program with only $250 <u>and no commissions</u>. (It's an ideal gift idea.)

Before we tear off this month's goody box, though, let's take a few minutes to see why the government's war on savers isn't going to let up anytime soon—certainly not before Election Day—and how you can wriggle out of the low-yield handcuffs the Federal Reserve has clapped on your money.

PLOTTING YOUR ESCAPE FROM LOW MONEY MARKET YIELDS

What sticks out in your mind about the summer of 1963? Dr. King's march on Washington? I remember catching a glimpse of President Kennedy's yacht, the <u>Honey Fitz</u>, tied up in Hyannis harbor. What else? It was 29 years ago that the nation's central bank—the Federal Reserve—last charged only 3% on overnight loans to commercial banks!

This <u>discount rate</u> (and the companion <u>federal funds rate</u>, also controlled by

Income Investing

Richard E. Band's Profitable Investing is published monthly and supplemented by a weekly telephone hotline update. Prior to starting his own publication, Band for several years was co-editor of *Personal Finance* (with Adrian Day, who now also has his own publication, *Adrian Day's Investment Analyst*, reviewed elsewhere in this book). The HFD began following *Richard E. Band's Profitable Investing* at the beginning of 1991.

Band's newsletter takes a broader perspective than most investment newsletters, trying to put individual recommendations in the context of an investor's entire assets. He calls his model portfolio his "Total-Return" portfolio, and it is well diversified among stocks, bonds and cash. His asset allocation approach isn't designed to hit the home runs that other newsletters will when they are fully invested in a few hot stocks, but by the same token Band's approach is far less risky. The HFD calculates that his portfolio has about 40% less volatility than the market as a whole.

Given this low risk, it is impressive that Band has come as close to the market's rate of return: Over the 18 months through mid-1992, his portfolio gained 28.5%, in contrast to the Wilshire 5000's 32.3%. On a risk-adjusted basis, in fact, Band has significantly outperformed the market and is in 11th place (out of 118) among the newsletters the HFD followed over this period.

Richard E. Band's Profitable Investing

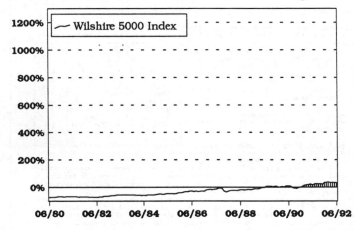

	Gain/Loss
1/1/91 to 6/30/92	+28.5%
(Second Quintile)	
1/1/89 to 6/30/92	(n/a)
1/1/87 to 6/30/92	(n/a)
1/1/85 to 6/30/92	(n/a)
1/1/83 to 6/30/92	(n/a)
6/30/80 to 6/30/92	(n/a)

Risk: 62% of market

The Ruff Times

Address
4457 Willow Rd.
Suite 200
Pleasanton, CA 94588

Editor
Howard Ruff

Phone Number
510-463-2200

Subscription Rates
$149.00/year

Telephone Hotline
Yes

Money Management
No

The Ruff Times

Volume XVIII   Issue 12 $5.00 Per Issue   July 6, 1992

MARKET INDICATORS

7/2	London Gold (Second Fix)	347.10
	68 wk OMA	353.76
7/2	Handy & Harman Silver	4.04
	60 wk OMA	4.10
7/2	Gold/Silver Ratio	85.92:1
7/1	N.Y.M. Platinum	386.00
	59 wk OMA	360.54
7/1	Trade Weighted Dollar	83.87
	83 wk OMA	88.76
7/1	Dow Jones Industrials	3354.10
	47 wk OMA	3158.42
7/1	Standard & Poors 500	412.88
	50 wk OMA	399.61
7/1	S&P Gold Mining Index	159.76
	54 wk OMA	158.71
7/1	DJ Spot Comm. Index	118.74
	55 wk OMA	117.78
7/1	CRB Index	208.12
	64 wk OMA	212.07
7/1	Dow Jones 20 Bonds	99.93
	58 wk OMA	97.63

COMING EVENTS

Howard Ruff Travel 1992

Oct — Holy Land, Egypt & Nile River Cruise

For information, call Fran Perry at
800-366-7833 or Bev Peterson at 800-777-2877

PEROT: OUR NATIONAL RORSCHACH INK-BLOT TEST

Howard Ruff

I have finally figured out Ross Perot. I now know what he means to America. He's an ink blot!

For those of you not privy to the arcane mysteries of psychology and psychiatry, the ink-blot test was developed by a man by the name of Rorschach. You make several big random blots of ink on paper, show them to patients, and ask them what each one brings to mind. The answers supposedly give you deep insights into the patient's innermost psychology.

The classic story is told of a man who was shown a bunch of ink blots by a psychiatrist and they all looked to him like men and women performing various unspeakable acts.

Finally, the psychiatrist said, "You're obsessed with sex." The man said, "Not me. You're the one with the dirty pictures." The essence of ink-blot analysis is that what you see depends on what you bring to the viewing. The ink blots aren't inherently anything.

Ross Perot is an ink blot. He attracts support from conservatives, liberals and people with no philosophy whatsoever, because they all see in him whatever they bring to the viewing.

One hyper-conservative splinter party in Utah is urging Ross Perot to run for the presidency (which he's going to do anyway). They either don't know or don't care that he's pro-abortion, pro-gun control, has made disparaging comments about the constitution, wants to boost taxes on the rich, and by some measures stands somewhere to the left of Bill Clinton.

On the other hand, many liberals are Perot supporters, not realizing that in the business area he is conservative and he has no sympathy with those who are pioneering the outer fringes of the sexual revolution. He sure wouldn't cultivate the gay vote.

But they see what they want to see. Why? Because everyone is so fed up with the current political landscape that they're looking for anyone as an alternative to the mediocre choices served up by the two parties.

They don't want Bush because they think he's weak. The Desert Storm euphoria has melted like the morning mist. They don't want Clinton because he's just another Democrat making the same promises to the same crowd. They want somebody new who will kick butt and take names. And they think Ross Perot is that man.

After all, a guy who started with $1,000 and is worth $3 billion must have some get-it-done talent. He's not tied to any special

---

The Ruff Times is published every other week by Howard Ruff and is supplemented by a telephone hotline that is updated twice each day. Most of those hotline updates are devoted to a summary of the day's financial developments, however, and not to making changes in Ruff's several portfolios.

Ruff became well known in the 1970s after he aggressively marketed his newsletter to smaller investors, many of whom never had subscribed to a newsletter before. Ruff was bucking the conventional financial wisdom at the time, especially by recommending gold, and he obviously struck a nerve among a cynical investment public. Much of his newsletter is devoted to wide-ranging philosophical, political and educational articles.

Ruff's newsletter also makes specific investment recommendations, though the clarity and completeness of his advice in this regard have waxed and waned over the years. When the HFD began following his performance in 1980, it rated his advice the lowest in clarity, but increased it to the highest clarity rating in late 1982 when Ruff initiated a specific model portfolio entitled the "Phantom Investor." This model portfolio lived for several years before it disappeared, at which time Ruff's clarity rating slipped once again. In 1986, in fact, the HFD did not attempt to calculate a performance figure for Ruff's advice, owing to its incompleteness and ambiguity.

In late 1986, however, Ruff's advice became clearer once again, and the HFD now rates three of his portfolios: one constructed out of the stocks and other securities listed on the back page of his newsletter, and the other two model mutual fund portfolios Ruff calls his "Optimum Switch Hitter" portfolios #1 and #2.

Overall for the entire 12 years through mid-1992, assuming that Ruff earned the T-Bill rate during 1986 when his advice was too vague and incomplete for the HFD to follow, he underperformed the Wilshire 5000 by a 38.2% to 432.7% margin.

The Ruff Times (Average)

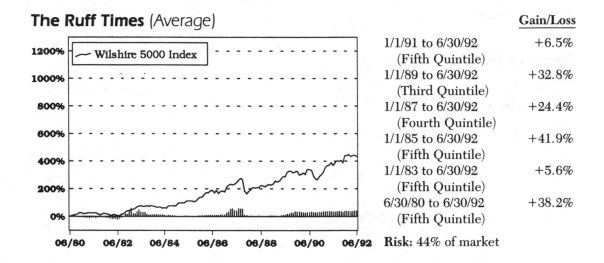

	Gain/Loss
1/1/91 to 6/30/92 (Fifth Quintile)	+6.5%
1/1/89 to 6/30/92 (Third Quintile)	+32.8%
1/1/87 to 6/30/92 (Fourth Quintile)	+24.4%
1/1/85 to 6/30/92 (Fifth Quintile)	+41.9%
1/1/83 to 6/30/92 (Fifth Quintile)	+5.6%
6/30/80 to 6/30/92 (Fifth Quintile)	+38.2%

Risk: 44% of market

The Ruff Times (Optimum Switch Hitter Portfolio #1)

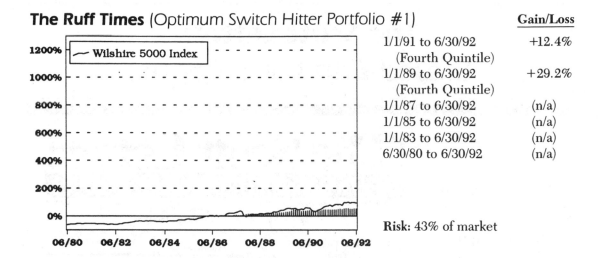

	Gain/Loss
1/1/91 to 6/30/92	+12.4%
(Fourth Quintile)	
1/1/89 to 6/30/92	+29.2%
(Fourth Quintile)	
1/1/87 to 6/30/92	(n/a)
1/1/85 to 6/30/92	(n/a)
1/1/83 to 6/30/92	(n/a)
6/30/80 to 6/30/92	(n/a)

Risk: 43% of market

The Ruff Times (Optimum Switch Hitter Portfolio #2)

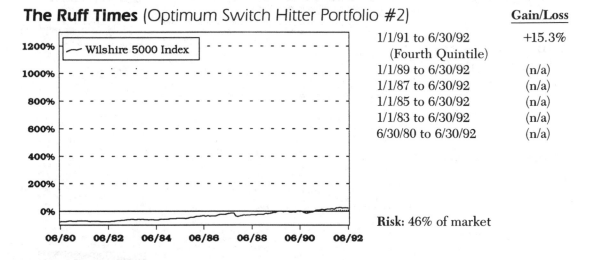

	Gain/Loss
1/1/91 to 6/30/92	+15.3%
(Fourth Quintile)	
1/1/89 to 6/30/92	(n/a)
1/1/87 to 6/30/92	(n/a)
1/1/85 to 6/30/92	(n/a)
1/1/83 to 6/30/92	(n/a)
6/30/80 to 6/30/92	(n/a)

Risk: 46% of market

The Ruff Times (The "Back Page" Portfolio)

	Gain/Loss
1/1/91 to 6/30/92	−7.6%
(Fifth Quintile)	
1/1/89 to 6/30/92	+29.9%
(Fourth Quintile)	
1/1/87 to 6/30/92	+20.0%
(Fourth Quintile)	
1/1/85 to 6/30/92	(n/a)
1/1/83 to 6/30/92	(n/a)
6/30/80 to 6/30/92	(n/a)

Risk: 84% of market

The Scott Letter:
Closed-End Fund Report

Address
Box 17800
Richmond, VA 23226

Editor
George Cole Scott

Phone Number
800-356-3508

Subscription Rates
$ 80.00/6 months
$135.00/year

Telephone Hotline
No

Money Management
No

The Scott Letter:
CLOSED-END FUND REPORT

Box 17800 Richmond, Virginia 23226   Published Monthly $135.00 per year   Vol. V Number 7   July/August, 1992
Registered under the S.E.C. Investment Advisers Act
The Newsletter of the Closed-End Fund Industry

Is Overseas Investing For You?

John Templeton says that by investing solely in the U.S. you are leaving out 2/3 of the world's economies and missing many opportunities for gain.

In a recent telephone conversation with us, Templeton said he isn't bothered by the fact that some markets, such as Hong Kong, are high. Even in this market, up nearly 50% in 1992, he sees bargains using measurements of value, the cornerstone of his philosophy.

Templeton looks for bargains in every country, a global rather than country fund approach to investing which has higher risks.

This report, the most comprehensive we have ever done, will look at the largest number of global, regional and country funds we have analyzed since our annual review a year ago.

Templeton told **The Scott Letter** he "still finds shares in Hong Kong selling at small fractions of what similar companies would sell for in other nations in terms of dividends, undervalued assets and other factors." This may be the reason three China funds are now in registration.

Foreign investment is too important. We can't ignore the other two thirds of the investment community especially now that we live in a more unified and interdependent world. Rather than researching individual companies, you just need to pick a manager who has the expertise to do the job you hire him to do. Good selection and a long-term view pays large dividends.

We asked Templeton about the merits of global investing versus choosing single or multi-country funds:

"Who in the world would want to limit themselves to America? If you look everywhere you get more opportunities. You may even find better opportunities, but you definitely get diversification which reduces your risk. Let the expert look for bargains in any country and not limit himself to one country."

Most of the Templeton closed-ends sell at premiums. This means that the best choices for us may still be in country or multi-country funds--a compromise for closed-end fund investors. The risks are higher, but so is the chance for gain.

Too much emphasis on growth stocks also brings volatility in net asset values. Prudent investors need to be aware of these factors in making their choices.

An additional factor in analysing overseas funds is for you to be aware that most managers, other than those who are value oriented, tend to pick high multiple growth stocks. Many chased the rising Japanese market in the late 1980s and were badly hurt when that market dropped 50%.

In this and other countries, it is easy to pick the more visible companies such as local telephone companies expecting that previous growth will continue(which often doesn't) rather than seeking undervalued companies which pay off in the long run to the patient investora--a must in this high stakes game. □

First Cuba Fund

Dreaming of a Big Return to Profit

In this 30th anniversary year of the Cuban Missile Crisis, U.S. citizens, according to press reports, will soon be able to invest in Cuba, one of the overlooked countries with a tremendous potential for growth when it is free of an aging Fidel Castro.

A Washington law firm, Shaw Pitman, Potts & Trowbridge, is planning to capitalize on increased trade when Cuba opens up. A newsletter, "Free Cuba", is being published quarterly by the firm in anticipation of this event. The latest issue reports on Congressional developments for possible changes and particularly how US firms planning to do business with Cuba can do so when the island nation opens up.

Anticipating this and after some research on the subject myself, we spoke to the well-known closed-end fund adviser, Thomas J. Herzfeld of Miami, who has registereed two Cuba funds with the Securities & Exchange Commission.

(continued on page 2)

The Scott Letter is published monthly by George Scott; it is not supplemented by a telephone hotline. Scott, a stockbroker, is co-author (with Albert Fredman) of a book about closed-end funds, *Investing in Closed-End Funds: Finding Value and Building Wealth* (New York Institute of Finance). Scott's opinion of a closed-end fund appears to be based on his fundamental analysis of its underlying value and whether or not it is trading at a discount or premium to its net asset value.

Scott's model portfolio really is just a list of recommended closed-end equity funds; he does not advise subscribers on what proportion of their portfolio ought to be kept in cash. Pursuant to its methodology on such matters, the HFD thus constructs a portfolio for *The Scott Letter* that is fully invested. The HFD began following *The Scott Letter* at the beginning of 1990, at which time Scott also had a model portfolio of closed-end bond funds. Though this has since been discontinued, its performance is included in what is reported for the newsletter's average. The remaining portfolio has above-average risk or volatility.

Over the two and one-half years that the HFD has tracked Scott's advice, he has been well rewarded for incurring this above-market risk. The HFD calculates that his newsletter produced a gain of 57.5% over this 30-month period, in contrast to 24.1% for the Wilshire 5000. This is sufficiently ahead of the market, so even after the newsletter's high risk is taken into account, it still is ahead of the market on a risk-adjusted basis.

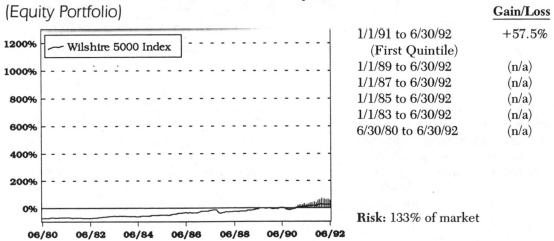

The Scott Letter: Closed-End Fund Report (Average)

	Gain/Loss
1/1/91 to 6/30/92	+57.5%
(First Quintile)	
1/1/89 to 6/30/92	(n/a)
1/1/87 to 6/30/92	(n/a)
1/1/85 to 6/30/92	(n/a)
1/1/83 to 6/30/92	(n/a)
6/30/80 to 6/30/92	(n/a)

Risk: 133% of market

The Scott Letter: Closed-End Fund Report
(Equity Portfolio)

	Gain/Loss
1/1/91 to 6/30/92	+57.5%
(First Quintile)	
1/1/89 to 6/30/92	(n/a)
1/1/87 to 6/30/92	(n/a)
1/1/85 to 6/30/92	(n/a)
1/1/83 to 6/30/92	(n/a)
6/30/80 to 6/30/92	(n/a)

Risk: 133% of market

The Sector Funds Newsletter

Address
P.O. Box 270048
San Diego, CA 92198

Editor
Cato B. Ohrn

Phone Number
619-748-0805

Subscription Rates
$ 44.00/3 months
$157.00/year

Telephone Hotline
Yes

Money Management
Yes

RELATIVE STRENGTH . . . the KEY TO WEALTH

THE SECTOR FUNDS NEWSLETTER™

P.O. BOX 270048 • SAN DIEGO, CALIFORNIA 92198-2048

EDITOR:
DR. CATO B. OHRN
(619) 748-0805

2nd and 4th week each month
June 30, 1992.

Global Health Sciences

The Global Health Sciences Fund is a closed end mutual fund that came public in Mid-January at $15 per share. It is listed on the New York Stock Exchange under the symbol GHS and is currently trading between $12 and $13a share.

This fund is managed by John Kaweske, whose claim to fame is being the manager of Financial Strategic Health Sciences, the #1 mutual fund for the 5 year period ending 12-31-91.

There are several reasons why you may want to buy this fund in addition to Financial Health. First of all, by having an international outlook, Global Health will own a higher percentage of foreign health care companies. This is considered highly desirable, because of lower Price/Earnings ratios in some cases, diversification across currencies and business cycles, and the recent political risks in the U.S. secondary to escalating healthcare costs.

Another attraction is the fact that Global Health, like many other closed ends, is trading at a discount from Net Asset Value. We expect this to turn into a premium when the current correction in medical stocks comes to an end.

There are certain other advantages that this fund shares with other closed end funds, the chief one being that the freedom from worry about redemptions allows for a truly long term strategy.

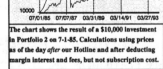

S&P500 Index weekly/14 week Rel.Strength Index

Sector Funds Newsletter Real Time Portfolio 2 (+400 % since 7-1-85) As of 6-15-92

S&P500(+ 113% since 7-1-85)

The chart shows the result of a $10,000 investment in Portfolio 2 on 7-1-85. Calculations using prices as of the day *after* our Hotline and after deducting margin interest and fees, but not subscription cost.

The Sector Funds Newsletter is published every two weeks by Cato Ohrn and is supplemented by a telephone hotline that is updated at least weekly (and more often when market conditions warrant).

Ohrn started his newsletter to capitalize on the growing number of mutual funds that con-centrate on individual industries or sectors. Since then, of course, many additional mutual fund newsletters have appeared on the scene. Ohrn's approach appears to be primarily technical, and he takes a relatively short-term approach to mutual fund investing. He also makes heavy use of margin in his model portfolios. (Though Ohrn's portfolios were heavily exposed in stocks during the October 1987 crash, he did succeed in getting off margin in the days just prior to the crash.)

The HFD has performance data for *The Sector Funds Newsletter* since 1987. One of the three model portfolios that Ohrn currently recommends—what he has christened "Portfolio 1"—has been in existence continuously since then; for the five and one-half years through mid-1992, it lost 20.9%, as compared to a 93.3% gain for the Wilshire 5000. One of the additional portfolios— "Portfolio 3," which is comprised solely of one or more of the Benham group's bond funds of targeted maturities—was discontinued in early 1987 and reinstated in 1988. Assuming that this portfolio earned the T-Bill rate during this hiatus, it gained 49.8% over this same five-and-one-half-year period—in contrast to 59.7% for the Shearson Lehman Treasury Index.

The third portfolio, named "Portfolio Number 2" and which Ohrn describes as a "Fidelity Funds Plus" portfolio, was begun more recently. Over the four and one-half years through mid-1992, this portfolio gained 39.8%, as compared to 89.0% for the Wilshire 5000. Averaging all three portfolios' performances, and taking into account the different periods of time each has been in existence, *The Sector Funds Newsletter* as a whole gained 22.5% over the five and one-half years through mid-1992, in contrast to the Wilshire 5000's 93.3%.

Both Ohrn's market timing and his fund selection bear responsibility for this below-market performance. For example, if each of the funds he recommended for his "Portfolio 1" had done as well as the Wilshire 5000 when owned by that portfolio, it would have performed significantly better—a gain of 31.9%, in contrast to a 20.9% loss. But it still wouldn't have equaled the 93.3% return of buying and holding.

Sector Funds Newsletter (Average)

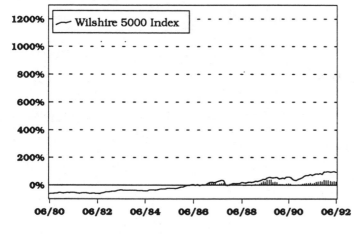

	Gain/Loss
1/1/91 to 6/30/92	+18.5%
(Third Quintile)	
1/1/89 to 6/30/92	+25.3%
(Fourth Quintile)	
1/1/87 to 6/30/92	+22.5%
(Fourth Quintile)	
1/1/85 to 6/30/92	(n/a)
1/1/83 to 6/30/92	(n/a)
6/30/80 to 6/30/92	(n/a)

Risk: 94% of market

Sector Funds Newsletter (Portfolio 1)

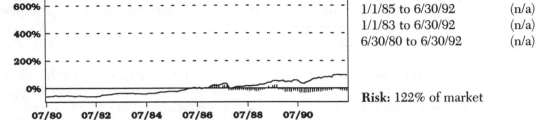

Gain/Loss

1/1/91 to 6/30/92 (Fourth Quintile)	+16.4%
1/1/89 to 6/30/92 (Fifth Quintile)	−0.6%
1/1/87 to 6/30/92 (Fifth Quintile)	−20.9%
1/1/85 to 6/30/92	(n/a)
1/1/83 to 6/30/92	(n/a)
6/30/80 to 6/30/92	(n/a)

Risk: 122% of market

Sector Funds Newsletter (Portfolio 2 ["Fidelity Funds Plus"])

Gain/Loss

1/1/91 to 6/30/92 (Fourth Quintile)	+16.1%
1/1/89 to 6/30/92 (Third Quintile)	+38.3%
1/1/87 to 6/30/92	(n/a)
1/1/85 to 6/30/92	(n/a)
1/1/83 to 6/30/92	(n/a)
6/30/80 to 6/30/92	(n/a)

Risk: 90% of market

Sector Funds Newsletter (Portfolio 3 [Mostly Bonds])

Gain/Loss

1/1/91 to 6/30/92 (Third Quintile)	+22.2%
1/1/89 to 6/30/92 (Third Quintile)	+31.6%
1/1/87 to 6/30/92 (Third Quintile)	+49.8%
1/1/85 to 6/30/92	(n/a)
1/1/83 to 6/30/92	(n/a)
6/30/80 to 6/30/92	(n/a)

Risk: 96% of market

Stockmarket Cycles

Address

P.O. Box 6873
Santa Rosa, CA
 95406-0873

Editor

Peter Eliades

Phone Number

707-579-8444

Subscription Rates

$198.00/year

Telephone Hotline

Yes

Money Management

Yes

$\bigwedge$ PETER ELIADES'
STOCKMARKET CYCLES
P.O. Box 6873 Santa Rosa, California 95406-0873 • (707) 579-8444

July 17, 1992	
End of Week #918	
DJIA	3331.64
CI	856
NCI	854
Ratio	1.003

Stockmarket Cycles <u>intra-day</u> telephone updates are now available throughout the market day giving the very latest cycle projections and trading recommendations. They are scheduled at 10 AM, 12:30, 3:00 and 5:00 PM EST and more often if market conditions require. The cost is only $2.00 per minute for the first minute and .45 for each additional minute and is billed by AT&T to your phone bill. The number is **(900) 909-5050.**

For those of you whose offices have blocked access to the 900 number, you may now receive these intra-day updates via computer and modem. This service is also available to those outside the United States. Call (707) 579-8444 for information.

NOTE: We remind all subscribers that the special anniversary offer of a full year of the newsletter with the daily telephone update for $360 expires July 31. You can renew or extend your subscription at that price regardless of expiration date, but letters must be postmarked by July 31 or call our office and renew by telephone.

—THE CYCLES—

It's a crazy wonderful business we are in, the business of attempting to predict or forecast the stock market. Most people are convinced it's impossible to predict any future event with accuracy or consistency. If they argue in favor of that point with you, pull out your local newspaper (if you live by the ocean) and read off the times for high and low tide to them. You might also try telling them exactly what time the sun will rise and set tomorrow. "Aha!" you might say, "but those predictions are based on events that occur with daily regularity and are not predictions at all but rather the result of scientific knowledge." We are not ready to claim that we have honed the stock market cycles down to the accuracy of tide tables or the times for sunrises and sunsets, but we would maintain that, for whatever reason, there are cycles of sentiment and psychology in the stock market which allow us to forecast future market events, sometimes with uncanny accuracy, other times with mixed results. Incidentally, if you think the tide tables are based on simple calculations, do some further research on them. You might be surprised how amazingly complex the calculations are and how much the analysis resembles cycle analysis for the markets.

We begin with that prologue because we believe many factors are coming together over the next few weeks that could allow us to make some potentially dramatic market forecasts. Later in this letter, we present a strong technical case for an important market top within the next 1-4 weeks. Before we begin that analysis how-

ever, let's examine some interesting long term stock market patterns.

One of the big reasons for believing the late 1970s and early 1980s would lead to a dramatic long term bull market was evidence of a 60 year cycle of market bottoms. The periods of resolution for that cycle were within 1-2 years of 1800, 1860, 1920, and 1980 (we can obviously now add 1980 as a successful resolution based on the spectacular rally from 729.95 to 3435.24).

Over the past two weeks we noticed another pattern of approximately 60 years —this one was a pattern of turning points. The first would have been June 1812 when the low seen was within 4% (the following year) of the lowest point in history from then until now. The next turning point occurred in May 1872 when a high was reached that was not exceeded significantly (by over 3%) for the next 15 years. Next came the July 1932 bottom, a very major trough that marked the lowest point for the stock market in the last 84 years.

Notice that so far we have seen a low (1812), a high (1872), and a low (1932). That takes us to July 1992 and although the prior results are not statistically significant we believe a case can be made for a very major high occurring in this time period. If it turns out to be as significant as the 1872 high, we would wait until 2007 or later before seeing this year's high significantly surpassed.

In our last issue we noted an argument could be made for a 276.8 week cycle top to occur the week ending

Stockmarket Cycles is published every three weeks by Peter Eliades and is supplemented by a daily telephone hotline. As his newsletter's name would suggest, Eliades is a technician.

Eliades recommends two separate model portfolios: one of stocks and the other of mu-

tual funds. Over the seven and one-half years through mid-1992, his mutual fund portfolio by far was the better performer, gaining 166.3%, as compared to a 20.8% loss for his stock portfolio. (The Wilshire 5000, in contrast, gained 197.6% over this same period.)

The HFD also has extracted from Eliades's

mutual fund portfolio a pure timing component and calculates that it essentially equaled a buy-and-hold strategy over these seven and one-half years, gaining 196.2%, in contrast to the market's 197.6%. Furthermore, because this timing-only portfolio was significantly less risky than the market, it handily beat the market on a risk-adjusted basis.

Eliades's timing performance would be even better than this but for the HFD's methodology on the treatment of switch signals in calculating performance on a pure timing basis. When measuring newsletters' abilities to time the market (as opposed to their abilities to pick individual stocks or mutual funds), the HFD endeavors to be relevant to the majority of fund investors who can buy or sell at only one price per day (the four o'clock NAV). Therefore, in these timing-only portfolios, the HFD executes all switches at the closing price on the day that a switch can take place.

This hurts Eliades's timing-only performance because he specifically gears his timing advice for Fidelity sector funds that have the luxury of hourly pricing, and because he often has bought and sold at prices better than the closing price. If the HFD were to give credit in Eliades's timing-only portfolio for the market's value at the hours he actually recommended that switches take place, his timing performance would be a gain of 217.6% over these seven and one-half years— ahead of the 196.2% gain assuming trades always take place at the close and ahead of the 197.6% for buying and holding.

Bear in mind that this methodological rule the HFD uses only applies to calculating newsletters' performances on a timing-only basis. The HFD ratings that reflect overall portfolio performance do *not* follow this methodological rule; that is, when Eliades recommends that a trade take place at a fund's 10 A.M. price, then the HFD's portfolio does so.

Stockmarket Cycles (Average)

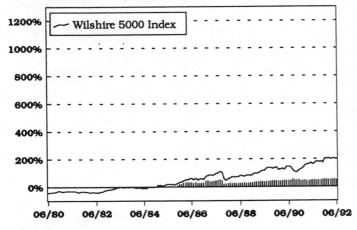

	Gain/Loss
1/1/91 to 6/30/92 (Fifth Quintile)	+6.9%
1/1/89 to 6/30/92 (Fifth Quintile)	+16.0%
1/1/87 to 6/30/92 (Fourth Quintile)	+17.6%
1/1/85 to 6/30/92 (Fourth Quintile)	+49.3%
1/1/83 to 6/30/92	(n/a)
6/30/80 to 6/30/92	(n/a)

Risk: 46% of market

Stockmarket Cycles (Model Stock Portfolio)

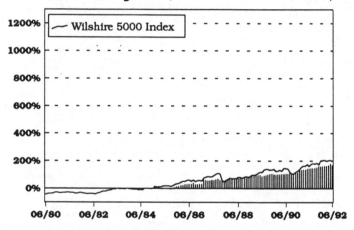

1200%	— Wilshire 5000 Index
1000%	
800%	
600%	
400%	
200%	
0%	

06/80 06/82 06/84 06/86 06/88 06/90 06/92

	Gain/Loss
1/1/91 to 6/30/92 (Fifth Quintile)	−8.8%
1/1/89 to 6/30/92 (Fifth Quintile)	−11.5%
1/1/87 to 6/30/92 (Fifth Quintile)	−35.2%
1/1/85 to 6/30/92 (Fifth Quintile)	−20.8%
1/1/83 to 6/30/92	(n/a)
6/30/80 to 6/30/92	(n/a)

Risk: 67% of market

Stockmarket Cycles (Mutual Fund Portfolio)

1200%	— Wilshire 5000 Index
1000%	
800%	
600%	
400%	
200%	
0%	

06/80 06/82 06/84 06/86 06/88 06/90 06/92

	Gain/Loss
1/1/91 to 6/30/92 (Third Quintile)	+24.4%
1/1/89 to 6/30/92 (Second Quintile)	+49.8%
1/1/87 to 6/30/92 (First Quintile)	+104.3%
1/1/85 to 6/30/92 (Second Quintile)	+166.3%
1/1/83 to 6/30/92	(n/a)
6/30/80 to 6/30/92	(n/a)

Risk: 63% of market

Strategic Investment

Address
824 E. Baltimore St.
Baltimore, MD
  21202-4799

Editors
James Davidson and
  William Rees-Mogg

Phone Number
410-234-0691

Subscription Rates
$59.00/year

Telephone Hotline
No

Money Management
Yes

The Eve of Depression — July 22, 1992

strategic investment

This Month

"Not a recovery"

"SI *continues to believe that there is less of a recovery than meets the eye. A big problem—payroll employment has not recovered at a pace compatible with recovery.*"
—Strategic Investment, *June 17, 1992*

That is what we told you last month. Now our intelligence bulletins from June are July's headlines about a surge in unemployment and the fizzling of the widely heralded recovery.

We told you what to expect in January. "As before, the key is money growth. Unless the money supply (M2 and M3) picks up sharply and nominal growth exceeds all expectations... there will be a surge and not a recovery in 1992."

In fact, the money supply has been shrinking for months. This has never happened in a recovery. Weakness in money and credit growth was one of the principal reasons cited by the Fed on July 2 in lowering the Discount Rate to 3%, the lowest rate since July 1963.

SI forecast at the beginning of the year that the Discount Rate would be even lower by now than it is. Greenspan and company *have been more cautious than we thought they might be.* But we also have been more convinced than other observers that the economy would not experience a normal business-cycle expansion.

The recovery may yet prove to be more than than "a figment of the imagination," as we called it months ago. A recent uptick in copper prices may be a prelude to a stronger third quarter. But I doubt it. With industrial production plunging in Japan, and Germany weakening, it is just as likely that we will see the deeper stage of depression that usually accompanies the unwinding of the credit cycle. That is what one would expect based on the patterns of the past, and so far, these patterns have been right.

Sincerely,

James Davidson

Depression looms in Japan. *The plunge of Japanese industrial production is a strong indicator that the U.S. has not bottomed. Only now, as Japan sinks into depression, is the full measure of credit cycle unwinding likely to be felt in the U.S.*

Playing the bungee-bounce in Tokyo

by Lord Rees-Mogg
(London) Investors with a sense of history are beginning to look with interest at the Tokyo market. The strange thing is that they are still bearish and expect the Tokyo Index to fall further. But they are becoming nervous lest the big bounce should escape them when it comes.

When a market has fallen as far as the Tokyo market, the bounce from the bottom—when it is reached—is proportionate to the scale of the fall. This happened in London in 1975; it happened more than once in recoveries on Wall Street after 1929; it happened in the violent swings of the German market in the 1920s.

It is almost a mathematical certainty. After a major fall, markets usually recover somewhere between a third and a half of the decline. When they have lost 30%, they are likely to recover 10% to 15%, which is a rise of 15% to 20% on the low point.

Tokyo has fallen by 60% from the high, suggesting that the recovery, if on the same scale, might be 20% to 30% of the original peak. But translate that to the rise from the low of 40 and it amounts to a recovery of from 50% to 75%. Suppose the Japanese market were to bottom out at 15,000 on the Nikkei Dow-Jones, it might recover quite quickly to 22,500—that seems inherently plausible. Supposing it made a low of 12,000, it could still recover to 20,000. That means that it would pay to buy Japanese shares at 16,000, even if they were to fall by another quarter, because the recovery might show a handsome profit.

These investors know that it is too late to buy into such a collapsed market if one waits for the final bottom and then tries to catch the rise. You have

Continued on page 12

Strategic Investment is published monthly by James Davidson and William Rees-Mogg. Davidson also provides a telephone hotline service, but because it is a separate service to which regular newsletter subscribers are not given access, the HFD does not take his hotline recommendations into account when tracking the newsletter's performance.

The newsletter recommends four model portfolios, two managed by Davidson and two by Steve Newby, a stockbroker who several times has won the *USA Today/FNN* National

Investment Challenge. (One of Newby's two portfolios wasn't inaugurated until the beginning of 1992 and isn't graphed separately in this book, though its performance is included in what is reported for the newsletter's average.) The investment approaches taken by these four portfolios are dramatically different: Whereas Newby's portfolios usually are fully invested in secondary stocks, Davidson's (as well as the editorial focus of the entire newsletter) are based on a fundamental bearishness about the U.S. economy in general and the U.S. stock market in particular.

On average the portfolios recommended by *Strategic Investment* have above-average risk. Newby's portfolios, by virtue of being fully invested in relatively thinly traded secondaries, have exhibited about three times as much volatility as the market as a whole. And one of Davidson's portfolios (his "Speculative Strategy") is about twice as volatile as the market as a whole (by virtue of his aggressive use of options and commodity futures contracts). The only exception is the second of Davidson's two portfolios (his "$100,000 Income" portfolio), which has barely more than half as much risk as the stock market as a whole.

Over the 18 months through mid-1992, this above-market risk was not rewarded: The "Speculative Strategy" lost 31.9%, "Newby's $25,000 Special" portfolio lost 11.9%, and the "$100,000 Income" portfolio gained 3.8%. This contrasts with a 32.3% gain for the Wilshire 5000 and a 17.8% gain for the Shearson Lehman Treasury Index.

Strategic Investment (Average)

	Gain/Loss
1/1/91 to 6/30/92	−15.6%
(Fifth Quintile)	
1/1/89 to 6/30/92	(n/a)
1/1/87 to 6/30/92	(n/a)
1/1/85 to 6/30/92	(n/a)
1/1/83 to 6/30/92	(n/a)
6/30/80 to 6/30/92	(n/a)

Risk: 118% of market

Strategic Investment (Newby's $25,000 Special Portfolio)

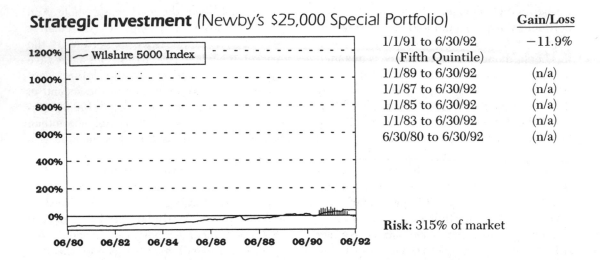

	Gain/Loss
1/1/91 to 6/30/92	−11.9%
(Fifth Quintile)	
1/1/89 to 6/30/92	(n/a)
1/1/87 to 6/30/92	(n/a)
1/1/85 to 6/30/92	(n/a)
1/1/83 to 6/30/92	(n/a)
6/30/80 to 6/30/92	(n/a)

Risk: 315% of market

Strategic Investment ($100,000 Income Portfolio)

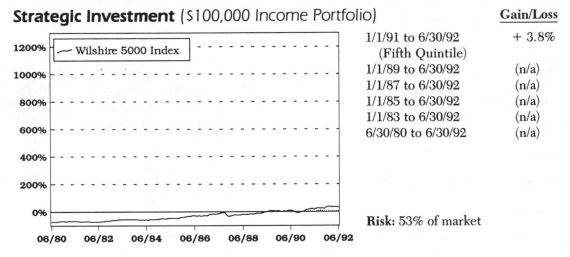

	Gain/Loss
1/1/91 to 6/30/92	+ 3.8%
(Fifth Quintile)	
1/1/89 to 6/30/92	(n/a)
1/1/87 to 6/30/92	(n/a)
1/1/85 to 6/30/92	(n/a)
1/1/83 to 6/30/92	(n/a)
6/30/80 to 6/30/92	(n/a)

Risk: 53% of market

Strategic Investment (Speculative Strategy)

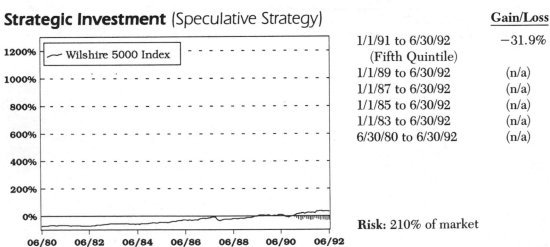

	Gain/Loss
1/1/91 to 6/30/92	−31.9%
(Fifth Quintile)	
1/1/89 to 6/30/92	(n/a)
1/1/87 to 6/30/92	(n/a)
1/1/85 to 6/30/92	(n/a)
1/1/83 to 6/30/92	(n/a)
6/30/80 to 6/30/92	(n/a)

Risk: 210% of market

Switch Fund Timing

Address
P.O. Box 25430
Rochester, NY 14625

Editor
David G. Davis

Phone Number
716-385-3122

Subscription Rates
$ 39.00/3 months
$119.00/year

Telephone Hotline
No

Money Management
Yes

SWITCH FUND TIMING ™

An Investment Newsletter, Focusing on Mutual Funds, Individual Stocks and Market Timing

Editor: *Dave Davis*

Published By:
Market Sentiment®
P.O. Box 25430
Rochester, New York 14625

Registered with the S.E.C. as an Investment Adviser

Issue 92-04	Dow 3318.52	June 30, 1992

SUMMARY and CURRENT ADVICE

The Dow Industrials finally decided to do a little catchup on the downside with the rest of the market. But the recent 120-point decline was only a beginning. The Dow is still up 5% year-to-date (YTD) while the OTC Composite is down 5% YTD and off 13% from its high of 645 reached in early February.

In every bull market, supply (of shares) always catches up with demand. And then the money runs out. During the past year there have been over 500 IPO's (initial public offerings) rapidly sucking up the available investment dollars. A new Fed easing should only move stocks higher for a brief period. Remain on the sidelines.

Recommended Exposure:

In Stocks...
0% Long
0% Short

In Gold.....
0% Long

In Funds....
0% Long

Are We Feeling the Effects of Tokyo, Finally ?

"Before the recent sharp decline in the Nikkei, explanations were rampant about why the Japanese stocks were not overvalued at 60 times earnings and yielding only .5%. Now, the same analysts are finding all sorts of reasons why a crash in Japanese stocks won't affect our markets. We didn't believe those pundits then, and we don't believe them now. The fact is, twenty-five years ago you could have bought many excellent Japanese companies for three times earnings. Now we don't suggest that these fine companies will decline to that lowly level again. But at a generous fifteen times earnings, the Nikkei would be at approximately 10000 -- which is about one-fourth the high and one-third of its present value. And since bear markets usually go to extreme on the downside, well, we'll leave the downside to your imagination."

The above paragraph was written by us on March 30th, 1990, when the Nikkei was at 30000. The accompanying graph shows where the Nikkei was when we made those comments, and what has happened since. At 30000, the Nikkei was only 23% and three months off its high of 39000. Today at 16000, the Nikkei is down nearly 60% from its high, and still falling.

We now believe 10000 may prove to be too optimistic because earnings have declined. Today, for the Nikkei to sell at 15 times earnings it would have to decline to less than 8000. This would represent an 80% decline.

Tokyo Stock Market
Nikkei average of 225 stock issues, week-end closes

the peak was reached in late 1989). The Japanese stock market clearly has further to go before the massive decline is over.

Crashes of this magnitude usually end in a panic. By definition, a panic involves high volume. But the decline so far has been on light volume of only 300 million shares a day (versus over one billion shares daily when

In our 3/30/90 issue, we also made the following observations: "But another Japanese bubble -- which may be ready to burst -- could be of even greater consequence. The real estate market in Japan is, in our opinion, a house of cards, challenged only by The Great Tulip Bulb Craze. When the Royal Palace is 'worth' more than Manhattan Island, something is screwy. And when the real estate of Japan is 'worth' more than the entire United States, we have to wonder how long this situation can exist.

(Continued on Page 2)

David G. Davis, Editor and Publisher

Switch Fund Timing is published monthly by David Davis and does not have a telephone hotline update. However, Davis will send out special one-page bulletins between issues when his market opinion changes.

As the name suggests, *Switch Fund Timing* is geared to investors interested in switching in and out of mutual funds, and the bulk of each letter is devoted to the timing and selection of funds. Nevertheless, the model portfolio in his newsletter that has existed for the longest time is a stock portfolio. Over the five and one-half years through mid-1992 for which the HFD has data, this model stock portfolio gained 78.7%, in contrast to 93.3% for the Wilshire 5000.

Only more recently has Davis inaugurated model mutual fund portfolios, and he now has three of them. Over the three and one-half years through mid-1992 for which the HFD has data for Davis's "Conservative" portfolio, it gained 32.2%, in contrast to 60.3% for the Wilshire 5000. Over the two and one-half years for which the HFD has data for his two other mutual fund portfolios, the "Conservative/Momentum" portfolio gained 19.0% (in contrast to 24.1% for the Wilshire 5000) and the "Gold" portfolio lost 1.3% (in contrast to a

14.4% loss for gold bullion itself). Overall, the HFD reports an average gain of 67.6% over the five and one-half years through mid-1992, in contrast to 93.3% for buying and holding.

The culprit in this market underperformance appears to be Davis's market timing rather than his stock or fund selection. In fact, his recommended stocks have performed better than the Wilshire 5000 during the times his stock portfolio owned them. And his recommended mutual funds have more or less equaled the market's performance during the times his fund portfolios have owned them.

Switch Fund Timing (Average)

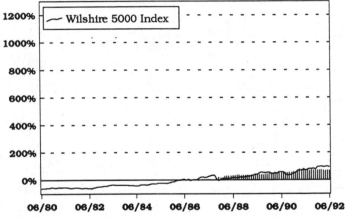

	Gain/Loss
1/1/91 to 6/30/92 (Fifth Quintile)	+6.1%
1/1/89 to 6/30/92 (Fourth Quintile)	+26.5%
1/1/87 to 6/30/92 (Second Quintile)	+67.6%
1/1/85 to 6/30/92	(n/a)
1/1/83 to 6/30/92	(n/a)
6/30/80 to 6/30/92	(n/a)

Risk: 75% of market

Switch Fund Timing (Model Stock Portfolio)

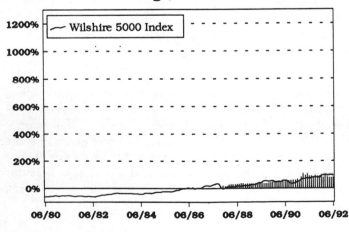

	Gain/Loss
1/1/91 to 6/30/92 (Fifth Quintile)	+7.7%
1/1/89 to 6/30/92 (Third Quintile)	+34.9%
1/1/87 to 6/30/92 (Second Quintile)	+78.7%
1/1/85 to 6/30/92	(n/a)
1/1/83 to 6/30/92	(n/a)
6/30/80 to 6/30/92	(n/a)

Risk: 172% of market

Switch Fund Timing (Conservative Model Portfolio)

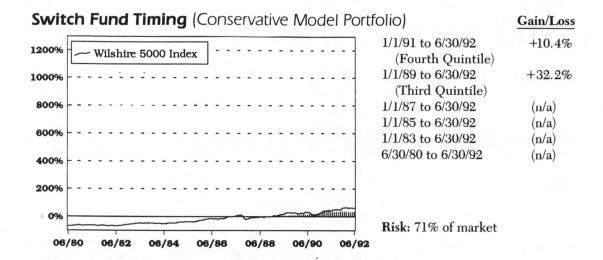

	Gain/Loss
1/1/91 to 6/30/92 (Fourth Quintile)	+10.4%
1/1/89 to 6/30/92 (Third Quintile)	+32.2%
1/1/87 to 6/30/92	(n/a)
1/1/85 to 6/30/92	(n/a)
1/1/83 to 6/30/92	(n/a)
6/30/80 to 6/30/92	(n/a)

Risk: 71% of market

Switch Fund Timing (Conservative/Momentum Portfolio)

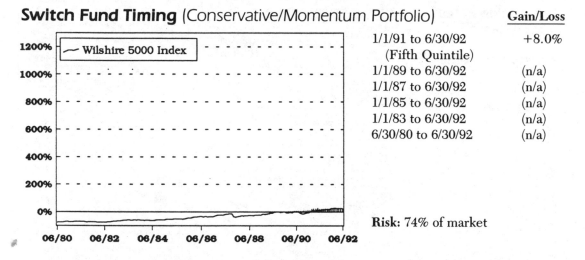

	Gain/Loss
1/1/91 to 6/30/92 (Fifth Quintile)	+8.0%
1/1/89 to 6/30/92	(n/a)
1/1/87 to 6/30/92	(n/a)
1/1/85 to 6/30/92	(n/a)
1/1/83 to 6/30/92	(n/a)
6/30/80 to 6/30/92	(n/a)

Risk: 74% of market

Switch Fund Timing (Gold Fund Portfolio)

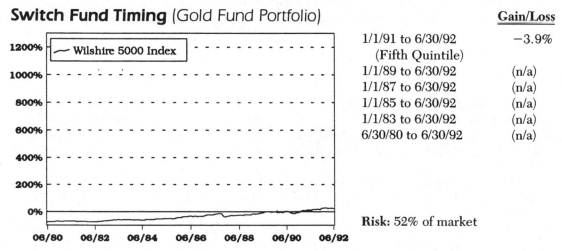

	Gain/Loss
1/1/91 to 6/30/92 (Fifth Quintile)	−3.9%
1/1/89 to 6/30/92	(n/a)
1/1/87 to 6/30/92	(n/a)
1/1/85 to 6/30/92	(n/a)
1/1/83 to 6/30/92	(n/a)
6/30/80 to 6/30/92	(n/a)

Risk: 52% of market

The Sy Harding Investor Forecasts

Address
P.O. Box 352016
Palm Coast, FL 32135

Editor
Sy Harding

Phone Number
904-446-0823

Subscription Rates
$195.00/year

Telephone Hotline
Yes

Money Management
Yes

The SY HARDING

INVESTOR FORECASTS ™

Our 5th Year

P.O. Box 352016 • Palm Coast, Florida 32135-2016 • A Confidential Investment Advisory For Traders and Investors

WHAT'S NEXT? OUR INDICATORS, INCLUDING THE DYNAMICS INDEX, REMAIN ON JUNE 29 BUY SIGNAL. INDICATORS ARE NOT YET IN RALLY CONTINUATION TERRITORY, SO MAY NOT LEAD TO AN EXTENDED SUMMER RALLY. BUT AT LEAST A TRADING RALLY.

1990- #2 Stock Market Timer in U.S.
1991- #2 Long Term Stock MarketTimer.
1991- #1 Gold Timer (Timer of the Year).
1992- #1 Long Term Stock Market Timer.
1992- #2 Market Timer last 6 months.
(Timer Digest, Greenwich, CT. June 22, 1992)

July 16, 1992.   DJIA 3345

THE VIEW FROM HERE:

Unlike most years, so far 1992 has not been a joyous year to be in the stock market.

Only the Dow is above it's Jan. high, and by just 2.1%. The S&P 500 and NYSE Index, after being down as much as 6%, are *still* down more than 1%. The Nasdaq, after being down 15% from its Feb. high, and after being the strongest sector in recent weeks, is *still* 9 1/2% off its high.

Confusion was the dominent characteristic of the market in the first half. Sectors were in constant rotation as economic expectations flipped back and forth between recovery and continuing recession. The confusion bred nervousness. Record amounts of unsophisticated new "CD" money flooded the market, and by its very inexperience is nervous. Most of this new money rushed into last year's big winners which were already overbought and ripe for correction. And correct they did. Biotech, computers, healthcare, and others of last year's big winners saw some issues correct 30, 40, even 60%. At the same time automotive issues, and a *few* special

situations like Disney saw *gains* of 30, 40, even 60%.

The result is that some sectors, and some individual stocks, are badly beaten down, perhaps on the bargain counter. Others remain or have become quite overextended.

So, what's in store for the second half?

With the market still overvalued by every historical method of valuation from P/E ratios and book value, to dividend yield, investor nervousness will continue to play an important role. Rallies will be met with skepticism. Pullbacks will be met with fear. Earnings disappointments and rumours will continue to cause share prices to plunge out of proportion to the news.

But unlike the first half, the second half begins with many sectors clearly beaten down. Many good stocks that were bid into the stratosphere have come back to reasonable, if not cheap, levels. And some sectors that have been asleep for years are due for an awakening. At the same time there are overextended sectors that must be avoided, just as biotech and technology were to be avoided in the first half.

The market remains overvalued, with earnings and dividends quite unlikely to catch up in time to bring valuations back to normal. Therefore sometime in the next 15 months we probably will see the more serious correction that so many have been waiting for since 1987. But we'll trust our indicators to have us on the sidelines at the right times as they have in the past.

With much of the market having corrected quite sharply in the first half, we expect better pickings in the second half. At the same time market timing remains important. It's no longer wise to buy and hold through corrections.

Stay tuned to the hotline!

INSIDE:

MARKET COMMENTARY
OUR MARKET TIMING INDICATORS !
LATEST NEWS ON OUR STOCKS!
PORTFOLIOS: BUY & HOLD
            SHORT TERM TRADER'S
            MUTUAL FUND SWITCHING
POTENTIAL OVERPERFORMER
POTENTIAL UNDERPERFORMER

The Sy Harding Investor Forecasts is published every three weeks by Sy Harding, who supplements the newsletter with a telephone hotline that is updated at least twice each week.

Harding's approach to market timing is based primarily on technical analysis, while his analysis of individual stocks and mutual funds focuses on a wide range of factors, fundamental as well as technical. As of mid-1992, Harding's letter contained three model portfolios: a "Buy & Hold" portfolio and a "Short-Term Trading" portfolio, both of which focus on individual stocks, and a "Mutual Fund

Switching" portfolio, which focuses just on mutual funds. Harding used to recommend a fourth portfolio (of options), but this was discontinued at the end of 1991. The performance of this now-discontinued portfolio is included in the newsletter's average, however. And in September 1992 Harding announced his intention to consolidate his "Buy & Hold" and "Short-Term Trading" portfolios into one, to be entitled his "Equities" portfolio.

Harding is a fairly active trader, so his "Buy & Hold" portfolio is appropriately named only in relation to his "Short-Term Trading" portfolio. In fact, his "Buy & Hold" portfolio will hold positions for as short a time as a few months. His "Mutual Fund Switching" portfolio also has been active, switching into and out of the market the equivalent of 11.5 times over the 18 months through mid-1992, or about once every six or seven weeks on average. For all his active trading, however, Harding has succeeded in lowering these portfolios' risk: Even his "Short-Term Trading" portfolio, for example, has one-third less risk than the market itself.

The HFD began following Harding's newsletter at the beginning of 1990, and over the subsequent two and one-half years it produced a gain of 4.1% (versus. 24.1% for the Wilshire 5000). This is sufficiently below the market that even when the gain is adjusted for the below-market risk, it still is below the market's gain.

Sy Harding Investor Forecasts (Average)

	Gain/Loss
1/1/91 to 6/30/92	+7.1%
(Fifth Quintile)	
1/1/89 to 6/30/92	(n/a)
1/1/87 to 6/30/92	(n/a)
1/1/85 to 6/30/92	(n/a)
1/1/83 to 6/30/92	(n/a)
6/30/80 to 6/30/92	(n/a)

Risk: 88% of market

Sy Harding Investor Forecasts (Portfolio 1: Buy & Hold)

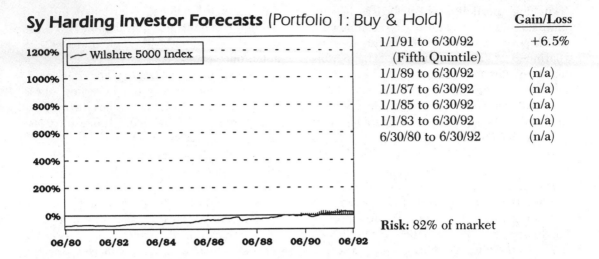

	Gain/Loss
1/1/91 to 6/30/92	+6.5%
(Fifth Quintile)	
1/1/89 to 6/30/92	(n/a)
1/1/87 to 6/30/92	(n/a)
1/1/85 to 6/30/92	(n/a)
1/1/83 to 6/30/92	(n/a)
6/30/80 to 6/30/92	(n/a)

Risk: 82% of market

Sy Harding Investor Forecasts (Portfolio 2: Short-Term Trading)

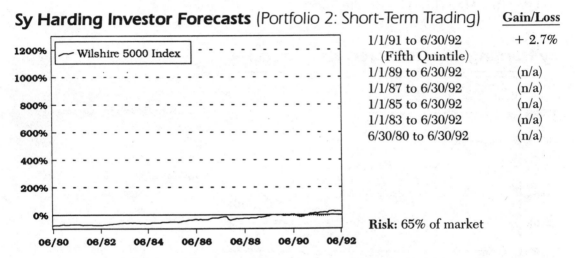

	Gain/Loss
1/1/91 to 6/30/92	+ 2.7%
(Fifth Quintile)	
1/1/89 to 6/30/92	(n/a)
1/1/87 to 6/30/92	(n/a)
1/1/85 to 6/30/92	(n/a)
1/1/83 to 6/30/92	(n/a)
6/30/80 to 6/30/92	(n/a)

Risk: 65% of market

Sy Harding Investor Forecasts (Portfolio 3: Fund Switching)

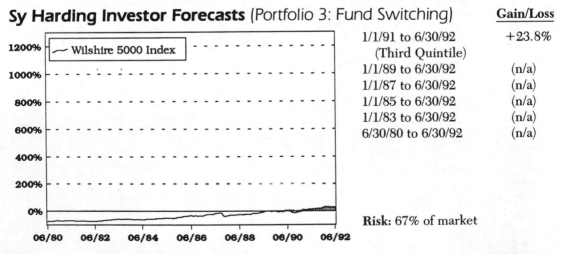

	Gain/Loss
1/1/91 to 6/30/92	+23.8%
(Third Quintile)	
1/1/89 to 6/30/92	(n/a)
1/1/87 to 6/30/92	(n/a)
1/1/85 to 6/30/92	(n/a)
1/1/83 to 6/30/92	(n/a)
6/30/80 to 6/30/92	(n/a)

Risk: 67% of market

Systems and Forecasts

Address
150 Great Neck Rd.
Great Neck, NY 11021

Editor
Gerald Appel

Phone Number
516-829-6444

Subscription Rates
$ 65.00/3 months
$125.00/6 months
$195.00/year

Telephone Hotline
Yes

Money Management
Yes

Gerald Appel's

SYSTEMS AND FORECASTS

SIGNALERT CORPORATION   150 GREAT NECK ROAD   GREAT NECK, N.Y. 11021

Volume 20   REGISTERED WITH THE S.E.C. AS AN INVESTMENT ADVISOR   Number 5

July 2, 1992

REMEMBER THE HOTLINE!

Those of you who call in regularly did receive the parameters necessary to produce the current buy signal.

We announce regularly Sunday and Wednesday evenings at 11 PM, and mid-week as necessary.

POWER TOOLS! -- Time to Review Your Tape and Manual......

Owners of Power Tools! should be reviewing their manuals at this time to check significant advance-decline levels required to generate thrust signals.

Even if the current advance fails, you should also be reviewing the videotape for those positive patterns which might emerge within 3 - 6 weeks that would signal the onset of a significant market advance.

Owners of the MACD videotape should also be reviewing patterns. MACD seems to have produced an excellent entry once again.

Subscribers who do not own the POWER TOOLS! Trading Seminar and/or the MACD videotape might want to telephone our office, 516-829-6444 to make inquiry. The same for those of you who do not own the Time-Trend III Trading Seminar and who might want to generate signals yourselves rather than to track via our hotline.

We have some very interesting research in progress. In some ways, too many projects which will require time to complete. Check out Open Trin on page 4, one of the items we are investigating.

THE STATE OF THE MARKET: A Time-Trend III buy signal was generated on June 23 with the NYSE Index at 221.99. As of the close last evening, we were ahead by 2.1% on the signal, which we have considered better placed than recent buy signals.

Bonds closed last week still on a buy. The status as of this week's close will be announced on the weekend hotline.

The advance does have a number of things going for it -- good initial market breadth, widespread pessimism, favorable interest rates, and support from a number of confirming indicators.

However, there is ample supply just above current levels and most stock charts do not show significant basing patterns. At this time, we expect not too much more than a tradeable rally, but the stock market will, of course, tell its own story.

And, of course, Time-Trend III remains the story teller. We will continue to follow its dictates.

That said, the good news includes favorable MACD patterns, positive new high - new low patterns, buy signals generated by volume readings, buy signals from STIX, high mutual fund cash positions, and some evidence that Ross Perot may be slipping in popularity.

The bad news remains as it has been -- stocks are expensive in terms of price-earnings ratios, and in terms of dividend payout, though not dividend payout in its relationship to current interest levels.

A significant uptrendline was violated on the recent downswing, but the line has since been repenetrated (unusual), so there is at least a fair chance of the major market indices swinging to new all time highs before the advance runs its course. As of this writing, the overhead at Dow 3350 - 3400 and at S & P 500 415 - 420 remains intact, but we estimate truer resistance at levels just above recent highs rather than just below.

Taken all in all, the technical picture has improved for the intermediate term, if not necessarily for the longer term. On a short term basis, the stock market is moving into extended territory. Here is where the test comes in. How much initial power can the stock market produce before the first minor correction? The more the better.

Keep tuned in. Maybe something really good will take place. We should all know soon enough....

Systems and Forecasts is published every three weeks by Gerald Appel and is supplemented by a telephone hotline that is updated sometimes as often as every day. Though Appel is a technician, his approach to technical analysis is significantly more statistical and sophisticated than that of other technicians.

The HFD has been following a portfolio for *Systems and Forecasts* since 1983. In 1990 Appel inaugurated two new portfolios. In addition to what he now calls his "Regular" portfolio, he created a "Jack White" portfolio (to be opened with the Jack White brokerage firm) and a "Futures and Options" portfolio.

The HFD didn't begin following these additional portfolios until 1991. Over the 18 months through mid-1992 for which the HFD has data for all three portfolios (over which time the Wilshire 5000 gained 32.3%), the best performer was the "Jack White" portfolio (+23.6%), followed by the "Regular" portfolio (+14.2%) and the "Futures & Options" portfolio (+10.5%).

While Appel's "Regular" and "Jack White" portfolios invest primarily in mutual funds, they frequently include index options as well. Appel used to have a portfolio exclusively devoted to mutual funds, this one concentrating on Fidelity's sector funds. However, Appel discontinued this portfolio when Fidelity imposed restrictions on the frequency of switching within their funds. The performance of this now-discontinued portfolio is included in what the HFD reports for this newsletter's average.

Appel's approach, while short-term, succeeds in keeping portfolio risk low. With this below-market risk we would expect Appel to underperform the market on a total-return basis, and indeed this was the case: Over the nine and one-half years through mid-1992, *Systems and Forecasts* produced a gain of 210.4%, in contrast to the Wilshire 5000's total return of 278.6%. However, when this newsletter's below-average risk is taken into account, it beats the market on a risk-adjusted basis.

Appel's best-known intermediate-timing indicator is entitled "Time Trend." It is a fairly active timing system, generating 135 signals over the nine and one-half years through mid-1992 (or over 14 per year on average). But it has paid off: An investor switching back and forth between hypothetical shares of the Wilshire 5000 and T-Bills on "Time Trend" signals would have done even better than Appel's model portfolios, gaining 392.9% over these nine and one-half years.

Appel also provides buy and sell signals for timing the bond market. It also is an active system, generating 52 signals over the seven and one-half years through mid-1992. While it is in first place among all bond timers the HFD followed over this period, it nevertheless underperformed a buy-and-hold.

Systems and Forecasts (Average)

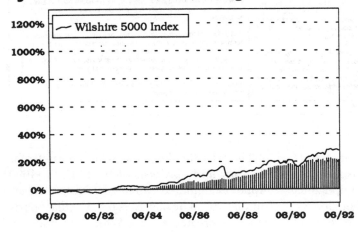

	Gain/Loss
1/1/91 to 6/30/92	+16.2%
(Fourth Quintile)	
1/1/89 to 6/30/92	+53.7%
(Second Quintile)	
1/1/87 to 6/30/92	+109.0%
(First Quintile)	
1/1/85 to 6/30/92	+172.8%
(Second Quintile)	
1/1/83 to 6/30/92	+210.4%
(First Quintile)	
6/30/80 to 6/30/92	(n/a)

Risk: 84% of market

Systems and Forecasts (The Regular Portfolio)

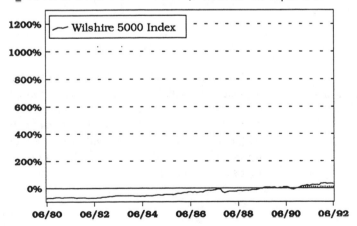

	Gain/Loss
1/1/91 to 6/30/92 (Fourth Quintile)	+14.2%
1/1/89 to 6/30/92 (Third Quintile)	+40.7%
1/1/87 to 6/30/92 (Second Quintile)	+86.7%
1/1/85 to 6/30/92 (Second Quintile)	+146.8%
1/1/83 to 6/30/92 (Second Quintile)	+180.8%
6/30/80 to 6/30/92	(n/a)

Risk: 76% of market

Systems and Forecasts (Jack White Portfolio)

	Gain/Loss
1/1/91 to 6/30/92 (Third Quintile)	+23.6%
1/1/89 to 6/30/92	(n/a)
1/1/87 to 6/30/92	(n/a)
1/1/85 to 6/30/92	(n/a)
1/1/83 to 6/30/92	(n/a)
6/30/80 to 6/30/92	(n/a)

Risk: 99% of market

Systems and Forecasts (Futures & Options Portfolio)

	Gain/Loss
1/1/91 to 6/30/92 (Fourth Quintile)	+10.5%
1/1/89 to 6/30/92	(n/a)
1/1/87 to 6/30/92	(n/a)
1/1/85 to 6/30/92	(n/a)
1/1/83 to 6/30/92	(n/a)
6/30/80 to 6/30/92	(n/a)

Risk: 93% of market

Telephone Switch Newsletter

Address
P.O. Box 2538
Huntington Beach, CA
92647

Editor
Douglas Fabian

Phone Number
800-950-8765

Subscription Rates
$ 99.00/8 months
$137.00/year

Telephone Hotline
Yes

Money Management
No

Fabians'
Telephone Switch Newsletter

"OUR OBJECTIVE IS TO HELP YOU BECOME WEALTHY."   JULY 8, 1992

MARKETS AT A GLANCE...
AS OF 7/2/92

INDEX	CURRENT READING	39WAR	+/- 39WD	FABIAN ALERT READINGS
MUTUAL FUND COMPOSITE PLAN:				
DJ 65 Comp	1172.06	1144.92	+ 2.37%	1205*
DJ Indust	3330.29	3193.35	+ 4.29%	3355*
DJ Trans	1324.74	1332.14	− 0.56%	1400*
MFC	39972	39632	+ 0.86%	41600*
MFC Dow−RSD			− 3.36%	

STATUS: We are currently in Equity Funds. We will switch to the Money Funds when both the MFC and the Dow Jones Composite move below their 39WARs. At present, a "spurt" is not in place.

GOLD FUND COMPOSITE PLAN:				
GFC	21247	21672	− 1.96%	20600*
Cash−RSD			− 3.27%	

STATUS: We are in the Money Funds. We will switch to the Gold Funds when the GFC moves above its 39WAR.

INT'L FUND COMPOSITE PLAN:				
IFC	35400	33947	+ 4.28%	35700*
Dow−RSD			− 0.13%	

STATUS: We are in the International Funds. We will switch to the Money Funds when the IFC moves below its 39WAR.

ASSET ALLOCATION TRADING PLAN:
STATUS: We have five invested positions.

OTCI	598.85	647.08	− 7.45%	680*
Dow−RSD			− 11.34%	
VLC	247.42	250.40	− 1.19%	263*
Dow−RSD			− 5.33%	

*An Alert Mode Exists

GENERAL MARKET: During the month of July, the Mutual Fund Composite (MFC) declined -2.62% and the Dow Jones Industrials (DJI) declined -2.31%. This type of movement did not have any effect on the DIVERGENCE that has existed between the DJI and the rest of the market.

Our relative strength calculation compares the action of each indicator in relation to the movement of the DJI. At the close of the market on Thursday, July 2nd, the Relative Strength Differential (RSD) readings for the market indicators we monitor continued to be negative. Current readings are virtually unchanged from last month for all of the indicators except the Over-the-Counter Industrials (OTCI). The OTCI declined 5.17% in June and its negative RSD reading has now increased to -11.34%.

The action of the daily Advance/Decline (A/D) line shows further evidence of divergence between the DJI and the rest of the market (See chart Page 8). During 1991, each new high recorded by the DJI was confirmed by yearly highs in the A/D. At the end of 1991, both the DJI and the A/D were at new yearly highs. Things changed for most of 1992. The new DJI high recorded on February 12, 1992 was not confirmed by the A/D. As a matter of fact, the current A/D reading is below its 39WAR.

Last month, we included a daily posted chart of the Value Line Composite covering the most recent ten-month period. To bring you up-to-date on the movement of the VLC during June, it broke below the rising bottoms line (C-D). It also went below its own 39WAR and it recorded a new low for the year on June 26th. It has since rebounded, but as of July 2nd, it was still below its 39WAR.

COMMENTARY: On Page 2, we show a daily posted chart of the Mutual Fund Composite covering all of 1991 and 1992 to date.

The MFC reached an all-time high on February 12, 1992, with a reading of 41851. For the next four months, it has been trending lower. During the month of June, it moved below and then above its 39WAR.

We felt it would be appropriate to discuss the working of the Mutual Fund Composite Trading Plan with reference to the chart.

Telephone Switch Newsletter is published monthly by Douglas and Richard Fabian (a son-and-father team). It is supplemented by a telephone hotline that is updated every Friday evening, and on other days in the event that a switch signal is generated.

This telephone hotline update schedule took on great significance during the October Massacre in 1987, because Fabian's system generated a switch out of equity funds on the Thursday prior to Black Monday. Those subscribers who called the special, unscheduled update that Thursday were told to get out on Friday, whereas those who waited until the regularly scheduled Friday-evening hotline to receive the "sell" advice were forced to sell into Monday's crash. The HFD's track record for *Telephone Switch Newsletter* is calculated assuming the investor got out of stock funds on Friday, October 16, since the telephone update was available to all subscribers. Nevertheless, the reader should be aware that many investors did not call that special update and thus achieved an inferior record to that which is reported here.

Fabian's approach to mutual fund investing is entirely technical and mechanical: Buy and sell signals are generated on the basis of whether the market is trading above or below its moving average. Though Fabian uses the 39-week moving average to time the stock market, there is nothing magical about 39 weeks in particular. In fact, Fabian has said that a 52-week moving average system would produce greater profits over the long run than a 39-week moving average. He sticks with the 39-week average, however, because he believes investors would not be willing to sit out the intermediate-term declines that a longer moving average would require.

This provides an insight into Fabian's contribution to the debate over different investment strategies. He argues that a newsletter with a great track record is of little importance if its approach is so risky, so complicated, or requires so much time to follow that no one actually follows the advice. Fabian admits that his system may not be the most profitable among all newsletters, but he insists it is one of the simplest, most understandable, and is one that investors actually can live with.

In any case, Fabian's system has been good enough to put his newsletter in seventh place for performance over the 12 years through mid-1992 (among all those newsletters the HFD tracks). Averaging his three portfolios' performance, his newsletter gained 335.4% over these 12 years, as compared to 432.7% for the Wilshire 5000. Because his newsletter achieved this rate of return with slightly less risk than that associated with the market as a whole, furthermore, its rank on a risk-adjusted basis jumps to fifth place (though slightly behind the Wilshire 5000).

Subscribers must keep in mind that Fabian's "Equity/Cash Switch Plan" (for which he is best known) is just one of three mutual fund switch plans offered by the newsletter. For the nine and one-half years through mid-1992 for which the HFD has data for Fabian's "Gold/Cash Switch Plan," it gained 25.3%, in contrast to a 23.3% loss for gold bullion. And for the eight-and-one-half years through mid-1992 for which the HFD has data for this newsletter's "International/Cash Switch Plan," it gained 189.0%, in contrast to 206.6% for the Wilshire 5000.

Fabian's timing signals for the stock market have done better than his "Equity/Cash Switch Plan." If each of this newsletter's recommended equity funds had performed as well as the Wilshire 5000 during the times this portfolio owned them, then the portfolio would gained 523.5% over the 12 years through mid-1992. This is good enough to rank the newsletter in first place over this period on a timing-only basis.

Telephone Switch Newsletter (Average)

	Gain/Loss
1/1/91 to 6/30/92 (Fourth Quintile)	+9.6%
1/1/89 to 6/30/92 (Fourth Quintile)	+30.9%
1/1/87 to 6/30/92 (Third Quintile)	+56.9%
1/1/85 to 6/30/92 (Third Quintile)	+126.3%
1/1/83 to 6/30/92 (Third Quintile)	+124.0%
6/30/80 to 6/30/92 (Third Quintile)	+335.4%

Risk: 43% of market

Telephone Switch Newsletter (Equity/Cash Switch Plan)

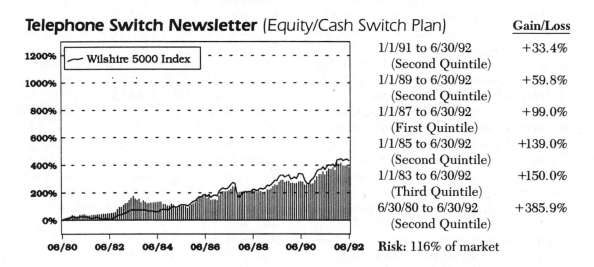

	Gain/Loss
1/1/91 to 6/30/92 (Second Quintile)	+33.4%
1/1/89 to 6/30/92 (Second Quintile)	+59.8%
1/1/87 to 6/30/92 (First Quintile)	+99.0%
1/1/85 to 6/30/92 (Second Quintile)	+139.0%
1/1/83 to 6/30/92 (Third Quintile)	+150.0%
6/30/80 to 6/30/92 (Second Quintile)	+385.9%

Risk: 116% of market

Telephone Switch Newsletter (Gold/Cash Switch Plan)

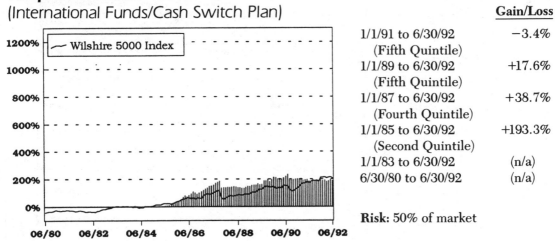

	Gain/Loss
1/1/91 to 6/30/92 (Fifth Quintile)	+0.1%
1/1/89 to 6/30/92 (Fifth Quintile)	+14.4%
1/1/87 to 6/30/92 (Fourth Quintile)	+29.2%
1/1/85 to 6/30/92 (Fifth Quintile)	+44.4%
1/1/83 to 6/30/92 (Fifth Quintile)	+25.3%
6/30/80 to 6/30/92	(n/a)

Risk: 70% of market

Telephone Switch Newsletter
(International Funds/Cash Switch Plan)

	Gain/Loss
1/1/91 to 6/30/92 (Fifth Quintile)	−3.4%
1/1/89 to 6/30/92 (Fifth Quintile)	+17.6%
1/1/87 to 6/30/92 (Fourth Quintile)	+38.7%
1/1/85 to 6/30/92 (Second Quintile)	+193.3%
1/1/83 to 6/30/92	(n/a)
6/30/80 to 6/30/92	(n/a)

Risk: 50% of market

The Timberline Investment Forecast

Address

Timberline Research, Inc.

4130 S.W. 117th Ave.

Suite 215

Beaverton, OR 97005

Editor

Mark West

Subscription Rates

$ 35.00/3 months

$135.00/year

Telephone Hotline

No

Money Management

No

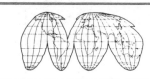

THE TIMBERLINE INVESTMENT FORECAST

Issue #34   Copyright 1992 Timberline Research, Inc.   July 17, 1992

SUMMARY

Only a few years into the 1990s, commentators have already dubbed it as the decade of fear. Mounting job losses, slow economic growth and impotent Fed monetary policy have instilled a dread among Americans. It has also raised doubts about predicating stock prices on a strong earnings rebound. Bonds, however, look positively attractive in this environment. Fixed income prospects will change when the politicians carry out plans to "help" the economy and inadvertently help precious metals investors instead. Expect a sharp rally in gold when programs to revitalize the economy proliferate.

THE ECONOMY

The current outlook makes one appreciate the old Chinese threat: "May you live in interesting times!" Almost everyone agrees that this is not a normal recovery. Some would argue that it is not a recovery at all but actually the start of a "triple dip" recession. By now, economic recovery should be engendering optimism rather than anxiety. Every age has a zeitgeist, a spirit that captures its essence. Rightly or wrongly, the 1980s were tagged the decade of greed; the 1990s may end up summarized as the decade of fear.

Unemployment dwarfs all the other sources of angst and remains the biggest concern for most people. The investment world got a shocker when the unemployment rate rose to 7.8% in June instead of declining as expected. Major corporations continue to announce layoffs in waves. Hughes Aircraft, the largest employer in California, recently announced 9,000 layoffs. Raytheon, Amoco, Mead and Aetna are just some companies where thousands of pink slips will be flying soon.

TOTAL RETURN FORECASTS			
	3 Months	6 Months	12 Months
STOCKS (Standard and Poor's 500)	⬇	⬇	⬇
BONDS (Long Term Treasury Bonds)	⬆	⬍	⬇
GOLD (London P.M. Fixing)	⬌	⬌	⬆

The Timberline Investment Forecast is published monthly by Mark West; there is no telephone hotline update. The newsletter's focus is on asset allocation between stocks, gold, bonds and cash. No specific security recommendations are provided, so the HFD is unable to construct any model portfolios to track its performance, and instead is limited to measuring just the service's asset allocation advice (see the chapter on asset allocation earlier in this volume).

West tailors three different asset allocations to subscribers of varying risk preferences: a "Conservative" portfolio, which is designed for investors with a low risk tolerance who are willing to hold for more than ten years; an "Average" portfolio, which is designed for medium-risk investors willing to hold between one and ten years; and an "Aggressive" portfolio, which is designed for high-risk investors whose investment time horizon is less than one year.

All three portfolios are very low risk, having less than a third as much volatility as the Wilshire 5000, for example. All three also are less risky than a portfolio that is equally divided among stocks, gold and bonds. However, the volatility of all three portfolios is quite similar, with the most volatile (by a hair) being West's "Conservative" portfolio.

Stocks were the best-performing of the major asset categories over the last several years, so it's hardly a surprise that portfolios such as West's did less well than the stock market. A fairer comparison would be with a portfolio that is divided equally among the major asset categories, and each of West's portfolios succeeded in beating it.

The Timberline Investment Forecast (Conservative Portfolio)

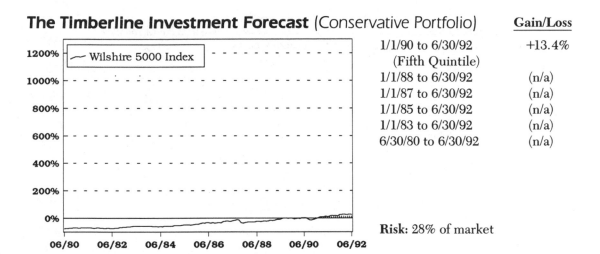

	Gain/Loss
1/1/90 to 6/30/92	+13.4%
(Fifth Quintile)	
1/1/88 to 6/30/92	(n/a)
1/1/87 to 6/30/92	(n/a)
1/1/85 to 6/30/92	(n/a)
1/1/83 to 6/30/92	(n/a)
6/30/80 to 6/30/92	(n/a)

Risk: 28% of market

The Timberline Investment Forecast (Average Risk Portfolio)

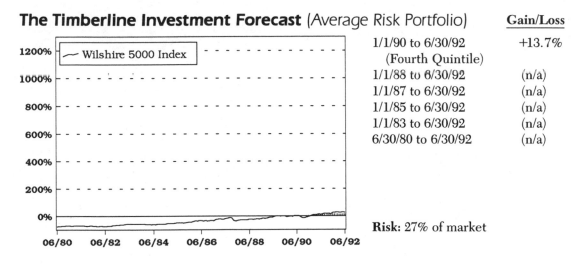

	Gain/Loss
1/1/90 to 6/30/92	+13.7%
(Fourth Quintile)	
1/1/88 to 6/30/92	(n/a)
1/1/87 to 6/30/92	(n/a)
1/1/85 to 6/30/92	(n/a)
1/1/83 to 6/30/92	(n/a)
6/30/80 to 6/30/92	(n/a)

Risk: 27% of market

The Timberline Investment Forecast
(Aggressive Portfolio)

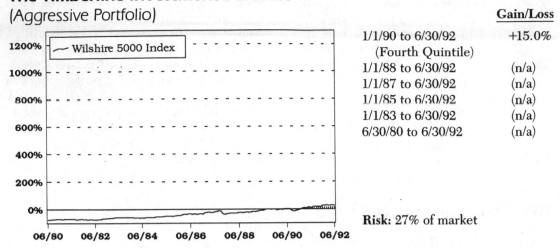

	Gain/Loss
1/1/90 to 6/30/92	+15.0%
(Fourth Quintile)	
1/1/88 to 6/30/92	(n/a)
1/1/87 to 6/30/92	(n/a)
1/1/85 to 6/30/92	(n/a)
1/1/83 to 6/30/92	(n/a)
6/30/80 to 6/30/92	(n/a)

Risk: 27% of market

Timer Digest

Address
P.O. Box 1688
Greenwich, CT
  06836-1688

Editor
Jim Schmidt

Phone Number
203-629-3503

Subscription Rates
$225.00/year

Telephone Hotline
Yes

Money Management
No

July 13, 1992

Timer
DIGEST

ISSUE NO. 190

#1 TOP TEN

THE GARSIDE FORECAST

#1 BONDS

SUTTON ADVISORY LETTER

#1 GOLD

DMC MARKET FAX

Mid Year Review

Timer Digest is published every three weeks by Jim Schmidt and supplemented by a telephone hotline that is updated at least twice each week.

Timer Digest rates the timing-only performances of market-timing newsletters and then uses the results of their ratings to construct a number of market-timing indicators of their own. Their methodology for measuring market-timing performance differs substantially from the HFD's, primarily in the pricing used for buy and sell signals. While the HFD insists on using the first closing price that a subscriber could have received upon acting on the buy or sell signal, *Timer Digest* typically uses the closing price that prevailed before the signal was announced.

This difference can lead to enormous differences. For example, some newsletters produced sell signals after the close on the Friday prior to 1987's Black Monday. Needless to say, any investor acting on that advice would have had to sell into the onslaught on Monday, October 19, but *Timer Digest* gave such newsletters credit for getting out of the market as of the close on Friday, October 16.

In any case, *Timer Digest* constructs a timing indicator out of the forecasts of the top ten stock market timers, as determined by their performance measurement. This indicator, which they call the "5 & 10 Consensus," has underperformed a buy-and-hold strategy. An investor who switched between hypothetical shares of the Wilshire 5000 and T-Bills on signals from the "5 & 10 Consensus" gained 65.2% over the four and one-half years through mid-1992, in contrast to 89.0% for buying and holding. If the investor actually went short upon a "5 & 10 Consensus" sell signal, instead of going into cash, he would have done even worse, gaining only 28.9%.

Timer Digest also constructs timing indicators according to the consensus of their top timers in the gold and bond arenas. These indicators added value to a buy-and-hold approach in the gold arena but failed to beat the market in bonds (see Appendix C).

Timer Digest also has a proprietary timing indicator of their own, which they call "Casper." This indicator also underperformed the market over these four and one-half years, gaining 58.0% or losing 7.3% depending on whether the investor went into cash or went short the market on receipt of a "Casper" sell signal.

Timer Digest also recommends three specific model portfolios, and two of them have beaten the market. Its model mutual fund portfolio (which trades exclusively in Fidelity's Select funds) gained 157.4% over these four and one-half years, handily beating the Wilshire 5000's 89.0%. And its "Dow Jones 30 Strategy" gained 50.4% over the two and one-half years through mid-1992 for which the HFD has data, well ahead of the Wilshire 5000's 24.1%. Its model stock portfolio, in contrast, underperformed the market over the four and one-half years through mid-1992, gaining just 66.9%, as compared with the Wilshire 5000's 89.0%.

Timer Digest (Average)

	Gain/Loss
1/1/91 to 6/30/92 (Second Quintile)	+40.1%
1/1/89 to 6/30/92 (First Quintile)	+88.7%
1/1/87 to 6/30/92	(n/a)
1/1/85 to 6/30/92	(n/a)
1/1/83 to 6/30/92	(n/a)
6/30/80 to 6/30/92	(n/a)

Risk: 130% of market

Timer Digest (Fidelity Select Portfolio)

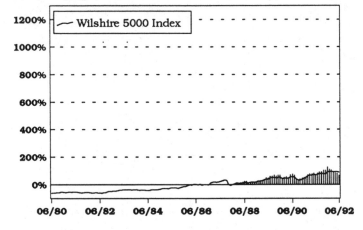

	Gain/Loss
1/1/91 to 6/30/92 (First Quintile)	+59.7%
1/1/89 to 6/30/92 (First Quintile)	+121.9%
1/1/87 to 6/30/92	(n/a)
1/1/85 to 6/30/92	(n/a)
1/1/83 to 6/30/92	(n/a)
6/30/80 to 6/30/92	(n/a)

Risk: 170% of market

Timer Digest (Model Stock Portfolio)

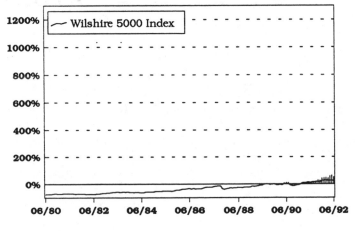

	Gain/Loss
1/1/91 to 6/30/92 (Fourth Quintile)	+11.0%
1/1/89 to 6/30/92 (Third Quintile)	+40.8%
1/1/87 to 6/30/92	(n/a)
1/1/85 to 6/30/92	(n/a)
1/1/83 to 6/30/92	(n/a)
6/30/80 to 6/30/92	(n/a)

Risk: 145% of market

Timer Digest (Dow Jones 30 Strategy)

	Gain/Loss
1/1/91 to 6/30/92 (First Quintile)	+51.7%
1/1/89 to 6/30/92	(n/a)
1/1/87 to 6/30/92	(n/a)
1/1/85 to 6/30/92	(n/a)
1/1/83 to 6/30/92	(n/a)
6/30/80 to 6/30/92	(n/a)

Risk: 129% of market

The Turnaround Letter

Address
New Generation
  Research, Inc.
225 Friend St.
Suite 801
Boston, MA 02114

Editor
George Putnam III

Phone Number
617-573-9550

Subscription Rates
$ 98.00/6 months
$195.00/year

Telephone Hotline
Yes

Money Management
No

The Turnaround Letter

Volume 7, Number 1   July 1992

MID-YEAR MARKET REVIEW

Although we do not believe in market timing (more on this at the end of this article), we do think it is useful to periodically review what is going on in the stock market as a whole. It is always helpful to understand the general investment environment, because even if it does not affect your decisions, it probably affects everyone else's.

So far this year, the stock market has been rather deceptive. If you just read the headlines, you would have the impression that the first half of 1992 has been a modestly profitable period for stock investors. In fact, many investors have been losing money.

Most headlines only track the Dow Jones Industrial average, which consists of 30 large, well-known and somewhat arbitrarily chosen industrial companies. The Dow is up about 3.6% for the year to date (through June 25), and it has set several new record highs over the past few months. On the other hand, the Standard & Poor's 500, which is a much broader index of large stocks, is down about 3.3%.

IN THIS ISSUE:

When you turn to the smaller capitalization stocks, the results are even gloomier. The NASDAQ Composite Index, representing a cross section of smaller stocks, is down 6.5%, and the NASDAQ Industrial Index is down 13%. The only bright spot among the smaller stocks is in the finance industry, with the NASDAQ Bank Index up 22.6%.

While there is no index for turnaround stocks, our sense is that, on the whole, they did reasonably well over the first half. After making large gains early in the year, a number of our recommended stocks have fallen back
(Continued on next page)

The Turnaround Letter is published monthly and edited by George Putnam III. It is supplemented by a telephone hotline that is updated once each month, at the time its monthly issue is mailed to subscribers.

As its title would suggest, the focus of *The Turnaround Letter* is on companies that Putnam believes will soon recover from a previous period of bad news and depressed prices. This sometimes leads to recommending stocks that are in bankruptcy proceedings.

Putnam segregates his recommendations into three risk categories ("Conservative/ Income," "Moderate Risk" and "Aggressive"), and in each issue he provides buy-hold-sell advice for each of his current recommendations. Because Putnam does not provide allocation advice on what portion of a subscriber's portfolio ought to be kept out of the market and in cash, the portfolios the HFD constructs to track these three categories are fully invested at all times in the securities that Putnam rates a "buy."

In several of the years the HFD has tracked *The Turnaround Letter*, one of Putnam's three portfolios has achieved huge gains while the other two have lagged the market by a large amount. In a classic illustration of the virtues of diversification, this was good enough for these portfolios' average performance nearly to beat the market as a whole: Over the four

and one-half years through mid-1992, the newsletter achieved an 85.6% gain, only barely behind the Wilshire 5000's 89.0%. The best-performing of the three is Putnam's "Aggressive" portfolio, which gained 145.6% over this period, followed by the "Moderate Risk" portfolio (+24.5%) and the "Conservative/Income" portfolio (+44.8%).

As might be expected, portfolios that are fully invested in "turnaround" situations will have much above-average risk, and this newsletter is no exception. The fact that the newsletter more or less equaled the market with more than double the risk means that on a risk-adjusted basis it significantly lagged a buy-and-hold strategy.

The Turnaround Letter (Average)

	Gain/Loss
1/1/91 to 6/30/92 (First Quintile)	+117.8%
1/1/89 to 6/30/92 (Second Quintile)	+50.3%
1/1/87 to 6/30/92	(n/a)
1/1/85 to 6/30/92	(n/a)
1/1/83 to 6/30/92	(n/a)
6/30/80 to 6/30/92	(n/a)

Risk: 275% of market

The Turnaround Letter (Moderate Risk Portfolio)

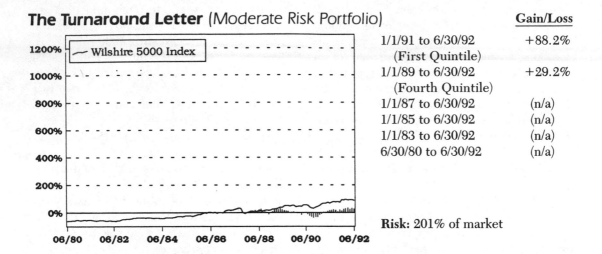

	Gain/Loss
1/1/91 to 6/30/92 (First Quintile)	+88.2%
1/1/89 to 6/30/92 (Fourth Quintile)	+29.2%
1/1/87 to 6/30/92	(n/a)
1/1/85 to 6/30/92	(n/a)
1/1/83 to 6/30/92	(n/a)
6/30/80 to 6/30/92	(n/a)

Risk: 201% of market

The Turnaround Letter (Conservative/Income Portfolio)

	Gain/Loss
1/1/91 to 6/30/92 (First Quintile)	+95.0%
1/1/89 to 6/30/92 (Second Quintile)	+69.0%
1/1/87 to 6/30/92	(n/a)
1/1/85 to 6/30/92	(n/a)
1/1/83 to 6/30/92	(n/a)
6/30/80 to 6/30/92	(n/a)

Risk: 203% of market

The Turnaround Letter (Aggressive Portfolio)

	Gain/Loss
1/1/91 to 6/30/92 (First Quintile)	+141.3%
1/1/89 to 6/30/92 (Fourth Quintile)	+21.4%
1/1/87 to 6/30/92	(n/a)
1/1/85 to 6/30/92	(n/a)
1/1/83 to 6/30/92	(n/a)
6/30/80 to 6/30/92	(n/a)

Risk: 557% of market

United & Babson Investment Report

Address
Babson-United
 Building
101 Prescott St.
Wellesley Hills, MA
 02181

Editor
Sidney McMath

Phone Number
617-235-0900

Subscription Rates
$134.00/6 months
$238.00/year

Telephone Hotline
No

Money Management
No

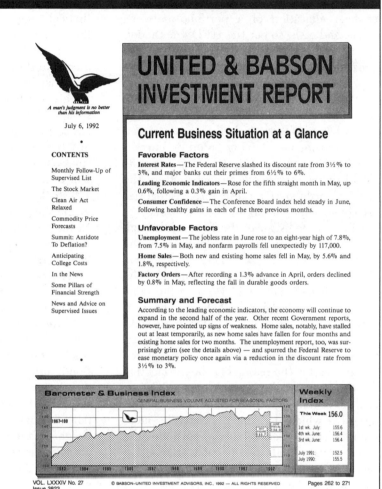

A man's judgment is no better than his information

July 6, 1992

•

CONTENTS

Monthly Follow-Up of
Supervised List

The Stock Market

Clean Air Act
Relaxed

Commodity Price
Forecasts

Summit: Antidote
To Deflation?

Anticipating
College Costs

In the News

Some Pillars of
Financial Strength

News and Advice on
Supervised Issues

•

UNITED & BABSON INVESTMENT REPORT

Current Business Situation at a Glance

Favorable Factors

Interest Rates — The Federal Reserve slashed its discount rate from 3½% to 3%, and major banks cut their primes from 6½% to 6%.

Leading Economic Indicators — Rose for the fifth straight month in May, up 0.6%, following a 0.3% gain in April.

Consumer Confidence — The Conference Board index held steady in June, following healthy gains in each of the three previous months.

Unfavorable Factors

Unemployment — The jobless rate in June rose to an eight-year high of 7.8%, from 7.5% in May, and nonfarm payrolls fell unexpectedly by 117,000.

Home Sales — Both new and existing home sales fell in May, by 5.6% and 1.8%, respectively.

Factory Orders — After recording a 1.3% advance in April, orders declined by 0.8% in May, reflecting the fall in durable goods orders.

Summary and Forecast

According to the leading economic indicators, the economy will continue to expand in the second half of the year. Other recent Government reports, however, have pointed up signs of weakness. Home sales, notably, have stalled out at least temporarily, as new home sales have fallen for four months and existing home sales for two months. The unemployment report, too, was surprisingly grim (see the details above) — and spurred the Federal Reserve to ease monetary policy once again via a reduction in the discount rate from 3½% to 3%.

Barometer & Business Index

GENERAL BUSINESS VOLUME ADJUSTED FOR SEASONAL FACTORS

1967=100

	Weekly Index
	This Week 156.0
1st wk. July:	155.6
4th wk. June:	156.4
3rd wk. June:	156.4
July 1991:	152.5
July 1990:	155.5

VOL. LXXXIV No. 27
Issue 3823

© BABSON–UNITED INVESTMENT ADVISORS, INC., 1992 — ALL RIGHTS RESERVED

Pages 262 to 271

United & Babson Investment Report is published weekly by Babson-United Investment Advisors, Inc., and is not supplemented by a telephone hotline. The *Report* is the successor publication to the *United Business & Investment Report*, which had been published since 1919. The new publication reflects the merger of United Business Service and *Babson's Reports* in the summer of 1986. (*Babson's Reports* had been founded in 1904.)

Both of the earlier publications, as well as the new one into which they merged, stressed fundamental analysis. The service maintains, and updates once each month, a "Supervised

List of Common Stocks," which is broken into three categories: "Stocks for Long-Term Growth," "Cyclical Stocks for Profit" and "Stocks for the Income-Minded." The service does not advise subscribers on the proper percentage allocation of a portfolio between stocks and cash, so per the HFD's methodology on such matters, the portfolios the HFD constructs to track their performance are kept fully invested at all times.

Within each of these categories of stocks on their "Supervised List," furthermore, a subset is defined of those "relatively best situated at present for new buying based on current market prices and other factors." Again per its established methodology on such matters, the HFD's portfolios for these three categories are constructed out of just these subsets.

Of the three lists over the 12 years through mid-1992, the "Income" list performed the best, gaining 123.2%. The "Long-Term Growth" portfolio gained 79.8% and the "Cyclical" portfolio gained 36.1% over the same period. (The Wilshire 5000, in contrast, gained 432.7% over this eight-year period.)

It is not immediately clear why these portfolios underperformed the market by such a margin. Part of the reason may be the fact that the composition of each list's subset of especially recommended stocks changed frequently, which led to a relatively large number of transactions in the portfolios the HFD constructed. Since each transaction caused commission costs to be deducted (1% each way, or 2% round-trip), this produced a not insignificant drag on performance.

How much of a difference does this make? In a study conducted over the first nine months of 1985, the HFD compared the portfolios constructed out of just this newsletter's most highly recommended stocks with hypothetical ones that were constructed out of all the stocks on their lists. The hypothetical ones gained an average of 11.5% over these nine months, as compared to 2.7% for the more narrowly constructed portfolios.

This isn't to say the HFD's methodology on such matters isn't proper. Presumably, this or any service doesn't downgrade a stock's status just because its potential falls behind other stocks by just 2% (which is the HFD's round-trip commission rate, equivalent to $1 on a $50 stock; see further discussion of this issue in the chapter on the HFD's methodology). Nevertheless, the HFD's performance figures suggest that the best way to take advantage of the service's recommendations is by concentrating on all the stocks on the newsletter's lists, not just those that they highlight as best situated for current purchase.

At the beginning of 1990, the HFD began following the convertible bonds and preferred stocks from this service's "Supervised List of Bonds and Preferred Stocks." As it did for the newsletter's other three "Supervised Lists," the HFD followed this list by constructing a portfolio that was fully invested and equally weighted among those securities rated most attractive for current purchase. Over the two and one-half years through mid-1992, this portfolio gained 6.5%, in contrast to 24.1% for the Wilshire 5000.

United & Babson Report (Average)

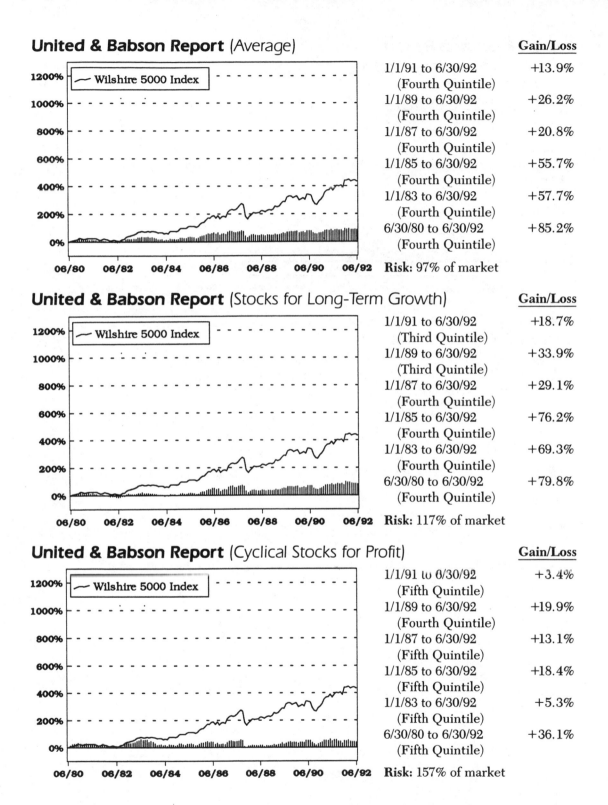

	Gain/Loss
1/1/91 to 6/30/92 (Fourth Quintile)	+13.9%
1/1/89 to 6/30/92 (Fourth Quintile)	+26.2%
1/1/87 to 6/30/92 (Fourth Quintile)	+20.8%
1/1/85 to 6/30/92 (Fourth Quintile)	+55.7%
1/1/83 to 6/30/92 (Fourth Quintile)	+57.7%
6/30/80 to 6/30/92 (Fourth Quintile)	+85.2%

Risk: 97% of market

United & Babson Report (Stocks for Long-Term Growth)

	Gain/Loss
1/1/91 to 6/30/92 (Third Quintile)	+18.7%
1/1/89 to 6/30/92 (Third Quintile)	+33.9%
1/1/87 to 6/30/92 (Fourth Quintile)	+29.1%
1/1/85 to 6/30/92 (Fourth Quintile)	+76.2%
1/1/83 to 6/30/92 (Fourth Quintile)	+69.3%
6/30/80 to 6/30/92 (Fourth Quintile)	+79.8%

Risk: 117% of market

United & Babson Report (Cyclical Stocks for Profit)

	Gain/Loss
1/1/91 to 6/30/92 (Fifth Quintile)	+3.4%
1/1/89 to 6/30/92 (Fourth Quintile)	+19.9%
1/1/87 to 6/30/92 (Fifth Quintile)	+13.1%
1/1/85 to 6/30/92 (Fifth Quintile)	+18.4%
1/1/83 to 6/30/92 (Fifth Quintile)	+5.3%
6/30/80 to 6/30/92 (Fifth Quintile)	+36.1%

Risk: 157% of market

United & Babson Report
(Stocks for the Income-Minded)

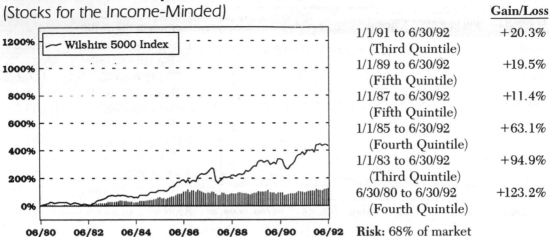

	Gain/Loss
1/1/91 to 6/30/92 (Third Quintile)	+20.3%
1/1/89 to 6/30/92 (Fifth Quintile)	+19.5%
1/1/87 to 6/30/92 (Fifth Quintile)	+11.4%
1/1/85 to 6/30/92 (Fourth Quintile)	+63.1%
1/1/83 to 6/30/92 (Third Quintile)	+94.9%
6/30/80 to 6/30/92 (Fourth Quintile)	+123.2%

Risk: 68% of market

United & Babson Report
(Supervised List of Convertible Bonds and Preferreds)

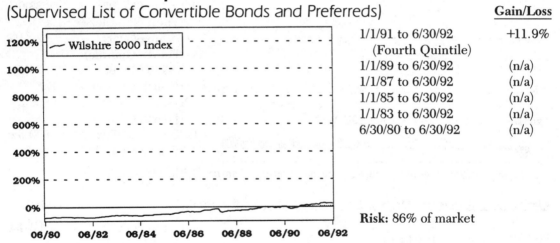

	Gain/Loss
1/1/91 to 6/30/92 (Fourth Quintile)	+11.9%
1/1/89 to 6/30/92	(n/a)
1/1/87 to 6/30/92	(n/a)
1/1/85 to 6/30/92	(n/a)
1/1/83 to 6/30/92	(n/a)
6/30/80 to 6/30/92	(n/a)

Risk: 86% of market

United Mutual Fund Selector

Address
Babson-United Building
101 Prescott St.
Wellesley Hills, MA
02181

Editor
Jack Walsh

Phone Number
617-235-0900

Subscription Rates
$ 7.00/3 issues
$125.00/year

Telephone Hotline
No

Money Management
No

Issue No. 588   June 30, 1992

Don't Switch Horses

While the first day of June's stock market trading set a new record for the *Dow* (3400+), the strength of the *Industrials* gave way to weakness as the month unfolded. To experience slippage in the wake of a record-setting performance is not unusual. In fact, the *Dow* set several intermittent highs during the first six months, and some profit taking has been a natural consequence. We regard profit taking as a healthy development, and not as a cause of concern.

Not all of the market barometers have been as vigorous as the *Dow*, and net asset value performances for many mutuals have been lackluster through the first five months. Nevertheless, we continue to anticipate more advances in the stock market this year, even allowing for occasional temporary dips. For the record, we feel the *Dow* could

In This Issue:
Supervised List Income Funds Reviewed
Changing Fees
Questions & Answers

touch 3600 before year's end. Having said that, we look forward to advancing net asset value comparisons for mutual funds, and would encourage not only *"staying the course"* but adding to your portfolio.

Mutual Fund Prospects — This *Selector* reviews the buys in the income category of our *Supervised List*. Those seeking income should consider buying one or more of the ten recommended funds. ■

The Changing Face Of Fees

Historically, fees or charges have been confusing for many mutual fund investors to sort out. High fees cut into investment returns, but help may be on the way. The *Securities and Exchange Commission* has proposed substantial changes with the hope of fostering price competition and cutting charges. However, these proposals/changes will require time to implement. In the meantime, fund companies are also attempting to foster business by changing the way fees are applied; and this may provide lower costs to some shareholders.

One recent example is part of the reorganization of the thirty-eight mutual funds of *Shearson Lehman Brothers Inc. Shearson* plans to introduce a new "variable or dual" fee program before the end of the year. Investors will chose whether to pay a traditional front-end sales commission or a back-end sales charge by buying A or B shares,

respectively. The A shares have no 12b-1 Plan fees. The B shares carry a contingent sales charge (i.e., the sales charge gradually declines, and is determined by how long you hold them), and a 12b-1 Plan fee. However, under the new dual fee structure, the B shares will automatically convert into A shares after eight years. And, at that time, the 12b-1 Plan fee would be eliminated. To the degree that new fee structures reduce the costs of mutual fund ownership, we applaud the changes whether by a fund family or by changing regulations.

Obviously, we continue to recommend that you "read the prospectus" because costs and expenses are spelled out there, and it is to your advantage to know them. Looking ahead, we expect more changes in fees; and for its part, the *Selector* will continue to analyze and point out the differences in expenses, costs and fees. ■

Vol. 24 No. 12   Babson-United Investment Advisors, Inc., 1992 — All rights reserved. Printed in U.S.A.   pages 133 through 144

The *United Mutual Fund Selector* is edited by Jack Walsh and published twice each month by Babson-United Investment Advisors, the same company that publishes *United & Babson Investment Report* (also reviewed in this *Guide*). A telephone hotline service is not provided.

The *Selector* is both a reference service on a large number of mutual funds (both load and no-load) as well as an advisory service focusing on the mutual fund selection decision. Once each month, for example, the service devotes eight or nine pages to reviewing the recent and long-term performance of all the funds on the list of those it follows, showing also those funds' current yield. In the alternate issue each month, the *Selector* updates its "Supervised List of Mutual Funds." This list is broken into four categories: "Aggressive Growth," "Growth," "Growth & Income" and "Income," and within each category, the newsletter indicates which fund(s) are "best suited for current purchase."

Though the *Selector* will comment on the stock market's prospects, those comments are not translated into allocation advice on the proper division of a portfolio between stocks and cash. Therefore, the portfolios the HFD constructs to track these four categories' performances always are fully invested.

These "Supervised Lists" contain both load and no-load funds. At times, however, the newsletter has told its subscribers that, other things being equal, there is no reason to choose a load fund over a no-load fund—and indeed that there is reason to choose the no-load fund instead. At other times, furthermore, the newsletter has said that in the event that subscribers don't know how long they will be holding a fund, they should buy only no-load funds. Therefore, per the HFD's methodology on such matters (which calls for including just those securities most highly rated by the service at any given time), the HFD constructs portfolios for their "Supervised Lists" out of those no-load or low-load funds that are rated "best suited for current purchase."

Over the six and one-half years through mid-1992, the average performance of these four portfolios was a gain of 92.4%, which contrasts with a 124.5% total return for the Wilshire 5000. The best performer was the newsletter's portfolio of "Aggressive Growth" funds, which gained 130.1% over these six and one-half years. The poorest performer was the newsletter's portfolio of "Income" funds, which gained 67.7%.

On average, this newsletter's lists of recommended mutual funds were less risky than the market as a whole. (Only the "Aggressive Growth" portfolio was riskier.) This partially explains the below-market performance, but not all: On a risk-adjusted basis, the newsletter still underperformed the market.

United Mutual Fund Selector (Average)

	Gain/Loss
1/1/91 to 6/30/92	+28.3%
(Second Quintile)	
1/1/89 to 6/30/92	+43.9%
(Second Quintile)	
1/1/87 to 6/30/92	+68.0%
(Second Quintile)	
1/1/85 to 6/30/92	(n/a)
1/1/83 to 6/30/92	(n/a)
6/30/80 to 6/30/92	(n/a)

Risk: 76% of market

United Mutual Fund Selector (Aggressive Growth Funds)

	Gain/Loss
1/1/91 to 6/30/92	+28.8%
(Second Quintile)	
1/1/89 to 6/30/92	+58.2%
(Second Quintile)	
1/1/87 to 6/30/92	+89.9%
(Second Quintile)	
1/1/85 to 6/30/92	(n/a)
1/1/83 to 6/30/92	(n/a)
6/30/80 to 6/30/92	(n/a)

Risk: 121% of market

United Mutual Fund Selector (Growth Funds)

	Gain/Loss
1/1/91 to 6/30/92	+31.9%
(Second Quintile)	
1/1/89 to 6/30/92	+42.7%
(Second Quintile)	
1/1/87 to 6/30/92	+60.3%
(Third Quintile)	
1/1/85 to 6/30/92	(n/a)
1/1/83 to 6/30/92	(n/a)
6/30/80 to 6/30/92	(n/a)

Risk: 94% of market

United Mutual Fund Selector (Growth & Income Funds)

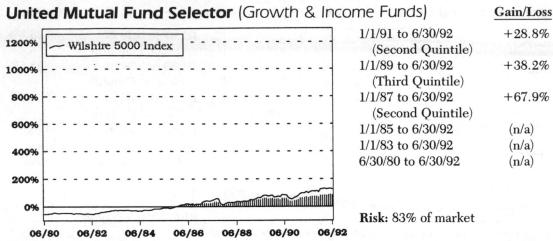

	Gain/Loss
1/1/91 to 6/30/92 (Second Quintile)	+28.8%
1/1/89 to 6/30/92 (Third Quintile)	+38.2%
1/1/87 to 6/30/92 (Second Quintile)	+67.9%
1/1/85 to 6/30/92	(n/a)
1/1/83 to 6/30/92	(n/a)
6/30/80 to 6/30/92	(n/a)

Risk: 83% of market

United Mutual Fund Selector (Income Funds)

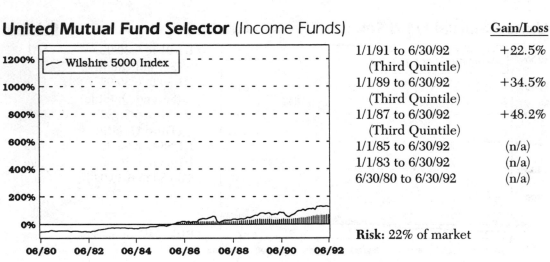

	Gain/Loss
1/1/91 to 6/30/92 (Third Quintile)	+22.5%
1/1/89 to 6/30/92 (Third Quintile)	+34.5%
1/1/87 to 6/30/92 (Third Quintile)	+48.2%
1/1/85 to 6/30/92	(n/a)
1/1/83 to 6/30/92	(n/a)
6/30/80 to 6/30/92	(n/a)

Risk: 22% of market

Value Line Convertibles

Address
711 Third Ave.
New York, NY 10017

Editor
Allan S. Lyons

Phone Number
800-634-3583

Subscription Rates
$ 39.50/8 issues
$475.00/year

Telephone Hotline
Yes

Money Management
Yes

Value Line Convertibles
...the all in one service for convertibles and warrants
Copyrighted 1992 by VALUE LINE PUBLISHING, INC 711 Third Avenue, New York, N.Y. 10017

VOL. 23 NO. 26 — PART I THE CONVERTIBLE STRATEGIST JULY 6, 1992

Break-Even Time

In our cover story this week, we look at how break-even time is calculated and its place in the evaluation of a convertible's attractiveness. Subscribers should note that, while we provide an issue's break-even time in the Spotlight section of Part I when it is especially recommended, the break-even time for every convertible covered in our service can be found in column 11 in Part II: The Convertible Evaluation Section.

Break-Even Time

In essence, break-even time measures the time required for a convertible's yield to offset its premium over conversion value. When investors choose a company's convertible rather than its common stock the choice usually involves a tradeoff. While the convertible will generally offer a higher current yield and more safety than its underlying common, it will also normally have less upside potential. Although a convertible will often trade at some premium over its conversion value (unless investors believe a call is likely), if the stock's price does not move much the premium can remain at a fairly constant level for a long time. In addition, as the common stock's price rises the premium over conversion value contracts, and the decrease in premium represents lost capital gains for the convertible holders. However, some investors assume that a high premium over conversion value translates into less profit potential than offered by the underlying stock. This is not necessarily the case as an issue trading at a high premium may provide a substantially higher yield. Take Seagate Technology, for example. Both the stock and the 6.75s2012 convertible bond are ranked 1 for performance, and the convertible is on our Especially Recommended List. Although the bond is 45% less risky, the question arises whether opting for the low risk of the bond is worth giving up the appreciation potential of the stock. In this case, the bond trades at a 112% premium over conversion value but offers a 9.5% current yield versus nil for the common. It will take 5.5 years for the higher coupon of the bond to offset the premium over conversion value. While it is true that in all likelihood investors who opt for the bond will fail to participate in 112% of

the rise in the common stock, over the next 5.5 years the bondholder would be fully compensated for the lost appreciation potential but also enjoy a 9.5% yield advantage during this time. Is this a good trade off? The ultimate decision will differ for each investor, but risk averse investors with a long term outlook might opt for the bond over the stock.

Calculating Break-Even Time

As shown in Figure 1, on page 188, the calculation of a convertible's break-even time is found by simply dividing the premium over conversion value by the difference in the convertible's annual income versus the common stock's. However, this calculation assumes that the common dividend stream will be constant and since common dividends can increase, decrease, or be eliminated completely, actual break-even times may differ from those calculated. As a result, investors should view the formula as only one step in the evaluation of a convertible which should always be used in conjunction with other information that is currently available.

In the figure, we calculate the break-even time of the Goodyear 6.875s2003 bond, currently on our Especially Recommended List. The bond is currently trading at $995.00, and is convertible into 12.461 common shares. With the common trading at $68.00, the bond has a conversion value of $847.35, and a premium over conversion value of about 17%. Since Goodyear pays a $0.40 yearly common dividend, the bond has a 6.3% yield advantage relative to the common (6.9% versus 0.6%). Using the formula in Figure 1 the breakeven of 2.35 years can be easily calculated. Again, for investors who purchase this Goodyear bond the break-even time

(Continued on Page 188)

NOTE: In keeping with our four-issue-per-month schedule, no issue was published last week. The last issue was published on June 22, 1992.

INSIDE

Factual material is obtained from sources believed to be reliable, but the publisher is not responsible for any errors or omissions contained herein.

Value Line Convertibles is published weekly by Value Line, Inc., which publishes a number of other investment newsletters as well (two of which are reviewed elsewhere in this *Guide*). The newsletter's Executive Editor is Allan Lyons. Beginning in 1987, the service inaugurated a weekly telephone hotline up-

date to give subscribers equal advance access to the buy and sell signals contained in the current issue.

The service is described as "the all-in-one service for convertibles and warrants." It rates and compares a universe of convertible bonds, convertible preferreds, and warrants, using a 1-to-5 rating scale (with "1" the best and "5" the worst). This rating system is broadly similar to, but not the same as, the more famous one that is employed by the *Value Line Investment Survey*.

In addition to rating its universe of securities on the 1-to-5 scale, the service highlights a subset of the securities rated "1" that "are likely to be easier to trade." This is an important additional criterion, because the bid-asked spreads on illiquid convertibles often are prohibitively high. The portfolio the HFD tracks to represent the newsletter's performance is constructed out of just these highlighted issues.

In addition, the newsletter does not advise subscribers on the proper division of a portfolio between the market and cash. Per the HFD's methodology on such matters, therefore, the HFD tracks a portfolio that is fully invested at all times. Over the six and one-half years through mid-1992, such a portfolio gained 188.2%, in contrast to 124.5% for the Wilshire 5000.

One of the theoretical advantages of investing in convertibles is that they provide downside protection. However, whatever other virtues this newsletter's approach may have, lessened downside protection doesn't seem to be one of them. During the month of the October 1987 crash, for example, the portfolio the HFD tracks for this newsletter lost more than the Wilshire 5000.

Value Line Convertibles

	Gain/Loss
1/1/91 to 6/30/92 (First Quintile)	+55.5%
1/1/89 to 6/30/92 (Second Quintile)	+63.0%
1/1/87 to 6/30/92 (First Quintile)	+115.8%
1/1/85 to 6/30/92	(n/a)
1/1/83 to 6/30/92	(n/a)
6/30/80 to 6/30/92	(n/a)

Risk: 74% of market

The Value Line Investment Survey

Address
711 Third Ave.
New York, NY 10017

Editor
Value Line, Inc.

Phone Number
800-634-3583

Subscription Rates
$ 55.00/10 issues
$525.00/year

Telephone Hotline
No

Money Management
Yes

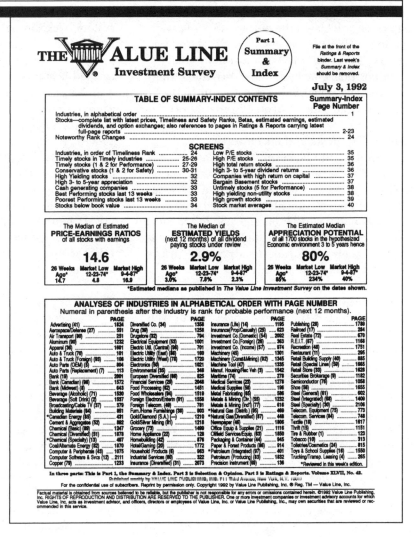

The *Value Line Investment Survey* has been published weekly since the 1930s, but its stock-rating system—which has received so much academic and investor attention—dates from the mid-1960s. In addition to providing ratings on a universe of about 1,700 stocks,

The *Value Line Investment Survey* is an encyclopedic reference source for those 1,700 companies.

Out of their 1,700-stock universe, *Value Line* selects 100 each week that it believes have the greatest performance potential over the ensuing 12 months; they receive a "1" rating for "Timeliness." (*Value Line* categorizes the remaining 1,600 stocks in its universe into four other groupings with progressively less upside potential.) *Value Line* has calculated the performance of a portfolio of "Group 1" stocks since the rating system's inception in 1965, assuming that its composition changed weekly as the ratings shifted. They claim that the "Group 1" stocks achieved an annual average price appreciation of 21.7%, far in excess of the average of the 1,700 stocks in their universe.

Significantly, however, the *Value Line* results do not take into account transaction costs, nor do they factor in the poorer executions an investor unfailingly gets when trying to act along with thousands of other subscribers. (Only recently did they begin to calculate their performance with the prices prevailing on the Fridays when most subscribers receive their issues.) The HFD's calculations, of course, do take commissions into account and the HFD uses prices that prevail after a newsletter's recommendations have hit the market. Not surprisingly, therefore, the HFD's performance figures are lower than what *Value Line* itself reports.

The HFD has calculated since 1983 the performance of a portfolio constructed out of the 100 stocks rated "1" for "Timeliness" by *Value Line*. This portfolio changed composition each week as a new issue of the newsletter was received: Those stocks downgraded from "Group 1" were sold and those newly upgraded were bought. It has been a fairly active portfolio, with a turnover ratio of 200% or more.

Owing to the fact that the HFD's figures over the post-1983 period came in at a fairly consistent discount to the figures *Value Line* itself calculated, and owing also to the fact that the HFD received numerous requests to report performance for *Value Line*'s ranking system back through 1980, the HFD has estimated what the newsletter's 1980-82 performance would have been had the HFD tracked it independently. The HFD took the average proportion by which its own figures came in below *Value Line*'s over the 1983-86 period, and applied that discount to their 1980-82 performance figures.

Beginning in 1988, *The Value Line Investment Survey* started providing allocation advice on the proper division of a portfolio between the stock market and cash. The HFD's figures from that point onward reflect this recommended division. Prior to then, the HFD assumed the portfolio was fully invested at all times.

For the entire 12 years through mid-1992, the HFD reports that *The Value Line Investment Survey* is in second place among all those newsletters followed over this period of time, with a gain of 620.7%. The Wilshire 5000, in comparison, gained 432.7% over this same period of time.

Value Line also reports on another way of using their ranking system which involves fewer transactions. This less active approach calls for buying the 100 "Group 1" stocks at the beginning of the year and then holding them for 12 months, even if the stocks are downgraded during the year. The HFD's data suggest that in most periods such an approach will perform about as well as the weekly rotating portfolio, and in some cases even better.

The Value Line Investment Survey

	Gain/Loss
1/1/91 to 6/30/92 (Second Quintile)	+38.7%
1/1/89 to 6/30/92 (Second Quintile)	+64.9%
1/1/87 to 6/30/92 (Second Quintile)	+86.9%
1/1/85 to 6/30/92 (Second Quintile)	+189.7%
1/1/83 to 6/30/92 (First Quintile)	+257.0%
6/30/80 to 6/30/92 (First Quintile)	+620.7%

Risk: 109% of market

The Value Line OTC Special Situations Service

Address
711 Third Ave.
New York, NY 10017

Editor
Peter A. Shraga

Phone Number
800-634-3583

Subscription Rates
$ 39.00/6 issues
$390.00/year

Telephone Hotline
No

Money Management
Yes

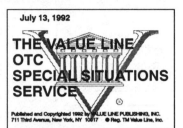

July 13, 1992

THE VALUE LINE OTC SPECIAL SITUATIONS SERVICE ®

Published and Copyrighted 1992 by VALUE LINE PUBLISHING, INC.
711 Third Avenue, New York, NY 10017 ● Reg. TM Value Line, Inc.

The 1019 Special Situations recommended in the 40 years since this service has been published — both successful and unsuccessful — have, on average, outperformed the Dow-Jones Industrial Average during comparable time periods by 135.7%.

Business: Fleet Call, Inc. is the second largest operator of Specialized Mobile Radio (SMR) systems in the United States, and the largest in Los Angeles, San Francisco, New York, Chicago, Dallas, and Houston. The company serves 136,000 subscribers on its SMR systems. Fleet Call is authorized by the FCC to build Digital Mobile networks which will provide high quality dispatch, mobile phone, data and paging services. President & C.E.O.: Brian D. McAuley. Address: 201 Route 17 North, Rutherford, NJ 07070 (201-438-1400).

CAPITAL STRUCTURE as of 3/31/92
Debt: $1.03 million   Pfd Stock: None
Shareholders' Equity $191.1 million (55,337,487 shares)

	1988	1989	1990	1991	1992
Revenues ($mill)	17.3	36.3	53.9	52.5	50
Profit Margin ●	--	--	--	--	--
Tax Rate	--	--	--	--	--
Earn'gs per sh ●	d.20	d.36	d.30	d.58	NMF
Shs Outst'g (mill)	21.2	21.2	21.2	55.3	59.0
Div'ds per sh	--	--	--	--	Nil
Book Value sh ●	.59	1.32	1.11	3.45	3.85
% Earn'd Tot Cap	--	--	--	--	--
% Earn'd Net W	--	--	--	--	--
W'rk'g Cap ($mill)	--	--	d8.03	2.71	
Current Ratio	--	--	.56	1.16	
Avg Ann'l P/E					

Fiscal Year Begins	QUARTERLY REVENUES ($mill.)				Full Fiscal Year
	June 30	Sept. 30	Dec. 31	Mar. 31	
1989					36.3
1990	13.5	14.4	14.2	11.8	53.9
1991	13.7	13.6	12.5	12.7	52.5
1992					50

Fiscal Year Begins	QUARTERLY EARNINGS (Per Share)				Full Fiscal Year
	June 30	Sept. 30	Dec. 31	Mar. 31	
1989					d.36
1990	d.11	d.05	.15	d.29	d.30
1991	d.21	d.15	d.14	d.08	d.58
1992					NMF

● -Pretax. ● -Excludes extraordinary charge: 8¢/sh. in 1989; 3¢/sh. in 1990; 47¢/sh. in 1991. ● -Includes intangibles: $3.38/sh. in 1988; $7.79/sh. in 1989; $8.19/sh. in 1990; $3.90/sh. in 1991.

Factual material is obtained from sources believed to be reliable, but the publisher is not responsible for any errors or omissions contained herein. ©1992 Value Line Publishing, Inc. RIGHTS OF REPRODUCTION AND DISTRIBUTION ARE RESERVED TO THE PUBLISHER. One or more investment companies or investment advisory accounts for which Value Line, Inc. acts as investment adviser, and officers, directors or employes of Value Line, Inc., or Value Line Publishing, Inc. may own securities which are reviewed or recommended in this service.

A- 919

NEW RECOMMENDATION • A-919 to A-922

FLEET CALL, INC.

Common Stock—Recent Price: 10⅛

Traded: OTC—CALL

The proliferation of wireless communications in this country has been quite dramatic. Cellular telephones, once an anomaly, are now commonplace. Though the first cellular systems became operational only in 1983, an estimated 6.4 million units were in use by mid-1991. This burgeoning industry traces its roots to a 1970 Federal Communications Commission (FCC) action that allocated a portion of the radio spectrum to cellular and other types of wireless communication services. Beyond spawning the cellular industry, this ruling gave rise to a type of private radio service known as Specialized Mobile Radio (SMR). While cellular has taken flight, SMR, due to a variety of technological shortcomings, has largely been resigned to use within private radio systems—"dispatch" networks—in which dispersed field personnel such as taxi drivers or service personnel communicate with a central dispatch point or with each other. With the emergence of digital technology, however, an SMR provider can now overcome these technological limitations and offer a full range of wireless communications services. This issue's New Recommendation, *Fleet Call, Inc.*, is poised to do just that.

Fleet Call is the nation's second largest SMR provider, with a current subscriber roster of 136,000. The company's services are concentrated in six major metropolitan areas: Los Angeles, San Francisco, New York, Chicago, Dallas, and Houston. To this point the company has expanded largely through acquisitions, finding many suitable candidates within the highly fragmented SMR industry.

Like other SMR providers, the company has hitherto been unable to offer cellular-like telephone service to the broader market due to the capacity limitations of analog SMR technology. In February of 1991, the company received authorization from the FCC to convert its six markets to more advanced "Digital Mobile" networks. With digital technology, a caller's voice is converted to a stream of digits, which are then compressed before being transmitted. The use of digital technology—and of two capacity-expanding techniques, time-division multiple access and frequency reuse—will, in the company's estimation, expand the capacity of its systems by at least 15 times. This added capacity will allow Fleet Call to offer a full range of wireless communications services, including cellular-like telephone service and paging in addition to the company's traditional dispatch services. To be sure, the cellular providers are also planning to convert their systems to digital technology over the next decade.

The Value Line OTC Special Situations Service is published twice each month by Value Line, Inc. (the publishers of a number of other investment newsletters as well, two of which are reviewed elsewhere in this Guide).

The service is not supplemented by a telephone hotline.

The *Service* takes an exclusively fundamental approach to analyzing companies. Each issue highlights one new special situation and provides follow-up advice on all previous special situations that have yet to be closed out. This follow-up includes a rating for each stock on a scale from "especially recommended" down to "hold" and "sell." The stocks recommended in this *Service* rarely are included in the 1,700-stock universe of its companion service, *The Value Line Investment Survey*, and their rating systems are quite different.

Beginning in 1988, the *Service* started providing allocation advice on the proper division of a portfolio between stocks and cash. The HFD's performance figures for this newsletter after that point reflect whatever allocation the newsletter recommended, and reflect a fully invested portfolio for the period prior to then.

Per its methodology on such matters, the HFD has constructed a portfolio for *The*

Value Line OTC Special Situations Service that invests in those stocks that they rate as "especially recommended." This portfolio did very well in the last half of 1980 (it was the number one performer during that period among those newsletters the HFD then was following) but lagged the market during the middle years of the decade of the 1980s. During the last years of the 1980s, however, the newsletter picked up steam again, such that for the entire 12 years through mid-1992, it was ahead of the market (498.5% versus 432.7%).

The approach taken by this letter is a risky one, though. In fact, after taking this high risk into account, its risk-adjusted performance actually was below the market's over these 12 years.

The Value Line OTC Special Situations Service

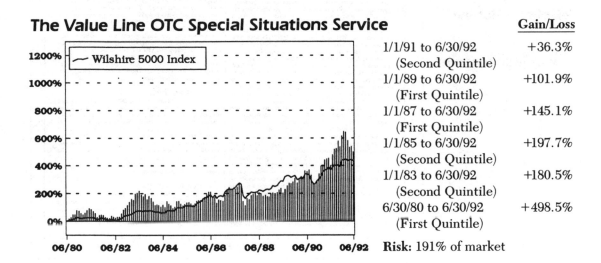

	Gain/Loss
1/1/91 to 6/30/92 (Second Quintile)	+36.3%
1/1/89 to 6/30/92 (First Quintile)	+101.9%
1/1/87 to 6/30/92 (First Quintile)	+145.1%
1/1/85 to 6/30/92 (Second Quintile)	+197.7%
1/1/83 to 6/30/92 (Second Quintile)	+180.5%
6/30/80 to 6/30/92 (First Quintile)	+498.5%

Risk: 191% of market

The Volume Reversal Survey

Address

P.O. Box 1451
Sedona, AZ 86336

Editor

Mark Leibovit

Phone Number

602-282-1275

Subscription Rates

$ 80.00/2 months
$360.00/year

Telephone Hotline

Yes

Money Management

No

Mark Leibovit

The Volume Reversal Survey ™
SINCE 1979

Prepared
On the Evening
Of: Sunday, June 28, 1992
VOLUME 14 NUMBER 438

A Comprehensive Guide to Volume Trends in the Major Markets

CALL <u>WALL STREET WEEK'S</u> #2 ELF (OCTOBER '91) FOR #1 ADVICE! AT 1-900-820-0877 FOR COMMENTARY ON STOCKS, OPTIONS, AND FUTURES. DON'T FORGET ABOUT THE 'WALL STREET BROKERAGE FIRM UPDATE' AT 11:15 A.M. (EASTERN). <u>$2.50 PER MINUTE.</u>

LONG AND WRONG!

1. STOCK MARKET -

If you're looking for an upbeat market newsletter, call Fidelity or Merrill Lynch or listen to my friend, John Templeton. You won't find it here! Stocks greeted the 8 week cycle on June 22 with a reaction low on declining volume and an uptick in some internal indicators. Except for the OEX, the June 22 lows held late last week in an apparent retest. Am I bullish? No! Can we rally. I suppose. Bearish sentiment has now taken hold. **My mid- January sell signal is looking awfully good.** Brokers phones stopped ringing, investors are now a little dismayed with the negative performance of their holdings this year, and the stock market is beginning to realize what I've known all year - talk of economic recovery is probably humbug. Fictitious government numbers, gullible financial reporters, overzealous money managers, greed. Yes, the answer is all of the above. As the expression goes, "in a bear market the bears are right". This means that negative sentiment isn't necessarily a contrary indicator. Using my 'inverted' Annual Forecast Model, we're due to bottom anywhere between now and late July and early August and experience a rally of indeterminate quality or amplitude into September. Beyond that, watch out below. In the meantime, it's 'slim pickens' trying to find stocks I like. I truly believe this tells us the true state of the market, i.e, lousy. Yes, IBM is rallying, but it's hard to imagine this stock providing anywhere near the kind of leadership the Street is hoping for. General Motors is losing money but finds plenty of buyers for its stock. Though technicals say they can both move higher, caveat emptor! This is also a time of potential great personal risk. Geophysical catastrophes, rioting, a level of tension rising in the country are all examples. Take care, my friends.

2. T-BONDS, T-BILLS, UTILITIES

I continue to remain bullish on these markets. Deflation, an extremely lethargic business climate, the need to keep interest payments on the national debt to a minimum, and election year (or should I say manipulative) forces should create the desired result. How low can interest rates go? There's a long way from 3 3/4% to zero. I long ago joked that we might have to PAY Uncle Sam to hold our money. With a real risk of an interest- suspension moratorium (commonly known as a default), it's not a joke anymore. Back to the day to day world. The most recent volume in the T-Bonds was positive on Wednesday/Thursday as we saw two days of increased volume to the upside. A breakout above 101/22 (the June 18 high) would be reassuring as volume slowed into that level and caused me some short-term concern. A close under 99/20 and, particularly, 98/15 could open up risks back down toward 9600 and throw a lot of cold water on my bullish forecast. I still feel new all-time highs (above 105/20) could be seen in the months ahead. T-Bills also experienced some indigestion as they touched 9639 on declining volume on June 18. Critical support lies at 9601. A close over 9639 and especially 9649 would be a big plus. The DOW Utilities continue to be hit with a series of negatives. In addition to the previously reported doubletop and Negative VR at the 215.00 level, two more Negative VRs were posted, one on June 17 off 216.26 and another one on June 24 off 214.25. The decline has carried this market to 206.00 and 199.67. Next support lies at 206.00 and 199.67. My bias remains for a positive resolution but, short-term, the tape says otherwise.

3. CURRENCIES -

The Dollar continued its free fall and volume remains negative. My analysis still points to the probability that we will not only take out the January low at 8387 but could work down toward the 7600 level over the intermediate term. It only makes sense to assume the D-Mark, Swiss Franc and Yen will trend higher in this environment. A late April upside projection points as high as 6900. A new upside projection was formed this past week toward 7400. Everything seems to be 'in-gear'. I'm continuing to use a best guess estimate for the Swiss Franc to 7500 and Yen to 8500 until more solid measurements are flashed in volume analysis.

4. GOLD & SILVER -

Gold reached $346.60 on June 23 but couldn't manage to stay there. Unfortunately, one of the reasons was a slowing of upside volume pointing to the loss of upside momentum. It's too early to tell whether this formation will have greater bearish consequences. Gold shares, with the exception of

The Volume Reversal Survey is published every three weeks by Mark Leibovit and is supplemented by a nightly telephone hotline update. Leibovit's approach to the market is almost exclusively technical, and "Volume Reversal" is the name of his particular approach to the analysis of price and volume statistics.

He is one of the "elves" whose market forecasts are polled each week by Public Television's "Wall Street Week With Louis Rukeyser."

Leibovit also has an additional "900"-number telephone hotline service that is updated several times during each business day.

The HFD does not track the recommendations made on this additional hotline because it is the HFD's policy not to call a hotline more than once per day. Up until mid-1990 this didn't pose a problem in tracking Leibovit's model portfolio, since the changes he recommended for that portfolio were made on his nightly hotline updates. In the summer of 1990 this changed, however, when Leibovit began using his "900"-number updates during the day to make changes to his portfolio. At that point the HFD was forced to stop following the portfolio. Over the period of time from the beginning of 1987 through the end of August 1990 for which the HFD has data, this portfolio lost 57.3%, in contrast to a 42.3% gain for the Wilshire 5000.

What accounts for this below-market performance? As far as the HFD data permit a conclusion, Leibovit's security selection is largely the cause. Had every one of the stocks Leibovit recommended for these three years and eight months performed exactly as the Wilshire 5000 did during the times they were owned, his portfolio would have gained 41.5%. The fact that this more or less equals the Wilshire 5000's return over this period means that Leibovit's security selections were largely responsible for the portfolio's 57.3% loss. Another contributing factor in Leibovit's big loss was commission costs, which can be traced to the fact that his portfolio's turnover rate was very high (over 300% in one of the months the HFD followed it, for example).

When the HFD was forced to discontinue its tracking of Leibovit's model portfolio, it began to focus instead on Leibovit's timing advice for investors in index mutual funds. On the occasions he has been bullish, Leibovit has recommended a position in the Vanguard Index 500 fund (sometimes on margin when he is particularly bullish). A portfolio that followed just Leibovit's index fund recommendations gained 93.4% over the five and one-half years through mid-1992, essentially equaling the 93.3% return of the Wilshire 5000. The fact that this portfolio did far better than his model portfolio suggests that the preferable way to follow Leibovit's newsletter is by focusing on his timing advice.

The Volume Reversal Survey (Average)

	Gain/Loss
1/1/91 to 6/30/92 (Third Quintile)	+22.4%
1/1/89 to 6/30/92 (Fifth Quintile)	+10.1%
1/1/87 to 6/30/92 (Fifth Quintile)	+4.9%
1/1/85 to 6/30/92	(n/a)
1/1/83 to 6/30/92	(n/a)
6/30/80 to 6/30/92	(n/a)

Risk: 59% of market

The Volume Reversal Survey (Index Fund Portfolio)

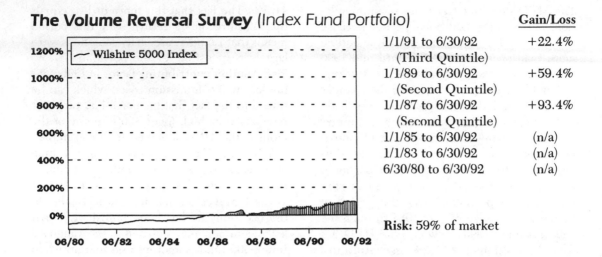

	Gain/Loss
1/1/91 to 6/30/92 (Third Quintile)	+22.4%
1/1/89 to 6/30/92 (Second Quintile)	+59.4%
1/1/87 to 6/30/92 (Second Quintile)	+93.4%
1/1/85 to 6/30/92	(n/a)
1/1/83 to 6/30/92	(n/a)
6/30/80 to 6/30/92	(n/a)

Risk: 59% of market

The Wall Street Digest

Address
One Sarasota Tower,
  #602
Two N. Tamiami Trail
Sarasota, FL 34236

Editor
Donald Rowe

Phone Number
813-954-5500

Subscription Rates
$150.00/year

Telephone Hotline
No

Money Management
No

THE WALL STREET DIGEST ONE SARASOTA TOWER   SARASOTA, FL 34236   813-954-5500

July 1992

TIMING MODEL PRODUCES SELL SIGNAL
PRIMARY MARKET TREND IS STILL UP

Our Carnegie Market Timing Model produced a -1 sell signal on Wednesday, June 17th. This sell signal is a temporary interruption of the strong primary uptrend of the market. We do not know when to expect a buy signal because nervousness about the Japanese Stock Market and the surging popularity of Ross Perot overwhelmed a growing number of very positive fundamental indicators that will eventually push the market much higher.

The Japanese market suddenly fell to a 5-1/2 year low and pulled all of the major global stock markets down. That was enough to produce selling on Wall Street.

Ross Perot adds another "uncertain factor" to Wall Street's nervousness because the polls say he could defeat President Bush and Governor Clinton today. Yet, no one knows what he plans to do about the major campaign issues. These are very temporary problems for the market. As investors, we have many reasons to be very optimistic.

Interest rates are low, the Fed is still accommodative, the recession is ending, and automotive and housing sales are increasing.

There is $3.7 trillion in cash equivalents in the U.S. financial system, money managers are nervously holding enough cash to push the market up another 100 to 150 points, and the U.S. is the only military and economic super power today with no challengers in sight.

The low U.S. dollar and an expensive Japanese yen will allow most Americans to substantially increase their living standards during the 1990s.

During the last two years while the yen was rising against the U.S. dollar, the Japanese Stock Market has lost over $1.8 trillion in value. The decline in Japanese real estate values may be even higher. Meanwhile, China, with one-fifth of the worlds' population, is booming. President Bush has very wisely maintained civil relations with China.

Exports to China are booming again, and American corporation are opening more doors to supply Western goods and services to the world's largest consumer market.

Encouraging things are happening in Europe, but they are inconsequential compared to what is quietly happening between China (population: 1.2 billion) and the U.S. (population: 250 million). The next great Super Boom has just begun. The next ten years will be the most prosperous period in American history.

The U.S. Stock Market is still the single best investment area, but wait for our buy signal.

WALL STREET'S MOST WIDELY READ INVESTMENT AND FINANCIAL SERVICE.

The Wall Street Digest is published monthly and is edited by Donald Rowe. Rowe also offers a telephone hotline update service to supplement his advice between issues of his newsletter, but it is provided to subscribers only for an additional subscription fee. Since the HFD's methodology on such matters is to follow hotline recommendations only in the event that they are provided to subscribers at no extra charge, Rowe's hotline is not monitored. Rowe also edits a mutual fund newsletter called *The Wall Street Digest Mutual Fund Advisor* (reviewed elsewhere in this *Guide*).

A substantial portion of each 16-page newsletter is devoted to discussing a broad range of financial-planning issues, everything from the purchase of real estate to tax planning. A couple of pages are devoted to specific recommendations, which since the beginning of 1985 (when the HFD began monitoring its performance) have primarily been in the stock market (but which also have included mutual funds and bonds). Rowe rates each stock on his recommended list a "buy," a "hold," or a "sell," and per its methodology on such matters, the HFD constructs a portfolio whose stock market portion includes just the "buy"-rated stocks.

In addition, Rowe recommends that all subscribers place a 15% trailing stop loss on each of his stock picks. The HFD's portfolio follows this advice faithfully, selling out any stock that drops 15% below the high reached since Rowe first recommended it. Inexplicably, Rowe catches only a minority of the occa-

sions on which these stops are triggered, so the HFD often is forced to repurchase stopped-out stocks upon receipt of subsequent issues and the discovery that Rowe still believes the stocks are in his portfolio. For the seven and one-half years through mid-1992, during which time the Wilshire 5000 gained 197.6%, *The Wall Street Digest*'s model stock portfolio gained just 33.7%, according to the HFD.

In 1989 *The Wall Street Digest* inaugurated a separate mutual fund portfolio. Over the three and one-half years through mid-1990, according to the HFD, this portfolio gained 31.6%, as compared to 60.3% for the Wilshire 5000. Overall, taking into account both portfolios and the fact that one has existed for less time than the other, the newsletter underperformed the Wilshire 5000 over the seven and one-half years through mid-1992 by a 42.8% to 197.6% margin.

The Wall Street Digest (Average)

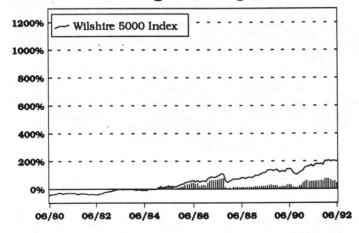

	Gain/Loss
1/1/91 to 6/30/92 (Fourth Quintile)	+13.4%
1/1/89 to 6/30/92 (Fourth Quintile)	+24.9%
1/1/87 to 6/30/92 (Fifth Quintile)	+15.7%
1/1/85 to 6/30/92 (Fifth Quintile)	+42.8%
1/1/83 to 6/30/92	(n/a)
6/30/80 to 6/30/92	(n/a)

Risk: 144% of market

The Wall Street Digest (Stock and Bond Portfolio)

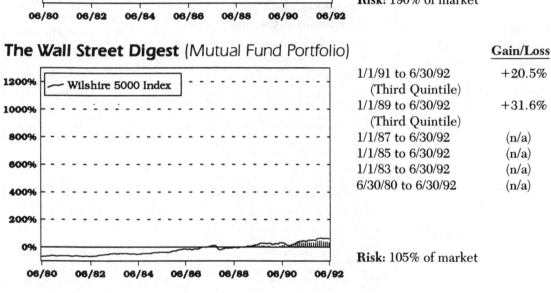

	Gain/Loss
1/1/91 to 6/30/92	+6.0%
(Fifth Quintile)	
1/1/89 to 6/30/92	+17.0%
(Fifth Quintile)	
1/1/87 to 6/30/92	+8.4%
(Fifth Quintile)	
1/1/85 to 6/30/92	+33.7%
(Fifth Quintile)	
1/1/83 to 6/30/92	(n/a)
6/30/80 to 6/30/92	(n/a)

Risk: 190% of market

The Wall Street Digest (Mutual Fund Portfolio)

	Gain/Loss
1/1/91 to 6/30/92	+20.5%
(Third Quintile)	
1/1/89 to 6/30/92	+31.6%
(Third Quintile)	
1/1/87 to 6/30/92	(n/a)
1/1/85 to 6/30/92	(n/a)
1/1/83 to 6/30/92	(n/a)
6/30/80 to 6/30/92	(n/a)

Risk: 105% of market

The Wall Street Digest
Mutual Fund Advisor

Address
One Sarasota Tower,
  #602
Two N. Tamiami Trail
Sarasota, FL 34236

Editors
Donald Rowe and
  Patricia M. Rowe

Phone Number
813-954-5500

Subscription Rates
$150.00/year

Telephone Hotline
No

Money Management
No

The Wall Street Digest   August 1992

Mutual Fund Advisor
——— THE TOP PERFORMING MUTUAL FUNDS ———

Cash Is Building On The Sidelines - An Upside Breakout Is Coming

Nervous institutions and money managers are building huge sums of cash while waiting for the market to signal the next move.

Aggressive growth fund managers have 20 - 26% cash, and they are nervous because they are not paid to manage cash.

The NASDAQ short interest is another positive factor. The number of OTC shares sold short in expectation of a market drop reached another record last week. Sentiment is bearish and that is another positive factor because the market seldom accommodates the majority.

If you examine the market factors that are usually in place before a major move up, you have to be bullish. The fundamentals are positive and still improving.

The technicals which include, but are not limited to negative momentum, advance/ declines and money flow will probably turn around and produce a buy signal in July when second quarter earnings are released.

GDP (Gross Domestic Product) growth was slower in the second quarter than the 2.7% gain in the first quarter. Even so, we doubt that growth was disappointing enough to produce a pullback to Dow 2000 as some analysts are forecasting.

Wall Street is nervous about the soaring federal debt, grid lock in Washington, and Mr. Perot's opposition to the free-trade agreement with Mexico.

In recent years U.S. exports to Mexico have grown from $12 billion to over $33 billion a year. This growth is just the beginning if we lower trade barriers. Mr. Perot says he is opposed to the free-trade agreement because it will cost too many American jobs. Mr. Perot does not understand that rising exports to Mexico serves to create U.S. jobs. How many American workers helped produce $33 billion in American made products to ship to Mexico? Wall Street thinks Mr. Perot is a protectionist and will not support him.

President Bush is doing all of the right things to open the doors to free trade around the globe which creates American jobs. For that reason alone, he will receive Wall Street's vote on Election Day.

In the meantime, the technicals are pointing to a higher stock market. All that is needed now is a catalyst to trigger the next rush into the market and "run the OTC shorts."

We think better than expected second quarter earnings will push the market 100 to 200 points higher. Now is the time to position your money in preparation for our buy signal which could come at any time.

No-Load Funds Generally Cheaper To Hold

The 100% No-Load Mutual Fund Council's study on fund expenses found that no-load funds as a group have lower expenses than either load funds or those that charge 12b-1 distribution fees.

As long as you are getting a decent return, why should you care about expenses? No one really knows, investors or money managers, what kind of return they will end the year with, especially in a stock fund. However, if you begin by assuming a certain rate of return, the effects of various expenses become clearer.

For example, $10,000 invested in a no-load fund with an average annual return of 15% would after 20 years generate $163,655 in total return (capital gains and dividends reinvested in fund). If a 0.25% 12b-1 fee is placed on the same fund, the total return would be reduced to $156,690, or $6975 less.

THE MUTUAL FUND ADVISOR One Sarasota Tower Sarasota, FL 34236   813-954-5500

The Wall Street Digest Mutual Fund Advisor is published monthly by Donald Rowe, who also publishes *The Wall Street Digest* (which is reviewed elsewhere in this volume). Rowe offers a separate telephone hotline update service to supplement his advice between issues of his newsletter, but it is provided only for an additional subscription fee. Pursuant to the HFD's methodology on such matters, therefore, this hotline is not monitored.

Though this newsletter focuses primarily on timing and fund selection within the equity markets, at times Rowe also will advise subscribers to invest a portion of their portfolios in bond funds. When the HFD began following the newsletter at the beginning of 1990, Rowe offered a total of nine portfolios: In addition to the six graphed here, he recommended a "Total Return," a "Global Equity," and an "International Equity" portfolio. Though these three have since been discontinued, their performances are included in the data for this newsletter's average.

Over the two and one-half years through mid-1992, the HFD calculates that the newsletter's portfolios gained an average of 6.1%, in contrast to 24.1% for the Wilshire 5000. Only a portion of this below-market performance can be accounted for by the fact that the newsletter's strategy has below-average risk. Thus, on a risk-adjusted basis as well, the newsletter underperformed the market.

The culprit in this underperformance appears to be the newsletter's fund selection. On a timing-only basis, for example, the HFD calculates that the newsletter slightly outperformed the market: A portfolio that alternated between hypothetical shares of the Wilshire 5000 and cash on Rowe's timing signals gained 26.1% over these 30 months, in contrast to 24.1% for the Wilshire 5000 and an average of 6.1% for Rowe's model portfolios. This means that the particular funds Rowe recommended underperformed the Wilshire 5000 during those times he advised subscribers to be invested in the stock market.

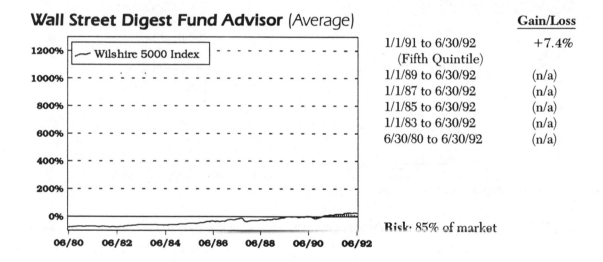

Wall Street Digest Fund Advisor (Average)

	Gain/Loss
1/1/91 to 6/30/92	+7.4%
(Fifth Quintile)	
1/1/89 to 6/30/92	(n/a)
1/1/87 to 6/30/92	(n/a)
1/1/85 to 6/30/92	(n/a)
1/1/83 to 6/30/92	(n/a)
6/30/80 to 6/30/92	(n/a)

Risk: 85% of market

Wall Street Digest Fund Advisor (Aggressive Growth)

Gain/Loss

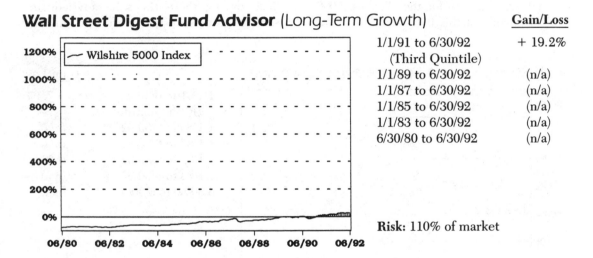

1/1/91 to 6/30/92	+ 14.3%
(Fourth Quintile)	
1/1/89 to 6/30/92	(n/a)
1/1/87 to 6/30/92	(n/a)
1/1/85 to 6/30/92	(n/a)
1/1/83 to 6/30/92	(n/a)
6/30/80 to 6/30/92	(n/a)

Risk: 124% of market

Wall Street Digest Fund Advisor (Long-Term Growth)

Gain/Loss

1/1/91 to 6/30/92	+ 19.2%
(Third Quintile)	
1/1/89 to 6/30/92	(n/a)
1/1/87 to 6/30/92	(n/a)
1/1/85 to 6/30/92	(n/a)
1/1/83 to 6/30/92	(n/a)
6/30/80 to 6/30/92	(n/a)

Risk: 110% of market

Wall Street Digest Fund Advisor (Growth & Income)

Gain/Loss

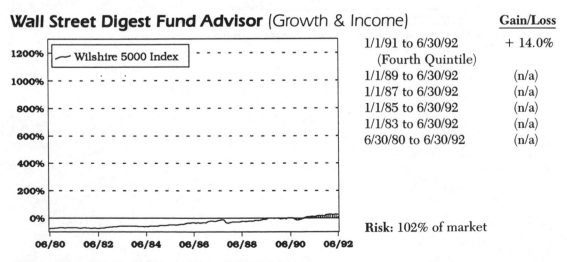

1/1/91 to 6/30/92	+ 14.0%
(Fourth Quintile)	
1/1/89 to 6/30/92	(n/a)
1/1/87 to 6/30/92	(n/a)
1/1/85 to 6/30/92	(n/a)
1/1/83 to 6/30/92	(n/a)
6/30/80 to 6/30/92	(n/a)

Risk: 102% of market

Wall Street Digest Fund Advisor (Sector)

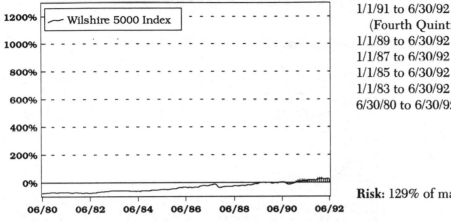

	Gain/Loss
1/1/91 to 6/30/92 (Fourth Quintile)	+ 14.1%
1/1/89 to 6/30/92	(n/a)
1/1/87 to 6/30/92	(n/a)
1/1/85 to 6/30/92	(n/a)
1/1/83 to 6/30/92	(n/a)
6/30/80 to 6/30/92	(n/a)

Risk: 129% of market

Wall Street Digest Fund Advisor (Income)

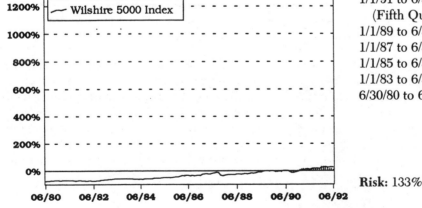

	Gain/Loss
1/1/91 to 6/30/92 (Fourth Quintile)	+ 16.4%
1/1/89 to 6/30/92	(n/a)
1/1/87 to 6/30/92	(n/a)
1/1/85 to 6/30/92	(n/a)
1/1/83 to 6/30/92	(n/a)
6/30/80 to 6/30/92	(n/a)

Risk: 79% of market

Wall Street Digest Fund Advisor (Top No-Loads)

	Gain/Loss
1/1/91 to 6/30/92 (Fifth Quintile)	+ 6.0%
1/1/89 to 6/30/92	(n/a)
1/1/87 to 6/30/92	(n/a)
1/1/85 to 6/30/92	(n/a)
1/1/83 to 6/30/92	(n/a)
6/30/80 to 6/30/92	(n/a)

Risk: 133% of market

The Wall Street Generalist

Address
MarketMetrics, Inc.
630 South Orange Ave.
Suite 104
Sarasota, FL 34236

Editor
Ray Hines

Phone Number
813-366-5645

Subscription Rates
$ 90.00/6 months
$160.00/year

Telephone Hotline
Yes

Money Management
Yes

THE WALL STREET Generalist

Editor - Ray Hines   Volume 10, No. 9 July 7, 1992

Rate Rally

Conditions appear in place for the market to do the unexpected soon, and stage a late summer rally up to the vicinity of the yearly highs. I say this because my work shows more underlying positives than is evident on the surface.

The Federal Reserve continues with extremely "easy" monetary policy, giving interest rates another notch lower since last issue. These lower rates will continue to put much pressure on short-term savings to move to attractive alternatives. I predict that by the end of the third quarter, money market and short-term CD rates will be below 3 per cent.

The very slow economic recovery present now is actually helping this process, because if economic recovery were more robust, more of these short-term savings would be invested in business projects. With the economy staying slow, funds are being parked in liquid financial assets more than usual early in this cycle. I believe this process has not run its course yet, and this excess liquidity should continue to feed into financial markets, perhaps noticeably.

The economy has lately been in a weak phase. With the massive monetary stimulation by the Fed, I believe this economic pause is temporary and may be caused in part by election uncertainty. An important side effect of this is that it will probably hasten long-term interest rates lower. Inflation remains well under control and a non-event in my economic work for some time to come. I do look for the economy in the

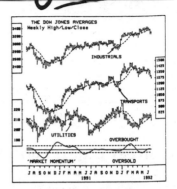

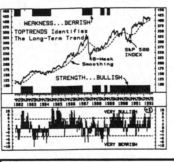

third quarter to be the most robust of the year, but believe it will be achieved with very low inflation. This combination of lower interest rates, low inflation, and modest business improvement should be beneficial for stock prices.

Speaking of stock prices, the analyst downgrades and accompanying "waterfall selling" by their institutional clients should be over with. I now look for a period of modest earnings improvement to unfold this month and give us "upgrades" for a change, as earnings are released. This should tend to give stock prices an upward bias for the next several weeks.

I also observe, with increasing interest, that the NASDAQ averages were finally down last week to important areas that should prove to be good support for the smaller stock averages. The decline from the January highs is on the order of 15 per cent, indicating the small company area has been pretty thoroughly "sold out" here. This leads me to believe that small stocks could be on the threshold of another period of strength in the last half of the year and surprise investors pleasantly.

My conclusion is that this month and possibly August have the underlying ingredients to see stocks stage a recovery move back to the vicinity of the yearly highs, in a fairly broad-based recovery. Watch for further global rate cuts.

—RAY—

MarketMetrics, Inc.
REGISTERED INVESTMENT ADVISOR

The Wall Street Generalist is published every three weeks by Ray Hines, who supplements his newsletter by a twice-weekly telephone hotline update.

Hines's approach involves a combination of both fundamental and technical analysis. He devotes several pages of each issue to a review of a number of technical, sentiment and monetary indicators and to an update of a large number of stocks on his recommended list. Of those stocks, Hines selects several to appear in either of his two model portfolios. One is a very aggressive portfolio for speculators, which utilizes margin and invests heavily in options (Hines calls this his "Select Trading" portfolio). The other portfolio is more conservative (Hines calls this his "Select Intermediate" portfolio). Hines's advice for both portfolios is very clear: He advises subscribers on exactly the number of shares which should be bought and sold, where to put the proceeds of sales and where to get the cash to make new purchases.

Hines's "Select Trading" portfolio sustained a big loss during the October 1987 crash. The portfolio was fully margined on Black Monday, in fact, owning two dollars of stock for each one dollar of net worth. As a result, this portfolio was the single largest loser in Octo-

ber 1987 among all those the HFD monitored, losing 70%. While this portfolio recovered some of this loss in the years following, it still is substantially in the red. For the five and one-half years through mid-1992, in fact, the HFD reports that this portfolio lost 87.0%, as compared to a 93.3% gain for the Wilshire 5000.

Hines's "Select Intermediate Portfolio" hasn't existed as long, and the HFD has data for it from the beginning of 1989. Over the subsequent three and one-half years through mid-1992, this portfolio gained 43.3%, in contrast to 60.3% for the Wilshire 5000.

The Wall Street Generalist (Average)

	Gain/Loss
1/1/91 to 6/30/92	+20.2%
(Third Quintile)	
1/1/89 to 6/30/92	−9.3%
(Fifth Quintile)	
1/1/87 to 6/30/92	−62.8%
(Fifth Quintile)	
1/1/85 to 6/30/92	(n/a)
1/1/83 to 6/30/92	(n/a)
6/30/80 to 6/30/92	(n/a)

Risk: 327% of market

The Wall Street Generalist (Select Trading Portfolio)

	Gain/Loss
1/1/91 to 6/30/92 (Fifth Quintile)	−5.8%
1/1/89 to 6/30/92 (Fifth Quintile)	−68.3%
1/1/87 to 6/30/92 (Fifth Quintile)	−87.0%
1/1/85 to 6/30/92	(n/a)
1/1/83 to 6/30/92	(n/a)
6/30/80 to 6/30/92	(n/a)

Risk: 531% of market

The Wall Street Generalist (Select Intermediate Portfolio)

	Gain/Loss
1/1/91 to 6/30/92 (Second Quintile)	+36.1%
1/1/89 to 6/30/92 (Second Quintile)	+43.3%
1/1/87 to 6/30/92	(n/a)
1/1/85 to 6/30/92	(n/a)
1/1/83 to 6/30/92	(n/a)
6/30/80 to 6/30/92	(n/a)

Risk: 152% of market

Weber's Fund Advisor

Address
P.O. Box 3490
New Hyde Park, NY
   11040

Editor
Ken Weber

Phone Number
516-466-1252

Subscription Rates
$39.00/4 months
$95.00/year

Telephone Hotline
Yes

Money Management
Yes

WEBER'S FUND ADVISOR

Information
and Strategy
for the
Mutual Fund
Investor

WHEN WILL THE BIG ONE HIT?

Just as people who reside along the San Andreas fault talk in hushed tones about The Big One, Wall Streeters also wait and wonder. Everyone knows that a tremor marking the start of a full-fledged bear market will hit sometime, but no one knows when.

Is it just coincidence that California has been hit with a series of quakes at the same time that a growing number of stock market analysts are warning us to head for safer ground? Whether those events on the two coasts are related or not, it is clear that the U.S. stock market is riddled with some serious faults.

Market seismologists adhering to the "Big One is Seriously Overdue" school say the Crash of 1987 doesn't count as a major quake - the market bounced back too quickly. And that makes it almost two decades since the start of the last major decline. For those of you who weren't fund shareholders when the earth moved back then, let us remind you that the bear market of 1973-74 took many growth mutual funds down 60% to 70%.

There are perpetually doom-sayers rampant in the financial world, but lately we're seeing them in greater quantity and of greater quality. Toss a pebble from a Wall Street window and chances are high you'll hit an analyst who's predicting a decline that takes the Dow down to at least the 2500 level. That's approximately a 25% drop in the Dow, but it would lop two-thirds off many star funds of the past few years.

If that sounds somewhat alarmist, consider this: the Dow is up a few percentage points for the year. Yet of the twenty-five growth funds with the best performance over the three years 1989-91, only *one* shows a gain, while the other twenty-four show an average loss of 13% this year.

Technical analysts term this separation of the Dow from the bulk of the market a "divergence," and they cite it as a serious squiggle on their Richter scale. For at some point, unless something extraordinarily bullish occurs, the broad market usually pulls the Dow-type stocks down to their level. And when the blue-chips stumble, the smaller stocks crumble.

Other signs that the financial bedrock is slipping: respected market-watchers are eschewing their normal wishy-washy predictions for clear-cut warnings. One prominent ad currently running in financial papers screams out the headline, "The End Is Near! Are You Prepared?" Right or wrong, there is a man who's not hedging his bets.

Many other analysts tell us that any revival of the market from here on out will be just a last-hurrah rally in the bull market that began in late 1974. As we've pointed out here previously, the public has been scooping up mutual fund shares at a record pace, largely as a refuge from 3% rates on bank CDs. But, one has to wonder, what will happen when the market declines and all the novice fund investors start to panic and dump their shares? Could that snowball into a rumbling avalanche?

Currently, mutual funds are holding an average 9% of their portfolios in cash, an amount slightly above the historical norm. That cash position would help cushion - but not stop - a runaway decline. Also, we think fund investors, recalling the bounce after 1987, will show more patience than most money pros expect.

Barron's quarterly poll of major institutional investors, released last week, shows that they have turned sharply more bearish, with almost 40% of the big money pros now saying there's at least a 50-50 chance of a "major market collapse" within 12 months. Happy days are here again?

Well, surely, you can count on that old standby, the election-year rally. Or maybe not. The Perot factor, among other unknowns, makes this a year without precedent. We think the only sure bet is that between now

July 15, 1992

Current Market:

Still Drifting

Current Go-With-The-Winner Strategy Signal:

Stay in Cash

Recommended Funds for the Go-With-The-Winner Strategy:

For Fidelity Investors:

Fidelity Cash Reserves

Date bought:
4/14/92
Price:
$1.00

Current Yield:
3.60%

For Schwab Investors:

Schwab Money Market

Date bought:
4/14/92
Price:
$1.00

Current Yield:
3.39%

(Continued, page three)

Weber's Fund Advisor is published monthly by Ken Weber. It is supplemented by a twice-weekly telephone hotline update. (Weber's hotline is one of the few within the newsletter industry that is toll-free.)

Weber entitles the strategy he advocates the "Go-With-the-Winner Strategy," and he describes it as "an aggressive, automatic mutual fund trading system." It is intended to keep subscribers invested in two of the better-performing mutual funds at any given time, and the system generates a switch whenever one of the funds falls sufficiently out of its top-performer status. On the occasion of any switch, Weber advises subscribers which new fund should replace the deleted one. All of the funds in Weber's universe participate in the mutual fund-switching service provided by Charles Schwab & Co., so executing his switch signals is especially easy.

The HFD has data for this strategy beginning in 1985 (Weber started his own model portfolio to follow this strategy on July 17, 1984). Over the seven and one-half years through mid-1992, according to the HFD, this portfolio gained 121.8%, as compared to 197.6% for the Wilshire 5000. This strategy achieved its gain with a risk level very close to the market's, so its risk-adjusted performance is below the market's by a very similar margin.

More recently, Weber introduced a second portfolio in his newsletter, entitled a "Low Risk/Low Switch" portfolio, and the HFD began following it at the beginning of 1989. Over the three and one-half years through mid-1992, this portfolio gained 34.2%, in contrast to the Wilshire 5000's 60.3%. In early 1990, Weber announced in his newsletter that he wanted his service to be ranked alongside others on the basis of his "Go-With-the-Winner" strategy alone, and not on the basis of an average of it and his "Low Risk/Low Switch" portfolio. For performance since then, therefore, what the HFD reports for the newsletter's average reflects just Weber's "Go-With-the-Winner" strategy.

What accounts for Weber's lagging the market? The primary factor appears to be fund selection. If each of the funds he recommended for his "Go-With-the-Winner" strategy had performed as well as the Wilshire 5000 during the times they were held by the portfolio, it would have gained 176.4% over the seven and one-half years through mid-1992. While this still is not equal to the Wilshire 5000's 197.6% return over this period, it is substantially better than the 121.8% the HFD reports for the portfolio's actual performance.

Weber's Fund Advisor (Average)

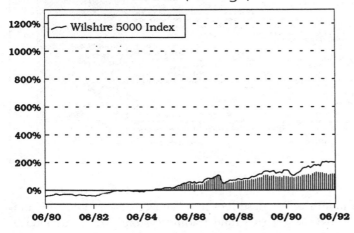

	Gain/Loss
1/1/91 to 6/30/92 (Fourth Quintile)	+8.5%
1/1/89 to 6/30/92 (Fourth Quintile)	+25.0%
1/1/87 to 6/30/92 (Third Quintile)	+53.8%
1/1/85 to 6/30/92 (Third Quintile)	+114.0%
1/1/83 to 6/30/92	(n/a)
6/30/80 to 6/30/92	(n/a)

Risk: 64% of market

Weber's Fund Advisor
("Go-With-the-Winner Strategy" Portfolio)

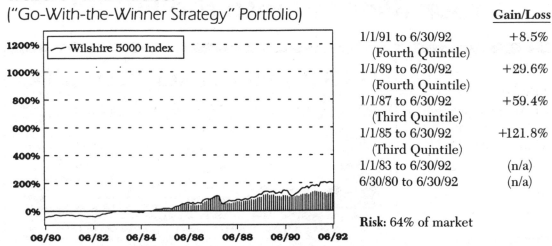

	Gain/Loss
1/1/91 to 6/30/92 (Fourth Quintile)	+8.5%
1/1/89 to 6/30/92 (Fourth Quintile)	+29.6%
1/1/87 to 6/30/92 (Third Quintile)	+59.4%
1/1/85 to 6/30/92 (Third Quintile)	+121.8%
1/1/83 to 6/30/92	(n/a)
6/30/80 to 6/30/92	(n/a)

Risk: 64% of market

Weber's Fund Advisor (Low Risk/Low Switch Portfolio)

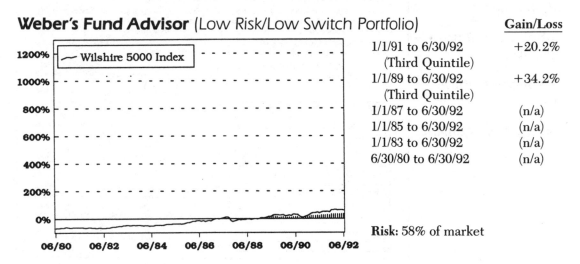

	Gain/Loss
1/1/91 to 6/30/92 (Third Quintile)	+20.2%
1/1/89 to 6/30/92 (Third Quintile)	+34.2%
1/1/87 to 6/30/92	(n/a)
1/1/85 to 6/30/92	(n/a)
1/1/83 to 6/30/92	(n/a)
6/30/80 to 6/30/92	(n/a)

Risk: 58% of market

Your Window Into the Future

Address
c/o Moneypower
P.O. Box 22400
Minneapolis, MN
55422

Editor
James Moore

Phone Number
612-537-8096

Subscription Rates •
$99.00/year

Telephone Hotline
No

Money Management
No

YOUR WINDOW INTO THE FUTURE

Advance Notice of Profitable Moves in Mutual Funds, Precious Metals, Bonds and Options. **$9.00**
Dedicated to investors who don't like to switch investments frequently.

EDITOR: JAMES H. MOORE   YEAR 11: MID-JULY 1992 ISSUE

While the Moneypower Indexes Box at lower left continues to measure market progress year-to-date (in column #1), for "buy-and-holders," I have altered column #2 to also measure progress from 4/29/92 (for cycle-investors). Unless we get a further, steep goldfund decline, 4/29 is the "compromise date" when the 34 mutual fund goldfunds hit their down-cycle low - and are now rebounding upward with our Inflation Predictor (page 6).

The *normal* cyclic profit-opposites to the goldfunds are the bonds, utilities and financial services. At cycle "turnaround" points, however, *all* four may move in the *same* direction... until the markets perceive the turnaround. Nevertheless, the items which are the *most* "correct" for the cycle (in this case, goldfunds) usually outprofit their normally-opposite - but paralleling - "competitors." So... we will want to closely watch how these indexes progress from 4/29.

LARGE INDEXES - SIX MONTHS TO DATE: Again, with the exception of financials, the first four categories have poor profits on the half year-to-date. Riskless T-Bonds have returned about 1.9%. The BULLION Precious Metals, combined, have moved somewhat better than stocks, bonds and utilities.

LARGE INDEXES - 2 MONTHS, SINCE 4/29: Bonds and financials are taking their final uptick-gasp, utilities continuing to stall, broad stocks eroding, and metals remaining strong. All these are early turnaround symptoms of an impending inflation upcycle... not yet recognized by most analysts.

SECTOR FUNDS - SIX MONTHS TO DATE: Here, again, we can note the results of all the poor financial advice to be in bonds and utilities since 12/91. In fact, only the financials have starred.

SECTOR FUNDS - TWO MONTHS, SINCE 4/29: Ahh, here we see the cycle beginning to "take hold." Although the goldfunds have not yet established *dominant oppositeness* they are already "leading" the other categories.

POSITIONS: If 4/29 indeed turns out to be the goldshares cyclic low, we entered seven weeks prematurely, on 3/12.

Portfolio "A": At June-end, here's how our two holdings in this portfolio are progressing since my anticipated 4/29 cycle low, and our premature 3/12 entry.

Item	Since 4/29	Since 3/12
Coeur D'Alene	+ 22.5%	+ 10.5%
Echo Bay	+ 9.1%	(-) 15.8%

Portfolio "B": Our single item, United Services Gold Shares, took a beating with the recent South African violence. This has happened before, and is usually rather temporary. When a subscriber called me on 6/23 - as it hit a $2.17 low - I simply said "buy more."

Item	Since 4/29	Since 3/12
Untd Svcs Gold Shrs	(-) 1.3%	(-) 7.2%

MONEYPOWER INDEXES 6/30/'92		
LARGE INDEXES	Year to Date	Since 4/29
Broad Stocks	(-) 1.2%	(-) 0.9%
Broad Financials	+ 4.0%	+ 3.0%
Broad Bonds	+ 1.4%	+ 2.7%
Broad Utilities	(-) 4.4%	0.0%
Broad Precious Metals	+ 3.8%	+ 4.4%
SECTOR FUNDS		
Mutual Fund Financials	+ 10.7%	+ 3.5%
Mutual Fund Long-Bond	(-) 3.9%	+ 5.2%
Mutual Fund Utilities	(-) 1.5%	+ 1.9%
Mutual Fund Goldfunds	(-)12.8%	+ 5.3%
POSITIONS		
MoneyPower 3-Portfolios	(-)28.3%	(-) 9.8%
Ratio "B"-Ben 2020+U.S.G.S.	+ 20.9%	+ 6.9%

Your Window Into the Future is published monthly by James Moore. For an additional subscription fee, Moore sells a service that regularly provides more frequent updates of his advice. Pursuant to its methodology on such matters, the HFD does not track the recommendations made by this additional service.

Moore devotes the bulk of his service to an analysis of inflation trends and the precious metals market. When the HFD began following Moore's newsletter in early 1986, he had one model portfolio, a mutual fund portfolio that switched from gold mutual funds into cash according to his signals. In late 1986 Moore created two additional portfolios. One of them ("Portfolio B: Conservative") invests in mutual funds, and the other ("Portfolio C: Speculative") often is invested in options. The original portfolio has been christened "Portfolio A: Aggressive."

Over the six and one-half years through mid-1992, the HFD reports that Moore's "Portfolio A" gained 86.9%, as compared to 124.5% for the Wilshire 5000. Over the five and one-half years through mid-1992 for which the HFD has data for Moore's other two portfolios, his "Portfolio B" gained 13.2% and his "Portfolio C" lost 100%. This compares to a 93.3% gain for the Wilshire 5000.

Moore's "Portfolio C" provides a good illustration of the risks inherent in options and how difficult it is to recover from big losses. Though the portfolio has done well during certain periods (gaining 164.2% during the first six months of 1990, for example), these gains are not enough to overcome the fact that it lost virtually everything in 1987 and again in 1988.

Moore's three portfolios also provide a good illustration of the HFD's approach to calculating average performances for newsletters that have more than one portfolio. Since the HFD gives equal weight to each portfolio each month, a portfolio that loses a lot of money over and over again will keep pulling down the newsletter's average. Moore's "Portfolio C" lost 100% in both 1988 and 1989, helping to explain why the HFD calculates a loss of 78.3% for the newsletters three portfolios over the entire period from the beginning of 1987 through mid-1992.

Your Window Into the Future (Average)

	Gain/Loss
1/1/91 to 6/30/92 (Fifth Quintile)	−27.3%
1/1/89 to 6/30/92 (Fifth Quintile)	−43.4%
1/1/87 to 6/30/92 (Fifth Quintile)	−78.3%
1/1/85 to 6/30/92	(n/a)
1/1/83 to 6/30/92	(n/a)
6/30/80 to 6/30/92	(n/a)

Risk: 307% of market

Your Window Into the Future (Portfolio A: Aggressive)

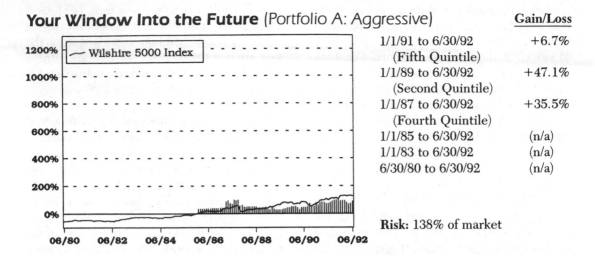

	Gain/Loss
1/1/91 to 6/30/92 (Fifth Quintile)	+6.7%
1/1/89 to 6/30/92 (Second Quintile)	+47.1%
1/1/87 to 6/30/92 (Fourth Quintile)	+35.5%
1/1/85 to 6/30/92	(n/a)
1/1/83 to 6/30/92	(n/a)
6/30/80 to 6/30/92	(n/a)

Risk: 138% of market

Your Window Into the Future (Portfolio B: Conservative)

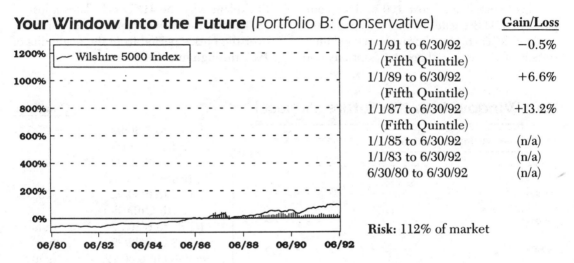

	Gain/Loss
1/1/91 to 6/30/92 (Fifth Quintile)	−0.5%
1/1/89 to 6/30/92 (Fifth Quintile)	+6.6%
1/1/87 to 6/30/92 (Fifth Quintile)	+13.2%
1/1/85 to 6/30/92	(n/a)
1/1/83 to 6/30/92	(n/a)
6/30/80 to 6/30/92	(n/a)

Risk: 112% of market

Your Window Into the Future (Portfolio C: Speculative)

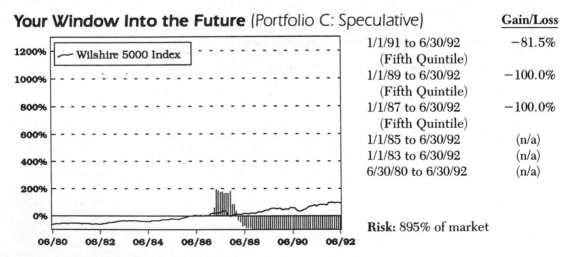

	Gain/Loss
1/1/91 to 6/30/92 (Fifth Quintile)	−81.5%
1/1/89 to 6/30/92 (Fifth Quintile)	−100.0%
1/1/87 to 6/30/92 (Fifth Quintile)	−100.0%
1/1/85 to 6/30/92	(n/a)
1/1/83 to 6/30/92	(n/a)
6/30/80 to 6/30/92	(n/a)

Risk: 895% of market

The Zweig Forecast

Address
P.O. Box 2900
Wantagh, NY 11793

Editor
Martin Zweig

Phone Number
516-785-1300

Subscription Rates
$155.00/6 months
$265.00/year

Telephone Hotline
Yes

Money Management
Yes

Vol. 22
Number 10
July 17, 1992

THE ZWEIG FORECAST

OUTLOOK AND STRATEGY

The Fed's recent cut in the Discount Rate is bullish as are the Monetary indicators in general. The short-term Sentiment readings are positive, although longer-term ones are not. The Tape action has improved to somewhat positive.

We're 58% Long in Stocks/42% Cash (T'Bills). We're also 10% Long in S&P Futures for a net Long position of 68% in Stocks.

DON'T FIGHT THE FED

Zweig Unweighted Price Indices
NYSE: 311.22
AMEX: 130.60
Dow: 3345

****
WALL $TREET WEEK WITH LOU RUKEYSER:
I'll be a panelist August 7. The guest is Robert Lloyd George.
****

INTERMEDIATE INDEX of 36 technical indicators has risen to a neutral 93. The MONETARY MODEL of 22 interest rate and Fed indicators rose to a bullish 79 points.

The Economic recovery has begun to sputter a bit. On July 2 the Unemployment report showed a jump from 7.4% up to 7.8%. With an election in sight, the Fed wasted no time by cutting the Discount Rate a half point to just 3.0%. It marked the seventh straight cut since late 1990 and it put the Discount Rate back to its lowest point since the 1960 to 1963 period. Immediately, pundits allowed that the Fed was fighting a futile battle, that it was too little too late, or that it was the end of easing anyhow and would not make much difference.

Since I hate to fight the Fed, I thought a check of the evidence was in order. Since 1970 there have been nine other times when the Fed responded to a rise in the Unemployment rate by cutting the Discount Rate the same day that the bad economic news appeared. In other words, that set up a classic battle between slumping business and the Fed's ability to pump things up. Well, just one month later the S&P 500 Index had risen by an average of 4.9%. Three months later stocks were up 9.6%; six months later the market was up 14.0% and a year later the S&P had risen 21.1%. So, at least over the past couple of decades, the Fed and those who follow the Fed have won.

I then checked back to 1928 on the theory that this may be the "last Discount Rate cut", which according to folklore implies that the easing is over and therefore stocks will falter. In that span there have been 15 "last cuts" (obviously, at the time there was no way to

THE ZWEIG FORECAST • P.O. BOX 2900, WANTAGH, NY 11793 • 516-785-1300

Published every 3 weeks plus special bulletins when conditions warrant. Includes hotline phone service.
Subscriptions: 6 months $155, 1 year $265, 2 years $445, (unlisted number sent to you separately).

The Zweig Forecast is published every three weeks by Martin Zweig and is supplemented by a telephone hotline that is updated as often as every day. Zweig also is publisher of the *Zweig Performance Ratings Report*, which is reviewed next in this volume.

Zweig has a Ph.D. in finance from Michi-gan State, an M.B.A. from the University of Miami and a B.S.E. from the Wharton School. This strong academic background provides a clue to his approach to investing, which is rigorous and objective. However, unlike other newsletter editors with a strong academic background, Zweig takes a much more short-term perspective on investing. Though the average holding period of his portfolio holdings today isn't as short as it was in the early 1980s (when it was less than two months), it remains well less than one year on average.

Zweig is very risk averse, and his approach shined during the October 1987 crash. Over the weeks prior to Black Monday, Zweig had whittled down the stocks in his portfolio, and in the days just prior had purchased a stock-index put option. This put option skyrocketed in value on October 19, more than making up for the losses in the stocks that did remain in his portfolio; on that day alone his portfolio gained some 9%. In fact, if we ignore October 1987 (not crediting Zweig for his gain that month and not debiting a buy-and-hold strategy for that month's big loss), then he is not ahead of the market over the 12 years through mid-1992. This is not to say that Zweig doesn't deserve credit for his advice in the Crash of 1987, for he surely does. But you need to be aware that his status as a market-beater over the last 12 years is heavily dependent on his success that month.

In any case, Zweig's newsletter is one of the few that beat the market over the 12 years through mid-1992. According to the HFD, Zweig's model portfolio gained 608.7% over this period, as compared to 432.7% for the Wilshire 5000. And because he beat the market with below-market risk, his risk-adjusted performance is even further ahead of the Wilshire 5000's.

When the HFD first began to monitor Zweig's performance, his portfolio invested exclusively in stocks and cash equivalents; when he saw the indicators changing, he quickly would buy or sell stocks. In the last several years, however, Zweig has held his stocks for longer periods of time, using stock-index futures contracts and options to change exposure quickly if and when needed. Subscribers should be aware that these non-stock portions of his portfolio have been a crucial part of its profitability.

The Zweig Forecast

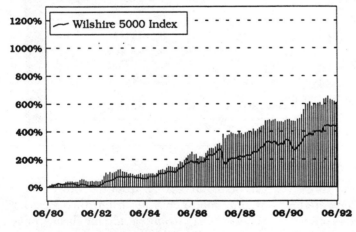

	Gain/Loss
1/1/91 to 6/30/92 (Third Quintile)	+19.6%
1/1/89 to 6/30/92 (Third Quintile)	+42.5%
1/1/87 to 6/30/92 (First Quintile)	+127.0%
1/1/85 to 6/30/92 (First Quintile)	+257.2%
1/1/83 to 6/30/92 (First Quintile)	+272.5%
6/30/80 to 6/30/92 (First Quintile)	+608.7%

Risk: 79% of market

Zweig Performance Ratings Report

Address
P.O. Box 2900
Wantagh, NY 11793

Editor
Timothy Clark

Phone Number
516-785-1300

Subscription Rates
$205.00/year

Telephone Hotline
No

Money Management
Yes

PUBLISHED TWICE A MONTH BY ZWEIG SECURITIES ADVISORY SERVICE, INC., P.O. BOX 2900, WANTAGH, NY 11793

NYSE EDITION

Zweig Performance Ratings Report

$205 Annually   July 1992

Zweig's Performance Ratings are computer-generated estimates of how stocks are expected to perform over the next 6 to 12 months relative to each other. The scale runs from 1, the best 5%, down to 9, the worst 5%. As seen in the performance table, there are more stocks in the middle ratings–fewer at the extremes. The Performance Ratings are derived from numerous technical and fundamental variables – each weighted by our proprietary formula. The most significant factors are *Earnings Momentum*, *Earnings Growth* and *Changes in Analysts Estimates*. Other factors include Institutional Trading Activity, Price

PERFORMANCE RATING RESULTS			
Performance Ratings	% of Stocks In Groups	Return for June	Return Since 5/76
1	5%	-4.8%	3634.9%
2	8%	-3.3%	2636.9%
3	12%	-4.1%	1114.1%
4	16%	-3.1%	950.6%
5	20%	-3.2%	562.9%
6	16%	-4.1%	368.6%
7	12%	-5.4%	269.0%
8	8%	-4.4%	148.7%
9	5%	-5.5%	3.9%
All Stocks		-4.4%	618.0%

Momentum, Relative P/Es, Book Value and Dividends.

The table shows the results that could have been earned since May 1976, by following the ratings published in this monthly service. These results assume that one switched portfolios each month so as always to remain in the Number 1 stocks (or Number 2, etc.).

Also seen in the report you are holding are P/E Ratios and Dividend Yields.

Please note: A "+" or "-" following the Performance Ratings denotes a change in the rating, either up or down, from the previous months rating.

Stocks of Interest

ENRON OIL & GAS CO. (EOG - $26.62) - This NYSE company has the highest "1" rating, placing it in the top 5% of companies covered. Enron is one of the largest U.S. independent oil and gas companies. Its principal activities include exploration, development and production. Properties are primarily located in Wyoming and Texas, with 90% of its reserves in the United States. Despite the depressed price of natural gas, sales and earnings results have been positive in recent quarters. For the most recent first quarter ended March, 1992, net income was $0.29 per share, an increase of 81% from the $0.16 reported for the same quarter last year. For the most recent 12 month period, sales were up 115% and net income was up 20%. In addition, sales revenue grew at a 39% rate over the past 5 years. The company is conservatively financed relative to other oil and gas companies, with a debt to equity ratio of .69. Also, institutions hold just 11.8% of the stock, leaving room for further accumulation and price appreciation. We recommend that shares of Enron be purchased. Stop at $21.25.

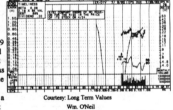

Courtesy: Long Term Values
Wm. O'Neil

The facts and statements here presented have been obtained or derived from original or recognized statistical sources which we believe to be reliable. We do not guarantee the accuracy of this information and it may possibly be condensed or incomplete.

The *Zweig Performance Ratings Report* is published twice each month by Zweig Securities Advisory Service, which also publishes *The Zweig Forecast* (reviewed on the previous pages). It is edited by Timothy Clark. The service does not include a telephone hotline update.

Each edition of the *Report* ranks all stocks in its universe on a "1" (best) to "9" (worst) scale that estimates their prospects over the ensuing 6 to 12 months. In addition, each edition highlights two or three "Stocks of Interest"; these are the service's recommendations, and follow-up advice is provided each month until they eventually are closed out. The service does not provide advice on the proper allocation of a portfolio between stocks and cash, so (per its established methodology on such matters) the HFD constructs a portfolio for the *Zweig Performance Ratings Report* that is fully invested in these "Stocks of Interest."

According to the newsletter, the stocks that its rating system has rated "1" have performed much better than the market and much better than those stocks rated "2," "3," and lower. Nevertheless, the *Report* chooses to highlight and recommend some stocks for the "Stocks of Interest" section that are not "1"-rated (as well as choosing to sell short some stocks that are not rated "9"). The newsletter does not explain what other factors are taken into account in selecting these "Stocks of Interest," and why, if those other factors are worth taking into account, they aren't incorporated into the rating system itself.

In any case, the HFD has not calculated the performance of a portfolio that is constructed out of just the "1"-rated stocks. Therefore, the HFD is not sure whether it is better for the investor to concentrate on the stocks rated "1" by the newsletter's rating system, or instead to concentrate on those highlighted as "Stocks of Interest."

Regardless of the answer to this question, however, there is little doubt that the "Stocks of Interest" have performed very well indeed. For the nine and one-half years through mid-1992, the portfolio the HFD constructed out of these stocks gained 315.5%, as compared to 278.6% for the Wilshire 5000, good enough that it is one of just two newsletters (out of 36 the HFD tracked over this period) to beat the market. Furthermore, owing to the fact that this performance was turned in with below-market risk, the newsletter's risk-adjusted rank is in first place over this period.

Investors should note that this performance was slightly better than that of Zweig's companion service, *The Zweig Forecast*, despite the fact that the *Zweig Performance Ratings Report* has no telephone hotline and its recommendations don't include options or futures contracts. For that reason, those interested in following Zweig's advice without the need to call a daily telephone hotline or purchase these non-stock positions ought to focus on this service instead.

Zweig Performance Ratings Report

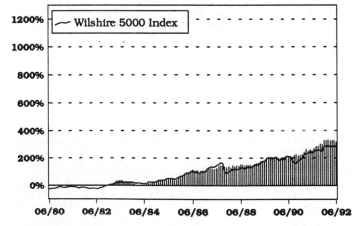

	Gain/Loss
1/1/91 to 6/30/92 (Second Quintile)	+31.3%
1/1/89 to 6/30/92 (First Quintile)	+69.2%
1/1/87 to 6/30/92 (First Quintile)	+99.7%
1/1/85 to 6/30/92 (First Quintile)	+234.0%
1/1/83 to 6/30/92 (First Quintile)	+315.5%
6/30/80 to 6/30/92	(n/a)

Risk: 78% of market

APPENDIX A

Newsletter Performance

The following tables rank newsletters on the basis of their total returns and risk-adjusted performances from mid-1980 through mid-1992. Several different periods of comparison were chosen not only because some newsletters do better in some markets than others, but also because not every newsletter monitored by *The Hulbert Financial Digest* has been in existence since mid-1980 (when the HFD began monitoring newsletter performance). Obviously, if a newsletter is not included in one of the rankings that follow, you can draw no conclusion about how it would have done; likewise, a newsletter that is included and is ranked #1 should be considered only in the context of the other newsletters also monitored over the same period of time. A #1-ranked adviser is not necessarily the best performer among *all* advisers, but rather just among those also monitored for that same period of time.

The periods of time covered in the following rankings are:

Appendix A-1. June 30, 1980 to June 30, 1992   *12 YRS*
Appendix A-2. January 1, 1983 to June 30, 1992   *9.5 YRS*
Appendix A-3. January 1, 1985 to June 30, 1992   *7.5*
Appendix A-4. January 1, 1987 to June 30, 1992   *5.5*
Appendix A-5. January 1, 1989 to June 30, 1992   *3.5*
Appendix A-6. January 1, 1991 to June 30, 1992   *1.5*

Within each of the Appendices A-1 through A-6, the rankings that appear on the left-hand pages are based on total return, while those appearing opposite them on the right-hand pages are based on risk-adjusted performance (which is explained further below).

Furthermore, in each of the various rankings, you will find the listings for two additional "portfolios": one for the Wilshire 5000's Value-Weighted Index (with dividends reinvested) and another for a portfolio constantly invested in 90-day Treasury bills.

All performances included in these appendices were calculated by *The Hulbert Financial Digest* according to its established methodology. Please refer to the chapter on the

HFD's methodology earlier in this *Guide* for a complete description of the rules and procedures the HFD followed.

Newsletters that recommend more than one portfolio are ranked on the basis of an average of their several portfolios. Such averages are calculated assuming an equal weighting of each of the individual portfolios, unless an unequal weighting is specifically recommended by the newsletter.

Risk-Adjusted Performance

As mentioned above, each of the rankings that appear on the right-hand pages of these appendices are based on risk-adjusted performances. The figures that appear in these rankings show the *average monthly return per unit of risk*. A figure of 0.30%, for example, can be interpreted as follows: On average each month, such a newsletter earns 0.30% more than the 90-day Treasury bill rate for each unit of risk. Even if the numbers in the following rankings don't have that much meaning for you in the abstract, you still can use them as the basis for comparing different strategies according to how well they have been able to exploit risk.

Since an investor can earn the Treasury bill rate for taking no risk at all, the calculations of risk-adjusted performance give a newsletter credit for taking risk only in the event that it makes more than the T-Bill rate. A negative number in the following rankings thus means that the newsletter did not, for the period under comparison, make as much money as the T-Bill rate. Since the risk-adjusted performance of T-Bills is 0.0 (by definition), it is not listed in the risk-adjusted rankings.

To calculate the risk-adjusted performance figures, the HFD uses the following procedure:

1. From each newsletter's average monthly performance the HFD subtracts the average monthly T-Bill performance over the same period of time. The result is the average monthly premium each newsletter has earned for undertaking risk.
2. The HFD then calculates the standard deviation of each newsletter's monthly performance. This is a statistical measure of volatility, with a lower number denoting less volatility. (For a description of what a standard deviation means in the context of investment performance, please refer to the discussion in the first section of this *Guide* about newsletters and risk).
3. The HFD then divides the number arrived at in Step 1 by the standard deviation arrived at in Step 2. The result is the average monthly performance per unit of risk. This is the number you will find in the tables that follow.

Interpreting the Risk-Adjusted Ratings

The risk-adjusted ratings have the most meaning in relation to each other. If newsletter ABC has a risk-adjusted performance of 0.50% in contrast to XYZ's 0.25%, then this means that ABC has done twice as good a job of exploiting risk. One comparison that you always should make is with the market: Has the newsletter made more, per unit of risk, than the market itself?

The reason to adjust performance for risk is because risk is something we want to avoid, if at all possible. And since risk cannot be eliminated altogether, then we should receive something in return for incurring it. From these basic principles, it follows that (1) of two letters with the same riskiness, the one that has made the most money is the better bet; and (2) of two newsletters with the same performance, the one that achieved that performance with the lower risk is the better bet.

The risk-adjusted performance ratings make these comparisons automatically. Newsletter #1 cannot score higher than newsletter #2 on a risk-adjusted basis simply by incurring more risk. If it performs twice as well with twice as much risk, then the two newsletters' risk-adjusted performances will be equal. Only if newsletter #1 outperforms newsletter #2 by a greater amount than it is riskier than newsletter #2 will it do better on a risk-adjusted basis (if, for example, it doubled the performance of newsletter #2 with just 50% more risk).

Newsletter	Individual Portfolio	Overall Average
1. The Chartist (Average)		+665.2%
a. Actual Cash Account	+514.0%	
2. The Value Line Investment Survey		+620.7%
3. The Zweig Forecast		+608.7%
4. The Value Line OTC Special Situations Service		+498.5%
Wilshire 5000 Value-Weighted Total Return Index		+432.7%
5. The Prudent Speculator		+428.9%
6. Growth Stock Outlook		+417.4%
7. Telephone Switch Newsletter (Average)		+335.4%
a. Equity/Cash Switch Plan	+385.9%	
8. **NoLoad Fund*X (Average)		+334.7%
a. Portfolio of "Class 3" Funds (Higher Quality Growth Funds)	+632.6%	
b. Portfolio of "Class 2" Funds (Speculative Growth Funds)	+373.3%	
c. Portfolio of "Class 1" Funds (Most Speculative Growth Funds)	+129.5%	
9. Market Logic (Average)		+299.7%
a. Master (Stock) Portfolio	+339.2%	
b. Actual Option Portfolio	+217.4%	
10. Dow Theory Forecasts (Average)		+280.1%
a. Investment List	+419.5%	
b. Income List	+404.7%	
c. Growth List	+280.3%	
d. Speculative List	+215.9%	
11. Growth Fund Guide (Average)		+277.3%
a. Special Situations Mutual Fund Portfolio	+378.6%	
b. Growth Mutual Fund Portfolio	+296.2%	
c. Quality Growth Mutual Fund Portfolio	+237.0%	
d. Aggressive Growth Mutual Fund Portfolio	+200.9%	
12. The Outlook (Average)		+266.0%
The Riskless Rate of Return: A T-Bill Portfolio		+159.4%
13. Kinsman's Telephone Growth & Income Service (Average)		+131.4%
a. Growth & Income Portfolio	+134.9%	
14. United & Babson Investment Report (Average)		+85.2%
a. Stocks for The Income-Minded	+123.2%	
b. Stocks for Long-Term Growth	+79.8%	
c. Cyclical Stocks for Profit	+36.1%	
15. The International Harry Schultz Letter (Average)		+84.2%
a. U.S. Stocks on the "List"	+55.3%	
16. The Professional Tape Reader (Average)		+67.0%
a. Model Stock Portfolio	+48.5%	

Appendix A-1: Risk-Adjusted Performance from 6/30/80 to 6/30/92

Newsletter	Individual Portfolio	Overall Average
1. Growth Stock Outlook		+0.19%
2. The Zweig Forecast		+0.18%
3. The Chartist (Average)		+0.16%
a. Actual Cash Account	+0.15%	
4. The Value Line Investment Survey		+0.15%
Wilshire 5000 Value-Weighted Total Return Index		+0.13%
5. Telephone Switch Newsletter (Average)		+0.12%
a. Equity/Cash Switch Plan	+0.12%	
6. The Value Line OTC Special Situations Service		+0.11%
7. The Prudent Speculator		+0.11%
8. **NoLoad Fund*X (Average)		+0.10%
a. Portfolio of "Class 3" Funds (Higher Quality Growth Funds)	+0.20%	
b. Portfolio of "Class 2" Funds (Speculative Growth Funds)	+0.11%	
c. Portfolio of "Class 1" Funds (Most Speculative Growth Funds)	+0.02%	
9. Market Logic (Average)		+0.09%
a. Master (Stock) Portfolio	+0.09%	
b. Actual Option Portfolio	+0.09%	
10. Growth Fund Guide (Average)		+0.09%
a. Special Situations Mutual Fund Portfolio	+0.13%	
b. Growth Mutual Fund Portfolio	+0.10%	
c. Quality Growth Mutual Fund Portfolio	+0.08%	
d. Aggressive Growth Mutual Fund Portfolio	+0.05%	
11. Dow Theory Forecasts (Average)		+0.08%
a. Income List	+0.14%	
b. Investment List	+0.13%	
c. Growth List	+0.08%	
d. Speculative List	+0.05%	
12. The Outlook (Average)		+0.08%
13. The Granville Market Letter (Average)		+0.01%
a. Traders' Stock Portfolio	−0.14%	
14. The Dines Letter (Average)		−0.03%
a. Long-Term Growth Portfolio	+0.12%	
b. Short-Term Trading Portfolio	−0.02%	
15. Kinsman's Telephone Growth & Income Service (Average)		−0.03%
a. Growth & Income Portfolio	−0.03%	
16. United & Babson Investment Report (Average)		−0.03%
a. Stocks for The Income-Minded	−0.01%	
b. Stocks for Long-Term Growth	−0.02%	
c. Cyclical Stocks for Profit	−0.04%	

Newsletter	Individual Portfolio	Overall Average
17. The Dines Letter (Average)		+38.3%
a. Long-Term Growth Portfolio	+558.2%	
b. Short-Term Trading Portfolio	−66.9%	
18. The Ruff Times (Average)		+38.2%
19. The Holt Advisory (Average)		−62.4%
20. The Granville Market Letter (Average)		−93.1%
a. Traders' Stock Portfolio	−51.8%	

Newsletter	Individual Portfolio	Overall Average
17. The International Harry Schultz Letter (Average)		−0.03%
a. U.S. Stocks on the "List"	−0.05%	
18. The Ruff Times (Average)		−0.05%
19. The Professional Tape Reader (Average)		−0.09%
a. Model Stock Portfolio	−0.11%	
20. The Holt Advisory (Average)		−0.18%

9.5 yrs

Appendix A-2: Gain from 1/1/83 to 6/30/92

Newsletter	Individual Portfolio	Overall Average
1. The Chartist (Average)		+417.2%
a. Traders Portfolio	+498.1%	
b. Actual Cash Account	+315.0%	
2. Zweig Performance Ratings Report		+315.5%
Wilshire 5000 Value-Weighted Total Return Index		+278.6%
3. The Zweig Forecast		+272.5%
4. The Value Line Investment Survey		+257.0%
5. Dessauer's Journal		+255.5%
6. Systems and Forecasts (Average)		+210.4%
a. The Regular Portfolio	+180.8%	
7. The Value Line OTC Special Situations Service		+180.5%
8. Growth Stock Outlook		+178.6%
9. **NoLoad Fund*X (Average)		+176.8%
a. Portfolio of "Class 3" Funds (Higher Quality Growth Funds)	+330.6%	
b. Portfolio of "Class 2" Funds (Speculative Growth Funds)	+184.9%	
c. Portfolio of "Class 1" Funds (Most Speculative Growth Funds)	+73.7%	
10. The Prudent Speculator		+172.7%
11. Dow Theory Forecasts (Average)		+168.7%
a. Income List	+298.1%	
b. Investment List	+246.6%	
c. Growth List	+156.7%	
d. Speculative List	+132.2%	
12. The Addison Report (Average)		+164.4%
a. Speculative Portfolio	+174.8%	
b. Conservative Portfolio	+155.8%	
13. The Princeton Portfolios (Average)		+146.7%
a. Long-Term Portfolio #1	+140.9%	
b. Long-Term Portfolio #2	+129.8%	
14. Growth Fund Guide (Average)		+139.6%
a. Special Situations Mutual Fund Portfolio	+187.4%	
b. Quality Growth Mutual Fund Portfolio	+160.3%	
c. Growth Mutual Fund Portfolio	+122.7%	
d. Aggressive Growth Mutual Fund Portfolio	+92.4%	
15. Market Logic (Average)		+139.4%
a. Master (Stock) Portfolio	+141.2%	
b. Actual Option Portfolio	+108.5%	
16. The Outlook (Average)		+138.7%
17. Telephone Switch Newsletter (Average)		+124.0%
a. Equity/Cash Switch Plan	+150.0%	
b. Gold/Cash Switch Plan	+25.3%	
18. Emerging & Special Situations		+121.6%

Appendix A-2: Risk-Adjusted Performance from 1/1/83 to 6/30/92

Newsletter	Individual Portfolio	Overall Average
1. Zweig Performance Ratings Report		+0.20%
2. The Chartist (Average)		+0.18%
a. Actual Cash Account	+0.17%	
b. Traders Portfolio	+0.17%	
3. The Zweig Forecast		+0.17%
4. Systems and Forecasts (Average)		+0.16%
a. The Regular Portfolio	+0.14%	
Wilshire 5000 Value-Weighted Total Return Index		+0.15%
5. Growth Stock Outlook		+0.15%
6. Dessauer's Journal		+0.14%
7. The Value Line Investment Survey		+0.12%
8. **NoLoad Fund*X (Average)		+0.09%
a. Portfolio of "Class 3" Funds (Higher Quality Growth Funds)	+0.19%	
b. Portfolio of "Class 2" Funds (Speculative Growth Funds)	+0.09%	
c. Portfolio of "Class 1" Funds (Most Speculative Growth Funds)	+0.02%	
9. The Prudent Speculator		+0.09%
10. Dow Theory Forecasts (Average)		+0.09%
a. Income List	+0.19%	
b. Investment List	+0.13%	
c. Growth List	+0.07%	
d. Speculative List	+0.06%	
11. The Addison Report (Average)		+0.08%
a. Conservative Portfolio	+0.08%	
b. Speculative Portfolio	+0.08%	
12. The Value Line OTC Special Situations Service		+0.08%
13. Growth Fund Guide (Average)		+0.07%
a. Quality Growth Mutual Fund Portfolio	+0.12%	
b. Special Situations Mutual Fund Portfolio	+0.11%	
c. Growth Mutual Fund Portfolio	+0.05%	
d. Aggressive Growth Mutual Fund Portfolio	+0.02%	
14. The Outlook (Average)		+0.06%
15. Market Logic (Average)		+0.06%
a. Master (Stock) Portfolio	+0.06%	
b. Actual Option Portfolio	+0.06%	
16. The Princeton Portfolios (Average)		+0.06%
a. Long-Term Portfolio #1	+0.06%	
b. Long-Term Portfolio #2	+0.05%	
17. Telephone Switch Newsletter (Average)		+0.05%
a. Equity/Cash Switch Plan	+0.07%	
b. Gold/Cash Switch Plan	−0.04%	
18. Emerging & Special Situations		+0.05%

Newsletter	Individual Portfolio	Overall Average
19. The Peter Dag Investment Letter (Average)		+108.1%
a. Model Vanguard Fund Portfolio	+127.0%	
20. Harry Browne's Special Reports (Average)		+107.5%
a. Variable [Speculative] Portfolio	+80.2%	
21. The Big Picture (Average)		+102.8%
a. Trading Portfolio	+123.9%	
The Riskless Rate of Return: A T-Bill Portfolio		+93.5%
22. The Cabot Market Letter (Average)		+80.0%
a. Model Stock Portfolio	+42.8%	
23. Kinsman's Telephone Growth & Income Service (Average)		+72.1%
a. Growth & Income Portfolio	+74.7%	
24. The International Harry Schultz Letter (Average)		+67.3%
a. U.S. Stocks on the "List"	+41.0%	
25. New Issues		+58.5%
26. United & Babson Investment Report (Average)		+57.7%
a. Stocks for The Income-Minded	+94.9%	
b. Stocks for Long-Term Growth	+69.3%	
c. Cyclical Stocks for Profit	+5.3%	
27. California Technology Stock Letter		+40.6%
28. Professional Timing Service (Average)		+29.8%
29. The Dines Letter (Average)		+18.1%
a. Long-Term Growth Portfolio	+335.2%	
b. Short-Term Trading Portfolio	−66.6%	
30. The Professional Tape Reader (Average)		+12.0%
a. Model Stock Portfolio	−0.4%	
31. The Ruff Times (Average)		+5.6%
32. The R.H.M. Survey of Warrants, Options & Low-Price Stocks		−45.3%
33. The Holt Advisory (Average)		−57.9%
34. On Markets		−63.1%
35. The Option Advisor (Average)		−65.2%
a. Conservative Portfolio	−71.9%	
b. Aggressive Portfolio	−92.3%	
36. The Granville Market Letter (Average)		−90.7%
a. Traders' Stock Portfolio	−35.9%	

Newsletter	Individual Portfolio	Overall Average
19. The Peter Dag Investment Letter (Average)		+0.05%
a. Model Vanguard Fund Portfolio	+0.12%	
20. Harry Browne's Special Reports (Average)		+0.04%
a. Variable [Speculative] Portfolio	−0.01%	
21. The Big Picture (Average)		+0.03%
a. Trading Portfolio	+0.05%	
22. The Granville Market Letter (Average)		+0.03%
a. Traders' Stock Portfolio	−0.11%	
23. The Cabot Market Letter (Average)		+0.02%
a. Model Stock Portfolio	0.00%	
24. New Issues		+0.01%
25. California Technology Stock Letter		−0.01%
26. The Option Advisor (Average)		−0.01%
a. Conservative Portfolio	+0.01%	
b. Aggressive Portfolio	−0.03%	
27. The Dines Letter (Average)		−0.02%
a. Long-Term Growth Portfolio	+0.13%	
b. Short-Term Trading Portfolio	−0.01%	
28. The International Harry Schultz Letter (Average)		−0.02%
a. U.S. Stocks on the "List"	−0.04%	
29. United & Babson Investment Report (Average)		−0.02%
a. Stocks for The Income-Minded	+0.02%	
b. Stocks for Long-Term Growth	0.00%	
c. Cyclical Stocks for Profit	−0.05%	
30. Kinsman's Telephone Growth & Income Service (Average)		−0.04%
a. Growth & Income Portfolio	−0.04%	
31. The Ruff Times (Average)		−0.07%
32. Professional Timing Service (Average)		−0.09%
33. The R.H.M. Survey of Warrants, Options & Low-Price Stocks		−0.09%
34. On Markets		0.10%
35. The Holt Advisory (Average)		−0.16%
36. The Professional Tape Reader (Average)		−0.17%
a. Model Stock Portfolio	−0.18%	

7.5 YRs

Newsletter	Individual Portfolio	Overall Average
1. MPT Review (Average)		+821.7%
a. $200,000 Aggressive Portfolio	+947.8%	
b. $800,000 Moderately Aggressive Portfolio	+940.0%	
c. $400,000 Aggressive Portfolio	+908.2%	
d. $800,000 Aggressive Portfolio	+904.5%	
e. $800,000 Conservative Portfolio	+736.7%	
f. $200,000 Moderately Aggressive Portfolio	+710.7%	
g. $400,000 Moderately Aggressive Portfolio	+646.9%	
h. $400,000 Conservative Portfolio	+645.9%	
i. $200,000 Conservative Portfolio	+573.6%	
2. BI Research		+497.5%
3. Medical Technology Stock Letter (Average)		+413.6%
a. Model Portfolio	+358.5%	
4. The Chartist (Average)		+287.7%
a. Traders Portfolio	+330.7%	
b. Actual Cash Account	+228.5%	
5. The Zweig Forecast		+257.2%
6. The Mutual Fund Strategist (Average)		+234.1%
7. Zweig Performance Ratings Report		+234.0%
8. The Princeton Portfolios (Average)		+208.4%
a. Long-Term Portfolio #1	+203.4%	
b. Long-Term Portfolio #2	+192.2%	
9. The Value Line OTC Special Situations Service		+197.7%
Wilshire 5000 Value-Weighted Total Return Index		+197.6%
10. Dessauer's Journal		+193.9%
11. The Value Line Investment Survey		+189.7%
12. The Investment Reporter (Average)		+175.1%
a. Portfolio of Speculative Stocks	+226.0%	
b. Portfolio of Conservative Stocks	+134.8%	
c. Portfolio of Higher Risk Stocks	+134.7%	
d. Portfolio of Average Risk Stocks	+112.7%	
e. Portfolio of Very Conservative Stocks	+112.5%	
13. Systems and Forecasts (Average)		+172.8%
a. The Regular Portfolio	+146.8%	
14. Personal Finance (Average)		+166.4%
a. Income Portfolio	+208.0%	
b. Growth Portfolio	+128.9%	
15. California Technology Stock Letter		+165.6%

Appendix A-3: Risk-Adjusted Performance from 1/1/85 to 6/30/92

Newsletter	Individual Portfolio	Overall Average
1. MPT Review (Average)		+0.27%
a. $800,000 Moderately Aggressive Portfolio	+0.29%	
b. $200,000 Aggressive Portfolio	+0.28%	
c. $800,000 Conservative Portfolio	+0.27%	
d. $800,000 Aggressive Portfolio	+0.27%	
e. $400,000 Aggressive Portfolio	+0.26%	
f. $200,000 Moderately Aggressive Portfolio	+0.25%	
g. $200,000 Conservative Portfolio	+0.25%	
h. $400,000 Conservative Portfolio	+0.23%	
i. $400,000 Moderately Aggressive Portfolio	+0.22%	
2. Zweig Performance Ratings Report		+0.26%
3. The Zweig Forecast		+0.25%
4. Systems and Forecasts (Average)		+0.23%
a. The Regular Portfolio	+0.20%	
5. The Mutual Fund Strategist (Average)		+0.21%
6. BI Research		+0.20%
7. The Chartist (Average)		+0.20%
a. Actual Cash Account	+0.20%	
b. Traders Portfolio	+0.18%	
8. Medical Technology Stock Letter (Average)		+0.17%
a. Model Portfolio	+0.16%	
9. Dessauer's Journal		+0.17%
Wilshire 5000 Value-Weighted Total Return Index		+0.16%
10. Personal Finance (Average)		+0.16%
a. Income Portfolio	+0.21%	
b. Growth Portfolio	+0.10%	
11. The Investment Reporter (Average)		+0.15%
a. Portfolio of Speculative Stocks	+0.15%	
b. Portfolio of Conservative Stocks	+0.11%	
c. Portfolio of Higher Risk Stocks	+0.10%	
d. Portfolio of Very Conservative Stocks	+0.09%	
e. Portfolio of Average Risk Stocks	+0.08%	
12. Growth Stock Outlook		+0.15%
13. Fund Exchange (Average)		+0.14%
a. Fixed Income Bond Portfolio	+0.35%	
b. Conservative Growth Margined Mutual Fund Portfolio	+0.13%	
c. Aggressive Growth Margined Mutual Fund Portfolio	+0.13%	
d. Aggressive Growth Mutual Fund Portfolio	+0.12%	
e. Growth/Income Mutual Fund Portfolio	+0.11%	
f. Gold Mutual Funds Portfolio	0.00%	
14. The Value Line Investment Survey		+0.14%
15. InvesTech Market Analyst		+0.13%

Appendix A-3: Gain from 1/1/85 to 6/30/92 (continued)

Newsletter	Individual Portfolio	Overall Average
16. **NoLoad Fund*X (Average)		+142.8%
a. Portfolio of "Class 3" Funds (Higher Quality Growth Funds)	+214.3%	
b. Portfolio of "Class 2" Funds (Speculative Growth Funds)	+133.7%	
c. Portfolio of "Class 1" Funds (Most Speculative Growth Funds)	+101.2%	
17. InvesTech Market Analyst		+141.8%
18. Dow Theory Forecasts (Average)		+131.6%
a. Investment List	+193.2%	
b. Income List	+192.8%	
c. Growth List	+146.6%	
d. Speculative List	+118.2%	
19. Telephone Switch Newsletter (Average)		+126.3%
a. International Funds/Cash Switch Plan	+193.3%	
b. Equity/Cash Switch Plan	+139.0%	
c. Gold/Cash Switch Plan	+44.4%	
20. Fund Exchange (Average)		+125.5%
a. Aggressive Growth Margined Mutual Fund Portfolio	+182.2%	
b. Conservative Growth Margined Mutual Fund Portfolio	+161.5%	
c. Fixed Income Bond Portfolio	+126.6%	
d. Aggressive Growth Mutual Fund Portfolio	+124.4%	
e. Growth/Income Mutual Fund Portfolio	+105.9%	
f. Gold Mutual Funds Portfolio	+41.3%	
21. The Marketarian Letter (Average)		+121.4%
a. Model Portfolio	+62.4%	
22. The Insiders		+118.9%
23. Emerging & Special Situations		+118.0%
24. The Cabot Market Letter (Average)		+117.2%
a. Model Stock Portfolio	+72.2%	
25. Weber's Fund Advisor (Average)		+114.0%
a. "Go-With-the-Winner Strategy" Portfolio	+121.8%	
26. Market Logic (Average)		+107.0%
a. Master (Stock) Portfolio	+118.4%	
b. Actual Option Portfolio	+73.6%	
27. New Issues		+104.8%
28. The Big Picture (Average)		+102.3%
a. Trading Portfolio	+123.2%	
29. Growth Stock Outlook		+102.2%
30. The Outlook (Average)		+101.4%
31. LaLoggia's Special Situation Report (Average)		+99.8%
a. Master List of Recommended Stocks	+131.9%	

Newsletter	Individual Portfolio	Overall Average
16. Telephone Switch Newsletter (Average)		+0.13%
a. International Funds/Cash Switch Plan	+0.19%	
b. Equity/Cash Switch Plan	+0.12%	
c. Gold/Cash Switch Plan	0.00%	
17. The Princeton Portfolios (Average)		+0.13%
a. Long-Term Portfolio #1	+0.12%	
b. Long-Term Portfolio #2	+0.12%	
18. The Value Line OTC Special Situations Service		+0.13%
19. **NoLoad Fund*X (Average)		+0.12%
a. Portfolio of "Class 3" Funds (Higher Quality Growth Funds)	+0.19%	
b. Portfolio of "Class 2" Funds (Speculative Growth Funds)	+0.11%	
c. Portfolio of "Class 1" Funds (Most Speculative Growth Funds)	+0.07%	
20. The Peter Dag Investment Letter (Average)		+0.12%
a. Model Vanguard Fund Portfolio	+0.22%	
21. California Technology Stock Letter		+0.12%
22. Dow Theory Forecasts (Average)		+0.11%
a. Income List	+0.20%	
b. Investment List	+0.16%	
c. Growth List	+0.11%	
d. Speculative List	+0.09%	
23. The Marketarian Letter (Average)		+0.10%
a. Model Portfolio	+0.02%	
24. Weber's Fund Advisor (Average)		+0.10%
a. "Go-With-the-Winner Strategy" Portfolio	+0.11%	
25. The Insiders		+0.09%
26. Growth Fund Guide (Average)		+0.09%
a. Special Situations Mutual Fund Portfolio	+0.12%	
b. Quality Growth Mutual Fund Portfolio	+0.11%	
c. Aggressive Growth Mutual Fund Portfolio	+0.06%	
d. Growth Mutual Fund Portfolio	+0.05%	
27. The Cabot Market Letter (Average)		+0.08%
a. Model Stock Portfolio	+0.05%	
28. Emerging & Special Situations		+0.08%
29. The Prudent Speculator		+0.08%
30. Market Logic (Average)		+0.08%
a. Master (Stock) Portfolio	+0.09%	
b. Actual Option Portfolio	+0.07%	
31. Harry Browne's Special Reports (Average)		+0.08%
a. Variable [Speculative] Portfolio	+0.01%	

Newsletter	Individual Portfolio	Overall Average
32. Growth Fund Guide (Average)		+94.7%
a. Special Situations Mutual Fund Portfolio	+124.7%	
b. Quality Growth Mutual Fund Portfolio	+96.2%	
c. Aggressive Growth Mutual Fund Portfolio	+81.8%	
d. Growth Mutual Fund Portfolio	+76.6%	
33. The Peter Dag Investment Letter (Average)		+86.1%
a. Model Vanguard Fund Portfolio	+103.0%	
34. Harry Browne's Special Reports (Average)		+84.5%
a. Variable [Speculative] Portfolio	+60.3%	
35. The Prudent Speculator		+81.6%
36. Bob Nurock's Advisory (Average)		+80.7%
a. Model Portfolio	+71.3%	
37. Margo's Market Monitor (Average)		+80.3%
a. Common Stock Portfolio	+53.5%	
38. The Addison Report (Average)		+74.3%
a. Conservative Portfolio	+89.9%	
b. Speculative Portfolio	+67.8%	
39. The Professional Tape Reader (Average)		+62.6%
a. Model Stock Portfolio	+44.6%	
The Riskless Rate of Return: A T-Bill Portfolio		+61.7%
40. United & Babson Investment Report (Average)		+55.7%
a. Stocks for Long-Term Growth	+76.2%	
b. Stocks for The Income-Minded	+63.1%	
c. Cyclical Stocks for Profit	+18.4%	
41. Plain Talk Investor (Average)		+54.1%
a. "Personal-Best" Stock Portfolio	+109.5%	
b. High Risk/High Reward Portfolio	+8.7%	
42. Stockmarket Cycles (Average)		+49.3%
a. Mutual Fund Portfolio	+166.3%	
b. Model Stock Portfolio	−20.8%	
43. Kinsman's Telephone Growth & Income Service (Average)		+47.2%
a. Growth & Income Portfolio	+49.4%	
44. Financial World (Average)		+44.6%
a. Stocks Rated A+	+86.2%	
45. The International Harry Schultz Letter (Average)		+43.9%
a. U.S. Stocks on the "List"	+28.6%	
b. Portfolio constructed from gold/silver trading advice (no margin)	+22.6%	
46. The Wall Street Digest (Average)		+42.8%
a. Stock and Bond Portfolio	+33.7%	
47. The Ruff Times (Average)		+41.9%
48. Professional Timing Service (Average)		+30.8%
a. Gold Futures Trading Portfolio	+31.2%	

Newsletter	Individual Portfolio	Overall Average
32. The Outlook (Average)		+0.08%
33. The Big Picture (Average)		+0.08%
a. Trading Portfolio	+0.09%	
34. LaLoggia's Special Situation Report (Average)		+0.08%
a. Master List of Recommended Stocks	+0.10%	
35. New Issues		+0.07%
36. Bob Nurock's Advisory (Average)		+0.05%
a. Model Portfolio	+0.04%	
37. Margo's Market Monitor (Average)		+0.05%
a. Common Stock Portfolio	+0.03%	
38. The Addison Report (Average)		+0.04%
a. Conservative Portfolio	+0.06%	
b. Speculative Portfolio	+0.03%	
39. The Granville Market Letter (Average)		+0.04%
a. Options Portfolio	+0.06%	
b. Traders' Stock Portfolio	−0.06%	
40. The Option Advisor (Average)		+0.02%
a. Conservative Portfolio	+0.03%	
b. Aggressive Portfolio	0.00%	
41. The Wall Street Digest (Average)		+0.02%
a. Stock and Bond Portfolio	+0.01%	
42. The Professional Tape Reader (Average)		+0.01%
a. Model Stock Portfolio	−0.03%	
43. United & Babson Investment Report (Average)		+0.01%
a. Stocks for Long-Term Growth	+0.05%	
b. Stocks for The Income-Minded	+0.02%	
c. Cyclical Stocks for Profit	−0.02%	
44. Plain Talk Investor (Average)		+0.01%
a. "Personal-Best" Stock Portfolio	+0.09%	
b. High Risk/High Reward Portfolio	−0.05%	
45. Financial World (Average)		+0.01%
a. Stocks Rated A+	+0.06%	
46. Stockmarket Cycles (Average)		0.00%
a. Mutual Fund Portfolio	+0.16%	
b. Model Stock Portfolio	−0.14%	
47. The Ruff Times (Average)		−0.01%
48. The International Harry Schultz Letter (Average)		−0.03%
a. U.S. Stocks on the "List"	−0.03%	
b. Portfolio constructed from gold/silver trading advice (no margin)	−0.12%	

Appendix A-3: Gain from 1/1/85 to 6/30/92 (continued)

Newsletter	Individual Portfolio	Overall Average
49. The Option Advisor (Average)		+3.8%
a. Conservative Portfolio	−32.8%	
b. Aggressive Portfolio	−64.0%	
50. The R.H.M. Survey of Warrants, Options & Low-Price Stocks		−13.0%
51. The Dines Letter (Average)		−16.5%
a. Long-Term Growth Portfolio	+136.6%	
b. Short-Term Trading Portfolio	−86.2%	
52. The Garside Forecast		−35.4%
53. On Markets		−51.9%
54. The Holt Advisory (Average)		−54.0%
55. The Granville Market Letter (Average)		−88.8%
a. Traders' Stock Portfolio	−16.7%	
b. Options Portfolio	−100.0%	

Newsletter	Individual Portfolio	Overall Average
49. Kinsman's Telephone Growth & Income Service (Average)		−0.04%
a. Growth & Income Portfolio	−0.04%	
50. The R.H.M. Survey of Warrants, Options & Low-Price Stocks		−0.05%
51. The Dines Letter (Average)		−0.06%
a. Long-Term Growth Portfolio	+0.09%	
b. Short-Term Trading Portfolio	−0.13%	
52. Professional Timing Service (Average)		−0.08%
a. Gold Futures Trading Portfolio	−0.06%	
53. On Markets		−0.09%
54. The Garside Forecast		−0.15%
55. The Holt Advisory (Average)		−0.20%

5.5 YR

Newsletter	Individual Portfolio	Overall Average
1. BI Research		+302.0%
2. MPT Review (Average)		+261.7%
a. $200,000 Aggressive Portfolio	+311.1%	
b. $400,000 Aggressive Portfolio	+286.8%	
c. $800,000 Conservative Portfolio	+255.4%	
d. $800,000 Moderately Aggressive Portfolio	+252.7%	
e. $800,000 Aggressive Portfolio	+240.1%	
f. $400,000 Conservative Portfolio	+235.4%	
g. $400,000 Moderately Aggressive Portfolio	+227.9%	
h. $200,000 Moderately Aggressive Portfolio	+207.7%	
i. $200,000 Conservative Portfolio	+192.5%	
2A. OTC Insight (Average)*		+170.3%
3. Medical Technology Stock Letter (Average)		+163.7%
a. Model Portfolio	+135.4%	
4. The Chartist (Average)		+147.6%
a. Traders Portfolio	+153.4%	
b. Actual Cash Account	+130.8%	
5. California Technology Stock Letter		+147.3%
6. The Value Line OTC Special Situations Service		+145.1%
7. Fidelity Monitor (Average)		+127.7%
a. Growth Mutual Funds Portfolio	+132.3%	
b. Select System Mutual Funds Portfolio	+114.3%	
8. The Zweig Forecast		+127.0%
9. Value Line Convertibles		+115.8%
10. Investment Quality Trends		+114.8%
11. Systems and Forecasts (Average)		+109.0%
a. The Regular Portfolio	+86.7%	
12. The Mutual Fund Strategist (Average)		+105.5%
13. Investors Intelligence (Average)		+101.4%
a. Fidelity Switch Fund (Equity) Portfolio	+125.3%	
14. Zweig Performance Ratings Report		+99.7%
15. Mutual Fund Forecaster		+95.9%
16. InvesTech Mutual Fund Advisor		+95.6%
Wilshire 5000 Value-Weighted Total Return Index		+93.3%

* Based on period from August 1987 through mid-1992; included for comparison purposes only.

Appendix A-4: Risk-Adjusted Performance from 1/1/87 to 6/30/92

Newsletter	Individual Portfolio	Overall Average
1. Systems and Forecasts (Average)		+0.25%
a. The Regular Portfolio	+0.20%	
2. BI Research		+0.23%
3. The Zweig Forecast		+0.21%
4. InvesTech Mutual Fund Advisor		+0.21%
5. MPT Review (Average)		+0.20%
a. $200,000 Aggressive Portfolio	+0.23%	
b. $800,000 Conservative Portfolio	+0.21%	
c. $800,000 Moderately Aggressive Portfolio	+0.20%	
d. $400,000 Aggressive Portfolio	+0.20%	
e. $800,000 Aggressive Portfolio	+0.19%	
f. $400,000 Conservative Portfolio	+0.18%	
g. $200,000 Moderately Aggressive Portfolio	+0.18%	
h. $200,000 Conservative Portfolio	+0.17%	
i. $400,000 Moderately Aggressive Portfolio	+0.17%	
6. Zweig Performance Ratings Report		+0.20%
7. California Technology Stock Letter		+0.19%
8. Investors Intelligence (Average)		+0.18%
a. Fidelity Switch Fund (Equity) Portfolio	+0.24%	
9. Investment Quality Trends		+0.18%
10. The Chartist (Average)		+0.17%
a. Actual Cash Account	+0.18%	
b. Traders Portfolio	+0.15%	
10A. OTC Insight (Average)		+0.16%
11. Fidelity Monitor (Average)		+0.16%
a. Growth Mutual Funds Portfolio	+0.18%	
b. Select System Mutual Funds Portfolio	+0.13%	
12. Value Line Convertibles		+0.15%
13. InvesTech Market Analyst		+0.15%
14. The Mutual Fund Strategist (Average)		+0.15%
15. Fund Exchange (Average)		+0.14%
a. Fixed Income Bond Portfolio	+0.36%	
b. Aggressive Growth Margined Mutual Fund Portfolio	+0.15%	
c. Aggressive Balanced Mutual Fund Portfolio	+0.13%	
d. Aggressive Growth Mutual Fund Portfolio	+0.13%	
e. Growth/Income Mutual Fund Portfolio	+0.12%	
f. Conservative Growth Margined Mutual Fund Portfolio	+0.10%	
g. Conservative Balanced Mutual Fund Portfolio	+0.10%	
h. Gold Mutual Funds Portfolio	0.00%	
16. The Value Line OTC Special Situations Service		+0.14%

* Based on period from August 1987 through mid-1992; included for comparison purposes only.

Newsletter	Individual Portfolio	Overall Average
17. Fundline (Average)		+92.4%
18. The Investment Reporter (Average)		+91.5%
a. Portfolio of Speculative Stocks	+190.2%	
b. Portfolio of Higher Risk Stocks	+68.0%	
c. Portfolio of Very Conservative Stocks	+63.6%	
d. Portfolio of Conservative Stocks	+54.6%	
e. Portfolio of Average Risk Stocks	+15.2%	
19. New Issues		+91.3%
20. The Value Line Investment Survey		+86.9%
21. InvesTech Market Analyst		+78.3%
22. The Big Picture (Average)		+76.6%
a. Trading Portfolio	+110.5%	
b. Model Portfolio	+42.8%	
23. Fund Exchange (Average)		+74.9%
a. Aggressive Growth Margined Mutual Fund Portfolio	+128.5%	
b. Aggressive Growth Mutual Fund Portfolio	+75.5%	
c. Conservative Growth Margined Mutual Fund Portfolio	+75.1%	
d. Fixed Income Bond Portfolio	+74.3%	
e. Aggressive Balanced Mutual Fund Portfolio	+67.2%	
f. Growth/Income Mutual Fund Portfolio	+65.1%	
g. Conservative Balanced Mutual Fund Portfolio	+54.3%	
h. Gold Mutual Funds Portfolio	+30.0%	
24. Dessauer's Journal		+72.4%
25. The Insiders		+71.2%
26. United Mutual Fund Selector (Average)		+68.0%
a. Aggressive Growth Funds	+89.9%	
b. Growth & Income Funds	+67.9%	
c. Growth Funds	+60.3%	
d. Income Funds	+48.2%	
27. Better Investing		+67.7%
28. Switch Fund Timing (Average)		+67.6%
a. Model Stock Portfolio	+78.7%	
29. Cabot's Mutual Fund Navigator (Average)		+65.6%
a. Growth Portfolio	+43.9%	
30. The No-Load Fund Investor (Average)		+60.7%
a. Wealth Builder Portfolio	+69.8%	
b. Pre-Retirement Portfolio	+61.6%	
c. Retirement Portfolio	+59.8%	
31. Personal Finance (Average)		+60.1%
a. Growth Portfolio	+70.0%	
b. Income Portfolio	+54.0%	
32. Emerging & Special Situations		+60.0%

Newsletter	Individual Portfolio	Overall Average
17. Medical Technology Stock Letter (Average)		+0.14%
a. Model Portfolio	+0.13%	
18. The Granville Market Letter (Average)		+0.12%
a. Options Portfolio	+0.14%	
b. Traders' Stock Portfolio	+0.02%	
Wilshire 5000 Value-Weighted Total Return Index		+0.12%
19. The Investment Reporter (Average)		+0.12%
a. Portfolio of Speculative Stocks	+0.19%	
b. Portfolio of Higher Risk Stocks	+0.07%	
c. Portfolio of Very Conservative Stocks	+0.07%	
d. Portfolio of Conservative Stocks	+0.05%	
e. Portfolio of Average Risk Stocks	−0.02%	
20. Mutual Fund Forecaster		+0.11%
21. Fundline (Average)		+0.11%
22. Switch Fund Timing (Average)		+0.11%
a. Model Stock Portfolio	+0.10%	
23. The Value Line Investment Survey		+0.10%
24. Growth Stock Outlook		+0.10%
25. New Issues		+0.10%
26. The Big Picture (Average)		+0.09%
a. Trading Portfolio	+0.12%	
b. Model Portfolio	+0.03%	
27. United Mutual Fund Selector (Average)		+0.09%
a. Aggressive Growth Funds	+0.11%	
b. Growth & Income Funds	+0.09%	
c. Growth Funds	+0.06%	
d. Income Funds	+0.05%	
28. Dessauer's Journal		+0.09%
29. Cabot's Mutual Fund Navigator (Average)		+0.08%
a. Growth Portfolio	+0.03%	
30. The Insiders		+0.08%
31. Better Investing		+0.08%
32. The No-Load Fund Investor (Average)		+0.07%
a. Wealth Builder Portfolio	+0.08%	
b. Retirement Portfolio	+0.08%	
c. Pre-Retirement Portfolio	+0.07%	

Newsletter	Individual Portfolio	Overall Average
33. Telephone Switch Newsletter (Average)		+56.9%
a. Equity/Cash Switch Plan	+99.0%	
b. International Funds/Cash Switch Plan	+38.7%	
c. Gold/Cash Switch Plan	+29.2%	
34. Donoghue's Moneyletter (Average)		+55.1%
a. "Venturesome" Model Portfolio	+59.2%	
35. Weber's Fund Advisor (Average)		+53.8%
a. "Go-With-the-Winner Strategy" Portfolio	+59.4%	
36. The Mutual Fund Letter (Average)		+53.4%
a. Growth & Income Portfolio	+61.3%	
b. Highly Aggressive Portfolio	+53.1%	
c. Moderately Aggressive Portfolio	+50.2%	
d. Income Portfolio	+48.6%	
37. The Marketarian Letter (Average)		+53.1%
a. Mutual Fund Portfolio for Traders	+92.2%	
b. Model Portfolio	+12.4%	
38. Dow Theory Forecasts (Average)		+52.8%
a. Growth List	+80.4%	
b. Investment List	+74.6%	
c. Income List	+64.0%	
d. Speculative List	+52.3%	
e. Low-Priced Stocks & Special Situations List	−2.6%	
39. Bob Brinker's Marketimer (Average)		+52.7%
a. Long-Term Growth Mutual Fund Portfolio	+66.3%	
b. Aggressive Growth Mutual Fund Portfolio	+48.5%	
c. Balanced Portfolio	+39.0%	
40. Growth Stock Outlook		+51.0%
41. Investment Horizons		+50.1%
42. **NoLoad Fund*X (Average)		+48.2%
a. Portfolio of "Class 3" Funds (Higher Quality Growth Funds)	+61.8%	
b. Portfolio of "Class 2" Funds (Speculative Growth Funds)	+47.0%	
c. Portfolio of "Class 4" Funds (Total Return Funds)	+45.5%	
d. Portfolio of "Class 1" Funds (Most Speculative Growth Funds)	+42.9%	
43. The Professional Tape Reader (Average)		+47.6%
a. Mutual Fund Portfolio	+61.3%	
b. Model Stock Portfolio	+34.4%	
44. The Cabot Market Letter (Average)		+46.3%
a. Model Stock Portfolio	+16.0%	
45. Plain Talk Investor (Average)		+46.3%
a. High Risk/High Reward Portfolio	+44.9%	
b. "Personal-Best" Stock Portfolio	+44.4%	

Newsletter	Individual Portfolio	Overall Average
33. Personal Finance (Average)		+0.07%
a. Growth Portfolio	+0.08%	
b. Income Portfolio	+0.06%	
34. Emerging & Special Situations		+0.06%
35. The Mutual Fund Letter (Average)		+0.06%
a. Growth & Income Portfolio	+0.11%	
b. Income Portfolio	+0.06%	
c. Highly Aggressive Portfolio	+0.05%	
d. Moderately Aggressive Portfolio	+0.05%	
36. Telephone Switch Newsletter (Average)		+0.06%
a. Equity/Cash Switch Plan	+0.15%	
b. International Funds/Cash Switch Plan	+0.01%	
c. Gold/Cash Switch Plan	0.00%	
37. Donoghue's Moneyletter (Average)		+0.06%
a. "Venturesome" Model Portfolio	+0.06%	
38. Weber's Fund Advisor (Average)		+0.05%
a. "Go-With-the-Winner Strategy" Portfolio	+0.06%	
39. The Marketarian Letter (Average)		+0.05%
a. Mutual Fund Portfolio for Traders	+0.14%	
b. Model Portfolio	−0.06%	
40. Bob Brinker's Marketimer (Average)		+0.05%
a. Long-Term Growth Mutual Fund Portfolio	+0.08%	
b. Aggressive Growth Mutual Fund Portfolio	+0.04%	
c. Balanced Portfolio	+0.02%	
41. Dow Theory Forecasts (Average)		+0.05%
a. Growth List	+0.10%	
b. Investment List	+0.09%	
c. Income List	+0.08%	
d. Speculative List	+0.05%	
c. Low-Priced Stocks & Special Situations List	−0.07%	
42. The Professional Tape Reader (Average)		+0.05%
a. Mutual Fund Portfolio	+0.16%	
b. Model Stock Portfolio	−0.02%	
43. Investment Horizons		+0.05%
44. **NoLoad Fund*X (Average)		+0.04%
a. Portfolio of "Class 3" Funds (Higher Quality Growth Funds)	+0.07%	
b. Portfolio of "Class 1" Funds (Most Speculative Growth Funds)	+0.04%	
c. Portfolio of "Class 2" Funds (Speculative Growth Funds)	+0.04%	
d. Portfolio of "Class 4" Funds (Total Return Funds)	+0.03%	
45. The Option Advisor (Average)		+0.04%
a. Aggressive Portfolio	+0.06%	
b. Conservative Portfolio	−0.01%	

Newsletter	Individual Portfolio	Overall Average
46. The Peter Dag Investment Letter (Average)		+43.6%
a. Model Vanguard Fund Portfolio	+56.6%	
47. The Princeton Portfolios (Average)		+42.6%
a. Long-Term Portfolio #1	+70.2%	
b. Long-Term Portfolio #2	+16.8%	
48. Market Logic (Average)		+41.9%
a. Master (Stock) Portfolio	+41.3%	
b. Actual Option Portfolio	+32.2%	
The Riskless Rate of Return: A T-Bill Portfolio		+41.7%
49. The Outlook (Average)		+41.3%
50. Mutual Fund Investing (Average)		+40.5%
a. Portfolio II (Balanced Growth)	+48.9%	
b. Portfolio I (Growth With Income)	+43.1%	
51. The Granville Market Letter (Average)		+37.5%
a. Traders' Stock Portfolio	+24.8%	
b. Options Portfolio	−94.7%	
52. The Addison Report (Average)		+37.0%
a. Speculative Portfolio	+45.3%	
b. Conservative Portfolio	+36.5%	
53. LaLoggia's Special Situation Report (Average)		+36.1%
a. Master List of Recommended Stocks	+60.7%	
b. Other Recommended Stocks	+10.8%	
54. Harry Browne's Special Reports (Average)		+36.1%
a. Variable [Speculative] Portfolio	+18.2%	
55. Equities Special Situations		+34.3%
56. Growth Fund Guide (Average)		+29.0%
a. Special Situations Mutual Fund Portfolio	+39.6%	
b. Quality Growth Mutual Fund Portfolio	+37.3%	
c. Aggressive Growth Mutual Fund Portfolio	+23.9%	
d. Growth Mutual Fund Portfolio	+16.5%	
57. Margo's Market Monitor (Average)		+25.8%
a. Fidelity Select Funds Portfolio	+42.2%	
b. Common Stock Portfolio	+0.9%	
58. Kinsman's Telephone Growth & Income Service (Average)		+25.1%
a. Growth & Income Portfolio	+23.6%	
59. The Ruff Times (Average)		+24.4%
a. The Back Page Portfolio	+20.0%	
60. The Sector Funds Newsletter (Average)		+22.5%
a. Model Mutual Fund Portfolio 3 (Mostly Bonds)	+49.8%	
b. Model Mutual Fund Portfolio 1	−20.9%	

Newsletter	Individual Portfolio	Overall Average
46. The Cabot Market Letter (Average)		+0.04%
a. Model Stock Portfolio	−0.01%	
47. The Princeton Portfolios (Average)		+0.04%
a. Long-Term Portfolio #1	+0.07%	
b. Long-Term Portfolio #2	0.00%	
48. Plain Talk Investor (Average)		+0.03%
a. High Risk/High Reward Portfolio	+0.04%	
b. "Personal-Best" Stock Portfolio	+0.03%	
49. The Prudent Speculator		+0.03%
50. Market Logic (Average)		+0.03%
a. Master (Stock) Portfolio	+0.03%	
b. Actual Option Portfolio	−0.15%	
51. The Outlook (Average)		+0.02%
52. The Peter Dag Investment Letter (Average)		+0.02%
a. Model Vanguard Fund Portfolio	+0.14%	
53. LaLoggia's Special Situation Report (Average)		+0.02%
a. Master List of Recommended Stocks	+0.07%	
b. Other Recommended Stocks	−0.02%	
54. The Wall Street Generalist (Average)		+0.02%
a. Select Trading Portfolio	+0.02%	
55. Equities Special Situations		+0.02%
56. The Addison Report (Average)		+0.01%
a. Speculative Portfolio	+0.03%	
b. Conservative Portfolio	+0.01%	
57. Mutual Fund Investing (Average)		0.00%
a. Portfolio II (Balanced Growth)	+0.05%	
b. Portfolio I (Growth With Income)	+0.02%	
58. The Wall Street Digest (Average)		−0.01%
a. Stock and Bond Portfolio	−0.01%	
59. The Ruff Times (Average)		−0.01%
a. The Back Page Portfolio	−0.01%	
60. Margo's Market Monitor (Average)		−0.02%
a. Fidelity Select Funds Portfolio	+0.02%	
b. Common Stock Portfolio	−0.04%	

Newsletter	Individual Portfolio	Overall Average
61. United & Babson Investment Report (Average)		+20.8%
a. Stocks for Long-Term Growth	+29.1%	
b. Cyclical Stocks for Profit	+13.1%	
c. Stocks for The Income-Minded	+11.4%	
62. The International Harry Schultz Letter (Average)		+20.2%
a. Portfolio constructed from gold/silver trading advice (no margin)	+25.5%	
b. Foreign Stocks on the "List"	+14.1%	
c. U.S. Stocks on the "List"	+10.7%	
63. Stockmarket Cycles (Average)		+17.6%
a. Mutual Fund Portfolio	+104.3%	
b. Model Stock Portfolio	−35.2%	
64. The Wall Street Digest (Average)		+15.7%
a. Stock and Bond Portfolio	+8.4%	
65. The Option Advisor (Average)		+14.3%
a. Aggressive Portfolio	+6.5%	
b. Conservative Portfolio	−65.5%	
66. Financial World (Average)		+13.3%
a. Stocks Rated A+	+45.9%	
67. Professional Timing Service (Average)		+11.9%
a. Mutual Fund Model Portfolio	+92.2%	
b. Gold Futures Trading Portfolio	+4.7%	
68. Bob Nurock's Advisory (Average)		+8.9%
a. Model Portfolio	+3.2%	
69. The Volume Reversal Survey (Average)		+4.9%
a. Index Fund Portfolio	+93.4%	
70. The Prudent Speculator		−4.2%
71. The R.H.M. Survey of Warrants, Options & Low-Price Stocks		−29.7%
72. On Markets		−36.8%
73. The Dines Letter (Average)		−39.5%
a. Long-Term Growth Portfolio	+70.1%	
b. Short-Term Trading Portfolio	−91.1%	
74. The Holt Advisory (Average)		−45.2%
75. The Garside Forecast		−49.7%
76. The Wall Street Generalist (Average)		−62.8%
a. Select Trading Portfolio	−87.0%	
77. Your Window Into the Future (Average)		−78.3%
a. Portfolio A: Aggressive Portfolio	+35.5%	
b. Portfolio B: Conservative Portfolio	+13.2%	
c. Portfolio C: Speculative Portfolio	−100.0%	

Appendix A-4: Risk-Adjusted Performance from 1/1/87 to 6/30/92 (continued)

Newsletter	Individual Portfolio	Overall Average
61. The Sector Funds Newsletter (Average)		−0.02%
a. Model Mutual Fund Portfolio 3 (Mostly Bonds)	+0.04%	
b. Model Mutual Fund Portfolio 1	−0.07%	
62. Financial World (Average)		−0.02%
a. Stocks Rated A+	+0.04%	
63. Harry Browne's Special Reports (Average)		−0.02%
a. Variable [Speculative] Portfolio	−0.08%	
64. United & Babson Investment Report (Average)		−0.03%
a. Stocks for Long-Term Growth	0.00%	
b. Cyclical Stocks for Profit	−0.01%	
c. Stocks for The Income-Minded	−0.09%	
65. Growth Fund Guide (Average)		−0.05%
a. Special Situations Mutual Fund Portfolio	+0.01%	
b. Quality Growth Mutual Fund Portfolio	−0.02%	
c. Aggressive Growth Mutual Fund Portfolio	−0.08%	
d. Growth Mutual Fund Portfolio	−0.11%	
66. Your Window Into the Future (Average)		−0.06%
a. Portfolio A: Aggressive Portfolio	+0.03%	
b. Portfolio B: Conservative Portfolio	−0.02%	
c. Portfolio C: Speculative Portfolio	−0.07%	
67. The International Harry Schultz Letter (Average)		−0.06%
a. Foreign Stocks on the "List"	−0.03%	
b. U.S. Stocks on the "List"	−0.05%	
c. Portfolio constructed from gold/silver trading advice (no margin)	−0.07%	
68. On Markets		−0.06%
69. The Volume Reversal Survey (Average)		−0.07%
a. Index Fund Portfolio	+0.15%	
70. Stockmarket Cycles (Average)		−0.07%
a. Mutual Fund Portfolio	+0.18%	
b. Model Stock Portfolio	−0.25%	
71. Kinsman's Telephone Growth & Income Service (Average)		−0.07%
a. Growth & Income Portfolio	−0.10%	
72. The R.H.M. Survey of Warrants, Options & Low-Price Stocks		−0.08%
73. Bob Nurock's Advisory (Average)		−0.08%
a. Model Portfolio	−0.06%	
74. Professional Timing Service (Average)		−0.12%
a. Mutual Fund Model Portfolio	+0.15%	
b. Gold Futures Trading Portfolio	−0.15%	
75. The Dines Letter (Average)		−0.16%
a. Long-Term Growth Portfolio	+0.07%	
b. Short-Term Trading Portfolio	−0.26%	
76. The Holt Advisory (Average)		−0.18%
77. The Garside Forecast		−0.23%

3.5YR

Newsletter	Individual Portfolio	Overall Average
1. Medical Technology Stock Letter (Average)		+289.1%
a. Aggressive Portfolio	+311.1%	
b. Model Portfolio	+247.4%	
2. The Granville Market Letter (Average)		+270.3%
a. Options Portfolio	+211.8%	
b. Traders' Stock Portfolio	+24.6%	
3. OTC Insight (Average)		+231.8%
a. $200,000 Aggressive Portfolio	+284.5%	
b. $800,000 Aggressive Portfolio	+252.5%	
c. $400,000 Aggressive Portfolio	+235.3%	
d. $400,000 Conservative Portfolio	+234.9%	
e. $200,000 Conservative Portfolio	+234.1%	
f. $200,000 Moderately Aggressive Portfolio	+223.3%	
g. $800,000 Moderately Aggressive Portfolio	+216.2%	
h. $800,000 Conservative Portfolio	+211.4%	
i. $400,000 Moderately Aggressive Portfolio	+206.4%	
4. BI Research		+205.5%
5. The Oberweis Report		+191.5%
6. MPT Review (Average)		+154.0%
a. $50,000 Aggressive Portfolio	+204.6%	
b. $800,000 Conservative Portfolio	+176.4%	
c. $400,000 Aggressive Portfolio	+163.1%	
d. $50,000 Moderately Aggressive Portfolio	+162.5%	
e. $800,000 Aggressive Portfolio	+155.8%	
f. $200,000 Aggressive Portfolio	+155.0%	
g. $800,000 Moderately Aggressive Portfolio	+153.9%	
h. $50,000 Conservative Portfolio	+149.7%	
i. $400,000 Moderately Aggressive Portfolio	+148.2%	
j. $400,000 Conservative Portfolio	+137.7%	
k. $200,000 Conservative Portfolio	+115.1%	
l. $200,000 Moderately Aggressive Portfolio	+114.3%	
7. The Chartist (Average)		+136.6%
a. Traders Portfolio	+160.8%	
b. Actual Cash Account	+107.0%	
8. Fidelity Monitor (Average)		+107.9%
a. Select System Mutual Funds Portfolio	+130.0%	
b. Growth Mutual Funds Portfolio	+81.7%	
9. The Value Line OTC Special Situations Service		+101.9%
10. Timer Digest (Average)		+88.7%
a. Fidelity Select Portfolio	+121.9%	
b. Model Stock Portfolio	+40.8%	

Appendix A-5: Risk-Adjusted Performance from 1/1/89 to 6/30/92

Newsletter	Individual Portfolio	Overall Average
1. BI Research		+0.33%
2. Blue Chip Values (Average)		+0.31%
a. Income & Growth Model Portfolio	+0.38%	
b. Growth Model Portfolio	+0.25%	
3. Medical Technology Stock Letter (Average)		+0.30%
a. Model Portfolio	+0.30%	
b. Aggressive Portfolio	+0.28%	
4. Fidelity Monitor (Average)		+0.30%
a. Select System Mutual Funds Portfolio	+0.30%	
b. Growth Mutual Funds Portfolio	+0.23%	
5. Zweig Performance Ratings Report		+0.28%
6. The Chartist (Average)		+0.28%
a. Actual Cash Account	+0.27%	
b. Traders Portfolio	+0.26%	
7. Fidelity Insight (Average)		+0.28%
a. Growth Portfolio	+0.35%	
b. Growth & Income Fund Portfolio	+0.32%	
c. Income & Preservation Fund Portfolio	+0.31%	
d. Speculative Portfolio	+0.15%	
8. OTC Insight (Average)		+0.28%
a. $200,000 Aggressive Portfolio	+0.31%	
b. $800,000 Aggressive Portfolio	+0.29%	
c. $400,000 Conservative Portfolio	+0.29%	
d. $200,000 Conservative Portfolio	+0.28%	
e. $400,000 Aggressive Portfolio	+0.28%	
f. $200,000 Moderately Aggressive Portfolio	+0.27%	
g. $800,000 Moderately Aggressive Portfolio	+0.27%	
h. $800,000 Conservative Portfolio	+0.27%	
i. $400,000 Moderately Aggressive Portfolio	+0.26%	
9. The Oberweis Report		+0.28%
10. MPT Review (Average)		+0.25%
a. $50,000 Aggressive Portfolio	+0.30%	
b. $800,000 Conservative Portfolio	+0.28%	
c. $50,000 Moderately Aggressive Portfolio	+0.27%	
d. $800,000 Moderately Aggressive Portfolio	+0.25%	
e. $800,000 Aggressive Portfolio	+0.25%	
f. $50,000 Conservative Portfolio	+0.25%	
g. $200,000 Aggressive Portfolio	+0.24%	
h. $400,000 Aggressive Portfolio	+0.24%	
i. $400,000 Moderately Aggressive Portfolio	+0.23%	
j. $400,000 Conservative Portfolio	+0.22%	
k. $200,000 Conservative Portfolio	+0.20%	
l. $200,000 Moderately Aggressive Portfolio	+0.20%	

Appendix A-5: Gain from 1/1/89 to 6/30/92 (continued)

Newsletter	Individual Portfolio	Overall Average
11. The Chartist Mutual Fund Timer		+81.6%
12. Investment Quality Trends		+76.7%
13. Fundline (Average)		+76.3%
14. Mutual Fund Forecaster		+74.4%
15. Zweig Performance Ratings Report		+69.2%
16. New Issues		+67.3%
17. The Value Line Investment Survey		+64.9%
18. Fidelity Insight (Average)		+63.3%
a. Growth Portfolio	+79.6%	
b. Growth & Income Fund Portfolio	+70.1%	
c. Speculative Portfolio	+52.1%	
d. Income & Preservation Fund Portfolio	+51.7%	
19. The Big Picture (Average)		+63.0%
a. Trading Portfolio	+93.9%	
b. Model Portfolio	+33.4%	
20. Value Line Convertibles		+63.0%
Wilshire 5000 Value-Weighted Total Return Index		+60.3%
21. MPT Fund Review (Average)		+59.3%
a. Optimal Aggressive Strategy	+70.2%	
b. Optimal Selective Strategy	+48.4%	
c. Optimal Balanced Strategy	+42.5%	
22. Blue Chip Values (Average)		+59.0%
a. Income & Growth Model Portfolio	+59.5%	
b. Growth Model Portfolio	+58.3%	
23. Systems and Forecasts (Average)		+53.7%
a. The Regular Portfolio	+40.7%	
24. F.X.C. Investors Corp.		+53.1%
25. Dessauer's Journal		+51.4%
26. The Turnaround Letter (Average)		+50.3%
a. Conservative/Income Portfolio	+69.0%	
b. Moderate Risk Portfolio	+29.2%	
c. Aggressive Portfolio	+21.4%	
27. Emerging & Special Situations		+49.4%
28. Personal Finance (Average)		+49.3%
a. Growth Portfolio	+65.2%	
b. Mutual Fund Portfolio (Short-Term)	+45.9%	
c. Mutual Fund Portfolio (Long-Term)	+45.2%	
d. Income Portfolio	+40.7%	
29. The No-Load Fund Investor (Average)		+48.9%
a. Wealth Builder Portfolio	+52.7%	
b. Retirement Portfolio	+47.0%	
c. Pre-Retirement Portfolio	+46.3%	

Newsletter	Individual Portfolio	Overall Average
11. The Chartist Mutual Fund Timer		+0.25%
12. Investment Quality Trends		+0.23%
13. F.X.C. Investors Corp.		+0.23%
14. The Granville Market Letter (Average)		+0.22%
a. Options Portfolio	+0.26%	
b. Traders' Stock Portfolio	+0.02%	
15. Timer Digest (Average)		+0.22%
a. Fidelity Select Portfolio	+0.27%	
b. Model Stock Portfolio	+0.08%	
16. Fundline (Average)		+0.20%
17. The Value Line OTC Special Situations Service		+0.20%
18. Systems and Forecasts (Average)		+0.20%
a. The Regular Portfolio	+0.13%	
19. Value Line Convertibles		+0.19%
20. InvesTech Mutual Fund Advisor		+0.19%
21. Mutual Fund Forecaster		+0.18%
22. Personal Finance (Average)		+0.18%
a. Growth Portfolio	+0.18%	
b. Mutual Fund Portfolio (Long-Term)	+0.18%	
c. Income Portfolio	+0.16%	
d. Mutual Fund Portfolio (Short-Term)	+0.12%	
23. Growth Stock Outlook		+0.17%
24. The No-Load Fund Investor (Average)		+0.17%
a. Retirement Portfolio	+0.21%	
b. Pre-Retirement Portfolio	+0.16%	
c. Wealth Builder Portfolio	+0.15%	
25. The Value Line Investment Survey		+0.17%
Wilshire 5000 Value-Weighted Total Return Index		+0.16%
26. The Big Picture (Average)		+0.14%
a. Trading Portfolio	+0.18%	
b. Model Portfolio	+0.06%	
27. New Issues		+0.14%
28. Bob Brinker's Marketimer (Average)		+0.14%
a. Fixed-Income Model Mutual Fund Portfolio	+0.28%	
b. Long-Term Growth Mutual Fund Portfolio	+0.13%	
c. Aggressive Growth Mutual Fund Portfolio	+0.10%	
d. Balanced Portfolio	+0.08%	
29. MPT Fund Review (Average)		+0.14%
a. Optimal Aggressive Strategy	+0.16%	
b. Optimal Selective Strategy	+0.10%	
c. Optimal Balanced Strategy	+0.10%	

Appendix A-5: Gain from 1/1/89 to 6/30/92 (continued)

Newsletter	Individual Portfolio	Overall Average
30. The Mutual Fund Strategist (Average)		+48.1%
a. Sector Portfolio	+53.3%	
b. Diversified Growth Portfolio	+47.9%	
31. The Clean Yield		+46.4%
32. **NoLoad Fund*X (Average)		+45.5%
a. Portfolio of "Class 1" Funds (Most Speculative Growth Funds)	+67.9%	
b. Portfolio of "Class 3" Funds (Higher Quality Growth Funds)	+44.9%	
c. Portfolio of "Class 2" Funds (Speculative Growth Funds)	+41.9%	
d. Portfolio of "Class 4" Funds (Total Return Funds)	+39.4%	
33. InvesTech Mutual Fund Advisor		+44.4%
34. Better Investing		+44.2%
35. United Mutual Fund Selector (Average)		+43.9%
a. Aggressive Growth Funds	+58.2%	
b. Growth Funds	+42.7%	
c. Growth & Income Funds	+38.2%	
d. Income Funds	+34.5%	
36. Bob Brinker's Marketimer (Average)		+43.3%
a. Long-Term Growth Mutual Fund Portfolio	+47.4%	
b. Fixed-Income Model Mutual Fund Portfolio	+44.9%	
c. Aggressive Growth Mutual Fund Portfolio	+43.5%	
d. Balanced Portfolio	+34.6%	
37. The Zweig Forecast		+42.5%
38. The PAD System Report (Average)		+40.9%
a. Model Portfolio C (The Conservative Version)	+91.1%	
b. Model Portfolio A (The Aggressive Version)	+19.6%	
39. Donoghue's Moneyletter (Average)		+39.2%
a. "Venturesome" Model Portfolio	+42.9%	
b. Conservative Mutual Fund Portfolio	+39.0%	
c. Signal Portfolio	+37.8%	
d. Moderate Mutual Fund Portfolio	+34.6%	
40. The Investor's Guide to Closed-End Funds (Average)		+39.0%
a. Managed Portfolio I: Balanced	+37.9%	
41. The Insiders		+38.6%
42. InvesTech Market Analyst		+36.7%

Newsletter	Individual Portfolio	Overall Average
30. The Zweig Forecast		+0.13%
31. Dessauer's Journal		+0.13%
32. The Mutual Fund Letter (Average)		+0.12%
a. Income Portfolio	+0.21%	
b. Growth & Income Portfolio	+0.18%	
c. Highly Aggressive Portfolio	+0.09%	
d. All Weather Portfolio	+0.09%	
e. Moderately Aggressive Portfolio	+0.07%	
33. United Mutual Fund Selector (Average)		+0.12%
a. Income Funds	+0.15%	
b. Aggressive Growth Funds	+0.14%	
c. Growth Funds	+0.10%	
d. Growth & Income Funds	+0.09%	
34. The Mutual Fund Strategist (Average)		+0.11%
a. Sector Portfolio	+0.12%	
b. Diversified Growth Portfolio	+0.11%	
35. **NoLoad Fund*X (Average)		+0.11%
a. Portfolio of "Class 1" Funds (Most Speculative Growth Funds)	+0.14%	
b. Portfolio of "Class 4" Funds (Total Return Funds)	+0.11%	
c. Portfolio of "Class 3" Funds (Higher Quality Growth Funds)	+0.11%	
d. Portfolio of "Class 2" Funds (Speculative Growth Funds)	+0.09%	
36. The Clean Yield		+0.11%
37. The Investor's Guide to Closed-End Funds (Average)		+0.11%
a. Managed Portfolio I: Balanced	+0.09%	
38. InvesTech Market Analyst		+0.11%
39. Fund Exchange (Average)		+0.10%
a. Fixed Income Bond Portfolio	+0.42%	
b. Aggressive Growth Margined Mutual Fund Portfolio	+0.18%	
c. Aggressive Growth Mutual Fund Portfolio	+0.11%	
d. Growth/Income Mutual Fund Portfolio	+0.10%	
e. Aggressive Balanced Mutual Fund Portfolio	+0.08%	
f. Conservative Growth Margined Mutual Fund Portfolio	+0.08%	
g. International Mutual Funds Portfolio	+0.03%	
h. Conservative Balanced Mutual Fund Portfolio	0.00%	
i. Gold Mutual Funds Portfolio	−0.09%	
40. Donoghue's Moneyletter (Average)		+0.10%
a. Conservative Mutual Fund Portfolio	+0.18%	
b. "Venturesome" Model Portfolio	+0.11%	
c. Moderate Mutual Fund Portfolio	+0.08%	
d. Signal Portfolio	+0.07%	
41. Emerging & Special Situations		+0.10%
42. Better Investing		+0.09%

Newsletter	Individual Portfolio	Overall Average
43. The Addison Report (Average)		+35.9%
a. Speculative Portfolio	+48.3%	
b. Conservative Portfolio	+31.8%	
44. The Mutual Fund Letter (Average)		+35.3%
a. Growth & Income Portfolio	+38.1%	
b. Income Portfolio	+37.7%	
c. Highly Aggressive Portfolio	+36.0%	
d. All Weather Portfolio	+34.0%	
e. Moderately Aggressive Portfolio	+30.1%	
45. Fund Exchange (Average)		+35.0%
a. Aggressive Growth Margined Mutual Fund Portfolio	+70.8%	
b. Fixed Income Bond Portfolio	+44.2%	
c. Aggressive Growth Mutual Fund Portfolio	+37.5%	
d. Conservative Growth Margined Mutual Fund Portfolio	+36.6%	
e. Growth/Income Mutual Fund Portfolio	+34.3%	
f. Aggressive Balanced Mutual Fund Portfolio	+31.7%	
g. International Mutual Funds Portfolio	+28.3%	
h. Conservative Balanced Mutual Fund Portfolio	+24.8%	
i. Gold Mutual Funds Portfolio	+6.4%	
46. Cabot's Mutual Fund Navigator (Average)		+34.1%
a. Income Portfolio	+51.9%	
b. Growth & Income Portfolio	+34.5%	
c. Growth Portfolio	+16.6%	
47. Graphic Fund Forecaster (Average)		+33.5%
a. Financial Strategic Funds Portfolio	+35.6%	
b. Growth/International Portfolio #1	+30.4%	
c. Fidelity Select Fund Portfolio #1	+30.2%	
d. Growth/International Portfolio #2	+22.1%	
48. Plain Talk Investor (Average)		+33.1%
a. "Personal-Best" Stock Portfolio	+32.8%	
b. High Risk/High Reward Portfolio	+31.4%	
49. The Ruff Times (Average)		+32.8%
a. The Back Page Portfolio	+29.9%	
b. "Optimum Switch Hitter" Mutual Fund Portfolio #1	+29.2%	
50. Growth Stock Outlook		+31.7%
51. The Outlook (Average)		+31.6%
a. Stock Appreciation Ranking System (5-Stars)	+31.6%	
52. Market Logic (Average)		+31.0%
a. Master (Stock) Portfolio	+30.9%	
b. Actual Option Portfolio	+25.3%	

Newsletter	Individual Portfolio	Overall Average
43. The Turnaround Letter (Average)		+0.09%
a. Conservative/Income Portfolio	+0.12%	
b. Aggressive Portfolio	+0.06%	
c. Moderate Risk Portfolio	+0.05%	
44. The PAD System Report (Average)		+0.08%
a. Model Portfolio C (The Conservative Version)	+0.27%	
b. Model Portfolio A (The Aggressive Version)	+0.02%	
45. The Addison Report (Average)		+0.07%
a. Speculative Portfolio	+0.12%	
b. Conservative Portfolio	+0.05%	
46. The Ruff Times (Average)		+0.07%
a. "Optimum Switch Hitter" Mutual Fund Portfolio #1	+0.04%	
b. The Back Page Portfolio	+0.04%	
47. The Insiders		+0.07%
48. Cabot's Mutual Fund Navigator (Average)		+0.07%
a. Income Portfolio	+0.25%	
b. Growth & Income Portfolio	+0.07%	
c. Growth Portfolio	−0.02%	
49. Graphic Fund Forecaster (Average)		+0.06%
a. Financial Strategic Funds Portfolio	+0.07%	
b. Growth/International Portfolio #1	+0.05%	
c. Fidelity Select Fund Portfolio #1	+0.04%	
d. Growth/International Portfolio #2	0.00%	
50. The Prudent Speculator		+0.06%
51. Telephone Switch Newsletter (Average)		+0.06%
a. Equity/Cash Switch Plan	+0.18%	
b. International Funds/Cash Switch Plan	−0.03%	
c. Gold/Cash Switch Plan	−0.04%	
52. Plain Talk Investor (Average)		+0.05%
a. "Personal Best" Stock Portfolio	+0.06%	
b. High Risk/High Reward Portfolio	+0.05%	

Newsletter	Individual Portfolio	Overall Average
53. Telephone Switch Newsletter (Average)		+30.9%
a. Equity/Cash Switch Plan	+59.8%	
b. International Funds/Cash Switch Plan	+17.6%	
c. Gold/Cash Switch Plan	+14.4%	
54. Financial World (Average)		+30.4%
a. Stocks Rated A+	+67.9%	
55. Investors Intelligence (Average)		+30.2%
a. Fidelity Switch Fund (Equity) Portfolio	+45.6%	
56. The Cabot Market Letter (Average)		+30.1%
a. Model Stock Portfolio	+14.4%	
57. Dow Theory Forecasts (Average)		+29.4%
a. Growth List	+57.5%	
b. Investment List	+49.9%	
c. Income List	+41.3%	
d. Speculative List	+21.0%	
e. Low-Priced Stocks & Special Situations List	−13.4%	
58. The Peter Dag Investment Letter (Average)		+28.7%
a. Model Vanguard Fund Portfolio	+40.5%	
59. The Investment Reporter (Average)		+28.4%
a. Portfolio of Speculative Stocks	+80.6%	
b. Portfolio of Very Conservative Stocks	+11.0%	
c. Portfolio of Higher Risk Stocks	+6.4%	
d. Portfolio of Conservative Stocks	+1.9%	
e. Portfolio of Average Risk Stocks	−5.8%	
60. Investment Horizons		+27.3%
61. The Marketarian Letter (Average)		+26.8%
a. Mutual Fund Portfolio for Traders	+29.3%	
b. Model Portfolio	+15.7%	
62. Switch Fund Timing (Average)		+26.5%
a. Model Stock Portfolio	+34.9%	
b. Conservative Model Mutual Fund Portfolio	+32.2%	
63. United & Babson Investment Report (Average)		+26.2%
a. Stocks for Long-Term Growth	+33.9%	
b. Cyclical Stocks for Profit	+19.9%	
c. Stocks for The Income-Minded	+19.5%	
64. California Technology Stock Letter		+25.7%
65. Mutual Fund Investing (Average)		+25.7%
a. Portfolio I (Growth With Income)	+32.6%	
b. Portfolio II (Balanced Growth)	+28.7%	
66. The Prudent Speculator		+25.3%

Newsletter	Individual Portfolio	Overall Average
53. The Outlook (Average)		+0.05%
a. Stock Appreciation Ranking System (5-Stars)	+0.05%	
54. The Peter Dag Investment Letter (Average)		+0.05%
a. Model Vanguard Fund Portfolio	+0.26%	
55. The Wall Street Generalist (Average)		+0.05%
a. Select Intermediate Portfolio	+0.08%	
b. Select Trading Portfolio	+0.04%	
56. Market Logic (Average)		+0.05%
a. Master (Stock) Portfolio	+0.05%	
b. Actual Option Portfolio	0.00%	
57. Investors Intelligence (Average)		+0.05%
a. Fidelity Switch Fund (Equity) Portfolio	+0.14%	
58. Financial World (Average)		+0.05%
a. Stocks Rated A+	+0.13%	
59. The Cabot Market Letter (Average)		+0.04%
a. Model Stock Portfolio	+0.01%	
60. Dow Theory Forecasts (Average)		+0.04%
a. Growth List	+0.15%	
b. Investment List	+0.12%	
c. Income List	+0.11%	
d. Speculative List	0.00%	
e. Low-Priced Stocks & Special Situations List	−0.28%	
61. The Investment Reporter (Average)		+0.03%
a. Portfolio of Speculative Stocks	+0.19%	
b. Portfolio of Very Conservative Stocks	−0.06%	
c. Portfolio of Higher Risk Stocks	−0.07%	
d. Portfolio of Average Risk Stocks	−0.08%	
e. Portfolio of Conservative Stocks	−0.12%	
62. Investment Horizons		+0.03%
63. The Marketarian Letter (Average)		+0.03%
a. Mutual Fund Portfolio for Traders	+0.04%	
b. Model Portfolio	−0.03%	
64. The Sector Funds Newsletter (Average)		+0.03%
a. Model Mutual Fund Portfolio 2 ("Fidelity Funds Plus" Portfolio)	+0.07%	
b. Model Mutual Fund Portfolio 3 (Mostly Bonds)	+0.05%	
c. Model Mutual Fund Portfolio 1	−0.03%	
65. United & Babson Investment Report (Average)		+0.02%
a. Stocks for Long-Term Growth	+0.06%	
b. Cyclical Stocks for Profit	+0.01%	
c. Stocks for The Income-Minded	−0.02%	
66. Fast Track Funds		+0.02%

Appendix A-5: Gain from 1/1/89 to 6/30/92 (continued)

Newsletter	Individual Portfolio	Overall Average
67. The Sector Funds Newsletter (Average)		+25.3%
a. Model Mutual Fund Portfolio 2 ("Fidelity Funds Plus" Portfolio)	+38.3%	
b. Model Mutual Fund Portfolio 3 (Mostly Bonds)	+31.6%	
c. Model Mutual Fund Portfolio 1	−0.6%	
The Riskless Rate of Return: A T-Bill Portfolio		+25.3%
68. Weber's Fund Advisor (Average)		+25.0%
a. Low Risk/Low Switch Portfolio	+34.2%	
b. "Go-With-the-Winner Strategy" Portfolio	+29.6%	
69. The Wall Street Digest (Average)		+24.9%
a. Mutual Fund Portfolio	+31.6%	
b. Stock and Bond Portfolio	+17.0%	
70. The Ney Report (Average)		+24.8%
a. Income Fund Portfolio	+26.2%	
b. Growth & Income Fund Portfolio	+24.3%	
c. Growth Fund Portfolio	+23.8%	
71. The Professional Tape Reader (Average)		+24.7%
a. Mutual Fund Portfolio	+30.9%	
b. Model Stock Portfolio	+18.2%	
72. Fast Track Funds		+24.7%
73. Growth Fund Guide (Average)		+22.9%
a. "Valueratio" Equities & Cash Portfolio	+34.0%	
b. "Valueratio" Equities, Cash & Leverage Portfolio	+30.4%	
c. "Valueratio" Fully Invested Portfolio	+26.7%	
d. Quality Growth Mutual Fund Portfolio	+25.7%	
e. Aggressive Growth Mutual Fund Portfolio	+23.3%	
f. Selected Core Account	+23.2%	
g. Special Situations Mutual Fund Portfolio	+21.7%	
h. Growth Mutual Fund Portfolio	+21.6%	
i. Growth Model Account	+13.7%	
j. Aggressive Model Account	+9.7%	
74. Professional Timing Service (Average)		+19.4%
a. Mutual Fund Model Portfolio	+85.2%	
b. Gold Futures Trading Portfolio	−13.1%	
75. The International Harry Schultz Letter (Average)		+18.7%
a. U.S. Stocks on the "List"	+21.8%	
b. Portfolio constructed from gold/silver trading advice (no margin)	+21.0%	
c. Foreign Stocks on the "List"	+8.5%	
76. LaLoggia's Special Situation Report (Average)		+17.7%
a. Master List of Recommended Stocks	+28.1%	
b. Other Recommended Stocks	+5.6%	

Newsletter	Individual Portfolio	Overall Average
67. The Wall Street Digest (Average)		+0.02%
a. Mutual Fund Portfolio	+0.05%	
b. Stock and Bond Portfolio	0.00%	
68. Switch Fund Timing (Average)		+0.02%
a. Conservative Model Mutual Fund Portfolio	+0.08%	
b. Model Stock Portfolio	+0.06%	
69. California Technology Stock Letter		+0.02%
70. Mutual Fund Investing (Average)		+0.01%
a. Portfolio I (Growth With Income)	+0.20%	
b. Portfolio II (Balanced Growth)	+0.05%	
71. Weber's Fund Advisor (Average)		+0.01%
a. Low Risk/Low Switch Portfolio	+0.08%	
b. "Go-With-the-Winner Strategy" Portfolio	+0.04%	
72. The Ney Report (Average)		+0.01%
a. Income Fund Portfolio	+0.02%	
b. Growth & Income Fund Portfolio	0.00%	
c. Growth Fund Portfolio	0.00%	
73. Your Window Into the Future (Average)		0.00%
a. Portfolio A: Aggressive Portfolio	+0.09%	
b. Portfolio C: Speculative Portfolio	−0.01%	
c. Portfolio B: Conservative Portfolio	−0.07%	
74. The Professional Tape Reader (Average)		0.00%
a. Mutual Fund Portfolio	+0.10%	
b. Model Stock Portfolio	−0.06%	
75. The Option Advisor (Average)		−0.01%
a. Aggressive Portfolio	+0.07%	
b. Option Income Portfolio	−0.03%	
c. Conservative Portfolio	−0.06%	
76. Equities Special Situations		−0.02%

Newsletter	Individual Portfolio	Overall Average
77. Kinsman's Telephone Growth & Income Service (Average)		+17.2%
a. Mutual Fund Switch Portfolio	+18.2%	
b. Growth & Income Portfolio	+16.0%	
78. Stockmarket Cycles (Average)		+16.0%
a. Mutual Fund Portfolio	+49.8%	
b. Model Stock Portfolio	−11.5%	
79. Harry Browne's Special Reports (Average)		+14.1%
a. Permanent Portfolio	+26.3%	
b. Variable [Speculative] Portfolio	+1.9%	
80. Equities Special Situations		+10.6%
81. The Volume Reversal Survey (Average)		+10.1%
a. Index Fund Portfolio	+59.4%	
82. The Princeton Portfolios (Average)		+6.5%
a. Long-Term Portfolio #1	+28.2%	
b. Long-Term Portfolio #2	−12.7%	
83. Bob Nurock's Advisory (Average)		+6.5%
a. Index Mutual Funds Portfolio	+20.7%	
b. Sector Mutual Funds Portfolio	+20.1%	
c. Model Portfolio	+0.9%	
84. The Option Advisor (Average)		−5.2%
a. Aggressive Portfolio	+31.1%	
b. Option Income Portfolio	+18.3%	
c. Conservative Portfolio	−74.6%	
85. Margo's Market Monitor (Average)		−6.4%
a. Common Stock Portfolio	−3.3%	
b. Fidelity Select Funds Portfolio	−11.6%	
86. The Wall Street Generalist (Average)		−9.3%
a. Select Intermediate Portfolio	+43.3%	
b. Select Trading Portfolio	−68.3%	
87. Futures Hotline Mutual Fund Timer (Average)		−13.1%
a. Asset Allocation Portfolio	+32.6%	
b. Model Futures Portfolio	−61.1%	
88. The Dines Letter (Average)		−18.4%
a. Good Grade Portfolio	+34.9%	
b. Long-Term Growth Portfolio	+33.6%	
c. Precious Metals Portfolio	+13.7%	
d. Short-Term Trading Portfolio	−85.5%	

Newsletter	Individual Portfolio	Overall Average
77. The Princeton Portfolios (Average)		−0.02%
a. Long-Term Portfolio #1	+0.04%	
b. Long-Term Portfolio #2	−0.09%	
78. The Volume Reversal Survey (Average)		−0.05%
a. Index Fund Portfolio	+0.21%	
79. Futures Hotline Mutual Fund Timer (Average)		0.05%
a. Asset Allocation Portfolio	+0.07%	
b. Model Futures Portfolio	−0.06%	
80. The International Harry Schultz Letter (Average)		−0.05%
a. U.S. Stocks on the "List"	0.00%	
b. Portfolio constructed from gold/silver trading advice (no margin)	−0.03%	
c. Foreign Stocks on the "List"	−0.06%	
81. Growth Fund Guide (Average)		−0.05%
a. "Valueratio" Equities & Cash Portfolio	+0.13%	
b. "Valueratio" Equities, Cash & Leverage Portfolio	+0.08%	
c. "Valueratio" Fully Invested Portfolio	+0.02%	
d. Quality Growth Mutual Fund Portfolio	+0.02%	
e. Aggressive Growth Mutual Fund Portfolio	−0.04%	
f. Special Situations Mutual Fund Portfolio	−0.07%	
g. Selected Core Account	−0.10%	
h. Growth Mutual Fund Portfolio	−0.15%	
i. Aggressive Model Account	−0.20%	
j. Growth Model Account	−0.21%	
82. Professional Timing Service (Average)		−0.06%
a. Mutual Fund Model Portfolio	+0.38%	
b. Gold Futures Trading Portfolio	−0.27%	
83. LaLoggia's Special Situation Report (Average)		−0.07%
a. Master List of Recommended Stocks	+0.03%	
b. Other Recommended Stocks	−0.11%	
84. Stockmarket Cycles (Average)		−0.08%
a. Mutual Fund Portfolio	+0.17%	
b. Model Stock Portfolio	−0.29%	
85. Kinsman's Telephone Growth & Income Service (Average)		−0.08%
a. Mutual Fund Switch Portfolio	−0.07%	
b. Growth & Income Portfolio	−0.09%	
86. On Markets		−0.09%
87. Harry Browne's Special Reports (Average)		−0.11%
a. Permanent Portfolio	+0.02%	
b. Variable [Speculative] Portfolio	−0.14%	
88. The R.H.M. Survey of Warrants, Options & Low-Price Stocks		−0.14%

Newsletter	Individual Portfolio	Overall Average
89. The R.H.M. Survey of Warrants, Options & Low-Price Stocks		−25.7%
90. The Holt Advisory (Average)		−29.8%
91. On Markets		−37.5%
92. The Garside Forecast		−41.5%
93. Your Window Into the Future (Average)		−43.4%
a. Portfolio A: Aggressive Portfolio	+47.1%	
b. Portfolio B: Conservative Portfolio	+6.6%	
c. Portfolio C: Speculative Portfolio	−100.0%	
94. Harmonic Research (Average)		−48.1%
a. Futures Portfolio	−50.0%	

Newsletter	Individual Portfolio	Overall Average
89. The Dines Letter (Average)		−0.16%
a. Good Grade Portfolio	+0.06%	
b. Long-Term Growth Portfolio	+0.05%	
c. Precious Metals Portfolio	−0.01%	
d. Short-Term Trading Portfolio	−0.34%	
90. Bob Nurock's Advisory (Average)		−0.17%
a. Index Mutual Funds Portfolio	−0.04%	
b. Sector Mutual Funds Portfolio	−0.06%	
c. Model Portfolio	−0.07%	
91. Margo's Market Monitor (Average)		−0.20%
a. Common Stock Portfolio	−0.10%	
b. Fidelity Select Funds Portfolio	−0.29%	
92. Harmonic Research (Average)		−0.22%
a. Futures Portfolio	−0.23%	
93. The Holt Advisory (Average)		−0.29%
94. The Garside Forecast		−0.38%

1.54RS

Appendix A-6: Gain from 1/1/91 to 6/30/92

Appendix A-6: Gain from 1/1/91 to 6/30/92

Newsletter	Individual Portfolio	Overall Average
1. The Granville Market Letter (Average)		+164.9%
a. Options Portfolio	+297.6%	
b. Traders' Stock Portfolio	+41.5%	
c. Investors' Stock Portfolio	+36.9%	
2. BI Research		+135.5%
3. The Turnaround Letter (Average)		+117.8%
a. Aggressive Portfolio	+141.3%	
b. Conservative/Income Portfolio	+95.0%	
c. Moderate Risk Portfolio	+88.2%	
4. AgBiotech Stock Letter		+109.8%
5. OTC Insight (Average)		+104.5%
a. $150,000 Aggressive Portfolio	+111.3%	
b. $25,000 Aggressive Portfolio	+111.1%	
c. $75,000 Aggressive Portfolio	+108.3%	
d. $150,000 Conservative Portfolio	+108.0%	
e. $150,000 Moderately Aggressive Portfolio	+107.6%	
f. $200,000 Conservative Portfolio	+107.3%	
g. $75,000 Moderately Aggressive Portfolio	+105.8%	
h. $400,000 Conservative Portfolio	+105.3%	
i. $25,000 Conservative Portfolio	+104.7%	
j. $400,000 Aggressive Portfolio	+104.2%	
k. $200,000 Aggressive Portfolio	+103.5%	
l. $75,000 Conservative Portfolio	+103.2%	
m. $800,000 Aggressive Portfolio	+102.8%	
n. $400,000 Moderately Aggressive Portfolio	+102.2%	
o. $800,000 Moderately Aggressive Portfolio	+100.4%	
p. $800,000 Conservative Portfolio	+99.6%	
q. $200,000 Moderately Aggressive Portfolio	+98.5%	
r. $25,000 Moderately Aggressive Portfolio	+89.7%	
6. The Prudent Speculator		+103.1%
7. Individual Investor Special Situations Report		+101.8%
8. Hussman Econometrics (Average)		+98.5%
a. Select Stock Portfolio	+135.3%	
b. Diversified Stock Portfolio	+129.2%	
c. Multi-Fund Portfolio	+56.8%	
9. The Oberweis Report		+85.7%
10. The Insiders		+72.5%
11. The Chartist (Average)		+69.3%
a. Traders Portfolio	+86.1%	
b. Actual Cash Account	+52.0%	
12. Medical Technology Stock Letter (Average)		+66.0%
a. Model Portfolio	+82.9%	
b. Aggressive Portfolio	+48.8%	

448   Appendix A: Newsletter Performance

Appendix A-6: Risk-Adjusted Performance from 1/1/91 to 6/30/92

Newsletter	Individual Portfolio	Overall Average
1. Value Line Convertibles		+0.75%
2. BI Research		+0.67%
3. Fidelity Insight (Average)		+0.66%
a. Income & Preservation Fund Portfolio	+0.87%	
b. Growth Portfolio	+0.76%	
c. Growth & Income Fund Portfolio	+0.63%	
d. Speculative Portfolio	+0.37%	
4. F.X.C. Investors Corp.		+0.57%
5. Dessauer's Journal		+0.53%
6. Investment Quality Trends		+0.46%
7. The Investor's Guide To Closed-End Funds (Average)		+0.46%
a. Managed Portfolio IV: U.S. Equity Funds	+0.60%	
b. Managed Portfolio I: Balanced	+0.49%	
c. Managed Portfolio III: Overseas Investment	+0.31%	
d. Managed Portfolio II: Income	+0.29%	
8. The No-Load Fund Investor (Average)		+0.45%
a. Retirement Portfolio	+0.44%	
b. Wealth Builder Portfolio	+0.44%	
c. Pre-Retirement Portfolio	+0.43%	
9. The Scott Letter: Closed-End Fund Report (Average)		+0.44%
a. Equity Portfolio	+0.44%	
10. The Marketarian Letter (Average)		+0.44%
a. Mutual Fund Portfolio for Traders	+0.37%	
b. Model Portfolio	+0.36%	
c. Mutual Fund Portfolio for Investors	+0.35%	
11. Richard E. Band's Profitable Investing		+0.43%
12. The Contrarian's View (Average)		+0.43%
a. Present & Future Income Portfolio	+0.58%	
b. Crapshooter's Folly Portfolio	+0.33%	
c. IRA Portfolio	+0.19%	
d. Hedger's Delight Portfolio	+0.02%	

Newsletter	Individual Portfolio	Overall Average
13. New Issues		+63.0%
✓14. MPT Review (Average)		+60.9%
a. $400,000 Aggressive Portfolio	+68.5%	
b. $200,000 Aggressive Portfolio	+65.7%	
c. $800,000 Conservative Portfolio	+64.7%	
d. $400,000 Conservative Portfolio	+63.6%	
e. $50,000 Aggressive Portfolio	+62.4%	
f. $200,000 Conservative Portfolio	+62.1%	
g. $400,000 Moderately Aggressive Portfolio	+61.2%	
h. $800,000 Aggressive Portfolio	+58.1%	
i. $800,000 Moderately Aggressive Portfolio	+56.6%	
j. $200,000 Moderately Aggressive Portfolio	+56.4%	
k. $50,000 Moderately Aggressive Portfolio	+55.5%	
l. $50,000 Conservative Portfolio	+52.3%	
15. The Scott Letter: Closed-End Fund Report (Average)		+57.5%
a. Equity Portfolio	+57.5%	
16. Value Line Convertibles		+55.5%
17. Dessauer's Journal		+50.6%
18. Mutual Fund Forecaster		+48.9%
19. The Contrarian's View (Average)		+47.6%
a. Crapshooter's Folly Portfolio	+98.5%	
b. Present & Future Income Portfolio	+70.7%	
c. IRA Portfolio	+19.1%	
d. Hedger's Delight Portfolio	+7.9%	
20. Fundline (Average)		+46.7%
a. $100,000 No-Timing Portfolio	+62.4%	
b. $100,000 Timing Portfolio	+39.4%	
21. Equities Special Situations		+46.2%
22. Market Logic (Average)		+45.7%
a. Master (Stock) Portfolio	+50.4%	
b. Actual Option Portfolio	+7.6%	

Newsletter	Individual Portfolio	Overall Average
13. The Turnaround Letter (Average)		+0.43%
a. Conservative/Income Portfolio	+0.47%	
b. Moderate Risk Portfolio	+0.45%	
c. Aggressive Portfolio	+0.30%	
14. Hussman Econometrics (Average)		+0.42%
a. Select Stock Portfolio	+0.47%	
b. Diversified Stock Portfolio	+0.45%	
c. Multi-Fund Portfolio	+0.33%	
15. Mutual Fund Forecaster		+0.42%
16. Fidelity Monitor (Average)		+0.42%
a. Growth Mutual Funds Portfolio	+0.45%	
b. Select System Mutual Funds Portfolio	+0.30%	
17. The Chartist (Average)		+0.41%
a. Traders Portfolio	+0.42%	
b. Actual Cash Account	+0.34%	
18. OTC Insight (Average)		+0.41%
a. $400,000 Conservative Portfolio	+0.42%	
b. $200,000 Conservative Portfolio	+0.42%	
c. $25,000 Conservative Portfolio	+0.42%	
d. $25,000 Aggressive Portfolio	+0.42%	
e. $150,000 Conservative Portfolio	+0.41%	
f. $75,000 Aggressive Portfolio	+0.41%	
g. $400,000 Moderately Aggressive Portfolio	+0.41%	
h. $400,000 Aggressive Portfolio	+0.41%	
i. $800,000 Aggressive Portfolio	+0.40%	
j. $150,000 Aggressive Portfolio	+0.40%	
k. $200,000 Aggressive Portfolio	+0.40%	
l. $75,000 Conservative Portfolio	+0.40%	
m. $75,000 Moderately Aggressive Portfolio	+0.40%	
n. $150,000 Moderately Aggressive Portfolio	+0.40%	
o. $200,000 Moderately Aggressive Portfolio	+0.39%	
p. $800,000 Moderately Aggressive Portfolio	+0.39%	
q. $800,000 Conservative Portfolio	+0.38%	
r. $25,000 Moderately Aggressive Portfolio	+0.38%	
19. The Insiders		+0.40%
20. Fundline (Average)		+0.39%
a. $100,000 No-Timing Portfolio	+0.40%	
b. $100,000 Timing Portfolio	+0.36%	
21. The Oberweis Report		+0.39%
22. Blue Chip Values (Average)		+0.39%
a. Income & Growth Model Portfolio	+0.44%	
b. Growth Model Portfolio	+0.35%	

Newsletter	Individual Portfolio	Overall Average
23. Fidelity Monitor (Average)		+45.2%
a. Growth Mutual Funds Portfolio	+45.8%	
b. Select System Mutual Funds Portfolio	+41.1%	
24. Emerging & Special Situations		+45.0%
25. The Cabot Market Letter (Average)		+44.4%
a. Growth and Income Portfolio	+46.9%	
b. Model Stock Portfolio	+39.9%	
26. Investment Quality Trends		+41.5%
27. Timer Digest (Average)		+40.1%
a. Fidelity Select Portfolio	+59.7%	
b. Dow Jones 30 Strategy	+51.7%	
c. Model Stock Portfolio	+11.0%	
✓ 28. The Value Line Investment Survey		+38.7%
29. The Marketarian Letter (Average)		+38.0%
a. Model Portfolio	+33.9%	
b. Mutual Fund Portfolio for Traders	+33.1%	
c. Mutual Fund Portfolio for Investors	+32.9%	
30. F.X.C. Investors Corp.		+36.8%
31. The Big Picture (Average)		+36.8%
a. Trading Portfolio	+51.4%	
b. Model Portfolio	+22.1%	
32. MPT Fund Review (Average)		+36.5%
a. Optimal Index-Plus Strategy	+50.6%	
b. Optimal Aggressive Strategy	+40.6%	
c. Optimal Selective Strategy	+32.5%	
d. Optimal Balanced Strategy	+22.6%	
33. The Value Line OTC Special Situations Service		+36.3%
34. Cabot's Mutual Fund Navigator (Average)		+33.7%
a. Growth Portfolio	+34.8%	
b. Income Portfolio	+33.4%	
c. Growth & Income Portfolio	+32.2%	
Wilshire 5000 Value-Weighted Total Return Index		+32.3%
35. Zweig Performance Ratings Report		+31.3%
36. Fidelity Insight (Average)		+30.5%
a. Growth & Income Fund Portfolio	+34.0%	
b. Growth Portfolio	+33.5%	
c. Income & Preservation Fund Portfolio	+28.5%	
d. Speculative Portfolio	+26.9%	
37. The No-Load Fund Investor (Average)		+30.5%
a. Wealth Builder Portfolio	+38.3%	
b. Pre-Retirement Portfolio	+28.2%	
c. Retirement Portfolio	+25.0%	

Newsletter	Individual Portfolio	Overall Average
23. Personal Finance (Average)		+0.39%
a. Mutual Fund Portfolio (Long-Term)	+0.42%	
b. Income Portfolio	+0.42%	
c. Growth Portfolio	+0.41%	
d. Mutual Fund Portfolio (Short-Term)	+0.29%	
24. Market Logic (Average)		+0.39%
a. Master (Stock) Portfolio	+0.39%	
b. Actual Option Portfolio	0.00%	
25. Zweig Performance Ratings Report		+0.39%
26. L/G No-Load Fund Analyst (Average)		+0.39%
a. Portfolio A: Conservative/Income Oriented	+0.62%	
b. Portfolio B: Conservative/Not Income Oriented	+0.46%	
c. Portfolio C: Long-Term Conservative Growth	+0.33%	
d. Portfolio D: Long-Term Aggressive Growth	+0.29%	
27. The Prudent Speculator		+0.39%
28. AgBiotech Stock Letter		+0.37%
29. Cabot's Mutual Fund Navigator (Average)		+0.37%
a. Income Portfolio	+0.52%	
b. Growth & Income Portfolio	+0.33%	
c. Growth Portfolio	+0.29%	
30. The Value Line Investment Survey		+0.36%
31. The Granville Market Letter (Average)		+0.36%
a. Options Portfolio	+0.37%	
b. Traders' Stock Portfolio	+0.30%	
c. Investors' Stock Portfolio	+0.27%	
32. Individual Investor Special Situations Report		+0.36%
33. Bob Brinker's Marketimer (Average)		+0.36%
a. Fixed-Income Model Mutual Fund Portfolio	+0.63%	
b. Balanced Portfolio	+0.36%	
c. Aggressive Growth Mutual Fund Portfolio	+0.30%	
d. Long-Term Growth Mutual Fund Portfolio	+0.29%	
34. United Mutual Fund Selector (Average)		+0.35%
a. Income Funds	+0.88%	
b. Growth Funds	+0.34%	
c. Growth & Income Funds	+0.33%	
d. Aggressive Growth Funds	+0.24%	
35. New Issues		+0.35%
36. InvesTech Mutual Fund Advisor		+0.34%
37. Emerging & Special Situations		+0.33%

Newsletter	Individual Portfolio	Overall Average
38. The PAD System Report (Average)		+29.4%
a. Model Portfolio C (The Conservative Version)	+42.5%	
b. Model Portfolio A (The Aggressive Version)	+14.2%	
39. The Clean Yield		+29.3%
40. The Investor's Guide To Closed-End Funds (Average)		+28.9%
a. Managed Portfolio IV: U.S. Equity Funds	+40.4%	
b. Managed Portfolio I: Balanced	+35.6%	
c. Managed Portfolio III: Overseas Investment	+26.3%	
d. Managed Portfolio II: Income	+14.3%	
41. Equity Fund Outlook (Average)		+28.8%
a. Moderate Risk Portfolio	+31.2%	
b. Aggressive Portfolio	+29.1%	
c. Conservative Portfolio	+28.7%	
42. Richard E. Band's Profitable Investing		+28.5%
43. United Mutual Fund Selector (Average)		+28.3%
a. Growth Funds	+31.9%	
b. Aggressive Growth Funds	+28.8%	
c. Growth & Income Funds	+28.8%	
d. Income Funds	+22.5%	
44. Czeschin's Mutual Fund Outlook & Recommendations (Average)		+27.4%
a. Long-Term Growth Portfolio	+36.0%	
b. Income Portfolio	+29.0%	
c. Jaguar Portfolio	+15.5%	
45. Ford Investment Review		+26.9%

Newsletter	Individual Portfolio	Overall Average
38. The Volume Reversal Survey (Average)		+0.33%
a. Index Fund Portfolio	+0.33%	
39. No-Load Portfolios (Average)		+0.33%
a. Income Portfolio	+0.72%	
b. Conservative Portfolio	+0.24%	
c. Aggressive Growth Portfolio	+0.21%	
40. Timer Digest (Average)		+0.32%
a. Dow Jones 30 Strategy	+0.42%	
b. Fidelity Select Portfolio	+0.37%	
c. Model Stock Portfolio	+0.06%	
Wilshire 5000 Value-Weighted Total Return Index		+0.32%
41. Czeschin's Mutual Fund Outlook & Recommendations (Average)		+0.31%
a. Income Portfolio	+0.65%	
b. Long-Term Growth Portfolio	+0.33%	
c. Jaguar Portfolio	+0.10%	
42. The Outlook (Average)		+0.31%
a. Stock Appreciation Ranking System (5-Stars)	+0.31%	
43. The Big Picture (Average)		+0.31%
a. Trading Portfolio	+0.30%	
b. Model Portfolio	+0.25%	
44. Bob Nurock's Advisory (Average)		+0.31%
a. Model Portfolio	+0.39%	
b. Index Mutual Funds Portfolio	+0.14%	
c. Sector Mutual Funds Portfolio	−0.15%	
45. Investors Intelligence (Average)		+0.30%
a. Fidelity Switch Fund (Bond) Portfolio	+0.94%	
b. Long-Term Portfolio	+0.27%	
c. Low-Priced Portfolio	+0.26%	
d. Fidelity Switch Fund (Equity) Portfolio	−0.04%	
e. Fidelity Switch Fund (International) Portfolio	−0.06%	

Newsletter	Individual Portfolio	Overall Average
46. InvesTech Mutual Fund Advisor		+26.6%
47. Fund Kinetics (Average)		+26.5%
a. Weekly "Erfer" Report	+18.6%	
48. The Chartist Mutual Fund Timer		+26.5%
49. Bob Brinker's Marketimer (Average)		+26.3%
a. Aggressive Growth Mutual Fund Portfolio	+35.8%	
b. Long-Term Growth Mutual Fund Portfolio	+29.0%	
c. Balanced Portfolio	+22.0%	
d. Fixed-Income Model Mutual Fund Portfolio	+17.7%	
50. Better Investing		+26.1%
51. **NoLoad Fund*X (Average)		+25.9%
a. Portfolio of "Class 1" Funds (Most Speculative Growth Funds)	+65.6%	
b. Portfolio of "Class 2" Funds (Speculative Growth Funds)	+26.9%	
c. Portfolio of "Class 3" Funds (Higher Quality Growth Funds)	+25.9%	
d. Portfolio of "Class 4" Funds (Total Return Funds)	+21.9%	
52. Blue Chip Values (Average)		+25.8%
a. Growth Model Portfolio	+26.4%	
b. Income & Growth Model Portfolio	+25.1%	
53. L/G No-Load Fund Analyst (Average)		+25.6%
a. Portfolio D: Long-Term Aggressive Growth	+28.1%	
b. Portfolio C: Long-Term Conservative Growth	+26.8%	
c. Portfolio A: Conservative/Income Oriented	+24.7%	
d. Portfolio B: Conservative/Not Income Oriented	+22.4%	
54. Mutual Fund Technical Trader (Average)		+25.4%
a. Aggressive Growth/High Risk Portfolio	+37.7%	
b. Growth/Short-Term Risk Portfolio	+32.3%	
c. Conservative Income & Growth/Moderate Risk Portfolio	+22.6%	
55. The Outlook (Average)		+25.3%
a. Stock Appreciation Ranking System (5-Stars)	+25.3%	

Newsletter	Individual Portfolio	Overall Average
46. MPT Review (Average)		+0.30%
a. $800,000 Conservative Portfolio	+0.34%	
b. $50,000 Aggressive Portfolio	+0.32%	
c. $200,000 Aggressive Portfolio	+0.31%	
d. $400,000 Aggressive Portfolio	+0.31%	
e. $400,000 Conservative Portfolio	+0.30%	
f. $800,000 Moderately Aggressive Portfolio	+0.30%	
g. $400,000 Moderately Aggressive Portfolio	+0.29%	
h. $50,000 Moderately Aggressive Portfolio	+0.29%	
i. $200,000 Conservative Portfolio	+0.29%	
j. $800,000 Aggressive Portfolio	+0.29%	
k. $200,000 Moderately Aggressive Portfolio	+0.27%	
l. $50,000 Conservative Portfolio	+0.27%	
47. The Cabot Market Letter (Average)		+0.30%
a. Growth and Income Portfolio	+0.38%	
b. Model Stock Portfolio	+0.22%	
48. MPT Fund Review (Average)		+0.30%
a. Optimal Index-Plus Strategy	+0.37%	
b. Optimal Aggressive Strategy	+0.30%	
c. Optimal Selective Strategy	+0.24%	
d. Optimal Balanced Strategy	+0.21%	
49. Adrian Day's Investment Analyst		+0.29%
50. The Mutual Fund Letter (Average)		+0.29%
a. Income Portfolio	+0.60%	
b. Growth & Income Portfolio	+0.40%	
c. All Weather Portfolio	+0.24%	
d. Highly Aggressive Portfolio	+0.19%	
e. Moderately Aggressive Portfolio	+0.18%	
51. Equities Special Situations		+0.28%
52. Equity Fund Outlook (Average)		+0.20%
a. Conservative Portfolio	+0.37%	
b. Moderate Risk Portfolio	+0.29%	
c. Aggressive Portfolio	+0.24%	
53. No-Load Mutual Fund Selections & Timing Newsletter (Average)		+0.28%
a. Intermediate Term Portfolio	+0.39%	
b. Asset Allocations Model Portfolio	+0.28%	
c. Sector Funds Portfolio	+0.11%	
54. The Clean Yield		+0.27%
55. **NoLoad Fund*X (Average)		+0.27%
a. Portfolio of "Class 1" Funds (Most Speculative Growth Funds)	+0.41%	
b. Portfolio of "Class 4" Funds (Total Return Funds)	+0.31%	
c. Portfolio of "Class 3" Funds (Higher Quality Growth Funds)	+0.27%	
d. Portfolio of "Class 2" Funds (Speculative Growth Funds)	+0.22%	

Newsletter	Individual Portfolio	Overall Average
56. The Investment Reporter (Average)		+24.8%
a. Portfolio of Speculative Stocks	+49.3%	
b. Portfolio of Average Risk Stocks	+12.1%	
c. Portfolio of Higher Risk Stocks	+7.1%	
d. Portfolio of Very Conservative Stocks	+5.2%	
e. Portfolio of Conservative Stocks	−1.5%	
57. Investors Intelligence (Average)		+23.8%
a. Low-Priced Portfolio	+55.6%	
b. Long-Term Portfolio	+26.5%	
c. Fidelity Switch Fund (Bond) Portfolio	+23.5%	
d. Fidelity Switch Fund (International) Portfolio	+6.0%	
e. Fidelity Switch Fund (Equity) Portfolio	+5.8%	
58. Personal Finance (Average)		+23.5%
a. Growth Portfolio	+33.5%	
b. Mutual Fund Portfolio (Short-Term)	+26.7%	
c. Mutual Fund Portfolio (Long-Term)	+20.2%	
d. Income Portfolio	+13.6%	
59. Futures Hotline Mutual Fund Timer (Average)		+23.2%
a. Model Futures Portfolio	+41.4%	
b. Asset Allocation Portfolio	+4.0%	
60. No-Load Mutual Fund Selections & Timing Newsletter (Average)		+22.6%
a. Intermediate Term Portfolio	+33.5%	
b. Asset Allocations Model Portfolio	+21.0%	
c. Sector Funds Portfolio	+13.7%	
61. Donoghue's Moneyletter (Average)		+22.5%
a. Signal Portfolio	+33.2%	
b. "Venturesome" Model Portfolio	+22.2%	
c. Moderate Mutual Fund Portfolio	+18.1%	
d. Conservative Mutual Fund Portfolio	+15.8%	
62. The Volume Reversal Survey (Average)		+22.4%
a. Index Fund Portfolio	+22.4%	
63. Adrian Day's Investment Analyst		+21.3%
64. Dow Theory Forecasts (Average)		+20.9%
a. Growth List	+39.0%	
b. Investment List	+24.1%	
c. Income List	+16.9%	
d. Speculative List	+16.6%	
e. Low-Priced Stocks & Special Situations List	+7.5%	
65. The Wall Street Generalist (Average)		+20.2%
a. Select Intermediate Portfolio	+36.1%	
b. Select Trading Portfolio	−5.8%	

Newsletter	Individual Portfolio	Overall Average
56. Medical Technology Stock Letter (Average)		+0.27%
a. Model Portfolio	+0.31%	
b. Aggressive Portfolio	+0.21%	
57. The Investment Reporter (Average)		+0.26%
a. Portfolio of Speculative Stocks	+0.34%	
b. Portfolio of Average Risk Stocks	+0.07%	
c. Portfolio of Higher Risk Stocks	+0.01%	
d. Portfolio of Very Conservative Stocks	−0.03%	
e. Portfolio of Conservative Stocks	−0.13%	
58. Income & Safety		+0.26%
59. Growth Stock Outlook		+0.25%
60. The Addison Report (Average)		+0.24%
a. Speculative Portfolio	+0.29%	
b. Conservative Portfolio	+0.18%	
61. Dow Theory Forecasts (Average)		+0.24%
a. Growth List	+0.33%	
b. Investment List	+0.22%	
c. Income List	+0.21%	
d. Speculative List	+0.13%	
e. Low-Priced Stocks & Special Situations List	0.00%	
62. Professional Timing Service (Average)		+0.24%
a. Mutual Fund Model Portfolio	+0.48%	
b. Gold Futures Trading Portfolio	−0.51%	
63. Mutual Fund Technical Trader (Average)		+0.24%
a. Growth/Short-Term Risk Portfolio	+0.27%	
b. Aggressive Growth/High Risk Portfolio	+0.25%	
c. Conservative Income & Growth/Moderate Risk Portfolio	+0.20%	
64. Donoghue's Moneyletter (Average)		+0.24%
a. Signal Portfolio	+0.25%	
b. Conservative Mutual Fund Portfolio	+0.24%	
c. "Venturesome" Model Portfolio	+0.21%	
d. Moderate Mutual Fund Portfolio	+0.19%	
65. The PAD System Report (Average)		+0.24%
a. Model Portfolio C (The Conservative Version)	+0.41%	
b. Model Portfolio A (The Aggressive Version)	+0.08%	

Newsletter	Individual Portfolio	Overall Average
66. InvesTech Market Analyst		+19.9%
67. The Zweig Forecast		+19.6%
68. The Addison Report (Average)		+19.6%
a. Speculative Portfolio	⌐29.7%	
b. Conservative Portfolio	+16.9%	
69. The Sector Funds Newsletter (Average)		+18.5%
a. Model Mutual Fund Portfolio 3 (Mostly Bonds)	+22.2%	
b. Model Mutual Fund Portfolio 1	+16.4%	
c. Model Mutual Fund Portfolio 2 ("Fidelity Funds Plus" Portfolio)	+16.1%	
70. Bob Nurock's Advisory (Average)		+17.6%
a. Model Portfolio	+37.8%	
b. Index Mutual Funds Portfolio	+12.3%	
c. Sector Mutual Funds Portfolio	+4.1%	
71. No-Load Portfolios (Average)		+17.4%
a. Income Portfolio	+18.9%	
b. Aggressive Growth Portfolio	+17.0%	
c. Conservative Portfolio	+15.9%	
72. Fund Exchange (Average)		+17.1%
a. Aggressive Growth Margined Mutual Fund Portfolio	+43.4%	
b. Conservative Growth Margined Mutual Fund Portfolio	+21.7%	
c. Fixed Income Bond Portfolio	+20.1%	
d. Aggressive Growth Mutual Fund Portfolio	+19.4%	
e. Growth/Income Mutual Fund Portfolio	+16.9%	
f. Aggressive Balanced Mutual Fund Portfolio	+14.4%	
g. Conservative Balanced Mutual Fund Portfolio	+10.9%	
h. International Mutual Funds Portfolio	+9.0%	
i. Gold Mutual Funds Portfolio	+0.8%	
73. The Mutual Fund Letter (Average)		+16.5%
a. Income Portfolio	+18.4%	
b. Highly Aggressive Portfolio	+17.1%	
c. Growth & Income Portfolio	+16.8%	
d. All Weather Portfolio	+16.6%	
e. Moderately Aggressive Portfolio	+13.0%	
74. Systems and Forecasts (Average)		+16.2%
a. Jack White Portfolio	+23.6%	
b. The Regular Portfolio	+14.2%	
c. Futures & Options Portfolio	+10.5%	
75. Investment Horizons		+15.9%
76. Global Fund Timer (Average)		+15.1%
a. U.S. Portfolio	+21.1%	
b. Global Portfolio	+15.0%	
c. Conservative Portfolio	+14.4%	
d. Zero Bond Portfolio	+9.0%	

Newsletter	Individual Portfolio	Overall Average
66. Fund Exchange (Average)		+0.23%
a. Fixed Income Bond Portfolio	+0.69%	
b. Aggressive Growth Margined Mutual Fund Portfolio	+0.32%	
c. Growth/Income Mutual Fund Portfolio	+0.23%	
d. Aggressive Growth Mutual Fund Portfolio	+0.22%	
e. Aggressive Balanced Mutual Fund Portfolio	+0.19%	
f. Conservative Growth Margined Mutual Fund Portfolio	+0.18%	
g. Conservative Balanced Mutual Fund Portfolio	+0.13%	
h. International Mutual Funds Portfolio	+0.04%	
i. Gold Mutual Funds Portfolio	−0.15%	
67. Ford Investment Review		+0.22%
68. The Chartist Mutual Fund Timer		+0.22%
69. Growth Fund Guide (Average)		+0.22%
a. Quality Growth Mutual Fund Portfolio	+0.55%	
b. Special Situations Mutual Fund Portfolio	+0.37%	
c. "Valueratio" Equities & Cash Portfolio	+0.28%	
d. "Valueratio" Equities, Cash & Leverage Portfolio	+0.25%	
e. "Valueratio" Fully Invested Portfolio	+0.18%	
f. Aggressive Growth Mutual Fund Portfolio	+0.18%	
g. Growth Mutual Fund Portfolio	+0.03%	
h. Growth Model Account	−0.02%	
i. Selected Core Account	−0.08%	
j. Aggressive Model Account	−0.12%	
70. The Value Line OTC Special Situations Service		+0.22%
71. The Ney Report (Average)		+0.22%
a. Growth & Income Fund Portfolio	+0.22%	
b. Income Fund Portfolio	+0.22%	
c. Growth Fund Portfolio	+0.20%	
72. Fund Kinetics (Average)		+0.21%
a. Weekly "Eifer" Report	+0.13%	
73. The Zweig Forecast		+0.21%
74. Better Investing		+0.21%
75. InvesTech Market Analyst		+0.20%
76. Harry Browne's Special Reports (Average)		+0.20%
a. Variable [Speculative] Portfolio	+0.16%	
b. Permanent Portfolio	+0.12%	

Newsletter	Individual Portfolio	Overall Average
77. Morningstar Mutual Funds (Average)		+14.7%
a. Equity & Hybrid Funds (5-Star)	+18.4%	
b. Bond Funds (5-Star)	+10.6%	
78. The Blue Chip Correlator		+14.4%
79. Harry Browne's Special Reports (Average)		+14.0%
a. Variable [Speculative] Portfolio	+16.6%	
b. Permanent Portfolio	+10.9%	
80. United & Babson Investment Report (Average)		+13.9%
a. Stocks for the Income-Minded	+20.3%	
b. Stocks for Long-Term Growth	+18.7%	
c. Supervised List of Convertible Bonds and Preferreds	+11.9%	
d. Cyclical Stocks for Profit	+3.4%	
81. Professional Timing Service (Average)		+13.6%
a. Mutual Fund Model Portfolio	+38.7%	
b. Gold Futures Trading Portfolio	−7.9%	
82. The Wall Street Digest (Average)		+13.4%
a. Mutual Fund Portfolio	+20.5%	
b. Stock and Bond Portfolio	+6.0%	
83. Plain Talk Investor (Average)		+13.3%
a. "Personal-Best" Stock Portfolio	+18.6%	
b. High Risk/High Reward Portfolio	+7.3%	
84. Graphic Fund Forecaster (Average)		+13.3%
a. Fidelity Select Fund Portfolio #2	+27.2%	
b. Fidelity Select Fund Portfolio #1	+12.1%	
c. Financial Strategic Funds Portfolio	+11.4%	
d. Growth/International Portfolio #2	+8.4%	
e. Growth/International Portfolio #1	+6.8%	
85. Financial World (Average)		+12.6%
a. Stocks Rated A+	+44.9%	
b. Balanced Fund Portfolio	+21.6%	
c. Aggressive Growth Fund Portfolio	+21.5%	
d. Corporate Bond Fund Portfolio	+21.2%	
e. Long-Term Growth Fund Portfolio	+20.1%	
f. US Gov't Bonds Fund Portfolio	+12.9%	
g. Growth & Income Fund Portfolio	+11.9%	
h. Sector Funds Portfolio	+9.3%	
i. International Stock Fund Portfolio	+2.5%	
j. International Bond Fund Portfolio	+2.4%	
86. Growth Stock Outlook		+11.6%
87. The Professional Tape Reader (Average)		+11.3%
a. Mutual Fund Portfolio	+13.6%	
b. Model Stock Portfolio	+8.7%	

Newsletter	Individual Portfolio	Overall Average
77. Futures Hotline Mutual Fund Timer (Average)		+0.19%
a. Model Futures Portfolio	+0.22%	
b. Asset Allocation Portfolio	−0.12%	
78. Morningstar Mutual Funds (Average)		+0.19%
a. Bond Funds (5-Star)	+0.27%	
b. Equity & Hybrid Funds (5-Star)	+0.16%	
79. Investment Horizons		+0.19%
80. Global Fund Timer (Average)		+0.17%
a. U.S. Portfolio	+0.21%	
b. Conservative Portfolio	+0.16%	
c. Global Portfolio	+0.14%	
d. Zero Bond Portfolio	+0.04%	
81. The Sector Funds Newsletter (Average)		+0.17%
a. Model Mutual Fund Portfolio 3 (Mostly Bonds)	+0.21%	
b. Model Mutual Fund Portfolio 2 ("Fidelity Funds Plus" Portfolio)	+0.14%	
c. Model Mutual Fund Portfolio 1	+0.12%	
82. Systems and Forecasts (Average)		+0.15%
a. Jack White Portfolio	+0.22%	
b. The Regular Portfolio	+0.13%	
c. Futures & Options Portfolio	+0.06%	
83. The Blue Chip Correlator		+0.13%
84. Kinsman's Telephone Growth & Income Service (Average)		+0.11%
a. Mutual Fund Switch Portfolio	+0.14%	
b. Growth & Income Portfolio	+0.07%	
85. The Wall Street Generalist (Average)		+0.11%
a. Select Intermediate Portfolio	+0.26%	
b. Select Trading Portfolio	+0.06%	
86. The Professional Tape Reader (Average)		+0.11%
a. Mutual Fund Portfolio	+0.19%	
b. Model Stock Portfolio	+0.03%	
87. Graphic Fund Forecaster (Average)		+0.11%
a. Fidelity Select Fund Portfolio #2	+0.25%	
b. Financial Strategic Funds Portfolio	+0.07%	
c. Fidelity Select Fund Portfolio #1	+0.07%	
d. Growth/International Portfolio #2	+0.03%	
e. Growth/International Portfolio #1	0.00%	

Newsletter	Individual Portfolio	Overall Average
88. Kinsman's Telephone Growth & Income Service (Average)		+11.2%
a. Mutual Fund Switch Portfolio	+12.7%	
b. Growth & Income Portfolio	+9.6%	
89. Fast Track Funds		+10.5%
90. The Peter Dag Investment Letter (Average)		+10.5%
a. Model Vanguard Fund Portfolio	+20.5%	
91. Growth Fund Guide (Average)		+10.0%
a. "Valueratio" Fully Invested Portfolio	+13.2%	
b. "Valueratio" Equities & Cash Portfolio	+13.1%	
c. Quality Growth Mutual Fund Portfolio	+12.4%	
d. "Valueratio" Equities, Cash & Leverage Portfolio	+12.3%	
e. Special Situations Mutual Fund Portfolio	+12.1%	
f. Aggressive Growth Mutual Fund Portfolio	+11.2%	
g. Growth Mutual Fund Portfolio	+7.7%	
h. Growth Model Account	+7.1%	
i. Selected Core Account	+6.9%	
j. Aggressive Model Account	+4.1%	
92. Income & Safety		+9.9%
93. Telephone Switch Newsletter (Average)		+9.6%
a. Equity/Cash Switch Plan	+33.4%	
b. Gold/Cash Switch Plan	+0.1%	
c. International Funds/Cash Switch Plan	−3.4%	
94. Mutual Fund Investing (Average)		+9.3%
a. Portfolio II (Balanced Growth)	+10.5%	
b. Portfolio I (Growth With Income)	+9.6%	
c. Portfolio III (IRA/Long Term Growth)	+7.5%	
95. The Ney Report (Average)		+9.0%
a. Growth & Income Fund Portfolio	+9.3%	
b. Income Fund Portfolio	+9.2%	
c. Growth Fund Portfolio	+8.6%	
96. Weber's Fund Advisor (Average)		+8.5%
a. Low Risk/Low Switch Portfolio	+20.2%	
b. "Go-With-the-Winner Strategy" Portfolio	+8.5%	
The Riskless Rate of Return: A T-Bill Portfolio		+7.5%
97. The Wall Street Digest Mutual Fund Advisor (Average)		+7.4%
a. Long-Term Growth Funds	+19.2%	
b. Income Funds	+16.4%	
c. Aggressive Growth Funds	+14.3%	
d. Sector Funds	+14.1%	
e. Growth & Income Funds	+14.0%	
f. Top No-Load Funds	+6.0%	

Newsletter	Individual Portfolio	Overall Average
88. Financial World (Average)		+0.11%
a. Corporate Bond Fund Portfolio	+0.46%	
b. Stocks Rated A¢	+0.25%	
c. US Gov't Bonds Fund Portfolio	+0.24%	
d. Balanced Fund Portfolio	+0.20%	
e. Long-Term Growth Fund Portfolio	+0.17%	
f. Aggressive Growth Fund Portfolio	+0.16%	
g. Growth & Income Fund Portfolio	+0.08%	
h. Sector Funds Portfolio	+0.04%	
i. International Stock Fund Portfolio	−0.08%	
j. International Bond Fund Portfolio	−0.10%	
89. United & Babson Investment Report (Average)		+0.10%
a. Stocks for the Income-Minded	+0.25%	
b. Stocks for Long-Term Growth	+0.14%	
c. Supervised List of Convertible Bonds and Preferreds	+0.08%	
d. Cyclical Stocks for Profit	−0.01%	
90. Plain Talk Investor (Average)		+0.08%
a. "Personal-Best" Stock Portfolio	+0.17%	
b. High Risk/High Reward Portfolio	+0.03%	
91. The Wall Street Digest (Average)		+0.08%
a. Mutual Fund Portfolio	+0.18%	
b. Stock and Bond Portfolio	+0.02%	
92. The Peter Dag Investment Letter (Average)		+0.08%
a. Model Vanguard Fund Portfolio	+0.48%	
93. Telephone Switch Newsletter (Average)		+0.07%
a. Equity/Cash Switch Plan	+0.29%	
b. Gold/Cash Switch Plan	−0.14%	
c. International Funds/Cash Switch Plan	−0.30%	
94. Mutual Fund Investing (Average)		+0.07%
a. Portfolio I (Growth With Income)	+0.15%	
b. Portfolio II (Balanced Growth)	+0.12%	
c. Portfolio III (IRA/Long Term Growth)	+0.01%	
95. Fast Track Funds		+0.06%
96. Weber's Fund Advisor (Average)		+0.03%
a. Low Risk/Low Switch Portfolio	+0.29%	
b. "Go-With-the-Winner Strategy" Portfolio	+0.03%	
97. The Mutual Fund Strategist (Average)		+0.02%
a. Sector Portfolio	+0.02%	
b. Diversified Growth Portfolio	+0.01%	

Newsletter	Individual Portfolio	Overall Average
98. The Sy Harding Investor Forecasts (Average)		+7.1%
a. Portfolio 3: Mutual Fund Switching Portfolio	+23.8%	
b. Portfolio 1: Buy & Hold	+6.5%	
c. Portfolio 2: Short-Term Trading Portfolio	+2.7%	
99. Stockmarket Cycles (Average)		+6.9%
a. Mutual Fund Portfolio	+24.4%	
b. Model Stock Portfolio	−8.8%	
100. The Ruff Times (Average)		+6.5%
a. "Optimum Switch Hitter" Mutual Fund Portfolio#2	+15.3%	
b. "Optimum Switch Hitter" Mutual Fund Portfolio#1	+12.4%	
c. The Back Page Portfolio	−7.6%	
101. The Mutual Fund Strategist (Average)		+6.3%
a. Sector Portfolio	+6.5%	
b. Diversified Growth Portfolio	+5.8%	
102. Switch Fund Timing (Average)		+6.1%
a. Conservative Model Mutual Fund Portfolio	+10.4%	
b. Conservative/Momentum Model Fund Portfolio	+8.0%	
c. Model Stock Portfolio	+7.7%	
d. Gold Fund Portfolio	−3.9%	
103. The Option Advisor (Average)		+5.9%
a. Option Income Portfolio	+19.4%	
b. Aggressive Portfolio	−3.3%	
c. Conservative Portfolio	−7.2%	
104. LaLoggia's Special Situation Report (Average)		+4.7%
a. Master List of Recommended Stocks	+23.9%	
b. Other Recommended Stocks	−12.8%	
105. The International Harry Schultz Letter (Average)		+4.4%
a. Foreign Stocks on the "List"	+20.6%	
b. Portfolio constructed from gold/silver trading advice (no margin)	+8.8%	
c. U.S. Stocks on the "List"	−14.7%	
106. California Technology Stock Letter		+3.0%
107. The Princeton Portfolios (Average)		+1.2%
a. Long-Term Portfolio#1	+27.0%	
b. Long-Term Portfolio#2	−20.4%	
108. The R.H.M. Survey of Warrants, Options & Low-Price Stocks		−1.8%

Newsletter	Individual Portfolio	Overall Average
98. The Option Advisor (Average)		+0.02%
a. Option Income Portfolio	+0.25%	
b. Conservative Portfolio	−0.01%	
c. Aggressive Portfolio	−0.02%	
99. The Wall Street Digest Mutual Fund Advisor (Average)		+0.01%
a. Income Funds	+0.16%	
b. Long-Term Growth Funds	+0.16%	
c. Growth & Income Funds	+0.10%	
d. Aggressive Growth Funds	+0.09%	
e. Sector Funds	+0.09%	
f. Top No-Load Funds	+0.01%	
100. The Sy Harding Investor Forecasts (Average)		+0.01%
a. Portfolio 3: Mutual Fund Switching Portfolio	+0.32%	
b. Portfolio 1: Buy & Hold	0.00%	
c. Portfolio 2: Short-Term Trading Portfolio	−0.09%	
101. The Princeton Portfolios (Average)		−0.01%
a. Long-Term Portfolio #1	+0.16%	
b. Long-Term Portfolio #2	−0.16%	
102. Stockmarket Cycles (Average)		−0.01%
a. Mutual Fund Portfolio	+0.35%	
b. Model Stock Portfolio	−0.34%	
103. The R.H.M. Survey of Warrants, Options & Low-Price Stocks		−0.01%
104. Switch Fund Timing (Average)		−0.01%
a. Conservative Model Mutual Fund Portfolio	+0.07%	
b. Model Stock Portfolio	+0.03%	
c. Conservative/Momentum Model Fund Portfolio	+0.02%	
d. Gold Fund Portfolio	−0.30%	
105. The Ruff Times (Average)		−0.03%
a. "Optimum Switch Hitter" Mutual Fund Portfolio #2	+0.23%	
b. "Optimum Switch Hitter" Mutual Fund Portfolio #1	+0.16%	
c. The Back Page Portfolio	−0.25%	
106. LaLoggia's Special Situation Report (Average)		−0.10%
a. Master List of Recommended Stocks	+0.41%	
b. Other Recommended Stocks	−0.28%	
107. The International Harry Schultz Letter (Average)		−0.11%
a. Foreign Stocks on the "List"	+0.23%	
b. Portfolio constructed from gold/silver trading advice (no margin)	+0.05%	
c. U.S. Stocks on the "List"	−0.33%	
108. The Dines Letter (Average)		−0.11%
a. Long-Term Growth Portfolio	+0.07%	
b. Good Grade Portfolio	−0.09%	
c. Precious Metals Portfolio	−0.19%	
d. Short-Term Trading Portfolio	−0.19%	

Newsletter	Individual Portfolio	Overall Average
109. Margo's Market Monitor (Average)		−4.4%
a. Common Stock Portfolio	+1.8%	
b. Fidelity Select Funds Portfolio	−11.2%	
110. The Dines Letter (Average)		−5.8%
a. Long-Term Growth Portfolio	+13.0%	
b. Good Grade Portfolio	−5.0%	
c. Precious Metals Portfolio	−6.1%	
d. Short-Term Trading Portfolio	−28.3%	
111. The Holt Advisory (Average)		−14.6%
a. Balanced Hedge Strategy	−21.9%	
112. Strategic Investment (Average)		−15.6%
a. $100,000 Income Portfolio	+3.8%	
b. Newby's $25,000 Special Portfolio	−11.9%	
c. Speculative Strategy	−31.9%	
113. The Garside Forecast		−24.8%
114. Your Window Into the Future (Average)		−27.3%
a. Portfolio A: Aggressive Portfolio	+6.7%	
b. Portfolio B: Conservative Portfolio	−0.5%	
c. Portfolio C: Speculative Portfolio	−81.5%	
115. On Markets		−33.7%
116. P.Q. Wall Forecast, Inc.		−38.7%
117. Harmonic Research (Average)		−39.2%
a. Futures Portfolio	−39.2%	
118. Overpriced Stock Service		−94.0%

Newsletter	Individual Portfolio	Overall Average
109. California Technology Stock Letter		−0.13%
110. Your Window Into the Future (Average)		−0.13%
a. Portfolio A: Aggressive Portfolio	+0.02%	
b. Portfolio B: Conservative Portfolio	−0.08%	
c. Portfolio C: Speculative Portfolio	−0.13%	
111. Overpriced Stock Service		−0.15%
112. On Markets		−0.15%
113. Margo's Market Monitor (Average)		−0.19%
a. Common Stock Portfolio	−0.03%	
b. Fidelity Select Funds Portfolio	−0.52%	
114. Strategic Investment (Average)		−0.27%
a. Newby's $25,000 Special Portfolio	−0.04%	
b. $100,000 Income Portfolio	−0.09%	
c. Speculative Strategy	−0.27%	
115. P.Q. Wall Forecast, Inc.		−0.52%
116. The Garside Forecast		−0.56%
117. The Holt Advisory (Average)		−0.67%
a. Balanced Hedge Strategy	−0.61%	
118. Harmonic Research (Average)		−0.98%
a. Futures Portfolio	−0.98%	

APPENDIX B

Mutual Fund
Newsletter Performance

Over the past several years there has been an explosion in the number of newsletters devoted just to mutual funds. *The Hulbert Financial Digest* receives numerous calls from subscribers wanting to know which mutual fund letters have done the best. That is, they aren't interested in which letter is ranked tops among all investment newsletters, but just among those that are devoted exclusively to mutual funds. The rankings that appear in this appendix are designed to respond to these subscribers' requests.

Because most mutual fund newsletters are relatively new, however, these rankings that follow are not as extensive as those that appear in Appendix A. Instead, the following rankings begin no earlier than 1985. This isn't to say that no mutual fund newsletter existed prior to that, but if you want to know how a particular mutual fund newsletter did over a longer period of time, and the HFD does have data for it, you will need to refer to Appendix A. In general, since the rankings in Appendix B are subsets of those appearing in Appendix A, you can refer back to those earlier rankings to obtain a fuller picture.

As is the case with Appendix A, the rankings that appear on the left-hand pages of this appendix are based on total return, while those appearing on the right-hand pages are based on risk-adjusted performances. For a description of the process used to adjust performance for risk, please refer to the introduction to Appendix A.

While the rankings that follow can be of help in choosing a mutual fund newsletter, they are by no means the last word on the matter. For example, as discussed at length in the chapter on market timing at the front of this *Guide*, some of the best newsletters for market timing are not mutual fund newsletters as such, since they also recommend individual stocks and other securities as well. Appendix C lists the best market timers over various periods, and you definitely should examine it in conjunction with this appendix.

Appendix B-1: Mutual Fund Performance
from 1/1/85 to 6/30/92 (Total Return)

Newsletter	Individual Portfolio	Overall Average
1. The Mutual Fund Strategist (Average)		+234.1% ①
Wilshire 5000 Value-Weighted Total Return Index		+197.6%
2. Stockmarket Cycles (Mutual Fund Portfolio)		+166.3%
3. **NoLoad Fund*X (Average)		+142.8%
a. Portfolio of "Class 3" Funds (Higher Quality Growth Funds)	+214.3%	
b. Portfolio of "Class 2" Funds (Speculative Growth Funds)	+133.7%	
c. Portfolio of "Class 1" Funds (Most Speculative Growth Funds)	+101.2%	
4. Telephone Switch Newsletter (Average)		+126.3%
a. International Funds/Cash Switch Plan	+193.3%	
b. Equity/Cash Switch Plan	+139.0%	
c. Gold/Cash Switch Plan	+44.4%	
5. Fund Exchange (Average)		+125.5%
a. Aggressive Growth Margined Mutual Fund Portfolio	+182.2%	
b. Conservative Growth Margined Mutual Fund Portfolio	+161.5%	
c. Fixed Income Bond Portfolio	+126.6%	
d. Aggressive Growth Mutual Fund Portfolio	+124.4%	
e. Growth/Income Mutual Fund Portfolio	+105.9%	
f. Gold Mutual Funds Portfolio	+41.3%	
6. Weber's Fund Advisor (Average)		+114.0%
a. "Go-With-the-Winner Strategy" Portfolio	+121.8%	
7. The Peter Dag Investment Letter (Model Vanguard Fund Portfolio)		+103.0%
8. Growth Fund Guide (Average)		+94.7%
a. Special Situations Mutual Fund Portfolio	+124.7%	
b. Quality Growth Mutual Fund Portfolio	+96.2%	
c. Aggressive Growth Mutual Fund Portfolio	+81.8%	
d. Growth Mutual Fund Portfolio	+76.6%	
The Riskless Rate of Return: A T-Bill Portfolio		+61.7%

TOP M.F   +234.1%
TOP STOCK +821.7%

Appendix B-1: Mutual Fund Newsletter Performance
from 1/1/85 to 6/30/92 (Risk-Adjusted)

Newsletter	Individual Portfolio	Overall Average
1. The Peter Dag Investment Letter (Model Vanguard Fund Portfolio)		+0.22%
2. The Mutual Fund Strategist (Average)		+0.21%
Wilshire 5000 Value-Weighted Total Return Index		+0.16%
3. Stockmarket Cycles (Mutual Fund Portfolio)		+0.16%
4. Fund Exchange (Average)		+0.14%
a. Fixed Income Bond Portfolio	+0.35%	
b. Conservative Growth Margined Mutual Fund Portfolio	+0.13%	
c. Aggressive Growth Margined Mutual Fund Portfolio	+0.13%	
d. Aggressive Growth Mutual Fund Portfolio	+0.12%	
e. Growth/Income Mutual Fund Portfolio	+0.11%	
f. Gold Mutual Funds Portfolio	0.00%	
5. Telephone Switch Newsletter (Average)		+0.13%
a. International Funds/Cash Switch Plan	+0.19%	
b. Equity/Cash Switch Plan	+0.12%	
c. Gold/Cash Switch Plan	0.00%	
6. **NoLoad Fund*X (Average)		+0.12%
a. Portfolio of "Class 3" Funds (Higher Quality Growth Funds)	+0.19%	
b. Portfolio of "Class 2" Funds (Speculative Growth Funds)	+0.11%	
c. Portfolio of "Class 1" Funds (Most Speculative Growth Funds)	+0.07%	
7. Weber's Fund Advisor (Average)		+0.10%
a. "Go-With-the-Winner Strategy" Portfolio	+0.11%	
8. Growth Fund Guide (Average)		+0.09%
a. Special Situations Mutual Fund Portfolio	+0.12%	
b. Quality Growth Mutual Fund Portfolio	+0.11%	
c. Aggressive Growth Mutual Fund Portfolio	+0.06%	
d. Growth Mutual Fund Portfolio	+0.05%	

5.5YR

Appendix B-2: Mutual Fund Newsletter Performance
from 1/1/87 to 6/30/92 (Total Return)

Newsletter	Individual Portfolio	Overall Average
1. Fidelity Monitor (Average)		+127.7% ①
a. Growth Mutual Funds Portfolio	+132.3%	
b. Select System Mutual Funds Portfolio	+114.3%	
2. Investors Intelligence (Fidelity Switch Fund (Equity) Portfolio)		+125.3%
3. The Mutual Fund Strategist (Average)		+105.5%
4. Stockmarket Cycles (Mutual Fund Portfolio)		+104.3%
5. Mutual Fund Forecaster		+95.9%
6. InvesTech Mutual Fund Advisor		+95.6%
7. The Volume Reversal Survey (Index Fund Portfolio)		+93.4%
Wilshire 5000 Value-Weighted Total Return Index		+93.3%
8. Fundline (Average)		+92.4%
9. Professional Timing Service (Mutual Fund Model Portfolio)		+92.2%
10. The Marketarian Letter (Mutual Fund Portfolio for Traders)		+92.2%
11. Fund Exchange (Average)		+74.9%
a. Aggressive Growth Margined Mutual Fund Portfolio	+128.5%	
b. Aggressive Growth Mutual Fund Portfolio	+75.5%	
c. Conservative Growth Margined Mutual Fund Portfolio	+75.1%	
d. Fixed Income Bond Portfolio	+74.3%	
e. Aggressive Balanced Mutual Fund Portfolio	+67.2%	
f. Growth/Income Mutual Fund Portfolio	+65.1%	
g. Conservative Balanced Mutual Fund Portfolio	+54.3%	
h. Gold Mutual Funds Portfolio	+30.0%	
12. United Mutual Fund Selector (Average)		+68.0%
a. Aggressive Growth Funds	+89.9%	
b. Growth & Income Funds	+67.9%	
c. Growth Funds	+60.3%	
d. Income Funds	+48.2%	
13. Cabot's Mutual Fund Navigator (Average)		+65.6%
a. Growth Portfolio	+43.9%	
14. The Professional Tape Reader (Mutual Fund Portfolio)		+61.3%
15. The No-Load Fund Investor (Average)		+60.7%
a. Wealth Builder Portfolio	+69.8%	
b. Pre-Retirement Portfolio	+61.6%	
c. Retirement Portfolio	+59.8%	
16. Telephone Switch Newsletter (Average)		+56.9%
a. Equity/Cash Switch Plan	+99.0%	
b. International Funds/Cash Switch Plan	+38.7%	
c. Gold/Cash Switch Plan	+29.2%	
17. The Peter Dag Investment Letter (Model Vanguard Fund Portfolio)		+56.6%

① Top M.F 127.7%
Top Stocks 302.0

Appendix B-2: Mutual Fund Newsletter Performance
from 1/1/87 to 6/30/92 (Risk-Adjusted)

Newsletter	Individual Portfolio	Overall Average
1. Investors Intelligence (Fidelity Switch Fund [Equity] Portfolio)		+0.24%
2. InvesTech Mutual Fund Advisor		+0.21%
3. Stockmarket Cycles (Mutual Fund Portfolio)		+0.18%
4. Fidelity Monitor (Average)		+0.16%
a. Growth Mutual Funds Portfolio	+0.18%	
b. Select System Mutual Funds Portfolio	+0.13%	
5. The Professional Tape Reader (Mutual Fund Portfolio)		+0.16%
6. Professional Timing Service (Mutual Fund Model Portfolio)		+0.15%
7. The Volume Reversal Survey (Index Fund Portfolio)		+0.15%
8. The Mutual Fund Strategist (Average)		+0.15%
9. Fund Exchange (Average)		+0.14%
a. Fixed Income Bond Portfolio	+0.36%	
b. Aggressive Growth Margined Mutual Fund Portfolio	+0.15%	
c. Aggressive Balanced Mutual Fund Portfolio	+0.13%	
d. Aggressive Growth Mutual Fund Portfolio	+0.13%	
e. Growth/Income Mutual Fund Portfolio	+0.12%	
f. Conservative Growth Margined Mutual Fund Portfolio	+0.10%	
g. Conservative Balanced Mutual Fund Portfolio	+0.10%	
h. Gold Mutual Funds Portfolio	0.00%	
10. The Marketarian Letter (Mutual Fund Portfolio for Traders)		+0.14%
11. The Peter Dag Investment Letter (Model Vanguard Fund Portfolio)		+0.14%
Wilshire 5000 Value-Weighted Total Return Index		+0.12%
12. Mutual Fund Forecaster		+0.11%
13. Fundline (Average)		+0.11%
14. United Mutual Fund Selector (Average)		+0.09%
a. Aggressive Growth Funds	+0.11%	
b. Growth & Income Funds	+0.09%	
c. Growth Funds	+0.06%	
d. Income Funds	+0.05%	
15. Cabot's Mutual Fund Navigator (Average)		+0.08%
a. Growth Portfolio	+0.03%	
16. The No-Load Fund Investor (Average)		+0.07%
a. Wealth Builder Portfolio	+0.08%	
b. Retirement Portfolio	+0.08%	
c. Pre-Retirement Portfolio	+0.07%	
17. The Mutual Fund Letter (Average)		+0.06%
a. Growth & Income Portfolio	+0.11%	
b. Income Portfolio	+0.06%	
c. Highly Aggressive Portfolio	+0.05%	
d. Moderately Aggressive Portfolio	+0.05%	

Newsletter	Individual Portfolio	Overall Average
18. Donoghue's Moneyletter (Average)		+55.1%
a. "Venturesome" Model Portfolio	+59.2%	
19. Weber's Fund Advisor (Average)		+53.8%
a. "Go-With-the-Winner Strategy" Portfolio	+59.4%	
20. The Mutual Fund Letter (Average)		+53.4%
a. Growth & Income Portfolio	+61.3%	
b. Highly Aggressive Portfolio	+53.1%	
c. Moderately Aggressive Portfolio	+50.2%	
d. Income Portfolio	+48.6%	
21. Bob Brinker's Marketimer (Average)		+52.7%
a. Long-Term Growth Mutual Fund Portfolio	+66.3%	
b. Aggressive Growth Mutual Fund Portfolio	+48.5%	
c. Balanced Portfolio	+39.0%	
22. **NoLoad Fund*X (Average)		+48.2%
a. Portfolio of "Class 3" Funds (Higher Quality Growth Funds)	+61.8%	
b. Portfolio of "Class 2" Funds (Speculative Growth Funds)	+47.0%	
c. Portfolio of "Class 4" Funds (Total Return Funds)	+45.5%	
d. Portfolio of "Class 1" Funds (Most Speculative Growth Funds)	+42.9%	
23. Margo's Market Monitor (Fidelity Select Funds Portfolio)		+42.2%
The Riskless Rate of Return: A T-Bill Portfolio		+41.7%
24. Mutual Fund Investing (Average)		+40.5%
a. Portfolio II (Balanced Growth)	+48.9%	
b. Portfolio I (Growth With Income)	+43.1%	
25. Growth Fund Guide (Average)		+29.0%
a. Special Situations Mutual Fund Portfolio	+39.6%	
b. Quality Growth Mutual Fund Portfolio	+37.3%	
c. Aggressive Growth Mutual Fund Portfolio	+23.9%	
d. Growth Mutual Fund Portfolio	+16.5%	
26. The Sector Funds Newsletter (Average)		+22.5%
a. Model Mutual Fund Portfolio 3 (Mostly Bonds)	+49.8%	
b. Model Mutual Fund Portfolio 1	−20.9%	
27. Your Window Into the Future (Portfolio B: Conservative Portfolio)		+13.2%

Newsletter	Individual Portfolio	Overall Average
18. Telephone Switch Newsletter (Average)		+0.06%
a. Equity/Cash Switch Plan	+0.15%	
b. International Funds/Cash Switch Plan	+0.01%	
c. Gold/Cash Switch Plan	0.00%	
19. Donoghue's Moneyletter (Average)		+0.06%
a. "Venturesome" Model Portfolio	+0.06%	
20. Weber's Fund Advisor (Average)		+0.05%
a. "Go-With-the-Winner Strategy" Portfolio	+0.06%	
21. Bob Brinker's Marketimer (Average)		+0.05%
a. Long-Term Growth Mutual Fund Portfolio	+0.08%	
b. Aggressive Growth Mutual Fund Portfolio	+0.04%	
c. Balanced Portfolio	+0.02%	
22. **NoLoad Fund*X (Average)		+0.04%
a. Portfolio of "Class 3" Funds (Higher Quality Growth Funds)	+0.07%	
b. Portfolio of "Class 1" Funds (Most Speculative Growth Funds)	+0.04%	
c. Portfolio of "Class 2" Funds (Speculative Growth Funds)	+0.04%	
d. Portfolio of "Class 4" Funds (Total Return Funds)	+0.03%	
23. Margo's Market Monitor (Fidelity Select Funds Portfolio)		+0.02%
24. Mutual Fund Investing (Average)		0.00%
a. Portfolio II (Balanced Growth)	+0.05%	
b. Portfolio I (Growth With Income)	+0.02%	
25. Your Window Into the Future (Portfolio B: Conservative Portfolio)		−0.02%
26. The Sector Funds Newsletter (Average)		−0.02%
a. Model Mutual Fund Portfolio 3 (Mostly Bonds)	+0.04%	
b. Model Mutual Fund Portfolio 1	−0.07%	
27. Growth Fund Guide (Average)		−0.05%
a. Special Situations Mutual Fund Portfolio	+0.01%	
b. Quality Growth Mutual Fund Portfolio	−0.02%	
c. Aggressive Growth Mutual Fund Portfolio	−0.08%	
d. Growth Mutual Fund Portfolio	−0.11%	

3,5 yr

Appendix B-3: Mutual Fund Newsletter Performance
from 1/1/89 to 6/30/92 (Total Return)

Newsletter	Individual Portfolio	Overall Average
1. Timer Digest (Fidelity Select Portfolio)	⊗	+121.9%
2. Fidelity Monitor (Average)		+107.9%
a. Select System Mutual Funds Portfolio	+130.0%	
b. Growth Mutual Funds Portfolio	+81.7%	
3. Professional Timing Service (Mutual Fund Model Portfolio)		+85.2%
4. The Chartist Mutual Fund Timer		+81.6%
5. Fundline (Average)		+76.3%
6. Mutual Fund Forecaster		+74.4%
7. Fidelity Insight (Average)		+63.3%
a. Growth Portfolio	+79.6%	
b. Growth & Income Fund Portfolio	+70.1%	
c. Speculative Portfolio	+52.1%	
d. Income & Preservation Fund Portfolio	+51.7%	
Wilshire 5000 Value-Weighted Total Return Index		+60.3%
8. The Volume Reversal Survey (Index Fund Portfolio)		+59.4%
9. Stockmarket Cycles (Mutual Fund Portfolio)		+49.8%
10. The No-Load Fund Investor (Average)		+48.9%
a. Wealth Builder Portfolio	+52.7%	
b. Retirement Portfolio	+47.0%	
c. Pre-Retirement Portfolio	+46.3%	
11. The Mutual Fund Strategist (Average)		+48.1%
a. Sector Portfolio	+53.3%	
b. Diversified Growth Portfolio	+47.9%	
12. Investors Intelligence (Fidelity Switch Fund (Equity) Portfolio)		+45.6%
13. Personal Finance (Average)		+45.5%
a. Mutual Fund Portfolio (Short-Term)	+45.9%	
b. Mutual Fund Portfolio (Long-Term)	+45.2%	
14. **NoLoad Fund*X (Average)		+45.5%
a. Portfolio of "Class 1" Funds (Most Speculative Growth Funds)	+67.9%	
b. Portfolio of "Class 3" Funds (Higher Quality Growth Funds)	+44.9%	
c. Portfolio of "Class 2" Funds (Speculative Growth Funds)	+41.9%	
d. Portfolio of "Class 4" Funds (Total Return Funds)	+39.4%	
15. InvesTech Mutual Fund Advisor		+44.4%
16. United Mutual Fund Selector (Average)		+43.9%
a. Aggressive Growth Funds	+58.2%	
b. Growth Funds	+42.7%	
c. Growth & Income Funds	+38.2%	
d. Income Funds	+34.5%	

⊗ Top M.F. 121.9 %
Top STOCKS 289.1 %

Appendix B-3: Mutual Fund Newsletter Performance
from 1/1/89 to 6/30/92 (Risk-Adjusted)

Newsletter	Individual Portfolio	Overall Average
1. Professional Timing Service (Mutual Fund Model Portfolio)		+0.38%
2. Fidelity Monitor (Average)		+0.30%
a. Select System Mutual Funds Portfolio	+0.30%	
b. Growth Mutual Funds Portfolio	+0.23%	
3. Fidelity Insight (Average)		+0.28%
a. Growth Portfolio	+0.35%	
b. Growth & Income Fund Portfolio	+0.32%	
c. Income & Preservation Fund Portfolio	+0.31%	
d. Speculative Portfolio	+0.15%	
4. Timer Digest (Fidelity Select Portfolio)		+0.27%
5. The Peter Dag Investment Letter (Model Vanguard Fund Portfolio)		+0.26%
6. The Chartist Mutual Fund Timer		+0.25%
7. The Volume Reversal Survey (Index Fund Portfolio)		+0.21%
8. Fundline (Average)		+0.20%
9. InvesTech Mutual Fund Advisor		+0.19%
10. Mutual Fund Forecaster		+0.18%
11. Stockmarket Cycles (Mutual Fund Portfolio)		+0.17%
12. The No-Load Fund Investor (Average)		+0.17%
a. Retirement Portfolio	+0.21%	
b. Pre-Retirement Portfolio	+0.16%	
c. Wealth Builder Portfolio	+0.15%	
Wilshire 5000 Value-Weighted Total Return Index		+0.16%
13. Personal Finance (Average)		+0.15%
a. Mutual Fund Portfolio (Long-Term)	+0.18%	
b. Mutual Fund Portfolio (Short-Term)	+0.12%	
14. Investors Intelligence (Fidelity Switch Fund [Equity] Portfolio)		+0.14%
15. Bob Brinker's Marketimer (Average)		+0.14%
a. Fixed-Income Model Mutual Fund Portfolio	+0.28%	
b. Long-Term Growth Mutual Fund Portfolio	+0.13%	
c. Aggressive Growth Mutual Fund Portfolio	+0.10%	
d. Balanced Portfolio	+0.08%	
16. The Mutual Fund Letter (Average)		+0.12%
a. Income Portfolio	+0.21%	
b. Growth & Income Portfolio	+0.18%	
c. Highly Aggressive Portfolio	+0.09%	
d. All Weather Portfolio	+0.09%	
e. Moderately Aggressive Portfolio	+0.07%	

Newsletter	Individual Portfolio	Overall Average
17. Bob Brinker's Marketimer (Average)		+43.3%
a. Long-Term Growth Mutual Fund Portfolio	+47.4%	
b. Fixed-Income Model Mutual Fund Portfolio	+44.9%	
c. Aggressive Growth Mutual Fund Portfolio	+43.5%	
d. Balanced Portfolio	+34.6%	
18. The Peter Dag Investment Letter (Model Vanguard Fund Portfolio)		+40.5%
19. Donoghue's Moneyletter (Average)		+39.2%
a. "Venturesome" Model Portfolio	+42.9%	
b. Conservative Mutual Fund Portfolio	+39.0%	
c. Signal Portfolio	+37.8%	
d. Moderate Mutual Fund Portfolio	+34.6%	
20. The Investor's Guide to Closed-End Funds (Average)		+39.0%
a. Managed Portfolio I: Balanced	+37.9%	
21. The Mutual Fund Letter (Average)		+35.3%
a. Growth & Income Portfolio	+38.1%	
b. Income Portfolio	+37.7%	
c. Highly Aggressive Portfolio	+36.0%	
d. All Weather Portfolio	+34.0%	
e. Moderately Aggressive Portfolio	+30.1%	
22. Fund Exchange (Average)		+35.0%
a. Aggressive Growth Margined Mutual Fund Portfolio	+70.8%	
b. Fixed Income Bond Portfolio	+44.2%	
c. Aggressive Growth Mutual Fund Portfolio	+37.5%	
d. Conservative Growth Margined Mutual Fund Portfolio	+36.6%	
e. Growth/Income Mutual Fund Portfolio	+34.3%	
f. Aggressive Balanced Mutual Fund Portfolio	+31.7%	
g. International Mutual Funds Portfolio	+28.3%	
h. Conservative Balanced Mutual Fund Portfolio	+24.8%	
i. Gold Mutual Funds Portfolio	+6.4%	
23. Cabot's Mutual Fund Navigator (Average)		+34.1%
a. Income Portfolio	+51.9%	
b. Growth & Income Portfolio	+34.5%	
c. Growth Portfolio	+16.6%	
24. Graphic Fund Forecaster (Average)		+33.5%
a. Financial Strategic Funds Portfolio	+35.6%	
b. Growth/International Portfolio #1	+30.4%	
c. Fidelity Select Fund Portfolio #1	+30.2%	
d. Growth/International Portfolio #2	+22.1%	
25. Switch Fund Timing (Conservative Model Mutual Fund Portfolio)		+32.2%

Newsletter	Individual Portfolio	Overall Average
17. United Mutual Fund Selector (Average)		+0.12%
a. Income Funds	+0.15%	
b. Aggressive Growth Funds	+0.14%	
c. Growth Funds	+0.10%	
d. Growth & Income Funds	+0.09%	
18. The Mutual Fund Strategist (Average)		+0.11%
a. Sector Portfolio	+0.12%	
b. Diversified Growth Portfolio	+0.11%	
19. **NoLoad Fund*X (Average)		+0.11%
a. Portfolio of "Class 1" Funds (Most Speculative Growth Funds)	+0.14%	
b. Portfolio of "Class 4" Funds (Total Return Funds)	+0.11%	
c. Portfolio of "Class 3" Funds (Higher Quality Growth Funds)	+0.11%	
d. Portfolio of "Class 2" Funds (Speculative Growth Funds)	+0.09%	
20. The Investor's Guide to Closed-End Funds (Average)		+0.11%
a. Managed Portfolio I: Balanced	+0.09%	
21. Fund Exchange (Average)		+0.10%
a. Fixed Income Bond Portfolio	+0.42%	
b. Aggressive Growth Margined Mutual Fund Portfolio	+0.18%	
c. Aggressive Growth Mutual Fund Portfolio	+0.11%	
d. Growth/Income Mutual Fund Portfolio	+0.10%	
e. Aggressive Balanced Mutual Fund Portfolio	+0.08%	
f. Conservative Growth Margined Mutual Fund Portfolio	+0.08%	
g. International Mutual Funds Portfolio	+0.03%	
h. Conservative Balanced Mutual Fund Portfolio		
i. Gold Mutual Funds Portfolio	−0.09%	
22. Donoghue's Moneyletter (Average)		+0.10%
a. Conservative Mutual Fund Portfolio	+0.18%	
b. "Venturesome" Model Portfolio	+0.11%	
c. Moderate Mutual Fund Portfolio	+0.08%	
d. Signal Portfolio	+0.07%	
23. The Professional Tape Reader (Mutual Fund Portfolio)		+0.10%
24. Switch Fund Timing (Conservative Model Mutual Fund Portfolio)		+0.08%
25. Cabot's Mutual Fund Navigator (Average)		+0.07%
a. Income Portfolio	+0.25%	
b. Growth & Income Portfolio	+0.07%	
c. Growth Portfolio	−0.02%	

Newsletter	Individual Portfolio	Overall Average
26. The Wall Street Digest (Mutual Fund Portfolio)		+31.6%
27. The Professional Tape Reader (Mutual Fund Portfolio)		+30.9%
28. Telephone Switch Newsletter (Average)		+30.9%
a. Equity/Cash Switch Plan	+59.8%	
b. International Funds/Cash Switch Plan	+17.6%	
c. Gold/Cash Switch Plan	+14.4%	
29. The Marketarian Letter (Mutual Fund Portfolio for Traders)		+29.3%
30. The Ruff Times ("Optimum Switch Hitter" Mutual Fund Portfolio #1)		+29.2%
31. Mutual Fund Investing (Average)		+25.7%
a. Portfolio I (Growth With Income)	+32.6%	
b. Portfolio II (Balanced Growth)	+28.7%	
32. The Sector Funds Newsletter (Average)		+25.3%
a. Model Mutual Fund Portfolio 2 ("Fidelity Funds Plus" Portfolio)	+38.3%	
b. Model Mutual Fund Portfolio 3 (Mostly Bonds)	+31.6%	
c. Model Mutual Fund Portfolio 1	−0.6%	
The Riskless Rate of Return: A T-Bill Portfolio		+25.3%
33. Weber's Fund Advisor (Average)		+25.0%
a. Low Risk/Low Switch Portfolio	+34.2%	
b. "Go-With-the-Winner Strategy" Portfolio	+29.6%	
34. The Ney Report (Average)		+24.8%
a. Income Fund Portfolio	+26.2%	
b. Growth & Income Fund Portfolio	+24.3%	
c. Growth Fund Portfolio	+23.8%	
35. Fast Track Funds		+24.7%
36. Growth Fund Guide (Average)		+22.9%
a. "Valueratio" Equities & Cash Portfolio	+34.0%	
b. "Valueratio" Equities, Cash & Leverage Portfolio	+30.4%	
c. "Valueratio" Fully Invested Portfolio	+26.7%	
d. Quality Growth Mutual Fund Portfolio	+25.7%	
e. Aggressive Growth Mutual Fund Portfolio	+23.3%	
f. Selected Core Account	+23.2%	
g. Special Situations Mutual Fund Portfolio	+21.7%	
h. Growth Mutual Fund Portfolio	+21.6%	
i. Growth Model Account	+13.7%	
j. Aggressive Model Account	+9.7%	
37. Bob Nurock's Advisory (Average)		+20.4%
a. Index Mutual Funds Portfolio	+20.7%	
b. Sector Mutual Funds Portfolio	+20.1%	

Newsletter	Individual Portfolio	Overall Average
26. Graphic Fund Forecaster (Average)		+0.06%
a. Financial Strategic Funds Portfolio	+0.07%	
b. Growth/International Portfolio #1	+0.05%	
c. Fidelity Select Fund Portfolio #1	+0.04%	
d. Growth/International Portfolio #2	0.00%	
27. Telephone Switch Newsletter (Average)		+0.06%
a. Equity/Cash Switch Plan	+0.18%	
b. International Funds/Cash Switch Plan	−0.03%	
c. Gold/Cash Switch Plan	−0.04%	
28. The Wall Street Digest (Mutual Fund Portfolio)		+0.05%
29. The Ruff Times ("Optimum Switch Hitter" Mutual Fund Portfolio #1)		+0.04%
30. The Marketarian Letter (Mutual Fund Portfolio for Traders)		+0.04%
31. The Sector Funds Newsletter (Average)		+0.03%
a. Model Mutual Fund Portfolio 2 ("Fidelity Funds Plus" Portfolio)	+0.07%	
b. Model Mutual Fund Portfolio 3 (Mostly Bonds)	+0.05%	
c. Model Mutual Fund Portfolio 1	−0.03%	
32. Fast Track Funds		+0.02%
33. Mutual Fund Investing (Average)		+0.01%
a. Portfolio I (Growth With Income)	+0.20%	
b. Portfolio II (Balanced Growth)	+0.05%	
34. Weber's Fund Advisor (Average)		+0.01%
a. Low Risk/Low Switch Portfolio	+0.08%	
b. "Go-With-the-Winner Strategy" Portfolio	+0.04%	
35. The Ney Report (Average)		+0.01%
a. Income Fund Portfolio	+0.02%	
b. Growth & Income Fund Portfolio	0.00%	
c. Growth Fund Portfolio	0.00%	
36. Bob Nurock's Advisory (Average)		−0.05%
a. Index Mutual Funds Portfolio	−0.04%	
b. Sector Mutual Funds Portfolio	−0.06%	
37. Growth Fund Guide (Average)		−0.05%
a. "Valueratio" Equities & Cash Portfolio	+0.13%	
b. "Valueratio" Equities, Cash & Leverage Portfolio	+0.08%	
c. "Valueratio" Fully Invested Portfolio	+0.02%	
d. Quality Growth Mutual Fund Portfolio	+0.02%	
e. Aggressive Growth Mutual Fund Portfolio	−0.04%	
f. Special Situations Mutual Fund Portfolio	−0.07%	
g. Selected Core Account	−0.10%	
h. Growth Mutual Fund Portfolio	−0.15%	
i. Aggressive Model Account	−0.20%	
j. Growth Model Account	−0.21%	

Newsletter	Individual Portfolio	Overall Average
38. Kinsman's Telephone Growth & Income Service (Mutual Fund Switch Portfolio)		+18.2%
39. Your Window Into the Future (Portfolio B: Conservative Portfolio)		+6.6%
40. Margo's Market Monitor (Fidelity Select Funds Portfolio)		−11.6%

Appendix B-3: Mutual Fund Newsletter Performance
from 1/1/89 to 6/30/92 (Risk-Adjusted) (continued)

Newsletter	Individual Portfolio	Overall Average
38. Your Window Into the Future (Portfolio B: Conservative Portfolio)		−0.07%
39. Kinsman's Telephone Growth & Income Service (Mutual Fund Switch Portfolio)		−0.07%
40. Margo's Market Monitor (Fidelity Select Funds Portfolio)		−0.29%

1.5 YRS

Appendix B-4: Mutual Fund Newsletter Performance
from 1/1/91 to 6/30/92 (Total Return)

Newsletter	Individual Portfolio	Overall Average
1. Timer Digest (Fidelity Select Portfolio)		+59.7%
2. The Scott Letter: Closed-End Fund Report (Equity Portfolio)		+57.5%
3. Hussman Econometrics (Multi-Fund Portfolio)		+56.8%
4. Mutual Fund Forecaster		+48.9%
5. Fundline (Average)		+46.7%
a. $100,000 No-Timing Portfolio	+62.4%	
b. $100,000 Timing Portfolio	+39.4%	
6. Fidelity Monitor (Average)		+45.2%
a. Growth Mutual Funds Portfolio	+45.8%	
b. Select System Mutual Funds Portfolio	+41.1%	
7. Professional Timing Service (Mutual Fund Model Portfolio)		+38.7%
8. Cabot's Mutual Fund Navigator (Average)		+33.7%
a. Growth Portfolio	+34.8%	
b. Income Portfolio	+33.4%	
c. Growth & Income Portfolio	+32.2%	
9. The Marketarian Letter (Average)		+33.0%
a. Mutual Fund Portfolio for Traders	+33.1%	
b. Mutual Fund Portfolio for Investors	+32.9%	
Wilshire 5000 Value-Weighted Total Return Index		+32.3%
10. Fidelity Insight (Average)		+30.5%
a. Growth & Income Fund Portfolio	+34.0%	
b. Growth Portfolio	+33.5%	
c. Income & Preservation Fund Portfolio	+28.5%	
d. Speculative Portfolio	+26.9%	
11. The No-Load Fund Investor (Average)		+30.5%
a. Wealth Builder Portfolio	+38.3%	
b. Pre-Retirement Portfolio	+28.2%	
c. Retirement Portfolio	+25.0%	
12. The Investor's Guide to Closed-End Funds (Average)		+28.9%
a. Managed Portfolio IV: U.S. Equity Funds	+40.4%	
b. Managed Portfolio I: Balanced	+35.6%	
c. Managed Portfolio III: Overseas Investment	+26.3%	
d. Managed Portfolio II: Income	+14.3%	
13. Equity Fund Outlook (Average)		+28.8%
a. Moderate Risk Portfolio	+31.2%	
b. Aggressive Portfolio	+29.1%	
c. Conservative Portfolio	+28.7%	

Top M.F. 59.7%
top STOCKS 164.9

Appendix B-4: Mutual Fund Newsletter Performance
from 1/1/91 to 6/30/92 (Risk-Adjusted)

Newsletter	Individual Portfolio	Overall Average
1. Fidelity Insight (Average)		+0.66%
a. Income & Preservation Fund Portfolio	+0.87%	
b. Growth Portfolio	+0.76%	
c. Growth & Income Fund Portfolio	+0.63%	
d. Speculative Portfolio	+0.37%	
2. The Peter Dag Investment Letter (Model Vanguard Fund Portfolio)		+0.48%
3. Professional Timing Service (Mutual Fund Model Portfolio)		+0.48%
4. The Investor's Guide to Closed-End Funds (Average)		+0.46%
a. Managed Portfolio IV: U.S. Equity Funds	+0.60%	
b. Managed Portfolio I: Balanced	+0.49%	
c. Managed Portfolio III: Overseas Investment	+0.31%	
d. Managed Portfolio II: Income	+0.29%	
5. The No-Load Fund Investor (Average)		+0.45%
a. Retirement Portfolio	+0.44%	
b. Wealth Builder Portfolio	+0.44%	
c. Pre-Retirement Portfolio	+0.43%	
6. The Scott Letter: Closed-End Fund Report		+0.44%
7. Mutual Fund Forecaster		+0.42%
8. Fidelity Monitor (Average)		+0.42%
a. Growth Mutual Funds Portfolio	+0.45%	
b. Select System Mutual Funds Portfolio	+0.30%	
9. Fundline (Average)		+0.39%
a. $100,000 No-Timing Portfolio	+0.40%	
b. $100,000 Timing Portfolio	+0.36%	
10. L/G No-Load Fund Analyst (Average)		+0.39%
a. Portfolio A: Conservative/Income Oriented	+0.62%	
b. Portfolio B: Conservative/Not Income Oriented	+0.46%	
c. Portfolio C: Long-Term Conservative Growth	+0.33%	
d. Portfolio D: Long-Term Aggressive Growth	+0.29%	
11. Timer Digest (Fidelity Select Portfolio)		+0.37%
12. Cabot's Mutual Fund Navigator (Average)		+0.37%
a. Income Portfolio	+0.52%	
b. Growth & Income Portfolio	+0.33%	
c. Growth Portfolio	+0.29%	
13. The Marketarian Letter (Average)		+0.36%
a. Mutual Fund Portfolio for Traders	+0.37%	
c. Mutual Fund Portfolio for Investors	+0.35%	

Newsletter	Individual Portfolio	Overall Average
14. United Mutual Fund Selector (Average)		+28.3%
a. Growth Funds	+31.9%	
b. Aggressive Growth Funds	+28.8%	
c. Growth & Income Funds	+28.8%	
d. Income Funds	+22.5%	
15. InvesTech Mutual Fund Advisor		+26.6%
16. Fund Kinetics (Average)		+26.5%
a. Weekly "Erfer" Report	+18.6%	
17. The Chartist Mutual Fund Timer		+26.5%
18. Bob Brinker's Marketimer (Average)		+26.3%
a. Aggressive Growth Mutual Fund Portfolio	+35.8%	
b. Long-Term Growth Mutual Fund Portfolio	+29.0%	
c. Balanced Portfolio	+22.0%	
d. Fixed-Income Model Mutual Fund Portfolio	+17.7%	
19. **NoLoad Fund*X (Average)		+25.9%
a. Portfolio of "Class 1" Funds (Most Speculative Growth Funds)	+65.6%	
b. Portfolio of "Class 2" Funds (Speculative Growth Funds)	+26.9%	
c. Portfolio of "Class 3" Funds (Higher Quality Growth Funds)	+25.9%	
d. Portfolio of "Class 4" Funds (Total Return Funds)	+21.9%	
20. L/G No-Load Fund Analyst (Average)		+25.6%
a. Portfolio D: Long-Term Aggressive Growth	+28.1%	
b. Portfolio C: Long-Term Conservative Growth	+26.8%	
c. Portfolio A: Conservative/Income Oriented	+24.7%	
d. Portfolio B: Conservative/Not Income Oriented	+22.4%	
21. Mutual Fund Technical Trader (Average)		+25.4%
a. Aggressive Growth/High Risk Portfolio	+37.7%	
b. Growth/Short-Term Risk Portfolio	+32.3%	
c. Conservative Income & Growth/Moderate Risk Portfolio	+22.6%	
22. Stockmarket Cycles (Mutual Fund Portfolio)		+24.4%
23. The Sy Harding Investor Forecasts (Portfolio 3: Mutual Fund Switching Portfolio)		+23.8%
24. Personal Finance (Average)		+23.4%
a. Mutual Fund Portfolio (Short-Term)	+26.7%	
b. Mutual Fund Portfolio (Long-Term)	+20.2%	
25. No-Load Mutual Fund Selections & Timing Newsletter (Average)		+22.6%
a. Intermediate Term Portfolio	+33.5%	
b. Asset Allocations Model Portfolio	+21.0%	
c. Sector Funds Portfolio	+13.7%	

Newsletter	Individual Portfolio	Overall Average
14. Personal Finance (Average)		+0.36%
a. Mutual Fund Portfolio (Long-Term)	+0.42%	
b. Mutual Fund Portfolio (Short-Term)	+0.29%	
15. Bob Brinker's Marketimer (Average)		+0.36%
a. Fixed-Income Model Mutual Fund Portfolio	+0.63%	
b. Balanced Portfolio	+0.36%	
c. Aggressive Growth Mutual Fund Portfolio	+0.30%	
d. Long-Term Growth Mutual Fund Portfolio	+0.29%	
16. United Mutual Fund Selector (Average)		+0.35%
a. Income Funds	+0.88%	
b. Growth Funds	+0.34%	
c. Growth & Income Funds	+0.33%	
d. Aggressive Growth Funds	+0.24%	
17. Stockmarket Cycles (Mutual Fund Portfolio)		+0.35%
18. InvesTech Mutual Fund Advisor		+0.34%
19. Hussman Econometrics (Multi-Fund Portfolio)		+0.33%
20. The Volume Reversal Survey (Index Fund Portfolio)		+0.33%
21. No-Load Portfolios (Average)		+0.33%
a. Income Portfolio	+0.72%	
b. Conservative Portfolio	+0.24%	
c. Aggressive Growth Portfolio	+0.21%	
Wilshire 5000 Value-Weighted Total Return Index		+0.32%
22. The Sy Harding Investor Forecasts (Portfolio 3: Mutual Fund Switching Portfolio)		+0.32%
23. The Mutual Fund Letter (Average)		+0.29%
a. Income Portfolio	+0.60%	
b. Growth & Income Portfolio	+0.40%	
c. All Weather Portfolio	+0.24%	
d. Highly Aggressive Portfolio	+0.19%	
e. Moderately Aggressive Portfolio	+0.18%	
24. Investors Intelligence (Average)		+0.28%
a. Fidelity Switch Fund (Bond) Portfolio	+0.94%	
b. Fidelity Switch Fund (Equity) Portfolio	−0.04%	
c. Fidelity Switch Fund (International) Portfolio	−0.06%	
25. Equity Fund Outlook (Average)		+0.28%
a. Conservative Portfolio	+0.37%	
b. Moderate Risk Portfolio	+0.29%	
c. Aggressive Portfolio	+0.24%	

Newsletter	Individual Portfolio	Overall Average
26. Donoghue's Moneyletter (Average)		+22.5%
a. Signal Portfolio	+33.2%	
b. "Venturesome" Model Portfolio	+22.2%	
c. Moderate Mutual Fund Portfolio	+18.1%	
d. Conservative Mutual Fund Portfolio	+15.8%	
27. The Volume Reversal Survey (Index Fund Portfolio)		+22.4%
28. The Peter Dag Investment Letter (Model Vanguard Fund Portfolio)		+20.5%
29. The Wall Street Digest (Mutual Fund Portfolio)		+20.5%
30. The Sector Funds Newsletter (Average)		+18.5%
a. Model Mutual Fund Portfolio 3 (Mostly Bonds)	+22.2%	
b. Model Mutual Fund Portfolio 1	+16.4%	
c. Model Mutual Fund Portfolio 2 ("Fidelity Funds Plus" Portfolio)	+16.1%	
31. No-Load Portfolios (Average)		+17.4%
a. Income Portfolio	+18.9%	
b. Aggressive Growth Portfolio	+17.0%	
c. Conservative Portfolio	+15.9%	
32. Fund Exchange (Average)		+17.1%
a. Aggressive Growth Margined Mutual Fund Portfolio	+43.4%	
b. Conservative Growth Margined Mutual Fund Portfolio	+21.7%	
c. Fixed Income Bond Portfolio	+20.1%	
d. Aggressive Growth Mutual Fund Portfolio	+19.4%	
e. Growth/Income Mutual Fund Portfolio	+16.9%	
f. Aggressive Balanced Mutual Fund Portfolio	+14.4%	
g. Conservative Balanced Mutual Fund Portfolio	+10.9%	
h. International Mutual Funds Portfolio	+9.0%	
i. Gold Mutual Funds Portfolio	+0.8%	
33. The Mutual Fund Letter (Average)		+16.5%
a. Income Portfolio	+18.4%	
b. Highly Aggressive Portfolio	+17.1%	
c. Growth & Income Portfolio	+16.8%	
d. All Weather Portfolio	+16.6%	
e. Moderately Aggressive Portfolio	+13.0%	

Newsletter	Individual Portfolio	Overall Average
26. No-Load Mutual Fund Selections & Timing Newsletter (Average)		+0.28%
a. Intermediate Term Portfolio	+0.39%	
b. Asset Allocations Model Portfolio	+0.28%	
c. Sector Funds Portfolio	+0.11%	
27. **NoLoad Fund*X (Average)		+0.27%
a. Portfolio of "Class 1" Funds (Most Speculative Growth Funds)	+0.41%	
b. Portfolio of "Class 4" Funds (Total Return Funds)	+0.31%	
c. Portfolio of "Class 3" Funds (Higher Quality Growth Funds)	+0.27%	
d. Portfolio of "Class 2" Funds (Speculative Growth Funds)	+0.22%	
28. Income & Safety		+0.26%
29. Mutual Fund Technical Trader (Average)		+0.24%
a. Growth/Short-Term Risk Portfolio	+0.27%	
b. Aggressive Growth/High Risk Portfolio	+0.25%	
c. Conservative Income & Growth/Moderate Risk Portfolio	+0.20%	
30. Donoghue's Moneyletter (Average)		+0.24%
a. Signal Portfolio	+0.25%	
b. Conservative Mutual Fund Portfolio	+0.24%	
c. "Venturesome" Model Portfolio	+0.21%	
d. Moderate Mutual Fund Portfolio	+0.19%	
31. Fund Exchange (Average)		+0.23%
a. Fixed Income Bond Portfolio	+0.69%	
b. Aggressive Growth Margined Mutual Fund Portfolio	+0.32%	
c. Growth/Income Mutual Fund Portfolio	+0.23%	
d. Aggressive Growth Mutual Fund Portfolio	+0.22%	
e. Aggressive Balanced Mutual Fund Portfolio	+0.19%	
f. Conservative Growth Margined Mutual Fund Portfolio	+0.18%	
g. Conservative Balanced Mutual Fund Portfolio	+0.13%	
h. International Mutual Funds Portfolio	+0.04%	
i. Gold Mutual Funds Portfolio	−0.15%	
32. The Chartist Mutual Fund Timer		+0.22%
33. Growth Fund Guide (Average)		+0.22%
a. Quality Growth Mutual Fund Portfolio	+0.55%	
b. Special Situations Mutual Fund Portfolio	+0.37%	
c. "Valueratio" Equities & Cash Portfolio	+0.28%	
d. "Valueratio" Equities, Cash & Leverage Portfolio	+0.25%	
e. "Valueratio" Fully Invested Portfolio	+0.18%	
f. Aggressive Growth Mutual Fund Portfolio	+0.18%	
g. Growth Mutual Fund Portfolio	+0.03%	
h. Growth Model Account	−0.02%	
i. Selected Core Account	−0.08%	
j. Aggressive Model Account	−0.12%	

Appendix B-4: Mutual Fund Newsletter Performance
from 1/1/91 to 6/30/92 (Total Return) (continued)

Newsletter	Individual Portfolio	Overall Average
34. Global Fund Timer (Average)		+15.1%
a. U.S. Portfolio	+21.1%	
b. Global Portfolio	+15.0%	
c. Conservative Portfolio	+14.4%	
d. Zero Bond Portfolio	+9.0%	
35. Morningstar Mutual Funds (Average)		+14.7%
a. Equity & Hybrid Funds (5-Star)	+18.4%	
b. Bond Funds (5-Star)	+10.6%	
36. The Ruff Times (Average)		+13.8%
a. "Optimum Switch Hitter" Mutual Fund Portfolio #2	+15.3%	
b. "Optimum Switch Hitter" Mutual Fund Portfolio #1	+12.4%	
37. Financial World (Average)		+13.7%
b. Balanced Fund Portfolio	+21.6%	
c. Aggressive Growth Fund Portfolio	+21.5%	
d. Corporate Bond Fund Portfolio	+21.2%	
e. Long-Term Growth Fund Portfolio	+20.1%	
f. US Gov't Bonds Fund Portfolio	+12.9%	
g. Growth & Income Fund Portfolio	+11.9%	
h. Sector Funds Portfolio	+9.3%	
i. International Stock Fund Portfolio	+2.5%	
j. International Bond Fund Portfolio	+2.4%	
38. The Professional Tape Reader (Mutual Fund Portfolio)		+13.6%
39. Graphic Fund Forecaster (Average)		+13.3%
a. Fidelity Select Fund Portfolio #2	+27.2%	
b. Fidelity Select Fund Portfolio #1	+12.1%	
c. Financial Strategic Funds Portfolio	+11.4%	
d. Growth/International Portfolio #2	+8.4%	
e. Growth/International Portfolio #1	+6.8%	
40. Kinsman's Telephone Growth & Income Service (Mutual Fund Switch Portfolio)		+12.7%
41. Investors Intelligence (Average)		+11.8%
c. Fidelity Switch Fund (Bond) Portfolio	+23.5%	
d. Fidelity Switch Fund (International) Portfolio	+6.0%	
e. Fidelity Switch Fund (Equity) Portfolio	+5.8%	
42. Fast Track Funds		+10.5%

Appendix B-4: Mutual Fund Newsletter Performance
from 1/1/91 to 6/30/92 (Risk-Adjusted) (continued)

Newsletter	Individual Portfolio	Overall Average
34. The Ney Report (Average)		+0.22%
a. Growth & Income Fund Portfolio	+0.22%	
b. Income Fund Portfolio	+0.22%	
c. Growth Fund Portfolio	+0.20%	
35. Fund Kinetics (Average)		+0.21%
a. Weekly "Erfer" Report	+0.13%	
36. The Ruff Times (Average)		+0.19%
a. "Optimum Switch Hitter" Mutual Fund Portfolio #2	+0.23%	
b. "Optimum Switch Hitter" Mutual Fund Portfolio #1	+0.16%	
37. The Professional Tape Reader (Mutual Fund Portfolio)		+0.19%
38. Morningstar Mutual Funds (Average)		+0.19%
a. Bond Funds (5-Star)	+0.27%	
b. Equity & Hybrid Funds (5-Star)	+0.16%	
39. The Wall Street Digest (Mutual Fund Portfolio)		+0.18%
40. Global Fund Timer (Average)		+0.17%
a. U.S. Portfolio	+0.21%	
b. Conservative Portfolio	+0.16%	
c. Global Portfolio	+0.14%	
d. Zero Bond Portfolio	+0.04%	
41. The Sector Funds Newsletter (Average)		+0.17%
a. Model Mutual Fund Portfolio 3 (Mostly Bonds)	+0.21%	
b. Model Mutual Fund Portfolio 2 ("Fidelity Funds Plus" Portfolio)	+0.14%	
c. Model Mutual Fund Portfolio 1	+0.12%	
42. Kinsman's Telephone Growth & Income Service (Mutual Fund Switch Portfolio)		+0.14%

Appendix B: Mutual Fund Newsletter Performance   493

Newsletter	Individual Portfolio	Overall Average
43. Growth Fund Guide (Average)		+10.0%
a. "Valueratio" Fully Invested Portfolio	+13.2%	
b. "Valueratio" Equities & Cash Portfolio	+13.1%	
c. Quality Growth Mutual Fund Portfolio	+12.4%	
d. "Valueratio" Equities, Cash & Leverage Portfolio	+12.3%	
e. Special Situations Mutual Fund Portfolio	+12.1%	
f. Aggressive Growth Mutual Fund Portfolio	+11.2%	
g. Growth Mutual Fund Portfolio	+7.7%	
h. Growth Model Account	+7.1%	
i. Selected Core Account	+6.9%	
j. Aggressive Model Account	+4.1%	
44. Income & Safety		+9.9%
45. Telephone Switch Newsletter (Average)		+9.6%
a. Equity/Cash Switch Plan	+33.4%	
b. Gold/Cash Switch Plan	+0.1%	
c. International Funds/Cash Switch Plan	−3.4%	
46. Mutual Fund Investing (Average)		+9.3%
a. Portfolio II (Balanced Growth)	+10.5%	
b. Portfolio I (Growth With Income)	+9.6%	
c. Portfolio III (IRA/Long Term Growth)	+7.5%	
47. The Ney Report (Average)		+9.0%
a. Growth & Income Fund Portfolio	+9.3%	
b. Income Fund Portfolio	+9.2%	
c. Growth Fund Portfolio	+8.6%	
48. Weber's Fund Advisor (Average)		+8.5%
a. Low Risk/Low Switch Portfolio	+20.2%	
b. "Go-With-the-Winner Strategy" Portfolio	+8.5%	
49. Bob Nurock's Advisory (Average)		+8.2%
a. Index Mutual Funds Portfolio	+12.3%	
b. Sector Mutual Funds Portfolio	+4.1%	
The Riskless Rate of Return: A T-Bill Portfolio		+7.5%
50. The Wall Street Digest Mutual Fund Advisor (Average)		+7.4%
a. Long-Term Growth Funds	+19.2%	
b. Income Funds	+16.4%	
c. Aggressive Growth Funds	+14.3%	
d. Sector Funds	+14.1%	
e. Growth & Income Funds	+14.0%	
f. Top No-Load Funds	+6.0%	
51. The Mutual Fund Strategist (Average)		+6.3%
a. Sector Portfolio	+6.5%	
b. Diversified Growth Portfolio	+5.8%	

Newsletter	Individual Portfolio	Overall Average
43. Financial World (Average)		+0.13%
a. Corporate Bond Fund Portfolio	+0.46%	
b. US Gov't Bonds Fund Portfolio	+0.24%	
c. Balanced Fund Portfolio	+0.20%	
d. Long-Term Growth Fund Portfolio	+0.17%	
e. Aggressive Growth Fund Portfolio	+0.16%	
f. Growth & Income Fund Portfolio	+0.08%	
g. Sector Funds Portfolio	+0.04%	
h. International Stock Fund Portfolio	−0.08%	
i. International Bond Fund Portfolio	−0.10%	
44. Graphic Fund Forecaster (Average)		+0.11%
a. Fidelity Select Fund Portfolio #2	+0.25%	
b. Financial Strategic Funds Portfolio	+0.07%	
c. Fidelity Select Fund Portfolio #1	+0.07%	
d. Growth/International Portfolio #2	+0.03%	
e. Growth/International Portfolio #1	0.00%	
45. Telephone Switch Newsletter (Average)		+0.07%
a. Equity/Cash Switch Plan	+0.29%	
b. Gold/Cash Switch Plan	−0.14%	
c. International Funds/Cash Switch Plan	−0.30%	
46. Mutual Fund Investing (Average)		+0.07%
a. Portfolio I (Growth With Income)	+0.15%	
b. Portfolio II (Balanced Growth)	+0.12%	
c. Portfolio III (IRA/Long Term Growth)	+0.01%	
47. Fast Track Funds		+0.06%
48. Weber's Fund Advisor (Average)		+0.03%
a. Low Risk/Low Switch Portfolio	+0.29%	
b. "Go-With-the-Winner Strategy" Portfolio	+0.03%	
49. The Mutual Fund Strategist (Average)		+0.02%
a. Sector Portfolio	+0.02%	
b. Diversified Growth Portfolio	+0.01%	
50. The Wall Street Digest Mutual Fund Advisor (Average)		+0.01%
a. Income Funds	+0.16%	
b. Long-Term Growth Funds	+0.16%	
c. Growth & Income Funds	+0.10%	
d. Aggressive Growth Funds	+0.09%	
e. Sector Funds	+0.09%	
f. Top No-Load Funds	+0.01%	
51. Bob Nurock's Advisory (Average)		−0.01%
a. Index Mutual Funds Portfolio	+0.14%	
b. Sector Mutual Funds Portfolio	−0.15%	

Newsletter	Individual Portfolio	Overall Average
52. Switch Fund Timing (Average)		+4.8%
a. Conservative Model Mutual Fund Portfolio	+10.4%	
b. Conservative/Momentum Model Fund Portfolio	+8.0%	
d. Gold Fund Portfolio	−3.9%	
53. Your Window Into the Future (Portfolio B: Conservative Portfolio)		−0.5%
54. Margo's Market Monitor (Fidelity Select Funds Portfolio)		−11.2%

Newsletter	Individual Portfolio	Overall Average
52. Switch Fund Timing (Average)		−0.05%
a. Conservative Model Mutual Fund Portfolio	+0.07%	
c. Conservative/Momentum Model Fund Portfolio	+0.02%	
d. Gold Fund Portfolio	−0.25%	
53. Your Window Into the Future (Portfolio B: Conservative Portfolio)		−0.08%
54. Margo's Market Monitor (Fidelity Select Funds Portfolio)		−0.52%

APPENDIX C

Market Timing

The rankings that appear in this appendix are based on newsletters' abilities to time their switches into and out of the stock, bond and gold markets—and nothing but those abilities. Unlike the performances reported in Appendices A and B, which take into account all aspects of a newsletter's advice, both timing and security selection, these appendices report performances on a pure-timing basis.

Within each market, each newsletter earned the same rate of return when in the market and the same rate of return when in cash. As the proxy for the stock market, these calculations used the Wilshire 5000 Value-Weighted Total Return Index. The proxy for the bond market was the Shearson Lehman Treasury Index. And the proxy for the gold market was London's P.M. fixing price. Cash was credited with the 90-day T-Bill rate.

Since the tables were designed in particular to assist the mutual fund switcher, two timing-only ratings were calculated for those newsletters that recommend actually going short upon receipt of a sell signal (which is something a mutual fund investor can't do). The first of the two ratings for such newsletters assumed that the investor did go short, but the second assumed that he went into cash (as would a mutual fund investor). In addition, the transactions reflected below were made at the closing prices on the days subscribers would have been able to act on the advice. No commissions or taxes were debited. For a more complete description of what these rankings measure, please refer to the section on market-timing newsletters that appears in the front section of this *Guide*.

The right-most column in these rankings lists the number of switches generated by each newsletter's timing system during that period. A switch into or out of the market is counted as one switch, so a round-trip counts as two.

As in Appendices A and B, the rankings that appear on the left-hand pages are based on total return, while those appearing on the right-hand pages are based on risk-adjusted performances. For a description of the process used to adjust performance for risk, please refer to the introduction to Appendix A.

Appendices C-1 through C-6 report stock-market timing, and correspond to the same time periods covered by Appendices A-1 through A-6. Appendices C-7 through C-10 report gold-market timing, and Appendices C-11 through C-14 report bond-market timing.

Appendix C-1: Stock Market Timing From 6/30/80 to 6/30/92 (Total Return)

Newsletter	X	Gain/Loss	Number of Switches
1. Telephone Switch Newsletter (Equity/Cash Timing Model)		+523.5%	20.0
2. Bob Nurock's Advisory (Technical Market Index—100% Cash on Sells)		+499.9%	7.0
3. Market Logic (Recommended Exposure to Stock Market)		+478.2%	1.4
4. Professional Timing Service ("Supply/Demand Formula"—100% Cash on Sells)		+436.5%	41.0
5. The Elliott Wave Theorist (Investors—100% Cash on Sells)		+434.0%	19.0
Wilshire 5000 Value-Weighted Total Return Index		+432.7%	
6. The Value Line Investment Survey (Market Timing Model—100% Cash on Sells)		+395.2%	4.5
7. Dow Theory Letters (Grading of Primary Trend—100% Cash on Sells)		+344.2%	16.0
8. The Dines Letter (Short-Term Model—100% Cash on Sells)		+339.3%	40.0
9. The Granville Market Letter (100% Cash on Sells)		+329.8%	19.6
10. Growth Fund Guide (Mutual Fund Allocation)		+304.0%	2.9
11. Bob Nurock's Advisory (Technical Market Index—100% Short on Sells)		+265.4%	7.0
12. The Professional Tape Reader (Mutual Fund Timing Model)		+238.9%	38.9
T-Bill Portfolio		+159.4%	
13. Professional Timing Service ("Supply/Demand Formula"—Shorting Allowed)		+45.4%	42.0
14. The Dines Letter (Short-Term Model—100% Short on Sells)		+31.1%	40.0
15. The Granville Market Letter (100% Short on Sells)		+11.1%	33.2

TOP STOCK SWITCH   523.5%
TOP STOCKS   665.2

Appendix C-1: Stock Market Timing From 6/30/80 to 6/30/92 (Risk-Adjusted)

Newsletter	Gain/Loss	Number of Switches
1. Telephone Switch Newsletter (Equity/Cash Timing Model)	+0.19%	20.0
2. The Elliott Wave Theorist (Investors—100% Cash on Sells)	+0.18%	19.0
3. Professional Timing Service ("Supply/Demand Formula"—100% Cash on Sells)	+0.17%	41.0
4. Bob Nurock's Advisory (Technical Market Index—100% Cash on Sells)	+0.17%	7.0
5. Market Logic (Recommended Exposure to Stock Market)	+0.16%	1.4
6. Dow Theory Letters (Grading of Primary Trend—100% Cash on Sells)	+0.15%	16.0
7. The Value Line Investment Survey (Market Timing Model—100% Cash on Sells)	+0.13%	4.5
8. The Dines Letter (Short-Term Model—100% Cash on Sells)	+0.13%	40.0
Wilshire 5000 Value-Weighted Total Return Index	+0.13%	
9. The Professional Tape Reader (Mutual Fund Timing Model)	+0.12%	38.9
10. The Granville Market Letter (100% Cash on Sells)	+0.11%	19.6
11. Growth Fund Guide (Mutual Fund Allocation)	+0.10%	2.9
12. Bob Nurock's Advisory (Technical Market Index—100% Short on Sells)	+0.08%	7.0
13. Professional Timing Service ("Supply/Demand Formula"—Shorting Allowed)	−0.06%	42.0
14. The Dines Letter (Short-Term Model—100% Short on Sells)	−0.08%	40.0
15. The Granville Market Letter (100% Short on Sells)	−0.10%	33.2

9.5 yrs

Appendix C-2: Stock Market Timing From 1/1/83 to 6/30/92 (Total Return)

Newsletter	Gain/Loss	Number of Switches
1. Systems and Forecasts ("Time Trend" Timing Model—100% Cash on Sells)	+392.9%	135.0
2. Market Logic (Seasonality Timing System)	+366.6%	302.0
3. Systems and Forecasts ("Time Trend" Timing Model—100% Short on Sells)	+334.3%	135.0
4. The Elliott Wave Theorist (Investors—100% Cash on Sells)	+313.2%	11.0
5. Professional Timing Service ("Supply/Demand Formula"—100% Cash on Sells)	+301.4%	34.0
6. Market Logic (Recommended Exposure to Stock Market)	+293.2%	0.9
Wilshire 5000 Value-Weighted Total Return Index	+278.6%	
7. Telephone Switch Newsletter (Equity/Cash Timing Model)	+264.2%	18.0
8. Bob Nurock's Advisory (Technical Market Index—100% Cash on Sells)	+245.0%	5.0
9. The Big Picture (Short-Term Trading Guide (SGA)—100% Cash on Sells)	+234.6%	78.0
10. The Value Line Investment Survey (Market Timing Model—100% Cash on Sells)	+230.0%	3.5
11. Dow Theory Letters (Grading of Primary Trend—100% Cash on Sells)	+203.8%	14.0
12. The Dines Letter (Short-Term Model—100% Cash on Sells)	+188.9%	35.0
13. Growth Fund Guide (Mutual Fund Allocation)	+187.1%	2.9
14. The Granville Market Letter (100% Cash on Sells)	+181.7%	18.6
15. The Professional Tape Reader (Mutual Fund Timing Model)	+156.7%	22.9
16. Bob Nurock's Advisory (Technical Market Index—100% Short on Sells)	+156.6%	5.0
T-Bill Portfolio	+93.5%	
17. Professional Timing Service ("Supply/Demand Formula"—Shorting Allowed)	+93.5%	35.0
18. The Dines Letter (Short-Term Model—100% Short on Sells)	+35.4%	35.0
19. The Big Picture (Short-Term Trading Guide (SGA)—Shorting Allowed)	+24.4%	78.0
20. The Granville Market Letter (100% Short on Sells)	+11.1%	32.2

Appendix C-2: Stock Market Timing From 1/1/83 to 6/30/92 (Risk-Adjusted)

Newsletter	Gain/Loss	Number of Switches
1. Market Logic (Seasonality Timing System)	+0.36%	302.0
2. The Elliott Wave Theorist (Investors—100% Cash on Sells)	+0.27%	11.0
3. Systems and Forecasts ("Time Trend" Timing Model—100% Cash on Sells)	+0.26%	135.0
4. Professional Timing Service ("Supply/Demand Formula"—100% Cash on Sells)	+0.21%	34.0
5. The Big Picture (Short-Term Trading Guide (SGA)—100% Cash on Sells)	+0.20%	78.0
6. Systems and Forecasts ("Time Trend" Timing Model—100% Short on Sells)	+0.20%	135.0
7. The Professional Tape Reader (Mutual Fund Timing Model)	+0.19%	22.9
8. Telephone Switch Newsletter (Equity/Cash Timing Model)	+0.17%	18.0
9. Market Logic (Recommended Exposure to Stock Market)	+0.17%	0.9
10. Dow Theory Letters (Grading of Primary Trend—100% Cash on Sells)	+0.16%	14.0
Wilshire 5000 Value-Weighted Total Return Index	+0.15%	
11. Bob Nurock's Advisory (Technical Market Index—100% Cash on Sells)	+0.15%	5.0
12. The Value Line Investment Survey (Market Timing Model—100% Cash on Sells)	+0.13%	3.5
13. The Dines Letter (Short-Term Model—100% Cash on Sells)	+0.12%	35.0
14. Growth Fund Guide (Mutual Fund Allocation)	+0.11%	2.9
15. The Granville Market Letter (100% Cash on Sells)	+0.10%	18.6
16. Bob Nurock's Advisory (Technical Market Index—100% Short on Sells)	+0.08%	5.0
17. Professional Timing Service ("Supply/Demand Formula"—Shorting Allowed)	+0.03%	35.0
18. The Dines Letter (Short-Term Model—100% Short on Sells)	−0.05%	35.0
19. The Big Picture (Short-Term Trading Guide (SGA)—Shorting Allowed)	−0.07%	78.0
20. The Granville Market Letter (100% Short on Sells)	−0.08%	32.2

Appendix C-3: Stock Market Timing From 1/1/85 to 6/30/92
(Total Return)

Newsletter	Gain/Loss	Number of Switches
1. Systems and Forecasts ("Time Trend" Timing Model—100% Cash on Sells)	+244.1%	114.0
2. Market Logic (Seasonality Timing System)	+244.1%	238.0
3. Market Logic (Recommended Exposure to Stock Market)	+209.0%	0.9
4. The Big Picture (Short-Term Trading Guide (SGA)—100% Cash on Sells)	+208.0%	59.0
5. Systems and Forecasts ("Time Trend" Timing Model—100% Short on Sells)	+202.8%	114.0
Wilshire 5000 Value-Weighted Total Return Index	+197.6%	
6. Stockmarket Cycles (Mutual Fund Switching Advice)*	+196.2%	50.0
7. The Mutual Fund Strategist (Intermediate Timing Model)	+188.9%	67.0
8. Marketarian Letter (Long-Term Investor in Mutual Funds—100% Cash on Sells)	+185.9%	27.0
9. The Elliott Wave Theorist (Investors—100% Cash on Sells)	+183.1%	7.0
10. The Value Line Investment Survey (Market Timing Model—100% Cash on Sells)	+181.4%	2.5
11. Telephone Switch Newsletter (Equity/Cash Timing Model)	+178.3%	15.0
12. Weber's Fund Advisor (Mutual Fund Allocation Advice)	+176.4%	18.0
13. Professional Timing Service ("Supply/Demand Formula"—100% Cash on Sells)	+170.1%	29.0
14. Investors Intelligence (Timing Advice for Switch Fund Traders)	+163.8%	17.1
15. Dow Theory Letters (Grading of Primary Trend—100% Cash on Sells)	+151.4%	11.0
16. The Zweig Forecast ("Short-Term Trend Indicator"—100% Cash on Sells)	+144.7%	121.0
17. InvesTech Mutual Fund Advisor (Mutual Fund Timing Model)	+143.6%	12.4
18. The Dines Letter (Short-Term Model—100% Cash on Sells)	+142.9%	26.0
19. Bob Nurock's Advisory (Technical Market Index—100% Cash on Sells)	+134.3%	3.0
20. Fund Exchange (Fund Timing Model)	+133.3%	19.3
21. Growth Fund Guide (Mutual Fund Allocation)	+125.7%	2.9
22. The Granville Market Letter (100% Cash on Sells)	+116.2%	16.6
23. The Professional Tape Reader (Mutual Fund Timing Model)	+105.8%	13.6
24. The Garside Forecast (Bell Ringer—100% Cash on Sells)	+91.2%	28.0
25. Bob Nurock's Advisory (Technical Market Index—100% Short on Sells)	+78.1%	3.0
T-Bill Portfolio	+61.7%	
26. The Big Picture (Short-Term Trading Guide (SGA)—Shorting Allowed)	+60.3%	59.0
27. Professional Timing Service ("Supply/Demand Formula"—Shorting Allowed)	+44.8%	30.0

Appendix C-3: Stock Market Timing From 1/1/85 to 6/30/92
(Risk-Adjusted)

Newsletter	Gain/Loss	Number of Switches
1. Market Logic (Seasonality Timing System)	+0.41%	238.0
2. The Big Picture (Short-Term Trading Guide (SGA)—100% Cash on Sells)	+0.29%	59.0
3. The Elliott Wave Theorist (Investors—100% Cash on Sells)	+0.27%	7.0
4. Stockmarket Cycles (Mutual Fund Switching Advice)*	+0.27%	50.0
5. Systems and Forecasts ("Time Trend" Timing Model—100% Cash on Sells)	+0.26%	114.0
6. Investors Intelligence (Timing Advice for Switch Fund Traders)	+0.25%	17.1
7. The Mutual Fund Strategist (Intermediate Timing Model)	+0.22%	67.0
8. The Professional Tape Reader (Mutual Fund Timing Model)	+0.22%	13.6
9. InvesTech Mutual Fund Advisor (Mutual Fund Timing Model)	+0.21%	12.4
10. Systems and Forecasts ("Time Trend" Timing Model—100% Short on Sells)	+0.19%	114.0
11. Dow Theory Letters (Grading of Primary Trend—100% Cash on Sells)	+0.19%	11.0
12. Marketarian Letter (Long-Term Investor in Mutual Funds—100% Cash on Sells)	+0.19%	27.0
13. Market Logic (Recommended Exposure to Stock Market)	+0.19%	0.9
14. Telephone Switch Newsletter (Equity/Cash Timing Model)	+0.18%	15.0
15. Professional Timing Service ("Supply/Demand Formula"—100% Cash on Sells)	+0.17%	29.0
Wilshire 5000 Value-Weighted Total Return Index	+0.16%	
16. The Value Line Investment Survey (Market Timing Model—100% Cash on Sells)	+0.16%	2.5
17. The Zweig Forecast ("Short-Term Trend Indicator"—100% Cash on Sells)	+0.16%	121.0
18. Weber's Fund Advisor (Mutual Fund Allocation Advice)	+0.16%	18.0
19. Fund Exchange (Fund Timing Model)	+0.15%	19.3
20. The Dines Letter (Short-Term Model—100% Cash on Sells)	+0.15%	26.0
21. Bob Nurock's Advisory (Technical Market Index—100% Cash on Sells)	+0.12%	3.0
22. The Garside Forecast (Bell Ringer—100% Cash on Sells)	+0.12%	28.0
23. Growth Fund Guide (Mutual Fund Allocation)	+0.12%	2.9
24. The Granville Market Letter (100% Cash on Sells)	+0.10%	16.6
25. Bob Nurock's Advisory (Technical Market Index—100% Short on Sells)	+0.05%	3.0
26. The Big Picture (Short-Term Trading Guide (SGA)—Shorting Allowed)	+0.02%	59.0
27. Professional Timing Service ("Supply/Demand Formula"—Shorting Allowed)	0.00%	30.0

Newsletter	Gain/Loss	Number of Switches
28. The Dines Letter (Short-Term Model—100% Short on Sells)	+31.1%	26.0
29. The Granville Market Letter (100% Short on Sells)	+28.3%	30.2
30. The Zweig Forecast ("Short-Term Trend Indicator"—100% Short on Sells)	+27.8%	121.0
31. The Elliott Wave Theorist (Traders—May Go Short on Sells)	−2.9%	47.0
32. The Garside Forecast (Bell Ringer—100% Short on Sells)	−55.6%	28.0

*Stockmarket Cycles' performance over this period would be 217.6% if the HFD were to give credit to the hourly prices at which trades were to take place. See the write-up for this newsletter earlier in this book.

Newsletter	Gain/Loss	Number of Switches
28. The Granville Market Letter (100% Short on Sells)	−0.03%	30.2
29. The Dines Letter (Short-Term Model—100% Short on Sells)	−0.03%	26.0
30. The Zweig Forecast ("Short-Term Trend Indicator"—100% Short on Sells)	−0.04%	121.0
31. The Elliott Wave Theorist (Traders—May Go Short on Sells)	−0.12%	47.0
32. The Garside Forecast (Bell Ringer—100% Short on Sells)	−0.18%	28.0

*Stockmarket Cycles' performance over this period would be 0.28% if the HFD were to give credit to the hourly prices at which trades were to take place. See the write-up for this newsletter earlier in this book.

Appendix C-4: Stock Market Timing From 1/1/87 to 6/30/92
(Total Return)

Newsletter	Gain/Loss	Number of Switches
1. Market Logic (Seasonality Timing System)	+192.6%	180.0
2. Systems and Forecasts ("Time Trend" Timing Model—100% Short on Sells)	+152.1%	95.0
3. Systems and Forecasts ("Time Trend" Timing Model—100% Cash on Sells)	+146.7%	95.0
4. Investors Intelligence (Timing Advice for Switch Fund Traders)	+136.1%	15.9
5. The Big Picture (Short-Term Trading Guide (SGA)—100% Cash on Sells)	+114.3%	40.0
6. Market Logic (Recommended Exposure to Stock Market)	+100.8%	0.9
7. The Volume Reversal Survey (Index Fund Portfolio)	+95.3%	19.0
8. Telephone Switch Newsletter (Equity/Cash Timing Model)	+94.7%	12.0
Wilshire 5000 Value-Weighted Total Return Index	+93.3%	
9. Mutual Fund Forecaster (Recommended Exposure to Stock Market)	+91.1%	0.5
10. The Mutual Fund Strategist (Intermediate Timing Model)	+87.1%	44.0
11. Fidelity Monitor (Growth Portfolio)	+85.9%	0.8
12. The Value Line Investment Survey (Market Timing Model—100% Cash on Sells)	+82.8%	2.5
13. Stockmarket Cycles (Mutual Fund Switching Advice)*	+82.4%	39.0
14. Dow Theory Letters (Grading of Primary Trend—100% Cash on Sells)	+82.2%	6.0
15. The Professional Tape Reader (Short-Term Model—100% Cash on Sells)	+79.9%	66.0
16. Weber's Fund Advisor (Mutual Fund Allocation Advice)	+79.6%	18.0
17. The Granville Market Letter (100% Cash on Sells)	+78.8%	9.6
18. Professional Timing Service ("Supply/Demand Formula"—100% Cash on Sells)	+78.0%	27.0
19. Personal Finance (Mutual Fund Switching Model)	+77.9%	19.0
20. The Marketarian Letter (Long-Term Investor in Mutual Funds—100% Cash on Sells)	+77.7%	19.0
21. The Zweig Forecast ("Short-Term Trend Indicator"—100% Cash on Sells)	+76.9%	92.0
22. InvesTech Mutual Fund Advisor (Mutual Fund Timing Model)	+74.1%	7.0
23. The Professional Tape Reader (Intermediate-Term Model—100% Cash on Sells)	+73.8%	13.0
24. Fund Exchange (Fund Timing Model)	+73.6%	13.3
25. The Elliott Wave Theorist (Investors—100% Cash on Sells)	+70.8%	3.0
26. The Garside Forecast (Bell Ringer—100% Cash on Sells)	+67.6%	28.0
27. Professional Timing Service (Mutual Fund "Dynamo" Model)	+67.2%	54.2
28. Bob Brinker's Marketimer (100% Cash on Sells)	+66.2%	2.7
29. The Professional Tape Reader (Mutual Fund Timing Model)	+63.1%	9.5

Appendix C-4: Stock Market Timing From 1/1/87 to 6/30/92
(Risk-Adjusted)

Newsletter	Gain/Loss	Number of Switches
1. Market Logic (Seasonality Timing System)	+0.52%	180.0
2. Investors Intelligence (Timing Advice for Switch Fund Traders)	+0.32%	15.9
3. Systems and Forecasts ("Time Trend" Timing Model—100% Cash on Sells)	+0.28%	95.0
4. The Big Picture (Short-Term Trading Guide (SGA)—100% Cash on Sells)	+0.27%	40.0
5. Systems and Forecasts ("Time Trend" Timing Model—100% Short on Sells)	+0.24%	95.0
6. The Professional Tape Reader (Mutual Fund Timing Model)	+0.21%	9.5
7. Dow Theory Letters (Grading of Primary Trend—100% Cash on Sells)	+0.18%	6.0
8. Stockmarket Cycles (Mutual Fund Switching Advice)*	+0.18%	39.0
9. The Volume Reversal Survey (Index Fund Portfolio)	+0.17%	19.0
10. InvesTech Mutual Fund Advisor (Mutual Fund Timing Model)	+0.17%	7.0
11. The Elliott Wave Theorist (Investors—100% Cash on Sells)	+0.16%	3.0
12. The Mutual Fund Strategist (Intermediate Timing Model)	+0.16%	44.0
13. Switch Fund Timing (Conservative Fund Timing Model)	+0.16%	9.0
14. Telephone Switch Newsletter (Equity/Cash Timing Model)	+0.15%	12.0
15. Market Logic (Recommended Exposure to Stock Market)	+0.14%	0.9
16. The Garside Forecast (Bell Ringer—100% Cash on Sells)	+0.14%	28.0
17. Fund Exchange (Fund Timing Model)	+0.14%	13.3
18. The Professional Tape Reader (Short-Term Model—100% Cash on Sells)	+0.14%	66.0
19. The Professional Tape Reader (Intermediate-Term Model—100% Cash on Sells)	+0.14%	13.0
20. The Zweig Forecast ("Short-Term Trend Indicator"—100% Cash on Sells)	+0.13%	92.0
Wilshire 5000 Value-Weighted Total Return Index	+0.12%	
21. Mutual Fund Forecaster (Recommended Exposure to Stock Market)	+0.12%	0.5
22. The Value Line Investment Survey (Market Timing Model—100% Cash on Sells)	+0.11%	2.5
23. Fidelity Monitor (Growth Portfolio)	+0.11%	0.8
24. The Marketarian Letter (Long-Term Investor in Mutual Funds—100% Cash on Sells)	+0.11%	19.0
25. Professional Timing Service ("Supply/Demand Formula"—100% Cash on Sells)	+0.11%	27.0
26. Personal Finance (Mutual Fund Switching Model)	+0.11%	19.0
27. Weber's Fund Advisor (Mutual Fund Allocation Advice)	+0.10%	18.0
28. The Granville Market Letter (100% Cash on Sells)	+0.10%	9.6
29. Professional Timing Service (Mutual Fund "Dynamo" Model)	+0.09%	54.2

Newsletter	Gain/Loss	Number of Switches
30. Switch Fund Timing (Conservative Fund Timing Model)	+62.6%	9.0
31. Margo's Market Monitor (Mutual Fund Portfolio)	+61.3%	19.4
32. The Dines Letter (Short-Term Model—100% Cash on Sells)	+61.1%	21.0
33. Bob Nurock's Advisory (Technical Market Index—100% Cash on Sells)	+52.2%	3.0
34. Growth Fund Guide (Mutual Fund Allocation)	+46.6%	2.9
T-Bill Portfolio	+41.7%	
35. The Big Picture (Short-Term Trading Guide (SGA)—Shorting Allowed)	+37.4%	40.0
36. The Granville Market Letter (100% Short on Sells)	+32.6%	16.2
37. Bob Nurock's Advisory (Technical Market Index—100% Short on Sells)	+15.7%	3.0
38. The Zweig Forecast ("Short-Term Trend Indicator"—100% Short on Sells)	+12.0%	92.0
39. The Professional Tape Reader (Long-Term Model—100% Cash on Sells)	+10.4%	7.0
40. Professional Timing Service ("Supply/Demand Formula"—Shorting Allowed)	+9.0%	28.0
41. The Professional Tape Reader (Short-Term Model—100% Short on Sells)	+7.3%	66.0
42. The Dines Letter (Short-Term Model—100% Short on Sells)	−5.3%	21.0
43. The Professional Tape Reader (Intermediate-Term Model—100% Short on Sells)	−18.8%	13.0
44. The Garside Forecast (Bell Ringer—100% Short on Sells)	−21.6%	28.0
45. The Elliott Wave Theorist (Traders—May Go Short on Sells)	−40.7%	42.0
46. The Professional Tape Reader (Long-Term Model—100% Short on Sells)	−66.6%	7.0

Stockmarket Cycles' performance over this period would be 89.1% if the HFD were to give credit to the hourly prices at which trades were to take place. See the write-up for this newsletter earlier in this book.

Newsletter	Gain/Loss	Number of Switches
30. Margo's Market Monitor (Mutual Fund Portfolio)	+0.09%	19.4
31. The Dines Letter (Short-Term Model—100% Cash on Sells)	+0.08%	21.0
32. Bob Brinker's Marketimer (100% Cash on Sells)	+0.08%	2.7
33. Bob Nurock's Advisory (Technical Market Index—100% Cash on Sells)	+0.05%	3.0
34. Growth Fund Guide (Mutual Fund Allocation)	+0.03%	2.9
35. The Big Picture (Short-Term Trading Guide (SGA)—Shorting Allowed)	+0.01%	40.0
36. The Granville Market Letter (100% Short on Sells)	+0.01%	16.2
37. Bob Nurock's Advisory (Technical Market Index—100% Short on Sells)	−0.04%	3.0
38. Professional Timing Service ("Supply/Demand Formula"—Shorting Allowed)	−0.05%	28.0
39. The Zweig Forecast ("Short-Term Trend Indicator"—100% Short on Sells)	−0.06%	92.0
40. The Professional Tape Reader (Short-Term Model—100% Short on Sells)	−0.07%	66.0
41. The Professional Tape Reader (Long-Term Model—100% Cash on Sells)	−0.08%	7.0
42. The Garside Forecast (Bell Ringer—100% Short on Sells)	−0.09%	28.0
43. The Dines Letter (Short-Term Model—100% Short on Sells)	−0.11%	21.0
44. The Professional Tape Reader (Intermediate-Term Model—100% Short on Sells)	−0.16%	13.0
45. The Elliott Wave Theorist (Traders—May Go Short on Sells)	−0.33%	42.0
46. The Professional Tape Reader (Long-Term Model—100% Short on Sells)	−0.35%	7.0

Stockmarket Cycles' performance over this period would be 0.17% if the HFD were to give credit to the hourly prices at which trades were to take place. See the write-up for this newsletter earlier in this book.

Appendix C-5: Stock Market Timing From 1/1/89 to 6/30/92
(Total Return)

Newsletter	Gain/Loss	Number of Switches
1. Professional Timing Service ("Supply/Demand Formula"—100% Cash on Sells)	+94.4%	19.0
2. The Granville Market Letter (100% Cash on Sells)	+84.2%	5.0
3. Professional Timing Service ("Supply/Demand Formula"— Shorting Allowed)	+78.5%	20.0
4. Professional Timing Service (Mutual Fund "Dynamo" Model)	+73.9%	41.0
5. Systems and Forecasts ("Time Trend" Timing Model—100% Cash on Sells)	+72.6%	62.0
6. Market Logic (Seasonality Timing System)	+72.0%	116.0
7. Systems and Forecasts ("Time Trend" Timing Model—100% Short on Sells)	+68.3%	62.0
8. The Granville Market Letter (100% Short on Sells)	+66.7%	11.6
9. The Big Picture (Master Key—No Shorting)	+65.8%	10.0
10. Investors Intelligence (Timing Advice for Switch Fund Traders)	+61.6%	8.8
11. The Volume Reversal Survey (Index Fund Portfolio)	+60.9%	13.0
12. Fidelity Monitor (Growth Portfolio)	+60.3%	0.0
Wilshire 5000 Value-Weighted Total Return Index	+60.3%	
13. Market Logic (Recommended Exposure to Stock Market)	+58.6%	0.5
14. Telephone Switch Newsletter (Equity/Cash Timing Model)	+58.5%	6.0
15. Mutual Fund Forecaster (Recommended Exposure to Stock Market)	+58.4%	0.5
16. The Wall Street Generalist ("Short-Term Indicator Consensus"— 100% Cash on Sells)	+57.1%	2.0
17. The Dines Letter (Long-Term Model—100% Cash on Sells)	+55.4%	2.0
18. The Chartist Mutual Fund Timer	+54.7%	17.0
19. The Wall Street Generalist (Long-Term Fund Timing)	+54.5%	2.6
20. The Wall Street Generalist (Intermediate Term Fund Timing)	+54.4%	4.2
21. Fidelity Insight (Growth Portfolio)	+53.9%	1.6
22. Personal Finance (Mutual Fund Switching Model)	+52.9%	16.5
23. The Value Line Investment Survey (Market Timing Model—100% Cash on Sells)	+52.4%	2.1
24. The Wall Street Generalist ("Short-Term Indicator Consensus"— 100% Short on Sells)	+52.2%	2.0
25. Kinsman's Telephone Growth & Income Service (Mutual Fund Allocation)	+51.8%	4.4
26. The Dines Letter (Intermediate-Term Model—100% Cash on Sells)	+49.7%	8.0
27. Weber's Fund Advisor (Mutual Fund Allocation Advice)	+49.4%	15.0
28. Timer Digest ("5& 10Consensus"—100% Cash on Sells)	+48.6%	44.0
29. Bob Brinker's Marketimer (100% Cash on Sells)	+47.5%	1.7
30. Crawford Perspectives (100% Cash on Sells)	+46.8%	18.0

Appendix C-5: Stock Market Timing From 1/1/89 to 6/30/92
(Risk-Adjusted)

Newsletter	Gain/Loss	Number of Switches
1. Market Logic (Seasonality Timing System)	+0.40%	116.0
2. Professional Timing Service ("Supply/Demand Formula"—100% Cash on Sells)	+0.39%	19.0
3. Professional Timing Service (Mutual Fund "Dynamo" Model)	+0.35%	41.0
4. The Granville Market Letter (100% Cash on Sells)	+0.33%	5.0
5. Investors Intelligence (Timing Advice for Switch Fund Traders)	+0.25%	8.8
6. Systems and Forecasts ("Time Trend" Timing Model—100% Cash on Sells)	+0.25%	62.0
7. The Professional Tape Reader (Mutual Fund Timing Model)	+0.24%	2.6
8. The Granville Market Letter (100% Short on Sells)	+0.22%	11.6
9. Professional Timing Service ("Supply/Demand Formula"— Shorting Allowed)	+0.22%	20.0
10. Systems and Forecasts ("Time Trend" Timing Model—100% Short on Sells)	+0.22%	62.0
11. The Big Picture (Master Key—No Shorting)	+0.22%	10.0
12. The Volume Reversal Survey (Index Fund Portfolio)	+0.22%	13.0
13. InvesTech Mutual Fund Advisor (Mutual Fund Timing Model)	+0.20%	1.1
14. Telephone Switch Newsletter (Equity/Cash Timing Model)	+0.18%	6.0
15. The Dines Letter (Long-Term Model—100% Cash on Sells)	+0.18%	2.0
16. Kinsman's Telephone Growth & Income Service (Mutual Fund Allocation)	+0.17%	4.4
17. The Chartist Mutual Fund Timer	+0.17%	17.0
18. The Value Line Investment Survey (Market Timing Model—100% Cash on Sells)	+0.17%	2.1
19. Fidelity Insight (Growth Portfolio)	+0.17%	1.6
20. Market Logic (Recommended Exposure to Stock Market)	+0.16%	0.5
21. Mutual Fund Forecaster (Recommended Exposure to Stock Market)	+0.16%	0.5
22. Fidelity Monitor (Growth Portfolio)	+0.16%	0.0
Wilshire 5000 Value-Weighted Total Return Index	+0.16%	
23. The Wall Street Generalist (Long-Term Fund Timing)	+0.15%	2.6
24. The Wall Street Generalist (Intermediate Term Fund Timing)	+0.15%	4.2
25. The Wall Street Generalist ("Short-Term Indicator Consensus"— 100% Cash on Sells)	+0.15%	2.0
26. Personal Finance (Mutual Fund Switching Model)	+0.15%	16.5
27. The Outlook (Market Allocation)	+0.14%	0.6
28. Weber's Fund Advisor (Mutual Fund Allocation Advice)	+0.14%	15.0
29. The Wall Street Generalist ("Short-Term Indicator Consensus"— 100% Short on Sells)	+0.13%	2.0
30. Bob Brinker's Marketimer (100% Cash on Sells)	+0.13%	1.7

Newsletter	Gain/Loss	Number of Switches
31. Bob Nurock's Advisory (Elves Short-Term Predictor—No Shorting)	+43.9%	9.0
32. InvesTech Mutual Fund Advisor (Mutual Fund Timing Model)	+42.9%	1.1
33. The Wall Street Generalist ("Top Trends"—100% Cash on Sells)	+42.8%	3.0
34. The Outlook (Market Allocation)	+42.6%	0.6
35. The Wall Street Digest (Mutual Fund Portfolio)	+41.6%	9.6
36. The Mutual Fund Strategist (Intermediate Timing Model)	+40.3%	14.0
37. Cabot's Mutual Fund Navigator (Growth Portfolio)	+39.6%	3.0
38. Donoghue's Moneyletter (Signal Portfolio)	+39.0%	2.3
39. Fund Exchange (Fund Timing Model)	+37.7%	10.7
40. Timer Digest ("Casper" Timing Model—100% Cash on Sells)	+36.9%	41.0
41. The Ruff Times (Mutual Fund Portfolio #1)	+36.5%	10.3
42. The Dines Letter (Intermediate-Term Model—100% Short on Sells)	+36.1%	8.0
43. The Addison Report (Mutual Fund Allocation)	+35.6%	8.8
44. The Big Picture (Short-Term Trading Guide (SGA)—100% Cash on Sells)	+35.4%	27.0
45. Switch Fund Timing (Conservative Fund Timing Model)	+34.9%	6.0
46. Stockmarket Cycles (Mutual Fund Switching Advice)*	+34.3%	24.0
47. Futures Hotline Mutual Fund Timer (Stock Fund Model—Cash on Sells)	+33.6%	35.2
48. The Professional Tape Reader (Mutual Fund Timing Model)	+33.3%	2.6
49. The Zweig Forecast ("Short-Term Trend Indicator"—100% Cash on Sells)	+33.0%	63.0
50. The Professional Tape Reader (Intermediate-Term Model—100% Cash on Sells)	+31.9%	8.0
51. Growth Fund Guide (Mutual Fund Allocation)	+30.7%	1.4
52. Margo's Market Monitor (Mutual Fund Portfolio)	+29.8%	11.4
53. The Garside Forecast (Bell Ringer—100% Cash on Sells)	+29.0%	24.0
54. The Dines Letter (Long-Term Model—100% Short on Sells)	+28.6%	2.0
55. The Professional Tape Reader (Short-Term Model—100% Cash on Sells)	+28.3%	45.0
56. Timer Digest ("5 & 10 Consensus"—100% Short on Sells)	+27.9%	44.0
57. The Dines Letter (Short-Term Model—100% Cash on Sells)	+27.0%	12.0
58. Bob Nurock's Advisory (Technical Market Index—100% Cash on Sells)	+26.2%	3.0
59. Dow Theory Letters (Grading of Primary Trend—100% Cash on Sells)	+26.1%	5.0
T-Bill Portfolio	+25.3%	
60. Crawford Perspectives (Shorting Allowed)	+23.4%	22.0
61. The Marketarian Letter (Switching Advice for Mutual Fund Traders)	+22.8%	14.0
62. Graphic Fund Forecaster (Growth/International Portfolio #1)	+22.5%	93.0

Newsletter	Gain/Loss	Number of Switches
31. Crawford Perspectives (100% Cash on Sells)	+0.13%	18.0
32. The Dines Letter (Intermediate-Term Model—100% Cash on Sells)	+0.13%	8.0
33. Timer Digest ("5& 10Consensus"—100% Cash on Sells)	+0.12%	44.0
34. Fund Exchange (Fund Timing Model)	+0.12%	10.7
35. Bob Nurock's Advisory (Elves Short-Term Predictor—No Shorting)	+0.12%	9.0
36. Switch Fund Timing (Conservative Fund Timing Model)	+0.12%	6.0
37. The Wall Street Digest (Mutual Fund Portfolio)	+0.11%	9.6
38. The Mutual Fund Strategist (Intermediate Timing Model)	+0.10%	14.0
39. The Wall Street Generalist ("Top Trends"—100% Cash on Sells)	+0.10%	3.0
40. Stockmarket Cycles (Mutual Fund Switching Advice)*	+0.09%	24.0
41. Timer Digest ("Casper" Timing Model—100% Cash on Sells)	+0.09%	41.0
42. Cabot's Mutual Fund Navigator (Growth Portfolio)	+0.09%	3.0
43. The Big Picture (Short-Term Trading Guide (SGA)—100% Cash on Sells)	+0.09%	27.0
44. The Ruff Times (Mutual Fund Portfolio #1)	+0.09%	10.3
45. Donoghue's Moneyletter (Signal Portfolio)	+0.08%	2.3
46. Growth Fund Guide (Mutual Fund Allocation)	+0.08%	1.4
47. The Professional Tape Reader (Intermediate-Term Model—100% Cash on Sells)	+0.08%	8.0
48. The Addison Report (Mutual Fund Allocation)	+0.08%	8.8
49. The Dines Letter (Intermediate-Term Model—100% Short on Sells)	+0.07%	8.0
50. Futures Hotline Mutual Fund Timer (Stock Fund Model—Cash on Sells)	+0.07%	35.2
51. The Zweig Forecast ("Short-Term Trend Indicator"—100% Cash on Sells)	+0.06%	63.0
52. Margo's Market Monitor (Mutual Fund Portfolio)	+0.05%	11.4
53. The Garside Forecast (Bell Ringer—100% Cash on Sells)	+0.05%	24.0
54. The Dines Letter (Long-Term Model—100% Short on Sells)	+0.04%	2.0
55. The Professional Tape Reader (Short-Term Model—100% Cash on Sells)	+0.03%	45.0
56. Timer Digest ("5& 10Consensus"—100% Short on Sells)	+0.03%	44.0
57. The Dines Letter (Short-Term Model—100% Cash on Sells)	+0.03%	12.0
58. Bob Nurock's Advisory (Technical Market Index—100% Cash on Sells)	+0.02%	3.0
59. Dow Theory Letters (Grading of Primary Trend—100% Cash on Sells)	+0.02%	5.0
60. Crawford Perspectives (Shorting Allowed)	+0.01%	22.0
61. The Marketarian Letter (Switching Advice for Mutual Fund Traders)	+0.01%	14.0
62. The Marketarian Letter (Long-Term Investor in Mutual Funds—100% Cash on Sells)	0.00%	6.5

Appendix C-5: Stock Market Timing From 1/1/89 to 6/30/92
(Total Return) (continued)

Newsletter	Gain/Loss	Number of Switches
63. Bob Nurock's Advisory (Sector Funds Portfolio)	+22.4%	9.5
64. The Marketarian Letter (Long-Term Investor in Mutual Funds—100% Cash on Sells)	+20.4%	6.5
65. The Wall Street Generalist ("Top Trends"—100% Short on Sells)	+20.1%	3.0
66. Bob Nurock's Advisory (Index Funds Portfolio)	+20.1%	7.0
67. The Elliott Wave Theorist (Investors—100% Cash on Sells)	+19.5%	2.0
68. Fast Track Funds	+17.4%	45.6
69. The Ney Report (Growth Fund Portfolio)	+16.6%	2.2
70. The Professional Tape Reader (Long-Term Model—100% Cash on Sells)	+13.8%	5.0
71. Bob Nurock's Advisory (Technical Market Index—100% Short on Sells)	−4.1%	3.0
72. Bob Nurock's Advisory (Elves Short-Term Predictor—Shorting)	−6.7%	9.0
73. The Zweig Forecast ("Short-Term Trend Indicator"—100% Short on Sells)	−10.5%	63.0
74. Timer Digest ("Casper" Timing Model—100% Short on Sells)	−12.7%	41.0
75. The Big Picture (Short-Term Trading Guide (SGA)—Shorting Allowed)	−15.2%	27.0
76. Futures Hotline Mutual Fund Timer (Intermediate-Term Model—100% Short on Sells)	−16.6%	81.0
77. The Dines Letter (Short-Term Model—100% Short on Sells)	−19.9%	12.0
78. The Professional Tape Reader (Short-Term Model—100% Short on Sells)	−28.9%	45.0
79. The Professional Tape Reader (Intermediate-Term Model—100% Short on Sells)	−32.0%	8.0
80. The Garside Forecast (Bell Ringer—100% Short on Sells)	−33.6%	24.0
81. The Professional Tape Reader (Long-Term Model—100% Short on Sells)	−47.6%	5.0
82. The Elliott Wave Theorist (Traders—May Go Short on Sells)	−51.6%	34.0

*Stockmarket Cycles' performance over this period would be 30.8% if the HFD were to give credit to the hourly prices at which trades were to take place. See the write-up for this newsletter earlier in this book.

Newsletter	Gain/Loss	Number of Switches
63. The Wall Street Generalist ("Top Trends"—100% Short on Sells)	0.00%	3.0
64. Graphic Fund Forecaster (Growth/International Portfolio #1)	0.00%	93.0
65. Bob Nurock's Advisory (Sector Funds Portfolio)	−0.03%	9.5
66. Fast Track Funds	−0.03%	45.6
67. Bob Nurock's Advisory (Index Funds Portfolio)	−0.05%	7.0
68. The Ney Report (Growth Fund Portfolio)	−0.05%	2.2
69. The Professional Tape Reader (Long-Term Model—100% Cash on Sells)	−0.13%	5.0
70. Bob Nurock's Advisory (Elves Short-Term Predictor—Shorting)	−0.14%	9.0
71. The Elliott Wave Theorist (Investors—100% Cash on Sells)	−0.16%	2.0
72. Timer Digest ("Casper" Timing Model—100% Short on Sells)	−0.16%	41.0
73. Bob Nurock's Advisory (Technical Market Index—100% Short on Sells)	−0.18%	3.0
74. The Big Picture (Short-Term Trading Guide (SGA)—Shorting Allowed)	−0.19%	27.0
75. The Zweig Forecast ("Short-Term Trend Indicator"—100% Short on Sells)	−0.20%	63.0
76. Futures Hotline Mutual Fund Timer (Intermediate-Term Model—100% Short on Sells)	−0.20%	81.0
77. The Professional Tape Reader (Short-Term Model—100% Short on Sells)	−0.29%	45.0
78. The Dines Letter (Short-Term Model—100% Short on Sells)	−0.29%	12.0
79. The Professional Tape Reader (Intermediate-Term Model—100% Short on Sells)	−0.31%	8.0
80. The Garside Forecast (Bell Ringer—100% Short on Sells)	−0.32%	24.0
81. The Professional Tape Reader (Long-Term Model—100% Short on Sells)	−0.45%	5.0
82. The Elliott Wave Theorist (Traders—May Go Short on Sells)	−0.58%	34.0

*Stockmarket Cycles' performance over this period would be 0.06% if the HFD were to give credit to the hourly prices at which trades were to take place. See the write-up for this newsletter earlier in this book.

Appendix C-6: Stock Market Timing From 1/1/91 to 6/30/92
(Total Return)

Newsletter	Gain/Loss	Number of Switches
1. Professional Timing Service ("Supply/Demand Formula"— Shorting Allowed)	+50.9%	5.0
2. Hussman Econometrics (Mutual Fund Portfolio)	+47.7%	3.4
3. Professional Timing Service ("Supply/Demand Formula"—100% Cash on Sells)	+45.2%	5.0
4. Bob Nurock's Advisory (Elves Short-Term Predictor—Shorting)	+39.1%	4.0
5. Bob Nurock's Advisory (Elves Short-Term Predictor—No Shorting)	+38.7%	4.0
6. Crawford Perspectives (100% Cash on Sells)	+37.3%	7.0
7. The Granville Market Letter (100% Short on Sells)	+36.9%	1.0
8. Crawford Perspectives (Shorting Allowed)	+36.3%	9.0
9. No-Load Mutual Fund Selections & Timing Newsletter (Intermediate-Term Model—100% Cash on Sells)	+36.0%	21.0
10. Telephone Switch Newsletter (Equity/Cash Timing Model)	+33.3%	1.0
11. No-Load Mutual Fund Selections & Timing Newsletter (Intermediate-Term Model—100% Short on Sells)	+33.3%	26.0
12. Bob Brinker's Marketimer (100% Cash on Sells)	+32.6%	0.1
13. Fund Kinetics	+32.3%	0.0
14. Donoghue's Moneyletter (Signal Portfolio)	+32.3%	0.0
15. Fidelity Monitor (Growth Portfolio)	+32.3%	0.0
16. The Wall Street Generalist ("Top Trends"—100% Cash on Sells)	+32.3%	0.0
17. The Wall Street Generalist ("Top Trends"—100% Short on Sells)	+32.3%	0.0
18. The Wall Street Generalist ("Short-Term Indicator Consensus"— 100% Cash on Sells)	+32.3%	0.0
19. The Wall Street Generalist ("Short-Term Indicator Consensus"— 100% Short on Sells)	+32.3%	0.0
Wilshire 5000 Value-Weighted Total Return Index	+32.3%	
20. The Wall Street Generalist (Intermediate Term Fund Timing)	+32.2%	1.9
21. The Contrarian's View (TIAA/CREF Switch Plan)	+32.2%	18.0
22. The Granville Market Letter (100% Cash on Sells)	+31.1%	3.5
23. Personal Finance (Mutual Fund Switching Model)	+31.0%	7.2
24. Market Logic (Recommended Exposure to Stock Market)	+30.9%	0.5
25. Mutual Fund Forecaster (Recommended Exposure to Stock Market)	+30.7%	0.5
26. The Wall Street Generalist (Long-Term Fund Timing)	+30.4%	1.5
27. Dow Theory Forecasts (Grading of Primary Trend)	+30.0%	1.0
28. Cabot's Mutual Fund Navigator (Growth Portfolio)	+29.1%	0.8
29. The Marketarian Letter (Switching Advice for Mutual Fund Traders)	+29.1%	7.0
30. Investors Intelligence (Timing Advice for Switch Fund Traders)	+29.0%	4.2
31. Timer Digest ("5& 10Consensus"—100% Cash on Sells)	+28.9%	12.0
32. Equity Fund Outlook (Aggressive Portfolio)	+28.8%	4.2

Appendix C-6: Stock Market Timing From 1/1/91 to 6/30/92
(Risk-Adjusted)

Newsletter	Gain/Loss	Number of Switches
1. No-Load Mutual Fund Selections & Timing Newsletter (Intermediate-Term Model—100% Cash on Sells)	+0.50%	21.0
2. Professional Timing Service ("Supply/Demand Formula"—100% Cash on Sells)	+0.46%	5.0
3. Bob Nurock's Advisory (Elves Short-Term Predictor—Shorting)	+0.46%	4.0
4. Bob Nurock's Advisory (Elves Short-Term Predictor—No Shorting)	+0.44%	4.0
5. Investors Intelligence (Timing Advice for Switch Fund Traders)	+0.44%	4.2
6. Professional Timing Service ("Supply/Demand Formula"—Shorting Allowed)	+0.44%	5.0
7. The Contrarian's View (TIAA/CREF Switch Plan)	+0.43%	18.0
8. Crawford Perspectives (100% Cash on Sells)	+0.43%	7.0
9. No-Load Mutual Fund Selections & Timing Newsletter (Intermediate-Term Model—100% Short on Sells)	+0.41%	26.0
10. Crawford Perspectives (Shorting Allowed)	+0.41%	9.0
11. Futures Hotline Mutual Fund Timer (Stock Fund Model—Cash on Sells)	+0.40%	11.4
12. Professional Timing Service (Mutual Fund "Dynamo" Model)	+0.39%	16.0
13. Market Logic (Recommended Exposure to Stock Market)	+0.38%	0.5
14. The Granville Market Letter (100% Short on Sells)	+0.38%	1.0
15. Mutual Fund Forecaster (Recommended Exposure to Stock Market)	+0.38%	0.5
16. No-Load Mutual Fund Selections & Timing Newsletter (Intermediate Portfolio)	+0.38%	10.9
17. The Market Mania Newsletter (Long-Term Mutual Fund Investor)	+0.37%	0.5
18. P. Q. Wall Forecast, Inc. (Mutual Fund Model—100% Cash on Sells)	+0.36%	12.0
19. Hussman Econometrics (Mutual Fund Portfolio)	+0.36%	3.4
20. The Professional Tape Reader (Mutual Fund Timing Model)	+0.36%	2.0
21. The Wall Street Generalist (Intermediate Term Fund Timing)	+0.36%	1.9
22. The Volume Reversal Survey (Index Fund Portfolio)	+0.35%	5.0
23. The Value Line Investment Survey (Market Timing Model—100% Cash on Sells)	+0.35%	1.2
24. The Sy Harding Investor Forecasts (Mutual Fund Switching Model)	+0.34%	11.5
25. The Blue Chip Correlator	+0.34%	3.0
26. The Wall Street Generalist (Long-Term Fund Timing)	+0.34%	1.5
27. Personal Finance (Mutual Fund Switching Model)	+0.34%	7.2
28. Telephone Switch Newsletter (Equity/Cash Timing Model)	+0.33%	1.0
29. Bob Brinker's Marketimer (100% Cash on Sells)	+0.32%	0.1
30. Fidelity Monitor (Growth Portfolio)	+0.32%	0.0
31. Fund Kinetics	+0.32%	0.0
32. Donoghue's Moneyletter (Signal Portfolio)	+0.32%	0.0

Newsletter	Gain/Loss	Number of Switches
33. The Sy Harding Investor Forecasts (Mutual Fund Switching Model)	+28.6%	11.5
34. P. Q. Wall Forecast, Inc. (Mutual Fund Model—100% Cash on Sells)	+28.5%	12.0
35. Systems and Forecasts ("Time Trend" Timing Model—100% Cash on Sells)	+28.5%	24.0
36. No-Load Mutual Fund Selections & Timing Newsletter (Intermediate Portfolio)	+27.7%	10.9
37. The Value Line Investment Survey (Market Timing Model—100% Cash on Sells)	+26.9%	1.2
38. The Marketarian Letter (Long-Term Investor in Mutual Funds—100% Cash on Sells)	+26.8%	1.0
39. Kinsman's Telephone Growth & Income Service (Mutual Fund Allocation)	+26.3%	2.1
40. Professional Timing Service (Mutual Fund "Dynamo" Model)	+26.2%	16.0
41. The Blue Chip Correlator	+26.0%	3.0
42. The Market Mania Newsletter (Long-Term Mutual Fund Investor)	+24.9%	0.5
43. No-Load Mutual Fund Selections & Timing Newsletter (Primary Trend Model—100% Cash on Sells)	+24.3%	2.0
44. The Wall Street Digest (Mutual Fund Portfolio)	+24.3%	4.6
45. The Volume Reversal Survey (Index Fund Portfolio)	+24.3%	5.0
46. Futures Hotline Mutual Fund Timer (Stock Fund Model—Cash on Sells)	+24.2%	11.4
47. Systems and Forecasts ("Time Trend" Timing Model—100% Short on Sells)	+23.1%	24.0
48. Fidelity Insight (Growth Portfolio)	+23.0%	0.6
49. Timer Digest ("5 & 10 Consensus"—100% Short on Sells)	+23.0%	12.0
50. InvesTech Mutual Fund Advisor (Mutual Fund Timing Model)	+22.6%	0.6
51. Mutual Fund Technical Trader (Aggressive Growth/High Risk Portfolio)	+22.0%	2.0
52. The Dines Letter (Long-Term Model—100% Cash on Sells)	+21.8%	1.0
53. The Dines Letter (Intermediate-Term Model—100% Cash on Sells)	+21.7%	5.0
54. The Garside Forecast (Bell Ringer—100% Cash on Sells)	+21.4%	18.0
55. The Big Picture (Master Key—No Shorting)	+21.4%	5.0
56. The Ruff Times (Mutual Fund Portfolio #1)	+21.2%	5.3
57. The Outlook (Market Allocation)	+20.7%	0.2
58. No-Load Mutual Fund Selections & Timing Newsletter (Primary Trend Model—100% Short on Sells)	+20.6%	5.0
59. Fundline (Timing Portfolio)	+20.2%	7.3
60. The Chartist Mutual Fund Timer	+20.2%	3.0
61. Fund Exchange (Fund Timing Model)	+19.0%	3.8
62. Market Logic (Seasonality Timing System)	+18.8%	48.0

Newsletter	Gain/Loss	Number of Switches
33. The Wall Street Generalist ("Top Trends"—100% Short on Sells)	+0.32%	0.0
34. The Wall Street Generalist ("Top Trends"—100% Cash on Sells)	+0.32%	0.0
35. The Wall Street Generalist ("Short-Term Indicator Consensus"—100% Short on Sells)	+0.32%	0.0
36. The Wall Street Generalist ("Short-Term Indicator Consensus"—100% Cash on Sells)	+0.32%	0.0
Wilshire 5000 Value-Weighted Total Return Index	+0.32%	
37. Growth Fund Guide (Mutual Fund Allocation)	+0.32%	0.7
38. The Marketarian Letter (Switching Advice for Mutual Fund Traders)	+0.32%	7.0
39. The Granville Market Letter (100% Cash on Sells)	+0.31%	3.5
40. Equity Fund Outlook (Aggressive Portfolio)	+0.31%	4.2
41. Systems and Forecasts ("Time Trend" Timing Model—100% Cash on Sells)	+0.31%	24.0
42. InvesTech Mutual Fund Advisor (Mutual Fund Timing Model)	+0.30%	0.6
43. Dow Theory Forecasts (Grading of Primary Trend)	+0.30%	1.0
44. The Outlook (Market Allocation)	+0.30%	0.2
45. Kinsman's Telephone Growth & Income Service (Mutual Fund Allocation)	+0.30%	2.1
46. Market Logic (Seasonality Timing System)	+0.30%	48.0
47. The Wall Street Digest (Mutual Fund Portfolio)	+0.29%	4.6
48. The Garside Forecast (Bell Ringer—100% Cash on Sells)	+0.29%	18.0
49. Cabot's Mutual Fund Navigator (Growth Portfolio)	+0.29%	0.8
50. Timer Digest ("5& 10Consensus"—100% Cash on Sells)	+0.28%	12.0
51. The Ruff Times (Mutual Fund Portfolio #2)	+0.28%	4.8
52. The Professional Tape Reader (Intermediate-Term Model—100% Cash on Sells)	+0.28%	4.0
53. The Big Picture (Master Key—No Shorting)	+0.27%	5.0
54. The Marketarian Letter (Long-Term Investor in Mutual Funds—100% Cash on Sells)	+0.26%	1.0
55. The Ruff Times (Mutual Fund Portfolio #1)	+0.26%	5.3
56. Systems and Forecasts ("Time Trend" Timing Model—100% Short on Sells)	+0.25%	24.0
57. Fundline (Timing Portfolio)	+0.25%	7.3
58. Fund Exchange (Fund Timing Model)	+0.25%	3.8
59. No-Load Mutual Fund Selections & Timing Newsletter (Primary Trend Model—100% Cash on Sells)	+0.24%	2.0
60. Fidelity Insight (Growth Portfolio)	+0.23%	0.6
61. The Dines Letter (Intermediate-Term Model—100% Cash on Sells)	+0.22%	5.0
62. The Dines Letter (Long-Term Model—100% Cash on Sells)	+0.22%	1.0

Newsletter	Gain/Loss	Number of Switches
63. The Ruff Times (Mutual Fund Portfolio #2)	+18.8%	4.8
64. The Professional Tape Reader (Intermediate-Term Model—100% Cash on Sells)	+18.1%	4.0
65. The Addison Report (Mutual Fund Allocation)	+16.9%	2.6
66. Timer Digest ("Casper" Timing Model—100% Cash on Sells)	+16.0%	16.0
67. Weber's Fund Advisor (Mutual Fund Allocation Advice)	+15.0%	7.0
68. Global Fund Timer (U.S. Portfolio)	+14.9%	10.9
69. The Professional Tape Reader (Mutual Fund Timing Model)	+14.2%	2.0
70. P. Q. Wall Forecast, Inc. (Stock Timing Model—Shorting Allowed)	+14.0%	18.0
71. Growth Fund Guide (Mutual Fund Allocation)	+13.6%	0.7
72. Switch Fund Timing (Conservative Fund Timing Model)	+13.3%	4.5
73. Stockmarket Cycles (Mutual Fund Switching Advice)*	+13.1%	11.0
74. No-Load Mutual Fund Selections & Timing Newsletter (Aggressive Growth Portfolio)	+13.0%	2.8
75. Bob Nurock's Advisory (Index Funds Portfolio)	+12.5%	2.0
76. The Mutual Fund Strategist (Intermediate Timing Model)	+12.5%	5.0
77. The Dines Letter (Short-Term Model—100% Cash on Sells)	+11.8%	7.0
78. The Zweig Forecast ("Short-Term Trend Indicator"—100% Cash on Sells)	+11.6%	26.0
79. Fast Track Funds	+11.4%	20.1
80. Switch Fund Timing (Conservative/Momentum Timing Model)	+11.2%	5.0
81. Dow Theory Letters (Grading of Primary Trend—100% Cash on Sells)	+10.8%	3.0
82. Margo's Market Monitor (Mutual Fund Portfolio)	+10.7%	5.4
83. The Professional Tape Reader (Short-Term Model—100% Cash on Sells)	+10.7%	22.0
84. Bob Nurock's Advisory (Sector Funds Portfolio)	+10.3%	2.5
85. The Dines Letter (Long-Term Model—100% Short on Sells)	+9.7%	1.0
86. The Big Picture (Short-Term Trading Guide (SGA)—100% Cash on Sells)	+8.4%	13.0
87. The Ney Report (Growth Fund Portfolio)	+8.1%	1.0
88. The Big Picture (Master Key—Shorting Allowed)	+8.0%	12.0
89. The Elliott Wave Theorist (Investors—100% Cash on Sells)	+7.5%	0.0
90. Bob Nurock's Advisory (Technical Market Index—100% Short on Sells)	+7.5%	0.0
91. Bob Nurock's Advisory (Technical Market Index—100% Cash on Sells)	+7.5%	0.0
T-Bill Portfolio	+7.5%	
92. Graphic Fund Forecaster (Growth/International Portfolio #1)	+7.1%	57.0
93. The Professional Tape Reader (Long-Term Model—100% Cash on Sells)	+6.1%	3.0

Newsletter	Gain/Loss	Number of Switches
63. The Addison Report (Mutual Fund Allocation)	+0.21%	2.6
64. Timer Digest ("5 & 10 Consensus" 100% Short on Sells)	+0.21%	12.0
65. Mutual Fund Technical Trader (Aggressive Growth/High Risk Portfolio)	+0.20%	2.0
66. No-Load Mutual Fund Selections & Timing Newsletter (Primary Trend Model—100% Short on Sells)	+0.19%	5.0
67. The Ney Report (Growth Fund Portfolio)	+0.18%	1.0
68. The Chartist Mutual Fund Timer	+0.17%	3.0
69. Timer Digest ("Casper" Timing Model—100% Cash on Sells)	+0.17%	16.0
70. Stockmarket Cycles (Mutual Fund Switching Advice)*	+0.17%	11.0
71. Margo's Market Monitor (Mutual Fund Portfolio)	+0.16%	5.4
72. No-Load Mutual Fund Selections & Timing Newsletter (Aggressive Growth Portfolio)	+0.16%	2.8
73. Global Fund Timer (U.S. Portfolio)	+0.16%	10.9
74. Bob Nurock's Advisory (Index Funds Portfolio)	+0.15%	2.0
75. Weber's Fund Advisor (Mutual Fund Allocation Advice)	+0.14%	7.0
76. Switch Fund Timing (Conservative Fund Timing Model)	+0.13%	4.5
77. P. Q. Wall Forecast, Inc. (Stock Timing Model—Shorting Allowed)	+0.12%	18.0
78. The Dines Letter (Short-Term Model—100% Cash on Sells)	+0.11%	7.0
79. Bob Nurock's Advisory (Sector Funds Portfolio)	+0.10%	2.5
80. Switch Fund Timing (Conservative/Momentum Timing Model)	+0.09%	5.0
81. The Mutual Fund Strategist (Intermediate Timing Model)	+0.09%	5.0
82. The Zweig Forecast ("Short-Term Trend Indicator"—100% Cash on Sells)	+0.09%	26.0
83. Dow Theory Letters (Grading of Primary Trend—100% Cash on Sells)	+0.08%	3.0
84. Fast Track Funds	+0.07%	20.1
85. The Professional Tape Reader (Short-Term Model—100% Cash on Sells)	+0.06%	22.0
86. The Dines Letter (Long-Term Model—100% Short on Sells)	+0.05%	1.0
87. The Big Picture (Short-Term Trading Guide (SGA)—100% Cash on Sells)	+0.03%	13.0
88. The Big Picture (Master Key—Shorting Allowed)	+0.02%	12.0
89. Graphic Fund Forecaster (Growth/International Portfolio #1)	0.00%	57.0
90. The Elliott Wave Theorist (Investors—100% Cash on Sells)	0.00%	0.0
91. Bob Nurock's Advisory (Technical Market Index—100% Short on Sells)	0.00%	0.0
92. Bob Nurock's Advisory (Technical Market Index—100% Cash on Sells)	0.00%	0.0
93. The Dines Letter (Intermediate-Term Model—100% Short on Sells)	0.00%	5.0

Newsletter	Gain/Loss	Number of Switches
94. The Dines Letter (Intermediate-Term Model—100% Short on Sells)	+6.0%	5.0
95. The Garside Forecast (Bell Ringer—100% Short on Sells)	+1.0%	18.0
96. The Professional Tape Reader (Intermediate-Term Model—100% Short on Sells)	−6.9%	4.0
97. Timer Digest ("Casper" Timing Model—100% Short on Sells)	−7.0%	16.0
98. Futures Hotline Mutual Fund Timer (Intermediate-Term Model—100% Short on Sells)	−7.8%	32.0
99. The Dines Letter (Short-Term Model—100% Short on Sells)	−11.1%	7.0
100. The Zweig Forecast ("Short-Term Trend Indicator"—100% Short on Sells)	−11.3%	26.0
101. The Professional Tape Reader (Short-Term Model—100% Short on Sells)	−16.2%	22.0
102. The Big Picture (Short-Term Trading Guide (SGA)—Shorting Allowed)	−19.9%	13.0
103. The Professional Tape Reader (Long-Term Model—100% Short on Sells)	−23.1%	3.0
104. The Elliott Wave Theorist (Traders—May Go Short on Sells)	−32.2%	10.0

*Stockmarket Cycles' performance over this period would be 12.6% if the HFD were to give credit to the hourly prices at which trades were to take place. See the write-up for this newsletter earlier in this book.

Newsletter	Gain/Loss	Number of Switches
94. The Professional Tape Reader (Long-Term Model—100% Cash on Sells)	−0.03%	3.0
95. The Garside Forecast (Bell Ringer—100% Short on Sells)	−0.08%	18.0
96. The Professional Tape Reader (Intermediate-Term Model—100% Short on Sells)	−0.16%	4.0
97. Timer Digest ("Casper" Timing Model—100% Short on Sells)	−0.19%	16.0
98. Futures Hotline Mutual Fund Timer (Intermediate-Term Model—100% Short on Sells)	−0.20%	32.0
99. The Professional Tape Reader (Short-Term Model—100% Short on Sells)	−0.28%	22.0
100. The Zweig Forecast ("Short-Term Trend Indicator"—100% Short on Sells)	−0.29%	26.0
101. The Dines Letter (Short-Term Model—100% Short on Sells)	−0.30%	7.0
102. The Big Picture (Short-Term Trading Guide (SGA)—Shorting Allowed)	−0.35%	13.0
103. The Professional Tape Reader (Long-Term Model—100% Short on Sells)	−0.45%	3.0
104. The Elliott Wave Theorist (Traders—May Go Short on Sells)	−0.50%	10.0

Stockmarket Cycles' performance over this period would be 0.15% if the HFD were to give credit to the hourly prices at which trades were to take place. See the write-up for this newsletter earlier in this book.

7.5 yr

Appendix C-7: Gold Market Timing From 1/1/85 to 6/30/92 (Total Return)

Newsletter	Gain/Loss	Number of Switches
1. The Ruff Times (Short-Term Model—100% Cash on Sells)	+68.6%	19.0
T-Bill Portfolio	+61.7%	
2. The Elliott Wave Theorist (Investors—100% Cash on Sells)	+55.9%	1.0
3. The Garside Forecast (Bell Ringer—100% Short on Sells)	+50.1%	15.0
4. The Garside Forecast (Bell Ringer—100% Cash on Sells)	+43.8%	15.0
5. The Zweig Forecast (Gold Model—100% Cash on Sells)	+37.5%	28.0
6. Telephone Switch Newsletter (Gold/Cash Switch Plan—100% Cash on Sells)	+22.4%	22.0
7. Fund Exchange (Gold Mutual Fund Switching Model)	+16.3%	36.0
London P.M. Gold Fixing Price	+11.1%	
8. Market Logic (Gold Model—100% Cash on Sells)	+4.8%	13.0
9. The Dines Letter (Short-Term Model—100% Cash on Sells)	+3.2%	20.0
10. The Zweig Forecast (Gold Model—100% Short on Sells)	−4.4%	28.0
11. The Elliott Wave Theorist (Traders—Shorting Allowed)	−15.9%	29.5
12. The Dines Letter (Short-Term Model—100% Short on Sells)	−39.4%	20.0
13. Market Logic (Gold Model—100% Short on Sells)	−42.6%	13.0

top GOLD   68.6%
top STOCKS   821.7

Newsletter	Gain/Loss	Number of Switches
1. The Ruff Times (Short-Term Model—100% Cash on Sells)	+0.03%	19.0
2. The Garside Forecast (Bell Ringer—100% Short on Sells)	0.00%	15.0
3. The Garside Forecast (Bell Ringer—100% Cash on Sells)	−0.02%	15.0
4. The Zweig Forecast (Gold Model—100% Cash on Sells)	−0.05%	28.0
London P.M. Gold Fixing Price	−0.08%	
5. The Elliott Wave Theorist (Investors—100% Cash on Sells)	−0.09%	1.0
6. Telephone Switch Newsletter (Gold/Cash Switch Plan—100% Cash on Sells)	−0.11%	22.0
7. The Zweig Forecast (Gold Model—100% Short on Sells)	−0.13%	28.0
8. Fund Exchange (Gold Mutual Fund Switching Model)	−0.14%	36.0
9. The Dines Letter (Short-Term Model—100% Cash on Sells)	−0.16%	20.0
10. Market Logic (Gold Model—100% Cash on Sells)	−0.16%	13.0
11. The Dines Letter (Short-Term Model—100% Short on Sells)	−0.23%	20.0
12. The Elliott Wave Theorist (Traders—Shorting Allowed)	−0.24%	29.5
13. Market Logic (Gold Model—100% Short on Sells)	−0.25%	13.0

Appendix C-8: Gold Market Timing From 1/1/87 to 6/30/92 (Total Return)

Newsletter	Gain/Loss	Number of Switches
1. Your Window Into the Future (Gold Mutual Fund Signals—100% Cash on Sells)	+44.0%	9.0
T-Bill Portfolio	+41.7%	
2. The Ruff Times (Short-Term Model—100% Cash on Sells)	+40.3%	15.0
3. The Elliott Wave Theorist (Investors—100% Cash on Sells)	+36.6%	1.0
4. Telephone Switch Newsletter (Gold/Cash Switch Plan—100% Cash on Sells)	+21.7%	17.0
5. Fund Exchange (Gold Mutual Fund Switching Model)	+14.2%	23.0
6. The Zweig Forecast (Gold Model—100% Cash on Sells)	+9.0%	20.0
7. The Garside Forecast (Bell Ringer—100% Short on Sells)	+7.4%	12.0
8. The Garside Forecast (Bell Ringer—100% Cash on Sells)	+4.3%	12.0
9. The Dines Letter (Short-Term Model—100% Cash on Sells)	+0.5%	16.0
10. The Elliott Wave Theorist (Traders—Shorting Allowed)	−5.2%	16.5
11. The Zweig Forecast (Gold Model—100% Short on Sells)	−11.2%	20.0
12. The Dines Letter (Short-Term Model—100% Short on Sells)	−11.9%	16.0
London P.M. Gold Fixing Price	−12.2%	
13. Market Logic (Gold Model—100% Cash on Sells)	−14.4%	9.0
14. Market Logic (Gold Model—100% Short on Sells)	−40.1%	9.0

Appendix C-8: Gold Market Timing From 1/1/87 to 6/30/92 (Risk-Adjusted)

Newsletter	Gain/Loss	Number of Switches
1. Your Window Into the Future (Gold Mutual Fund Signals—100% Cash on Sells)	+0.02%	9.0
2. The Ruff Times (Short-Term Model—100% Cash on Sells)	0.00%	15.0
3. The Garside Forecast (Bell Ringer—100% Short on Sells)	−0.08%	12.0
4. Telephone Switch Newsletter (Gold/Cash Switch Plan—100% Cash on Sells)	−0.09%	17.0
5. The Elliott Wave Theorist (Investors—100% Cash on Sells)	−0.10%	1.0
6. The Garside Forecast (Bell Ringer—100% Cash on Sells)	−0.12%	12.0
7. Fund Exchange (Gold Mutual Fund Switching Model)	−0.13%	23.0
8. The Zweig Forecast (Gold Model—100% Cash on Sells)	−0.13%	20.0
9. The Dines Letter (Short-Term Model—100% Cash on Sells)	−0.15%	16.0
10. The Dines Letter (Short-Term Model—100% Short on Sells)	−0.16%	16.0
11. The Zweig Forecast (Gold Model—100% Short on Sells)	−0.17%	20.0
London P.M. Gold Fixing Price	−0.18%	
12. The Elliott Wave Theorist (Traders—Shorting Allowed)	−0.21%	16.5
13. Market Logic (Gold Model—100% Cash on Sells)	−0.24%	9.0
14. Market Logic (Gold Model—100% Short on Sells)	−0.32%	9.0

Appendix C-9: Gold Market Timing From 1/1/89 to 6/30/92
(Total Return)

Newsletter	Gain/Loss	Number of Switches
1. Professional Timing Service (Gold Futures Trading Advice—Shorting Allowed)	+41.2%	37.5
2. Futures Hotline Mutual Fund Timer (Intermediate-Term Model—100% Short on Sells)	+40.5%	57.0
3. Professional Timing Service (Gold Mutual Fund Allocation—100% Cash on Sells)	+36.6%	33.5
4. The Market Mania Newsletter (Gold Model—100% Short on Sells)	+25.5%	9.0
T-Bill Portfolio	+25.3%	
5. Bob Brinker's Marketimer (Gold Mutual Fund Allocation)	+25.2%	0.0
6. The Market Mania Newsletter (Gold Model—100% Cash on Sells)	+25.2%	8.0
7. The Addison Report (Gold Mutual Fund Allocation)	+22.8%	9.5
8. The Ruff Times (Short-Term Model—100% Cash on Sells)	+21.7%	13.0
9. The Elliott Wave Theorist (Investors—100% Cash on Sells)	+20.8%	1.0
10. The Elliott Wave Theorist (Traders—Shorting Allowed)	+20.3%	7.5
11. Your Window Into the Future (Gold Mutual Fund Signals—100% Cash on Sells)	+18.7%	4.0
12. Futures Hotline Mutual Fund Timer (Mutual Fund Model—100% Cash on Sells)	+18.2%	29.0
13. The Professional Tape Reader (Long-Term Model—100% Cash on Sells)	+15.4%	2.0
14. The Mutual Fund Strategist (Gold Model)	+13.2%	66.0
15. Timer Digest (Consensus of Top Timers—100% Cash on Sells)	+10.8%	42.0
16. Telephone Switch Newsletter (Gold/Cash Switch Plan—100% Cash on Sells)	+8.2%	8.0
17. The Professional Tape Reader (Long-Term Model—100% Short on Sells)	+8.0%	2.0
18. The Zweig Forecast (Gold Model—100% Cash on Sells)	+7.7%	13.0
19. Timer Digest (Consensus of Top Timers—100% Short on Sells)	+6.1%	42.0
20. The Professional Tape Reader (Short-Term Model—100% Cash on Sells)	+3.8%	43.0
21. The Zweig Forecast (Gold Model—100% Short on Sells)	+0.2%	13.0
22. Fund Exchange (Gold Mutual Fund Switching Model)	−3.6%	15.0
23. The Dines Letter (Short-Term Model—100% Cash on Sells)	−5.4%	10.0
24. The Professional Tape Reader (Short-Term Model—100% Short on Sells)	−7.4%	43.0
25. The Garside Forecast (Bell Ringer—100% Cash on Sells)	−11.1%	6.0
26. The Dines Letter (Short-Term Model—100% Short on Sells)	−11.8%	10.0
27. Market Logic (Gold Model—100% Cash on Sells)	−14.3%	6.0

Appendix C-9: Gold Market Timing From 1/1/89 to 6/30/92
(Risk-Adjusted)

Newsletter	Gain/Loss	Number of Switches
1. Professional Timing Service (Gold Futures Trading Advice— Shorting Allowed)	+0.14%	37.5
2. Professional Timing Service (Gold Mutual Fund Allocation— 100% Cash on Sells)	+0.11%	33.5
3. Futures Hotline Mutual Fund Timer (Intermediate-Term Model— 100% Short on Sells)	+0.09%	57.0
4. The Market Mania Newsletter (Gold Model—100% Short on Sells)	+0.02%	9.0
5. The Market Mania Newsletter (Gold Model—100% Cash on Sells)	0.00%	8.0
6. Bob Brinker's Marketimer (Gold Mutual Fund Allocation)	0.00%	0.0
7. The Ruff Times (Short-Term Model—100% Cash on Sells)	−0.03%	13.0
8. The Addison Report (Gold Mutual Fund Allocation)	−0.04%	9.5
9. The Elliott Wave Theorist (Traders—Shorting Allowed)	−0.04%	7.5
10. Futures Hotline Mutual Fund Timer (Mutual Fund Model—100% Cash on Sells)	−0.06%	29.0
11. Your Window Into the Future (Gold Mutual Fund Signals—100% Cash on Sells)	−0.06%	4.0
12. The Mutual Fund Strategist (Gold Model)	−0.08%	66.0
13. The Professional Tape Reader (Long-Term Model—100% Cash on Sells)	−0.09%	2.0
14. The Professional Tape Reader (Long-Term Model—100% Short on Sells)	−0.09%	2.0
15. Timer Digest (Consensus of Top Timers—100% Short on Sells)	−0.12%	42.0
16. Timer Digest (Consensus of Top Timers—100% Cash on Sells)	−0.13%	42.0
17. The Zweig Forecast (Gold Model—100% Cash on Sells)	−0.13%	13.0
18. The Elliott Wave Theorist (Investors—100% Cash on Sells)	−0.13%	1.0
19. Telephone Switch Newsletter (Gold/Cash Switch Plan—100% Cash on Sells)	−0.14%	8.0
20. The Zweig Forecast (Gold Model—100% Short on Sells)	−0.14%	13.0
21. The Professional Tape Reader (Short-Term Model—100% Short on Sells)	−0.17%	43.0
22. The Professional Tape Reader (Short-Term Model—100% Cash on Sells)	−0.19%	43.0
23. The Dines Letter (Short-Term Model—100% Short on Sells)	−0.19%	10.0
24. The Dines Letter (Short-Term Model—100% Cash on Sells)	−0.20%	10.0
25. The Garside Forecast (Bell Ringer—100% Short on Sells)	−0.24%	6.0
26. The Wall Street Generalist (Short-Term Gold Model—100% Cash on Sells)	−0.26%	0.0
27. The Wall Street Generalist (Short-Term Gold Model—100% Short on Sells)	−0.26%	0.0

Newsletter	Gain/Loss	Number of Switches
28. The Garside Forecast (Bell Ringer—100% Short on Sells)	−14.3%	6.0
29. The Wall Street Generalist (Short-Term Gold Model—100% Short on Sells)	−16.3%	0.0
30. The Wall Street Generalist (Short-Term Gold Model—100% Cash on Sells)	−16.3%	0.0
London P.M. Gold Fixing Price	−16.3%	
31. Market Logic (Gold Model—100% Short on Sells)	−31.5%	6.0

Newsletter	Gain/Loss	Number of Switches
London P.M. Gold Fixing Price	−0.26%	
28. Fund Exchange (Gold Mutual Fund Switching Model)	−0.27%	15.0
29. The Garside Forecast (Bell Ringer—100% Cash on Sells)	−0.28%	6.0
30. Market Logic (Gold Model—100% Cash on Sells)	−0.34%	6.0
31. Market Logic (Gold Model—100% Short on Sells)	−0.35%	6.0

Appendix C-10: Gold Market Timing From 1/1/91 to 6/30/92
(Total Return)

Newsletter	Gain/Loss	Number of Switches
1. Futures Hotline Mutual Fund Timer (Intermediate-Term Model—100% Short on Sells)	+17.7%	28.0
2. The Professional Tape Reader (Long-Term Model—100% Short on Sells)	+12.7%	0.0
3. Your Window Into the Future (Gold Mutual Fund Signals—100% Cash on Sells)	+8.0%	2.0
4. The Elliott Wave Theorist (Traders—Shorting Allowed)	+7.8%	1.0
5. Market Logic (Gold Model—100% Short on Sells)	+7.6%	2.0
T-Bill Portfolio	+7.5%	
6. The Professional Tape Reader (Long-Term Model—100% Cash on Sells)	+7.5%	0.0
7. Bob Brinker's Marketimer (Gold Mutual Fund Allocation)	+7.5%	0.0
8. The Market Mania Newsletter (Gold Model—100% Short on Sells)	+6.2%	5.0
9. The Mutual Fund Strategist (Gold Model)	+4.8%	27.0
10. Telephone Switch Newsletter (Gold/Cash Switch Plan—100% Cash on Sells)	+4.3%	2.0
11. The Elliott Wave Theorist (Investors—100% Cash on Sells)	+3.8%	1.0
12. Market Logic (Gold Model—100% Cash on Sells)	+3.6%	2.0
13. Switch Fund Timing (Gold Portfolio)	+2.9%	2.0
14. Professional Timing Service (Gold Futures Trading Advice—Shorting Allowed)	+2.5%	17.5
15. The Market Mania Newsletter (Gold Model—100% Cash on Sells)	+1.8%	4.0
16. Futures Hotline Mutual Fund Timer (Mutual Fund Model—100% Cash on Sells)	+1.5%	12.0
17. Professional Timing Service (Gold Mutual Fund Allocation—100% Cash on Sells)	+1.0%	14.5
18. The Addison Report (Gold Mutual Fund Allocation)	+0.4%	5.5
19. No-Load Mutual Fund Selections & Timing Newsletter (100% Short on Sells)	−0.4%	21.0
20. The Professional Tape Reader (Short-Term Model—100% Short on Sells)	−1.2%	12.0
21. Fund Exchange (Gold Mutual Fund Switching Model)	−1.4%	6.0
22. The Ruff Times (Short-Term Model—100% Cash on Sells)	−1.4%	9.0
23. No-Load Mutual Fund Selections & Timing Newsletter (100% Cash on Sells)	−2.0%	18.0
24. The Professional Tape Reader (Short-Term Model—100% Cash on Sells)	−2.3%	12.0
25. The Zweig Forecast (Gold Model—100% Cash on Sells)	−3.6%	6.0
26. The Zweig Forecast (Gold Model—100% Short on Sells)	−4.5%	6.0

Appendix C-10: Gold Market Timing From 1/1/91 to 6/30/92
(Risk-Adjusted)

Newsletter	Gain/Loss	Number of Switches
1. Futures Hotline Mutual Fund Timer (Intermediate-Term Model—100% Short on Sells)	+0.23%	28.0
2. The Professional Tape Reader (Long-Term Model—100% Short on Sells)	+0.13%	0.0
3. Your Window Into the Future (Gold Mutual Fund Signals—100% Cash on Sells)	+0.03%	2.0
4. The Elliott Wave Theorist (Traders—Shorting Allowed)	+0.02%	1.0
5. Market Logic (Gold Model—100% Short on Sells)	+0.01%	2.0
6. Professional Tape Reader (Long-Term Model—100% Cash on Sells)	0.00%	0.0
7. Bob Brinker's Marketimer (Gold Mutual Fund Allocation)	0.00%	0.0
8. The Market Mania Newsletter (Gold Model—100% Short on Sells)	−0.02%	5.0
9. The Mutual Fund Strategist (Gold Model)	−0.13%	27.0
10. Professional Timing Service (Gold Futures Trading Advice—Shorting Allowed)	−0.19%	17.5
11. Futures Hotline Mutual Fund Timer (Mutual Fund Model—100% Cash on Sells)	−0.19%	12.0
12. Telephone Switch Newsletter (Gold/Cash Switch Plan—100% Cash on Sells)	−0.19%	2.0
13. The Elliott Wave Theorist (Investors—100% Cash on Sells)	−0.21%	1.0
14. Market Logic (Gold Model—100% Cash on Sells)	−0.21%	2.0
15. No-Load Mutual Fund Selections & Timing Newsletter (100% Short on Sells)	−0.26%	21.0
16. The Professional Tape Reader (Short-Term Model—100% Short on Sells)	−0.26%	12.0
17. The Market Mania Newsletter (Gold Model—100% Cash on Sells)	−0.28%	4.0
18. Professional Timing Service (Gold Mutual Fund Allocation—100% Cash on Sells)	−0.29%	14.5
19. No-Load Mutual Fund Selections & Timing Newsletter (100% Cash on Sells)	−0.32%	18.0
20. The Zweig Forecast (Gold Model—100% Short on Sells)	−0.34%	6.0
21. Fund Exchange (Gold Mutual Fund Switching Model)	−0.34%	6.0
22. Switch Fund Timing (Gold Portfolio)	−0.35%	2.0
23. The Ruff Times (Short-Term Model—100% Cash on Sells)	−0.36%	9.0
24. The Professional Tape Reader (Short-Term Model—100% Cash on Sells)	−0.39%	12.0
25. The Garside Forecast (Bell Ringer—100% Short on Sells)	−0.39%	4.0
26. The Addison Report (Gold Mutual Fund Allocation)	−0.42%	5.5

Newsletter	Gain/Loss	Number of Switches
27. P. Q. Wall Forecast, Inc. (Gold Model—100% Short on Sells)	−7.6%	5.0
28. P. Q. Wall Forecast, Inc. (Gold Model—100% Cash on Sells)	−8.3%	5.0
29. The Garside Forecast (Bell Ringer—100% Short on Sells)	−10.3%	4.0
30. Timer Digest (Consensus of Top Timers—100% Cash on Sells)	−10.9%	25.0
31. The Garside Forecast (Bell Ringer—100% Cash on Sells)	−11.2%	4.0
32. The Wall Street Generalist (Short-Term Gold Model—100% Cash on Sells)	−12.2%	0.0
33. The Wall Street Generalist (Short-Term Gold Model—100% Short on Sells)	−12.2%	0.0
London P.M. Gold Fixing Price	−12.2%	
34. The Dines Letter (Short-Term Model—100% Cash on Sells)	−12.8%	3.0
35. The Dines Letter (Short-Term Model—100% Short on Sells)	−15.5%	3.0
36. Timer Digest (Consensus of Top Timers—100% Short on Sells)	−16.4%	25.0

Appendix C-10: Gold Market Timing From 1/1/91 to 6/30/92
(Risk-Adjusted) (continued)

Newsletter	Gain/Loss	Number of Switches
27. The Garside Forecast (Bell Ringer—100% Cash on Sells)	−0.42%	4.0
28. The Zweig Forecast (Gold Model—100% Cash on Sells)	−0.43%	6.0
London P.M. Gold Fixing Price	−0.46%	
29. The Wall Street Generalist (Short-Term Gold Model—100% Cash on Sells)	−0.46%	0.0
30. The Wall Street Generalist (Short-Term Gold Model—100% Short on Sells)	−0.46%	0.0
31. The Dines Letter (Short-Term Model—100% Cash on Sells)	−0.51%	3.0
32. P. Q. Wall Forecast, Inc. (Gold Model—100% Short on Sells)	−0.54%	5.0
33. P. Q. Wall Forecast, Inc. (Gold Model—100% Cash on Sells)	−0.54%	5.0
34. The Dines Letter (Short-Term Model—100% Short on Sells)	−0.59%	3.0
35. Timer Digest (Consensus of Top Timers—100% Cash on Sells)	−0.60%	25.0
36. Timer Digest (Consensus of Top Timers—100% Short on Sells)	−0.65%	25.0

12 YRS

Newsletter	Gain/Loss	Number of Switches
Shearson Lehman Treasury Index	+124.0%	
1. Systems and Forecasts (Long-Term Bond Model—100% Cash on Sells)	+105.4%	52.0
2. Fund Exchange (Bond Mutual Fund Timing Model—100% Cash on Sells)	+94.3%	38.0
3. The Garside Forecast (Bell Ringer—100% Cash on Sells)	+82.0%	12.0
4. The Elliott Wave Theorist (Investors—100% Cash on Sells)	+76.4%	10.5
5. The Marketarian Letter (Bond Model)	+75.7%	35.6
T-Bill Portfolio	+61.7%	
6. Systems and Forecasts (Long-Term Bond Model—100% Short on Sells)	+31.0%	52.0
7. The Elliott Wave Theorist (Traders—May Go Short on Sells)	−16.1%	46.0
8. The Garside Forecast (Bell Ringer—100% Short on Sells)	−32.6%	12.0

TOP BONDS   125.0
TOP STOCKS   665.2

Appendix C-11: Bond Market Timing From 1/1/85 to 6/30/92 (Risk-Adjusted)

Newsletter	Gain/Loss	Number of Switches
Shearson Lehman Treasury Index	+0.24%	
1. Systems and Forecasts (Long-Term Bond Model—100% Cash on Sells)	+0.21%	52.0
2. The Elliott Wave Theorist (Investors—100% Cash on Sells)	+0.21%	10.5
3. The Garside Forecast (Bell Ringer—100% Cash on Sells)	+0.17%	12.0
4. Fund Exchange (Bond Mutual Fund Timing Model—100% Cash on Sells)	+0.16%	38.0
5. The Marketarian Letter (Bond Model)	+0.13%	35.6
6. The Elliott Wave Theorist (Traders—May Go Short on Sells)	−0.01%	46.0
7. Systems and Forecasts (Long-Term Bond Model—100% Short on Sells)	−0.13%	52.0
8. The Garside Forecast (Bell Ringer—100% Short on Sells)	−0.46%	12.0

Appendix C-12: Bond Market Timing From 1/1/87 to 6/30/92 (Total Return)

Newsletter	Gain/Loss	Number of Switches
Shearson Lehman Treasury Index	+59.7%	
1. The Garside Forecast (Bell Ringer—100% Cash on Sells)	+59.5%	12.0
2. Systems and Forecasts (Long-Term Bond Model—100% Cash on Sells)	+57.8%	38.0
3. Fund Exchange (Bond Mutual Fund Timing Model—100% Cash on Sells)	+56.2%	24.0
4. The Marketarian Letter (Bond Model)	+49.5%	31.3
5. The Elliott Wave Theorist (Investors—100% Cash on Sells)	+43.6%	5.0
T-Bill Portfolio	+41.7%	
6. Systems and Forecasts (Long-Term Bond Model—100% Short on Sells)	+15.4%	38.0
7. The Garside Forecast (Bell Ringer—100% Short on Sells)	+1.5%	12.0
8. The Elliott Wave Theorist (Traders—May Go Short on Sells)	−11.3%	32.0

Appendix C-12: Bond Market Timing From 1/1/87 to 6/30/92 (Risk-Adjusted)

Newsletter	Gain/Loss	Number of Switches
1. The Garside Forecast (Bell Ringer—100% Cash on Sells)	+0.20%	12.0
2. Systems and Forecasts (Long-Term Bond Model—100% Cash on Sells)	+0.16%	38.0
3. Fund Exchange (Bond Mutual Fund Timing Model—100% Cash on Sells)	+0.15%	24.0
Shearson Lehman Treasury Index	+0.14%	
4. The Marketarian Letter (Bond Model)	+0.10%	31.3
5. The Elliott Wave Theorist (Investors—100% Cash on Sells)	+0.08%	5.0
6. The Elliott Wave Theorist (Traders—May Go Short on Sells)	0.00%	32.0
7. Systems and Forecasts (Long-Term Bond Model—100% Short on Sells)	−0.20%	38.0
8. The Garside Forecast (Bell Ringer—100% Short on Sells)	−0.27%	12.0

Newsletter	Gain/Loss	Number of Switches
Shearson Lehman Treasury Index	+46.3%	
1. The Wall Street Generalist (Short-Term Bond Model—100% Cash on Sells)	+42.4%	5.0
2. Systems and Forecasts (Long-Term Bond Model—100% Cash on Sells)	+41.8%	25.0
3. The Addison Report (Bond Mutual Fund Allocation)	+41.6%	12.8
4. Fund Exchange (Bond Mutual Fund Timing Model—100% Cash on Sells)	+38.4%	13.0
5. Timer Digest (Consensus of Top Timers—100% Cash on Sells)	+38.2%	35.0
6. The Professional Tape Reader (Long-Term Model—100% Cash on Sells)	+38.0%	6.0
7. The Mutual Fund Strategist (Bond Model—100% Cash on Sells)	+38.0%	19.0
8. The Market Mania Newsletter (100% Cash on Sells)	+36.4%	11.0
9. The Dines Letter (Bond Model—100% Cash on Sells)	+36.3%	2.0
10. The Big Picture ("Master Key For Bonds"—100% Cash on Sells)	+35.7%	9.0
11. The Professional Tape Reader (Short-Term Model—100% Cash on Sells)	+34.9%	42.0
12. Futures Hotline Mutual Fund Timer (Long-Term Asset Allocation Model)	+34.8%	2.0
13. The Marketarian Letter (Bond Model)	+34.7%	20.8
14. Professional Timing Service ("Supply/Demand" Formula—100% Cash on Sells)	+34.6%	7.0
15. Futures Hotline Mutual Fund Timer (Asset Allocation Model)	+33.3%	29.5
16. The Garside Forecast (Bell Ringer—100% Cash on Sells)	+30.8%	6.0
17. The Elliott Wave Theorist (Investors—100% Cash on Sells)	+26.9%	4.0
18. The Wall Street Generalist (Short-Term Bond Model—100% Short on Sells)	+25.5%	5.0
T-Bill Portfolio	+25.3%	
19. The Big Picture ("Master Key For Bonds"—Shorting Allowed)	+16.2%	12.0
20. Systems and Forecasts (Long-Term Bond Model—100% Short on Sells)	+15.7%	25.0
21. Timer Digest (Consensus of Top Timers—100% Short on Sells)	+12.3%	35.0
22. The Dines Letter (Bond Model—100% Short on Sells)	+12.0%	2.0
23. The Professional Tape Reader (Long-Term Model—100% Short on Sells)	+10.7%	6.0
24. The Market Mania Newsletter (100% Short on Sells)	+6.5%	11.0
25. Professional Timing Service ("Supply/Demand" Formula—Shorting Allowed)	+0.5%	8.0
26. The Professional Tape Reader (Short-Term Model—100% Short on Sells)	−0.1%	42.0

Appendix C-13: Bond Market Timing From 1/1/89 to 6/30/92
(Risk-Adjusted)

Newsletter	Gain/Loss	Number of Switches
1. The Addison Report (Bond Mutual Fund Allocation)	+0.30%	12.8
Shearson Lehman Treasury Index	+0.30%	
2. Systems and Forecasts (Long-Term Bond Model—100% Cash on Sells)	+0.29%	25.0
3. The Wall Street Generalist (Short-Term Bond Model—100% Cash on Sells)	+0.28%	5.0
4. Fund Exchange (Bond Mutual Fund Timing Model—100% Cash on Sells)	+0.23%	13.0
5. The Market Mania Newsletter (100% Cash on Sells)	+0.22%	11.0
6. The Mutual Fund Strategist (Bond Model—100% Cash on Sells)	+0.21%	19.0
7. The Professional Tape Reader (Long-Term Model—100% Cash on Sells)	+0.21%	6.0
8. Timer Digest (Consensus of Top Timers—100% Cash on Sells)	+0.21%	35.0
9. The Marketarian Letter (Bond Model)	+0.21%	20.8
10. Futures Hotline Mutual Fund Timer (Long-Term Asset Allocation Model)	+0.21%	2.0
11. Futures Hotline Mutual Fund Timer (Asset Allocation Model)	+0.19%	29.5
12. The Professional Tape Reader (Short-Term Model—100% Cash on Sells)	+0.19%	42.0
13. Professional Timing Service ("Supply/Demand" Formula—100% Cash on Sells)	+0.19%	7.0
14. The Big Picture ("Master Key For Bonds"—100% Cash on Sells)	+0.18%	9.0
15. The Dines Letter (Bond Model—100% Cash on Sells)	+0.18%	2.0
16. The Garside Forecast (Bell Ringer—100% Cash on Sells)	+0.16%	6.0
17. The Elliott Wave Theorist (Investors—100% Cash on Sells)	+0.11%	4.0
18. The Wall Street Generalist (Short-Term Bond Model—100% Short on Sells)	+0.01%	5.0
19. The Big Picture ("Master Key For Bonds"—Shorting Allowed)	−0.13%	12.0
20. Systems and Forecasts (Long-Term Bond Model—100% Short on Sells)	−0.13%	25.0
21. The Dines Letter (Bond Model—100% Short on Sells)	−0.16%	2.0
22. Timer Digest (Consensus of Top Timers—100% Short on Sells)	−0.17%	35.0
23. The Professional Tape Reader (Long-Term Model—100% Short on Sells)	−0.18%	6.0
24. The Market Mania Newsletter (100% Short on Sells)	−0.24%	11.0
25. Professional Timing Service ("Supply/Demand" Formula—Shorting Allowed)	−0.33%	8.0
26. The Professional Tape Reader (Short-Term Model—100% Short on Sells)	−0.42%	42.0

Newsletter	Gain/Loss	Number of Switches
27. Futures Hotline Mutual Fund Timer (Intermediate-Term Model—100% Short on Sells)	−4.8%	70.0
28. The Elliott Wave Theorist (Traders—May Go Short on Sells)	−13.6%	19.0
29. The Garside Forecast (Bell Ringer—100% Short on Sells)	−17.5%	6.0

Newsletter	Gain/Loss	Number of Switches
27. Futures Hotline Mutual Fund Timer (Intermediate-Term Model—100% Short on Sells)	−0.50%	70.0
28. The Garside Forecast (Bell Ringer—100% Short on Sells)	−0.58%	6.0
29. The Elliott Wave Theorist (Traders—May Go Short on Sells)	−0.91%	19.0

Appendix C-14: Bond Market Timing From 1/1/91 to 6/30/92
(Total Return)

Newsletter	Gain/Loss	Number of Switches
1. The Wall Street Generalist (Short-Term Bond Model—100% Short on Sells)	+19.5%	2.0
2. The Wall Street Generalist (Short-Term Bond Model—100% Cash on Sells)	+19.2%	2.0
3. Bob Brinker's Marketimer (Bond Model)	+17.8%	0.0
Shearson Lehman Treasury Index	+17.8%	
4. Fund Exchange (Bond Mutual Fund Timing Model—100% Cash on Sells)	+16.7%	4.0
5. Timer Digest (Consensus of Top Timers—100% Cash on Sells)	+16.3%	14.0
6. The Dines Letter (Bond Model—100% Cash on Sells)	+15.9%	1.0
7. Investors Intelligence (Bond Portfolio)	+15.7%	0.9
8. The Big Picture ("Master Key For Bonds"—100% Cash on Sells)	+15.5%	7.0
9. Systems and Forecasts (Long-Term Bond Model—100% Cash on Sells)	+15.3%	14.0
10. The Professional Tape Reader (Short-Term Model—100% Cash on Sells)	+14.9%	15.0
11. The Addison Report (Bond Mutual Fund Allocation)	+14.7%	4.8
12. The Marketarian Letter (Bond Model)	+14.1%	7.0
13. No-Load Mutual Fund Selections & Timing Newsletter (100% Cash on Sells)	+13.8%	13.0
14. Futures Hotline Mutual Fund Timer (Asset Allocation Model)	+13.5%	10.0
15. The Mutual Fund Strategist (Bond Model—100% Cash on Sells)	+13.3%	8.0
16. Futures Hotline Mutual Fund Timer (Long-Term Asset Allocation Model)	+12.6%	1.0
17. The Dines Letter (Bond Model—100% Short on Sells)	+12.6%	1.0
18. Global Fund Timer (Zero-Bond Fund Portfolio)	+12.3%	8.0
19. The Professional Tape Reader (Long-Term Model—100% Cash on Sells)	+12.1%	4.0
20. P. Q. Wall Forecast, Inc. (Bond Model—100% Cash on Sells)	+11.8%	5.0
21. Timer Digest (Consensus of Top Timers—100% Short on Sells)	+11.7%	14.0
22. The Market Mania Newsletter (100% Cash on Sells)	+11.5%	4.0
23. Systems and Forecasts (Long-Term Bond Model—100% Short on Sells)	+10.4%	14.0
24. No-Load Mutual Fund Selections & Timing Newsletter (100% Short on Sells)	+10.0%	19.0
25. The Big Picture ("Master Key For Bonds"—Shorting Allowed)	+9.3%	10.0
26. Professional Timing Service ("Supply/Demand" Formula—100% Cash on Sells)	+8.1%	4.0
27. The Garside Forecast (Bell Ringer—100% Cash on Sells)	+7.8%	5.0
28. Income & Safety	+7.6%	1.0

Appendix C-14: Bond Market Timing From 1/1/91 to 6/30/92
(Risk-Adjusted)

Newsletter	Gain/Loss	Number of Switches
1. The Addison Report (Bond Mutual Fund Allocation)	+0.58%	4.8
2. The Wall Street Generalist (Short-Term Bond Model—100% Short on Sells)	+0.55%	2.0
3. The Wall Street Generalist (Short-Term Bond Model—100% Cash on Sells)	+0.54%	2.0
4. Futures Hotline Mutual Fund Timer (Long-Term Asset Allocation Model)	+0.49%	1.0
Shearson Lehman Treasury Index	+0.47%	
5. Bob Brinker's Marketimer (Bond Model)	+0.47%	0.0
6. The Marketarian Letter (Bond Model)	+0.46%	7.0
7. No-Load Mutual Fund Selections & Timing Newsletter (100% Cash on Sells)	+0.45%	13.0
8. The Big Picture ("Master Key For Bonds"—100% Cash on Sells)	+0.45%	7.0
9. Futures Hotline Mutual Fund Timer (Asset Allocation Model)	+0.43%	10.0
10. Timer Digest (Consensus of Top Timers—100% Cash on Sells)	+0.43%	14.0
11. Fund Exchange (Bond Mutual Fund Timing Model—100% Cash on Sells)	+0.42%	4.0
12. The Professional Tape Reader (Short-Term Model—100% Cash on Sells)	+0.40%	15.0
13. Investors Intelligence (Bond Portfolio)	+0.40%	0.9
14. The Market Mania Newsletter (100% Cash on Sells)	+0.37%	4.0
15. The Dines Letter (Bond Model—100% Cash on Sells)	+0.37%	1.0
16. Systems and Forecasts (Long-Term Bond Model—100% Cash on Sells)	+0.37%	14.0
17. Global Fund Timer (Zero-Bond Fund Portfolio)	+0.31%	8.0
18. P. Q. Wall Forecast, Inc. (Bond Model—100% Cash on Sells)	+0.31%	5.0
19. The Mutual Fund Strategist (Bond Model—100% Cash on Sells)	+0.27%	8.0
20. The Professional Tape Reader (Long-Term Model—100% Cash on Sells)	+0.21%	4.0
21. The Dines Letter (Bond Model—100% Short on Sells)	+0.20%	1.0
22. Timer Digest (Consensus of Top Timers—100% Short on Sells)	+0.18%	14.0
23. No-Load Mutual Fund Selections & Timing Newsletter (100% Short on Sells)	+0.15%	19.0
24. Systems and Forecasts (Long-Term Bond Model—100% Short on Sells)	+0.12%	14.0
25. The Big Picture ("Master Key For Bonds"—Shorting Allowed)	+0.09%	10.0
26. The Garside Forecast (Bell Ringer—100% Cash on Sells)	+0.07%	5.0
27. Professional Timing Service ("Supply/Demand" Formula—100% Cash on Sells)	+0.06%	4.0
28. Income & Safety	+0.02%	1.0

Appendix C-14: Bond Market Timing From 1/1/91 to 6/30/92
(Total Return) (continued)

Newsletter	Gain/Loss	Number of Switches
T-Bill Portfolio	+7.5%	
29. The Elliott Wave Theorist (Investors—100% Cash on Sells)	+7.5%	0.0
30. The Professional Tape Reader (Short-Term Model—100% Short on Sells)	+4.4%	15.0
31. The Professional Tape Reader (Long-Term Model—100% Short on Sells)	+2.9%	4.0
32. P. Q. Wall Forecast, Inc. (Bond Model—100% Short on Sells)	+0.9%	7.0
33. Futures Hotline Mutual Fund Timer (Intermediate-Term Model—100% Short on Sells)	−1.4%	35.0
34. The Market Mania Newsletter (100% Short on Sells)	−4.6%	4.0
35. Professional Timing Service ("Supply/Demand" Formula—Shorting Allowed)	−5.3%	5.0
36. The Elliott Wave Theorist (Traders—May Go Short on Sells)	−13.7%	4.0
37. The Garside Forecast (Bell Ringer—100% Short on Sells)	−15.0%	5.0

Newsletter	Gain/Loss	Number of Switches
29. The Elliott Wave Theorist (Investors—100% Cash on Sells)	0.00%	0.0
30. The Professional Tape Reader (Short-Term Model—100% Short on Sells)	−0.12%	15.0
31. The Professional Tape Reader (Long-Term Model—100% Short on Sells)	−0.16%	4.0
32. P. Q. Wall Forecast, Inc. (Bond Model—100% Short on Sells)	−0.23%	7.0
33. Futures Hotline Mutual Fund Timer (Intermediate-Term Model—100% Short on Sells)	−0.42%	35.0
34. The Market Mania Newsletter (100% Short on Sells)	−0.44%	4.0
35. Professional Timing Service ("Supply/Demand" Formula—Shorting Allowed)	−0.50%	5.0
36. The Garside Forecast (Bell Ringer—100% Short on Sells)	−0.97%	5.0
37. The Elliott Wave Theorist (Traders—May Go Short on Sells)	−1.74%	4.0

APPENDIX D

Newsletter Directory

This appendix lists the addresses and subscription rates for the investment newsletters that have been scrutinized in this book. If we have the information, we also list the name of the newsletter's editor, its phone number, whether or not the newsletter supplements its issues with a telephone hotline, and whether or not the newsletter also manages clients' money.

As you will see, most letters have relatively inexpensive trial offers that allow you to become exposed to them at very little cost. As discussed earlier in this book, we recommend that, in the final stages of choosing among various newsletters, you take out a trial subscription to them. Only in that way can you be sure that you are comfortable with the investment philosophy and clarity provided in them. Look to see if your chosen newsletter makes sense to you. Do you find yourself agreeing with the arguments and conclusions drawn? If not, you are unlikely to feel comfortable following the newsletter—no matter how good its past performance. Do you find that the newsletter has a habit of not mentioning past recommendations that have turned out to be losers? A lack of honesty does not mean that all of that adviser's recommendations are losers, but this trait surely is worth keeping in mind as you contemplate subscribing to the newsletter.

Every effort was made to insure that the addresses and rates were current as of October 1992, but we cannot guarantee that these rates will be the ones you can get. Some advertise more inexpensive offers, especially in the pages of the financial press (especially in *Barron's* and *Investor's Business Daily*), and in many instances a little checking is all you will need to do to discover even better offers than those listed here.

As a rule, few public libraries subscribe to many investment newsletters. However, some of the larger ones do subscribe to several, so a visit might be worthwhile. The newsletters most often subscribed to by libraries are Standard & Poor's *Outlook, Dow Theory Forecasts, United & Babson Investment Report,* and those published by Value Line, Inc.

A final note concerning telephone hotlines. The following directory indicates whether or not each newsletter gives its regular subscribers access to a telephone hotline at no additional subscription cost. This does not mean that all recommendations made on these hotlines were taken into account by the HFD in measuring these newsletters' performance, however—though in most cases it does. As discussed at greater length in the chapter on the HFD's methodology earlier in this *Guide*, the HFD does not take a newsletter's hotline into account if its editor updates it more than once a day per portfolio. To find out for sure whether or not the HFD has been tracking the recommendations made over a particular hotline, consult the write-up that accompanies that newsletter's entry earlier in this *Guide*.

Name	Yearly Price	6-Month Price	Trial Subscription Price	Hot Line	Manages Money
The Addison Report P.O. Box 402 Franklin, MA 02038 (Andrew L. Addison) 508-528-8678	$175.00	$ 95.00	$ 35.00/3 months	X	X
Adrian Day's Investment Analyst Agora, Inc. 824 E. Baltimore St. Baltimore, MD 21202 (Adrian Day) 800-433-1528	$ 49.00			X	X
AgBiotech Stock Letter P.O. Box 40460 Berkeley, CA 94704 (Jim McCamant) 510-843-1842	$165.00				
BI Research P.O. Box 133 Redding, CT 06875 (Tom Bishop)	$ 80.00				
Better Investing National Association of Investors Corporation 1515 E. Eleven Mile Rd. Royal Oak, MI 48067 (Donald Danko) 313-543-0612	$ 17.00		$ 2.00/1 issue		
The Big Picture KCI Communications, Inc. 1101 King St. Suite 400 Alexandria, VA 22314 2980 (Stephen Leeb and Walter Pierce) 703-548-2400	$127.00			X	X
The Blue Chip Correlator P.O. Box 3576 Newport Beach, CA 92659 (Steven G. Check) 714-641-3579	$179.00			X	X
Blue Chip Values 680 N. Lake Shore Dr. Tower Suite 2038 Chicago, IL 60611 (Gerald Perritt) 312-649-6940	$195.00				

Name	Yearly Price	6-Month Price	Trial Subscription Price	Hot Line	Manages Money
Bob Brinker's Marketimer P.O. Box 7005 Princeton, NJ 08543 (Robert Brinker) 908-359-8838	$185.00				X
Bob Nurock's Advisory P.O. Box 988 Paoli, PA 19301 (Robert Nurock) 800-227-8883	$247.00	$ 97.00		X	
The Cabot Market Letter P.O. Box 3044 Salem, MA 01970 (Carlton Lutts) 508-745-5532	$250.00	$145.00		X	X
Cabot's Mutual Fund Navigator P.O. Box 3044 Salem, MA 01970 (Timothy W. Lutts) 508-745-5532	$ 86.00			X	X
California Technology Stock Letter Murenove, Inc. P.O. Box 308 Half Moon Bay, CA 94019 (Lissa Morgenthaler and Michael Murphy) 415-726-8495	$270.00		$ 49.00/6 issues	X	X
The Chartist P.O. Box 758 Seal Beach, CA 90740 (Dan Sullivan) 310-596-2385	$150.00	$ 80.00		X	X
The Chartist Mutual Fund Timer P.O. Box 758 Seal Beach, CA 90740 (Dan Sullivan) 310-596-2385	$100.00	$ 55.00		X	X
The Clean Yield Clean Yield Publications, Ltd. P.O. Box 1880 Greensboro Bend, VT 05842 (Rian Fried) 802-533-7178	$ 85.00		$ 3.50/1 issue		X

Name	Yearly Price	6-Month Price	Trial Subscription Price	Hot Line	Manages Money
The Contrarian's View 132 Moreland St. Worcester, MA 01609 (Nick Chase) 508-757-2881	$ 39.00			X	
Crawford Perspectives 1456 Second Ave Suite 145 New York, NY 10021 (Arch Crawford) 212-744-6973	$250.00		$ 85.00/3 issues		
Czeschin's Mutual Fund Outlook & Recommendations P.O. Box 1423 Baltimore, MD 21203-1423 (Robert Czeschin) 410-558-1699	$147.00			X	
Dessauer's Journal P.O. Box 1718 Orleans, MA 02653 (John Dessauer and Susanna Graham) 508-255-1651	$195.00	$105.00	$ 35.00/2 months	X	X
The Dines Letter P.O. Box 22 Belvedere, CA 94920 (James Dines)	$195.00	$115.00			X
Donoghue's Moneyletter 290 Elliot St. Box 91004 Ashland, MA 01721-9104 (Ann Needle) 508-881-2800	$127.00	$ 49.00		X	X
Dow Theory Forecasts 7412 Calumet Ave. Hammond, IN 46324-2692 (Charles Carlson) 219-931-6480	$233.00				
Dow Theory Letters P.O. Box 1759 La Jolla, CA 92038 (Richard Russell) 619-454-0481	$250.00	$150.00			

Name	Yearly Price	6-Month Price	Trial Subscription Price	Hot Line	Manages Money
The Elliott Wave Theorist P.O. Box 1618 Gainesville, GA 30503 (Robert Prechter) 404-536-0309	$233.00		$ 55.00/2 months		
Emerging & Special Situations Standard & Poor's Corp. 25 Broadway New York, NY 10004 (Robert Natale) 800-852-1641	$210.00		$ 45.00/3 months	X	
Equities Special Situations P.O. Box 1708 Riverton, NJ 08077 (Robert J. Flaherty) 800-237-8400 Ext. 61	$150.00				
Equity Fund Outlook P.O. Box 1040 Boston, MA 02117 (Thurman Smith) 617-397-6844	$ 95.00				X
F.X.C. Investors Corp. 62-19 Cooper Ave. Glendale, Queens, NY 11385 (Francis X. Curzio) 800-392-0992	$290.00		$ 48.00/3 months		X
Fast Track Funds 5536 Temple City Blvd. Temple City, CA 91780 (Eli Pereira)	$107.00			X	
Fidelity Insight Mutual Fund Investors Association P.O. Box 9135 Wellesley Hills, MA 02181-9135 (Eric Kobren) 617-235-4432	$ 99.00		$ 39.00/4 months	X	X
Fidelity Monitor P.O. Box 1294 Rocklin, CA 95677-7294 (Jack Bowers) 800-397-3094	$ 96.00		$ 48.00/5 months	X	

Name	Yearly Price	6-Month Price	Trial Subscription Price	Hot Line	Manages Money
Financial World P.O. Box 10750 Des Moines, IA 50340 800-666-6639	$ 37.50				
Ford Investment Review 11722 Sorrento Valley Rd. Suite I San Diego, CA 92121 (Ford Investor Services) 800-842-0207	$120.00				
Fund Exchange 1200 Westlake Ave. N. Suite 700 Seattle, WA 98109-3530 (Paul Merriman) 800-423-4893	$ 99.00	$ 49.00		X	X
Fund Kinetics 17525 NE 40th St. Suite E123 Redmond, WA 98052 (Byron B. McCann) 800-634-6790	$175.00		$ 45.00 6 weeks	X	
Fundline P.O. Box 663 Woodland Hills, CA 91365 (David Menashe) 818-346-5637	$127.00		$ 47.00/4 months	X	X
Futures Hotline Mutual Fund Timer P.O. Box 6275 Jacksonville, FL 32236 (Craig Corcoran) 904-693-0355	$295.00			X	
The Garside Forecast P.O. Box 1812 Santa Ana, CA 92702 (Ben Garside) 714-259-1670	$125.00	$ 75.00		X	
Global Fund Timer P.O. Box 77330 Baton Rouge, LA 70879 (Greg Cook) 800-256-3136	$ 96.00			X	

Name	Yearly Price	6-Month Price	Trial Subscription Price	Hot Line	Manages Money
The Granville Market Letter P.O. Drawer 413006 Kansas City, MO 64141 (Joe Granville) 816-474-5353	$250.00	$150.00	$ 85.00/3 months		
Graphic Fund Forecaster 6 Pioneer Circle P.O. Box 673 Andover, MA 01810 (Fred W. Hohn) 508-470-3511	$145.00		$ 30.00 2 months	X	X
Growth Fund Guide Growth Fund Research Building Box 6600 Rapid City, SD 57709 (Walter Rouleau) 605-341-1971	$ 89.00	$ 54.00		X	
Growth Stock Outlook P.O. Box 15381 Chevy Chase, MD 20825 (Charles Allmon) 301-654-5205	$195.00		$ 75.00/3 months	X	X
Harmonic Research 650 Fifth Ave. New York, NY 10019 (Mason S. Sexton) 212-484-2065	$720.00			X	X
Harry Browne's Special Reports P.O. Box 5586 Austin, TX 78763 (Harry Browne) 800-531-5142	$225.00		$ 5.00/1 issue	X	
The Holt Advisory P.O. Box 2923 West Palm Beach, FL 33409 (Thomas J. Holt and Frank Ventura) 800-289-9222	$185.00				X
The Hulbert Financial Digest 316 Commerce St. Alexandria, VA 22314 (Mark Hulbert) 703-683-5905	$135.00		$ 37.50/5 months		

Name	Yearly Price	6-Month Price	Trial Subscription Price	Hot Line	Manages Money
Hussman Econometrics P.O. Box 3199 Farmington Hills, MI 48333 (John Hussman) 800-487-7626	$195.00		$ 99.00/6 months	X	
Income & Safety The Institute for Econometric Research 3471 N. Federal Hwy. Ft. Lauderdale, FL 33306 (Norman Fosback and Glen King Parker) 800-327-6720	$ 49.00			X	
Individual Investor Special Situations Report 38 E. 29th St. 4th Floor New York, NY 10016 (Gordon Anderson) 212-689-2777	$165.00		$ 12.50/1 issue		
The Insiders The Institute for Econometric Research 3471 N. Federal Hwy. Ft. Lauderdale, FL 33306 (Norman Fosback and Glen King Parker) 800-327-6720	$ 49.00			X	
The International Harry Schultz Letter P.O. Box 622 FERC CH-1001, Lausanne Switzerland (Harry Schultz) 32 16 533684	$275.00				
InvesTech Market Analyst 2472 Birch Glen Whitefish, MT 59937-3349 (James B. Stack) 406-862-7777	$175.00		$ 99.00/7 months	X	
InvesTech Mutual Fund Advisor 2472 Birch Glen Whitefish, MT 59937-3349 (James B. Stack) 406-862-7777	$175.00		$ 99.00/7 months	X	

Name	Yearly Price	6-Month Price	Trial Subscription Price	Hot Line	Manages Money
Investment Horizons 680 N. Lake Shore Dr. Tower Suite 2038 Chicago, IL 60611 (Gerald Perritt) 800-326-6941	$195.00				X
Investment Quality Trends 7440 Girard Ave. Suite 4 La Jolla, CA 92037 (Geraldine Weiss) 619-459-3818	$275.00	$175.00			
The Investment Reporter 133 Richmond St. W. #700 Toronto, Ontario Canada, M5H 3M8 (Canadian Business Service) 416-869-1177	$257.00			X	
The Investor's Guide to Closed-End Funds Thomas J. Herzfeld Advisors, Inc. P.O. Box 161465 Miami, FL 33116 (Thomas J. Herzfeld) 305-271-1900	$325.00		$ 60.00/2 months		X
Investors Intelligence Chartcraft, Inc. P.O. Box 2046 30 Church St. New Rochelle, NY 10801 (Michael Burke) 914-632-0422	$175.00		$ 30.00/2 months	X	
Kinsman's Telephone Growth & Income Service P.O. Box 2107 Sonoma, CA 95476-2107 (Robert Kinsman) 707-935-6504	$145.00			X	X
L/G No-Load Fund Analyst 300 Montgomery St. Suite 621 San Francisco, CA 94104 (Ken Gregory and Craig Litman) 415-989-8513	$169.00				X

Name	Yearly Price	6-Month Price	Trial Subscription Price	Hot Line	Manages Money
LaLoggia's Special Situation Report P.O. Box 167 Rochester, NY 14601 (Charles LaLoggia) 716-232-1240	$230.00	$125.00			
MPT Fund Review P.O. Box 5695 Incline Village, NV 89450 (Bruno Terkaly and Treanna Allbaugh) 702-831-1396	$ 95.00		$ 39.00/2 month		X
MPT Review P.O. Box 5695 Incline Village, NV 89450 (Louis Navellier) 702-831-1396	$245.00		$ 59.00/2 months	X	X
Margo's Market Monitor P.O. Box 642 Lexington, MA 02173 (Bill Doane) 617-861-0302	$125.00		$ 25.00/4 issues		X
Market Logic The Institute for Econometric Research 3471 N. Federal Hwy. Ft. Lauderdale, FL 33306 (Norman Fosback and Glen King Parker) 800-327-6720	$ 95.00			X	
The Market Mania Newsletter P.O. Box 1234 Pacifica, CA 94044 (Glenn Cutler) 415-952-8853	$119.00			X	
The Marketarian Letter P.O. Box 1283 Grand Island, NE 68802 (Gerald Theisen and Jeff Helleberg) 800-658-4325	$225.00	$125.00		X	X
Medical Technology Stock Letter P.O. Box 40460 Berkeley, CA 94704 (Jim McCamant) 510-843-1857	$320.00		$ 65.00/3 months	X	

Name	Yearly Price	6-Month Price	Trial Subscription Price	Hot Line	Manages Money
Morningstar Mutual Funds 53 West Jackson Blvd. Suite 460 Chicago, IL 60604 (John Rekenthaler) 800-876-5005	$395.00				
Mutual Fund Forecaster The Institute for Econometric Research 3471 N. Federal Hwy. Ft. Lauderdale, FL 33306 (Norman Fosback and Glen King Parker) 800-327-6720	$ 49.00			X	
Mutual Fund Investing 7811 Montrose Rd. Potomac, MD 20854 (Jay Schabacker) 800-777-5005	$177.00			X	X
The Mutual Fund Letter 680 N. Lake Shore Dr. Tower Suite 2038 Chicago, IL 60611 (Gerald Perritt) 800-326-6941	$ 99.00				X
The Mutual Fund Strategist P.O. Box 446 Burlington, VT 05402 (Charlie Hooper) 802-658-3513	$149.00	$ 94.00	$ 52.00/3 months	X	X
Mutual Fund Technical Trader P.O. Box 4560 Burlington, VT 05406-4560 (Stephen Parker) 802-658-5500	$ 48.00			X	X
New Issues The Institute for Econometric Research 3471 N. Federal Hwy. Ft. Lauderdale, FL 33306 (Norman Fosback and Glen King Parker) 800-327-6720	$ 95.00			X	
The Ney Report P.O. Box 92223 Pasadena, CA 91109 (Richard Ney) 818-441-2222	$295.00	$195.00		X	X

Name	Yearly Price	6-Month Price	Trial Subscription Price	Hot Line	Manages Money
**NoLoad Fund*X 235 Montgomery St. Suite 662 San Francisco, CA 94104 (Burton Berry and Janet Brown) 415-986-7979	$114.00		$ 27.00/3 months		X
The No-Load Fund Investor P.O. Box 283 Hastings-on-Hudson, NY 10706 (Sheldon Jacobs) 914-693-7420	$105.00				X
No-Load Mutual Fund Selections & Timing Newsletter 1120 Empire Central Pl. Suite 315 Dallas, TX 75247 (Stephen L. McKee) 800-800-6563	$180.00		$ 50.00/3 months	X	X
No-Load Portfolios 8635 W. Sahara Suite 420 The Lakes, NV 89117 (William Corney and Leonard Goodall)	$ 69.00			X	
OTC Insight Insight Capital Management, Inc. P.O. Box 127 Moraga, CA 94556 (James Collins) 800-955-9566	$195.00		$ 39.00/2 months	X	X
The Oberweis Report 841 N. Lake Aurora, IL 60506 (James D. Oberweis) 708-801-4766	$ 99.00		$249.00/1 year by fax	X	X
On Markets 31 Melkhout Crescent Hout Bay 7800 South Africa (Tony Henfrey) +27 21 7904259	$185.00	$100.00	$ 50.00/3 months		
The Option Advisor Box 46709 Cincinnati, OH 45246 (Bernard Schaeffer and Robert Bergen) 800-327-8833	$ 99.00	$ 66.00		X	

Name	Yearly Price	6-Month Price	Trial Subscription Price	Hot Line	Manages Money
The Outlook Standard & Poor's Corp. 25 Broadway New York, NY 10004 (Arnold Kaufman) 800-852-1641	$280.00		$ 29.95/12 issues		
Overpriced Stock Service Murenove, Inc. P.O. Box 308 Half Moon Bay, CA 94019 (Michael Murphy and Lissa Morgenthaler) 415-726-8495	$495.00			X	X
P. Q. Wall Forecast, Inc. P.O. Box 480601 Denver, CO 80248-0601 (P. Q. Wall) 303-455-1523	$198.00		$ 99.00/3 months	X	X
The PAD System Report P.O. Box 554 Oxford, OH 45056 (Daniel Alan Seiver) 513-529-2863	$195.00		$ 35.00/3 months	X	
Personal Finance 1101 King St. Suite 400 Alexandria, VA 22314 (Stephen Leeb) 703-548-2400	$ 39.00			X	X
The Peter Dag Investment Letter 65 Lakefront Dr. Akron, OH 44319 (George Dagnino) 800-833-2782	$250.00		$ 75.00/3 months		X
Plain Talk Investor 1500 Skokie Blvd Suite 203 Northbrook, IL 60062 (Fred Gordon) 708-564-1955	$135.00				

Name	Yearly Price	6-Month Price	Trial Subscription Price	Hot Line	Manages Money
The Princeton Portfolios 301 N. Harrison Suite 229 Princeton, NJ 08540 (Michael Gianturco) 212-288-8424	$225.00			X	X
The Professional Tape Reader P.O. Box 2407 Hollywood, FL 33022 (Stan Weinstein)	$350.00	$210.00		X	
Professional Timing Service P.O. Box 7483 Missoula, MT 59807 (Curtis Hesler) 406-543-4131	$185.00	$100.00		X	
The Prudent Speculator P.O. Box 1767 Santa Monica, CA 90406-1767 (Al Frank) 310-315-9888	$175.00		$ 45.00/3 months		X
The R.H.M. Survey of Warrants, Options & Low-Price Stock 172 Forest Ave. Glen Cove, NY 11542 (Mark Fried) 516-759-2904	$280.00	$150.00			
Richard E. Band's Profitable Investing 7811 Montrose Rd. Potomac, MD 20854 (Richard Band) 301-424-3700	$ 99.00			X	
The Ruff Times 4457 Willow Rd. Suite 200 Pleasanton, CA 94588 (Howard Ruff) 510-463-2200	$149.00			X	
The Scott Letter: Closed-End Fund Report Box 17800 Richmond, VA 23226 (George Cole Scott) 800-356-3508	$135.00	$ 80.00			

Name	Yearly Price	6-Month Price	Trial Subscription Price	Hot Line	Manages Money
The Sector Funds Newsletter P.O. Box 270048 San Diego, CA 92198 (Cato B. Ohrn) 619-748-0805	$157.00		$ 44.00/3 months	X	X
Stockmarket Cycles P.O. Box 6873 Santa Rosa, CA 95406-0873 (Peter Eliades) 707-579-8444	$198.00			X	X
✓Strategic Investment 824 E. Baltimore St. Baltimore, MD 21202-4799 (James Davidson and William Rees-Mogg) 410-234-0691	$ 59.00				X
Switch Fund Timing P.O. Box 25430 Rochester, NY 14625 (David G. Davis) 716-385-3122	$119.00		$ 39.00/3 months		X
The Sy Harding Investor Forecasts P.O. Box 352016 Palm Coast, FL 32135 (Sy Harding) 904-446-0823	$195.00			X	X
Systems and Forecasts 150 Great Neck Rd. Great Neck, NY 11021 (Gerald Appel) 516-829-6444	$195.00	$125.00	$ 65.00/3 months	X	X
Telephone Switch Newsletter P.O. Box 2538 Huntington Beach, CA 92647 (Douglas Fabian) 800-950-8765	$137.00		$ 99.00/8 months	X	
The Timberline Investment Forecast Timberline Research, Inc. 4130 S.W. 117th Ave Suite 215 Beaverton, OR 97005	$135.00		$ 35.00/3 months		
Timer Digest P.O. Box 1688 Greenwich, CT 06836-1688 (Jim Schmidt) 203-629-3503	$225.00			X	

Name	Yearly Price	6-Month Price	Trial Subscription Price	Hot Line	Manages Money
The Turnaround Letter New Generation Research, Inc. 225 Friend St Suite 801 Boston, MA 02114 (George Putnam III) 617-573-9550	$195.00	$ 98.00		X	
United & Babson Investment Report Babson-United Building 101 Prescott St. Wellesley Hills, MA 02181 (Sidney McMath) 617-235-0900	$238.00	$134.00			
United Mutual Fund Selector Babson-United Building 101 Prescott St. Wellesley Hills, MA 02181 (Jack Walsh) 617-235-0900	$125.00		$ 7.00/3 issues		
Value Line Convertibles 711 Third Ave. New York, NY 10017 (Allan S. Lyons) 800-634-3583	$475.00		$ 39.50/8 issues	X	X
The Value Line Investment Survey 711 Third Ave. New York, NY 10017 (Value Line, Inc.) 800-634-3583	$525.00		$ 55.00/10 issues		X
The Value Line OTC Special Situations Service 711 Third Ave. New York, NY 10017 (Peter A. Shraga) 800-634-3583	$390.00		$ 39.00/6 issues		X
The Volume Reversal Survey P.O. Box 1451 Sedona, AZ 86336 (Mark Leibovit) 602-282-1275	$360.00		$ 80.00/2 months	X	

Name	Yearly Price	6-Month Price	Trial Subscription Price	Hot Line	Manages Money
The Wall Street Digest One Sarasota Tower, #602 Two N. Tamiami Trail Sarasota, FL 34236 (Donald Rowe) 813-954-5500	$150.00				
The Wall Street Digest Mutual Fund Advisor One Sarasota Tower, #602 Two N. Tamiami Trail Sarasota, FL 34236 (Donald Rowe and Patricia M. Rowe) 813-954-5500	$150.00				
The Wall Street Generalist MarketMetrics, Inc. 630 South Orange Ave. Suite 104 Sarasota, FL 34236 (Ray Hines) 813-366-5645	$160.00	$ 90.00		X	X
Weber's Fund Advisor P.O. Box 3490 New Hyde Park, NY 11040 (Ken Weber) 516-466-1252	$ 95.00		$ 39.00/4 months	X	X
Your Window Into the Future c/o Moneypower P.O. Box 22400 Minneapolis, MN 55422 (James Moore) 612-537-8096	$ 99.00				
The Zweig Forecast P.O. Box 2900 Wantagh, NY 11793 (Martin Zweig) 516-785-1300	$265.00	$155.00		X	X
Zweig Performance Ratings Report P.O. Box 2900 Wantagh, NY 11793 (Timothy Clark) 516-785-1300	$205.00				X

Index

Weiss, Geraldine, 207–8
Weiss, Martin, 186, 187
West, Mark, 356–57

SPECIAL INTRODUCTORY OFFER
TO READERS OF THIS BOOK

The Hulbert Financial Digest
316 Commerce Street
Alexandria, VA 22314
Phone: 703-683-5905

This book—*The Hulbert Guide to Financial Newsletters* (Fifth Edition)—is the most comprehensive overview of investment newsletters ever written, covering performance over a twelve-year period (through mid-1992).

Those of you who would like on-going and updated information will find it in Mark Hulbert's monthly newsletter, *The Hulbert Financial Digest*. In every issue he provides subscribers with current information on newsletters' performance, analyses of which strategies are working, a sentiment index that reports the consensus opinion on stocks, bonds and gold of over 135 advisers, and a list of which stocks and mutual funds are currently recommended by the greatest number of newsletters (and which are being sold by the greatest number).

If you're interested, I encourage you to take out an introductory subscription to *The Hulbert Financial Digest*. Below you'll find an offer for a five-month trial. Together with this book, a subscription to the HFD ensures that never again will you have to rely on advertising hype to determine how much you would make (or lose) by following a newsletter's recommendations. Subscribe now and receive the cold hard facts yourself on a regular basis.

Sincerely,

Donna Westemeyer

Donna Westemeyer
Business Manager,
The Hulbert Financial Digest

Please return the form below

_____ Yes! Sign me up for a five-month trial to *The Hulbert Financial Digest* for $37.50.

_____ My payment is enclosed   _____ Please bill my Mastercard or Visa

Card # _____ Exp. Date: _____

Signature _____

Name: _____

Address: _____

City, State, Zip: _____

ED5

The Hulbert Financial Digest • 316 Commerce Street • Alexandria, VA 22314 • 703-683-5905